The Way of Complete Perfection

The Way of Complete Perfection

A Quanzhen Daoist Anthology

Selected, translated, and with an introduction by

Louis Komjathy

SUNY PRESS

Published by State University of New York Press, Albany

For information, contact State University of New York Press, Albany, NY
www.sunypress.edu

Production by Ryan Morris
Marketing by Fran Keneston

Library of Congress Cataloging-in-Publication Data

The way of complete perfection : a Quanzhen Daoist anthology / selected, translated, and with an introduction by Louis Komjathy.
    pages cm
Includes bibliographical references and index.
ISBN 978-1-4384-4651-6 (hc : alk. paper)–978-1-4384-4652-3 (pb : alk. paper)
1. Quan zhen jiao.   I. Komjathy, Louis, 1971–

BL1943.C55W39 2013
299.5'1482—dc23   2012023545

10 9 8 7 6 5 4 3 2 1

For
Chen Yuming 陳宇明,
child of Huashan,
and
dedicated Quanzhen Daoists
throughout the world

學書之道，不可尋文而亂目。當宜探意以合心。捨
書探意採理。捨理採趣。採得趣，則可以牧之入心。

The way to study texts is not to strive after literary merit, and thereby confuse your eyes. Instead, you must extract the meaning as it harmonizes with the heart-mind. Abandon texts after you have extracted their meaning and grasped their principle. Abandon principle after you have realized the fundamental ground. After you realize the fundamental ground, attend to it until it completely enters the heart-mind.

—Wang Chongyang 王重陽

道家留丹經子書，千經萬論，可一言以蔽之曰清淨。

As transmitted within the Daoist tradition, the alchemical classics and texts of various masters, the thousand scriptures and ten thousand treatises may all be covered with a single phrase: "clarity and purity."

—Ma Danyang 馬丹陽

Contents

Illustrations

Figures

Tables

Preface

The present book is an anthology of primary Quanzhen (Ch'üan-chen; Complete Perfection) Daoist texts, which were originally written in classical Chinese and are here rendered into English translations. It is the first such anthology, and one of only a few sourcebooks of Daoist literature available in the Western world. To date, only three early Quanzhen texts have been translated, one of which appeared in my *Cultivating Perfection: Mysticism and Self-transformation in Early Quanzhen Daoism* (Brill, 2007). The present volume aims to fill this lacuna in academic research on Daoism. It includes complete and partial translations of twenty-one Quanzhen Daoist texts, the majority of which have never been translated or even studied in relevant scholarly literature. In addition to providing a general introduction to Quanzhen, the anthology follows a standardized format, with each chapter consisting of historical and topical discussions of the texts and corresponding translations with scholarly annotations.

Quanzhen is one of the most important Daoist movements in Chinese history. Associated with Wang Chongyang (1113–1170) and his first-generation disciples, Quanzhen began as a small ascetic and eremitic community in eastern Shandong and eventually became a monastic order with national distribution. It became the dominant form of monastic Daoism in mainland China and continues to occupy a central position in contemporary Chinese society and throughout the modern world, especially in its Longmen (Lung-men; Dragon Gate) lineage. The present anthology provides a glimpse into the religious world of Quanzhen, especially as documented in the literature written by the first-generation adherents.

The Way of Complete Perfection serves as a companion volume to my *Cultivating Perfection*, which is one of only three Western-language studies of Quanzhen. The present anthology provides access to Daoist literature through reliable, annotated English translations. It may serve as a sourcebook of Daoist literature in general and as a primer of Quanzhen Daoism in particular. Scholars and students of Chinese religion, Daoism, and religious studies as well as individuals interested in Daoism will find *The Way of Complete Perfection* to be a unique opportunity to access Daoist literature in reliable English translation. Readers will find Quanzhen writings to be a profound expression of the Daoist religious tradition.

Acknowledgments

Every book has a story. Every book recounts various moments in the process of its composition. Some of these are visible, others hidden. This is not simply the case for the trees that now appear as white sheets, but also for the hours, days, months, and years that were offered for its completion. In the case of the present book, the background story includes conversations over tea; mountain peaks; distant monasteries; friendships found, lost, and recovered; and continual travel.

The initial idea for the present book began while I was a graduate student at Boston University. While working on my Ph.D. dissertation, published as *Cultivating Perfection: Mysticism and Self-transformation in Early Quanzhen Daoism* (Brill, 2007), I read and translated portions of the early Quanzhen textual corpus.

After receiving my Ph.D., I had the good fortune to receive a Chiang Ching-kuo Foundation (CCKF) grant and an associate professorship in the Institute of Religion, Science and Social Studies (IRSSS) of Shandong University (PRC). It was during my academic year in China (2005–2006) that I began substantial work on the translations and annotations that form the majority of selections herein. I am grateful to the CCKF for its generous support of my archeological and ethnographic fieldwork on Quanzhen Daoism in Shandong and on contemporary Quanzhen Daoist monasticism. In addition to providing the opportunity for some of my translation work, my time in China helped me better understand the importance of community and place in Daoism as well as the reality of regional variation among Daoists. During this time, I also benefited from my close working relationship with colleagues at IRSSS, especially my mentor and friend Jiang Sheng, the director of IRSSS. I am particularly grateful for his friendship and support. Conducting archaeological research on Shandong Daoism there clarified many dimensions of early Quanzhen Daoism, including geography, distribution, material culture, and so forth. I also engaged in participant-observation at the monasteries of Taiqing gong (Palace of Great Clarity), the base-monastery at Laoshan (Mount Lao; near Qingdao, Shandong) and of Yuquan yuan (Temple of the Jade Spring), the base-monastery at Huashan (Mount Hua; near Huayin, Shaanxi). I am grateful to the monks at these monasteries for their generosity and hospitality. In particular, I benefited from many conversations with Chen Yuming, former vice-abbot of Yuquan yuan and member of the Huashan lineage, and Yu Yuanhui, a senior monk of Yuquan yuan and member of the Longmen lineage. They deepened my understanding of Quanzhen religious praxis and clarified which texts were most essential for inclusion in the present anthology. In addition to deepening knowledge of Quanzhen Daoism, I hope that this book may also support the revitalization of Daoism as a religious path in the contemporary world.

In addition to consultation of the few previous translations of Quanzhen texts mentioned in the pages that follow, the present book benefited from various colleagues and friends who provided critical comments and suggestions. In particular, I am grateful to Suzanne Cahill (University of

California, San Diego) for her careful reading of my translations of the hagiographies contained in chapter 6. Stephen Eskildsen (University of Tennessee, Chattanooga) was also generous with his time; his suggestions on some of the poems in chapter 1 and hagiographies in chapter 6 were especially helpful. The late Monica Esposito (1962–2011; Kyoto University) provided important comments on chapter 7 and on the translation of the monastic manuals contained there. I especially benefited from her expertise on late imperial Daoism in general and Longmen in particular. I dedicate the translation of the *Chuzhen jie* to her memory. My translations of some of the poetry, discourse records, hagiographies, and monastic manuals also were refined through Livia Kohn's critical reading and helpful suggestions. My ability to translate Daoist texts and my understanding of the Daoist tradition are deeply indebted to her mentorship. Elena Valussi (Loyola University) read and commented on the poems by Sun Buer, and I thank her for her suggestions. Finally, I am grateful to the two anonymous SUNY Press reviewers for their helpful suggestions and for their endorsement, and to Nancy Ellegate and other members of SUNY Press for their willingness to publish such a complex book, especially in a cultural moment that seems to presage postliteracy.

Academic work, and translation work in particular, is often a lonely undertaking. This is especially the case with such an obscure undertaking as translating classical Chinese Daoist texts, texts that only a handful of people in the modern world have read in the original Chinese and texts that challenge most of the assumptions of Western connoisseurs of "Daoism." My work has been sustained by various relationships, especially the concern and support of community members of the Daoist Foundation and the Gallagher Cove Daoist Association (Olympia, Washington). I am especially grateful to Paul Dreisbach, Greg Hart, Steve Plaza, Jackal Tanelorn, Ruth Urand, and Kevin Wagner for their friendship and steadfastness. Our "conversations on the Dao" have given sustenance throughout the years documented in this book.

Finally, I'm grateful to my wife and life-partner, Kate Townsend, for her enduring love and support. As always, she dedicated a great deal of time to reading, discussing, and editing my work. From her, I continue to learn the importance of embracing stillness and constant acceptance. She remains clear as others fade.

As I expressed in my previous saunters into perfection, no one acknowledged here bears any responsibility for this study, except to the extent that they deem it a sign of respect and an honor. All of us are, after all, fundamentally responsible. The imperfections that remain are my own.

So concludes my search for complete perfection.

Abbreviations

DZ   *Daozang* 道藏. Refers to the *Zhengtong daozang* 正統道藏 (Daoist Canon of the Zhengtong Reign), the Ming-dynasty (1368–1644) Daoist Canon of 1445, including the 1607 supplement. Numbers follow *Title Index to Daoist Collections* (Komjathy 2002), which parallel *Concordance du Tao-tsang* (CT) (Schipper 1975).

JH   *Daozang jinghua* 道藏精華 (Essential Blossoms of the Daoist Canon). Numbers follow *Title Index to Daoist Collections* (Komjathy 2002).

JY   *Daozang jiyao* 道藏集要 (Collected Essentials of the Daoist Canon). Numbers follow *Title Index to Daoist Collections* (Komjathy 2002).

T.   *Taishō shinshū daizōkyō* 大正新脩大藏經 (Taisho Buddhist Canon). Cited by number in Taisho edition, followed by volume number, page, and column.

TY   *Daozang tiyao* 道藏提要 (Descriptive Notes on the Daoist Canon) (Ren and Zhong 1991). Numbers follow *Title Index to Daoist Collections* (Komjathy 2002).

ZW   *Zangwai daoshu* 藏外道書 (Daoist Books Outside the Canon). Numbers follow *Title Index to Daoist Collections* (Komjathy 2002).

Orientations

The present work is an anthology of primary Quanzhen (Ch'üan-chen; Complete Perfection) texts, which were originally written in classical Chinese and are here rendered into English translations. Quanzhen is one of the most important Daoist movements in Chinese history and remains the dominant form of monastic Daoism in the modern world, especially in its Longmen (Lung-men; Dragon Gate) lineage.[1] Giving particular attention to works composed within the early religious community, by the founder Wang Chongyang (1113–1170) and his first-generation disciples, this study is the first historically accurate sourcebook of Quanzhen literature. It includes complete and partial translations of twenty-one Daoist texts, the majority of which have never been translated or even studied in relevant scholarly literature. The translations include representative works from every major genre of Quanzhen literature, from poetry and discourse records to didactic texts, commentaries, and hagiographies. As major transitions occurred toward the beginning of the Yuan dynasty (1279–1368) and Qing dynasty (1644–1911), specifically the systematization of Quanzhen monasticism, I have also included translations of two late medieval monastic manuals and one late imperial one. In the present introduction, I discuss Quanzhen history and practice, Quanzhen literature, scripture study and contemplative reading, the structure and contents of the anthology, and scholarly conventions utilized in *The Way of Complete Perfection*. The introduction is followed by seven chapters arranged topically and thematically with corresponding annotated translations.

Quanzhen History and Practice[2]

In the first year of the Dading reign period (1161), at the age of forty-eight, a failed Chinese literati and foot soldier named Wang Yunqing—also known as Wang Zhongfu—abandoned his

---

1. Although there can be little debate about the central position of Quanzhen Daoism in Chinese history and in the modern world, it is important to keep in mind that it was only one major Daoist movement among many. Other key movements include Taiping (Great Peace); Tianshi (Celestial Masters), also known as Zhengyi (Orthodox Unity); Taiqing (Great Clarity); Shangqing (Highest Clarity); Lingbao (Numinous Treasure); and so forth. Among these, Zhengyi is the other main movement that survives into the modern world. For some reliable English-language introductions to Daoism see Kohn 2001; 2009; Miller 2003; Kirkland 2004; Komjathy forthcoming. See also Kohn 2000a; Schipper and Verellen 2004; Pregadio 2008.

2. This section aims to be a fairly nontechnical introduction to the history of Quanzhen Daoism, meaning that I have not cited all of the primary and secondary scholarly literature to support my account. The present account is based on my previous academic study of the movement (Komjathy 2007a), especially chapter 1. For specific biographical details on the early Quanzhen adherents see chapter 6 in this volume. For an attempt to reconstruct the religious system of early Quanzhen see Komjathy 2007a. For readily available English-language studies of Quanzhen more generally see Katz 1999; Eskildsen 2004; Marsone 2010; and the special issue of the *Journal of Chinese Religions* 29 (2001). These studies include fairly comprehensive references to international and multilingual scholarship on Quanzhen. Much of that literature is also cited in the pages that follow this introduction and is contained in the bibliography of this book. There is also the interesting phenomenon of research groups and organizations dedicated to Quanzhen studies, including the Shandong Muping Quanzhen Religious Culture Forum (www.muping.gov.cn/qz; Shandong) and Center for Quanzhen Research (www.daoist. org/quanzhen/qzmp.htm; Hong Kong). See also the Center for the Study of Qi-Lu Culture (www.qlwh.com; Shandong).

family and the desire for worldly recognition. In the summer of that year, he had a mystical encounter with one or more Daoist immortals, sometimes identified as Zhongli Quan (Zhengyang [Aligned Yang]; second c. CE?) and his spiritual disciple Lü Dongbin (Chunyang [Purified Yang]; b. 798?). This occurred on a bridge in Ganhe (near present-day Huxian, Shaanxi). Following this event, Wang completely embraced a Daoist religious way of life, specifically the life of a solitary renunciant and internal alchemist. He thereupon changed his names, possibly under divine inspiration: his given name became Zhe (Wise), his personal name Zhiming (Knowing Illumination), and his religious name Chongyang (Redoubled Yang). Such was the pivotal spiritual moment for Wang Chongyang, the eventual founder of the Quanzhen (Complete Perfection) religious community.

In a nearby village named Nanshi, Wang Chongyang dug himself a "grave" that he named "Tomb for Reviving the Dead" (*huo siren mu*). This was a mound of dirt several feet high, with a ten-foot-high ceiling dug under it. Near the entrance to this underground enclosure Wang placed a plaque that read, "Wang Haifeng" (Lunatic Wang). Wang spent three years in this enclosure, engaging in ascetic practices, practicing internal alchemy, and exchanging poetry with those who came to visit him.

In the autumn of 1163, Wang Chongyang filled in his meditation enclosure and moved to the village of Liujiang (present-day Huxian), about three miles from Nanshi. Located in the Zhongnan mountains,[3] Liujiang was home to a small Daoist eremitic community. There Wang trained with two hermits, He Dejin (Yuchan [Jade Toad]; d. 1170) and Li Lingyang (Lingyang [Numinous Yang]; d. 1189). It seems that the three renunciants lived on a small piece of land near a stream, where each had a separate grass hut.

Figure 1. Approximation of an Early Quanzhen Hermitage[4]

---

3. The places of Wang's early life were in close proximity to the Zhongnan mountains, a famous location in Daoist history more generally, where Laozi was believed to have transmitted the *Daode jing* to Yin Xi (see Kohn 1997) and where Louguan (Lookout Tower Monastery), the first Daoist monastery, was established (see Kohn 2003a). The Zhongnan mountains would later become home to a number of important Quanzhen sacred sites. The site of Wang Chongyang's early hermitage and the eremitic community of Liujiang is now named Chongyang gong (Palace of Chongyang).

4. For a discussion of the architectural layout and characteristics of early Quanzhen hermitages and meditation enclosures see Komjathy 2007a, 157–66. In terms of meditation enclosures (*huandu*), *du*, in its earliest usage, refers to a specific spatial measurement. A *huandu* refers to a small square hut measuring four *du* on each side, with one *du* equaling approximately one *zhang*. During the Song-Jin period this approximately equaled three meters (Goossaert 1997, 172–76; Eskildsen 2004, 212, n. 90; see also Goossaert 1999). A *huandu*, or meditation enclosure, was thus about nine-feet square. In the present anthology see section 4ab of the *Danyang yulu* (DZ 1057; trl. in chapter 2) and section 2b–3a of the *Chongyang lijiao shiwu lun* (DZ 1233; trl. in chapter 3).

Wang engaged in solitary Daoist religious praxis, focusing on asceticism and internal alchemy (*neidan*). It was also at this time that Wang accepted his two earliest-known disciples: Shi Chuhou (Dongyang [Cavernous Yang]; 1102–1174) and Yan Chuchang (1111–1183).

After spending four years in the eremitic community of Liujiang and engaging in intensive religious practice, Wang Chongyang burned down his hut, dancing while he watched it burn to the ground. This occurred in the summer of 1167, when Wang was fifty-four years old. Thereupon, Wang began traveling eastward. After arriving in Shandong Province, he accepted Liu Tongwei (Moran [Silent Suchness]; d. 1196) as a disciple; Liu was Wang's first Shandong disciple. Liu thereupon retraced Wang Chongyang's steps westward to join the eremitic community at Liujiang in Shaanxi. Simultaneously, Wang Chongyang made his way to Ninghai (present-day Muping, Shandong). About a month after arriving in Shandong's eastern peninsula, Wang visited the estate of a local official named Fan Mingshu (fl. 1160s), who was entertaining a group of guests. There Wang met and attracted the interest of Ma Yu (Danyang [Elixir Yang]; 1123–1184), who would become one of his most influential students. Ma agreed to allow Wang to build a meditation hut on his property. This hut was the Quanzhen an (Hermitage of Complete Perfection), where Wang lived until the following spring. While spending much of his time in seclusion, Wang also wrote poetry and began attracting disciples. His earliest Shandong converts were Qiu Chuji (Changchun [Perpetual Spring]; 1148–1227), Tan Chuduan (Changzhen [Perpetual Perfection]; 1123–1185), and Wang Chuyi (Yuyang [Jade Yang]; 1142–1217).[5] In order to become a fully recognized disciple, one had to commit to the life of a renunciant (*chujia*; lit., "leave the family"), which included forsaking intoxicants, sexual activity, greed and material accumulation, as well as anger. Under Wang Chongyang's influence, Tan Changzhen separated from his wife and all three disciples accepted Wang's ascetic requirements. Following Ma Danyang's conversion in 1168, after which he separated from his wife Sun Buer and handed over his property to his son, Wang Chongyang took his disciples to the Kunyu mountains (near Yantai and Weihai in eastern Shandong), where they established Yanxia dong (Cavern of Misty Vapors).[6] There Wang, overseeing the religious practice of Ma, Qiu, Tan, and Wang Yuyang, initiated a program of intensive training that included sleep deprivation, exposure to extreme heat and cold, scoldings, and beatings when their diligence faltered. Wang Chongyang also required them to beg for alms in their hometowns. In the final years of his life (1168–1170), Wang Chongyang accepted Hao Datong (Guangning [Expansive Serenity]; 1140–1213), Sun Buer (Qingjing [Clear Stillness]; 1119–1183), and Liu Chuxuan (Changsheng [Perpetual Life]; 1147–1203). These seven early Shandong adherents (Hao, Liu, Ma, Qiu, Sun, Tan, and Wang) would later become identified in the Quanzhen tradition as the so-called Seven Perfected (*qizhen*).

Wang Chongyang and his seven primary Shandong disciples in turn established and ministered to the communities of five eastern Shandong Daoist associations (*wuhui*). These included Yuhua hui (Association of Jade Flower; Dengzhou), Qibao hui (Association of Seven Treasures; Wendeng), Jinlian hui (Association of Gold Lotus; Ninghai), Sanguang hui (Association of Three Radiances; Fushan), and Pingdeng hui (Association of Equal Rank; Laizhou). These meetinghouses were foundational for

---

5. It seems that Wang Yuyang's widowed mother, maiden name Zhou, became a renunciant at Yanxia dong as well. Wang Chongyang gave her the personal name Deqing (Inner Power Purified) and religious name Xuanjing (Mysterious Stillness) (*Jinlian xiangzhuan*, DZ 174, 36a–36b). If this was the case, Wang Chongyang would have had at least two formally recognized female disciples.

6. During summer of 2008, the site was being renovated. Author's field observations. See also Mou et al. 2005; Shandong 2005; Ding et al. 2007.

the formation of Quanzhen as a regional Daoist religious movement and for establishing patterns of lay patronage.

In late 1169, Wang Chongyang left Shandong and traveled west. He was accompanied by Ma Danyang, Tan Changzhen, Liu Changsheng, and Qiu Changchun. While it seems that Wang intended to establish and disseminate Quanzhen in his native region of Shaanxi, the group took lodging in an inn in Bianliang (present-day Kaifeng, Henan), most likely due to the onset of illness. Wang Chongyang died in Bianliang in 1170, about two months later, and leadership responsibilities were transferred to Ma Danyang. After burying Wang's body in Bianliang, the four disciples honored Wang's request and made their way to Shaanxi. There they met with He Dejin and Li Lingyang—Wang's earlier companions—and Shi Chuhou, Yan Chuchang, and Liu Tongwei—Wang's earlier disciples. The nine adepts constructed a tomb and small temple (*an*) at the very site in Liujiang village where Wang had burned down his meditation hut. They then retrieved Wang's body from Bianliang and interred it in the Liujiang temple. This temple was known as the Zuting (Ancestral Hall), which was later renamed Chongyang gong (Palace of Redoubled Yang) and Lingxu guan (Monastery of Numinous Emptiness). After spending three years in mourning at Zuting, Ma, Tan, Liu, and Qiu parted ways to pursue their own training and ministerial work

All of the first-generation Quanzhen adherents engaged in solitary ascetic training, most often in mountain locales and hermitages. Hao Guangning lived as a mendicant in Wozhou and practiced under the famous Zhaozhou Bridge (Zhaoxian, Hebei) for six years (1175–1181). Liu Changsheng lived as a wandering ascetic in the Luoyang environs (1171–1175). Ma Danyang practiced *huandu* throughout his life, and in his final two years he spent time in seclusion in the Jinyu an (Hermitage of Gold and Jade; in Huangxian, Shandong). Qiu Changchun did solitary practice first at Panxi (1173–1181) and then in the mountainous gorges of Longmen dong (near present-day Xinjichuan and Longxian, Shaanxi), training at various times for possibly the next ten years. Sun Buer moved to Luoyang in 1179, where she trained with a female Daoist recluse from Henan named Feng Xiangu (Immortal Maiden Feng; fl. 1145–1179).[7] According to the *Lishi tongjian houji*, Feng lived in an "upper cave" (*shangdong*) and had Sun live in the lower one. Sun practiced and taught there until her death in 1183. After the three-year mourning period for Wang Chongyang (1170–1173), Tan Changzhen lived as an urban recluse in Luoyang, Henan, spending time in both Chaoyuan gong (Palace for Attending to the Origin) and the more remote Yunxi an (Hermitage of Cloudy Ravines). Finally, Wang Yuyang engaged in intensive ascetic practice for nine years (1168–1177) in Yunguang dong (Grotto of Cloud-like Radiance) of Tiecha shan (Mount Tiecha; Wendeng, Shandong). Extant Quanzhen hagiographies contain various stories and miraculous deeds related to the early adepts during these times and in these places (see chapter 6 in this volume). Here it should mentioned that these bio-geographical (geo-biographical) moments included spiritual direction of disciples as well as the composition of voluminous amounts of poetry.

The early Quanzhen religious community was, thus, focused on ascetic and alchemical practice. In particular, intensive, solitary, and eremitic training occupied a central place in the lives of the first-generation adherents. This included "meditation enclosure" (*huandu*) (see Goossaert 1997, 171–219; 1999; Komjathy 2007a, 157–66) and *wugeng* training (Goossaert 2000; Komjathy 2007a, 175–79). The former involved intensive solitary practice in a small hut usually for one hundred days with an attendant to provide basic necessities.[8] The latter involved engaging in meditation and internal

---

7. *Jinlian ji*, DZ 173, 5.10ab; *Lishi tongjian houji*, DZ 298, 6.17b–18a. See also Despeux and Kohn 2003, 142–49.

8. See, e.g., *Jinlian xiangzhuan*, DZ 174, 24b–25a; *Danyang yulu*, DZ 1057, 4ab.

alchemy practice during the five night-watches. These are the five periods of darkness, and each is associated with a specific branch-time correspondence: (1) *xu* (7 p.m.–9 p.m.), (2) *hai* (9 p.m.–11 p.m.), (3) *zi* (11 p.m.–1 a.m.), (4) *chou* (1 a.m.–3 a.m.), and (5) *yin* (3 a.m.–5 a.m.). Seclusion, meditation, and internal alchemy practice were primary. Emphasis was also placed on quietistic meditation, focusing on cultivating clarity and stillness, and, to a lesser degree, on scripture study.

On the level of institutional history, each of the first-generation adherents contributed to the growth of Quanzhen as a religious movement and subsequent monastic order. With Shaanxi and Shandong as the early centers of religious activity, they trained their own disciples; guided lay believers; formed working relationships with local magistrates; secured patronage from all segments of the Chinese population; built and renovated hermitages and temples; and became increasingly recognized by imperial courts. Primarily under the direction of Qiu Changchun, the third patriarch and successor of Ma Danyang as national leader, and his disciples, the second-generation Quanzhen adherents, Quanzhen became a nationwide monastic order with increasing diversity with respect to demographics, doctrine, and training models. This growth and transformation benefited greatly from Qiu Changchun's famous westward journey to meet Chinggis Qan (Genghis Khan; ca. 1162–1227; r. 1206–1227) during the years of 1220 to 1223. Qiu was accompanied by nineteen select disciples, including individuals who would play a major role in the growth and flourishing of the Quanzhen monastic order. The meeting, actually a series of meetings, occurred in the Hindu Kush (near present-day Kabul, Afghanistan) and resulted in the Qan granting Qiu, and the Quanzhen order by extension, *de facto* control of the whole of northern China's monastic communities, Buddhists included.[9] Upon his return to northern China in 1223, Qiu was installed as abbot of the newly restored Tianchang guan (Monastery of Celestial Perpetuity), which was later renamed Changchun gong (Palace of Perpetual Spring) and then Baiyun guan (White Cloud Monastery) (see Koyanagi 1934; Marsone 1999; Li 2003; also Yoshioka 1979).[10] During the last four years of Qiu's life, Quanzhen was transformed from a regional religious movement to a nationwide monastic order, growing enormously in membership. Qiu continued to follow the pattern established by Wang Chongyang, Ma Danyang, and Wang Yuyang, that is, meeting halls for lay patrons in support of hermitages and monasteries. We know that while residing in Tianchang guan Qiu Changchun was involved in the establishment of eight associations, all affiliated with Tianchang guan (see *Xiyou ji*, DZ 1429, 2.16a; Komjathy 2007a, 58). All of these events occurred during the Jurchen-Jin dynasty (1115–1234) and Southern Song dynasty (1127–1279), and within the foreign-controlled northern regions of China.

A pivotal moment in Quanzhen history of course corresponds to the death of Qiu Changchun, the last first-generation adherent, in 1227. Qiu was succeeded as Quanzhen Patriarch and national religious leader by his disciple Yin Zhiping (Qinghe [Clear Harmony]; 1169–1251), who in turn transferred leadership to Li Zhichang (Zhenchang [Perfect Constancy]; 1193–1256), another one of Qiu's direct disciples, in 1238.[11] With the help of other second-generation Quanzhen luminaries,

9. This resulted in an influx of Buddhist monks into the Quanzhen order and in Quanzhen gaining control of some Buddhist temples, though how many were occupied remains debated. While more research needs to be conducted, there was clearly cross-pollination between Quanzhen and Chan Buddhism. For example, members of the Quanzhen monastic order adopted dimensions of Chan Buddhism, including monastery layout, monastic structure, and monastic rules.

10. This temple in Yanjing (present-day Beijing) would become the primary monastic headquarters of the Quanzhen order and its Longmen lineage from the Qing dynasty (1644–1911) into the contemporary period.

11. For lineage charts of the early Quanzhen movement and the first six patriarchs see Komjathy 2007a, 378–81. On the second- and third-generations see Ren 2001, 2.728; Li 2003, 460–61.

such as Wang Zhijin (Qiyun [Perched-in-Clouds]; 1178–1263) and Song Defang (Piyun [Wrapped-in-Clouds]; 1183–1247),[12] the Quanzhen monastic order became a nationwide religious movement with large numbers of adherents, both monastic and lay. Particularly noteworthy in the present context is the fact that Song Defang and his disciple Qin Zhian (Shuli [Useless Timber]; 1188–1244) were instrumental in the compilation and editing of the *Xuandu baozang* (Precious Canon of the Mysterious Metropolis), which was completed in 1244 at their editorial headquarters of Xuandu guan (Monastery of the Mysterious Metropolis) in Pingyang (Shanxi). This Jin-dynasty Daoist Canon was the only such project in history initiated and carried out by an individual Daoist subtradition without government sponsorship. The *Xuandu baozang* contained some 7,800 *juan* and was the largest Daoist Canon ever compiled.

Quanzhen continued to gain power and increase in membership during the years of 1222 to 1280, partially due to its attraction as the primary tax-exempt religious institution during the Mongol Yuan dynasty (1279–1368).[13] Quanzhen monasteries and temples were established throughout northern China and its clerical membership grew, so that by the late thirteenth century there were some four thousand Quanzhen sacred sites and twenty thousand monks and nuns (Goossaert 2001, 114–18).[14] However, Buddho-Daoist court debates were held in 1258 and 1281, the loss of which by the Daoist side resulted in a series of anti-Daoist edicts by Qubilai Qan (Khubilai Khan; Emperor Shizu; r. 1260–1294) of the Mongol Yuan dynasty. This culminated in the burning and destruction of Daoist texts, textual collections, and printing blocks in 1281 (only the *Daode jing* was to be spared) (see Yao 1980a; Zheng 1995; Goossaert 2001). Although devastating at the time, these events did not prevent Quanzhen's long-term development as a monastic order. "In fact, it had already gained recognition as an 'orthodox,' valuable part of Taoist religious tradition, and secured its place in the institutional and ideological construction of Taoism as an ascetic order devoted to both individual self-cultivation and communal disciplines" (Goossaert and Katz 2001, 92). Quanzhen temple construction and restoration continued throughout the Yuan dynasty, and the commission and erection of steles remained fairly constant from 1230 through 1350 (Goossaert 1997, 11). Moreover, in 1310 Emperor Wuzong (r. 1308–1311) bestowed honorary posthumous titles on major Quanzhen figures (see *Jinlian xiangzhuan*, DZ 174, 3b–9a).

---

12. Hagiographies of three of these second-generation adherents appear in the *Zhongnan neizhuan* (DZ 955): (1) Yin Zhiping (3.1a–6b); (2) Li Zhichang (3.6b–13a); and (3) Song Defang (3.20b–23b). On Wang, see his disciple Huang Zutai's preface to the *Panshan Qiyun Wang zhenren yulu* (DZ 1059); also Goossaert 1997, 500–6. The latter source also contains important research on the lives and activities of most of these Quanzhen adepts.

13. Various dates are given for the establishment of the Yuan dynasty, but it was in 1279 that the Southern Song was finally defeated and the Mongols gained control of the whole of China. The Mongol Yuan dynasty was the first non-Chinese-ruled dynasty to have nationwide control. Although such historical patterns date back to the Toba-Wei dynasty (386–534), the Mongols set a precedent for national rule of the indigenous Chinese population by a foreign people that prepared the way for the Manchu Qing dynasty (1644–1911). Interestingly, the Manchus were the later descendants of the Jurchens.

14. Like Daoist monasticism more generally (see Kohn 1997; 2003a; 2004a; Reiter 1998), Quanzhen monasticism is understudied. The most comprehensive study is Vincent Goossaert's dissertation (1997; see also Zheng 1995), and one hopes that it will eventually be published. Some important work on late imperial and early modern Quanzhen has also appeared in print. See Hackmann 1920; 1931; Yoshioka 1979; Esposito 1993; 2000; 2001; 2004; Goossaert 2004; 2007; Liu 2004a; 2004b; Komjathy 2008b; 2009. On modern Quanzhen monasticism see Herrou 2005.

The thirteenth and early fourteenth centuries were thus the height of early Quanzhen monasticism, that is, the monastic order that developed under the leadership of Qiu Changchun and his disciples and that became the dominant form of Daoist monasticism during the Yuan dynasty.[15] In its late medieval monastic expression, Quanzhen adherence and practice represented the institutionalization of its earlier ascetic and eremitic commitments. This included incorporating rows of meditation hermitages in monastic architectural layout, instituting ordination rituals and a standardized lineage-based name system, and developing monastic regulations (Goossaert 1997, 113–342; 2001). During the Yuan dynasty, Quanzhen Daoists, both monks and nuns, thus entered a more fully developed ordination process and monastic system. This involved living in formal monasteries and temples with a regimented schedule that included ethical guidelines and monastic regulations, solitary and communal meditation, as well as communal ritual.[16] The early Quanzhen emphasis on abstinence from the Four Hindrances (alcohol, sex, wealth, and anger) also became codified in monastic rules, which incorporated a shift toward vegetarianism.[17] Quietistic meditation and internal alchemy remained the primary forms of meditation, though the Quanzhen monastic communities also adopted a form of communal meditation centering on the bowl-clepsydra (see chapter 7).

By the beginning of the Ming dynasty (1368–1644), Quanzhen was eclipsed by the Zhengyi (Orthodox Unity) movement as the preferred and imperially sanctioned form of Daoism (see De Bruyn 2000). Quanzhen regained national prominence during the Qing dynasty (1644–1911) (see Esposito 1993, 2000, 2001). The Qing-dynasty monastic order and its Longmen (Dragon Gate) lineage were codified under the leadership of Wang Changyue (Kunyang [Paradisiacal Yang]; 1594?– 1680). Wang was the lineage-disciple of Zhao Fuyang (fl. 1600–1640), the sixth Longmen patriarch and heir of the Longmen Discipline (Vinaya) Masters (lüshi) line. Wang Changyue eventually emerged as a major monastic leader, becoming appointed as abbot of Baiyun guan (White Cloud Monastery; Beijing) in 1655 and commencing the public ordination of novices in 1656.

---

15. It was during this period of Chinese history that Quanzhen incorporated more adherents of the so-called Southern School (Nanzong) of internal alchemy as well as more features derived from Chan Buddhism. These and other dimensions of intra- and interreligious interaction deserve further study.

16. A thorough study of early Quanzhen ritual has yet to be undertaken. Preliminary research indicates that members of the early Quanzhen religious community accepted liturgical performance as relevant to Daoist religious life. Having been trained by unnamed, "non-Quanzhen" Daoists, they performed and participated in the two primary forms of Daoist ritual, namely, zhai-purification and jiao-offering rites. Mature Quanzhen ritual accepted the standardized form of Lingbao (Numinous Treasure) Daoist ritual, but also quickly incorporated the major new, late medieval ritual and exorcistic traditions, such as Tianxin (Celestial Heart), Wulei (Five Thunder), and so forth. See Tsui 1991, 26–27; Goossaert 1997, 162–68; 2001; Eskildsen 2004, 171–93. Unfortunately, there are no early or late medieval Quanzhen ritual and liturgical manuals. See Schipper and Verellen 2004. Information on earlier Quanzhen ritual must be gleaned from stele inscriptions and hagiographies. The only relatively early Quanzhen liturgical works are a simple birthday celebration for Zhongli Quan and Lü Dongbin (Jindan dayao xianpai, DZ 1070, 3a–10b; trl. Eskildsen 1989, 395–408) and a brief Salvation-through-Sublimation (liandu) rite (Daofa huiyuan, DZ 1220, 210).

17. My preliminary research indicates that vegetarianism was not universally adopted or advocated in the early Quanzhen community. This would make sense in terms of geography, as seafood is one of the primary forms of sustenance in Shandong. Of the first-generation adherents, it seems that Ma Danyang and Qiu Changchun were the most committed to vegetarianism as an expression of wisdom and compassion.

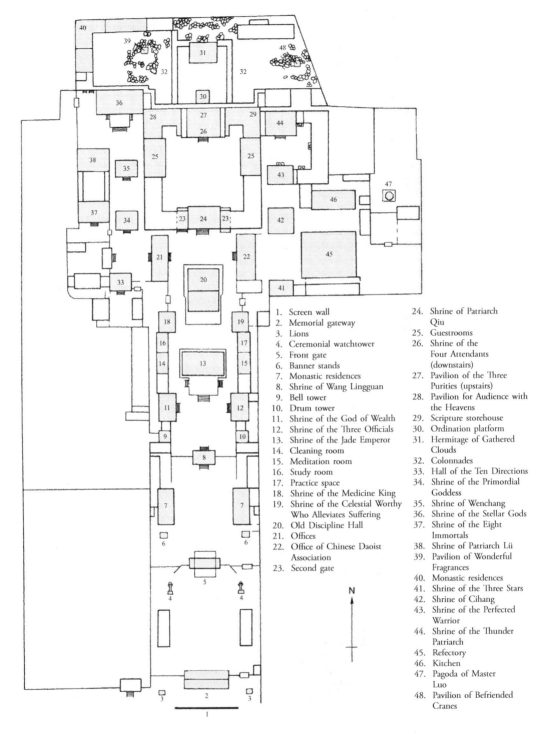

1. Screen wall
2. Memorial gateway
3. Lions
4. Ceremonial watchtower
5. Front gate
6. Banner stands
7. Monastic residences
8. Shrine of Wang Lingguan
9. Bell tower
10. Drum tower
11. Shrine of the God of Wealth
12. Shrine of the Three Officials
13. Shrine of the Jade Emperor
14. Cleaning room
15. Meditation room
16. Study room
17. Practice space
18. Shrine of the Medicine King
19. Shrine of the Celestial Worthy Who Alleviates Suffering
20. Old Discipline Hall
21. Offices
22. Office of Chinese Daoist Association
23. Second gate
24. Shrine of Patriarch Qiu
25. Guestrooms
26. Shrine of the Four Attendants (downstairs)
27. Pavilion of the Three Purities (upstairs)
28. Pavilion for Audience with the Heavens
29. Scripture storehouse
30. Ordination platform
31. Hermitage of Gathered Clouds
32. Colonnades
33. Hall of the Ten Directions
34. Shrine of the Primordial Goddess
35. Shrine of Wenchang
36. Shrine of the Stellar Gods
37. Shrine of the Eight Immortals
38. Shrine of Patriarch Lü
39. Pavilion of Wonderful Fragrances
40. Monastic residences
41. Shrine of the Three Stars
42. Shrine of Cihang
43. Shrine of the Perfected Warrior
44. Shrine of the Thunder Patriarch
45. Refectory
46. Kitchen
47. Pagoda of Master Luo
48. Pavilion of Befriended Cranes

N

Figure 2. Modern Temple Layout of White Cloud Monastery[18] (cf. Yoshioka 1979, 250–52; Qiao 2001, 142)

18. Based on my field observations in June of 2011. Not depicted here is the Daoist Seminary (Daojiao xueyuan) located to the east and outside the central axis and the Daoist Medical Clinic located to the west and outside the central axis.

As standardized by Wang Changyue, Quanzhen monastic life centered on the study and application of the three core Longmen precept texts, namely, *Chuzhen jie* (Precepts of Initial Perfection; JY 292; ZW 404), *Zhongji jie* (Precepts of Medium Ultimate; JY 293; ZW 405), and *Tianxian jie* (Precepts of Celestial Immortality; JY 291; ZW 403). As Monica Esposito has pointed out, "[Wang] established a precepts program centered on rules of proper behavior which also included spiritual teachings and exhibited signs of Chan inspiration. His teaching was combined with strong Confucian ethics and Buddhist soteriology" (2001, 191–92; see also 2001, 197, and 2000, 629). The late imperial Longmen system also placed emphasis on quietistic meditation, internal alchemy, scripture study, and communal ritual. Wang Changyue's formalized, "orthodox" Longmen lineage became the dominant Quanzhen monastic system to the present day.

On a political level, late imperial Longmen was characterized by relatively close connections with the Qing imperial elite and by strict governmental control (see Esposito 2000). For example, following the bureaucratic structure of the Ming, religious administration was a function of the Board of Rites (*libu*), one of the six boards of the central administration. Daoism was specifically governed by the Daolu si (Central Daoist Registry), "a central government agency responsible for certifying and disciplining Daoist religious practitioners throughout the empire" (Hacker 1985, 489; Esposito 2000, 623). It controlled corresponding boards and officers on the provincial, departmental, prefectural, and county levels. Following Wang Changyue's revitalization and systematization of Quanzhen monasticism, specifically as embodied in its Longmen branch, major new voices in the religious tradition emerged. Some important figures include the eleventh-generation patriarchs Min Yide (Lanyun [Lazy Cloud]; 1758–1836), a disciple of Shen Yibing (Qingyun [Light Cloud]; 1708–1786), and Liu Yiming (Wuyuan [Awakening to the Origin]; 1734–1821),[19] a disciple of a number of obscure Daoist hermits. Interestingly, Min Yide compiled one of the most important extra-canonical textual collections, namely, the *Daozang xubian* (Supplemental Collection to the Daoist Canon; 1834) (see Komjathy 2002; Esposito 2001, 221–24). This collection includes important works on late imperial *neidan* and female alchemy. Slightly later, a new Longmen sublineage was formed under the name Wu-Liu, associated with Wu Shouyang (Chongxu [Infused Emptiness]; 1574–1644) and Liu Huayang (Chuanlu [Transmission Vessel]; 1735–1799), a Chan Buddhist monk.[20] The works of these individuals became highly influential in late imperial and modern Daoist (and non-Daoist) circles.

With Baiyun guan as its monastic headquarters, Quanzhen maintained its political and religious supremacy throughout the Qing dynasty and into the modern period (see Goossaert 2007). However, members of Quanzhen in particular and organized Daoism more generally suffered major challenges with the end of imperial rule in 1912, which corresponds to the so-called Republican period (1912–1949; 1949–present). This resulted in a disruption of traditional patronage patterns and monastic life. On a social and political level, there was a corresponding disparagement of traditional Chinese culture and religious commitment. At the same, Chen Mingbin (1854–1936), the abbot of Baiyun guan, initiated the formation of the first national Daoist association, called the Daojiao hui, in 1912 (Qing et al. 1995, 4.291; Goossaert 2007, 74–80). This was the predecessor organization to the Zhongguo daojiao xiehui (Chinese Daoist Association), which was founded in 1957. The trend toward secularization and Westernization, specifically under the influence of Western political ideologies and

---

19. Thomas Cleary (1986a; 1991) has published a variety of general-audience translations based on Liu Yiming's *Daoshu shier zhong* (Twelve Daoist Works), collected as a variety of separate works in volume 8 of the *Zangwai daoshu*.

20. Eva Wong (1998) has published a general-audience translation of some texts from the *Wu-Liu xianzong* (Immortal Tradition of Wu and Liu), which also appear as separate texts in volume 7 of the *Daozang jiyao* and volume 5 of the *Zangwai daoshu*.

belief systems, culminated in the Communist revolution, the establishment of the People's Republic of China in 1949, and the so-called Cultural Revolution (1966–1976). Many Quanzhen monastics were forced to return to lay life and to renounce Daoist religious beliefs, and most Quanzhen monasteries and sacred sites were converted into governmental holdings, and military posts and storage facilities. It was not until the economic and social reforms of Deng Xiaoping (1904–1997) beginning in 1978 that mainland Chinese Quanzhen commenced a gradual process of revitalization. Under the national leadership of members of the Chinese Daoist Association and its regional and local affiliates, Quanzhen Daoists have initiated and supported a variety of important projects. One of the most noteworthy was the compilation, editing, and publication of the *Zhonghua daozang* (Chinese Daoist Canon; abbr. ZH) in 2005. Edited by Wang Ka of the Chinese Academy of Social Sciences and nominally by Zhang Jiyu (b. 1962), a prominent Zhengyi priest and the vice-president of the Chinese Daoist Association, the *Zhonghua daozang* is the first punctuated edition of the Ming-dynasty Daoist Canon; it also contains punctuated versions of the Dunhuang manuscripts, but omits most extra-canonical and post-Ming-dynasty texts (see Komjathy 2002). Major restoration of Quanzhen temples and monasteries has also been initiated and completed. In terms of contemporary Daoism, the major provincial centers of Quanzhen include Hubei, Shaanxi, and Sichuan. Important sacred sites and temples in mainland China include Baxian gong (Eight Immortals Palace; Xi'an, Shaanxi), Baiyun guan (White Cloud Monastery; Beijing), Chongyang gong (Palace of Chongyang; Huxian, Shaanxi), Huashan (Mount Hua; near Huayin, Shaanxi), Kunyu shan (Kunyu Mountains; near Yantai and Weihai, Shandong), Longmen dong (Dragon Gate Grotto; near Longxian, Shaanxi), Louguan tai (Lookout Tower Monastery; Zhouzhi, Shaanxi), Laoshan (Mount Lao; near Qingdao, Shandong), Qingcheng shan (Azure Wall Mountain; Guanxian, Sichuan), Qingyang gong (Azure Ram Palace; Chengdu, Sichuan), Wudang shan (Mount Wudang; near Shiyan, Hubei), and Yongle gong (Palace of Eternal Joy; Ruicheng, Shanxi).[21] With decreasing centralized political and religious control from the late 1990s to the present, members of Quanzhen have also become more public about differences in practice models and lineage affiliations. This has resulted in the revitalization of other, "non-Longmen" lineages, including Huashan, Jinshan, Wudang, and so forth (author's field observations). The Longmen lineage emphasizes precept study and application; Huashan focuses on quietistic meditation, lineage-specific *neidan* techniques, and mountain contemplation; Jinshan involves lineage-specific *neidan* methods and martial arts; and Wudang is most well known for martial arts, specifically its synthesis of Bagua zhang (Eight Trigram Palm), Taiji quan (Yin-yang Boxing), and Xingyi quan (Form Intent Boxing).[22] Contemporary Quanzhen has also witnessed the ascendancy of Quanzhen nuns (*kundao*; *nüguan*) as monastic leaders, especially in Hunan and Sichuan, and a corresponding emphasis on female alchemy (*nüdan*). In contemporary Quanzhen monasteries, the primary form of communal religious practice centers on recitation of the morning and evening liturgy, which is titled *Xuanmen risong zaowan gongke* (Morning and Evening Liturgy of the Mysterious Gate for Daily Recitation) or *Quanzhen zaowan tan gongke* (Morning and Evening Liturgy of Complete Perfection).[23]

---

21. For some insights on Daoist sacred sites see Hahn 2000; Qiao 2001.

22. The Wudang lineage is more complex, as it is not necessarily Quanzhen or Quanzhen in all cases. Since the rise of Mount Wudang as a Daoist center from the Yuan dynasty (1279–1368) to the present, the mountain has been characterized by the coexistence of both Zhengyi and Quanzhen, and Zhengyi was actually dominant there in Yuan-Ming times. See, e.g., Lagerwey 1992; De Bruyn 2004; 2010.

23. For a Chinese Quanzhen commentary on the Quanzhen liturgy see Min et al. 2000. For a rudimentary academic study see Kim 2006.

With the social and cultural disruptions caused by the Communist takeover and Cultural Revolution, Quanzhen has also become a global religious tradition in the contemporary period. Although understudied, there are Quanzhen religious communities in Australia, Brazil, Canada, France, Hong Kong, Italy, Singapore, Switzerland, Taiwan, and the United States.[24] Most of these groups and organizations are affiliated with the Longmen and Wudang lineages, at least in name.[25] With the global dissemination and transformation of Quanzhen, there are increasing disjunctures and incongruities between the official mainland monastic order and its associated diaspora and convert communities. For example, in the case of Longmen, many of the groups are lay and do not adhere to core Longmen ethical requirements, including vegetarianism, abstinence from intoxicants, and celibacy. Differences in beliefs and practices are related to issues regarding identity, affiliation, and connection. The globalization of Longmen is complicated, and perhaps ironically supported, by the decentralized nature of Quanzhen religious leadership. Major global Quanzhen organizations include the Ching Chung Taoist Association (Hong Kong, Australia, Canada), British Taoist Association, French Taoist Association, Italian Taoist Association, and Swiss Taoist Association.[26] Most of these groups model themselves on the Chinese Daoist Association (CDA/CTA), which, it should be recognized, is primarily a political organization. More research, in turn, needs to be done on the actual lineage connections and historical origins of the given communities. For the global Quanzhen community, perhaps this book may deepen their understanding, connection, and practice in conversation with some of the source texts of the tradition.

Based on this brief overview of Quanzhen Daoist history, from its origins in the life and teachings of Wang Chongyang to its diverse expressions in the contemporary world, we may, for heuristic purposes and developing my earlier periodization (Komjathy 2007a, 33–36; cf. Yao 1980a; Goossaert 1997), identify a variety of historical phases: (1) formative (1161–1167); (2) incipient organized (1167–1173); (3) organized (1173–1223); (4) expansive (1223–1368); (5) resurgent (1655–1911); (6) modern (1912–1978); (7) contemporary (1978–present). The formative phase dates from Wang Chongyang's decision to fully commit to a Daoist religious way of life and his gathering of the first-generation disciples. The incipient organized phase dates from the coalescing of the early religious community, including the establishment of the five Shandong associations, to the completion of the three-year mourning period following Wang Chongyang's death. The organized phase corresponds to the early ministerial work of the first-generation adherents, the formation of the Quanzhen patriarchate, and the meeting of Qiu Changchun with Chinggis Qan. The expansive phase dates from Chinggis Qan's recognition of Qiu Changchun and Qiu's ascendancy to the position of abbot of Tianchang guan, including the institutionalization and growth of Quanzhen monasticism, to the loss of imperial favor at the end of the Yuan dynasty. The resurgent phase includes Wang

---

24. On Quanzhen Daoism in Hong Kong see Tsui 1991; You 2002; Li et al. 2007. For some academic studies of American Daoism see Komjathy 2003a; 2003b; 2004; 2006. Other important information may be found on the Center for Daoist Studies website (www.daoistcenter.org).

25. There are a variety of ways to determine the validity of modern Quanzhen religious affiliation: ordination certificates, ordination registers, lineage names based on lineage poems (*paishi*), and ethnographic fieldwork involving interviews with teachers. On the religious side, the matter is complicated by the central importance of self-cultivation, revelation, and mystical experience in Daoism. On the sociopolitical and economic side, one must be aware of the increasing and troubling practice of selling ordination certificates to foreigners by some mainland Chinese monastics. This is most common among non-temple-based Daoists in Beijing, Hubei, and Sichuan as well as in the Wudang shan and Longhu shan environs.

26. Like the CDA, most of these groups have websites.

Changyue's revitalization and standardization of Quanzhen monasticism, his formulation of an official Longmen lineage, and the eventual patronage of the Qing imperial elite. The modern phase includes the end of dynastic rule and imperial patronage, including a movement toward increasing secularization, modernization, and detraditionalization. Finally, the contemporary phase begins with Deng Xiaoping's social and economic reforms (1978) and extends to the recent revitalization and globalization of Quanzhen.

Quanzhen Literature

Quanzhen literature includes any text that was composed by or is associated with a Quanzhen religious adherent; they are literary works whose authors have affiliation with the Quanzhen tradition and which originate in a Quanzhen religious context (see Schipper and Verellen 2004, 1130–31).[27] By definition, no Quanzhen text can predate the life of Wang Chongyang (1113–1170), the movement's founder. Such pre-Quanzhen works, usually earlier Daoist scriptures (*daojing*), became part of the religious tradition, but they are not Quanzhen in origin or content. Taken as a whole, the Quanzhen literary corpus consists of the following genres: poetry, as contained in anthologies (*ji*); discourse records / recorded sayings (*yulu*); instructions (*jue*); discourses (*lun*); commentaries (*zhu*); records (*lu/ji*); hagiographies (*zhuan*); precepts (*jie/lü*); and pure regulations (*qinggui*). In my own research, I have found the following typology to be helpful: (1) literary anthologies; (2) discourse records; (3) didactic texts; (4) scriptures and exegeses; (5) histories, hagiographies, and epigraphy; (6) gazetteers and topographies; (7) precept texts and monastic manuals; (8) ritual and liturgical texts; and (9) encyclopedias.[28]

In an attempt to create congruence with the previous historical periodization, we may make a distinction between four periods of Quanzhen literary production: early (Jin dynasty [1115–1234]), corresponding to the formative, incipient organized, and organized phases; late medieval (late Jin and Yuan [1279–1368]), corresponding to the expansive phase; late imperial (Ming [1368–1644] and Qing [1644–1991]), corresponding to the resurgent phase; and modern (1912–present), corresponding to

---

27. This methodology is complicated by the fact that there are a variety of texts authored by obscure figures and anonymous works in the Ming-dynasty Daoist Canon that seem to originate in Quanzhen religious communities. In the Yuan dynasty and Ming dynasty, there is also the increasing presence of Wang Chongyang and the so-called Seven Perfected in (non-Quanzhen) plays, theater, and popular novels. See, for example, Hawkes 1981; Wong 1990; Idema 1993; Goossaert 2001; Katz 2001. That is, "Quanzhen content" became part of mainstream Chinese culture. As is the case with the category of "Daoist art," such developments bring the issue of origin/context in relation to content/concerns into high relief.

28. Other typologies have been proposed. Judith Boltz (1987), who covers a much broader timeframe and set of Daoist sub-traditions, divides Daoist texts as a whole into revelation and ritual; hagiography; topographic, epigraphic, and historiographic treatises; literary anthologies and dialogic treatises (*yulu*); and exegeses and encyclopedic compilations. Vincent Goossaert (1997, 406–61), influenced by Boltz, utilizes the following: Anthologies littéraires, Les entretiens (*yulu*), Textes didactiques, Classiques et commentaires, and Hagiographie. Yao Tao-chung (2000, 573–581) discusses the early Quanzhen textual corpus in terms of anthologies, cultivation texts, inner alchemy, annotations, hagiographies, and records (specifically of Qiu Chang-chun's meeting with Chinggis Qan). Finally, the section on Quanzhen in *A Historical Companion to the Daozang* (Schipper and Verellen 2004) divides the extant textual corpus into hagiography and biography, *logia* (*yulu*) and collected works, rules and organization, and individual practice. Some later Daoist texts categorized as "Quanzhen" in that work deserve more care-ful reflection. Boltz, Yao, and the contributors to the *Daozang tiyao* (Ren and Zhong 1991) and *A Historical Companion to the Daozang* (Schipper and Verellen 2004) provide details concerning each text. Most of the entries on the early Quanzhen textual corpus in the *Historical Companion* were contributed by Florian Reiter.

the modern and contemporary phases.[29] The early Quanzhen textual corpus, that is, the works associated with the first-generation adherents, consists of about thirty-two extant and "canonical" texts, either independent or anthologized works (see Komjathy 2007a, 382–422). The preferred genre among the early community was poetry; this was followed in prominence by discourse records and, to a lesser extent, by commentaries. According to the contributors to *A Historical Companion to the Daozang* (Schipper and Verellen 2004, 1127–88; see also Goossaert 1997, 412–21), the Ming-dynasty Daoist Canon contains roughly sixty Quanzhen texts in total. Examining these with the intent of identifying patterns, we find that late medieval Quanzhen literature, the works associated with the second-, third-, and fourth-generation adherents, continued to be comprised largely of literary anthologies and discourse records. However, as discussed in chapter 7, members of the Quanzhen monastic order began utilizing new genres, specifically monastic manuals. This was also the time when most of the earliest Quanzhen epigraphic collections and hagiographies were compiled (see chapter 6). Late imperial Quanzhen literature, or more specifically the Longmen literary tradition, is dominated by the works attributed by Wang Changyue (see chapter 7), although much of his work derives from early Daoist sources (see Kohn 2004b). Another interesting dimension of that period of Quanzhen textual production is the composition of *neidan* manuals (see Esposito 2000; 2001), including texts on female alchemy (*nüdan*). These works follow the late imperial trend toward simplification, popularization, and demystification; they provide relatively direct explanations of *neidan* symbolic terminology and methods, often with accompanying illustrations. Although beyond the realm of textual production, it is also noteworthy that members of the late imperial monastic order commissioned major objects of Daoist material culture. Perhaps most famous among these are the steles associated with the Longmen monk and court eunuch Liu Chengyin (Suyun (Pure Cloud; d. 1894), namely, the *Neijing tu* (Diagram of Internal Pathways) (see Komjathy 2008b; 2009) and *Xiuzhen tu* (Diagram of Cultivating Perfection) (see Despeux 1994). Although their writings lack the same degree of cultural capital and religious standing as the earlier literature, members of the modern Quanzhen tradition continue to produce important works. Among the most representative and influential are the late Min Zhiting's (Yuxi [Jade Rivulet]; 1924–2004) monastic manual, titled *Daojiao yifan* (Daoist Religious Models; 1990; cf. Chen Yaoting 2003), and Ren Farong's (b. 1936) commentaries on the *Daode jing* and *Yinfu jing*. To date, no attention has been given to contemporary, international Quanzhen writings, although the Center for Daoist Studies has begun important archival work on this topic.

As discussed in detail later, the present anthology gives primary consideration to the early Quanzhen textual corpus. Here it should be mentioned that there are other important, though less well-known materials relevant for the study of Quanzhen. These include epigraphy (stele inscriptions) and gazetteers (geographical directories and place-specific histories). The most important early epigraphic collection is the late-thirteenth-century *Ganshui xianyuan lu* (Record of the Immortal Stream of Ganshui; DZ 973) by Li Daoqian (Hefu [Harmonious Beginning]; 1219–1296). Many of the hagiographies are based on epigraphic sources in this collection. Relevant materials are also contained in the modern collection *Daojia jinshi lue* (Collection of Daoist Epigraphy; 1988) by Chen Yuan (1880–1971) and colleagues. The most detailed study of Quanzhen social and institutional history based on epigraphy is Vincent Goossaert's dissertation (1997). That work also contains a

---

29. As not much research has been done on post-Ming and "extra-canonical" Quanzhen texts, this account must be taken as tentative, preliminary, and subject to revision.

fairly comprehensive catalogue of relevant inscriptions, totaling about 270 in number (531–57; see also Goossaert 2001; Wang 2005), including sources not collected by Chen. Through the Daoist Studies Research Group of the Institute of Religion, Science, and Social Studies, Professor Jiang Sheng and I have begun collecting materials related to Shandong Daoism; in the course of this research, members have discovered previously unknown sacred sites and steles related to Quanzhen history and religious activity. These materials will eventually be published in a large-format book, which is tentatively titled *Shandong daojiao zhi* (Record of Shandong Daoism; cf. Mou et al. 2005; Shandong 2005; Zhao 2009).

Voluminous amounts of Quanzhen literature have also been lost. As documented in my notes to the hagiographies in chapter 6, there are some twenty-seven lost works associated with the first-generation adepts. Vincent Goossaert (1997, 424–32) has identified a total of eighty-one lost works from the formative phase to the expansive phase of Quanzhen history, from 1170 to 1368 in his study. A wider variety of Quanzhen literature also exists in extra-canonical collections and uncollected manuscripts. With respect to the pre-imperial textual corpus, the following are some important works not contained in the Ming-dynasty Daoist Canon:

1. *Laojun bashiyi hua tu* (Illustrations of the Eighty-one Transformations of Lord Lao) by Shi Zhijing (1202–1275), which is extant in three Ming-dynasty editions (see Reiter 1990b)

2. *Qizhen xianzhuan* (Immortal Biographies of the Seven Perfected; 1417), which expands on an earlier work by Wang Cui (d. 1243)

3. *Quanzhen zongyan fangwai xuanyan* (Mysterious Words from the Realm of Ancestral Perceptions of Quanzhen), which is a later and slightly altered version of the *Minghe yuyin* (Lingering Overtones of the Calling Crane; DZ 1400; 1347) edited by Peng Zhizhong

4. *Xiyou lu* (Record of Westward Travels; 1229) by Yelü Chucai (1190–1244) (see de Rachewiltz 1962)

5. *Xuanfeng qinghui tu* (Illustrations of Celebrated Meetings of Mysterious Currents; 1274/1305) by Shi Zhijing (1202–1275) (see Katz 2001)

In terms of imperial and modern Quanzhen literature, a thorough study of extra-canonical textual collections, that is, collections that postdate the Ming-dynasty Daoist Canon (see Komjathy 2002), will reveal historically significant works of enduring value. Interestingly, there are a number of works attributed to the first-generation disciples. The actual provenance of these compositions awaits further research, but the titles are as follows: *Wupian lingwen* (Numinous Writings in Five Sections; JY 202; ZW 866) attributed to Wang Chongyang, and the *Qiuzu quanshu jieji* (Complete Collated Works of Patriarch Qiu; JH 45), attributed to Qiu Changchun. Other unexplored or underutilized works include the *Qinggui xuanmiao* (Pure Regulations, Mysterious and Wondrous; ZW 361), *Quanzhen yaodao* (Essential Way of Complete Perfection; JH), and *Qunxian ji* (Anthology of Various Immortals; ZW 707). Utilizing the extra-canonical collections, especially the *Daozang jiyao* and *Daozang xubian*, major work on the resurgent phase and late imperial Quanzhen literature has been conducted by Monica Esposito (2000; 2001); Esposito's research emphasizes the literary productions of Wang Changyue (Kunyang [Paradisiacal Yang]; 1594?–1680), Min Yide (Lanyun [Lazy Cloud]; 1758–1836), and Liu

Yiming (Wuyuan [Awakening to the Origin]; 1734–1821). Unfortunately, almost none of this literature has been rendered into sound translations with appropriate historical contextualization, exegesis, and annotation. With respect to manuscripts, many relatively unknown and perhaps undiscovered works are housed in the collection of the Zhongguo guojia tushuguan (National Library of China) and in Japanese collections, both private and public.[30] No doubt future research will reveal a history of textual production and a textual corpus even more complex than this brief account suggests.

When one considers the Quanzhen textual corpus as a whole, especially as expressed in the early literature that became formative for the Quanzhen literary tradition, it is difficult to make general comments or to identify general characteristics. Among scholars of Quanzhen, Vincent Goossaert has, perhaps, been the most daring in characterizing Quanzhen literature. For example,

> Our lack of a fundamental text defining a Quanzhen identity is not an effect of faulty transmission. There was indeed no such thing as a specific Quanzhen scriptural tradition, because there is no Quanzhen revealed scripture. Of course, Wang Zhe, later Quanzhen masters, as well as a number contemporary religious seekers not belonging to the order met with immortals and received from them poems and oral instructions. These revelations, however, were of a personal nature and were not meant to be the basis of a written tradition. . . . The ultimate authority within the early Quanzhen order was not a fundamental text but the action and speech of the patriarchs and masters. . . . [T]he huge majority of Quanzhen literature is either performative or narrative: it proposes a detailed pedagogy in action, by exhorting adepts and telling the exemplary story of the order's patriarchs and former masters. It aims at convincing auditors and readers to join the order and imitate its patriarchs. As such, this literature can be considered a huge repertory of fragments of contextualized teachings that together form a Quanzhen lore. (2001, 120–21; see also Boltz 1987, 137–39)

Similarly, the general introduction to Quanzhen texts in *A Historical Companion to the Daozang* contains the following statement:

> The major problem with Quanzhen writings lies in their unsystematic nature. Quanzhen is not a revelation, and there is no founding scripture on which the whole tradition can be said to rest. The fact that the school produced no classic was considered a blemish by the early Ming theoretician Zhao Yizhen [d. 1382]. For a school with a deep sense of its unity and mission, the corpus left by Quanzhen is dispersed and heterogeneous. (Schipper and Verellen 2004, 1130; see also 1132, 1134–35, 1142–43, 1167–69)

We may accept Goossaert's characterizations, specifically his insight regarding the lack of a "founding scripture"[31] and the contextualized nature of Quanzhen writings. The poetry, discourse records, and

---

30. Like Daoist material culture more generally, the history, politics, and ethics of these and similar collections deserve further study. Those responsible for every collection should provide information on the sources and contexts of acquisition.

31. This claim, however, deserves some qualification. While Quanzhen, unlike most of the other major Daoist movements in Chinese history, was not based upon revealed scriptures, it was still rooted in revelation and mystical experience on some level. For example, Wang Chongyang supposedly received a series of secret transmissions from the immortals Zhongli Quan and Lü Dongbin (see Komjathy 2007a; chapter 6 herein). Many of the early adepts also received spirit transmissions from Wang Chongyang (see chapter 6 herein). In addition, Quanzhen "canonized" a variety of earlier Daoist scriptures as part of the movement's doctrinal foundation (see chapter 5 herein).

didactic texts in particular document Quanzhen adherents as intensely focused on their own inner cultivation and on directing the spiritual development of other dedicated practitioners and lay supporters. Their teachings addressed the specific needs and concerns of a given disciple, inquirer, or community. However, the "ultimate authority" within the early Quanzhen movement was not simply based on the guidance of teachers; it also rested in each individual's personal study, practice, and experience. Here one may note the central importance of mystical experience and spiritual realization in the early community (see Komjathy 2007a, 216–61). Diversity is evident in the writings of the first-, second-, and third-generation adherents themselves. While this "heterogeneity" may be a "major problem" for some, apparently subverting the Quanzhen commitment to "unity," from a different perspective it may have been respect for that very diversity—diversity emerging through personal practice, understanding, and realization—which created a greater sense of unity. The unity was not bound by fixed doctrine and dogma, but by a commitment to a Daoist religious path that aimed at complete self-transformation and mystical union. Moreover, when we add late medieval and late imperial precept texts and monastic manuals, we also discover a movement toward systematization and standardization. At the same time, members of Quanzhen, whether living during the expansive or resurgent periods, remained committed to Quanzhen models of practice and attainment. With respect to the writings of the first-generation adherents, early Quanzhen literature documents a religious community dedicated to a soteriological system that involved asceticism, seclusion, internal alchemy, alchemical transformation, and mystical experience and being (see Komjathy 2007a). Such commitments have remained primary defining characteristics of Quanzhen throughout its history, even if more systematized and institutionalized. They are documented in the surviving literature from every historical period and in the lives of dedicated members of the Quanzhen movement.

A final point concerns the place of Quanzhen literature in history and practice, both religious and secular. Specifically, one may wonder about the influence of Quanzhen literature on Daoist adherents and communities and on Chinese society and culture more generally. Preliminary study indicates that later Quanzhen adepts, especially members of its core spiritual elite, revered earlier patriarchs and masters as embodiments of Daoist practice and attainment, as models for their own inward potential, and as ideals deserving emulation. Those individuals expressed and inspired each adept's own aspirations for spiritual realization and immortality. Moreover, the central importance of a master-father (shifu) and oral instructions (koujue), direct one-to-one transmission and spiritual direction, has been constant throughout Quanzhen history. Thus, the lived religiosity documented in the poetry, discourse records, and hagiographies, as well as in the oral histories derived from them, served less to establish rigid doctrinal conformity than to inspire consistent and prolonged Daoist training. When analyzed in terms of intertextuality, references to the early textual corpus in the writings of later adepts are relatively scarce. For example, in their associated discourse records (DZ 1310; DZ 1059), Yin Zhiping (Qinghe [Clear Harmony]; 1169–1251) and Wang Zhijin (Qiyun [Residing-among-Clouds]; 1178–1263), both disciples of Qiu Changchun, are more content to recount the oral teachings and experiences of their masters than to cite their writings. Considering the Quanzhen corpus as a whole, authors most often cite canonical Daoist scriptures (e.g., *Daode jing*, *Qingjing jing*), rather than the works of Quanzhen masters.

When one turns to the larger contours of Chinese history and elite culture, one finds an even stronger lack of interest in Quanzhen literature. Specifically, there are very few Yuan and Ming editions of Quanzhen works that survive in independent editions. Quanzhen anthologies were rarely found in large private libraries, and Quanzhen poetry was infrequently included in imperial anthologies of classical poetry. Moreover, only thirty-six Quanzhen works are listed in bibliographic catalogues of the Ming and Qing, with the literary anthologies being underrepresented (Goossaert 1997, 436–38; Schipper and Verellen 2004, 1133; see also Yao 1977; van der Loon 1984; Katz 2001, 169–74).

Here I would also apply the distinction between "texts in general circulation" and "texts in internal circulation" in a slightly different way than advocated in *A Historical Companion to the Daozang*, wherein the former refers to works that circulated throughout Chinese society (e.g., *Daode jing* and *Zhuangzi*) and the latter designates works composed within specific Daoist movements. One would like to know more about Quanzhen views concerning Quanzhen texts. Certain texts indicate that Quanzhen adherents circulated and studied texts only within the confines of Quanzhen communities; that they considered it inappropriate and even perilous to disseminate them outside the monastic order; and that they believed certain writings were only relevant for individuals committed to a Daoist religious path aimed at spiritual realization, self-transformation, and numinous pervasion.[32] Whether this was a matter of sacrality, secrecy, and esotericism or intended to establish and maintain the parameters of religious affiliation is an open question. In any case, "internal circulation" might be taken as texts only circulated *within* the Quanzhen religious community, specifically among ordained and lineage-based members of the tradition. There are some writings understood as "inner texts." What these and similar comments do not account for is the practice of engraving Quanzhen poems on stone cliffs and boulders. Although yet to be fully documented, an excellent example of this practice exists in the courtyard of Taiqing gong (Palace of Great Clarity), the base-temple at Laoshan (Mount Lao; near Qingdao, Shandong). These are ten poems written by Qiu Changchun when he visited the temple in 1209 (*Panxi ji*, DZ 1159, 2.14a–15a). In terms of contemporary mainland Chinese Quanzhen, it is noteworthy that Min Zhiting included selections from many of the early discourse records in his *Daojiao yifan* (240–56). The *Chongyang lijiao shiwu lun* (DZ 1233; trl. in chapter 3) has also been circulated as a free pocket-size booklet throughout mainland China, and a recently engraved stele was erected in the monastic compound of Yuquan yuan (Temple of the Jade Spring), the base-temple of Huashan (Mount Hua; near Huayin, Shaanxi). The stele is located in front of the Qizhen dian (Shrine to the Seven Perfected).

Scripture Study and Contemplative Reading

Daoist scriptures (*daojing*)[33] exerted a formative influence on Wang Chongyang and the first-generation Quanzhen adherents, and they continued to occupy a central place during every period of Quanzhen history. The most influential texts include the fourth-century BCE *Daode jing* (Scripture

---

32. See, for example, section 23a of the *Jinguan yusuo jue* (DZ 1156; trl. Komjathy 2007a); section 6a of the *Chongyang lijiao shiwu lun* (DZ 1233; trl. in chapter 3 herein); section 21ab of the "Hao Taigu zhenren yulu," as contained in the *Zhenxian zhizhi yulu* (DZ 1256, 1.19a–22b; trl. in chapter 2 herein); and section 2.10b of the *Dadan zhizhi* (DZ 244; trl. in chapter 4 herein).

33. Note that "scripture" is a specific, technical category for Daoist texts. The character *jing*, which in other contexts may be rendered as "canon" or "classic," consists of the *mi* ("silk") radical with *jing* ("watercourse"). Considered poetically, scriptures are threads and streams that form and re-form networks of connection. They connect the Daoist practitioner to both the unnamable mystery that is the Dao and the Daoist tradition, the community of adepts that preceded one, as an energetic and historical continuum.

on the Dao and Inner Power), fourth- to second-century BCE *Nanhua zhenjing* (Perfect Scripture of Southern Florescence; a.k.a. *Zhuangzi*), sixth-century CE *Yinfu jing* (Scripture on the Hidden Talisman; DZ 31), eighth-century *Qingjing jing* (Scripture on Clarity and Stillness; DZ 620), tenth-century *Chuandao ji* (Anthology on the Transmission of the Dao; 263, j. 14–16), as well as other Zhong-Lü texts and the early twelfth-century *Jin zhenren yulu* (Discourse Record of Perfected Jin; DZ 1056). Certain Buddhist scriptures, especially the third-century CE *Xinjing* (Heart Sūtra; T. 250–57) and *Jingang jing* (Vajracchedikā Sūtra; Diamond Sūtra; T. 235–37, 273, 2734), which may date to the second century CE, also received a place of veneration. Of these, the *Daode jing*, *Qingjing jing*, and *Yinfu jing* were especially venerated.

Here I would also draw attention to the fact that members of the monastic order were probably responsible for the composition of new Daoist scriptures.[34] Some likely examples include the following thirteenth-century works:

1. *Yuanshi tianzun shuo dedao liaoshen jing* (Scripture on Realizing the Dao and Understanding Self as Revealed by the Celestial Worthy of Original Beginning; DZ 25; abbr. *Dedao liaoshen jing*; Schipper and Verellen 2004, 1173)

2. *Yuanshi tianzun shuo taigu jing* (Scripture on Great Antiquity as Revealed by the Celestial Worthy of Original Beginning; DZ 102; abbr. *Taigu jing*; Schipper and Verellen 2004, 710–11)

3. *Taishang chiwen donggu jing* (Great High Scripture on Profound Antiquity Written in Red; DZ 106; DZ 107; abbr. *Donggu jing*; Schipper and Verellen 2004, 711), which is an alternatively titled duplicate of the *Taigu jing*

4. *Taishang dongxuan lingbao tianzun datong jing* (Scripture on Great Pervasion as Revealed by the Great High Celestial Worthy of Numinous Treasure and Cavern Mystery; DZ 327; cf. DZ 105; abbr. *Datong jing*; Schipper and Verellen 2004, 744)

The fact that these scriptures almost always appear with Quanzhen commentaries and are included in Quanzhen collections—even to the present day—adds support for a Quanzhen provenance (Schipper and Verellen 2004, 1132). The presentation of these texts as "Lingbao (Numinous Treasure) scriptures" probably represents an attempt to provide legitimacy to their composition; as discussed briefly earlier, Quanzhen adopted the standardized Lingbao Daoist ritual, which included the use of scriptures from the Lingbao canon. In terms of noteworthy commentaries, Li Daochun (Yingchan [Shimmering Toad]; fl. 1288–1306), a lineage-descendant (second-generation) of Bai Yuchan (1134–1229), wrote commentaries on the *Datong jing* and *Donggu jing* (DZ 105; DZ 107). The scriptures are cited in section 14b of the *Chuzhen jie* as well (trl. in chapter 7). There are also two additional scriptures that bear the imprint of Quanzhen: the *Taishang laojun nei riyong miaojing* (Wondrous Scripture for Daily Internal Practice of the Great High Lord Lao; DZ 645; also *Qunxian yaoyu zuanji*, DZ 1257, 1.1ab; abbr. *Nei riyong jing*; trl. Kohn 2000; Komjathy 2008a) and the *Taishang laojun wai riyong miaojing* (Wondrous Scripture for Daily External Practice of the Great High Lord Lao; DZ

---

34. This fact does contradict the earlier point about there being no "founding Quanzhen scriptural tradition," as these scriptures derive from a later moment in Quanzhen religious history.

646; abbr. *Wai riyong jing*; trl. Kohn 2000). The *Wai riyong jing* was engraved in stone in 1352 and erected at Louguan tai (Lookout Tower Monastery; Zhouzhi, Shaanxi) (Schipper and Verellen 2004, 1187–88).[35] The *Nei riyong jing* continues to be studied and applied in contemporary Quanzhen monastic communities (author's field observations). The importance of scripture study in Quanzhen Daoism is confirmed by the large number of Quanzhen commentaries, both extant and lost (see chapter 5).[36]

Formal scripture study (*jingxue*) was a central practice of the early Quanzhen community and remained so throughout the various periods when the monastic order flourished. This is also the case in contemporary Quanzhen monastic communities, with the *Daode jing*, *Qingjing jing*, and *Yinfu jing* being primary.[37] Among the early Quanzhen adepts, we find a variety of perspectives on the relative importance of scripture study. For example, in an oft-quoted poem Wang Chongyang explains,

> [To practice spiritual refinement] you must fully understand the three hundred characters of the *Yinfu jing* and read up on the five thousand words of the *Daode jing*. (*Quanzhen ji*, DZ 1153, 13.7b–8a)

On a more general level, Wang Chongyang gives the following advice on reading and understanding Daoist texts:

> The way to study texts is not to strive after literary merit, and thereby confuse your eyes. Instead, you must extract the meaning as it harmonizes with the heart-mind. Abandon texts after you have extracted their meaning and grasped their principle. Abandon principle after you have realized the fundamental ground. After you realize the fundamental ground, then attend to it until it completely enters the heart-mind. (*Chongyang lijiao shiwu lun*, DZ 1233, 1b–2a)

For Wang, and this view is clearly representative of the early Quanzhen adepts as a whole, the aspiring adept must reflect on the place of scripture study in his or her own life and practice. The relevance

---

35. Here I refer to the sacred site as "Louguan tai" for convenience's sake. Technically speaking, this is anachronistic. From the Tang dynasty (618–907) to 1862, there were two main Daoist temples in the Zhongnan mountains near the historical Louguan: Zongsheng gong (Palace of the Ancestral Sage) and Shuojing tai (Terrace of the Revealed Scripture). The designation of "Louguan" either referred to the temple compound consisting of the two temples and others, or denoted Zongsheng gong specifically. There was no Louguan tai yet. It was only after 1862 when Zongsheng gong was destroyed in wars that the name "Louguan tai" appeared. This situation has continued to the present day.

36. On lost Quanzhen texts see Goossaert 1997, 424–32; nine commentaries from early and late medieval Quanzhen literature are no longer extant. Unfortunately, *A Historical Companion to the Daozang* does not include Quanzhen commentaries on Daoist scriptures in the Quanzhen section. Rather, they appear in the commentary entries to the specific texts, which are often problematically categorized as "philosophy." Relevant works include the following: DZ 100 (723), DZ 101 (724), DZ 102 (710–11), DZ 105 (710), DZ 106 (711), DZ 107 (711), DZ 122 (696–97), DZ 126 (699–700), DZ 137 (1174), DZ 313 (725), DZ 401 (789), DZ 727 (686–87), DZ 755 (728), DZ 699 (659), DZ 760 (730), DZ 974 (730), and DZ 1336 (718–19). DZ 122, DZ 137, and DZ 974 are translated in chapter 5 in the present anthology.

37. This is so much the case that these texts are included in a modern list of "five scriptures" (*wujing*) and "four books" (*sishu*) of Daoism, which are canonical designations adopted from Confucianism. With respect to internal cultivation, the former include the *Daode jing*, *Huangting jing*, *Yinfu jing*, *Qingjing jing*, and *Longhu jing*, while the latter refer to the *Cantong qi*, *Wuzhen pian*, *Sanhuang yujue*, and *Qinghua miwen*. Min and Li 1994, 945.

of scripture study is relative to the individual practitioner, and such relevance is based on his or her affinities and commitments. Reading and study (and translation) may support Daoist practice, or they may become a distraction. In a Quanzhen context, the point of reading and study is to deepen practice. One endeavors to apply a given text's insights to one's daily life. Scripture study thus is not only an intellectual exercise; it is also a spiritual one.[38] According to Wang, one must focus on the transformational experience and influence of reading Daoist scriptures. Here there is a complex interplay among study, practice, and experience. Study without practice and experience may lead to a lack of discernment concerning relevance; practice and experience without study may lead to various forms of self-delusion. From a Daoist perspective, this is because scriptures (*jing*) are, etymologically and theologically speaking, threads and watercourses that form and re-form networks of connection. They connect the Daoist adherent to both the unnamable mystery that is the Dao and the Daoist tradition, the community of adepts that preceded one, as a historical and energetic continuum. It is that community and tradition that may correct mistaken views and egoistic distortions. This is so much the case that Daoists frequently refer to the external Three Treasures (*wai sanbao*): the Dao, the scriptures, and the teachers (*shi*).

Other members of the early Quanzhen community also commented on the relative importance of scripture study. Two statements from Ma Danyang will help to qualify any definitive statements about Quanzhen views on reading Daoist texts.[39] On one occasion, Ma confronted his disciple Wang Yizhong (see chapter 3 in this volume) on the potential detrimental effects of excessive reading:

> "Now, the Dao wants to form a contract with the heart-mind. If you can attain such a condition through literature, when is it time to awaken? Therefore, in terms of awakening to the Dao, [reading] the *Nanhua* is delusion becoming even more deluded." (DZ 1057, 3b)[40]

This is not an authoritarian statement on either the *Zhuangzi* in particular or scripture study in general. It is a context-specific admonition for a Quanzhen adept who had become overly engaged in and attached to reading. In the same text but in a different context, Ma comments,

> "When studying the Dao, you should not read scriptures and books extensively. This confuses consciousness and obstructs Daoist training. If [you want to read], Heshang gong's commentary on the *Daode jing* and Master Jinling's commentary on the *Yinfu jing* [are best]. When you read these two texts, there will be no obstruction." (DZ 1057, 10a)

So, it is not scripture study per se that is the problem from Ma Danyang's perspective; rather, it is *excessive* and consumptive reading that becomes a hindrance to spiritual training. The Quanzhen practitioner is not to read for mere enjoyment or entertainment; the point of scripture study is to

---

38. Cf. the Catholic practice of *lectio divina* ("sacred reading").

39. For some additional references see *Jin zhenren yulu*, DZ 1056, 2a, 3b; *Jinyu ji*, DZ 1149, 1.7b–8a, 2.19b, 5.2a; *Shenguang can*, DZ 1150, 18a, 19a; *Quanzhen ji*, DZ 1153, 10.20b, 21a; *Jinguan yusuo jue*, DZ 1156, 3a, 3b, 4a, 5a, 13a, 16a, 19b; *Ershisi jue*, DZ 1158, 4ab; *Ganshui lu*, DZ 973, 1.8a. See also the hagiographies translated here in chapter 6.

40. See also *Jianwu ji*, DZ 1142, 2.32b.

clarify one's understanding and to deepen one's practice. Ma also emphasizes the importance of discernment when choosing which texts to study and apply.

Quanzhen scripture study involved both informal reading and more formal discipline, namely, the composition of commentaries. Like the work of literary and scholarly translation ("carrying over"), commentarial annotation involves close reading, deep reflection, and careful analysis. It also requires daring, dedication, and inspiration.

Whether or not one is aware of it, reading the texts in the present anthology is a form of scripture study, but there are different types and approaches to reading. In a contemporary American context, one finds oneself in a situation characterized by commodification and material accumulation, by planned obsolescence, instant gratification, and conspicuous consumption. Potential readers are inundated with mass-market publications, including popular "translations" of Daoist texts; walking into large-chain bookstores, one encounters "new fiction" and "new nonfiction," most of which are not worthy of the trees sacrificed for their printing. The writing, reading, and publication of books require care, and the present book has no place in the modern trend toward "consumptive" and "voracious reading." Whether these translations are read as historical artifacts or manifestations of the Dao, they will take time to read. They will need be to be read and probably reread slowly, deliberatively, contemplatively. You will need some degree of interest, commitment, and concentration. As was the case for its forging in various places at different times, reading this book requires consistent and prolonged engagement. This is perhaps even more the case for those, whether Daoist or not, who would read it for spiritual insights and guidance.

For those who choose to embrace the undertaking, Quanzhen literature offers many contributions. In the texts translated within these pages, we find expressions of a religious community committed to self-cultivation and transformation. This is not the spiritual athleticism, egotism, dilettantism, exhibitionism, and materialism that plague the modern world.[41] Members of the early religious community and late medieval monastic order understood religious practice as a lifelong undertaking, filled with challenges as well as exhilarations. There were moments of experiential confirmation, perhaps in the form of mystical encounters or numinous pervasion, but there were also times when one simply ground rocks into smoothened spheres in hidden caves unbeknownst to anyone else. The path toward realization and immortality involved radical self-responsibility and unwavering commitment. It required complete dedication to a Daoist religious path and way of life. Reading Quanzhen texts with an openness to their existential, soteriological, and theological insights may, if one dares, clarify one's own understanding, meaning, and purpose. Considered as a whole, Quanzhen literature provides insights into the underlying patterns of the cosmos and the characteristics of human existence. It provides insights in human psychology, especially from the perspective of spiritual discipline. Quanzhen texts contain detailed instructions on specific forms of Daoist meditation as well as more general admonitions concerning the necessity of daily, moment-to-moment internal practice. They also document the types of activities and forms of community organization conducive to human flourishing.

So, if one engages these texts as religious expressions and biographical dispensations, rather than as material or historical artifacts, one finds a new, perhaps hidden landscape. This involves taking seriously the approach to reading and scripture study advocated by members of the tradition. To read

41. For a counterpoint see Goossaert 2002. Cf. Liu 2004b.

with attentiveness, discernment, and application is to become open to the potential transformative effect of the texts themselves. Such is contemplative reading, a way of approaching texts as more than texts. Rather, they are documentations of individual and communal lifeworlds, expressions of lived religiosity, as well as offerings and petitions to those who follow.

Structure and Translations

The selection of Quanzhen texts translated in the following pages is ample and representative, though not comprehensive. My choices regarding the included texts emerged through years of study, research, and the actual work of translation. It has been informed by international academic research on the Quanzhen religious movement and subsequent monastic order. At various points, I have also discussed my choices with scholars and practicing Quanzhen Daoists in mainland China, Hong Kong, Europe, and the United States. I have also reflected upon the way in which it might become a sourcebook of the Quanzhen tradition, a primer for Quanzhen religious affiliation and commitment, and, perhaps, a seminary textbook to help establish a viable and tradition-based Quanzhen religious community in the West. It is my firm conviction that the texts selected are among the most historically significant and representative. They provide a clear glimpse into the primary concerns, worldviews, practices, goals, and ideals of the Quanzhen tradition. The selection of texts to be translated has been informed by my study of Quanzhen, and that study has, in turn, been influenced by the translation of Quanzhen texts. There is a dialectic at work. At the same time, the reader is well advised to remember that every selection, and every translation for that matter, is an interpretation. This is especially the case with the poetry, which is overwhelming in volume. As my sustained research convinces me that Quanzhen is, first and foremost, a soteriological system focusing on ascetic, alchemical, and mystical practice and realization, this anthology reflects that interpretation. It is not the definitive word on the tradition and cannot, of course, document the full complexity of the tradition.

The anthology gives primary attention to the early Quanzhen religious movement by focusing on texts composed in the formative, incipient organized, and organized phases of Quanzhen history. Generally speaking, these are works composed, with brush and ink on paper, by the first-generation adherents. Some of them were compiled by their direct disciples. The anthology, in turn, includes translations, many of them complete, from fifteen texts associated with the earliest Quanzhen adepts, what was referred to earlier as "early Quanzhen literature." There are also translations of five works from late medieval Quanzhen literature and the expansive phase of Quanzhen history, including the earliest hagiographical accounts of the first-generation adherents. Finally, one text comes from late imperial Quanzhen literature and the resurgent phase of Quanzhen history. The latter work has been included for three primary reasons: it is one of the most important precept texts and monastic manuals; it represents the core of Wang Changyue's Longmen standardization; and it remains one of the central texts of contemporary Longmen.

The book is organized into seven chapters. Chapter 1, "Poetic Insights," includes translations of poems by every first-generation adherent whose work is still extant. Especially significant are the four poem sequences by Sun Buer, which are the only extant writings that can be legitimately ascribed to Sun. The selected poems place primary emphasis on Quanzhen cultivational concerns, practice, and attainment. As mentioned earlier, the literary anthologies and corresponding poetry are the most diverse with respect to content. Many other organizing principles and selection criteria could have been utilized, including place-specific compositions (see Mou et al. 2005; Shandong 2005;

Ding et al. 2007; Komjathy 2010) as well as personal correspondences and social history. Chapter 2, "Direct Instruction," focuses on discourse records associated with the first-generation Quanzhen adherents. It includes complete translations of the following texts: *Jin zhenren yulu* (Discourse Record of Perfected Jin; DZ 1056, 1a–4b), associated with Jin Daocheng (Chongzhen [Exalted Perfection]; fl. 1110?); "Yuhua she shu" (Guidance for the Jade Flower Society; *Quanzhen ji*, DZ 1153, 10.20b–21a) by Wang Chongyang; *Danyang zhenren yulu* (Discourse Record of Perfected Danyang; DZ 1057), associated with Ma Danyang; and "Hao Taigu zhenren yu[lu]" (Discourse Record of Perfected Hao Taigu; abbr. *Zhenxian yulu*, DZ 1256, 1.19a–22b), associated with Hao Guangning. Chapter 3, "Daily Practice," follows the early Quanzhen distinction between "daily external practice" and "daily internal practice," namely, ethical reflection and application, and meditation and internal alchemy, respectively. With respect to the former, it includes two lists of Quanzhen practice principles and ethical commitments; they include the "Ten Admonitions" (*Xianle ji*, DZ 1141, 2.18ab) by Liu Changsheng and the "Ten Admonitions" (*Zhenxian yulu*, DZ 1256, 1.8b–9b) by Ma Danyang. Other works translated in chapter 7 could have been included here, specifically, the "Jiaozhu Chongyang dijun zefa bang" (Sovereign Lord Chongyang's List of Punishments; *Quanzhen qinggui*, DZ 1235, 11b–13a) and the "Chuzhen shijie" (Ten Precepts of Initial Perfection; *Chuzhen jie*, ZW 404, 9ab). With respect to daily internal practice, this chapter contains a translation of the *Chongyang lijiao shiwu lun* (Redoubled Yang's Fifteen Discourses to Establish the Teachings; DZ 1233), which is attributed to Wang Chongyang. Chapter 4, "Alchemical Transformation," includes a translation of the *Dadan zhizhi* (Direct Pointers to the Great Elixir; DZ 244), attributed to Qiu Changchun.

Chapter 5, "Scripture Study," includes translations of two commentaries by members of the first-generation and one commentary by a Quanzhen monk from the expansive phase of Quanzhen history. The texts translated are as follows: *Taishang laojun shuo chang qingjing jing songzhu* (Recitational Commentary on the *Taishang laojun shuo chang qingjing jing*; DZ 974) by Liu Tongwei; *Huangdi yinfu jing zhu* (Commentary on the *Huangdi yinfu jing*; DZ 122) by Liu Changsheng; and *Qingtian ge zhushi* (Commentary on the "Qingtian ge"; DZ 137) by Wang Jie (Daoyuan [Dao's Source]; Hunran [Primordial Suchness]; fl. 1331–1380). Liu Tongwei's text is especially significant because it represents the only extant work by this marginalized early member of the tradition; similarly, Wang Jie's commentary is noteworthy as the only such text focusing on an earlier Quanzhen work, namely, Qiu Changchun's poem titled "Qingtian ge" (Song of the Clear Sky; trl. in chapter 1). Chapter 6, "Hagiographical Ideals," includes translations of hagiographies contained in the *Jinlian zhengzong ji* (Record of the Orthodox Lineage of the Golden Lotus; DZ 173) by Qin Zhian (Shuli [Useless Timber]; 1188–1244) and the *Zhongnan shan Zuting xianzhen neizhuan* (Esoteric Biographies of Immortals and Perfected of the Ancestral Hall of the Zhongnan Mountains; DZ 955) by Li Daoqian (Hefu [Harmonious Beginning]; 1219–1296). Among the former, I have translated the entries on Wang Chongyang, He Dejin, Li Lingyang, and the so-called Seven Perfected; among the latter, the entries on Liu Tongwei, Shi Chuhou, and Yan Chuchang appear. The texts come from the expansive phase of Quanzhen history, and they contain the earliest extant Quanzhen hagiographies for each adherent, some of which are derived from slightly earlier epigraphic sources. The inclusion of members of early Quanzhen beyond the conventional parameters of Wang Chongyang and the Seven Perfected helps to fill in some historical gaps and restore a more integrated view of the early community. Finally, chapter 7, "Monastic Life," contains translations of two late medieval Quanzhen monastic manuals and one late imperial precept text and monastic manual. The translated texts include the *Quanzhen qinggui* (Pure Regulations of Complete Perfection; DZ 1235) by Lu Daohe (Tongxuan [Pervading Mystery]; fl. 1280–1360?); anonymous *Quanzhen zuobo jiefa* (Practical Methods for the

Sinking Bowl-clepsydra from Complete Perfection; DZ 1229); and *Chuzhen jie* (Precepts of Initial Perfection; JY 292; ZW 404) by Wang Changyue.

Each chapter includes a concise historical introduction, which discusses the date and authorship of the text as well as its relationship to other Daoist texts. I also provide information on the contents of the given work. As some texts are more complex and diverse, they require a greater degree of elucidation and mapping. The introductory material concludes with references to previous translations and studies. These introductions are followed by the translations proper, which include annotations when necessary. The most commonly occurring technical terminology appears in appendix 1, Quanzhen Technical Glossary. This is meant to be a concise and essential glossary; for a more technical version see Komjathy 2007a, 435–89. The glossary is followed by a second appendix, Quanzhen Texts Translated in *The Way of Complete Perfection*. The latter lists the twenty-one texts translated in this anthology with the corresponding chapters.

As indicated earlier and as briefly discussed in each chapter, the Quanzhen literary corpus, beginning with the formative phase and continuing to be produced in the contemporary period, is vast and diverse. A comprehensive anthology, which would provide a more accurate glimpse into the historical complexity of the tradition and possibly complexify some of the views that might derive from the present anthology, would actually result in multiple anthologies. It would also require many more years of life than this book represents. Some of those works are contained in the Ming-dynasty Daoist Canon; others exist in extra-canonical editions and manuscripts. Some are beginning to be investigated; others are known only to a few dedicated scholars, caretakers of private libraries, or Daoist archivists; still others have yet to be discovered. I hope that this anthology provides a model for anthologies on other important Daoist movements as well as a future anthology on later periods of Quanzhen history. One may also envision other studies involving alternative methodologies, including art history, ethnography, material culture studies, and so forth.

In any case, the texts translated in *The Way of Complete Perfection* do reveal some of the basic contours, central concerns, practice modalities, and models of attainment characteristic of Quanzhen Daoism. They also provide glimpses into the lives of its spiritual elite and into the communal contexts that supported its growth and development as a monastic order and the dominant form of Daoist monasticism in the modern world. Among the more interesting and relatively unknown contributions is communal Daoist meditation centering on the bowl-clepsydra (*zuobo*). As discussed in chapter 7, this practice became dominant in Quanzhen monasteries during the expansive phase, becoming instituted at the end of the thirteenth century. Quanzhen monastics gathered for a winter meditation retreat during which a sinking bowl-clepsydra marked the cosmological and energetic cycles. Contemplation of the object itself, the "sitting-bowl," becomes a symbol of Quanzhen study and practice, including the multiple layers of meaning and multiple dimensions of approach. For some, such a time-measuring device, with its corresponding metallurgy, might suggest "Daoist science." For others, the related communal, monastic practice, around which monks and nuns coalesced in a seasonal undertaking framed by monastic regulations, might reveal important dimensions of Quanzhen social and institutional history. From a different perspective, the bowl-clepsydra represents dedication to seated meditation and cosmological attunement. Still further, the object reveals an inner landscape of flowing watercourses and storehouses for vital substances.[42] The *zuobo* symbolizes and inspires the fusion of disparate elements into an integrated whole.

---

42. One Daoist reader of the book manuscript suggested the following: "Perhaps we could summarize Quanzhen practice as 'Make sure your bowl is clean.'"

On Translation and Scholarly Conventions

Etymologically speaking, speaking in terms of origins, "translation" relates to the Latin *translatio*, which in turn derives from the past participle stem of *transferre* (*Oxford English Dictionary*). Translation then involves a transference, a "carrying over." To translate is to endeavor to carry over, to transfer a text from one particular sociohistorical context into another. To translate is to transmit, to transport, to translocate. The translator's orientation is, in turn, rooted in an intimate relationship with a given text/context; the translator seeks to maintain this connection, while at the same time transmitting the original text into a new embodiment in a different cultural world. This invariably includes transformation and transfiguration, but it is the extent to which the original connection is maintained that (principally) determines the success of a given translation. This is the orientation of the translator, of "one who carries over."

The relationship between original text and imagined translation, between source language and target language, involves a complicated interplay: the interplay of imagination, of cultural worlds, of potentially irreconcilable languages (distinguished by alternate verb tenses, syntax, metaphor, breadth of vocabulary, etc.) and of projected possibilities. One of the primary concerns of translation involves the extent to which the translation (target language) adheres to or diverges from the original text (source language). The texts translated in *The Way of Complete Perfection* were composed in classical Chinese, a pictographic and ideogrammatic language that differs markedly from English and other Western languages, based as they are on alphabetic scripts in which the relationship between signifier (word) and signified (object) is much more arbitrary. In the case of English, a "dog" could thus be a "cat." In contrast, in classical Chinese and Daoist technical contexts, what is 靈 ("numinous") could not be 惡 ("perverse"), 邪 ("deviant"), or 逆 ("oppositional"). These considerations also bring the relationship between text and context into sharper focus. Every text originates in a specific sociohistorical context. While the extent to which translating a given text necessitating a larger historical knowledge base may vary, in certain cases historical contextualization is a necessary condition for accurate translation. This is especially so with regard to religious texts in general and Quanzhen works in particular.

Having reflected deeply on the actual requirements and applied practice of translation, it is my firm conviction that historical contextualization and scholarly annotation are indispensable for fully understanding a given Daoist text. Translation is close reading, and annotation is concentrated research. This conviction is documented throughout the pages of the present book, though I have done my best to provide only essential and concise notes. The motivating principle involves supplying necessary knowledge to deepen the experience of reading and the process of understanding. In engaging in historical contextualization and providing annotations, my goal has been to make the texts more accessible, to unfold their layers of intertextuality and technical specificity, as well as to open up the meaning-system and lifeworld of early Quanzhen Daoism. Simultaneously, I have attempted to preserve their radical alterity, to subvert the all-too-common process of domestication that occurs in translation. These texts come from completely different sociohistorical contexts and radically unfamiliar religious communities. My approach to translating Daoist texts seeks to preserve their unfamiliar textures and allow space for cognitive dissonance. This includes the commitment to provide *complete translations*, rather than dissections and anatomizations that are more recognizable and easily seen as "relevant" or "interesting" (see also Bokenkamp 2002, xxiii). Through a dialectical tension between accessibility and resistance, I hope that the reader will gain a greater appreciation of the text/context of early Quanzhen Daoism.

In my view, the ideal translation is, then, both literary (attentive to language) and scholarly (attentive to historical and cultural context). I have worked hard to convey the tone, style, and content of the source texts. This is challenged by the occasional hermeneutical openness of the texts—some works could be rendered in third- or first-person voice, including the possible use of imperatives directed at the reader. My standard translation methodology has been as follows: (1) initial rendering based on the primary Chinese text; (2) revision based on readability without consultation of the primary Chinese text; and (3) revision based on critical comments by specialist colleagues and comparison of my translation with the primary Chinese text.

The final point that deserves note involves specific scholarly conventions. I have used the original Chinese for personal names, place names, book titles, and so forth. At the first appearance, I provide Pinyin romanization and an English translation. From that point forward, only the Pinyin romanization is given. This stands in contrast to recent tendencies in Western-language publications to utilize English translations of Chinese text titles as though referring to the original texts (see, e.g., Bokenkamp 1997; Campany 2002; Kohn 2004b). My practice helps to remind us that we are reading translations of *Chinese texts* that were composed in *Chinese Daoist contexts*.

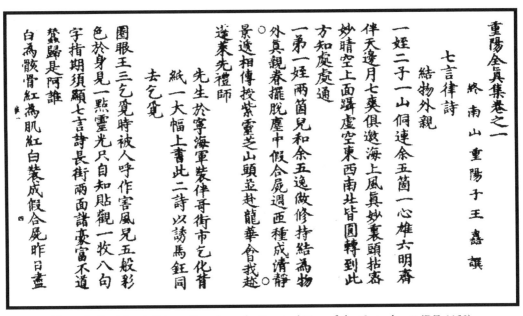

Figure 3. Traditional Chinese Page from the Received Text of the *Quanzhen ji* (DZ 1153)

These texts are not part of some imagined ahistorical, universal wisdom tradition; they are Daoist *religious* texts written in classical Chinese. As such, one would traditionally have read them in unpunctuated versions (originally handwritten manuscripts) with the characters arranged from top-to-bottom and right-to-left. For ease of use, I have also included English translations of the titles in the second appendix. In this way, readers without knowledge of Chinese may have a working equivalents sheet—from *Quanzhen ji* to *Anthology of Complete Perfection*, *Dadan zhizhi* to *Direct Pointers to the Great Elixir*, *Quanzhen qinggui* to *Pure Regulations of Complete Perfection*, and so forth.

In providing work numbers for Daoist textual collections, I utilize the standardized abbreviations and catalogue numbers established in *Title Index to Daoist Collections* (Komjathy 2002). Numbers for the Ming-dynasty Daoist Canon parallel those of Kristofer Schipper's earlier index and used in *A Historical Companion to the Daozang* (Schipper and Verellen 2004). All references to "extra-canonical" collections derive from my earlier reference work. I had hoped to include the original Chinese texts as an appendix, but length concerns precluded this. Except for the *Chuzhen jie*, which appears in the *Daozang jiyao* and *Zangwai daoshu*, all of the texts are contained in the Ming-dynasty Daoist Canon (see Schipper and Verellen 2004). This collection is becoming more readily available through electronic versions. Punctuated editions of pre-imperial Daoist texts are contained in the *Zhonghua daozang* (Chinese Daoist Canon; abbr. ZH; 2005). Punctuated editions of early Quanzhen texts, but with simplified characters, may be found in Bai 2005a and 2005b; Zhao 2005a and 2005b.

In preparation for reading the translations that follow, I invite you to pause and reflect upon the lives, communities, language, and work behind this anthology.

Chapter One

Poetic Insights

The early Quanzhen adepts wrote voluminous amounts of poetry, only a partial record of which survives. Poetry was by far the preferred means of expression in the early Quanzhen religious community. Wang Chongyang and his first-generation disciples employed all of the major Song-Jin genres of Chinese poetry, including lyrics (*ci*), songs (*ge*),[1] regulated verse (*lüshi*), and quatrains (*jueju*). Elegies (*zan*) are also included in some of the hagiographical collections (see chap. 6). While it is apparent that the early Quanzhen adherents studied and applied canonical Daoist scriptures (see chap. 5 herein), the preponderance of poetry and discourse records points toward the importance of context-specific teachings and personal spiritual direction. The extant poetry provides glimpses into the daily lives and activities of Quanzhen adherents as well as into their sociohistorical and communal contexts. Poems addressed to fellow adepts, lay people, and patrons reveal members of the Quanzhen community as engaged and committed teachers. There are also poems that address religious training in specific places at specific times (see Komjathy 2010). However, more often than not, it is difficult to determine the provenance of most poems contained in the literary anthologies.

The translation of Quanzhen poetry represents a major challenge, especially as so little Daoist poetry has been translated to date. One of the principal difficulties involves composing readable and sound English renderings. This challenge is complicated by the relative vagueness and hermeneutical openness of many of the poems. On the basis of literary merit, execution, and significance, few connoisseurs of Chinese poetry would probably designate Quanzhen poetry as worthy of "anthologization." It might simply be categorized as "devotional" or "religious poetry" (cf. Schipper and Verellen 2004, 1127–33, 1142–43). However, the poetry does provide glimpses into the lifeworlds of these religious practitioners. In addition to the challenges of creating readable English poems and interpreting the technical terminology in accurate ways, the syntactic and hermeneutical openness of the poetry allows a number of equally viable and accurate translations/ interpretations. Here it is important to note that I have translated certain poems using a personal voice (first-person; "I"), while others poems are presented as addressed to the reader, with frequent use of second-person pronouns ("you") and an imperative voice. The former provide a sense of the personal dedication among the early adepts with respect to their own self-cultivation; the latter suggest a larger communal context, including a concerned attempt to inspire others to embrace and remain committed to Daoist practice. A third challenge involves selecting representative works. Every selection is an interpretation, and one is well advised to remember the partial nature of

---

1. Technically, *ge*-songs are not an independent genre. Instead, they may be composed in other poetic forms. Nonetheless, as many of the extant Quanzhen poems are *ge*-songs, I use the category as a method of identification.

any presentation. As I understand early Quanzhen as an ascetic, alchemical, and mystical movement (see Komjathy 2007a), I have selected poems that emphasize religious praxis. The poems translated herein provide clear glimpses into and representative expressions of the early religious community.

In the present chapter, I have thus selected poems that express some of the primary concerns and commitments of the early adepts. These include a rejection of ordinary and mundane ways of life, in which dissipation, distortion, and disorientation are the primary defining characteristics. For the early Quanzhen adepts, a dedicated religious life required ascetic commitments, self-cultivation, and alchemical transformation. The present selection includes poems by most of the early adherents, specifically by Wang Chongyang and the so-called Seven Perfected. The poems cover such topics as skeletons and marionettes,[2] renunciation and seclusion, meditative and alchemical praxis, and spiritual realization. I have included some of the most famous and influential verses, such as the "Wuzhen ge" (Song on Awakening to Perfection) by Wang Chongyang and the "Qingtian ge" (Song of the Clear Sky) by Qiu Changchun. In addition, I have included all of the extant poems that can be reasonably and reliably attributed to Sun Buer, the only senior female member of early Quanzhen.[3]

In the first three poems on skeletons and marionettes, we find the early adepts emphasizing the dissipation and meaninglessness of leading an ordinary life. For these religious adherents, ordinary human beings, those not engaging in Daoist cultivation, resemble walking corpses and puppets. These translations are followed by Wang Chongyang's "Song on Awakening to Perfection," a poem that contains biographical details on the founder of Quanzhen and provides one of the clearest expressions of his motivations for becoming a Daoist adept. In the next poem on the Four Hindrances, Wang emphasizes the importance of abandoning such sources of dissipation. The two subsequent poems, "Cultivation and Practice" by Wang Chongyang and "Cultivating the Dao" by Qiu Changchun, provide glimpses into basic Quanzhen cultivational concerns. These are complemented by the four poems by Sun Buer, wherein one finds a strong emphasis on alchemical transformation. Note that these "poems" are *ci*-lyrics, meaning that they are written to particular musical tunes (*cipai*) that follow a standardized formal structure. The next poem is one of a series of poems on the "five night-watches" (*wugeng*), also referred to as the "five drum-soundings" (*wugu*). In the context of early Quanzhen, *wugeng* training involved engaging in intensive Daoist practice during the five double-hours of darkness (see Goossaert 2000; Komjathy 2007a, 175–79). Next, I offer translations of two series on Quanzhen alchemical praxis, one by Wang Yuyang and the other by Hao Guangning. Although abstract and often frequently difficult to decipher, they are among a rare group of writings that assist one in reconstructing the Quanzhen alchemical system. As Hao's thirty poems appear to

---

2. The frequent emphasis on "skulls" and "corpses" in early Quanzhen recalls chapter 18 of the *Zhuangzi* where Zhuangzi finds a skull in a field and has a subsequent dream-conversation about freedom from social identity.

3. There are a variety of other texts spuriously attributed to Sun Buer. Most of these date to the Ming (1368–1644) and Qing (1644–1911) dynasties, during which time female alchemy (*nüdan*) became more systematized and Sun Buer was elevated to the position of matriarch. Relevant texts include the *Sun Buer yuanjun fayu* (Dharma Sayings of Primordial Goddess Sun Buer; JY 212; ZW 370) and *Sun Buer yuanjun chuanshu dandao bishu* (Secret Writings on the Way of the Elixir Transmitted by Primordial Goddess Sun Buer; JY 213; ZW 371) (see Boltz 1987, 155–56; Despeux 1990, 170, 292–301; Yao 2000, 578; Despeux and Kohn 2003, 212–14, 241–43). Later poems attributed to Sun appear in various collections, including the *Sun Buer nüdan shi zhu* (Commentary on Sun Buer's Poetry on Female Alchemy; Chen 1934), *Nüdan hebian* (Collected Works on Female Alchemy; Tao 1989, 1–188), and *Nü jindan fayao* (Essential Methods of the Gold Elixir for Women; JH 48) (see Despeux 1990, 170, 291–302; 2000; Despeux and Kohn 2003, 206, 212–14). Sections of this text and the *Sun Buer yuanjun gongfu cidi* (Practices and Stages of Sun Buer; Tao 1989, 282–88) have been translated in Thomas Cleary's *Immortal Sisters: Secret Teachings of Taoist Women* (1989b). Readers should note, however, that none of these works were actually composed by Sun Buer.

be a sequential and integrated series, I have included them in their entirety. The technical details of Quanzhen alchemical praxis may be clarified by consulting my translation of the *Dadan zhizhi* (see chapter 4). The alchemical poems are supplemented by three selections on the fruition or attainment that was expected to come from Quanzhen religious practice. Among the latter, I have included "Elegy on Abandoning Form" by Ma Danyang, which is commonly identified as his "deathbed poem."

Some Quanzhen poetry has appeared in print previously, though readers of the present volume may be unfamiliar with those publications. Wilt Idema has published English translations of most of the poems on the theme of skeletons and marionettes (1993). As Idema has pointed out (1993, 197), the theme of skeletons, and the corresponding reflection on the fragility of human existence, finds a classical Daoist precedent in chapter 18 of the *Zhuangzi* (see Watson 1968, 193–94). Vincent Goossaert has published French translations of Quanzhen poems on the "five night-watches" (2000; also 1999). An English translation of the "Wuzhen ge" was also produced by Florian Reiter (1994). My own renderings have benefited from these earlier translations. In terms of technical terminology, I have provided essential annotations, but many of the commonly occurring terms will be found in the Quanzhen Technical Glossary at the back of the book (see appendix 1).

To the Tune "Groping for Fish" / Wang Chongyang[4]

I lament the skeleton
Lying in the open fields.
Your lonely white bones are scattered,
A vagrant from some unknown place.
There's no way to tell whether you're male or female;
You've been cast aside and completely abandoned.
This is because you did not practice cultivation in former lives,
But rather played around like a foolish monkey
And in this life you have now fallen down.
Wind-blown, rain-drenched, and sun-bleached,
You are beaten by the senseless herding boys.

I wish to inquire about how you came to such an end,
But I still have compassion for your suffering.
How could we converse about this anyway?
Your mouth is filled with mud and sand fills your eyes—
This is the way you will decay.
Forever, day and night,
You count the yearly change of autumn, winter,
Of spring and summer too—
Through all four seasons lonely and alone.[5]
Come to your senses, people old and young
And do not flaunt your smartness, flash your charms.

---

4. *Quanzhen ji*, DZ 1153, 3.8b.

5. "Lonely and alone" translates *gugua*, characters that have been used historically as a self-deprecating term by Chinese emperors.

The Skeleton / Tan Changzhen[6]

Skeleton, oh skeleton, your face is so ugly,
Only because in life you loved beauty and alcohol.
Cunningly smiling you became fattened on ideas and pleasures
So your blood and flesh gradually wasted away.
      Gradually wasting away—But you still continued to lust.
Through greed and avarice, you dissipated your vitality with no completion,
Your desires were without limit but your body had its term
And now today you have become a skeleton!
      Becoming a skeleton—Listen to me:
It is not easy to acquire a human body with Seven Treasures!
Realize that innate nature and life-destiny are like pulling-strings,
So do not blindly follow your emotions!
      That's why I have painted this form to show to you
And see whether or not you will today become awakened!

The Marionette / Ma Danyang[7]

Providing amply for my wife
And lusting for a living,
My body was like a marionette.
Led by fame and profit
I busily did my tricks.
Pulled in a thousand different ways
I was made to act out
All kinds of postures and mad behavior.
Flashing my style
I shook my head, played with my shadow,
And made a full display of my finest sides.

But then I encountered my teacher[8] who told me
My comportment was that of a walking corpse,
My tramping around that of running bones.
When anger resembles the pulling-strings,
How can there be no impermanence?
Hastily I recognized the clouds and streams within the gourd
And tapped the Mysterious Pass,
Where hemp and wheat smell so fragrant.
The dragon coils around the tiger,
And mercury and lead are refined:
When the elixir congeals, I'll become an immortal.

6. *Shuiyun ji*, DZ 1160, 1.18b–19a.

7. *Jinyu ji*, DZ 1149, 10.19b–20a.

8. Wang Chongyang.

Song on Awakening to Perfection / Wang Chongyang[9]

At the age of nine, I had no concern for provincial affairs—
My paternal grandfather dead and mourned at eighty-two years.
At the age of twenty-three, I flourished among glorious days—
My elder uncle dead and mourned at seventy-seven years.
At the age of thirty-three, I realized my greed and lust—
My loving father dead and mourned at seventy-three years.
From antiquity to today, a lifespan of one hundred or seventy years is rare;
Observing this, the sequential passing away, how can I bear it?
At the age of thirty-six, I was soundly asleep within my slumber—
I began demanding that my elder brother share his livelihood.
With overbearing vitality I rushed against heaven, giving rein to my passions;
Morning after morning, day in and day out, I ruined myself in drunkenness.
Taking advantage of the weak, and cheating people, I passed my time;
I slandered my brother, scolded my wife, and had contempt for heaven and earth.
Tending to neither my family's property nor my own person,[10]
I only considered and craved the empty fortunes and reputation of others.
Wealth slipped through my fingers like floating clouds
As the resentment and disdain of my wife and child rose as high as heaven.[11]
Selling off my property to obtain three portions of cash,
Two portions went to my food and clothing, one to my alcohol bill.
I was completely ignorant about what everyone else wore and ate;
I repaid my drinking debts and spoke about my great misfortune.
At the age of forty-eight, I took up contention and warfare—
Through contention, I carefully examined my entire person.
Suddenly, one morning, my heart broke apart;
I became insane,[12] giving myself over to madness.
I ceased being afraid of people ridiculing and laughing at me;
With my whole heart, I only feared obscuring the luminosity of the Three Radiances.
Stilling worries and purifying thoughts, I attended to my own body;
As soon as awakening came, I abandoned wife and child.
I used to love washing my face and, alas, arranging my hair;
People around me would say I was quick to follow prevailing fashions.
With my family's wealth completely squandered, excelling at carelessness,
I dreaded to work like horses and oxen, all for the sake of children and grandchildren.
At the age of fifty-two, light and shade were passing quickly—
To live to seventy years, how many days were really left?
The dangers of the road ahead correspond to the reincarnation cycle—
Old karma is difficult to disperse; to wait in idleness is to be lost.

---

9. *Quanzhen ji*, DZ 1153, 9.11b–12b.

10. "Not tending" translates the Chinese *buxiu*, which in Quanzhen technical terms would be rendered as "not cultivating."

11. It is unclear how many children Wang Chongyang had.

12. *Haifeng*, lit., "injurious wind."

Once one loses this human body, one will cease to be for ten thousand *kalpas*;
How can one find contentment under such circumstances?
We must know this before it's too late, listening while robust and strong—
Abandon grave and graveyard to wander among clouds and waters.[13]
Is anything more enjoyable than wandering among clouds and waters?
To be free from anxiety, free from thought, free from activity.
My only pillow is the clear wind, a consequence of a previous existence;
The luminous moon through one circuit, this is my connection to a former life.

The Four Hindrances / Wang Chongyang[14]

Alcohol

Alcohol, oh alcohol,
So hateful to the lips,
Plundering the mouth.
Innate nature overly obscured,
And spirit unable to flourish.
You injure and ruin the perfect and primordial;
You disperse and wear away longevity.
Half-intoxicated, anxiety fills the bowels;
Completely drunk, the heart-mind's direction is lost.
Toward oneself, unrestrained, mad and wild;
Toward others, not even the most basic dignity.
What is better than abandoning this and waking up to sobriety?
Free from injury, free from calamity, cultivate the double nine.

Sex

Sex, oh sex,
How much calamity,
Dissipating good fortune.
Injuring the golden essence,
Harming the jade fluids.
You diminish and destroy qi and spirit;
You spoil and ruin humaneness and virtue.
You cause the Three Fields to empty,
And make the five organs confused.
You ruin unified nature, numinous and bright;
You exhaust the strength of limbs and sinews.
What is better than abandoning this and becoming everlasting?
Free from injury, free from calamity, extend your attainment.

---

13. This recalls the second discourse of the *Shiwu lun*, where Wang Chongyang discusses "cloud wandering." See chapter 3.
14. *Quanzhen ji*, DZ 1153, 1.18a–19a.

Wealth

Wealth, oh wealth,
How you produce retribution,
Making gradual injury come.
You can only buy appearances;
You can claim cups and glasses.
Yet again you cause virtue to be dispersed,
And then you provoke retribution to arrive.
You increase and extend suffering in the Three Realms,
Making it difficult to escape the calamities of the Nine Subterrains.
You may increase family prosperity and fortune,
But how can such life evade the inevitability of reincarnation!
What is better than abandoning this and gaining constant joy?
Free from injury, free from calamity, every day there is freedom.

Anger

Anger, oh anger,
How you injure spirit,
Harming the stomach.
You invite wildness and ferocity,
And strong desires for worldly things rise up.
Before the Seven Cavities [of Hundun],[15]
The Two Luminants resembled a spring.
But now, the aspiration for the Dao cannot circulate,
And the imperial laws become subordinated to dread.
Quarreling and fighting expose the robber bands;
Contention and vying continue to make chaos and waste.
What is better than abandoning this and enjoying cessation?
Free from injury, free from calamity, you connect with worthiness.

Cultivation and Practice / Wang Chongyang[16]

—1—

No one understands this cultivation and practice;
From the beginning it is only this: recognize perfect compassion.
Both criminals and superior adepts wander among mountains and streams;

---

15. An allusion to chapter 7 of the *Zhuangzi* (Book of Master Zhuang): "The emperor of the South Sea was called Shu (Brevity), the emperor of the North Sea was called Hu (Suddenness), and the emperor of the central region was called Hundun (Primordial Chaos). Shu and Hu from time to time came together for a meeting in the territory of Hundun, and Hundun treated them very generously. Shu and Hu discussed how they could repay his kindness. 'All people,' they said, 'have seven openings so they can see, hear, eat, and breathe. But Hundun alone doesn't have any. Let's try boring him some!' Every day they bored another hole, and on the seventh day Hundun died" (adapted from Watson 1968, 97).

16. *Quanzhen ji*, DZ 1153, 1.14a–16b.

Both scholars and gentlemen have entered the Fiery Pond.
When the white horse neighs, the gold roars in response.
When the azure ox tills the fields, the jade is without flaws.
Between the celestial thoroughfare and terrestrial pillar, mists are luminous;
When elder and matron meet among the dragon's shelter, a child is born.

—2—

The great vessel, cultivated through practice, does not involve discarding the ornamental;
Precious gems, cast aside by the foolish and thoughtless, belong to my lineage.
Facing the clear winds within, I complete the perfect qi;
Raising my gaze to the luminous moon in front, I coalesce the precious sand.
Constantly hold fast to earlier practices, and constantly check their lists;
Then you may accept new developments, and select what's beneficial.
A single pervasion hurled into the space above the clear empyrean
Penetrates the empty Void and manifests in the appearance of sprouts.

—3—

The dragon hums, stretching and rising, while the tiger roars;
Snow and breakers unite as wind, a spiraling whirlpool cast forth.
Thoroughly purify the unified numen, increasing your effort until it is lustrous;
Harmonize and unite the two qi until they become mutually conjoined.
The raven and turtle move to face each other, playing within the ocean;
The crimson phoenix flies forth, taking roost above the summit.
Through one revolution, the luminous moon sends forth its own resplendence;
In its elevated location, the jade peak illuminates the Three Reeds.

—4—

Ever since my first attainment, I have seen the celestial Perfected;
On that very day I understood what the people of former times [knew].
Separated from the mundane and returning to daily activities, I was a guest beyond the
     clouds;
Casting off the dust and refraining from work, I was a visitor within the land.
This is because in the past I took hold of the vermilion mercury,
And because from the beginning I have stabilized the liquid silver.
A spark of numinous luminosity returns to the realm of stillness;
Peering into the perfect radiance within, I turn the golden wheel.

—5—

When the Mysterious Pass is obtained, there is no need to seek it out;
When refinement reaches redoubled yang, yin is completely dissipated.
From this point, you must urgently increase Fire over Wood;[17]

---

17. Associations unclear. In this combination, Wood may refer to the vital fluids in the heart (Fire). Another common association is Wood with innate nature and Fire with spirit. The line would thus suggest realizing the connection between innate nature and spirit.

From this point, you must once again decoct Metal in Water.[18]
The myriad spirits respond in kind and return to see who is there;
The single perfect numen alone naturally commands their respect.
When gathered it is form, and when scattered it is qi;
It comes and goes in the clear Void, eternally free of a heart-mind.

—6—

The womb-immortal dances and emerges, becoming a spirit immortal;
All of the other immortals henceforth obtain their proper arrangement.
How should one employ the elixir field when the golden tiger surrounds it?
Don't wait for the jade dragon to coil around the precious cauldron.
Urge on the circulation of lead and mercury according to clarity and stillness;
Change the positions of yin and yang to reach unexcelled joy and contentment.[19]
One part of red vapor is produced in the mountain summit;
Circulate radiance as a luminous lad who illumines the azure Luan-bird.

—7—

When you rend open the clouds, dispersing them completely, the moon becomes
    luminous;
Reverting the luminosity, the spirit transport moves to shoreline.
When Water and Fire encounter each other, you open the proper route;
When Wood and Metal are divided from each other, you stabilize perpetual life.
Black lead and crimson mercury divide into south and north;
The white tiger and azure dragon exchange [stem positions of] *jia* and *geng*.[20]
In accordance with this cultivation and ascesis, perfection is fully realized;
In emptiness, you weave and bind the jade silken fibers into an awning.

—8—

In this way, with clear illumination attained, you can abandon your search;
Then it will no longer be necessary for me to discuss "shallow" and "deep."
The principle of aligned sitting involves connecting *zi* and *wu*;[21]

---

18. Associations unclear. In this combination, Metal may refer to the perfect qi and original yang in the kidneys (Water). Another common association is Metal with emotionality and Water with vital essence. The line would suggest decreasing emotional reactivity and sexual arousal in order to stabilize one's foundational vitality.

19. Most likely refers to exchanging the yin and yang lines within the trigrams Kan-water ☵ and Li-fire ☲ to become Kun-earth ☷ and Qian-heaven ☰, respectively. This alchemical process involves a movement from differentiation to undifferentiation. Under one interpretation, the yin-line of Li-fire represents fluids, while the yang-line of Kan-water represents the qi in the kidneys. Through the exchange of these substances, the alchemist creates pure spirit in the head (Qian-heaven) and pure qi in the lower abdomen (Kun-earth). This is alternatively explained as attaining clarity and stillness by rooting the movement of vital essence and activating the movement of spirit.

20. In internal alchemy texts, this more often appears as *gengjia*, a combination of the seventh and first celestial stems, respectively. *Geng* usually refers to Metal and the western direction as well as to the emotions and the tiger; *jia* usually refers to Wood and the eastern direction as well as to innate nature and the dragon.

21. *Zi* and *wu* are the first and seventh terrestrial branches, respectively. In the present context, this most likely refers to aligning the body by becoming aware of the relationship between the sacrum (*zi*) and the crown (*wu*).

Circulate [qi] to the head and back again by observing *ding* and *ren*.[22]
Five kinds of variegated colors continually spread out;
At the single mysterious pivot, they beautifully encroach.
Take hold of the empty Void and the perfect and wondrous landscape;
Accordingly, grasp these realms to create an unsurpassed sound.

—9—

The patterns of respiration, exhalation and inhalation, are subtle and refined;
If nourished from the beginning, a single pearl becomes manifest.
With child and mother in mutual accord, there is a perfect brilliant coalescing;
Qi and spirit gather and assemble, and a strange radiant thing appears.
Invert and wed them to divide the mysterious causal mover;
Upper and lower become infused and harmonized, obtaining the essential pivot.
Adeptly face the deep mountains, residing in the most elevated place;
Now harmonized, you alone let loose the lunar, revolving solitude.

—10—

From the beginning altered and joined, you caught the wind's churnings;
Sown in the Turquoise Pond, the seeds became a jade lotus.
It produces and emerges as a single stem, its sides bright and pure;
It sways and opens as five petals, each one a perfect sphere.
In the past, you had the ability to awaken, pervading the mysterious and wondrous;
Today you have returned to understand how to realize suchness.
When no longer bound by the four seasons, hasten to depart;
Above the realm of perpetual spring, there is no ordering of years.

—11—

For cultivation and practice, you must employ the *Diagram of Nine Yang*;[23]
If you understand and grasp this map of yang, various affairs will be settled.
Those with wisdom know how to leap beyond the transformative process;
Those who are unenlightened have distorted understanding, becoming lost in lesser
    attainments.
If you can begin to investigate and uncover the being within Nonbeing,
After completion, it will seem as though being is actually Nonbeing.
Both the existence of Nonbeing and nonexistence of being lack actual form;[24]
When there are no forms within being, you have reached the thoroughfare of the heavens.

---

22. *Ding* and *ren* are the fourth and ninth celestial stems, respectively. Here *ding* relates to the southern direction and the front of the body, while *ren* relates to the northern direction and the back of the body. The context suggests circulating qi up the spine and down the front centerline of the body, or through the Governing and Conception vessels.

23. Reference unclear. Possibly the eleventh-century *Shangqing taixuan jiuyang tu* (DZ 154).

24. An allusion to the Buddhist *Heart Sūtra* (T. 250–57): "Form is emptiness; emptiness is form. Form does not differ from emptiness; emptiness does not differ from form. Whatever is emptiness, that is form. The same is true for sensation, perception, cognition, and consciousness."

—12—

If you know how bestowed guidance [enables] avoidance of the Three Defilements,
Cry out the realization that existed before you were this ordinary human being.
Entering the fire [of *saṃsāra*], select the teachings that reform the burning;
Crossing the river [of liberation], struggle to rescue the drowning.
Within the sun, refined splendor is perpetually born as luminescence;
Within the moon, the precious forest is eternally undecaying.
This is the great elixir returning to the realm beyond things;
Wandering carefree, coming and going, you enter the empty Void.

Cultivating the Dao / Qiu Changchun[25]

—1—

When the eyes and ears are divorced from sound and color,
The body and heart-mind withdraw from being and Nonbeing.
Abiding in suchness and pervading the transformative process,
Why bother discussing what is refined and what coarse?

—2—

Adepts refining qi and purifying the heart-mind
Seek out the floating clouds and root up mundane markings.
Their heart-minds become like mountains, unable to be moved;
Their qi becomes like an ocean, constant amid the currents.

—3—

The myriad karmic effects are like flickering candles,
And the Three Poisons are like melting ice.
When you discard the husk of yin and yang,
What's the point of discussing Greater and Lesser Vehicles?

—4—

The Five Visions in origin are the same substance;
The Three Bodies together are a single pillar.
A concentrated heart-mind is free from what follows "me";
Perfect realization becomes luminous when empty.

—5—

What is naturally born is in due course naturally destroyed;
What is free from shallowness also lacks depth.
If you don't realize that the body is not "mine,"
It will be difficult to understand how things *are* the heart-mind.

25. *Panxi ji*, DZ 1159, 4.13b–15a.

—6—

Taking steps to break open the world of emptiness,
You abruptly open the power of the transformative process.
The floating clouds collect in the realm of stillness;
The sun of wisdom illuminates the heaven of meditation.

—7—

Where can even a single word find a place to reside?
The myriad affairs have no enduring significance.
When the transformative process opens the Celestial Cavern,
Vital essence and spirit can withstand the years and winter's cold.

—8—

Even if the eyes have their times of application,
The ground of the heart-mind must remain at rest.
Then you face the dream of this entire life,
And accordingly wander among the myriad transformations.

—9—

The body resembles the narrowness of ten square-feet;
The heart-mind resembles the vastness of the great Void.
The Four Oceans are divided by a thousand peaks;
The Three Numinosities are observable in a single body.

—10—

Serene and dissolved in the space of no-mind,
Radiant luminosity illuminates the great Void.
The dim opaqueness contains a precious moon;
The woven network is threaded by a celestial pearl.

—11—

To ascend to Perfection, you must be free of turbid qi;
To transcend the mundane, you must have clear markings.
Quickly, urgently, separate yourself from the long night;
Silently, deeply, lift yourself to the Great Empyrean.

—12—

Inside the jade cauldron, the cinnabar sand issues forth;
Inside the gold vessel, the blue liquid becomes fragrant.
The heart-minds of ghosts and spirits are impossible to fathom;
The longevity of heaven and earth are difficult to measure.

—13—

As though in a dream, you separate yourself from glory and kingdom;
As spirit, you travel to the Heaven of the Purple Prefecture.

In splendor, you encounter the guests of the Three Islands;
In leisure, you visit the immortals of the ten continents.

—14—

Relying upon the Dao, you attain a condition free from affairs,
But acting according to phenomena produces a heart-mind.
If you liberate yourself and cast off the Three Poisons,
You can also abandon the Five Phases.

—15—

The Dao becomes manifest through nonaction,
And the heart-mind is born because of phenomena.
The Primordial Origin contains the myriad appearances;
The Great One arises from that which "Emptiness" names.

—16—

Motion is an effect of the motionless;
Nonaction leads to deliberate action.
The Three Radiances cannot illuminate this place;
The myriad appearances manifest when it becomes luminous.

—17—

Realization of the original self without a heart-mind—
How can this be exhausted by using awareness and thinking?
The Five Phases cannot reach this place;
Each of the myriad transformations returns at its time.

—18—

The moon rises, a glistening brilliance in the center of heaven;
The wind arrives, a clear purity in the middle of the night.
[Ordinary] humans cannot reach the grotto-heavens,
But guests free of mundane concerns naturally meet each other.

—19—

In the medicinal garden, the sprouting fields are pure;
On the gold altar, the jade canopy becomes replenished.
In the vessel, the heavens have no period of darkness;
Beyond external things, the landscape has a perpetual spring.

—20—

Among the ten caverns, the elevated Perfected are arrayed;
In the Three Heavens, the highest sages reside.
White clouds have the ability to escort any guest;
The oriole is released to transmit the sacred writings.

To the Tune "Casting Lots" / Sun Buer[26]

When you seal the fists and loosen your robes,[27]
The Water and Fire will immediately commingle and merge.
The misty vapors of the myriad districts manifest below the ocean;
With a single strike, the Three Passes become penetrated.
Immortal bliss continually expands
As you constantly drink the delicious wine.
The wondrous medicine is completely beyond time limits;
The nine-times-reverted cinnabar sand becomes complete.

To the Tune "Accentuating Slender Eyebrows" / Sun Buer[28]

—1—

Admonish people to awaken.
In cultivation and practice, renounce the suffering of the Three Roads.
Attain enlightened liberation,
And leap through the doorway.
[Remember] Tan, Ma, Qiu, Liu,
Sun, Wang, and Hao Taigu.
The ocean of divine law is a raft of compassion;
Inside the kingdom, there is universal salvation.

—2—

Transform ignorance and delusion.
Separate from husband and children in the Burning House.
Rely on wisdom and discernment,
And sever your ties to the Three Roads.
Distinctions between self and other are landslides;
The ocean of right and wrong results in personal decay.
Old karma must be expelled;
New misfortune must not be created.

—3—

Respond to the immortal offering.
Mercury and lead, the black and white, are the path to longevity.
Making progress from the beginning,
Attend to your work through bitter determination.

---

26. *Minghe yuyin*, DZ 1100, 5.7a.

27. "Seal the fists" (*wogu*), which literally means "grasp firmly," is an allusion to chapter 55 of the *Daode jing*. In alchemical practice, it refers to a specific sacred hand-gesture (Skt.: *mudrā*; Chin.: *shouyin*), wherein the tips of the thumbs touch the inside base of the ring finger and the other fingers fold over the thumbs.

28. *Minghe yuyin*, DZ 1100, 6.13a–15a.

Do not sleep day or night;
Coarse clothes and simple food are sufficient.
Beg and teach at the road heads;
Become a caretaker of the ten directions.

—4—

Be free from grief and anxiety.
A solitary cloud and wild crane [recluse] beyond constraint
Within a thatched hut,
Leisurely read the golden books.
Forests and streams outside the window,
At the edge of the rolling hills, water and bamboo.
Luminous moon and clear wind;
Become worthy to be their companion.

—5—

Nourish the original beginning.
The monkey-mind and horse-thought must be corralled and tied up.
With the Six Thieves completely exhausted,
Do not seek or be concerned about anything.
Vague and indistinct,
The place of darkness and silence.[29]
Deep and clear,
Innate nature settles and life-destiny resides.

—6—

Realize true progress.
The path to pervasive mysteriousness is between Wood and Metal.
Within the four symbols of the body,[30]
The Five Phases completely assemble.
Qi coalesces and spirit congeals,
While yin and yang naturally revert.
The whole body fills with a fragrant mist;
The fire of the Celestial Cycle is sufficient.

—7—

Break through the dark road.
When thunder shakes the earth, rain falls on mountain peaks.
The Yellow Sprouts grow,

29. The characters *yao, ming, hun,* and *mo* derive from the *Daode jing* where they are used to describe the Dao and the Daoist adept by extension. See, e.g., chapters 20 and 21.
30. The four directions.

And the White Snow floats down.
Dew descends as precious nectar,
While fragrant grasses fill the garden.
The Jade Stamen unfurls and diffuses;
The Gold Flower opens and reveals itself.

—8—

The landscape is covered by a map.
Soaring like clouds and streams, one traverses it
Above the winding Jiang River,
Flying birds and running rabbits.
The tiger encircles and the dragon coils;
Kan-water and Li-fire join together.
Revolving the wheel through the Celestial Pass;
You shift and move the Terrestrial Axle.

—9—

The Dharmic Wheel is roused.[31]
The Waterwheel is strong in its thirty spokes.
Shift the sun and moon[32]
So that they revolve to enter the gold furnace.
The jade cauldron becomes warm,
And the perfect fire of ninefold yang is decocted.
Misty vapors emerge from the myriad districts;[33]
A thousand-layered kingfisher-green mist.

—10—

Collect the luminous pearl.
Through refinement and completion, the immortal embryo dances.
In the Association of Perfect Blessings,
The Maiden completely gathers.
When thirsty, drink the precious nectar;
The jade zither naturally pacifies.
Its harmony stabilizes the immortal sound;
Pound the gold and strike the jade.

—11—

Nonbeing is within being.
Within Nonbeing, still other progeny are produced.
Inside being and Nonbeing,

---

31. An alternate name for the Celestial Cycle.

32. The left and right eye, respectively.

33. Compare Sun's lyric "To the Tune 'Casting Lots'" that appears earlier in this chapter.

Practice inward contemplation and selection;
Inside Nonbeing, store perfection;
Inside being, maintain resemblance to Nonbeing.
When being and Nonbeing are both forgotten,
One returns to merge with the great Void.

—12—

Practice and accomplishment become sufficient.
Among the Three Islands of Penglai, various immortals gather.
In the Association of the Turquoise Pond,
Sages and worthies are beyond number.
Each one completely cultivates perfection;
Study the Dao and become a companion of the arrayed immortals.
Focus on the elevated Perfected
And the sacred Queen Mother of the West.

—13—

Present offerings to the celestial offices.
When immortal robes are bestowed, you become transcendent.
Mount the ascending phoenix,
And be carefree and enjoy the pure metropolis.
Among the treasure hall and precious tower,
Gold spikes fill the vermillion portals.
Perpetual spring without nightfall,
There is no longer coming or going.

To the Tune "Tree Leaves Rustling" / Sun Buer[34]

—1—

Observing the white phoenix,
Watching the black raven,
I grope for fish and shrimp beneath the water.
Orioles thread the willow trees;
Butterflies seek out the flowers.
Shadowed in secluded retirement,
If not a disciple of clouds, no one can brag.

—2—

With the forest of thought regulated,
And by broadening compassion,
In the end one establishes a foundation.
With a rap of the staff,

---

34. *Minghe yuyin*, DZ 1100, 6.15a–16b.

One leaves behind the splayed covering.
Enjoying simple idiocy,
Painful discomfort seems totally unknown.

—3—

When the tortoise scales are shaken off,
And the rabbit's horn pierces,
The toad leaps toward heaven and flies.
The mud ox roars;
The wood horse neighs.
Few people know this—
They are taken away by the times and dissipate the Celestial Pivot.

—4—

Wheat contains flour,
Millet contains grains.
And even cotton leggings have legs inside.
Mountains contain stones,
While oceans contain water.
Discuss the perfectly real—
Establish a foundation among the limitlessness of cavern mists.

—5—

Capture the horse of thought;
Lock up the monkey of the mind;
Then spirit and qi are nourished and join in completion.
Do not put on coquettish airs,
But merge with suchness.
Embodying the silent mystery,
Dharma-vision leaps beyond the great multitude.

—6—

Bringing the mysterious and wondrous to rest,
Converting those among the cities and passes,
Each footprint is a step toward return.
The flower has a red space;
The willow has green throughout.
You do not have to fence yourself off—
The countenances of immortals and buddhas are everywhere.

—7—

The moon in the sky,
The moon aligned and whole,
Travels to heaven after passing through the earth.
Being and Nonbeing exist;

Inversion involves turning over.
The Wondrous is a twofold mystery;
For the orthodox Dao, you must seek oral transmission.

—8—

The moon in the sky,
The moon high and thin,
Mao and *you* are not empty transmissions.[35]
Eight *liang* of mercury,[36]
And eight *liang* of lead.
With one *jin* total,[37]
In enlightened breakthrough, one realizes three thousand reaches the multitude.

—9—

The moon in the sky,
The moon resonant and crescent,
The wondrousness of the perfect Dao is infinite.
The dragon takes hold of the tiger,
And the tiger takes hold of the dragon.
When these two meet each other,
They coalesce into a Gold Flower playing in the wind.

—10—

The moon in the sky,
The moon aligned in the south,
Forward and behind, each is three times three.
Li-fire is female;
Kan-water is male.
In discussing the wondrous and mysterious,
Do not speak about breakthrough, but teach people about what to consider.

—11—

The moon in the sky,
The moon resonant and blazing,
The lead and mercury reside in the cauldron.
Gold depends on the fire;
Refinement completes the pearl.
A single calabash—
Three hundred and eighty-four *zhu* in weight.[38]

---

35. *Mao* and *you* are the fourth and tenth terrestrial branches, respectively. In this combination, *mao* usually refers to the heart and spirit, while *you* refers to the kidneys and vital essence.

36. *Liang* is an ancient Chinese measurement for object mass and monetary objects, often translated as "ounce" or "tael."

37. *Jin* is an ancient Chinese measurement, consisting of sixteen *liang*. It is sometimes translated as "catty."

38. *Zhu* is an ancient Chinese measurement for weight, equaling one twenty-fourth of a *liang*.

To the Tune "Fragrance Filling the Courtyard" / Sun Buer[39]

The radiance of the mineral fire is hidden;
The human body does not last long;
When reckoning comes, one realizes that life and death are difficult to guard against.
Whether suddenly born or suddenly perishing,
It is just like the brilliance of a lightning strike.
Recognize and break through the provisional joining of physical form;
Endeavor to obtain this
And abandon the world for the immortal regions.
After thinking reaches its limits,
Turn the heart-mind back to the Dao
And seek to know the ruler within these phenomena.
Moment by moment constantly maintain these meetings—
Be unified in walking and in sitting;
Be unified in drinking the nectar of mists.
Be unified as a companion of the clear wind and luminous moon;
Be unified in a single aspiration;
Be unified in perceiving celestial radiance.
Be unified in mutually beneficial associations;
Be unified with your master in seeking the Dao;
Be unified in your singing as fragrance fills the courtyard.

The Five Night-watches / Ma Danyang[40]

At the first drum-sounding, I retire alone, guarded within.
With a cloud, I thoroughly till the precious landscape.
A mysterious kind of purple fungus sprouts;
Then my grotto-heaven is without dissipation.
Free from leakage, free from outflow,
The tiger of Kan-water and the dragon of Li-fire commingle.

At the second drum-sounding, I retire alone, guarded within.
With the cloud torn open, I align the celestial constellations.
The sun and moon exchange their radiance;
Then my precious jar is without dissipation.
Free from leakage, free from outflow,
Emerging from the earth, the dragon and snake engage in battle.

---

39. *Minghe yuyin*, DZ 1100, 6.16b–17a.

40. *Jianwu ji*, DZ 1142, 2.9b–10a.

At the third drum-sounding, I retire alone, guarded within.
I redouble my urgent tapping of the Mysterious Gate.
I summon myself as one of the initiated to awaken;
Then my Jade Pass is without dissipation.
Free from leakage, free from outflow,
The Maiden and the Child join hands.

At the fourth drum-sounding, I retire alone, guarded within.
Attentively, I take care to guard against the thieves.
Through wisdom and illumination, I disperse deviant demons;
Then the golden essence is without dissipation.
Free from leakage, free from outflow,
A spark of numinous radiance congeals.

At the fifth drum-sounding, I retire alone, guarded within.
Immersed in deep silence, I attain the presence within Nonbeing.
Resonating with beings, I reside in perfect constancy;
Then the spiritual elixir is without dissipation.
Free from leakage, free from outflow,
The immortal embryo, now manifest, is clear and flourishing.

Instructions on the Golden Elixir / Wang Yuyang[41]

Alcohol, sex, wealth, and anger must be abandoned![42]
Worldly affairs and pleasures must be removed!
The Three Death-bringers and yin-ghosts must be dissolved!
The Six Thieves and ten malevolent deeds must be destroyed!

Mountains of demons must be banished without end!
All desist from rebelliousness, convolutions, and contortions!
Just beg for your food, paper, cloth, and robes
And keep the monkey-mind in tight.

Unified intention not yet perfectly constant,
The knife of wisdom splits obstructions.
When both movement and stillness are forgotten,
Do not brag about your clarity and purity.

With innate nature and life-destiny firmly nourished and controlled,
Deeply store essence, qi, and blood.

41. *Yunguang ji*, DZ 1152, 3.20ab.

42. The Four Hindrances of Quanzhen practice.

Then the myriad spirits are joyful and in harmony
And numinous currents pervade your bones and joints.

Above, join the Palace of the Vermilion Numen;
Below, enter the Dragon-Tiger Cavern.
Guard and nourish qi, essence, and spirit,
But watch it, lest you carelessly dissipate the heart-mind.

The four oceans issue cloudlike radiance;
The three peaks release white snow.
Meet and merge them in the Palace of Mysterious Prime,
On and on, continuously without interruption.

Water and fire are spontaneously extracted and replenished,
The Celestial Cycle is spontaneously circulated in order.
Spirit and qi are spontaneously numinous,
And the Perfected and masters spontaneously give support.

With the hundred bones spontaneously open and expansive,
Your appearance spontaneously changes.
The sun and moon spontaneously revolve,
As the golden elixir spontaneously congeals.

The Child is spontaneously joyous;
The Maiden is spontaneously delighted.
The Five Qi spontaneously attend to the origin,
And the Four Elements unite in harmony.

Mysterious principle is spontaneously pervasive;
The myriad spirits are spontaneously transcendent.
With the great Dao spontaneously complete,
The solid earth spontaneously starts to change.

In proper *samādhi* you can find perfection.
In obscurity you can hold the clear mind's fragrance.
Let your light diffuse and transform into pure spirit—
Spirit radiance emerges like a bolt of lightning.

By forging and refining, you complete the great elixir,
Emerging like the moon over a row of houses.
In a single strike it passes through the Three Passes
Where ranks of immortals stand arrayed beyond the clouds.

Open and expansive, heaven and earth are clear
While the hidden numen whirls about, becoming vast and pervasive.
The sun and moon intermingle their light in their revolutions
As you join the freezing vastness of the Biluo Heaven.[43]

Your enlightened radiance fills the entire world,
Greatly joyful, yet also completely free from joy.
After nine revolutions, the great elixir is complete,
And once and forever you transcend all life and death.

A clear song rings through the great Void.
Feeling floodlike, you visit the Golden Tower.
With Chaos Prime [Lord Lao] pervading the Three Realms,
You reach out and beckon forth to everyone.

Poems on the Golden Elixir / Hao Guangning[44]

—1—

Within the cosmic canopy, some dedicated adepts,
Of spirit and of sacrality, mold themselves to the cosmic patterns.
In nonaction and virtue, they enter the nature of beings;
Dwell alone and open the furnace of creative transformation.
Unswayed by the eastern winds blowing the willow catkins,
They rest in the teachings, as the autumnal moon illuminates the vessel.
The golden elixir circulates to reach the Cavern of Niwan;[45]
From the beginning, their names are recorded in Jade Metropolis.

—2—

With the pure yang of double five attained, there is accomplishment;[46]
The great completion of Qian-heaven becomes your ancestor.
Descending into your body, it directly enters the cavern of boundlessness;
Mixed with substance, it extends to the center of dark vastness.
Present, it meets the male in Kan-water, riding the white deer;
Latent, it becomes the female in Li-fire, saddling the azure dragon.
Wait for them to have a single encounter in three thousand days—
The crane becomes a bird and tortoise, and the rock becomes a pine.

---

43. On the Biluo Heaven see Bokenkamp 1991.

44. *Taigu ji*, DZ 1161, 4.1a–8b.

45. *Niwan* (lit., "mudball") is most likely a Chinese transliteration of nirvana, although it may have originally emerged as a *neidan* modification of a *waidan* term. The Cavern of Niwan, also appearing as Niwan Palace, is usually identified as either the crown-point or the center of the head.

46. "Double five" (*wuwu*) usually refers to the fifth day of the fifth month, which roughly corresponds to June 8. Double five day occurs between the nodes of Bearded Grain and Summer Solstice, or just before the apex of yang.

—3—

The red mouse and black snake leap beyond the world's bizarreness,
This border between spirit immortality that dissipates the Celestial Pivot.[47]
The rumbling of thunder and a bolt of lightning—three mountains are split;
The sun emerging in unified radiance—the four oceans first appear.
It was told to an elder prostrating his silvery head;
It was also heard by a novice wearing azure robes.
The master referred to it as the diffusion of perfect principle;
Novices and masters conversing on the Dao come to attain this too late.

—4—

The yellow ram transforms to become a white gibbon;
The fierce tiger leaves his tracks, waiting for the crimson ox.
The rabbit dwells in the cave, and the fox is in the fire;
Mysterious pervasion and wondrous presence come from the Dao as Source.
Extending numinosity to descend in traces, it expands and circulates
Through twelve springs and also through sixty autumns.
The qi of the Dao returns to the body to the point of intimacy;
At the Association of Penglai,[48] you form a covenant with Yingzhou.[49]

—5—

Unified with the Seven Primes, nine times six years old—
From the beginning, I knew my fate did not reside in heaven.[50]
The warm winds in the cauldron dispersed the bright red snow;
The crescent moon in the furnace is refined into an auspicious lotus.
Reclining on a pillow by the winding Jiang River, I am waking up from sleep;
Crossing oceans and streams three times, I transform the mulberry fields.[51]
Thinking about my former days in Nanke[52] and the Yellow Millet Dream,[53]
I talk with Immortal Taigu[54] about our time in the Kunyu mountains.

---

47. Interestingly, in this line Hao Guangning uses the character *xie* ("to leak out"). This character consists of *shui* ("water") and *shi* ("world"), and thus parallels the occurrence of *shi* in the preceding line. It seems that Hao is giving a Daoist reading of *xie*, taking it as meaning the dissipation that comes from living in the ordinary world.

48. Possibly an actual Quanzhen community association in Penglai, located in the eastern peninsula of Shandong Province.

49. Yingzhou is one of the Three Islands, with the other two being Penglai and Fangzhang. The eastern paradise.

50. An allusion to the famous alchemist saying, "My fate is in me, not in the heavens" (*wo ming zai wo, buzai tian*).

51. A famous Chinese idiom: "Blue oceans [become] mulberry fields" (*canghai sangtian*). The phrase was made famous by Li Bo (Li Bai; 701–762), who drew his inspiration from the hagiography of Ma Gu (Hemp Maiden) in the *Shenxian zhuan* (Biographies of Spirit Immortals) (see Campany 2002, 262). The saying conventionally means "to witness great changes over time," but Hao seems to suggest his own process of alchemical transformation.

52. A reference to the "Dream of Nanke," in which a certain Chun Yufen dreams of being appointed as head magistrate of Nanke. He eventually fails in battle, his army defeated, his body wounded, and his beautiful wife killed. He then wakes up to find that it was a useless dream about an imaginary place.

53. A dream experienced by Lü Dongbin, which parallels that of Chun Yufen, that inspires him to become a disciple of Zhongli Quan and completely commit himself to alchemical praxis. See, for example, Kohn 1993, 126–32.

54. That is, Hao is talking to himself. There is also a play on his Daoist name here, and one could translate the phrase as "immortals of great antiquity."

—6—

The fixed stars are originally unmanifest, but then appear—
Through stillness, cessation, and serenity, they separate and fix their positions.
In four transformations, the Palace of Gen-mountain completes a wondrous substance;[55]
Invert form and take hold of life-destiny, completely realizing the perfect embryo.
Students must awaken to this and penetrate the seal of the heart-mind;
The awakened know it, and principle and innate nature become empowered.
Liberation and attainment become centered, like intention guiding an arrow's trajectory;
A thousand scriptures and ten thousand discourses—all equally opened.

—7—

For three months the thunder rumbles, first one and then two sounds;
When you begin to know the world, ghosts and spirits become frightened.
With wind as your carriage and clouds your support, you travel three thousand miles;
The tiger and the dragon are majestic through ninety thousand patternings.
Within the gate of myriad transformations, you alone are ruler;
Arranging the eight tassels of the phenomenal world, you are the director.
The secret symbol of Zhen-thunder intertwines with every movement;[56]
Through highest virtue, the sovereign lords engrave your names.

—8—

From cauldron and vessel there comes six and then three—
One extraction, one half-turn, and one fixed metal ring.
Connect the golden tripod rings and the jade material so that refinement increases;
By making offerings to the sacred and nourishing worthiness, you refine the elixir which
    has been given.
Through wind and fire, Daoist initiates are able to revert their luminosity;
By transforming form and substance, you can alter the stains of worldliness.
You must learn how decoction allows the completion of a new pattern;
As transmitted by and received from Zhongli [Quan], the Dao is not difficult.[57]

—9—

The family of Dui-lake has a hexagram called "returning ethereal soul";[58]
Inverting agedness and extending life, there is yet another gateway.

---

55. Gen-mountain ☶ is one of the eight trigrams. It is often associated with the bladder. In internal alchemy practice, it may refer to the heart emptied and stilled of emotional and intellectual activity, or the lower elixir field filled with perfect qi.

56. Zhen-thunder ☳ is one of the eight trigrams. It is often associated with the liver and the ethereal soul. In internal alchemy practice, it may refer to the circulation of perfect qi throughout the body.

57. Zhongli Quan is a pseudo-historical immortal of the Han dynasty. In internal alchemy circles, he was identified as the teacher of Lü Dongbin, and this relationship was codified through the so-called Zhong-Lü textual corpus (see Baldrian-Hussein 1984, especially 23–31; Boltz 1987, 139–43). The Quanzhen order eventually identified him as one of the so-called Five Patriarchs (*wuzu*). See *Jinlian ji*, DZ 173; *Jinlian xiangzhuan*, DZ 174.

58. "Returning ethereal soul" (*guihun*) hexagrams are those in which the upper and lower trigrams become the same when the yin-yang polarity of the fifth line is switched. The eight *guihun* hexagrams are 7, 8, 13, 14, 17, 18, 53, and 54. In the case of the Dui-lake trigram, this refers to hexagram 54.

When the young girl is betrothed, you must wait for new life to appear;
On the day when a grown son is wedded, you see important descendants.
When there is a serene mouth within your mouth, how can you speak?
When there is a body beyond the body, what is there to discuss?
When you are divorced from the Dao and spirit immortality, there is deep longing;
When you cast off form and forget your traces, the Dao constantly abides.

—10—

In the course of three thousand *jiazi* years, one immortal appears;[59]
The root of heaven and earth is the spirit of creative transformation.[60]
Take hold of yin and yang until everything is completely understood;
They revolve through every appearance, governing both the subtle and defiled.
Many respond by becoming fathers, with children as recompense for old age;
Control perverse and demonic thoughts, so that you may attain perfection.
Realize and attain the pivot of spirit and the principle of inversion;
Within the vessel, there is a space filled with laughter and joy.

—11—

For the azure dragon and fierce tiger, there is no enclosure;
The young girl is urged forward six times to meet the adolescent boy.
When they meet in the Yellow Court, make an urgent inspection;
In serenity become familiar with the Jade Portal, so that the silence may be contained.
When the precious vase is split open incessantly, a red lotus begins to bud;
When the lion begins to move, the black jade becomes vast and deep.
Committed adepts take hold of these so that they return to the cavern prefecture;
Then the myriad spirits spread out and vie to be the first to join.

—12—

If the eight trigrams are mutually ordered, ruler and guest become established;
If the Five Phases are produced and controlled, lord and minister become confirmed.
The azure Luan-bird rattles its bells and enters the cave of the fire dragon;
The crimson phoenix alights and swallows the body of the metal tiger.
Groom and bride are wedded and harmonized through regulated patterning;
Father and son are placed in accord so that they obtain centered purity.
In everything, accord with spirit and qi until you can constantly guard them;
When a single respiration becomes infused, you have the square-inch of Perfection.

—13—

If you want to identify the elixir sand, you must make two even divisions;
With west, south, and north established, match the three rarities.[61]

---

59. The *jiazi* year is the beginning of the sixty-year cycle in Chinese reckoning.

60. An allusion to chapter 6 of the *Daode jing*. "The gateway to the Mysterious Female is called the root of heaven and earth (*tiandi gen*)." Among Daoists, it is often interpreted as the nose or mouth.

61. The "three rarities" (*sanqi*) is probably an alternate name for the "three essentials" (*sanyao*) and "three treasures" (*sanbao*), namely, vital essence, qi, and spirit.

Within the Palace of Ninefold Yang, open the Gold Portal;[62]
In front of the Hall of Yin Six [Six Yin], stir up the Jade Pond.[63]
The *zhu*-weight may be determined as three hundred and eighty-four,
The *jin*-weight may be determined as sixteen—you must know these two divisions.
Before the double-hour of *wu* and after *zi*, follow the application times;
The individual rays of the myriad conditions are contained by the jade radiance.

—14—

The lead and mercury must be divided so that yang and yin are discernible;
One half *jin* of silver is matched with an equal measure of gold.
The fiery clouds alight and enter the nose of the Oxherder;[64]
The frigid moon passes through and opens the heart of the Weaving Maiden.[65]
When the spirit water is stored, the Golden Well becomes full;
When the source of the Dao is clear and luminous, the Jade Spring becomes deep.
Ascending and descending through the inversions, you illuminate Li-fire and Kan-water;
For those who are not yet awakened, how can they become familiar with this place?

—15—

The solar essence in the east is separated from the lunar florescence in the west;
In truth, they are the elixir heaven when strong and abundant.
Two and eight,[66] beautiful women with respectful and elegant bearing;
Nine and three,[67] superior persons with persuasive and enduring deportment.
Curtains of water crystal are suspended in front of the precious jade steps;
Streamers of weighted cornelian hang before the kingfisher-green screen.
Allow me to ask about the Origin: Where does one return to?
Above the Tower of Seven Stars,[68] there has never been separation.

—16—

The origin of the dose resides in every person and community;
The beginning of the crimson phoenix can be seen in the falling mists.
Above the cliff, one encounters grasses adding to auspicious appearances;
At the top of the sandbank, one meets with stones coalescing into numinous sand.
Within the northern vastness, how often does the saw-toothed rhinoceros horn appear?

---

62. The Palace of Ninefold Yang is the head, and the Gold Portal (*jinhu*; a.k.a. *jinque*) is one of the Nine Palaces, the mystical cranial locations in the head.

63. The Six Yin usually refers to six hexagrams in the *Yijing*. Here the context suggests an esoteric name for a head location, as Jade Pond refers to the mouth.

64. The Oxherder is usually associated with the heart region (see Komjathy 2008b, 2009). Based on the context, Oxherder may refer to the head.

65. The Weaving Maiden is usually associated with the kidneys (see Komjathy 2008b, 2009). Based on the context, Weaving Maiden may refer to the heart region.

66. Yin numbers.

67. Yang numbers.

68. The seven stars of the Northern Dipper (Ursa Major). Often associated with one's life-destiny or fate (*ming*) in Daoism.

Within the southern reaches, how frequently has someone been able to collect an
    elephant's tusks?
Venturing a further remark: Who deserves to find such a rare place?
Facing the inside of the Celestial Pool, let loose the Golden Flower.

—17—

Someone asked me about the most appropriate undertaking;
Take hold of spiritual accomplishment during the time of creative transformation.
The tiger hides in blue vastness, while the wind blows *hoo hoo.*
The dragon coils inside the vermilion grotto, while rain falls *shee shee.*
After the cloud wisps have dispersed, thunder comes to a rest;
After the dewdrops form, the dipper stars shine down their influence.
Simply wait in the east for the shifts in movement that occur in pure refinement;
When the issuing of the variegated clouds is contained, one revolution of daylight.

—18—

When the pure currents are elevated and expansive, the world becomes different;
You don't need to comprehend the obscure tenuity—stop talking about emptiness.
Realize that the meaning of poetic sensibilities is to have personal joyousness;
There are few people who can completely understand the heart-mind and expressions of
    the Dao.
Karmic effects take hold of innate nature, so it may be deluded or perfected;
If you completely disperse the pure currents, our teachings and movement become murky.
A seed of the golden elixir is contained within the furnace,
But ingredients without immortal bones are difficult to prepare and complete.

—19—

Within the Palace of Yang Nine there is a Buddhist monk of great realization;
With hands folded reverentially in aligned meditation, he chants the *Scripture on the
    Yellow Court.*[69]
Direct your spirit radiance to penetrate the storehouse of empty Nonbeing;
The auspicious qi becomes clear and coalesces, assembling the precious vessel.
Approaching and reposing in the grotto-heaven, offer petitions with dexterity;
With every material from the phenomenal world, exhort the regal numen.
From this you are able to understand and attain the aspiration of western arrival;
At the place before Primordial Chaos, how can form exist?

---

69. The third or fourth century CE *Huangting jing* (DZ 331; 332), which is most often associated with Shangqing (Highest Clarity) Daoism and read as a visualization manual. It exerted a strong influence on the esoteric and symbolic language of internal alchemy.

—20—

If you wish to study immortality, you must refine the golden elixir;[70]
Lead and mercury will come to take their places within the cauldron.
Applying fire through the Celestial Cycle, follow the sequential arrangement;
Increasing accomplishment through the times and seasons, do not become negligent.
To preserve spirit you must first cause the heart-mind to revert to stillness;
To nourish qi you must not allow the tongue to descend from Qian-heaven.
Throughout the twelve double-hours, do not be inconsistent or inattentive;
In suchness, innate nature and life-destiny are completely protected and nourished.

—21—

When the Five Qi occupy the same palace, they become a single family;
Circulating and governing in mutual support, mists rise from shorelines.
Attend to the carts without dissent, and you will have the way of perpetual serenity.
Constantly search for the precious substances, and the florescence of the cassia moon[71]
    will emerge.
When lead and mercury are mixed and fused, you attain the highest rank;
The numinous wisdom of qi and spirit coagulates as elixir sand.
The subtle application of Complete Perfection is the talisman of mysterious practice;
The flowing vapors of glistening infusions are the vapors of variegated clouds.

—22—

How can one attain the ability to swallow the dose?
It is accomplished without requiring a ram to be sacrificed.
When the mountain marshes are pervaded by qi, clouds emerge from the valleys;
When the earth and heavens are joined extensively, trees become ladders.
Through the commingling of Kan-water and Li-fire, you understand inversion;
Through the return of dragon and tiger, you manifest awakening through delusion.
When you realize this in the Center, you have the principle of ebb and flow;
Take care of the teachings and pacify the earth, so that you may tread on clouds and
    rainbows.

—23—

Constantly listen to the sound of the golden minerals within the pot;
Mundane emotions must be expelled so that the disposition of the Dao appears.
After the yang-spirit is complete, you will be completely free from obscuration;
When the yin corporeal soul is dispersed, you will once again realize clarity.

---

70. This line echoes Zhang Boduan's (d. 1082) *Wuzhen pian* (Chapters on Awakening to Perfection; DZ 263, 26–30; DZ 1017, 18; trl. Cleary 1987): "In studying immortality, you must study celestial immortality (*tianxian*). This alone is the most superior doctrine of the Golden Elixir (*jindan*)" (DZ 263, 26.9a).

71. The eighth month. The moon phases are often used as symbolic designations for stages of alchemical practice.

When the lotus blooms with fire, you become capable like this;
When a portion is seized within water, you will certainly become complete.
Complete the melding of these two substances so that there is constant association;
Then you will steadfastly ride a cloud-chariot and ascend to the Jade Capital.

—24—

Catch and lead the golden bird to rest in the lunar palace;
If you happen to learn how to enclose it, then it will completely coalesce.
With spirit radiance bright and penetrating, you acquire a body of numinous emptiness;
The thoroughfare to the wondrous Dao opens,[72] the net of the transformative process.
The consciousness of the heart-mind begins to understand how to be a guest in a humble
    abode;
The vision of wisdom then perceives how a ruler comes to be venerated.
In accordance with this you begin to realize that to be embodied is suffering;
And that not becoming attached to empty names is great pervasion.

—25—

Students of the Dao must first sever ties to external attractions;
Cultivate the Dao and nourish simplicity, then you will join the immortal lineage.
Forget emotions covered by activity—decoct the golden ye-fluids;
Stop worrying about every outcome—refine the purple sand.
Unify innate nature and attend to the Origin so that the Five Qi collect;
When the myriad spirits assemble at the peak, let loose the three flowers.
From this, you will completely connect with the path of perpetual life;
Forever facing the clear empyrean, you commingle with the variegated clouds.

—26—

Renunciants who wish to receive guidance concerning immortality
Must stay with a perfected master and receive oral instructions.[73]
Inside the furnace, let the lead fly until it is constantly strong and fine;
Inside the crucible, allow the mercury to coalesce until it is forever new and fresh.
The flowing gold produces powder that fuses into dragon bones;
The falling dew becomes frost that turns into the jade saliva.
Through a single polishing, the mind-mirror becomes luminous and discerning;
The face before our birth becomes naturally perfect.

---

72. An allusion to chapter 6 of the *Zhuangzi*, wherein Yan Hui describes his practice of sitting-in-forgetfulness (*zuowang*) to Kongzi (Master Kong; "Confucius"): "I smash up my limbs and body, drive out perception and intellect, cast off form, do away with understanding, and make myself identical with Great Pervasion. This is what I mean by sitting-in-forgetfulness" (adapted from Watson 1968, 90).

73. This echoes the guidance given in the first, second, and sixth sections of the *Chongyang lijiao shiwu lun* (Chongyang's Fifteen Discourses to Establish the Teachings). See chapter 3 herein.

—27—

When cultivation and practice no longer require effort, you may be carefree;
You do not have to face the empty room and guard silent aloneness.
From the Purple Storehouse do not allow sheep and tigers to quarrel;
From the Elixir Palace you can order the myriad spirits to show their respect.
Wandering the mountains in every direction—the path to the azure empyrean;
Crossing over the waters in constant ascent—the bridge of felled trees.
Gather and obtain the numinous fungus, urgently swallowing the outgrowths;
Why should baskets and gourds be suspended beneath the forests?

—28—

With three and one inside the vessel, luminosity takes on an extraordinary constancy;
Venerable Changmei sits looking at the pines and bamboo groves.[74]
Vermilion kernels six *zhu* in weight fill up the golden appearance;
Within the Twelve Storied Tower, drink the Jade Nectar.
A white crane at the edge of the tree-line—moving incessantly back and forth;
A bird and tortoise amid pond and shoreline—traversing up and down.
The numinous lad steps forward from Kan-water, coming to reside;
He makes offerings with the master in order to add to the broth of life-destiny.

—29—

When the original qi joins and completes the body of clear purity,
The variegated clouds suddenly emerge as vapors of the five directions.
After the golden elixir coalesces you follow the model of Master Chunyang;[75]
The jade *ye*-fluids pour through you and open a flower without night.
With the gate of unmanifest form, pile up the white snow;
Inside the storehouse of emptiness, tend to the Yellow Sprouts.
On the path of perpetual life, there are few people traveling;
The root resides in the immortal lineage and Daoist lineage.

—30—

The celestial currents blow, splitting open and dropping the yang blossoms;
When you see the universe as a mire, your thinking is not mistaken.
In leisure, gather the camellias, decocting their delicate stamens;
In stillness, collect the peonies, refining their flourishing blossoms.
Harmonize the two substances so that spirit and qi become clear;
Irrigate the Three Fields until barley and hemp outgrowths appear.
Take leave of the drinking of evening banquets and retire this very moment;
Take your seat on the white deer and enter the clouds and mists.

---

74. Changmei (Long Eyebrows) usually refers to Laozi, whose standard iconography includes long eyebrows, which indicate longevity and wisdom.

75. Chunyang (Purified Yang) is Lü Dongbin's (b. 798?) Daoist name.

Song of the Clear Sky / Qiu Changchun[76]

The clear sky:[77] nothing rises higher, floating clouds mere veil.
Clouds rise up and come to screen the myriad constellations.
Yet even then the stars form a dense network, warding off all perversities;
Their radiant luminosity never shines on the Demon King.

When I first opened empty space, heaven and earth were clear—
Ten thousand doors, a thousand gateways, I just sang of Great Peace.
And then there was a moment when a single black cloud appeared,
And each of the Nine Cavities and hundred bones lacked serenity.

When this occurred, I spread the teachings, making wisdom a strong current;
It extended through the Three Realms and ten directions as a great whirlwind.
When clouds disperse in emptiness, substance becomes naturally perfect;
It spontaneously manifests as a florescence in lineage after lineage.

So even now, below the moon, the square earth sustains the piping flutes—
A single sound, one brilliant note, it guards flourishing contentment.
It startles and awakens the jade lad of the eastern direction;
He staggers and then mounts a white stag like a starry steed.

Retiring and retreating, the sound is not like ordinary music—
It is neither the music of lithophones, nor that of horns.
When there are three feet of cloud chimes and twelve cords of lute,
Throughout the course of *kalpa*s, Chaos Prime was cut up.[78]

Jade resonates and chimes ring to sever vulgar songs;
Clear and light, penetrating everywhere, the sound passes through every mind.
Through them I attained my first realization, with ghosts and spirits in support;
Then I entered the earth and ascended to heaven, leaping beyond past and present.

Everywhere completely self-abiding, I am free from attachments and concerns.
My heart-mind has no cravings and no desire for fame, my body no defilement.
In seclusion, I sing a song about pure snow in the alchemical vessel.
Tranquil and harmonious, beyond the world, it is a tune of pure spring.

This song of my lineage is completely spontaneous;
It is produced by a flute without holes, a zither without strings.
Attain startled awakening and float above the dream of life;
Throughout day and night, a clear sound fills the grotto-heaven.

---

76. *Panxi ji*, DZ 1159, 3.1ab.

77. Or, "azure heaven."

78. An allusion to chapter 7 of the *Zhuangzi*. See note 15.

Quatrains on Immortal Bliss / Liu Changsheng[79]

—1—

By remembering the Dao and realizing perfect calmness,
Life-destiny becomes clear and you excel at refining the elixir.
Pervade heaven by completing utmost practice;
Leap beyond the barrier of life and death. (2.1a)

—2—

Free from affairs, one has neither desires nor pursuits;
Free from contention, one has neither discrimination nor separation.
Free from language, one only remembers the Dao;
Free from pleasure, one also becomes free from grief. (2.1b)

—3—

Support the country by establishing hermitages for immortals;
Make offerings with a desire for blessings from the Dao.
When discussing abilities, understand the myriad beings;
When coming in contact with them, distance yourself from the foolish. (2.1b)

—4—

Increase your practice to wondrously pervade heaven;
When the heart-mind is perfected, you subdue every type of error.
From the realized ones of antiquity and today,
Life-destiny is retained and the precious radiance is complete. (2.1b–2a)

—5—

You may eat strong-smelling vegetables, but do not kill living beings;
Your governance and regulation should be like a crystalline clarity.
When you have free time, read the *Zhuangzi* and *Laozi*;[80]
You will pervade heaven when your practice becomes complete. (2.2a)

—6—

Be free of selfish love and abandon feelings of hatred;
Through perfect constancy, spirit and qi become numinous.
The clear *gui*-water of life-destiny is resplendent;
After you penetrate principle, you will ascend naturally. (2.2b–3a)

—7—

From a grass-thatched shelter, wander among mountains and streams;
From a pure dwelling-place, set aside the affairs of the world.
In seclusion during the day, read and study the *Daode jing*.
In stillness during the night, listen to the flowing waters. (2.3a)

79. Selections from *Xianle ji*, DZ 1141, 2.1a–17a, 5.1a–20a.

80. Many of the "Quatrains on Immortal Bliss" speak about reading Daoist scriptures. Compare 5.9a, where Liu Changsheng recommends reading *Zhuangzi* and *Liezi*. Liu Changsheng was the early Quanzhen adept most committed to scripture study, as evidenced in his extant commentaries. See chapter 5 herein.

—8—

From a retired residence, enter the northern mountains;
Free from binding concerns, consider the domain of dust.
Attend to the Dao [by cultivating] the fields in three sections;
Nourish perfection so that hemp and wheat become your sustenance. (2.3b)

—9—

Forget the world and refrain from thoughts of contention;
With a heart-mind in seclusion, read Daoist texts.
When you realize perfection, you attain the state beyond life and death;
When you penetrate principle, you attain the luminosity of suchness. (2.5a)

—10—

By abandoning perversion, qi becomes clear and deep;
By forgetting emotions, you realize the water and metal.
By emptying the heart-mind, perfect unification occurs;
By embracing the Dao, ghosts and spirits become deferential. (2.5a)

—11—

Daily practice leads to the perfection of suchness;
Through infusion and harmony, qi nourishes spirit.
Life-destiny becomes pure and the gold radiance coalesces;
Returning [to the Source], you become an immortal. (2.5b)

—12—

Whether going out or staying in, remain in meditative enclosure;[81]
In perfect pervasion, both movement and stillness are forgotten.
By divining the changes, you sit and sleep in illumination;
Yin is completely transformed into pure yang. (2.5b)

—13—

The state of desirelessness resembles a clear sky;
In the state of suchness, the myriad appearances are illuminated.
Circulate the numen so that it harmonizes with the Dao;
Resonate with transformation so that your speaking is like a scripture. (2.5b–6a)

—14—

As early as possible you must awaken to the skeletons;
When life-destiny is pure, you may escape from the nine obscurities.
The gold child harmonizes with the jade maiden;
The perfect luster ascends to the pinnacle of clouds. (2.6a)

---

81. *Huandu*. See Goossaert 1999; Komjathy 2007a, 157–66.

—15—

Through daily practice, tie up the monkey of the mind;
When arousal arises, you must dispel the black clouds.
Through perfect constancy, you may develop the fruits of goodness;
When you return [to the Source], your name will be among the spirit immortals. (2.9b)

—16—

Through illumined emptiness, you can attend to perfection;
By descending the fire, you can transform the red silver.
With clear aspirations, beginning and end become penetrated;
You may cultivate and complete the body-beyond-the-body. (2.9b)

—17—

Through daily practice, abandon greed and anger;
Through perfect pervasion, attain the reasons for the Dao.
In subtle illumination, spirit and qi coalesce;
Beyond your own life-destiny there is no other relationship. (2.11a)

—18—

Illuminate the Dao so that innate nature attains perfect constancy;
Here turbid thoughts of greed and anger become forgotten.
Through clear pervasion, the Three Treasures coalesce;
Then you may cast off the husk and reach the immortal districts. (2.12a)

—19—

Through flexibility and yielding, you may awaken the perfect fire;
Free from thinghood, you may connect with your true self.
In sudden awakening you realize perfect cultivation;
Responding to beings, you complete the fruits of perfection. (2.13b)

—20—

Illuminating the One, stillness and clarity are constant;
Pervading subtlety, movement and stillness are forgotten.
The luminosity of virtue perfectly resonates with beings;
The wisdom of the Dao circulates as celestial radiance. (2.14a)

—21—

The great Dao originally is without name;
Earth and heaven return to stillness and clarity.
Solitary pervasion illuminates the myriad transformations;
By penetrating principle, practice and accomplishment are complete. (2.15a)

—22—

In clear pervasion, spirit and qi become numinous;
The highest adept awakens to a state without contention.

By penetrating principle, you can complete accomplishment and practice;
Among cerulean mists, you wander beyond the clouds. (5.1b)

—23—

Attain the Dao and become perfected naturally;
The azure lotus emerges from a muddy pond.
Even if obstructions hinder, the heart-mind is not obstructed;
Cast off form to manifest the body-beyond-the-body. (5.1b)

—24—

Through daily practice, the Six Roots are purified;
By awakening to perfection, the Dao's principle is illuminated.
Through suchness, you may complete the myriad practices;
You once again depart to wander among cerulean mists. (5.2b)

—25—

Abandon the mundane and clarify your aspirations;
Realize the Dao and nourish the Three Fields.
After a long time, the numinous sprouts develop;
When they become perfectly radiant, hemp and wheat proliferate. (5.5ab)

—26—

When the heart-mind dies, the radiance of innate nature emerges;
When you forget emotions, the life of realization resides.
The Dao is completed, and there is another body;
In perfect departure, it naturally ascends. (5.10b–11a)

—27—

In cultivating perfection, strong determination is essential;
In studying the Dao, the end is just like the beginning.
The sages and worthies of empty Nonbeing realize this—
Through innate nature and life-destiny one leaps beyond life and death. (5.14a)

The Heart-mind Is the Dao . . . / Wang Yuyang[82]

The heart-mind is the Dao; the Dao is the heart-mind;
With the heart-mind merged with the Dao, past and present are connected.
When the heart-mind transacts with the Dao, innate nature is naturally fragrant;
With even a spark of Perfection, one emerges in Mount Kun[lun].
When the heart-mind awakens, innate nature is numinous;
With Perfection spontaneously residing, one attains completion.

---

82. *Yunguang ji*, DZ 1152, 3.19b.

When the heart-mind is without images, innate nature is formless;
With spirit radiant, one circulates the golden essence.
When the heart-mind guards the Dao, innate nature is purified;
Whether in moving practice or meditation, one *is* Penglai.
When the heart-mind is realized, innate nature is relaxed;
With Perfection undissipated, one dwells in the distant realms.
When both people and self pass away, things and emotions cease;
By perfecting the great Dao, one realizes [a condition] beyond suffering.

Elegy on Abandoning Form / Ma Danyang[83]

Great is the ascent to Perfection!
The path leads into the clear darkness.
Unicorns follow the scarlet envoy banner.
Phoenixes pull my vermilion carriage.
With bells ringing and jade pieces dangling,
I wander through the Void and pace the clouds.
Rising above, I receive the declarations of the Perfected.[84]
I climb up to the Jade Imperial Dwelling.

---

83. *Jinyu ji*, DZ 1149, 6.8b–9a; *Lishi tongjian xupian*, DZ 297, 1.21b; Chen Y. 1988, 640.

84. Possibly an allusion to the *Zhen'gao* (Declarations of the Perfected; DZ 1016), an anthology of early Shangqing (Highest Clarity) revelations and texts compiled by Tao Hongjing (456–536). The implication is that Ma Danyang is entering the highest Daoist heavens, specifically the Three Heavens of Yuqing (Jade Clarity), Shangqing (Highest Clarity), and Taiqing (Great Clarity).

Chapter Two

Direct Instruction

This chapter contains discourse records (*yulu*) attributed to the early Quanzhen adepts. While most often associated with the Chan (Jpn.: Zen) tradition in the form of "recorded sayings," a "proto-*yulu*" genre in fact goes back to some of the earliest moments of Chinese and Daoist literary history. Here I am thinking specifically of the *Lunyu* (Analects) and the *Zhuangzi* (Book of Master Zhuang). In the case of classical Daoism, we find various dialogic exchanges in the *Zhuangzi.*[1] For example, in response to Huizi's inability to use a large gourd, Zhuangzi comments,

> "Now you had a gourd big enough to hold five shoulder-loads of weight. Why didn't you think of making it into a great tub so you could go floating around the rivers and lakes, instead of worrying because it was too big and unwieldy to dip into things! Obviously you still have a lot of underbrush in your head!" (Adapted from Watson 1968, 35)

Similarly, when Ququezi (Master Timid Magpie) inquires about the "activities of the wondrous Dao," Zhangwuzi (Master Elder Hibiscus) responds,

> "Right is not right; so is not so. If right were really right, it would differ so clearly from not right that there would be no need for argument. If so were really so, it would differ so clearly from not so that there would be no need for argument. Forget the years; forget distinctions. Leap into the boundless and make it your home!" (Adapted from Watson 1968, 48–49)

And, when Nanbo Zikui (Adept Sunflower of Southern Cypress) asks the female master Nüyu (Feminine Self-reliance) about Daoist practice, she recounts her instructions to Buliangyi (Divining Beam-support):

> "I began explaining and kept at him for three days, and after that he was able to put the world outside himself. When he had put the world outside himself, I kept at him for seven more days, and after that he was able to put things outside himself. When he had put things outside himself, I kept at him for nine more days, and after that he was able to put life outside himself. After he had put life outside himself, he was able

---

1. As I have suggested elsewhere (Komjathy 2007a), the *Zhuangzi* occupied a much more central place than commonly recognized in the study of Quanzhen Daoism. Here I would add that there is clear evidence for master-disciple lineages in the *Zhuangzi*. See Roth 1999; Schipper 2000.

to achieve the brightness of dawn, and when he had achieved the brightness of dawn, he could see his own aloneness. After he had managed to see his own aloneness, he could do away with past and present, and after he had done away with past and present, he was able to enter where there is no life and no death." (Adapted from Watson 1968, 82–83)[2]

Nonetheless, while these classical examples reveal historical precedents for the later emergence of the *yulu* genre, discourse records as a distinctive literary genre are a uniquely Chan innovation. At least generically speaking, Quanzhen discourse records are modeled on their Chan Buddhist counterparts. In terms of linguistic affinity as well as Buddhist influence on Quanzhen, the *yulu* genre is a Chan contribution.[3] However, as Quanzhen works do not explicitly cite any Chan discourse records, further research is required on specific influences, assuming that there are any.

In the context of early Quanzhen, discourse records were most often compiled by disciples in order to ensure that a given master's teachings were preserved and transmitted. The discourse records contain disparate and wide-ranging instructions. This is to be expected as the collected teachings derive from different contexts and biographical moments. In this respect, one is well advised to reflect on the ways in which the passage in question is directed at specific adepts, communities, and contexts. Take, for example, the following insights given by Wang Chongyang to the Jade Flower Association, an early Quanzhen religious community in Ninghai (present-day Muping, Shandong):

"Fellow adepts, if you long for perfect cultivation, simply eat when hungry and sleep when tired. There is no need to practice meditation or to study the Dao. You only need to separate yourself from the affairs of the mundane world. You only need to allow your heart-mind to be clear and pure. Anything beyond these two words [clarity and purity] is not cultivation." (*Quanzhen ji*, DZ 1153, 10.21a; cf. *Danyang yulu*, DZ 1057, 7a)

If one reads these instructions as authoritative and absolutist, one fails to understand the nuanced and sophisticated ways that Quanzhen teachers responded to the immediate questions, concerns, and spiritual requirements of a given adept or community. Wang Chongyang gave these teachings to a community largely composed of lay Quanzhen adherents and potential converts. Many, no doubt, had already committed themselves to meditation and study; they were individuals who had already embraced a Quanzhen way of life. One can imagine that some community members had become overly attached to study or practice, and Wang Chongyang was giving a necessary corrective, emphasizing freedom from mundane concerns and the cultivation of clarity and stillness in one's daily life. Quanzhen religious practice was not to be reduced to one specific activity, but rather

2. Based on these passages, one might compose some Daoist proto-*gong'an* (Jpn.: *kōan*): (1) Where's the gourd that contains rivers and lakes?; (2) Show me the suchness beyond argument; (3) What's the aloneness where birth and death do not encroach? For some Quanzhen adaptations of *gong'an*s see the late thirteenth-century *Qing'an Yingchanzi yulu* (DZ 1060) and the early fourteenth-century *Xuanjiao da gong'an* (DZ 1065). Another interesting textual connection is Gao Daokuan's (Yuanming [Complete Illumination]; 1195–1277) "Sanfa song" (Song of the Three Methods; *Shangsheng xiuzhen sanyao*, DZ 267, 1.2a–9a), which describes the purification of consciousness using the allegory of training a horse in a way that parallels the famous Ox-herding Pictures of Chan Buddhism.

3. On the historical development of Chan "recorded sayings" and "encounter dialogues" see Yanagida 1983; Berling 1987; Gardner 1991; McRae 1992; Dumoulin 1994; Gregory and Getz 1999; Poceski 2004. Few of these publications acknowledge the Chinese literary legacy that provided its kindling.

embraced as an all-pervasive existential approach. Others may have been ruminating about being incapable of Quanzhen religious training, believing that they would never make spiritual progress. In any case, Wang Chongyang provides necessary clarification and encouragement to his listeners. These instructions are neither the essentialized expression nor the culmination of early Quanzhen religious views and practice; in fact, the early training regimen, especially as embraced and applied by the Quanzhen spiritual elite, was quite complex. It was a comprehensive and integrated soteriological system (see Komjathy 2007a).

The first selection that follows is a translation of the opening section of *Jin zhenren yulu* (Discourse Record of Perfected Jin; DZ 1056, 1a–4b).[4] The text is not a Quanzhen text per se (see introduction to the present volume), but it has been included because of its influence on Wang Chongyang and his first-generation disciples.[5] Based on its resemblance to the "Chongzhen pian" (Chapters of Chongzhen; *Daoshu*, DZ 1017, 19.3b–4b), it is probable that the text contains the teachings of Jin Daocheng (Chongzhen [Exalted Perfection]; fl. 1110?), a shadowy historical figure.[6] Based on textual content, it appears that Perfected Jin adhered to the teachings and practices of the so-called Zhong-Lü lineage of internal alchemy (see Baldrian-Hussein 1984; Boltz 1987, 139–43), which is associated with various texts that also played some role in the formative phase of Quanzhen (see Komjathy 2007a). The *Jin zhenren yulu* provides a clear and concise discussion of Daoist cultivation, with emphasis placed on developing clarity and stillness; preserving the Three Treasures of vital essence, qi, and spirit; and attaining perfect practice and perfect accomplishment. The text cites the sixth-century *Yinfu jing* (2a) and the sixth-century *Xisheng jing* (3b), and mentions Lü Dongbin (b. 798?) by name (2b).

This is followed by a translation of the "Yuhua she shu" (Guidance for the Jade Flower Society), which appears in the *Quanzhen ji* (Anthology of Complete Perfection; DZ 1153, 10.20b–21a). This undated text represents instructions given by Wang Chongyang to the Yuhua hui (Jade Flower Association; Ninghai, Shandong). The Jade Flower Association was one of the five early Quanzhen religious communities in the eastern peninsula of Shandong. It is generally unclear who initiated such establishments, how many people participated, what types of activities occurred, and what, if any, lasting influence they had on the later development of Quanzhen as a formal monastic order. However, these meeting halls did provide a communal context for the early Quanzhen adepts, a place for potential adherents to become familiar with Quanzhen views and practices, and an opportunity for lay participation and involvement (see Katz 1999, 70; Goossaert 1997, 354–75).[7] Based upon the fact that Wang Chongyang lived in Shandong for the last three years of his life, from 1167–1170, the "Yuhua she shu" probably dates from that time. However, it is unclear if Wang presented his guidance as a public talk or as a written record. In terms of content, Wang Chongyang provides

---

4. Only this section corresponds to the title of the work. The remaining parts are later works spuriously attributed to some of the early Quanzhen adepts, including Wang Chongyang and Ma Danyang.

5. The text is cited by name in the following early Quanzhen texts: *Quanzhen ji*, DZ 1153, 10.21a; "Changzhen yulu" (*Zhenxian yulu*, DZ 1256, 1.10b). A comparison of the text's content reveals significant parallels with early Quanzhen cultivational concerns.

6. As far as my research goes, there are no extant hagiographies or historical sources on the life of Jin Daocheng.

7. Goossaert (1997, 371–75) suggests that laypeople received instruction on internal alchemy practice. While potentially true of certain dedicated individuals, this seems highly unlikely as a general phenomenon. I would surmise that the needs of householder congregants were met through charitable, devotional, and ritualistic activities. See Eskildsen 2004, 155–93.

basic instruction on the cultivation of innate nature and life-destiny, or adepts' spiritual capacities and foundational vitality. Wang suggests that attention to one's essential needs, specifically food and sleep, is the foundation of Daoist practice. He also advocates Daoist practice as an all-pervasive existential approach, wherein every moment is an opportunity to engage in self-cultivation. Wang cites the sixth-century *Yinfu jing* (20b) and the early twelfth-century *Jin zhenren yulu* (21a) as support for his instruction.

Next, I provide a complete translation of the *Danyang zhenren yulu* (Discourse Record of Perfected Danyang; DZ 1057; abbr. *Danyang yulu*).[8] This text was compiled by a disciple of Ma Danyang named Wang Yizhong (Lingyin [Numinous Hiddenness]; fl. 1183), who is principally remembered in Quanzhen history as the compiler and editor of this text.[9] After retiring from leadership of the Quanzhen religious community and transferring responsibilities to Qiu Changchun, Ma Danyang returned to his hometown of Ninghai (present-day Muping) at the age of fifty-nine. This occurred in the fourth lunar month of 1182, and it was partially determined by an imperial edict of 1181 by Jurchen-Jin Emperor Shizong (1123–1189; r. 1161–1189) requiring that all Daoists return to their hometowns (*Jinlian ji*, DZ 173, 3.6b; *Lishi tongjian xubian*, DZ 297, 1.18b–19a; *Ganshui lu*, DZ 973, 1.22b–23b). According to his own account, Wang Yizhong arrived in Ninghai from Dongwu (Hebei) in the third lunar month of 1183 with the intent of becoming Ma's disciple. After testing Wang's resolve, Ma accepted him (1a). The text thus contains some of the final teachings of Ma Danyang, who died nine months later. Based on the various Quanzhen hagiographies, we know that Ma traveled extensively during these years, providing guidance to various Quanzhen adepts and communities (see, e.g., *Jinlian ji*, DZ 173, 6b–11b). Wang Yizhong also notes that some of Ma's oral instructions derive from earlier teaching sessions (4b). The text, in turn, documents the specific locations where Ma taught (Dongmu [1b, 7a], Huating [3b], Jiaoma near Huangxian [4b], Laizhou [6b], Laiyang [10a], Dengjun [14a]) as well as the specific people who received the corresponding instructions (Cao and Liu [4b], Ren [4b], Jiang Xi [6b], Han Tao [6b], Cao and Lai [7a], Gong Daosheng [9b], Yu Qingfeng [9b], Cao and Zeng [12a]). Within the text, Ma admonishes Wang Yizhong for excessive reading of the *Zhuangzi* (3b) and recommends the Heshang gong commentary on the *Daode jing* and Tang Chun's commentary on the *Yinfu jing* (10a). Among other key names mentioned in the text, we find reference to Liu Biangong (Gaoshang [Exalted Eminence]; 1071–1143), an earlier Daoist ascetic in Shandong who emphasized solitary meditative praxis in a meditation enclosure (*huandu*) and who may have indirectly influenced the incorporation of that practice into the early Quanzhen religious community (see Goossaert 1997, 47–54; Goossaert 1999). The content of the *Danyang yulu* is quite diverse. Some key themes and concerns include purity (1b, 2b–3a, 8a); clarity and stillness (2b, 4a, 5a, 6a, 8a, 13b–14b); energetic integrity and nondissipation (4b, 5a, 6a, 11a, 15b); seclusion and meditation enclosure (4b, 8b, 12b); simplicity

---

8. There are three other discourse records associated with Ma Danyang, namely, (1) the *Danyang zhiyan* (Direct Sayings of Danyang; DZ 1234; 1179?), (2) the untitled opening section of the late thirteenth-century *Zhenxian yulu* (Discourse Records of Perfected Immortals; DZ 1256, 1.1a–2a), and (3) the "Danyang zhiyan" in the fourteenth-century *Qunxian yaoyu zuanji* (Collection of Essential Sayings from Various Immortals; DZ 1257, 2.15a–16a). The first text purports to be a transcription of an address that Ma Danyang gave to the Chongyang hui in the Longmen mountains (near Longxian, Shaanxi) (1a). The second text does not indicate its compiler and editor, but some of its content parallels the *Danyang yulu*. The third work, also anonymous, contains some parallel content with the *Danyang yulu*, but is completely distinct from DZ 1234. See Boltz 1987, 153–54; Schipper and Verellen 2004, 1144–45, 1162; Komjathy 2007a.

9. As far as my research goes, there is no extant hagiography of this second-generation Quanzhen adherent.

and voluntary poverty (5a, 10b–11a); no-mind (5ab, 7a, 8b, 9a); abstinence from alcohol, sex, and meat consumption (2b–3a, 12a, 13b–14b); as well as daily practice (11b).

The final selection is a translation of the *Hao Taigu zhenren yu[lu]* (Discourse Record of Perfected Hao Taigu; abbr. *Taigu yulu*), which is preserved in the thirteenth-century *Zhenxian zhizhi yulu* (Discourse Records and Direct Pointers of Perfected Immortals; DZ 1256, 1.19a–22b; abbr. *Zhenxian yulu*). The *Taigu yulu* does not mention a compiler or editor, but presents itself as oral teachings of Hao Guangning. Given the fact that the work is contained in a relatively late anthology, some reservations concerning authorial attribution are in order. The *Zhenxian yulu* also collects discourse records attributed to Tan Changzhen (1.9b–10b), Liu Changsheng (1.10b–12a), and Qiu Changchun (1.12a–19a).[10] With respect to dating, it is noteworthy that the discourse record attributed to Tan Changzhen also appears in his *Shuiyun ji* (Anthology of Water and Clouds; DZ 1160, 1.20b–21a), dating possibly to as early as 1187 or as late as 1220. The other *Zhenxian yulu* titles in general and our text in particular may thus be considered reliably attributed. The *Taigu yulu* is especially significant because so little of Hao Guangning's literary productions are extant. His only other surviving work is the fragmentary *Taigu ji* (Anthology of Taigu; 1161),[11] which consists of a commentary on the *Cantong qi* (Token for the Kinship of the Three; DZ 999; DZ 1004), thirty-three diagrammatic explanations of the *Yijing*, and a sequence of thirty "Jindan shi" (Poems on the Gold Elixir; translated in chapter 1 herein). The text contains allusions to the *Daode jing* and *Zhuangzi*. Within the pages of the *Taigu yulu*, we find Hao Guangning emphasizing the importance of renunciation and solitary practice (19a, 20a), alchemical transformation (19ab, 21–22b), clarity and stillness (19b), voluntary simplicity and poverty (19b), daily practice (20a), and five illnesses of the heart-mind (20b).

In addition to the aforementioned discourse records associated with the first-generation Quanzhen adepts, there are also various texts by later members of the tradition. Of particular note are the *Qinghe zhenren beiyou yulu* (Discourse Record of Perfected Qinghe during Northward Travels; DZ 1310; abbr. *Qinghe yulu*) and the *Panshan Qiyun Wang zhenren yulu* (Discourse Record of Perfected Wang Qiyun of Mount Pan; DZ 1059; abbr. *Qiyun yulu*). The *Qinghe yulu* collects the oral instructions of Yin Zhiping (Qinghe [Clear Harmony]; 1169–1251), a disciple first of Liu Changsheng and then of Qiu Changchun, who ascended to the position of Quanzhen Patriarch and national leader following the death of the latter in 1227. The *Qiyun yulu* contains the teachings of Wang Zhijin (Qiyun [Residing-among-Clouds]; 1178–1263), a disciple first of Hao Guangning and later of Qiu Changchun, with Wang being one of the most influential second-generation Quanzhen leaders. An anthology focusing on the later moments of Quanzhen history and the monastic order might include translations of these texts and other Quanzhen discourse records.[12]

No historically informed and contextually accurate translations of early Quanzhen discourse records have been published to date. However, in his dissertation (2002, 178–84), Paulino Belamide included a translation of the "Changchun Qiu zhenren ji Xizhou daoyou shu" (Writings of Perfected

10. These texts continue to receive wide circulation in contemporary Quanzhen monastic communities as they were included by the late Min Zhiting (1924–2004) in his *Daojiao yifan* (Daoist Religious Models; 1990).

11. The text was compiled by Fan Yuanxi (1178–1249) and includes prefaces by Hao, Fan, Feng Bi (1162–1240), and Liu Qi (1203–1250).

12. Many of the later Quanzhen discourse records are catalogued in *A Historical Companion to the Daozang* (Schipper and Verellen 2004; see also Goossaert 1997).

Qiu Changchun Sent to Daoist Friends in Xizhou), a text contained in the *Zhenxian yulu* (DZ 1256, 1.12a–19a). Vincent Goossaert has translated the prefaces to the *Qiyun yulu* in his dissertation (1997, 503–6). A popular translation of selections of the *Danyang yulu* (1b–2b, 6a–8a, 9a), complete with nonexistent section headings and decontextualized teachings, appears in Thomas Cleary's *Taoist Meditation* (2000, 106–11).

Discourse Record of Perfected Jin[13]

Compiled by Anonymous Disciples

The master said, "The opening has arrived this very day. This person is about to perish, so there is no time to wait. At this very moment, I am about to meet spirit immortals and to depart from the mundane world, facing the flourishing of the great Dao.

"Now, you may think that you are all part of the celestial community, but there are worthy and ignorant among you. These are not the same. The worthy face the Dao, while the ignorant turn their backs on the Dao. Facing the Dao, there is life; turning one's back on the Dao, there is death. The heart-mind clarified and thinking stilled is the road to the Celestial Hall. The heart-mind uncultivated and thinking chaotic is the gateway to the Earth Prison.

"You may think that I am asking whether it is better to ascend to the Celestial Hall or to enter the Earth Prison. But, in truth, as elders of the Dao and worthies of virtue, how can you think this way, engaging in such deluded and ignorant verbal expressions! Unless the Daoist teachings flourish in the present moment, there is no way for the celestial opportunity of clarity and purity to spread in the mundane world or to be received by illuminated and superior adepts."

The master said, "Those engaging in cultivation must first recognize that innate nature and life-destiny are the ancestor and the patriarch. Only on their basis can you cultivate perfection and protect life-destiny. This cultivation begins with preserving the Three, embracing the Origin, and guarding the One.[14] **[1b]** Preserving the Three means to work on the real Three Treasures of vital essence, qi, and spirit. Embracing the Origin means to embrace and guard the original yang and perfect qi. Guarding the One means to guard the unified, numinous spirit.

"Spirit is the original source; it resides in the heart. The heart is associated with the Fire [phase], the southern direction, and [the celestial stems of] *bingding*. Innate nature resides in the heart. Innate nature is associated with yang. The kidneys can give rise to the original yang and perfect qi. [The kidneys][15] are associated with the Water [phase], the northern direction, and [the celestial stems of] *rengui*. Water is life-destiny, and life-destiny is associated with yin.

---

13. *Jin zhenren yulu*, DZ 1056, 1a–4b.

14. "Embracing the Origin" (*baoyi*) and "guarding the One" (*shouyi*) echo classical Daoist technical terminology related to Daoist quietistic meditation. See chapters 5, 10, 16, 20, 22, and 28 of the *Daode jing* and chapters 5, 8, 14, 17, 19, 24, and 25 of the "Neiye" (Inward Training) section of the *Guanzi* (Book of Master Guan). On classical Daoist meditative praxis see Roth 1999. For a discussion of later Daoist meditation practices designated as "guarding the One" see Kohn 1989.

15. The text contains "qi" here. I have amended the text to parallel the earlier description of the heart.

"What I have said above concerning innate nature and life-destiny should be understood and disseminated. From ancient times to the present day, many people have not understood innate nature and life-destiny, but today these concepts are becoming clearer in the world."

The master said, "The study of the Dao originally has three [stages]. The first stage involves maintaining a unified heart-mind in all mental activities. This is done by focusing on the lower elixir field, the cavern of immortality. Do not allow the heart-mind and thinking to become scattered and chaotic. Embrace the original yang and perfect qi and you will attain long life. This is the root of the perfect Dao, the way of escaping death and entering life. It is the furnace of immortality in which the transformative process of yin and yang [occurs]. Inside this elixir field, purify the heart-mind and stabilize thinking.

"Dark and serene, [2a] subtle and uninterrupted, practice like this diligently for three to five years. Then the two qi will commingle inside your own alchemical furnace. They become warm and full, joining to form a single, unified qi. You complete this transformative process in emptiness, while the numinous embryo of immortality is formed in your inner vessel.

"As this happens, the spirit inside the heart becomes numinous. Leaping for joy, it spontaneously sings and dances. When spirit acquires qi it becomes numinous, and when qi acquires spirit it becomes clear. As the *Yinfu jing* (Scripture on the Hidden Talisman) says,[16] 'Sacred accomplishment is born here; spiritual illumination emerges from this.' Qi is the mother of spirit; spirit is the child of qi.[17] If you can constantly guard spirit and qi together, without allowing separation, with time spirit becomes stabilized naturally, and the way of immortality is completed.

"In the second stage, after stage one has been attained, you can let go of the four elements [of the body],[18] be without restraint, and practice at ease. The qi of the Dao[19] is naturally [present] within clarity and purity. Spirit ascends to the numinous palace. You are always active in your immediate situation, and never look back.

"In the third stage, once you have attained the stabilization of spirit and the harmonization of qi, you can go even farther and attain a celestial lifespan. Let the heart-mind be free in casual abandon and become independent by being carefree. Free from worldly affairs, you become clear and at ease. Through this, you realize the undifferentiated state of the great Dao. [2b] Clarity and purity reach their culmination. Your accomplishment becomes complete and your practice is fulfilled. The Jade Emperor will summon you to the [celestial] assembly, making sure that nothing obstructs your long life and happiness."

The master said, "As you study the Dao and engage in cultivation, sometimes your spirit may lack stability, your accomplishment is not yet complete, and you do not realize that your lifespan is

---

16. The anonymous sixth-century CE *Yinfu jing* (DZ 31). For a translation of Liu Changsheng's commentary see chapter 5 herein.

17. This sentence parallels the opening section of the seventh-century *Cunshen lianqi ming* (Inscription on Preserving Spirit and Refining Qi; DZ 834). See Kohn 1987, 119.

18. Here I have translated the "four greats" (*sida*) as the Four Elements of standard Indian cosmology borrowed from Buddhism. In this case it would refer to the body/self as a whole. This technical term may also refer to the four limbs. In the present context, it suggests not restricting one's physical activity.

19. *Daoqi*.

limited. In that case, practice embracing and guarding. Perfected Lü said,[20] 'Even without speaking about the great Dao, people naturally realize it. This is because they put forth right effort and are not self-centered.' "[21]

The master said, "Now, if you fail to be diligent in your practice, your effort will bear no fruit and your spirit will lack clarity. Restrain [this tendency] permanently and you will not lose perfect practice. Your heart-mind will not be labored, and your aspirations will not be wild. Your vital essence will not be lost, and your spirit will not become dispersed."

The master said, "Alas, as I look at people in the world seeking a teacher and inquiring about the Dao, [I find that] they are not willing to subordinate themselves to others. They only speak about everyone else as inferior to themselves. When it comes to cultivation, they are unwilling to be diligent and attentive, patient and forbearing. They merely engage in hollow speech and never even start the right effort toward perfection. Moreover, they are not truly committed to cultivation. When they see people in poverty, they also lack any inclination to be of assistance or to come to the rescue. [3a] With each successive step, they squander their efforts and practice until they utterly lose their hidden virtue and act in opposition to the Dao. Adepts like this who want to complete immortality and have confirmation of the Dao—how much more distant could they be!

"I will now briefly discuss the causes that lead to the fruits of the Dao. To ascend to the heavens only requires that you protect perfect accomplishment and perfect practice.[22] Doing so, you become a person of eminent virtue and can naturally attune your activities with the heavens and earth. As a scripture says, 'August heaven does not have relatives; virtue is the only support.'[23]

"If you want perfect accomplishment, purify your heart-mind and stabilize your thoughts, harness vital essence and control spirit. Without moving and without acting, in perfect clarity and perfect purity, embrace the Origin and guard the One, preserve spirit and solidify qi. This is perfect accomplishment.

"If you want perfect practice, cultivate kindness and virtue by relieving poverty and rescuing people from suffering. If you see people in difficulty, you should constantly give rise to the desire to help them. At times, [it may also be appropriate] to persuade worthy people to enter the Dao and engage in training. In everything you do, put others first and yourself last. Maintain selflessness in relations with the myriad beings. This is perfect practice."

The master said, "To engage in cultivation and nourish life-destiny, first accumulate practice and exert effort. [3b] If you put forth effort but fail to practice, the fruits of the Dao will not ripen. Only after accomplishment and practice are complete can one be called a Perfected."

The master said, "When you adepts speak with members of our community, emphasize the Great Awakening,[24] innate nature, and principle. Also explain how to deeply investigate the wondrous Dao

---

20. Lü Dongbin (b. 798?), who was identified as one of the so-called Five Patriarchs (*wuzu*) in Quanzhen.

21. Source unknown.

22. *Zhengong* and *zhenxing* may also be translated as "true merit" and "true good deeds," respectively. I have occasionally translated *gong* as "effort."

23. Source unknown.

24. Great Awakening (*dawu*) parallels the Chan (Zen) Buddhist emphasis on becoming spiritually realized or enlightened. However, the earliest reference, appearing as *dajue*, appears in chapter 2 of the *Zhuangzi*. See Watson 1968, 47.

and to set one's aspirations on engaging in cultivation and studying immortality. As the *Xisheng jing* (Scripture on the Western Ascension) says,[25]

> 'Get rid of all impurities and stop your thoughts;
> Purify the heart-mind and guard the One.
> When all impurities are gone, the myriad affairs are done.
> These are the essentials of my way.'

How amazing! It's totally incomparable!

"Generally speaking, whether acting or speaking, coming or going, illuminate and nourish the treasures within the body. Admonish people to follow the Way of Heaven and to accord with the celestial principle.[26] Do not slander the heavens or defile the earth. If you notice adepts of the deep abyss talking behind the backs of others with reckless speech, redirect the conversation to spiritual matters. Then you are truly one who has realized the Dao. But as long as you cling to the mundane you will never attain this."

The master said, "As you study the Dao, first unite the body through clarity and purity. Do not kill, take intoxicants, eat meat, break the precepts, or commit sexual transgressions. Each desire only entangles you more in the mundane and the myriad affairs, causing suffering for oneself and trouble for others. [4a] Sever all ties to hatred, anger, stinginess, and greed. Constantly practice patience under insult and forbearance; live simply and frugally. When you see people in difficulty, give rise to a disposition of assistance and liberation. When you see people in poverty, assist them by doing good. Always place others first and yourself last. Treat others respectfully regardless of social position. Respond to opposition with kindness. Do not concern yourself with the transgressions of others. Do not discuss the faults of others. Secretly accumulate hidden virtue, and do not seek recognition from others. Simply hope that the heavens will take notice and be a person committed to the Dao."

The master said, "The great Dao is without a set location. Its subtlety and wondrousness are immeasurable. The action of sages is embodied in daily practice.

"In their daily activities, the majority of people remain unaware of this. They turn their backs on the Dao and lose perfection. Their actions are influenced by death and dirt. They do not realize that humans in fact live in the Dao like fish in water. If fish lose water, they die; if humans lose the Dao, they perish."[27]

The master said, "Now, as I read through the scriptures and classics, [I find that] the meaning is often hidden and mysterious and that it is hard to find a good explanation. Thus today I have tried to use ordinary language to disperse delusion and point toward awakening. And if something is not yet clear, I leave it to adepts of later generations to seek out the teachings. [4b] Perhaps they can explain the meaning, put it into practice, and even transmit it to their disciples. Doing so, they

---

25. The late fifth- or early sixth-century *Xisheng jing* (DZ 666; DZ 726), most likely composed in the Louguan (Lookout Tower Monastery; Zhouzhi, Shaanxi) environs. The quotation comes from section 39.10–12/6.17ab; see Kohn 1991, 256, also 247 and 250.

26. An allusion to section 1a of the *Yinfu jing*. On the Way of Heaven see also chapter 13 of the *Zhuangzi*.

27. An allusion to section 32.1–3/6.1ab of the *Xisheng jing*. See Kohn 1991, 252.

can guard life-destiny and cultivate perfection, accumulate blessings that reach the far ends of the cosmos. Relieving the sickness and suffering of human beings becomes their most important practice. If you receive these writings, then suffering will be relieved up to nine generations. Your father and mother will receive benefit.

"If this discourse deceives people, may I forever reside in Yinshan (Dark Mountain) for endless *kalpa*s."[28]

Guidance for the Jade Flower Society[29]

Wang Zhe, Master Chongyang

Now, the Jade Flower is the ancestor of qi, while the Gold Lotus is the ancestor of spirit. When qi and spirit are bound together, we refer to this as "spirit immortality."

A commentary on the *Yinfu jing* says, "Spirit is the child of qi; qi is the mother of spirit."[30] When child and mother meet, you can become a spirit immortal.

The reason why I established the Jade Flower and Gold Lotus Societies in the two prefectures is because I wanted all adepts to recognize perfect innate nature.[31] If you do not understand the perfect source, you will only study the lesser techniques of subsidiary schools. Such methods may produce blessings and nourish the body, but they have nothing to do with the Way of Cultivating Immortality.

Considering the issue of innate nature and life-destiny, if you make even the slightest misstep, you may be led astray from the human path [through transmigration]. Fellow adepts, if you long for perfect cultivation, simply eat when hungry and sleep when tired. There is no need to practice meditation or to study the Dao. You only need to separate yourself from the affairs of the mundane world. You only need to allow your heart-mind to be clear and pure. Anything beyond these two words [clarity and purity] is not cultivation.

All adepts should cherish discernment and wisdom. Each day when you practice in the purification chamber remain continuously alert for awakening.[32] Do not become lost in other schools. For practice and accomplishment, [21a] there is nothing else beyond perfect accomplishment and perfect practice.

---

28. Compare the conclusion of the *Jinguan yusuo jue* (Instructions on the Gold Pass and Jade Lock; DZ 1156) as translated in Komjathy 2007a.

29. "Yuhua she shu." From *Quanzhen ji*, DZ 1153, 10.20b–21a.

30. Section 1b of the *Yinfu jing zhu* (Commentary on the *Yinfu jing*; DZ 121) by Tang Chun (Jinling daoren [Daoist of Nanjing]; eleventh c. CE?), which Eskildsen (2004, 36, 216, n. 43) points out was the preferred *Yinfu jing* commentary of the early Quanzhen movement. The passage in question appears in section 1b. According to the *Danyang yulu* (DZ 1057, 10a; translated herein), Daoist adherents should not read excessively, as it disturbs the heart-mind. When one does wish to study scriptures, Ma Danyang recommends Heshang gong's commentary on the *Daode jing* and Master Jinling's commentary on the *Yinfu jing*. See also Liu Changsheng's commentary (*Yinfu jing zhu*, DZ 144, 5b). A parallel passage also appears in section 1a of Sun Simiao's (581–682?) *Cunshen lianqi ming* (Inscription on Visualizing the Spirits and Refining Qi; DZ 834). See Kohn 1987, 119.

31. The Yuhua hui (Association of Jade Flower; Dengzhou, Shandong) and Jinlian hui (Association of Gold Lotus; Ninghai, Shandong), respectively.

32. Here "purification chamber" translates *zhaichang*. I am reading this as equivalent to "pure chamber" (*jingshi*) and "meditation enclosure" (*huandu*), or practicing solitary mediation in a secluded room or hut.

Perfected Jin said,[33] "If you long for perfect accomplishment, you must purify your heart-mind and stabilize your thinking. Discipline spirit and emotions. Free from movement and activity, this is perfect clarity and perfect purity. Embrace the Origin and guard the One. Preserve spirit and stabilize qi. This is perfect accomplishment.

"If you long for perfect practice, you must cultivate humaneness and accumulate virtue by alleviating poverty and relieving suffering. If you see people in difficult situations, constantly cultivate a heart-mind of assistance and liberation. At times, you should persuade suitable people to enter the Dao and engage in cultivation. In whatever you do, put others first and yourself last. Be selfless when relating to the myriad beings. This is perfect practice."

I humbly wish that all adepts may soon receive [these instructions] and [attain] clearness of apprehension.

Discourse Record of Perfected Danyang[34]

Compiled by Wang Yizhong, Master Lingyin

In the third month of *guimao* year of the Dading reign [1183], I paid obeisance to Master [Danyang] for the first time. This occurred to the south of Fan Mingshu's hermitage in Muping.[35]

The master asked, "Where did you come from?"

I replied, "I came from Dongwu in order to gaze upon the master's inner power.[36] Because I do not take material possessions and wealth to be valuable, and because I am content in my own quietness, I sit here [in hopes of] entering this path. When I heard about your movement, I became very happy. I wish to wait upon your kerchief and sandals, and now prostrate myself [hoping] to hear even a single word."

The master was satisfied with this and accordingly responded, "With each passing year, there are fewer people who have the heart to study the Dao. [Without this], you cannot realize it."

After pausing for a long time, he again spoke saying, "If you are hungry, you should eat and then leave. If you have already eaten, you should sleep and then leave."

One day the master saw me[37] standing reverently in front of him with my hands joined. At that moment he sighed and said, "Daoists only wish to be open and joyful, but beautiful physical appearances are destined to fade. A hermitage is not a palace, and you are not an official magistrate. If you merely preach about vulgar rituals, **[1b]** then take this opportunity. Those in ancient times

33. A reference to the *Jin zhenren yulu* (translated herein), most likely associated with Jin Daocheng (Chongzhen [Exalted Perfection]; fl. 1110?). The passage appears in section 3a.

34. *Danyang zhenren yulu*, DZ 1057. Cf. *Danyang zhiyan*, DZ 1234 and *Zhenxian yulu*, DZ 1256, 1.1a–2a.

35. Also known as Ninghai, Shandong. Fan Mingshu (fl. 1167) was a local official and wealthy landowner of Ninghai, and it was on his estate that Ma Danyang first met Wang Chongyang. See *Jinlian ji*, DZ 173, 3.4b; 5.1b (translated in chapter 6 herein). See also *Jinlian xiangzhuan*, DZ 174, 23b–24a.

36. Dongwu is located to the west of Jinan, in Hebei Province.

37. *Pu*, literally meaning "slave" or "servant." A conventional designation used in place of "I."

said, 'Among the three mountains there are companions whose emotions are dull; within the four oceans there is no Daoist lineage whose discernment is deep.'[38] Do not follow this pattern."

Every time the master transmitted teachings he would say, "Those who study the Dao must seek their own awakening. The reason why you are not awakened is because of obscuration. If you want to break through obscuration, you must first scour your heart-mind. Illuminated realization will be the result of cleansing and purification. When accomplishment is attained and completed, you must not seek direction from other people. Even I, a simpleton, can plainly understand this work."

When the master was practicing in the area above Dongmu,[39] Buddhists and Daoists would come to visit. Whether he recognized them or not, he was invariably the first to bow. His disciples accordingly increased. One posed the following question: "Through that and this, obscuration and mediocrity are produced. What is the use of bowing?"

The master said, "Through yielding and flexibility,[40] the Dao humbly descended to become the Source. Moreover, the Three Teachings are different windows inside the same gateway. Kongzi said, 'Even if it meant being a guard holding a whip,[41] I would do it.'[42] A sign of respect thus may be a personal affront."

[2a] The master said, "The Patriarch,[43] in purity, worked on [his own] literary writing. After he realized the Dao, he became very diligent about it. With regard to [the poems written in the form of] *cangtou chaizi*,[44] the hidden language strings together pearls. The underlying plan is not perplexing. Continually keeping tune with human poetry, there are poems that hide the rhymed characters. Each keeps tune with the others, but only the Patriarch had the end rhymes. Hence there is one that reads, 'Three hundred and sixty golden bones and joints.' Everyone laments [that we do not understand this], as we regard it as the words of a spirit immortal. At this time who can obtain it? With the exception of the adept of Panxi,[45] few understand the series."

---

38. Source unknown.

39. Near present-day Muping, Shandong, which was Wang Yuyang's birthplace.

40. *Rouruo* are foundational Daoist principles and values. The earliest occurrences appear in chapters 3, 10, 36, 40, 43, 52, 55, 76, and 78 of the *Daode jing*. They are also one of the so-called Nine Practices (*jiuxing*) of the early Celestial Masters. See Bokenkamp 1997, 49; Komjathy 2008a.

41. That is, being in a position of relatively low status.

42. An allusion to chapter 7 of the *Lunyu* (Analects). The entire passage reads as follows: "The Master said, 'If wealth were a permissible pursuit, I would be willing even to act as a guard holding a whip outside the market place. If it is not, I shall follow my own inclinations" (Lau 1992, 59).

43. Wang Chongyang.

44. "Opening line hiding a selected character." A poetic form in which one not only adopts the prescribed metrical pattern and rhyme scheme, but also evokes the opening character from the last character in the father verse. The "hidden head" (*cangtou*) refers to the fact that the first character of each verse is not supplied in the written poem (Boltz 1987, 146, 309, n. 353; also Eskildsen 2004, 240, n. 11). According to Eskildsen, the Ching Chung Taoist Association (Hong Kong) has published an edition of Quanzhen poetry that includes the missing characters.

45. Qiu Changchun. Panxi refers to the place by that name in Shaanxi Province where Qiu engaged in solitary religious practice. Panxi is located west of Xianyang and Xi'an.

The master said, "When the Patriarch was staying in Dengzhou,[46] he wore a bamboo rain hat with a tassel hanging like a quail's plume and carried a five-stringed lute and an iron bowl. These things made him appear strange and old. He begged for alms in the marketplaces, and the people of Dengzhou did not recognize him. One evening he returned to the monastery and wrote this stanza on the wall.

> As soon as I abandoned the waters, forests, and hamlets of Zhongnan,[47]
> My family had neither son and wife nor any grandchildren.[48]
> Beyond a thousand miles, I venture to encounter companions,
> Those who would extend themselves to enter the gate of perpetual life beyond dying.[49]

In the early morning he dusted off his clothes and began traveling east.

"After several days, a prefect with official regalia and eminent appearance went to the monastery [2b] and took note of the poem's theme. He sighed in respect. Then he accordingly composed a poem to the same tune:

> Separated from one's home for three years, abandoning the old hamlet,
> Everyone forgets the halls and forests, and sons and grandchildren grow up.
> At another time, I dusted off my sleeves and sought the lord who had departed,
> I responded with the promise of peace and leisure, a single rap on the gate."

The master spoke the following words, "Eating plainly nourishes qi. Abandoning anger nourishes innate nature. Abiding in a humble position nourishes inner power. Guarding the One, clarity and stillness, and calm tranquility nourish the Dao.[50]

"When your name is not written in official documents and registers, and your heart-mind is not bound to power and profit, you can cast off the shell of human being and become the companion of heaven."

The master said, "Alcohol is a draught that confuses innate nature. Meat is a substance that severs life-destiny.[51] Straightaway you must recognize that not consuming these is best. Still, the transgression of drinking alcohol and eating meat may be excused. However, if you transgress [the precept] against having sex, the punishment will not be less than death. Why is this? Because sex is more dangerous

---

46. Dengzhou is in the eastern peninsula of Shandong, northwest of Yantai. It was the location of the Yuhua hui (Association of Jade Flower).

47. Shaanxi.

48. The second line of the stanza uses the Chinese *jia*, which may refer to both one's actual family and one's religious lineage.

49. *Changsheng busi*, which more often appears as *changsheng bulao* ("perpetual life beyond aging"). It is a Daoist technical phrase that refers to longevity or immortality. A classical precedent, though with a completely different meaning, appears in chapter 33 of the *Daode jing*: "To die but not to perish is longevity" (*si er buwang zhe shou*).

50. These Daoist technical terms echo various passages from the *Daode jing*.

51. This is one of the clearest early Quanzhen precedents for a vegetarian diet. However, although the later Quanzhen monastic order required vegetarianism, it seems that the early community allowed for individual dietary choices. It seems that Ma Danyang and Qiu Changchun were the early adherents most committed to a vegetarian diet as a necessary precondition for spiritual realization and alchemical transformation. See Komjathy 2011a.

than wolves or tigers. It destroys a person's beautiful deeds and virtuous actions. **[3a]** Sex injures vital essence and disperses spirit. At the extreme, it leads to the death of the physical body. Thus, for Daoists it is a major transgression."

The master said, "To attain peace and a joyous life, nothing is better than seclusion. If Daoists are able to reside in a hermitage, they can decrease their level of fatigue by joining with one or two people as companions.[52] Together they can gather fur in order to make padded jackets and find tree-fall to make walking sticks. Moreover, they can sing and travel together, encountering amazing mountains and streams along the way. They can also admire Huan-trees together and ensure that each other avoid the path to avarice."

The master addressed me saying, "Those who study the Dao want there to be an end and a beginning, but you cannot divide the Dao in half and dispense with some aspect. Other people find this as a pretext for making jokes. Moreover, considering people who read books, how can they not know that only ordinary people attempt to establish character by engaging in mundane professions. Those who act through the Dao are adepts who truly establish personal character through the most important undertaking."

The master constantly would write large characters on a single scroll and address his Daoist companions as follows:[53] "Invite people to come to our mountain to attain liberation and inversion. **[3b]** They will quickly open the pathway into the Cavern of Dragon and Tiger."

I then asked, "When people find out about our mountain, who will have the courage to ask about the location of the Cavern of Dragon and Tiger?"

The master laughed and said, "The pivot of the heavens[54] has not yet dared to lighten its commands; one can thus note, in minute detail, whether the worthy are awakened or not."

One day the master yelled for me. After a long time he came out and asked, "Where did you go?" I responded, "At the hour of *wu* [11 a.m.–1 p.m.], I retire to my sleeping quarters, so that my spirit and emotions may attain deep serenity. A section of the *Zhuangzi* rests on the headboard of my bed because I enjoy reading various passages. Therefore, I was not here." The master said, "Now, the Dao wants to form a contract with the heart-mind.[55] If you can attain such a condition through

---

52. These teachings parallel the first and sixth discourses of the *Chongyang lijiao shiwu lun* attributed to Wang Chongyang. See the translation contained in chapter 3 herein.

53. It seems that some of the early adepts enjoyed writing calligraphy and using it as an opportunity for self-cultivation and communal instruction. For example, in Tan Changzhen's hagiography in the *Jinlian ji* (DZ 173, 4.2a), we are informed, "Every evening, Master Tan enjoyed writing the two characters *gui* ("turtle") and *she* ("snake")." See the translation in chapter 6 herein.

54. *Tianji*, also translated as "mechanism of heaven" or "celestial trigger." References to the "pivot of the heavens" appear in chapters 14 and 17 of the *Zhuangzi*. A more detailed discussion appears in the sixth-century *Yinfu jing*.

55. *Fu*, "talisman," "tally," or "contract," most often refers to an object used for imperial and military communications in ancient China. The tally was broken apart, with one section kept by each party. If a message was transmitted, it would be accompanied by the other section to confirm its authenticity. In Daoism, it becomes a symbol of communication and reunification with the Dao. The earliest Daoist occurrence appears in the title of chapter 5, "Talisman of Virtue Complete," of the *Zhuangzi*. Quanzhen Daoists would also recognize the allusion to the *Yinfu jing*.

literature, when is it time to awaken? Therefore, in terms of awakening to the Dao, [reading] the *Nanhua* [*Zhuangzi*] is delusion becoming even more deluded."[56]

When the master was residing in Huating he spoke the following:[57] "What kind of 'thing' is the Dao? It is the source of the ancestral qi. How can you not know this through the breath moving through your own nose? How can you not listen to the words of Master Guangcheng:[58] 'When the elixir furnace and Waterwheel cease toiling, [4a] the crane embryo and tortoise respiration naturally become subtle and fine.'"[59]

The master addressed the community: "If you can solely dedicate yourself to studying the Dao, then each of you will become an immortal. This is not the same as achieving recognition in the mundane world, which leads to degradation and dissipation. For Confucians, achievement in learning and official position are what they desire. For Daoists, simplicity and ease[60] are what we practice. Still more important, clarity and purity and nonaction are methods of the highest vehicle."

The master resided in a meditation enclosure[61] furnished only with a desk, long couch, brush, ink tablet, and sheepskin. It was empty of any extraneous objects. In the early morning he ate one bowl of rice porridge and at noon he ate one bowl of noodles.[62] Beyond this, meat and strong-smelling vegetables never entered his mouth.

One day he summoned me to enter the enclosure, asking me to sit for a while. I asked, "Does the way of my master make distinctions between either/or?"

The master said, "Wu![63] Even if songs and lyrics sing about dragon and tiger, Child and Maiden, these are simply words. Therefore, if you long for the wondrousness of the Dao, nothing is better

---

56. The *Nanhua zhenjing* (Perfect Scripture of Southern Florescence; DZ 670) is the Daoist honorific title given to the *Zhuangzi*. Note that Ma Danyang, like most of the early senior Quanzhen adepts, is giving context-specific instruction here; this is not an authoritarian statement about scripture study. For instance, later on in section 10a Ma Danyang recommends reading the Heshang gong commentary on the *Daode jing* and Tang Chun's commentary on the *Yinfu jing*. Cf. *Jianwu ji*, DZ 1142, 2.32b; *Jinyu ji*, DZ 1149, 1.7b–8a, 2.19b, 5.2a; *Shenguang can*, DZ 1150, 18a, 19a.

57. As Ma was living near his hometown of Ninghai (Muping) at this time, Huating (Flower Pavilion) must have been a local district or Ma's name for his residence. Based on the context, it cannot have been the place by that name northwest of Xi'an, Shaanxi. See also *Jinlian ji*, DZ 173, 3.8ab.

58. Guangchengzi (Master Expansive Completion) first appears in chapter 11 of the *Zhuangzi*, wherein he gives advice on Daoist cultivation to the Yellow Emperor. See Watson 1968, 118–20. Here Master Guangcheng emphasizes Daoist quietistic meditation, nonaction, and mystical union with the Dao, with his teachings paralleling chapters 14, 47, 52, and 56 of the *Daode jing*. Guangchengzi also becomes a central figure in early medieval immortality lore, with his hagiography appearing in the *Shenxian zhuan*. See Campany 2002, 159–61. By the Northern Song dynasty, Guangchengzi becomes identified as one of the so-called "transformations" (*bianhua*; manifestations) of Lord Lao, the deified Laozi. See Little 2000, 175–76. In the present context, Master Guangcheng teaches internal alchemy, a new religious modality.

59. The crane and tortoise are both symbols of longevity.

60. *Yi*, also translatable as changeability, in the sense of adaptation.

61. *Huandu*.

62. Following the Buddhist proscription against monastics eating after noon.

63. An allusion to the famous Chan *gong'an* (Jpn.: *kōan*) of Zhao Zhou (Jpn.: Jōshū; 778–897), better known through the Japanese Zen tradition as "Mu." The "case" appears in both the *Wumen guan* (Gateless Gate) and *Biyan lu* (Blue Cliff Record), which have been translated by Thomas Cleary. It reads as follows: A monk asked Zhaozhou, "Does a dog have Buddha-nature?" Zhaozhou replied, "Wu!" There are different interpretations, but here *wu* may be read as "nonbeing," rather than as "no" or "without." That is, true realization exists beyond the discrimination between "dog" and "Buddha-nature."

than nourishing qi. But people drift and drown in profit and reputation, and in the process squander and ruin their qi. **[4b]** Those who study the Dao do not concern themselves with anything other than nourishing qi. Now, if the *ye*-fluids in the heart descend and the qi in the kidneys ascends, eventually reaching the spleen, and the enlivening influence of original qi is not dispersed, then the elixir will coalesce.[64] [Organs] such as the liver and lungs are pathways through which [the fluids and qi] come and go. If you practice stillness for a long time, you yourself will know this. If you do not nourish qi, even if you carry Mount Tai under your arm and leap beyond the Northern Sea,[65] this is not the Dao."

This discussion occurred before my conversion and [the master] spoke these words over a period of ten days.

I stood outside the meditation enclosure with Cao and Liu,[66] my fellow adepts. [The master] suddenly came out saying, "Now, as for [cultivating] the Dao, it simply consists of the following: Maintain clarity and purity and practice nonaction. Remain carefree and become independent. Stay undefiled and unattached. If you can thoroughly digest these twelve characters,[67] you will be a Daoist who has fathomed the depths. Just believe this old man's words. If you practice this, you will certainly benefit. I am definitely not misleading you young people."[68]

When the master was staying in Jiaoma to the west Huangxian,[69] he sang from inside Ren's hermitage,[70] "Throughout the day[71] I scatter ten thousand ounces of yellow gold; **[5a]** coarse clothes and simple food are more than enough. Words and years pass away beyond the gate. When people chant these words, they will take joy in their underlying principle. Thus they will record them and not know who wrote them. They are originally mine, [but some will] say, 'These words are found in Elder Shun's *Wei-Jiang ji* (Anthology of Wei and Jiang).'"[72]

The master said, "Strange indeed are these words."

---

64. Cf. *Dadan zhizhi*, DZ 244, 7a.

65. An allusion to chapter 1 of the *Mengzi* (Book of Master Meng). See Lau 1984, 17. According to discourse 7 of the *Chongyang lijiao shiwu lun*, "To sit authentically, you must maintain a heart-mind like Mount Tai, remaining unmovable and unshakable throughout the entire day" (see chapter 3 herein).

66. As is the case for most of the *Danyang yulu*, the historical personages corresponding to the adepts mentioned are difficult to identify. The preface to the *Quanzhen ji* by Fan Yi (fl. 1185), the Superintendent of Schools in Ninghai (Shandong), mentions a number of later adepts who played major roles in the flourishing of the Quanzhen movement. Among their names, we find Cao Zhen (d. 1207) and Liu Zhenyi (Langran [Clear Suchness]; d. 1206) (DZ 1153, preface, 3b), who are sometimes identified as disciples of Liu Changsheng. Their hagiographies appear in sections 1.9a–11b and 1.13a–14b of the *Zhongnan neizhuan* (DZ 955). Brief biographical entries on these Daoists appear in Min and Li 1994. For lineage charts of major second-generation Quanzhen adherents see Ren 2001, 2.728; Li 2003, 460–61.

67. *Qingjing wuwei xiaoyao zizai buran buzhuo.*

68. Cf. *Jiaohua ji*, DZ 1154, 2.3b.

69. On the eastern peninsula of Shandong, northwest of Yantai, near Penglai.

70. Adept unidentified. If a scribal error occurred in the transcription of Ren's surname, the adept in question may be Ren Shouyi. Ren Shouyi's hagiography appears in the *Zhongnan neizhuan* (DZ 955, 2.1b–2b).

71. Reading *zhongri* for *zongri*.

72. Text unknown.

The master said, "Who are the ancestors of the Daoist movement? It has been transmitted from the lineage of Zhong[li Quan] and Lü [Dongbin]. An ode says,

> A spark of numinous radiance completely illuminates the Great Emptiness;
> The skilled artistry of cinnabar and azure are beyond anyone's production.
> Cessation nourishes the luminous moon, enclosing mutual association;
> There is a lookout tower above karma—how can you categorize me?

These words are a spearhead to pierce open and disperse the haze."

The master said, "Qi is difficult to harness; its movement is like a galloping horse. Only stillness makes this easy. Get rid of external considerations. If you observe the mixed panorama before your eyes as though you are deep in the mountains, this is the disposition of a Daoist. If you don't attain the ground of no-mind, you won't be able to govern anything. [5b] This is what I know about the Dao: its value resides in no-mind."

The master also said, "When the heart-mind is stable, emotions are forgotten. When the body is empty, qi circulates. When the heart-mind dies, spirit lives.[73] When yang flourishes, yin dissipates. These are the principles of suchness.

"Obscuration is ignorance. If you merely concern yourself with having children and grandchildren, when you return to study the Dao there will be no benefit or progress. How can you not deeply consider this?"

The master said, "When I was over forty years old, I happened to meet my master[74] and enter the Dao.[75] Thus, the hair on my temples was already graying. Inside my abdomen, there was a strange violet substance. What caused this? I kept my intention within the pass for over ten years in order to nourish spirit and qi. This is like sound in an empty valley: If you follow the sound and react to it, how can you separate yourself from things? Only emptiness as the center allows this. If you don't believe me, dedicate yourself to abiding in stillness and nourishing it. Then you yourself will know this."

The master spoke the following: "Master [Liu] Haichan was originally a minister in the land of Yan.[76] One morning he awakened to the Dao. Thereupon he severed his family entanglements. [6a] His poetry includes the following words:

---

73. Here Ma Danyang seems to be combining the *Zhuangzi's* notion of a "heart-mind of dead ashes" (*sihui xin*) (chap. 2) with the sixth-century *Yinfu jing's* (section 1b) view that concern for the external appearances disrupts one's spiritual integrity. The death of the ordinary heart-mind and habitual nature leads to a deeper connection with the Dao.

74. Wang Chongyang.

75. *Rudao*. It may have the general meaning of "to become a Daoist adherent" or the more technical meaning of formal initiation/ordination. See also the first discourse of the *Chongyang lijiao shiwu lun* (chapter 3 herein).

76. Liu Cao (Haichan [Oceanic Toad]; fl. 940–1030?) is most often identified as a disciple of Chen Tuan (Xiyi [Infinitesimal Subtlety]; d. 989) and a principal figure in the dissemination of *neidan* techniques during the Song dynasty. He was later recognized as a patriarch in the lineages of Quanzhen and the so-called Nanzong (Southern School) of internal alchemy. He appears as one of the Five Patriarchs of Quanzhen in the *Jinlian ji* (DZ 173) and *Jinlian xiangzhuan* (DZ 174).

> I abandoned the hearths and dwellings of three thousand people;
> I abandoned personal troops numbering one million.

After this he earned his livelihood by begging. Whenever he arrived in an open area, he would give a performance. He got to the point where he would go to brothels carrying barrels of liquor without feeling any embarrassment.

"Later on, when a certain kind of Daoist tells you that Liu came from wealth and privilege, you can compare his version to this Master Haichan and see that it is not the case."

The master said, "If people can understand the Way of Clarity and Stillness, then virtue and refinement will be complete. Thus a scripture reads, 'If people can be constantly clear and pure, heaven and earth will return.'[77] This 'heaven and earth' does not refer to the heaven and earth that enclose and sustain [human beings]. It refers to the heaven and earth within the human body. The area above the diaphragm is 'heaven'; the area below the diaphragm is 'earth.' If the qi of heaven descends and the meridians of earth become pervaded, the upper and lower areas will be connected and harmonized. Vital essence and qi will stabilize naturally. This is what the younger Immortal Ren has spoken."[78]

The master said, "The subtlety of guarding qi resides in keeping vital essence complete. It is most important to guard against [dissipation] when sleeping. **[6b]** When you are getting ready to sleep, keep appropriate mindfulness and get rid of anxieties. Lie on your [right] side, breathing softly through the nose. Make sure that your ethereal soul does not become unsettled on the inside, and that your spirit does not roam to the outside. If you can do this, your qi and vital essence will stabilize naturally."

The master said, "The Confucians use virtue as recompense for virtue, and use righteousness as recompense for people's mistakes. Perfected Xi[79] said, 'Use honesty to bind friends together, and use kindness as recompense for disdain.' We consider this best."

When the master was residing in Laizhou, there was a certain Jiang Xi who took the *Lügong zhuan* (Biography of Adept Lü) as an offering to him. The master read the following out loud: "Ordinary people regard reputation and profit as fundamental, not knowing that the body contains spirit. Chasing after material things without stopping, they completely dissipate celestial perfection. Who can they blame but themselves?" The master then rolled up the scroll and addressed Xi saying, "These words are precious and express the fundamental principle. Nevertheless, considering the fact that ordinary people lack awakening, such a path is difficult to practice."

There was a certain Han Tao, whose given name was Qingfu. He admired Tao Yuanming and Shao Yaofu as people,[80] so he established Anle yuan (Garden of Peaceful Joyousness) as a public park.

---

77. Section 1b of the eighth-century *Qingjing jing*.

78. Adept unidentified. However, the *Quanzhen ji* mentions that Wang Chongyang received instruction from a Buddhist monk named Ren. See *Quanzhen ji*, DZ 1153, 2.20b, 2.24b; Marsone 2001, 100.

79. Or, "a former Perfected."

80. The famous Chinese poets Tao Qian (365–427) and Shao Yong (1011–1077). The former is most often associated with an idyllic pastoral life centering on farming and drinking, while the latter played a major role in the development of Neo-Confucianism.

[7a] When the master was returning to Dongmu from Guanyou, the road passed through Jinan, where the master was invited to visit the garden and make offerings of vegetarian dishes. When he had finished, Han Tao prostrated himself before the master, tapping his head on the ground and saying, "From my youth I longed for the Dao. Today, having already grown old, I rejoice in the opportunity to meet my master. I long for the master to bestow some instruction, so that he may dispel my covering of ignorance."

The master responded, "The Dao becomes embodied through no-mind, and its application rests in forgetting words. Flexibility and yielding are the root; clarity and purity are the foundation.[81] For these to be put into action, people must regulate their drinking and eating and stop ruminating and worrying. Practice quiet sitting in order to harmonize the breath. Sleep peacefully in order to nourish qi. When the heart-mind does not race around, innate nature becomes stable. When the body is not belabored, vital essence becomes complete. When spirit is not disturbed, the elixir will coalesce. After this, extinguish feelings through emptiness and settle spirit in the absolute. This can be called realization of the subtle Dao without leaving your home."[82]

Han Tao thanked the master saying, "The great Dao is vast and nebulous,[83] absent of anything to grab hold of or restrain. Having heard your wondrous discourse just now, I wish to become your disciple and enter [the Dao]."

[7b] Adepts Cao and Lai were Confucian by birth,[84] but they discarded the Confucian tradition and studied the Dao. For many years, no one tried to oppose them. They were constantly dignified and unconcerned, so people would ask them questions: "When the master was west of the pass, how did he transact with the Dao?"[85]

Cao and Lai responded, "The master wore only a single cotton garment in winter and summer, being unconcerned about his clothes. He ate coarse food and ceased with sufficiency. In the cold of winter with its accompanying snowfall, he had no fire in his hut. He lived like this for ten years. If he did not have the qi of the Dao in his belly, he would not have been able to sustain himself."[86]

The master said, "Everything requires preparedness. Through preparation, you will be free of difficulty and suffering. Thus, those who practice the Dao control their emotions and desires when they are young and vigorous. Being prepared at the earliest possible moment, spirit immortality is possible.

---

81. Daoist technical terms derived from the *Daode jing*. See chapters 3, 10, 15, 16, 36, 40, 43, 45, 52, 55, 57, 76, and 78.

82. An allusion to chapter 47 of the *Daode jing*: "Without opening the door, one may know the world. Without looking outside the window, one may know the Way of Heaven." In the Daoist tradition, this is often interpreted as an admonition for internal cultivation, including the introspection of the inner landscape of the body.

83. *Hongmeng*, more commonly appearing with different characters, often refers to the original qi of suchness (*ziran yuanqi*).

84. If the earlier identification is viable, Adept Cao is Cao Zhen (a.k.a. Cao Tian). Adept Lai may be Lai Lingyu, whose hagiography appears in section 1.11b–12a of the *Zhongnan neizhuan* (DZ 955). His name also appears in the aforementioned preface to the *Quanzhen ji*.

85. This refers to an earlier time in Ma Danyang's life, specifically when he lived and practiced in Shaanxi Province from 1170 to 1182. Ma returned to his hometown of Ninghai (Muping) in 1182, following an imperial edict of 1181 requiring all Daoists to return to their place of birth.

86. See Ma's poems in the *Jianwu ji*, DZ 1142, 1.2b, 2.21b.

"If you wait until your hair is white and your head bowed,[87] your aspirations will be squandered and your qi will be exhausted. Beginning to study the Dao [at this age] may be compared to making a fur-lined coat after Great Cold[88] has already arrived. Is this not too late?"

[8a] The master said, "The thirty-six Daoyin exercises[89] and twenty-four reverted elixirs are but gradual gateways for entering the Dao. Do not mistake them for the great Dao itself.[90] If you exhaust yourself investigating stove and furnace or obtaining the symbolism of turtle and snake, you are creating issues where there aren't any and adding falseness to your innate nature. All of this is extremely misleading! Thus, as transmitted within the Daoist tradition, the alchemical classics and texts of various masters, the thousand scriptures and ten thousand treaties may all be covered with a single phrase: 'clarity and purity.' "[91]

The master said, "Considering clarity and purity, clarity refers to clarifying the source of the heart-mind, while purity refers to purifying the ocean of qi. When the source of the heart-mind is clear, external phenomena cannot disturb it. Through this, emotions settle and spiritual illumination emerges. When the ocean of qi is pure, deviant desires cannot affect it. Through this, vital essence becomes complete and the abdomen becomes full.

"Thus, you must purify the heart-mind as though purifying water, and nourish qi as though nourishing an infant. When qi flourishes, spirit become numinous. When spirit becomes numinous, qi becomes transformational. This is the result of clarity and purity.

"If you practice conscious, deliberate exercises, [8b] these are limited techniques. But if you practice the principle of no-mind and nonaction, this is unlimited clear emptiness."

The master said, "Nonaction means not thinking and not worrying. Even though you may have to exist in the midst of love, desire, anger, accumulation, gain and loss, constantly abide in nonaction. Even if you are wading through various affairs, constantly remain unconcerned. Moreover, if you become completely concentrated, clarifying the heart-mind, purifying your intentions, nourishing qi, and completing spirit, you will drift in the land of carefree wandering and enter the Village of Nothing-Whatsoever.[92]

The master said, "Liu Gaoshang (Liu the Sublime) lived in a meditation enclosure for forty years.[93] He freed himself from everything but emptying the heart-mind, filling the belly,[94] avoiding

---

87. Reading *chuiding* for *chuiling*.

88. One of the twenty-four nodes, approximately corresponding to January 21, or the extreme of winter.

89. The specific techniques are unknown. Daoyin (lit., "guided stretching"), sometimes translated as "calisthenics" or "gymnastics" and inaccurately referred to as "Daoist Yoga," is an ancient Chinese health and longevity practice. It usually involves a combination of stretching and breathwork. For general accounts of Daoyin see Despeux 1988; Kohn 2008.

90. Compare chapter 15 of the *Zhuangzi* for a classical Daoist critique of Daoyin.

91. Cf. *Dadan zhizhi*, DZ 244, 2.11b.

92. An allusion to chapter 1 of the *Zhuangzi*, wherein Zhuangzi chastises Huizi for his instrumentalist mentality: "Now you have this big tree and you're distressed because it's useless. Why don't you plant it in Not-Even-Anything Village, or the field of Broad-and-Boundless, relax and do nothing by its side, or lie down for a free and easy sleep under it? Axes will never shorten its life, nothing can ever harm it. If there's no use for it, how can it come to grief or pain?" (Watson 1968, 35).

93. Liu Biangong (Gaoshang [Exalted Eminence]; 1071–1143) was an earlier Daoist ascetic in Shandong who emphasized solitary meditative praxis in meditation enclosure (*huandu*). See Goossaert 1997, 47–54; Goossaert 1999.

94. An allusion to chapter 3 of the *Daode jing*.

ornamentation, forgetting reputation, abandoning profit, clarifying spirit, and completing qi. The elixir formed naturally, and immortality was completed naturally.

"Thus we have a *zan*-hymn that says, 'Block the openings and shut the gates.'[95] Earlier adepts chanted these instructions, but today we see people who regard them as irrelevant."

[9a] The master said, "[The state of] no-mind is not the same as the stupid mindlessness of cats and dogs. It means striving to keep your heart-mind in the realm of clarity and purity and being free of deviant states of consciousness. Thus ordinary people have no mind of clarity and purity, while Daoists have no mind of dust and defilement. But this is not complete mindlessness, and it is not like the condition of trees and rocks or cats and dogs."

The master said, "There is no birth and no extinction. When you observe the buddhas, and the moments of their awakening, they escaped [the mundane world] by casting off [the shell] and [sending out] the embryo. As Lord Qiu [Changchun] has said, 'In this way, I expel the yin-spirits. If I can reach the Celestial Hall, suddenly there will be a pair of florescences taking flight. Then the yang-spirit emerges.'[96] This, then, is the initial ground."

The master said, "For people of the great Dao, emotions are kept at a distance and nonaction is the subtle foundation. When residing in the mundane world, they are free from love of materiality, and vexations have no consequences."

The master said, "For those engaging in cultivation whose accomplishment and practice have not reached fulfillment, when the great boundary arrives, the sages and worthies will not have taught [them how] to die. **[9b]** If you do not engage in cultivation, when your death arrives, you will not be able to attain a condition wherein you are not reincarnated."

The master said, "One thought does not interrupt the serenity of a unified world."
Gong Daosheng asked,[97] "When constant silence becomes clear and deep, what is it like?"
The master replied, "If you come to harmonize with its clarity and depth, nothing is useful."

Yu Qingfeng posed the following question:[98] "After one has cultivated for several years, why is it that divine perception is still not luminous and the ground of the heart-mind is still not numinous?"
The master said, "Because you are not free from other concerns; practicing the Dao has not yet become essential."

The master said, "Every man and woman comes into being from Nonbeing. This is because there is affection, love, greed, and desire. [If not for these] they would not manifest in the world of

---

95. Chapters 52 and 56 of the *Daode jing*.

96. See *Dadan zhizhi*, DZ 244, 1.18a, 2.2ab, 2.4b–5a, 2.11b (herein).

97. Adept unidentified.

98. Yu Qingfeng may be Yu Zhidao (Dongzhen [Cavernous Perfection]; 1166–1250), who was Ma's disciple. His hagiography appears in section 3.13a–20b of the *Zhongnan neizhuan* (DZ 955). Among prominent second-generation adherents with the surname Yu, there was also Yu Zhike (Daoxian [Dao Manifest]; 1168–1232), who was Liu Changsheng's disciple, and Yu Tongqing (Zhenguang [Perfected Radiance]; 1162–1217). A hagiography of the latter appears in the *Zhongnan neizhuan* (DZ 955, 1.18a–20a). However, none of these individuals had Qingfeng (Clear Wind) as their Daoist name. Yu Qingfeng is also mentioned in the "Changchun shu" (*Zhenxian yulu*, DZ 1256, 1.13b).

samsāra. The embryo of each being is nourished and transformed, and the corresponding natural disposition follows from love and desire. This is how life is produced. When innate nature follows love, there is birth; when life-destiny follows desires, there is being. Both of these follow love and desire, and from them obstruction and prosperity arise. These produce jealousy, and reincarnation follows. There is no end.

"Buddhist teachings want us to purify the earth, [but] we should purify the heart-mind. If the heart-mind is clear and pure, **[10a]** reincarnation ends naturally."

The master was fond of making rice porridge. If it was the double-hour of *wu* [11 a.m.–1 p.m.], he would eat one bowl. When he had finished, he would discuss the Dao with people. After leading them through these instructions, he urged them on without getting tired. The master covered his innate nature with the compassion and goodness of a superior person.

When he was residing in Laiyang,[99] he composed sentences of varying lengths. One read, "After finishing a bowl of rice porridge, we must practice exercises in a complete manner." Those who study [the Dao] should examine this. After eating and drinking, we should practice formal sitting. Those who do not take the Dao as the [primary] pursuit should be reprimanded, so that they can know [what needs to be done].

The master said, "When studying the Dao, you should not read scriptures and books extensively. This confuses consciousness and obstructs Daoist training. If [you want to read], Heshang gong's commentary on the *Daode jing* (Scripture on the Dao and Inner Power)[100] and Master Jinling's commentary on the *Yinfu jing* (Scripture on the Hidden Talisman) [are best].[101] When you read these two texts, there will be no obstruction. If you abandon reading everything else, you can nourish qi in the land of Zuilu du (Metropolis of the Zui Blackness). This, above all, is the best undertaking."

[10b] The master said, "For those who study the Dao, whether walking, standing, sitting or lying down, there is not a single instant when their heart-minds are not focused on the Dao. When walking, they set foot on the path of levelness. When standing, they solidify their feelings in Great Emptiness. When sitting, they attune their breathing through the nose. When lying down, they embrace the pearl below the navel. After a long time of harmonizing the breath, there will be no disruption, and you will be like a simpleton throughout the entire day. This is the proper practice—it it has nothing to do with contrived activities."

The master said, "Generally speaking, when you begin studying the Dao, you get caught up in mundane concerns on a daily basis, unable to realize a suspended heart-mind. If even the slightest attachment has not been removed, the Dao will not be stable.

"After completing this, you will not think about previous occurrences or worry about future developments. Moreover, when something appears before your eyes, you will be free of human concerns."

---

99. Laiyang is located in the eastern peninsula of Shandong, southwest of Yantai.

100. The *Laozi zhangju* (Chapter-and-Verse Commentary on the *Laozi*; a.k.a. *Daode zhenjing zhu* [Commentary on the Perfect Scripture on the Dao and Inner Power]; DZ 682).

101. The *Yinfu jing zhu* (Commentary on the *Yinfu jing*; DZ 121) by Tang Chun (Jinling daoren [Daoist of Nanjing]; eleventh c. CE?).

The master said, "A Daoist must not dislike being poor. Poverty is the root of nourishing life.[102] If hungry, eat one bowl of rice porridge. If tired, spread out a grass mat. Pass the days and nights in tattered garments. [11a] This truly is the life of a Daoist. Thus, you must realize that the single matter of clarity and purity cannot be acquired by the wealthy."

When the master passed through a pure society,[103] he was invited to attend a meal. There were several Buddhist monks sitting there in patched robes. One monk was badgering them with extensive distinctions, using verbal expressions to examine difficulties. The master responded with the following refined expression: "What if you threw everything outside this very body, not concerning yourself with anything excessive?" The monk blushed, and then the color drained from his face. He no longer had any composition.

The master said, "Generally speaking, if you want to become a Daoist, you must be a person with enduring fortitude. You definitely cannot have doubts or be indecisive. Rather, focus on innate nature and life-destiny as your great concern. If you practice with determination and without ceasing, you will undoubtedly attain completion. If men and women have many emotions but few aspirations for mists and vapors,[104] then they cannot be called 'students of the Dao.'"

The master said, "The qi within the body should not be dispersed; the spirit within the heart-mind should not be obscured.
[11b] Someone asked, "How can we ensure that qi remains undispersed?"
The master said, "A body without effortful action."
Someone again asked, "How can we ensure that spirit remains unobscured?"
The master said, "A heart-mind without concerns."
Another question was raised, "If the body and heart-mind are like this, is it permissible to retreat to a hermitage?"
The master said, "After this, you can abide in a position of attainment or lowliness; even better, you can be content whether you stay or depart."

The master said, "The heart-mind and innate nature must be completely unaffected by the affairs of the mundane world. Being dragged through tall brambles and [watching people] ridicule the wind and praise the moon are a kiln for smelting emotion and innate nature. What becomes impossible? Supposing one goes on begging rounds in search of alms and meets with rejection or even theft, such opportunities are a Daoist's daily application of our lineage."[105]

The master said, "When each of you first arrives at the pass, you should beg for food until you obtain one meal, and then eat this amount. At the present moment, your accomplishment and practice

---

102. On voluntary poverty in early Quanzhen Daoism see Eskildsen 2004, 40–43.

103. *Qingshe*. Possibly the name of a place in Shandong. I have not been able to identify such a place on historical maps of the Jin dynasty.

104. Or, "the aspiration for Yanxia." A possible reference to Yanxia dong (Cavern of Misty Vapors). Here "mists and vapors" suggests solitary religious praxis in remote places, separation from mundane concerns, and immortality.

105. "Daily application" translates *riyong*. See chapter 3 herein.

are modest, so you must choose wisely where you reside as well as what you eat. When you come to complete the Dao, you will not tire. Still you must ask to repay your debts and then depart."

The master said, "When I first arrived at the pass,[106] I went begging for food. I eventually came to a tavern, where a drunk man was sitting. [12a] Amid his various insults, he punched me. I tried to run away, but he dragged me back and punched me again. All I could do was patiently accept it. Adepts Cao and Zeng, have you ever met with this kind of demonic obstruction?"[107]

    The disciples answered, "No."

    Master-father Ma said, "That's good. If you do encounter [such a situation], don't fight back."[108]

The master said, "The way of the Patriarch involved not acquiring nice clothes or eating good food. He sang songs while shaking bells.[109] He only wanted his heart-mind and head to be free of everything."

The master said, "When I was [living] among ordinary [people], I ate meat and drank alcohol. Today I have already abstained from them for several tens of years. If you drink alcohol and eat meat, but you also want to become a spirit immortal, you are only denying what is undeniable. If your heart-mind does not cherish the Dao, and you hanker for alcohol and crave the rank odor [of meat], only attending to your mouth and belly, suffering and hardship will be your recompense. In the end you will become some kind of lower ghost."

The master said, "The Patriarch guided four people; these were Qiu, Liu, Tan, and Ma. He read about the goodness and virtue of Master Renfeng.[110]

    [12b] "The Patriarch said, 'If you hear this, block and rend your ears. You should extend yourself toward realization, holding fast to what is precious and not daring to let go.'"

    Master-uncle Liu also heard him speak these words.[111]

The master said, "In the past, when I was living in meditation enclosure, I considered abstaining from speech. My discourse would then become a new kind of fruit. The Daoist community heard about this. The next day, they prepared melons and dumplings. They entered my enclosure and I ate three pieces. The consequence was that I could not eat for three days after."

The master said, "In the past the Patriarch made his disciples go to Ninghai and beg for small amounts of money and grain. I wanted to have another disciple go for me [and thus said], 'Have another elder or junior disciple go.'

    "Later [the Patriarch asked me,] 'Why?'

---

106. *Guanzhong* (lit., "inside the pass") usually refers to Shaanxi Province.

107. Cao would be the same adept mentioned earlier. I have not been able to locate a second-generation adept with the surname Zeng.

108. An application of *kṣānti*, or patience under insult, which is one of the Six Perfections (*pāramitā*) of Mahāyāna Buddhism.

109. Reading *ling* ("bell") for *ling* ("to command").

110. The identity of Renfengzi is unclear.

111. "Master-uncle" (*shishu*) indicates an adept of the same generation as one's "master-father" (*shifu*). The use of this phrase suggests that it is the editor, Wang Yizhong, writing. Here Liu refers to Ma's fellow first-generation adept Liu Changsheng.

"[I answered,] 'I, your disciple, don't want to go back to my home village [as a beggar].'[112]

"The Patriarch became furious and beat me continuously until dawn. Because of the many blows that I received, I had a regressing heart [and wanted to leave]. But Master-brother Qiu urged me to stay.[113] To the present time, neither of us has forgotten this."

[13a] The master said, "When we were staying in my home village, the Patriarch made us go to Laizhou and beg for food.[114] After several days, I was filled with doubts. At night I had a dream where the master said, 'In future days, when you are older, you will develop community[115] and help to establish order and happiness among the Han [people]. Travel the streets and develop community.'"

The master said, "When we returned to my home village and went [begging] in the streets for the first time, the Patriarch had us wear our hair in small horns and put face-powder on our faces. I thought to myself, 'I don't care if children and friends see me; I only fear running into my relatives.' While thinking this, I arrived at the house of Fan Mingshu and was about to have a brief rest. Then I saw my sister's father-in-law sitting there, and said to myself, 'This time I should stop being ashamed.'"

A disciple addressed the master, "According to the *Xu zhenjun shangsheng zhuan* (Biography on the Ascent of Perfected Lord Xu),[116] 'After one thousand, two hundred and forty years, there will be eight hundred people who ascend to become immortals.' Why is this?"

The master said, "The Patriarch taught that the sons of kings and immortals come from ten thousand unlearned people."

[13b] The master said, "Master Zhang Yan had a statement that was especially good:[117] 'Daoist statements come and go, but what is essential is that they illuminate the treasure of caring for and benefiting the body.'"

The master laughed to himself saying, "He spread out and passed on his discourse, but the fact is that he was encouraging others."

The master said, "'The song of a hundred don'ts, if it comes from [ordinary] thought, does not amount to ten admonitions.'[118] These indeed are words spoken by the Patriarch. If you adhere to them, they will be completed."

---

112. Here I am following Stephen Eskildsen's amendments (2004, 44).

113. "Master-brother" (*shixiong*) indicates an adept of the same generation as Ma Danyang. Qiu refers to Ma's fellow first-generation adept Qiu Changchun.

114. Laizhou is on the central-western edge of the eastern peninsula of Shandong.

115. Lit., "extend hands."

116. This may refer to the *Xishan Xu zhenjun bashiwu hualu*, DZ 448. The passage appears in section 1.17b. If one accepts the date of that work as the thirteenth century, then this is a later interpolation. See Schipper and Verellen 2004, 901–2. However, as there are several hagiographies of Perfected Lord Xu of the Six Dynasties (220–589) to the Song dynasty (960–1279), this may not be a later interpolation at all.

117. The identity of Zhang Yan is unclear.

118. Ma Danyang's "Ten Admonitions" (*shiquan*) appear in the *Zhenxian yulu*, DZ 1256, 1.8b–9b. They are translated in chapter 3 herein.

The master said, "Taken as a whole, there are many people who praise themselves and who can consider themselves superior. How infrequent is it that they will subordinate themselves to others."

The master said, "I picked up a donkey contract on the road.[119] The Patriarch beat me continuously until dawn. Some scars were left on my head and face."

The master said, "[Take the statement] 'no one is honest.' Suppose that Qingfeng says,[120] 'That's true.' He is an honest person." The master laughed at this. How great! He finished speaking, "The master was like this in his practice and then stopped. Everyone was honest."

Qingfeng said, "Through this single honesty, a single immortal. In the end, this is not honest."[121]

[14a] The master said, "Deeply storing the white snow should not become overemphasized; extensively amassing Yellow Sprouts should not be bound to greed." After saying this, he laughed and again spoke, "What good is there in this?"

He also said, "In a dream, one can finish casting metals without moulds for a sword; in the Dharma, one can depart while still having emotions in the heart-mind."

He also said, "Below Yaochi dian (Shrine of the Turquoise Pond) azure phoenixes dance; in Langyuan gong (Palace of Remote Wilds) white cranes fly."

When the master returned to the seaside, people respectfully received the proscriptions and precepts and joined the Five Associations. Then the master took his place among them. When the disciples heard that Master Ma was in Dengjun,[122] the association members, over one hundred in number, reverentially addressed the master saying, "Every one of your disciples abides in a state of purification and stillness, accepting the precepts against the [five] strong-smelling vegetables and alcohol.[123] It has already been seven days. We have accordingly cleaned the association and made sacrifices for prosperity, so that future karmic retribution will be dispersed."

The master said, "Good. You adepts have been clear and pure for seven days. You have honored my instructions and thus there is benefit. [14b] Each of the disciples of my lineage has been clear and pure for their entire lifetime [since conversion]. They have severed ties to lust and desire, and cut the bonds of proscribed food and alcohol. Thus prosperity has increased."

The entire community offered obeisance and sighed saying, "The teachings of clarity and stillness truly cannot be disputed. Thus people of the three provinces follow and accept the teachings. Gradually they spread to every area, so that people heard about our lineage and believe in its approach and guidance. The great teachings increase and flourish, and they began with our master."

---

119. "Donkey contract" translates *lüqi*. The historical meaning is unclear, but the context suggests that some type of lottery or gambling is involved.

120. Yu Qingfeng mentioned earlier in note 98.

121. Meaning unclear.

122. Most likely the Yuhua hui (Association of Jade Flower) in Dengzhou. Dengzhou designates the central part of the eastern peninsula of Shandong. Huangxian, Laizhou, Penglai, and Qixia are located within the borders of Dengzhou.

123. The five strong-smelling vegetables (*wuxin*) include onions, garlic, chives, shallots, and leeks. These are primarily vegetables in the modern *allium* (onion) genus, but ginger is also sometimes included.

The master addressed all of his disciples as follows: "How many watches are there in one day?"[124]

The disciples responded, "There are six."

The master asked, "Taken together, how many watches are there in day and night?"

The disciples said, "There are twelve."

The master said, "Within the twelve double-hours of day and night, the Way of Heaven circulates, revolving as the transformative process. Does it have a moment when it stops?"

The disciples said, "There is no cessation."

The master said, "Generally speaking, those who study the Dao must take the Way of Heaven as their pattern,[125] [observing] it revolving as a transformative process in their very own bodies. [15a] Throughout the twelve double-hours, be constantly clear and constantly pure.[126] Do not give rise to even a single defiled thought. Your only concern should be cultivation and practice. If throughout the daily progress and monthly advance there is no disruption in your practice, you will assuredly become a spirit immortal.

"[However,] if you are careless and squander your accomplishment and lose your practice, how can you attain realization? I have observed you during the twelve double-hours and there has not been a single hour when your focus is solely on the Dao. Even if you gain benefactors within the ten directions who make offerings and provide sustenance, how can you then repay this attainment?

"Suddenly you close your eyes, and then you again enter the cycle of reincarnation. When will you escape? At the present moment I reemphasize my instructions to you: simply cleanse your own heart-mind and banish desires. When the myriad karmic influences do not taint you, spirit and qi become infused and harmonized. This very condition is the Dao. If you follow this cultivation and practice, you will not become disoriented or confused. If you follow the riptide of pleasure, and your practice does not reach completion, it is not my fault. How can you fail to remember your seven ancestors? Before your birth, they created karma through their various misdeeds, receiving punishment and suffering in the underworld. They look forward to their descendants completing the Dao, so that they will be rescued and attain rebirth in the heavens. Each of you must remember this. Become unwavering with a firm heart-mind. [15b] Embrace the Dao and you will not die. This is what I wish for. Take care of yourselves!"

When the disciples had heard these compassionate words, they were joyous and content. They incited each other to find encouragement in them.

The master said, "The Dao is formless and nameless; it is the ancestor of spirit and qi. When original qi descends and transforms, spiritual illumination is naturally generated. If you refine spirit and merge with the Dao, this is 'cultivating perfection.' Any other name or appearance is confused, and difficulties correspondingly follow in measure. My memory has become your initiation into this great network.

"Now then, the essentials of cultivating this involve not allowing spirit and qi to separate. Spirit and qi are innate nature and life-destiny. Innate nature and life-destiny are the dragon and tiger. The dragon and tiger are lead and mercury. Lead and mercury are water and fire. Water and

---

124. "Watch" (*geng*) refers to each of the twelve double-hours.

125. A reference to the opening lines of the sixth-century *Yinfu jing*. Interestingly, chapter 13 of the *Zhuangzi* is titled "Tiandao" (The Way of Heaven).

126. An allusion to various sections of the eighth-century *Qingjing jing*.

fire are the Child and Maiden. The Child and Maiden are perfect yin and perfect yang. Perfect yin and perfect yang then are spirit and qi.[127] None of these various names and representations can fully express it. It is sufficient to be content with the two characters of spirit and qi.

"If you want to nourish qi and complete spirit, you must completely get rid of your various attachments. Be clear and pure externally and internally. If you remain concentrated and focused for a long time, spirit will coalesce and qi will infuse you. **[16a]** After three years without dissipation, the lower elixir [field] will become full. After six years without dissipation, the middle elixir [field] will become full. After nine years without dissipation, the upper elixir [field] will become full. This refers to the three elixir [fields] becoming complete; the accomplishment of the nine reversions becoming complete; the bones and marrow coalescing and transforming; the blood and meridians[128] becoming complete and perfected; the internal becoming complete and the external becoming abundant; radiant form gaining penetrating illumination; silent suchness being unagitated; and resonance being free from exhaustion. Through a thousand changes and ten thousand transformations, one meditates in a position of cessation. Thirty-six thousand divine numens leap and wander within the world, and the Three Worlds are managed and accepted. Within the eight difficult situations,[129] none of the thousand calamities or ten thousand poisons can destroy you. With regard to the transformations of the great *kalpa*, and its inflooding calamities and four perplexities, spirit fills the Great Emptiness. Indeed, there is nothing that it does not fill. Thus the heavens have their specific duration and then fall into ruin. The earth has its specific duration and then sinks into perishing. Mountains have their specific duration and then break down in collapse. Oceans have their specific duration and then become exhausted. Everything that exists ends in ruin.

"If students of the Dao reach the place where spirit and the Dao become merged, they will attain an eternal condition free from ruin. United by their accomplishment, their nine ancestors will ascend to [the heaven of] Shangqing (Highest Clarity)."

Discourse Record of Perfected Hao Taigu[130]

Compiled by Anonymous Disciples

Perfected Guangning said,[131] "When you become a renunciant,[132] you must forget grief and abandon worry. Know sufficiency and be constantly content.[133] In one day, there are two *sheng* of grain[134]—how

---

127. Compare the *Ershisi jue*, DZ 1158.

128. Or "blood vessels."

129. Traditionally speaking, the "eight difficult situations" (*banan*) is a Buddhist technical term referring to eight conditions or circumstances of incarnation wherein it is difficult to make progress toward liberation. In one formulation, they include in hells; as hungry ghosts; as animals; in Uttarakuru, the continent north of Mount Sumeru where pleasures dominate; in the heavens of long life; as deaf, blind, or mentally retarded; as a worldly philosopher; and between the period before a Buddha's birth or after his death. Soothill and Hodous 1995 (1937), 41.

130. *Hao Taigu zhenren yu[lu]*. From *Zhenxian zhizhi yulu*, DZ 1256, 1.19a–22b.

131. I have added this phrase to the translation.

132. *Chujia*, which literally means "leave the family" and often indicates becoming a monastic.

133. *Zhizu*, here translated as "knowing sufficiency," derives from the *Daode jing*. See chapters 28, 33, 44, and 46.

134. *Sheng* is an ancient Chinese weight measurement for grain. It is sometimes translated as "pint." One *dou* consists of ten *sheng*.

can you use it by storing it? In one year, there is a *duan* of cotton cloth[135]—how can you seek it outside the body? A day of seclusion is a day of immortality. When the Dao infuses you and you remain free from desire, spirit becomes stable and qi becomes harmonious. **[19b]** This is the source of the transformative process; it exhausts the reversal of yin and yang.

"The Dao is not distant from people, but people make themselves distant from the Dao. The sun and moon are not hurried, but people try to hurry them. When your resolve and determination are uncommitted, the heart-mind wavers and your thinking wanes. Wandering and traveling to various places is not as good as meditating alone and guarding the Dao. Being set adrift by fame and personal profit is not as good as carefree wandering and silent aloneness. Eating one's fill of precious delicacies is not as good as [being content with] coarse provisions and restricting your appetite. Having chests filled with bolts of fine silk is not as good as [being content with] simple garments and covering your body. Enjoying splendid banquet music is not as good as remaining beyond [the mundane world] and guarding stillness. Ascending towers in spring is not as good as [abiding in] calm seclusion and being unadorned.[136] Obtaining wealth by losing righteousness is not as good as accepting poverty and taking joy in yourself. Having the ability to argue and engage in disputation is not as good as remaining silent for an entire day.[137] Speaking about antiquity and discussing today is not as good as embracing the Source and guarding the One. Having a lot of skill and abilities is not as good as abandoning learning so that you may guard ignorance.[138] Constantly clinging to old shortcomings is not as good as purifying the heart-mind and repenting of transgressions.[139] When the qi of the Dao is subtle and fine, you may practice and attain immortality. **[20a]** Gaining awareness and forgetting language, you exit and enter its pure flowing. Among great Emptiness and the wondrous Source, you obtain the fish while forgetting the fish-trap.[140] Securely corral the horse of the will, and urgently settle the monkey of the mind. When you guard ignorance, the myriad beings become complete; when you guard the Dao, a thousand blessings naturally descend."

Perfected Guangning also said, "Daily practice involves refining qi when residing in quiet places and refining spirit when residing in noisy places. Walking, standing, sitting, and lying down *are* the Dao. Throughout day and night do not get confused by what appears before you. If you sleep for one hour, this is an hour lost. Practice day by day and you will gradually gain accomplishment. If you

---

135. *Duan* is an ancient Chinese length measurement for cloth. It is sometimes given as eighteen feet or six meters.

136. An allusion to chapter 20 of the *Daode jing*: "Most people are busy as though attending the Tailao feast, as though ascending a tower in spring; I alone am unmoving, showing no sign." In a Daoist context, this chapter is often read as providing instructions on quietistic meditation.

137. Hagiographies indicate that Hao Guangning did, in fact, practice voluntary silence. See the *Jinlian ji*, DZ 173, 5.7a (chapter 6 in the present volume), wherein we are told that the local people referred to Hao as "Master Speechless" (*buyu xiansheng*).

138. An allusion to chapter 20 of the *Daode jing*. See also chapter 19, 33, and 71.

139. *Huiguo.*

140. A reference to chapter 26 of the *Zhuangzi*: "The fish trap exists because of the fish; once you've gotten the fish, you can forget the trap. The rabbit snare exists because of the rabbit; once you've gotten the rabbit, you can forget the snare. Words exist because of meaning; once you've gotten the meaning, you can forget the words. Where can I find a man who has forgotten words so I can have a word with him?" (Watson 1968, 302). In the context of the *Zhuangzi*, "forgetting" is a meditation practice aimed at mystical union with the Dao as well as a state of consciousness that is contentless, nonconceptual, and nondualistic. See chapters 2, 4, and 6.

refrain from sleeping for one thousand days, your training will become complete. Do not believe others when they speak about 'bones of destiny.' "[141]

Perfected Guangning also said, "Considering adepts who are cultivating perfection, if they have not surrendered their heart-minds, even if they have been renunciants for many years, they will not know that there is a place beyond being and they will not realize innate nature.[142] If one does not realize innate nature, how can one nourish life-destiny? If innate nature and life-destiny are not prepared, how will one be able to complete perfection? The reason why it is like this is because of illnesses of the heart-mind. [20b] The first illness of the heart-mind involves seeing other people penetrating the principle of innate nature and life-destiny and wishing to gain it for oneself. One is unwilling to humble oneself, and other people are thus unwilling to discuss it. The heart-mind then gives rise to resentment and slander. The second illness of the heart-mind involves not considering the karma of other people, but [simply believing that] oneself alone will not have retribution. One is unable to convert others and produce goodness, so they only produce deviant thoughts. This squanders the karma of human incarnation. The third illness of the heart-mind involves seeing other people reading scriptures and various writings and, not understanding them oneself, giving rise to resentment in one's own heart-mind. Considering people in these categories, they will never attain great wisdom and understanding or become followers of the self-realization of celestial vision. The fourth illness of the heart-mind involves karma not yet becoming manifest, but forcing the arising of karma by acting toward the multitude of sentient beings. Such actions disturb and create chaos in other people. Such is the state of human beings who are depraved. The fifth illness of the heart-mind involves the heart-mind being insufficient, which again results in a chaotic state. Such is the state of human beings who are deficient.

"If you expel these five illnesses, humbling yourself, seeking counsel and making inquiries, you will certainly attain Perfection. If you are not yet able to abide in great stillness, you must at this very moment guard your original endowment. If you have not yet penetrated great principle, you should constantly study the scriptures and the teachings. If you are not yet able to inspire people, you should simply shut yourself off and guard stillness. In trying to diminish attaining even a slight amount of karma, do not forget innate nature and life-destiny. [21a] Those who can be like this approach the Dao and complete sagehood within a short period of time. Those who cannot accord with this will assuredly sink into Fengdu and will not be able to obtain a human body.[143] Perhaps they will take on feathers or horns, forever working among the six domestic animals.

---

141. *Sugu*, sometimes appearing as "immortal bones" (*xiangu*), is an earlier Daoist belief that immortality involved a personal dispensation or endowment from the cosmos. This stands in contrast with early Quanzhen views that diligent self-cultivation is the foundation of alchemical transformation. Perfection is not given; it is realized through dedicated and prolonged practice.

142. "Realize innate nature" translates *jianxing*. In the context of Chan (Zen) Buddhism, the term, better known through its Japanese pronunciation *kenshō*, often indicates enlightenment experiences with identifiable characteristics that may be confirmed by a Chan master.

143. Fengdu is one of the Chinese netherworlds or "hells." See Min and Li 1994, 1006; Hu 1995, 656, 1469; Chenivesse 1996, 1997a, 1997b; Nickerson 1997, 234–37. For a symbolic diagram see *Shangqing lingbao dafa*, DZ 1221, 17.22a. According to the "Changchun shu," associated with Qiu Changchun, "Perfected Danyang said, 'If the roots of karma (*yegen*) are deep and not completely eliminated, how can you expect to attain the Dao? Moreover, there is the [sexual] technique (*shu*) of extraction and battle in the bedroom, which exhausts and confuses vital essence and spirit. This undermines virtue and misleads people. Their names become placed in the ghost records (*guilu*), and they then sink into Fengdu'" (*Zhenxian yulu*, DZ 1256, 1.16b). See also *Jinguan yusuo jue*, DZ 1156, 23a; Komjathy 2007a, 366.

"Daily homage to the nine mysteries and seven ancestors causes one to ruin motivations of the Dao. Now, considering the discourses of the Seven Perfected and Five Patriarchs, all of them expound on the principles of innate nature and life-destiny. Many subsequent students have only sought inferior methods and deviant pathways. Some employ the heart-mind to direct qi, while others count breaths to forget the heart-mind. Some circulate water and fire so that they commingle. Still others focus on the dragon and tiger so that they merge. These myriad doctrines cannot fully contain the principles that have been conveyed by the patriarchs and masters of Complete Perfection. If they become extinguished, they will not appear again. So, my way takes opening pervasion as the foundation, realizing innate nature as the substance, and nourishing life-destiny as the application. It takes deferential harmony as virtue, withdrawing retreat as practice, and guarding one's endowment as accomplishment. After a long time of accumulation and development, celestial radiance manifests inwardly. The perfect qi infuses and flows forth, while form and spirit are mutually wondrous. Through the Dao, one merges with Perfection.

[21b] "Students of today do not distance their heart-minds from right and wrong, personal profit and injury, benefit and detriment, as well as greed and anger. When their heart-minds are like this, how can innate nature become stabilized? How can qi become harmonious? Suchness becomes lost, and one becomes distanced even farther from the Dao. Such people take a cloak trimmed with swan-down as worthless and our tradition's teachings as useless. When they see the lofty and illustrious, they become envious of their various distinctions. When they see the young and old, they make fun of their various appearances. If even a small amount of personal benefit is available, they use every effort to secure advantages for themselves. Such people may inquire into the great Dao, but their ears have become deaf and their eyes blind.

"Those who are cunning and clever, and those who engage in devious speech and have wild schemes should not be encouraged to leave the family.[144] They have no hope of becoming spirit immortals. They are unwilling to subdue the heart-mind, but rather throw off restraint and give rein to whatever their current emotional state happens to be. They have already become disciples of vulgarity, having failed to penetrate the meaning of the scriptures. Breathing like oxen and acting like horses, they do not know the principle of the Dao. They can make anything seem like its opposite.[145]

"Master [Chongyang] established our school in hopes that each and every adept would cultivate immortality. Today I have observed that many disciples of our tradition are accruing karma by speaking about abnormal and seductive occurrences such as entering dreams by sending out spirit. When building monasteries and restoring temple halls, people should simply record the master's surname and given name. They should introduce details about the profession of his paternal grandmother's side of the family and write several important things about his accomplishments. [22a] If people engage in foolish talk or gossip about others, simply close your eyes and seal your lips. Enlarge your heart-mind to transact with the Dao. For such people, delusion has suppressed what should be primary. A false wisdom has compelled them toward "knowledge," but they only know how to speak about "right" and "wrong." They neither understand punishment and blessing, nor think about transacting with the Dao. They give rein to a wayward heart-mind and do not perfect it. In the future, a yin-official will inflict retribution for their transgressions. He will examine each person's

---

144. That is, do not allow the unworthy and deficient to join the religious community.

145. Literally, "turn black into white."

behavior and recommend those [who are worthy]. Not rejecting faithful encouragement, but rather accepting direct instruction—this brings joy to cultivation and practice.

"If you wish to enter my tradition, you must first cultivate the heart-mind. When the heart-mind does not wander to the outside, spirit becomes stable naturally, and qi becomes harmonious naturally. When qi and spirit are harmonious, the Three Fields coalesce naturally. When the Three Fields coalesce, medicinal fungi and plants are produced naturally. If you want to complete this preparation, be diligent and attentive in your practice. Yin virtue subdues ghosts, while yang virtue subdues people.[146]

"When these two types of virtue are prepared, the fruits of the Dao become established and complete. In previous generations, such people were numerous and included immortal Li, immortal Wang of Xianyang, immortal Li of Longxi, immortal Wang of Chengdu, immortal Zhao of Xiangzhou, immortal Ma of Tengzhou, and immortal Lao of Xuzhou.[147] Their names include many more, but all of them were courageous disciples. [22b] After you enter the Dao, you must subordinate your heart-mind and thoughts.[148] If the heart-mind is distressed, strengthen your resolve. Revere your teachers like gods, and respect your fellow adepts like guests. Do not allow your mouth to issue trivial speech or your body to engage in sensuous activities. If you protect the teachers and revere the scriptures for twenty or thirty years for the purpose of bringing about realization, you will cast off form and gain immortal departure. You will become the eyes of our tradition. How can this not be considered a great accomplishment!

"Students of today do not revere their teachers or respect their fellow adepts. If they see a worthy person, their heart-minds are filled with resentment. If they see dimwitted people, their heart-minds are filled with disparaging ideas. They do not focus on good things, but merely produce feelings of superiority. These types of adepts become demon soldiers within the tradition. After they die, they become seeds of the Earth Prisons. Some have two horns and some have none. Some have tails a thousand lengths long, while others are ten thousand lengths long. The nine mysteries and seven ancestors in the end meet with mud and coal. In the frozen pond, they suffer in extreme coldness. In the boiling lake, they are distressed by extreme burning. In the tree of swords and the mountain of knives, they pass through a thousand lives and ten thousand deaths.[149] Do not wait until the time to repent arrives."

---

146. Here yin corresponds to a more passive or receptive attitude, while yang refers to a more active and effortful one.

147. The corresponding Daoist adepts are generally unclear. "Wang of Xianyang" of course refers to Wang Chongyang.

148. Cf. 19b.

149. References to the punishments of specific Earth Prisons.

Chapter Three

Daily Practice

Within the early Quanzhen religious community, there was a strong emphasis on daily practice. For the early adepts, daily practice did not simply mean training each day; it also meant viewing one's entire life as Daoist cultivation. As Stephen Eskildsen has shown (2004, 26–33), many of the early Quanzhen adherents referred to an all-pervasive existential approach toward self-cultivation and spiritual realization as "daily practice" (lit., "daily application"; *riyong*), translated by Eskildsen as "daily sustenance." Throughout the early Quanzhen textual corpus, one finds references to "daily practice," especially in the writings of Ma Danyang, Qiu Changchun, and Hao Guangning, three of Wang Chongyang's direct disciples.[1] As expressed by Ma Danyang,

> "Daily practice involves never deceiving or mocking heaven and earth. Always train yourself diligently. Cherish each moment. Do not pass the day in vain. Decrease your sleep, as this is something that [ordinary] people desire. You should rectify your misdeeds, but this is not to be done through seated meditation.[2] You should keep your heart-mind stable for a long time. Whether walking, standing, sitting, or lying down, follow the Dao. All adepts should quit giving rise to thoughts. Quickly seek out innate nature and life-destiny. If you can just purify the heart-mind and abandon desires, you will become a spirit immortal. Acknowledge nothing else and stop having doubts! These are proper and true words. You only need to be constantly clear and constantly pure."[3] (*Danyang zhiyan*, DZ 1234, 1a)

And in the same public talk, Ma Danyang admonishes,

> "Each day, you must not forget the matter of daily practice. Daily practice consists of two types: daily external practice (*wai riyong*) and daily internal practice (*nei riyong*).[4]

---

1. My translations of the relevant passages are indebted to those of Eskildsen.

2. Here Ma Danyang seems to suggest that direct action, rather than mental or energetic outreach, must be taken to rectify one's previous injurious behavior. Stated simply, one must apologize and make amends directly to the effected being. As is confirmed by his own life and the early Quanzhen training regimen, consistent and prolonged seated meditation, involving both quietistic meditation and internal alchemy, was considered essential.

3. This insight and admonition parallels section 1b–2a of the eighth-century *Qingjing jing* (DZ 620): "Constantly resonating, constantly still, there is constant clarity, constant stillness. When clarity and stillness are like this, you gradually enter the perfect Dao."

4. Interestingly, the Ming-dynasty Daoist Canon contains two related, anonymous works that may derive from a later, possibly thirteenth-century, Quanzhen context. These are the *Taishang laojun nei riyong miaojing* (Wondrous Scripture for Daily Internal Practice of the Great High Lord Lao; DZ 645; also *Qunxian yaoyu zuanji*, DZ 1257, 1.1ab; abbr. *Nei riyong jing*) and the *Taishang laojun wai riyong miaojing* (Wondrous Scripture for Daily External Practice of the Great High Lord Lao; DZ 646; abbr. *Wai riyong jing*). Both texts have been translated by Livia Kohn (2000a), while a translation of the former appears as Handbook 6 of my *Handbooks for Daoist Practice* (Komjathy 2008a). The *Nei riyong jing* emphasizes meditation practice, while the *Wai riyong jing* emphasizes morality and virtuous deeds.

"Considering daily external practice, you are strongly forbidden to see the faults of others, boast about your own virtue, envy the wise and talented, give rise to worldly thoughts that are the fire of ignorance, produce feelings of superiority over the masses, [discriminate] between self and other or right and wrong, or speak of hatred and affection.

"Considering daily internal practice, quit giving rise to doubtful thoughts. Never forget the internal. Whether wandering about or standing and sitting, you should clear the heart-mind and discard desires. Have nothing that hangs on or hinders [your progress]. Do not get defiled and do not become attached. In perfect clarity and perfect purity, remain carefree according to your aspirations.[5] Consistently throughout the day contemplate the Dao in the same way a hungry person thinks of food or a thirsty person of drink. If you become aware of the slightest imbalance, you must correct it. If you train yourself in this way, you will become a spirit immortal." (Ibid., 2a–2b)

Similarly, Hao Guangning advises the aspiring Quanzhen adept as follows:

"Daily practice involves refining qi when residing in quiet places and refining spirit when residing in noisy places. Walking, standing, sitting and lying down *are* the Dao. Throughout day and night do not get confused by what appears before you. If you sleep for one hour, this is an hour lost. Practice day by day and you will gradually gain accomplishment. If you refrain from sleeping for one thousand days, your training will become complete. Do not believe others when they speak about 'bones of destiny.'"[6] (*Zhenxian yulu*, DZ 1256, 1.20a)

Qiu Changchun also discusses daily internal and daily external practice, that is, personal and interpersonal cultivation, or the development of spiritual realization and ethical engagement.

"Abandon self and accord with others. Overcome yourself and return to ritual propriety. This is daily external practice. Forgive others and withstand insults.[7] Eliminate every thought and anxiety. Allow all things to come to rest in your heart-mind. This is daily internal practice. . . . Put others first and yourself last. Use yourself as the prescription for others. This is daily external practice. Through clarity and stillness, maintain your training. This is daily internal practice. . . . Constantly direct the heart-mind toward unity, purifying and cleansing yourself throughout the twelve double-hours. Each and every moment remain awake and attentive. Don't allow your innate nature to become

---

5. "Remain carefree" translates *xiaoyao*, a phrase which derives from the title of chapter 1 ("Xiaoyao you" [Carefree Wandering]) of the *Zhuangzi*.

6. "Bones of destiny" translates *sugu*, which also appears as *xiangu* ("immortal bones"). "Bones of destiny" refers to an earlier Daoist belief that immortality involved a personal dispensation or endowment from the cosmos. This stands in contrast with early Quanzhen views that diligent self-cultivation is the foundation of alchemical transformation. Perfection is not given; it is realized through dedicated and prolonged practice. A complete translation of the *Hao Taigu zhenren yu[lu]*, the text from which this passage derives, appears here in chapter 2.

7. This corresponds to patience under insult (*kṣānti*), one of the six perfections (*pāramitā*) of Mahāyāna Buddhism. The other five include generosity, ethics, diligence, concentration, and wisdom.

obscured. Make the heart-mind stable and your qi harmonious. This is real daily internal practice. Cultivate benevolence and amass virtue. Allow yourself to suffer for the benefit of others. This is real daily external practice." (*Zhenxian yulu*, DZ 1256, 1.15b)

In these passages, one encounters the early Quanzhen adepts giving clear guidance concerning Daoist practice. One's daily life becomes practice-realization; practice-realization becomes one's daily life. But how does one "attain" such an existential or ontological condition? According to the preceding insights, one cultivates clarity and stillness as an internal condition and selflessness and virtue as an external condition. Over time, one realizes that there is nothing to attain; one merges with the Dao.

Following Ma Danyang and Qiu Changchun, we may make a provisional distinction between "daily external practice," which includes ethical reflection and application, and "daily internal practice," which encompasses meditation and internal alchemy. With respect to the former, members of the early Quanzhen religious community embraced and advocated ethical commitments and application. On the most basic level, early Quanzhen ethics focus on avoidance of the Four Hindrances (*sihai*), namely, alcohol, sex, wealth, and anger. Alcohol refers to any ingested substance that leads to intoxication or obscuration of consciousness. Sex includes not only actual sexual activity, but all forms of sensuality. With respect to the latter, the early adepts were especially concerned about sexual fantasies, both conscious and unconscious, and, in the case of male practitioners, nocturnal seminal emission due to "demons of sleep" (*shuimo*) and "yin-ghosts" (*yingui*). Wealth consists of both avaricious thoughts and material accumulation, especially for personal profit. Finally, anger disrupts energetic vitality and integrity. In a traditional Chinese context, anger injures the liver, which is responsible for the smooth flow of qi throughout the body and thus for one's overall psychosomatic health. According to Wang Chongyang, alcohol obscures innate nature, retards spirit, squanders perfection, and exhausts longevity. Sexual activity dissipates vital essence, injures bodily fluids, spoils qi and spirit, and corrupts virtue. Through sexual activity, the Three Fields become empty and the five yin-organs are thrown into disorder. Wealth, or avarice, creates confusion, leads to excess, dissipates virtue, and brings about suffering. Finally, anger dissipates spirit, injures the stomach, generates contention, and allows emotions to supersede the Dao. Wang's senior disciples continued his emphasis on the dissipating effects of alcohol, sex, wealth, and anger (Komjathy 2007a, 105–6, 149–56, 241; see also chapter 1 in the present volume).[8]

We also find emphasis on performing good deeds (*xing*) and cultivating merit (*gong*), terms which in internal cultivation refer to practice and accomplishment, respectively. In the context of Quanzhen ethics, *xing* and *gong*, following technical Buddhist usage, often refer to beneficial and virtuous activity that purify one's karma and generate "merit," with increased levels of merit being required for rebirth into more karmically beneficial ontological conditions. Quanzhen ethics also incorporate a classical Daoist emphasis on "virtue" (*de*), including "hidden virtue" (*yinde*) that focuses on one's inward state over external recognition. Strictly speaking, ethics relates to external practice. This involves developing purity of thought, speech, and action, especially in terms of interpersonal relationships and engaged activity in the world. As Ma Danyang explains, "Considering daily external

---

8. Some other relevant occurrences of the "Four Hindrances" appear in the following: *Jianwu ji*, DZ 1142, 2.3a; *Jinyu ji*, 1149, 3.2b, 3.7a, 8.23a; *Shenguang can*, DZ 1150, 23a, 33a; *Yunguang ji*, DZ 1152, 3.20ab; *Quanzhen ji*, DZ 1153, 4.14a, 5.12a; *Fenli shihua ji*, DZ 1155, 1.8b; *Jinguan yusuo jue*, DZ 1156, 1a; *Shuiyun ji*, DZ 1160, 1.14a.

practice, you are strongly forbidden to see the faults of others, boast about your own virtue, envy the wise and talented, give rise to worldly thoughts that are the fire of ignorance, produce feelings of superiority over the masses, [discriminate] between self and other or right and wrong, or speak of hatred and affection" (*Danyang zhiyan*, DZ 1234, 2a). Similarly, Qiu Changchun urges aspiring Quanzhen adepts as follows: "Put others first and yourself last. Use yourself as the prescription for others. This is daily external practice" (*Zhenxian yulu*, DZ 1256, 1.15b). As we can see from these quotations, Quanzhen ethical commitments rest squarely on an internal orientation, on self-cultivation and transformation.[9]

With respect to specific ethical guidelines and precepts (*jielü*), the early Quanzhen textual corpus is generally silent. One possible explanation is that there was an assumed set of ethical commitments, or that this dimension of Quanzhen practice was articulated through direct oral instruction and communal exploration. In any case, there are some intriguing hints within the writings of the first-generation adherents. For example, during his time in Liujiang Wang Chongyang had some contact with a certain Buddhist Master Ren who taught repentance (*jiangchan*) and discussed eighteen precepts (*shiba jie*) (*Quanzhen ji*, DZ 1153, 2.20b, 2.24b; Marsone 2001, 100). Unfortunately, these eighteen precepts are not listed in any of Wang's extant works. However, in the *Jinguan yusuo jue*, a text attributed to the founder (see Komjathy 2007a; cf. Hachiya 1972), Wang Chongyang emphasizes the importance of virtue as foundational for Quanzhen religious praxis (DZ 1156, 1b; also 13a, 15a, 22b). In section 16a of the text, Wang specifically mentions the five precepts (*wujie*), which originally derive from Buddhism:

1. Do not kill

2. Do not steal

3. Do not commit sexual misconduct

4. Do not lie

5. Do not take intoxicants

The *Jinguan yusuo jue* also urges Quanzhen adepts to avoid the ten malevolent deeds (Chin.: *shi'e*; Skt.: *daśakuśala*), namely, killing, stealing, sexual misconduct, lying, slander, coarse language, equivocating, coveting, anger, and false views (see Soothill and Hodous 1995 [1937], 50; Ding 1939, 252, 2052; Xingyun 1989, 471).

Beyond this, there are two early lists of admonitions, which I have translated in the present chapter. The first is the "Ten Admonitions" (*shiquan*) by Liu Chuxuan (Changsheng [Perpetual Life]; 1147–1203). These are contained in his *Xianle ji* (Anthology of Immortal Bliss; DZ 1141, 2.18ab). The second is the "Ten Admonitions" by Ma Yu (Danyang [Elixir Yang]; 1123–1184). These are slightly more problematic in terms of dating and authorship, as they are preserved in the late thirteenth-century *Zhenxian yulu* (Discourse Records of Perfected Immortals; DZ 1256, 1.8b–9b). Based on my comparison of the content with other works of Ma, I am inclined to accept the attribution as legitimate.

With the transformation of Quanzhen from a regional ascetic and eremitic community to a national monastic order in the thirteenth century, members of the clerical elite began composing

---

9. Stephen Eskildsen has also emphasized the early Quanzhen commitment to compassionate activities. See Eskildsen 2004, 31–37, 110–14, 155–70.

monastic manuals. There was a corresponding systematization of Quanzhen ethical guidelines into monastic rules.[10] For example, there is the admittedly late "Jiaozhu Chongyang dijun zefa bang" (Sovereign Lord Chongyang's List of Prohibitions). This list is contained in the late thirteenth- or early fourteenth-century *Quanzhen qinggui* (Pure Regulations of Complete Perfection; DZ 1235, 11b–13a; see chapter 7 here). It provides insights into late medieval Quanzhen monastic life, including the rules and corresponding punishments for transgressions that framed that social organization.

The most systematic expression of Quanzhen precepts and monastic rules appears in late imperial works. The most significant and influential of these are attributed to Wang Changyue (Kunyang [Paradisiacal Yang]); 1594?–1680), who established the official, "orthodox" Longmen (Dragon Gate) lineage. According to Wang Changyue's formulation, there are three levels of ordination with corresponding precepts:

1. Ten Precepts of Initial Perfection, as contained in the *Chuzhen jie* (JY 292; ZW 404, 9ab)

2. Three Hundred Precepts of Medium Ultimate, as contained in the *Zhongji jie* (JY 293; ZW 405, 2a–36b)

3. Ten Virtues and Thirty-seven Virtuous Activities of Celestial Immortality, as contained in the *Tianxian jie* (JY 291; ZW 403)

A translation of the first text is included here in chapter 7. Interestingly, the *Chuzhen ji* indicates that Quanzhen adepts must become proficient in the five precepts and *Taishang ganying pian* (Great High Lord Lao's Treatise on Impulse and Response; DZ 1167; JY 94) before practicing the Ten Precepts of Initial Perfection. While the *Chuzhen jie* could be categorized as a "precept text," I believe that it is more accurately understood as a monastic manual. The relevant precepts are only one dimension of the text. It should also be added that in the context of late imperial, modern, and contemporary Quanzhen, ethical guidelines include celibacy, vegetarianism, and renunciation of intoxicants. Members of the early community are less consistent on the issue of killing and consuming animals, with Ma Danyang and Qiu Changchun seeming to be the most committed to vegetarianism (see Komjathy 2011a).

As the Daoist tradition is most frequently constructed in modern times as emphasizing a "naturalistic philosophy" and "spontaneous lifestyle," especially through selective reading of the texts of classical Daoism, very little attention has been given to its sophisticated ethical systems. The same is true of Quanzhen. In fact, Quanzhen Daoism and Daoist religious movements more generally emphasize the importance of virtue for spiritual attainment. Ethical commitments and application represent one connective tissue within the tradition as social body. The only Quanzhen precepts translated to date appear in Heinrich Hackmann's early German works (1920; 1931), a partial German translation of the *Chuzhen jie*; in Catherine Despeux's *Immortelles de la Chine ancienne* (1990), a French translation of the "Nine Precepts for Female Perfected" from the *Chuzhen jie*; and in Livia Kohn's *Cosmos and Community: The Ethical Dimensions of Daoism* (2004b). The latter work and its electronic supplement include translations of relevant selections from the *Chuzhen jie* and *Zhongji jie*.

Returning to the early Quanzhen textual corpus considered as a whole, one text in particular stands out with respect to daily internal practice. This is the *Chongyang lijiao shiwu lun* (Redoubled

---

10. For information on Quanzhen monastic regulations see Goossaert 1997, 259–301.

Yang's Fifteen Discourses to Establish the Teachings; DZ 1233; abbr. *Chongyang shiwu lun*, *Lijiao shiwu lun*, or *Shiwu lun*). In Western-language presentations of Quanzhen, specifically outside of the small academic community focusing on Quanzhen, the text has been held up as *the* representative expression of the early movement.[11] Such status is perhaps largely due to its accessibility and relative simplicity. However, the *Chongyang lijiao shiwu lun* also may be read as a manual for aspiring Quanzhen adepts and as a general introduction to foundational Quanzhen religious praxis.

As the title indicates, the text is attributed to Wang Chongyang, though reservations have been expressed by some specialists (see, e.g., Hachiya 1992; Goossaert 1997 and 2001; Marsone 2001; Schipper and Verellen 2004, 1127, 1168). When analyzed in content, taking into account the overall characteristics of early Quanzhen and the early textual corpus, the *Chongyang lijiao shiwu lun* expresses tenets and concerns from the movement's early phases. The main discrepancy in this respect is the section on preparing herbal medicines (Discourse 4), though a basic understanding of herbology on the part of hermits would likely have been part of common folklore at the time as well as a prerequisite for an eremitic lifestyle. The text appears to have originated in an early Quanzhen context and may, in fact, have been composed either by Wang Chongyang or other first-generation adepts in an attempt to provide direction for potential converts and new initiates.[12] In terms of internal textual evidence, the only clearly relevant aspect is citation of the sixth-century *Yinfu jing* (Scripture on the Hidden Talisman; DZ 31) (Discourse 11). Other hints include an allusion to the section on friendship (Discourse 6) in the *Danyang yulu* (DZ 1057, 3a; translated here in chapter 2) and in the *Zhenxian yulu* (DZ 1256, 1.8b–9b; translated in this chapter), and Ma Danyang's suggestion that Wang Chongyang wrote on the theme of "Wandering" (*Jinyu ji*, DZ 1149, 2.13a–13b; Schipper and Verellen 2004, 1170). Discourses 7, 8, 9, and 13 (3b–5b) appear in the fourteenth-century *Qunxian yaoyu zuanji* (Collection of Essential Sayings from Various Immortals; DZ 1257, 2.2b–4a) as a guide to Daoist meditation.

In terms of content, the text presents itself as "fifteen discourses" written or delivered by Wang Chongyang. They are as follows:

Table 1. Fifteen Discourses of the *Chongyang lijiao shiwu lun*

1. Living in Hermitages	9. Refining Innate Nature
2. Cloud Wandering	10. Joining the Five Qi
3. Studying Texts	11. Merging Innate Nature and Life-destiny
4. Preparing Medicinal Herbs	12. The Way of Sages
5. On Construction	13. Going Beyond the Three Realms
6. Companions of the Way	14. Methods for Nourishing the Body
7. Sitting in Meditation	15. Leaving the Mundane World
8. Controlling the Heart-mind	

---

11. As mentioned, prior to my translation of the *Jinguan yusuo jue* (Komjathy 2007a), the *Chongyang lijiao shiwu lun* was the only early Quanzhen work to appear in published translation and scholarship. There is also Waley's somewhat dated translation of the *Xiyou ji* (DZ 1429) (DZ 1931) as well as Peter Acker's recent translation of the *Yinfu jing zhu* (DZ 122) (2006). Some later Quanzhen, specifically Longmen, works have also been translated. See the introduction in this volume.

12. If the text dates from the formative moments of Quanzhen as a local Shandong religious community, then Wang Chongyang may have specifically written the text for use in the five Shandong religious associations (*wuhui*).

From these titles alone, one gains a glimpse into the religious worldview, spiritual orientation, and training regimens of the early Quanzhen movement. I have included the text in the present chapter because Wang Chongyang emphasizes the way in which the cultivation of clarity and stillness must become one's daily practice (Discourse 7).[13] The aspiring Quanzhen adept must not reduce "meditation" to a seated technique undertaken for a fixed duration; rather, the aspirant must cultivate contemplative presence as an all-pervasive existential approach. Also noteworthy is Wang's emphasis on the necessity of engaging in solitary and eremitic religious praxis, specifically in huts and hermitages (Discourses 1 and 5). This parallels both the early Quanzhen practice of "meditation enclosure" (*huandu*) (see Goossaert 1997, 171–219; 1999; Komjathy 2007a, 157–66) as well as the actual seclusion of the early adepts in such places as the Huo siren mu (Tomb for Reviving the Dead; near Huxian, Shaanxi), Quanzhen an (Hermitage of Complete Perfection; Muping, Shandong), Yanxia dong (Grotto of Misty Vapors; near Yantai and Weihai, Shandong), Jinyu an (Hermitage of Gold and Jade; Huangxian, Shandong), Longmen dong (Dragon Gate Grotto; near Longxian, Shaanxi), Yunxi an (Hermitage of Cloudy Ravines; Luoyang, Henan), Yunguang dong (Grotto of Cloud-like Radiance; Wendeng, Shandong), and so forth (see Komjathy 2010). If one accepts my translation/interpretation as viable, then Wang Chongyang seems to suggest that seclusion is a *prerequisite* for entrance into the early Quanzhen religious community: "All renunciants must first retreat to a hermitage. . . . Then you may enter the Way of Perfection" (Discourse 1). Wang also emphasizes the importance of the dual cultivation of innate nature (*xing*) and life-destiny (*ming*), or stillness practices (*jinggong*; e.g., meditation) that nourish one's spirit and movement practices (*donggong*; e.g., health and longevity techniques) that nourish one's basic vitality. In the context of the present volume, I would also draw attention to Wang Chongyang's advice on reading and studying texts:

> The way to study texts is not to strive after literary merit, and thereby confuse your eyes. Instead, you must extract the meaning as it harmonizes with the heart-mind. Abandon texts after you have extracted their meaning and grasped their principle. Abandon principle after you have realized the fundamental ground. After you realize the fundamental ground, then attend to it until it completely enters the heart-mind. (Discourse 3; see also chapter 5)

For those actually studying and applying the insights of Daoist texts, what is most important is to develop discernment about their relevance. Wang Chongyang emphasizes the interconnection among study, practice, and experience. He also suggests that reading and study may be a transformational experience.

The *Chongyang lijiao shiwu lun* has been translated into English numerous times (Yao 1980a, 73–85; Ebrey 1995 [1981]; Reiter 1985a; Cleary 1991, 130–35; Kohn 1993, 86–92). My own translation was previously published in my *Handbooks for Daoist Practice* (Komjathy 2008a). I am grateful to the Yuen Yuen Institute (Yuanxuan xueyuan) of Hong Kong for permission to reprint it. Here it should also be mentioned that the *Chongyang lijiao shiwu lun* continues to occupy a central place in contemporary Quanzhen monastic communities. It has been circulated as a free pocket-

---

13. Categorized in a more straightforward way, the *Chongyang lijiao shiwu lun* is a treatise or discourse. It is primarily didactic in intent. One could also reflect on the text as a proto-monastic manual. See chapter 7.

size booklet throughout mainland China, and a recently engraved stele was erected in the monastic compound of Yuquan yuan (Temple of the Jade Spring), the base-temple of Huashan (Mount Hua; near Huayin, Shaanxi). The stele is located in front of the Qizhen dian (Shrine to the Seven Perfected).

Ten Admonitions of Liu Changsheng[14]

Liu Chuxuan, Master Changsheng

1. Do not consider yourself right while criticizing the transgressions of others and despising them. Do not be dissolute in intention and unrepentant.

2. Do not lose self-control and wrongly rage against people or the Dao. Do not constantly give rise to thoughts of resentment.

3. Do not praise yourself for being right while constantly discussing the faults of others.

4. Do not be praise yourself as lofty while diminishing all others, especially those who have entered the Dao.

5. Do not, without relying on the scriptural teachings, talk about the Dao or universal principles.

6. Do not start things without bringing them to conclusion. Keep your mind and intention constantly as if you were just seeing them for the first time.

7. Do not constantly speak about the shortcomings of worldly people. You should only want to mention their admirable qualities.

8. Do not be without evenness when going about affairs. Do not regard someone who creates benefits for you with affection and someone who does not offer you benefits with jealousy.

9. Do not, when around people who practice *samādhi* and wisdom or other forms of cultivation, fail to observe quietude. And before you have reached principle and attained awakening, do not fail to study the scriptures.

10. Do not develop attachments to being and nonbeing.[15] Do not, before you reach awakening, fail to constantly maintain purity and stillness, whether standing, walking, sitting, or lying down.

Ten Admonitions of Ma Danyang[16]

Ma Yu, Master Danyang

1. Do not offend the laws of the country.

---

14. *Xianle ji*, DZ 1141, 2.18ab.

15. Or, "what you have and do not have."

16. *Zhenxian yulu*, DZ 1256, 1.8b–9b.

2. When encountering a fellow disciple, always be the first to bow. All men and women are like our father or mother because all become fathers and mothers as they pass through the six paths of transmigration.[17]

3. Give up all alcohol, sex, wealth, anger,[18] disputation, and egoism.

4. Discard worry, grief, planning, scheming, craving, karmic connections, selfish love, and thinking. If there is even a single thought, disperse it as soon as it arises. Throughout the twelve double-hours of the day, constantly examine your transgressions and the biases that diminish your realization, then immediately rectify them.

5. Meet positive situations with astonishment and never cheat good people or receive offerings from them.

6. Guard against ignorance and the fire of the karmic factors.[19] Constantly practice forbearance and shame so that, through this, grace will double and you will be free of self-interest toward the myriad beings.

7. Be cautious in speech, controlled in food and drink, and moderate in taking rich flavors.[20] Discard luxury and give up all love and hate.

8. Do not concern yourself with miraculous events or strange occurrences. Always work within your lot and only wish to strive earnestly to transform all beings toward life.

9. Live in a hut no larger than three bays with no more than three Companions of the Way.[21] If one of you is ill or in discomfort, you can mutually support each other. "If you die, I'll bury you; if I die, you'll bury me."[22] Or again, if one of you has an opinion but does not reach a conclusion, you can guide each other by pointing out the correct teaching. Do not give rise to a stranger's attitude with them.

10. Do not give rise to a dominating mind-set, but always practice expedient means, lessening yourself and benefiting others. Even if people live in a dank hovel, treat them as if they were sages or wise men. Employ clarity, simplicity, softness, and weakness, thereby always going along with the needs of others.

    Following your karmic connections, go a bit farther every day, giving up all greed and anger and attaining a state of being carefree and self-realized. Keep your aspiration on cultivation and practice, steady from beginning to end. Be careful not to get lazy or emotionally involved, but maintain a clear mind in a state of nonaction. This is perfection! Let your intention be pure and free from perversion and deviance. This is goodness!

---

17. "Six paths of transmigration" translates *liudao*, namely, gods (*deva*), demi-gods (*asura*), humans, animals, hungry ghosts, and hell-dwellers.

18. The Four Hindrances.

19. Thoughts, speech, and action.

20. This includes meat and sweets.

21. *Daoyou*.

22. This admonition parallels Discourse 6 of the *Chongyang lijiao shiwu lun* (DZ 1233). See later in this chapter.

Nourish your qi and make your spirit whole, always giving rise to sympathy and compassion. Secretly accumulate meritorious deeds, without letting others know about them but always expecting the scrutiny of the heavens.

Redoubled Yang's Fifteen Discourses to Establish the Teachings[23]

Wang Zhe, Master Chongyang

Discourse 1: Living in Hermitages

All renunciants must first retreat to a hermitage.[24] A hermitage is an enclosure, a place where the body may be attuned and entrusted. When the body is attuned and entrusted, the heart-mind gradually realizes serenity. Qi and spirit become harmonious and expansive. Then you may enter the Way of Perfection.[25]

Now, when movement and activity become necessary, you must not overdo things and exhaust yourself. If you overdo things and become exhausted, you will dissipate your qi. And yet, you cannot remain entirely inactive either. If you do not move, your qi and blood will become obstructed and weakened.

You should, therefore, find a middle way between movement and stillness. Only then can you guard constancy and be at peace with your endowments. This is the method of residing in serenity.

Discourse 2: Cloud Wandering

There are two kinds of wandering.[26]

The first involves viewing the brilliant scenery of mountains and rivers, the splendid colors of flowers and trees. Some people engaging in this kind of wandering delight in the variety and splendor of provinces or prefectures. Others enjoy the towers and pavilions of temples and monasteries. [1b] Some seek out friends to forget their concerns. Others indulge the heart-mind with fine clothing and food. People like this, even if they travel roads measuring ten thousand miles, exhaust their bodies and squander their strength. Regarding the sights of the world, their heart-minds become confused and their qi declines. Such people are engaging in empty cloud wandering.

---

23. *Chongyang lijiao shiwu lun*, DZ 1233.

24. In keeping with the early Quanzhen emphasis on solitary religious praxis and asceticism, "renunciants" translates *chujia* (lit., "leave the family"). After Quanzhen became a fully established form of Daoist monasticism in the early thirteenth century, *chujia* means to become a monastic, which usually involves an ordination ritual. We also find the parallel technical term "enter the Dao" (*rudao*) or "enter the gate" (*rumen*). See chapter 7.

25. Or, "enter the perfect Dao" (*ru zhendao*). The line may thus be interpreted as aligning oneself with the Dao or as becoming a formal member of the Quanzhen religious community. The phrase also appears in section 2a of the eighth-century *Qingjing jing* (DZ 620).

26. "Cloud wandering" (*yunyou*) most often refers to being an itinerant monastic, someone who travels from temple to temple and mountain to mountain in search of advanced training.

The second kind of wandering involves investigating innate nature and life-destiny and inquiring into the subtle and mysterious. Ascending high summits beyond peaks and gorges, such a person visits enlightened teachers without becoming exhausted. Crossing over distant waters of turbulent and roiling waves, one inquires into the Dao without becoming wearied. Then even a single phrase exchanged between teacher and disciple initiates complete illumination. Internally one realizes the great issue of life and death and comes to stand as an elder of Complete Perfection. Such people are engaging in authentic cloud wandering.

Discourse 3: Studying Texts

The way to study texts is not to strive after literary merit, and thereby confuse your eyes.[27] Instead, you must extract the meaning as it harmonizes with the heart-mind. Abandon texts after you have extracted their meaning and grasped their principle. Abandon principle after you have realized the fundamental ground. After you realize the fundamental ground, **[2a]** then attend to it until it completely enters the heart-mind.

Keep it in the heart-mind for a long time, and its essence and inner truth will become naturally present. The radiance of the heart-mind will be vast and abundant; wisdom and spirit will take flight and soar. There is no place that they will not pervade, nothing that you will not understand.

When you reach this stage, you should practice storing and nourishing such a condition. And yet, do not be overly enthusiastic or rush to accomplish this. Rather, simply fear losing innate nature and life-destiny.

There are also people who do not understand the root meaning of texts, but merely desire to memorize many concepts and become widely read. Such people converse and babble on in front of others, bragging about their outstanding talents. This is of no benefit to cultivation and practice. Instead, it injures spirit and qi. Although one reads more and more, what is the benefit in relation to the Dao?

Only by attaining the meaning of texts can you store them deep within.

Discourse 4: Preparing Medicinal Herbs

Medicinal herbs are the flourishing emanations of mountains and waterways, the essential florescence of plants and trees. One type is warming, while another is cooling. They can tonify or disperse. One type is thick, while another is thin. They can be applied externally or taken internally.

If one is willing to study them as essences, one can enliven the innate nature and life-destiny of people. However, if one is a deluded healer, one will injure the body and the physical constitution

---

27. The early Quanzhen adepts had diverse views on the relative importance of scripture study. For example, Ma Danyang admonishes his disciple Wang Yizhong for excessive study of the *Zhuangzi* (*Danyang yulu*, DZ 1057, 3b). In the same text, Ma instructs as follows: "If [you want to read], Heshang gong's commentary on the *Daode jing* and Master Jinling's commentary on the *Yinfu jing* [are best]. When you read these two texts, there will be no obstruction" (10a; translated here in chapter 2). Among the early adepts, Liu Changsheng was the most committed to consistent scripture study; he wrote commentaries on the *Daode jing* (lost), *Huangting jing* (DZ 401), and *Yinfu jing* (DZ 122; translated here in chapter 5). Similarly, Hao Guangning wrote a partial commentary on the *Cantong qi* and *Yijing* (*Taigu ji*, DZ 1161, j. 1–3), while Liu Tongwei composed one on the *Qingjing jing* (DZ 974; translated here in chapter 5). See also Wang Chongyang's comments from the *Quanzhen ji* cited further on.

of people. **[2b]** All those who study the Dao must fully understand this. If you do not understand herbal preparation, you will have no way to support the Dao.

You should also not develop attachments, because they will injure your hidden accomplishment. Externally, you may become greedy for wealth and expensive goods; internally, you may waste the ability to cultivate perfection. This not only leads to transgressions and errors in this life, but will also cause retribution in future lives. Elevated disciples within my gate, take care and be attentive!

Discourse 5: On Construction

Reed-thatched huts and grass-thatched shelters are essential for protecting the body.[28] To sleep in the open air or in the open fields offends the sun and moon.

On the other hand, living beneath carved beams and high eaves is also not the action of a superior adept. Great palaces and elevated halls—how can these be part of the living plan for followers of the Dao?

Felling trees severs the precious fluids of the earth's meridians; begging for goods and money, while performing religious activities, takes away the life-blood of the people.[29] Such people merely cultivate external accomplishment; they do not cultivate internal practice. This is like using painted cakes to satisfy hunger or storing snow for provisions[30]—one vainly expends great effort and in the end gains nothing.

Someone with strong determination must early on search for the precious palaces within his own body. **[3a]** Vermilion towers outside the body, no matter how unceasingly they are restored, will collapse and crumble. Perceptive and illuminated worthies should carefully examine this.

Discourse 6: Companions of the Way

Followers of the Dao join together as companions because they can assist each other in sickness and disease. "If you die, I'll bury you; if I die, you'll bury me."[31]

---

28. Many of the early Quanzhen adepts lived in specific hermitages: Wang Chongyang at the Hermitage of Complete Perfection, Ma Danyang at the Hermitage of Gold and Jade, and Tan Changzhen at the Hermitage of Cloudy Ravines.

29. This line seems to contradict Wang Chongyang's requirement that his Shandong disciples go begging in their hometowns. See, for example, *Danyang yulu*, DZ 1057, 2a, 12b, 13a (translated here in chapter 2); *Quanzhen ji*, DZ 1153, 1.7ab. The hagiographies (translated here in chapter 6) also contain relevant information. One possible explanation for the apparent discrepancy is that, in contrast to the Buddhist practice, Quanzhen begging was not a mendicant practice to secure food. Rather it was meant to free the early adepts from egoistic concerns, including a sense of personal reputation and social superiority.

30. An early Chan reference to "painted cakes" appears in chapter 11 of the *Jingde chuandeng lu* (Record of the Transmission of the Lamp during the Jingde Reign; T. 2076; 1004). Here Xiangyan Zhixian (d. 898) explains that "painted cakes cannot satisfy hunger." Interestingly, Eihei Dōgen's (1200–1253) *Shōbōgenzō* (Treasury of the True Dharma Eye) contains a text titled *Gabyō* (Painted Rice Cakes), wherein Dōgen challenges the conventional distinction between "rice cakes" and "painted rice cakes," between the former being real and the latter being illusory. There are various English-language translations of Dōgen's masterwork. For guidance see the online Soto Zen Text Project (hcbss.stanford.edu/research/projects/sztp).

31. This line parallels the ninth of the "Ten Admonitions" of Ma Danyang (translated earlier in this chapter): "Live in a hut no larger than three bays with no more than three companions in the Dao. If one of you is ill or in discomfort, you can mutually support each other. 'If you die, I'll bury you; if I die, you'll bury me.' Or again, if one of you has an opinion but does not reach a conclusion, you can guide each other by pointing out the correct teaching. Do not give rise to a stranger's attitude with them" (*Zhenxian yulu*, DZ 1256, 19a).

Therefore, you must first choose the right person and only then join with that person as a companion. Do not join with someone first and then consider him as a person.

Once this is accomplished, do not become overly attached to each other. Attachment between people ensnares the heart-mind.

At the same time, do not remain completely without attachment. A complete lack of attachment will cause your feelings to diverge. You should find a middle way between attachment and nonattachment.

There are three kinds of people with whom you should join and three whom you should avoid.[32] Join those with an illuminated heart-mind, wisdom, or strong determination. Avoid those who are ignorant concerning external projections of the heart-mind, who lack wisdom and are turbid in innate nature, or who lack determination and are inclined to quarrel.[33]

When establishing yourself in a monastery, completely accord with your own heart-mind and aspirations. Do not just follow your emotions or trust the outer appearance of others. Only choose the elevated and illumined. This is the supreme method.

Discourse 7: Sitting in Meditation

[3b] "Sitting in meditation" does not simply mean to sit with the body erect and the eyes closed. This is superficial sitting. To sit authentically, you must maintain a heart-mind like Mount Tai, remaining unmovable and unshakable throughout the entire day. [Maintain this practice] whether standing, walking, sitting, or lying down, whether in movement or stillness. Restrain and seal the Four Gates, namely, the eyes, ears, mouth, and nose. Do not allow the external world to enter in. If there is even the slightest trace of a thought about movement and stillness, this cannot be called quiet sitting.[34] If you can practice like this, although your body resides in the world of dust, your name will already be listed in the ranks of the immortals.

Then there is no need to travel great distances and consult others. Rather, worthiness and sagehood resides in this very body. After one hundred years, with accomplishment complete, you will cast off the husk and ascend to perfection. With a single pellet of elixir completed, spirit wanders through the eight outer realms.

Discourse 8: Controlling the Heart-mind

Let me explain the way of the heart-mind. If the heart-mind is constantly deep, then it remains unmoving. [4a] Obscure and dark,[35] it does not give attention to the ten thousand beings. Profound

---

32. Cf. *Danyang yulu* (DZ 1057, 3a; translated here in chapter 2), where Ma Danyang instructs, "To attain peace and a joyous life, nothing is better than seclusion. If Daoists are able to reside in a hermitage, they can decrease their level of fatigue by joining with one or two people as companions. Together they can gather fur in order to make padded jackets and find tree-fall to make walking sticks. Moreover, they can sing and travel together, encountering amazing mountains and streams along the way. They can also admire Huan-trees together and ensure that each other avoid the path to avarice."

33. These lines appear partially inspired by the *Lunyu* (Analects), where Kongzi (Master Kong; "Confucius") explains, "One benefits from three kinds of friends, while one becomes injured by three other types. To become friends with the direct, the trustworthy, and the well-informed brings benefit. To become friends with those who curry favor, are fond of appearances, and engage in flattery brings injury" (XVI.4; cf. Lau 1992 [1983], 163).

34. *Jingzuo.*

35. *Hunhun momo.* These characters are used by Daoists to describe the Dao. They derive from chapter 20 of the *Daode jing.*

and vague,[36] there is no such thing as internal or external. Not even the slightest trace of thought remains. This is the stabilized heart-mind.[37] It needs no control.

However, if the heart-mind is generated by pursuing external appearances, it becomes upset and overturned, searching for the head and chasing after the tail. This is called the chaotic heart-mind. You must urgently extract and expel it. Do not let it become unrestrained. Such a heart-mind ruins and spoils the Dao and inner power. It harms and diminishes innate nature and life-destiny.

Whether standing, walking, sitting, or lying down, [if the heart-mind] is constantly exhausted by hearing and seeing, knowing and perceiving, then there will only be sickness and suffering.

Discourse 9: Refining Innate Nature

Regulating innate nature is like harmonizing the strings of a zither. If they are too tight, they will snap. If they are too loose, they will not resonate. Find the middle place between taut and slack, and the zither will be harmonized.

This is also like casting a sword. If there is too much steel, it will break. If there is too much tin, it will bend. Find the harmonious mixture of steel and tin, and the sword will be useful.

To harmonize and refine innate nature, embrace these two methods. Then you yourself will become wondrous.[38]

Discourse 10: Joining the Five Qi

[4b] The Five Qi gather in the Central Palace;[39] the Three Primes collect at the top.[40]

The Azure Dragon breathes out crimson mist; the White Tiger exhales black smoke.

The myriad spirits array themselves in rows; the hundred meridians flow and become infused.

The cinnabar sand is radiant and becomes brilliant; the lead and mercury congeal and become purified.

The body may still reside in the human realm, but the spirit already wanders among the heavens.

---

36. *Mingming yaoyao*. These characters are also used by Daoists to describe the Dao. They derive from chapter 21 of the *Daode jing*.

37. *Dingxin*. *Ding*, translated as "stability" or "concentration," is used in a technical, meditative sense for the Sanskrit *samādhi*. In terms of the present context, it refers to stabilized stillness, meditative absorption, or concentration.

38. "Wondrous" translates *miao*, a character that invokes the Dao. For example, according to chapter 1 of the fourth-century BCE *Daode jing*: "Mysterious and again more mysterious—The gateway to all wonders." See also chapters 15 and 27.

39. In the present context, the Central Palace (*zhonggong*) most likely refers to the lower elixir field. Sections 1.18b–20b and 2.1a–3a of the *Dadan zhizhi* (DZ 244; translated here in chapter 4) contain illustrations and instructions on the corresponding *neidan* method. Interestingly, chapter 2 of the received *Huangdi neijing suwen* (Yellow Thearch's Inner Classic: Basic Questions; DZ 1018) is entitled "Siqi diaoshen lun" (Discourse on Harmonizing Spirit with the Four Qi).

40. The Three Primes (*sanyuan*) usually refer to the three elixir fields. Here they include the corresponding vital substances of vital essence, qi, and spirit.

Discourse 11: Merging Innate Nature and Life-destiny

Innate nature is spirit; life-destiny is qi. Innate nature meeting life-destiny is like wild birds obtaining the wind. They use it to float and soar, rising lightly. Saving their strength, they complete their flight with ease.

Thus the *Yinfu jing* (Scripture on the Hidden Talisman) says,[41] "The regulation of all beings resides with their qi." This is exactly it.

The adept cultivating perfection must rely on this, never allowing it to be disseminated to lesser adepts. One should fear that the spirits and luminaries will send down censure. Innate nature and life-destiny are the roots of cultivation and practice. You should attentively forge and refine them.

Discourse 12: The Way of Sages

[5a] To enter the way of sages, you must develop determination for many years, amassing accomplishments and binding yourself to practice. Only an adept of elevated illumination, an individual with excelling realization, can enter the way of sages.

Your body may reside in a single room, but innate nature will fill the heavens, earth, and whole cosmos. The multitude of sages silently protects and supports you. Immortal lords in limitless numbers invisibly encircle and surround you. Your name becomes recorded in Zigong (Purple Palace) and established among the ranked immortals. Your physical form may remain in the world of dust, but your heart-mind is already illuminated beyond all beings.

Discourse 13: Going Beyond the Three Realms

The Three Realms are the realm of desire, the realm of form, and the realm of formlessness.

When the heart-mind forgets planning and thinking, one goes beyond the realm of desire. When the heart-mind forgets mental projections, one goes beyond the realm of form. When the heart-mind does not manifest even a vision of emptiness, one goes beyond the realm of formlessness.

Abandoning these Three Realms, the spirit dwells in the country of immortals and sages. [5b] Innate nature resides in the region of Yuqing (Jade Clarity).[42]

---

41. Section 2a of the sixth-century *Yinfu jing*, a Daoist scripture that was accepted as canonical within the early Quanzhen movement. According to Wang Chongyang, "[To practice spiritual refinement] you must fully understand the three hundred characters of the *Yinfu jing* and read up on the five thousand words of the *Daode jing*" (*Quanzhen ji*, DZ 1153, 13.7b–8a). A translation of the text with Liu Changsheng's commentary appears here in chapter 5.

42. The highest of the Three Heavens, with the other two being Shangqing (Highest Clarity; middle) and Taiqing (Great Clarity; lowest).

Discourse 14: Methods for Nourishing the Body

The Dharma Body is a representation of formlessness.[43] It is neither emptiness nor existence, has neither after nor before. It is neither low nor high, neither long nor short.

When applied, there is nowhere that it does not pervade. When stored, it is dark and obscure without residual traces.

If you realize this way, you can appropriately nourish this body. The more you nourish it, the more accomplishment you attain. The less you nourish it, the less accomplishment you attain.

Do not desire to go back; do not yearn for the mundane world. Then you will depart and dwell in suchness.

Discourse 15: Leaving the Mundane World

Leaving the mundane world does not mean that the body departs. Instead, it refers to a condition of the heart-mind. The body is like the lotus root; the heart-mind is like the lotus blossom. The root is in mud, but the blossom is in the empty void.

[6a] For the person in realization of the Dao, the body may reside in the mundane world, but the heart-mind rests in the sacred realms. People of today desire to be eternally undying, and so "leaving the ordinary world" seems like a great absurdity. Such people have not fully understood the principle of the Dao.

I have spoken these fifteen discourses to admonish those within these gates with strong determination and sincere aspirations. Examine these principles profoundly and in detail so that you may know them.

---

43. The Dharma Body (*fashen*) is one of the Three Bodies (Skt.: *trikāya*; Chin.: *sanshen*) of a Buddha. These are the Dharmakāya, Sambhogakāya, and Nirmānakāya, that is, the dharma-body, bliss-body, and transformation-body. These correspond to (1) the body of a Buddha in its essential nature; (2) the body of a Buddha received for his own use and enjoyment; and (3) the body of a Buddha by which he can appear in any form. See Soothill and Hodous 1995 (1937), 77–78; Ding 1939, 302; Xingyun 1989, 555. In early Quanzhen, the Dharma Body is synonymous with the yang-spirit (*yangshen*) and body-beyond-the-body (*shenwai shen*) formed through internal alchemy practice. For example, according to the *Jinguan yusuo jue*, "If someone can fully comprehend these Three Transmissions, then he will transcend the Three Realms. The Three Realms are the realm of desire, the realm of form, and the realm of formlessness. The heart-mind, innate nature, and intention manifest as the Three Bodies. These are the Dharma Body of Clarity and Stillness, the Bliss Body of Enlightened Fullness, and the Transformation Body of Samādhi. These three each have a spirit of manifest traces" (DZ 1156, 12ab; trl. Komjathy 2007a). Similarly, the *Dadan zhizhi* explains, "Huangdi (Yellow Thearch) employs fire so that the dragon emerges in stillness. Transforming fire, the dragon leaps up. Spontaneously, there is a body-beyond-the-body; it is called the Dharma Body of Clarity and Purity" (DZ 244, 2.8b; translated here in chapter 4).

Chapter Four

Alchemical Transformation

Internal alchemy (*neidan*) was and remains a primary dimension of Quanzhen religious praxis. With respect to early Quanzhen *neidan* training, there is frequent use of alchemical language and symbolism. This is highly technical and esoteric terminology, and the literary anthologies, specifically the early poetry, are filled with it. Some examples include elder, maiden, matron, child, dragon, tiger, lead, mercury, and so forth (see appendix 1, Quanzhen Technical Glossary). Early Quanzhen poetry, in turn, often reads like a list of fairly standard late medieval *neidan* concerns (see chapter 1). A close reading allows one to understand the underlying philosophy and specific views informing Quanzhen internal alchemy. For example, with some work, one can reconstruct the correlative cosmology and views of self (see Komjathy 2007a, 98–146). However, the literary anthologies and poetry contain few references to specific techniques or detailed instructions on alchemical practice.

One is thus left with one of two methodologies, each of which has its limitations. The first approach involves attempting to reconstruct Quanzhen *neidan* practice through the literary anthologies. The benefit of this approach is that scholars generally consider the poetry to be the least problematic writings in terms of dating and provenance. However, there are also problems involved here. The poetry is not intended to provide systematic instruction on Quanzhen practice; it is, more often than not, inspired, highly personal, context-specific, and intended to encourage aspiring adepts. Quanzhen teachers most likely gave detailed *neidan* instruction, guidance on the specific methods, through direct master-disciple conversations and oral transmissions (see chapter 2). Moreover, in order to supplement the apparent omissions and gaps in the poetry, one must conjecture on assumed meanings based on reference to other, more problematic Quanzhen works or to contemporaneous *neidan* sources, sources that do not derive from a Quanzhen context. The second possible methodology focuses on exploration and analysis of other Quanzhen works, which are often of uncertain date and questionable attribution. These include the *Chongyang zhenren jinguan yusuo jue* (Perfected Chongyang's Instructions on the Gold Pass and Jade Lock; DZ 1156; abbr. *Jinguan yusuo jue*; trl. Komjathy 2007a); *Chongyang zhenren shou Danyang ershisi jue* (Twenty-four Instructions Transmitted from Perfected Chongyang to Danyang; DZ 1158; abbr. *Ershisi jue*); *Dadan zhizhi* (Direct Pointers to the Great Elixir; DZ 244); as well as some lesser-known texts attributed to Wang Chongyang (e.g., *Jin zhenren yulu*, DZ 1056, 4b–8b). Of these, the *Jinguan yusuo jue* reads more like a discourse record than a *neidan* treatise, while the *Ershi jue* is akin to a dictionary of *neidan* terminology.[1] Thus, if one wishes to gain some insight into the technical specifics of Quanzhen *neidan* training, one must turn to the *Dadan zhizhi*.

In the pages that follow, I provide a complete, annotated translation of the *Dadan zhizhi*, the only early Quanzhen text that can be accurately categorized as a manual of alchemical practice and transformation. The text is attributed to Qiu Chuji (Changchun [Perpetual Spring]; 1148–1227), the youngest of the first-generation adherents and the third Patriarch of Quanzhen. This attribution is clearly spurious: Qiu did not write the text, and the text was definitely compiled at a later date. However, this initial observation raises a related question: does the *Dadan zhizhi* have any actual association with the teachings of Qiu Changchun? It is beyond the confines of the present volume to provide a systematic discussion (see Komjathy 2007b), so some basic comments will have to suffice. In the opening section of the *Dadan zhizhi*, Qiu is identified as Changchun yandao zhujiao zhenren (Perfected Changchun, National Leader Expounding the Dao), a title bestowed by Qubilai Qan (Khubilai Khan; Emperor Shizu; 1215–1294; r. 1260–1294) in 1269 (*Jinlian xiangzhuan*, DZ 174, 2a–3b). However, Qiu's title lacks the additional honorific "perfected lord" (*zhenjun*) added by Emperor Wuzong (r. 1308–1311) in 1310 (DZ 174, 3b–10b; Boltz 1987, 160; Ren and Zhong 1991, 175). These details indicate that the text was compiled at least forty to sixty years after the death of Qiu. However, comparison with other teachings associated with Qiu Changchun (e.g., *Qinghe yulu*, DZ 1310, 2.5ab, 2.9a–10b, 2.14ab, 3.11b; *Xuanfeng lu*, DZ 176, 1b; *Zhenxian yulu*, DZ 1256, 1.14b, 2.5a) reveals some interesting parallels. These and similar passages provide an important clue concerning the association of the *Dadan zhizhi* with Qiu Changchun: Qiu was recognized and remembered by his disciples and acquaintances as an experienced Daoist practitioner who was proficient with not only alchemical techniques but also related experiences. It is also noteworthy that the "Changchun Qiu zhenren ji Xizhou daoyou shu" (Writings Sent by Perfected Qiu Changchun to Daoist Friends in Xizhou; abbr. "Changchun shu"; *Zhenxian yulu*, DZ 1256, 1.12a–19a), like other texts of the early Quanzhen textual corpus, presents itself as a transcription of oral instructions. Placed in the larger context of early Quanzhen religious praxis, one must admit the inevitable: specific transformative techniques were utilized. So, which techniques were employed by the early Quanzhen adherents and their disciples? The *Dadan zhizhi* provides some clues.

The *Dadan zhizhi* is thus a problematic text with respect to issues of dating and authorship. For all intents and purposes, it seems to be a mid to late thirteenth-century text, postdating the death of Qiu Changchun and most of his direct disciples. However, even this claim must be qualified. Apart from Qiu's honorific title, there is no internal evidence to date the text convincingly after 1227. Here it also must be noted that the format of the text only makes the matter more complex. The received text consists of primary, secondary, and even tertiary strata.[2] Certain layers are attributed to Qiu Changchun, while other sections are impossible to identify. In addition, there are commentaries

---

1. The following terms with Quanzhen definitions appear in the *Ershisi jue*: *zong* (1a), *zu* (1a), *xing* (1a), *ming* (1a), *gen* (1a), *ye* (1a), *long* (1ab), *hu* (1ab), *qian* (1b), *hong* (1b), *jingong* (1b), *huangpo* (1b), *yinger* (1b), *chanü* (1b), *xinyuan* (1b), *yima* (1b), *bin* (1b), *zhu* (1b), *long* (1b–2a), *she* (1b–2a), *sanbao* (2a), *taishang* (2a, 3b–4a), *chujia* (2a, 3b), *xiuxing* (2a), *changsheng busi* (2a–2b), *dao* (2b), *qingjing* (2b), *sanming* (2b–3a), *jiuxing* (3a), *jiuqiao* (3a), *sishi* (3a), *shuihuo* (3ab), *sancai* (3b), *choutian* (3b), *qifan* (4a). This is followed by quotations from a variety of classical Chinese and Daoist texts.

2. Following a similar format as the *Xishan ji* (DZ 246), the *Dadan zhizhi* frequently refers to the teachings of Shi Huayang, often without locatable, corresponding passages in the *Xishan ji*. It is difficult to know if we should read these references in the voice of Qiu Changchun or as a separate dimension of the text. Simply stated, the format of the *Dadan zhizhi* is as confounding as its content is fascinating.

on instructions that appear as a primary aspect of the text, while there are secondary commentaries (embedded in the text in smaller characters) that seem to be a later addition. From my perspective, these details suggest that the primary textual layers predate 1269/1300. Even a conservative evaluation would have to move the text much closer to the lifetime of Qiu Changchun. While the *Dadan zhizhi* was definitely not composed by Qiu, it may contain some material that was transmitted in Quanzhen monastic communities as oral instructions associated with Qiu. As far as my research goes, which aspects these might be is impossible to determine. For the purposes of the present study, the text does provide a glimpse into Quanzhen alchemical praxis as documented, remembered, and transmitted within a specific segment of the Quanzhen monastic community. Here personal meditation with the goal of self-transformation and immortality was primary.

The *Dadan zhizhi*, in turn, dates to a historical moment when Quanzhen had become a formal monastic order with national distribution. As such, one can imagine that it was distributed to certain Quanzhen adherents as a manual for alchemical praxis, possibly due to the absence of direct training under a teacher. The received text of the *Dadan zhizhi* is, in turn, organized as a series of instructions and illustrations with corresponding explanations. For simplicity's sake, we may begin by saying that *neidan* praxis is presented as a sequence of nine stages.[3] Generally speaking, each stage consists of illustrated instructions, followed by exegesis. In short, the *Dadan zhizhi* is an illustrated manual of Quanzhen *neidan* praxis. Here alchemical training is mapped out as a sequence, a stage-based process, which, if practiced correctly, will result in "immortality."

Table 2. Nine Stages of Quanzhen Alchemical Practice according to the *Dadan zhizhi*

1. Coupling the Dragon and Tiger and Inverting the Five Phases (1.6a–8b)
2. Firing Times of the Celestial Cycle and Inverting the Five Phases (1.8b–11b)
3. Reversion of the Three Fields and Flying the Gold Essence behind the Elbows (1.12a–14b)
4. Reversion of the Three Fields and the Reverted Elixir of the Gold *Ye*-fluids (1.14b–17b)
5. Five Qi Meeting the Origin and Refining Form into Greater Yang (1.18b–20b)
6. Union of Spirit and Qi and the Consummation of the Three Fields (1.20b–23b)[4]
7. Five Qi Meeting the Origin and Refining Spirit to Enter the Summit (2.1a–3a)[5]
8. Initiating the Fire through Inner Observation and Refining Spirit to Merge with the Dao (2.3a–5a)
9. Casting Off the Husk to Ascend to Immortality and Transcending the Mundane to Enter
   the Sacred (2.8a–11b)[6]

---

3. Paulino Belamide identifies nine stages (2002, 157), but then proceeds to only discuss eight (ibid., 158–65). The latter division is based on the isolated series of diagrams at the beginning of the *Dadan zhizhi* (3a–6a). In her entry on the text in *A Historical Companion to the Daozang*, Farzeen Baldrian-Hussein claims that there are ten stages (Schipper and Verellen 2004, 1171), thus paralleling the *Lingbao bifa* (DZ 1191), which she has translated and studied (1984). That number may derive from counting miscellaneous materials that are interspersed throughout the text.

4. In the beginning section of the text, this diagram is identified as the "union of spirit and water," rather than "union of spirit and qi."

5. This diagram is not listed at the beginning section of the text.

6. At the beginning of the text, this diagram is identified as the "Diagram of Transcending the Mundane to Enter the Sacred and Casting Off the Husk to Become an Immortal."

In addition to the nine primary illustrations, instructions, and explanations, the *Dadan zhizhi* contains sections on "signs of response" (*yingyan*) (i.e., experiential confirmation) (1.17b–18a) and "demonic influences" (*mojun*) (i.e., difficulties and hindrances to alchemical progress) (2.5a–8a), both of which parallel sections of the tenth-century *Chuandao ji* (Anthology on the Transmission of the Dao; *Xiuzhen shishu*, DZ 263, 14–16). There are other noteworthy internal textual dimensions as well. The *Dadan zhizhi* cites the following scriptures: sixth-century *Yinfu jing* (1.1a, 1.2b), *Beidou zhenjing* (1.1b), eighth-century *Qingjing jing* (1.4a), tenth-century *Xishan ji* (1.8a), ninth-century *Zhonghuang jing* (2.3a), and fourth-century *Huangting jing* (2.11a). The text also mentions major personages related to *neidan* practice, including Shi Huayang (1.8a, 1.10b, 1.12b, 1.17a, 2.2a), Liu Haichan (2.8b), Wang Chongyang (2.8b, 2.15a), and Zhongli Quan and Lü Dongbin (2.8b). With respect to the question of provenance, the most distinctive characteristic of the text is the reference to Shi Huayang and the Xishan (Western Mountain) lineage,[7] which contrasts with the rest of the early Quanzhen corpus.[8] Although the Xishan lineage has yet to be thoroughly studied, and the potential historical connection between Quanzhen and Xishan and its associated lineage is currently unclear, these details may indicate that the text derives from a Quanzhen monastic context in which members of the Xishan lineage had joined the Quanzhen order. It in turn appears that section 2.11b to the end of the text are later additions. In any case, the *Dadan zhizhi* represents a comprehensive manual on *neidan* practice, and it was probably composed for distribution to Quanzhen ascetic, eremitic, and monastic communities.

The *Dadan zhizhi* has been translated with basic annotations by Paulino Belamide in his dissertation (2002). Belamide's translation includes English versions of the corresponding diagrams. I have incorporated these images into my translation, and I am grateful to Dr. Belamide for permission to do so. My translation has also benefited from his rendering, though there are significant differences in our interpretations. The reader should note that different fonts have been used, with the following correspondences: primary textual layer (12-point font), primary commentary layer (11-point font), and subcommentary (9-point font), with the latter usually appearing embedded in the original Chinese text as smaller characters. I have provided essential annotations, but many of the commonly occurring terms will be found in appendix 1, Quanzhen Technical Glossary.

Direct Pointers to the Great Elixir[9]

Attributed to Qiu Chuji, Master Changchun

The immortal scripture says, "Observe the Way of Heaven, and attend to the activities of heaven, and that is all."[10] Embody the laws and images of heaven and then practice them. Heaven and earth are originally the unified qi of the great Void.

---

7. Not to be confused with the famous Tang literati, our Shi Huayang is identified as the transmitter of one version of the *Chuandao ji* (DZ 263, 14–16), while the *Xishan ji* is attributed to him, though it was compiled by his disciple Li Song. There is thus a connection with the so-called Zhong-Lü textual tradition.

8. For some later potential connections between Quanzhen and Xishan see *Suiji yinghua ji* (DZ 1076; Schipper and Verellen 2004, 1150) by He Daoquan (Wugou; d. 1399).

9. *Dadan zhizhi*, DZ 244.

10. Section 1a of the sixth-century *Yinfu jing* (Scripture on the Hidden Talisman; DZ 31). A translation with Liu Changsheng's commentary appears here in chapter 5. On the "Way of Heaven" (*tiandao*) see also chapters 1 and 2 of the *Huangdi neijing suwen* (DZ 1018) and chapter 13 of the *Zhuangzi*.

After stillness reaches its extreme, movement occurs. There is transformation, and then [the unified qi] becomes two. The light and clear ascends, becoming yang and heaven. The heavy and turbid descends, becoming yin and earth.[11] Even though they are separated and exist as two, they cannot to be still. Because the celestial qi moves first, it descends to unite with the terrestrial qi. After reaching its extreme, it ascends again. The terrestrial qi originally does not ascend, but through mixing and merging with the celestial qi it stretches out to ascend. After reaching its extreme, it descends again. The upper and lower need each other to transform and produce the myriad beings. Heaven transforms to become the sun, moon, and stars; earth transforms to become rivers, oceans, and mountains. One after another, the myriad beings are produced. Thus, the myriad beings come into being by obtaining the ascending and descending qi of yin and yang [1.1b] and become fully formed by obtaining the refinement of the essential florescence of the sun and moon. The sun and moon circulate and revolve, each according to its own pathway. If they did not obtain the central qi, they would not revolve. The central qi is associated with the location of the Northern Dipper. The direction of the Dipper handle (Note: The Great Sage of Central Heaven, not the northern direction) correspondingly points toward the Celestial Handle and shifts in accordance with the time. The sun, moon, and stars follow its direction as they move through their own circulations. According to the *Doujing* (Scripture on the Dipper),[12] "The Celestial Handle refers to the constant revolutions of day and night." The ascent and descent of heaven and earth, and the movement of the sun and moon do not lose their times. There is no end to the transformations of the myriad things.

Humans are endowed with unified sameness with heaven and earth. In the beginning, the qi of one's father and mother interacted, commingling to become a pearl. It was stored internally as the spark of original yang and perfect qi. It was externally wrapped in vital essence and blood. These circulated through the life-stem[13] of one's mother. After conceiving an embryo, the mother becomes aware that there is something [within her]. Each inhalation and exhalation moves between the different places [in the mother and embryo], and [the mother] is connected with the original qi of the embryo being conceived. The two kidneys develop first, and then the yin-organs and yang-organs are formed successively. [2a] By the tenth month, the embryo is complete and qi is sufficient. Before being born, while still in the mother's womb, the embryo covers its face with its hands. The Nine Cavities are not yet connected, but [the embryo] receives the mother's qi as nourishment. Vague and indistinct,[14] pure and unified without separation, it is the qi of Prior Heaven.[15]

---

11. An allusion to the beginning of chapter 3 of the *Huainanzi* (Book of the Huainan Masters; DZ 1184).

12. These lines come from the "Beidou zhou" (Invocation of the Northern Dipper), which is contained in the *Taishang xuanling beidou benming yansheng zhenjing* (DZ 622, 6a), a text of unknown provenance.

13. The umbilical cord.

14. *Hunhun dundun*. A reference to the mysteriousness of the Dao. See chapters 14 and 15 of the *Daode jing*.

15. *Xiantian qi*, which is sometimes translated as "prenatal qi" or "protocosmic qi." The qi of Prior Heaven refers to one's energetic endowment from the cosmos and one's ancestors.

It is not until qi, spirit, and vital essence become abundant inside the womb that [the embryo] no longer receives the qi and blood of the mother. When the mother's life-stem is separated, spirit and qi rise, while the head moves downward for birth. As soon as emerging from the mother's womb, the two hands open. Qi scatters to the Nine Cavities. Inhalation and exhalation enter and exit through the nose and mouth. This is the qi of Later Heaven.[16] One *cun* and three *fen* inside the navel is where the original yang and perfect qi are stored.[17] When [these types of qi] are not in a mutually beneficial relation, delusion causes you to forget your original face.[18] This eventually leads to dissipation and exhaustion and results in disease and early death, sorrow and anxiety, worry and vexation, joy and anger, as well as sorrow and happiness.

The navel at the center of the human body is called the Central Palace,[19] Repository of Life-destiny, Primordial Chaos, Spirit Chamber, Yellow Court, elixir field, Cavern of Spirit and Qi, Cavity of Returning to the Root, Pass of Retrieved Life-destiny, Cavity of the Primordial, [2b] Cavern of the Hundred Meetings, Gate of Life, Divine Furnace of the Great Monad,[20] and Original Face.[21] There are many other names as well. This location contains and stores vital essence and marrow. It connects the hundred meridians and nourishes the entire body. Completely pure and simple, it cannot be grasped.

Ordinary people are unable to get close to it because they are pulled along by the seven emotions and six desires. In confusion, they have forgotten this original place, and the qi from respiration only reaches the Ocean of Qi (Note: The Ocean of Qi is located above, in the repository of the diaphragm and lungs). Since it does not reach the Central Palace and Repository of Life-destiny to unite with the original qi and perfect qi, Metal and Wood remain separate. How then can the dragon and tiger commingle to generate the pure essence? In addition, they do not know the pivot of movement and circulation (Note: The *Yinfu jing* says, "This is heaven manifesting killing power").[22] How can the qi and *ye*-fluids flow and revolve to refine spirit and form?

The heart is associated with Fire. Its center stores the vital essence of aligned yang. It is called mercury, Wood, and the dragon. The kidneys are associated with Water. Their center stores original yang and perfect qi. It is called lead, Metal, and the tiger. First, guide the qi of water and fire to commingle by ascending and

---

16. *Houtian qi*, which is sometimes translated as "postnatal qi" or "deuterocosmic qi." This qi of Later Heaven refers to qi derived from food and breathing.

17. *Cun* is an ancient Chinese measurement for length, often translated as "inch." One *cun* consists of ten *fen*.

18. *Benlai mianmu*, which also appears as the "face before you were born." The phrase is associated with Chan Buddhism, wherein it most often designates one's inherent and original enlightenment.

19. Here and in other sections of the *Dadan zhizhi* (e.g., 1.6b–7a, 1.9a, 2.7a), the Central Palace (*zhonggong*) refers to the lower elixir field, the abdominal region. However, in other locations, it seems to designate the heart region (e.g., 1.10a, 2.7ab).

20. "Great Monad" translates *taiyi*.

21. Some of these Daoist technical terms and esoteric body location names derive from the third-century *Huangting jing* (Scripture on the Yellow Court; DZ 331; DZ 332).

22. *Yinfu jing*, DZ 31, 1a.

descending. **[3a]** When they rise and sink, joining together, use your intent to entice perfect essence and perfect qi to emerge. Mix and unite them in the Central Palace. Use the spirit fire for decoction, and guide the qi to circulate through the entire body. When qi is abundant and spirit is strong, you coalesce and complete the great elixir. This is not simply beneficial for prolonging life and increasing longevity. If

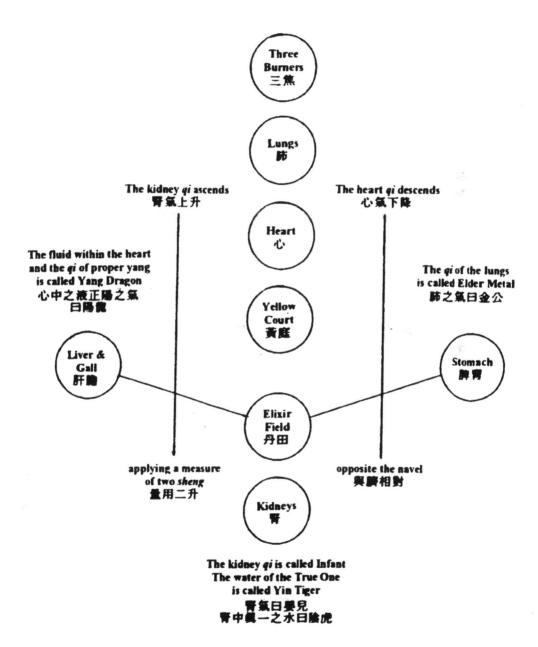

Figure 4. Diagram of Coupling the Dragon and Tiger and Inverting the Five Phases

accomplishment and practice are cultivated,[23] you may ascend to the position of the sages. More detailed instructions follow.

[3b] Every human being is sufficient; each of us is perfectly complete.

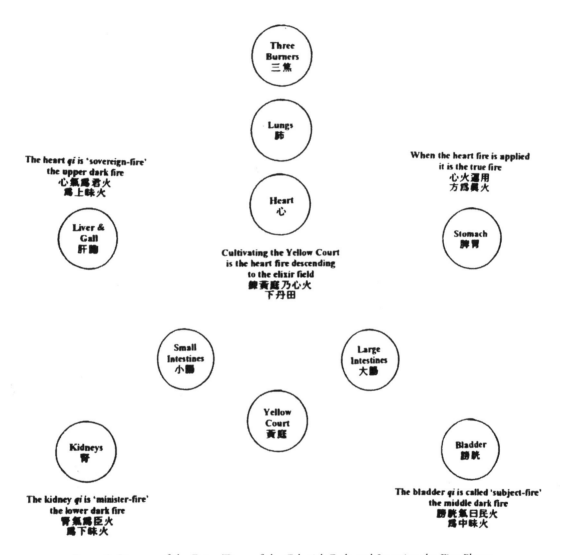

Figure 5. Diagram of the Firing Times of the Celestial Cycle and Inverting the Five Phases

23. Or, "merit and deeds."

Heaven and earth ascend and descend; the sun and moon come and go. At one moment closed, at another moment open, advancing and retreating, preserved and destroyed. The *Yijing* (Classic of Changes) says, "Only sages are able to know advance and retreat as well as preservation and destruction."

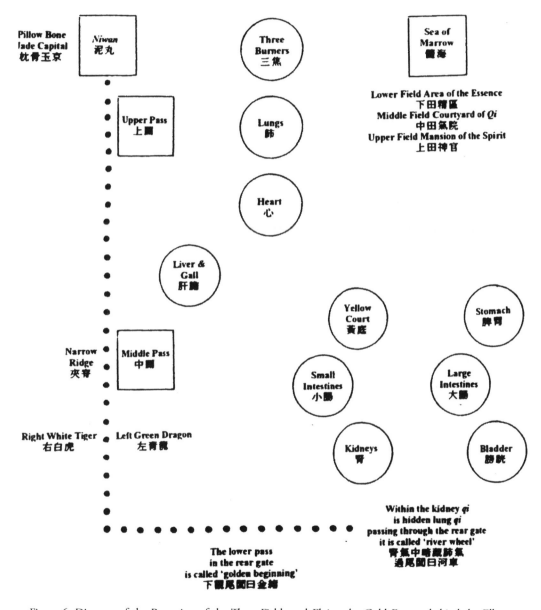

Figure 6. Diagram of the Reversion of the Three Fields and Flying the Gold Essence behind the Elbows

[4a] Vague and indistinct, the center contains something. Secluded and darkened, the center contains vital essence. Clarity is the source of turbidity—gradually enter the perfect Dao.[24]

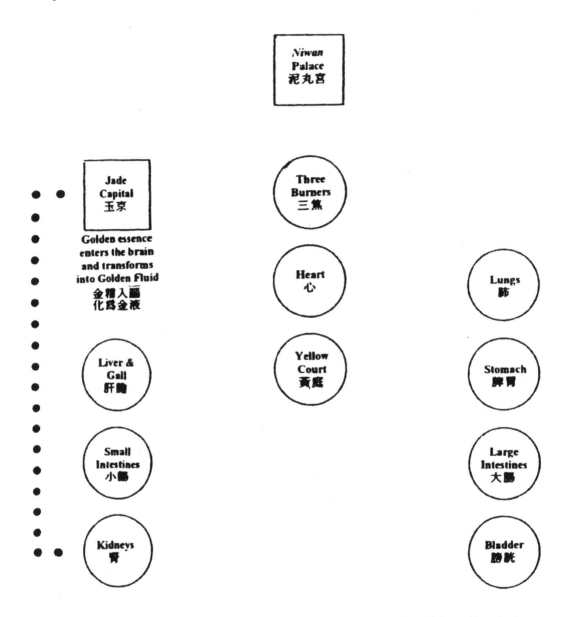

Figure 7. Diagram of the Reversion of the Three Fields and the Reverted Elixir of the Gold *Ye*-fluids

---

24. An allusion to section 1b–2a of the eighth-century *Qingjing jing* (Scripture on Clarity and Stillness; DZ 620). A translation with Liu Tongwei's commentary appears here in chapter 5. As in the *Chongyang lijiao shiwu lun* (see chapter 3), *zhendao* may be translated as the "Way of Perfection" in a Quanzhen context.

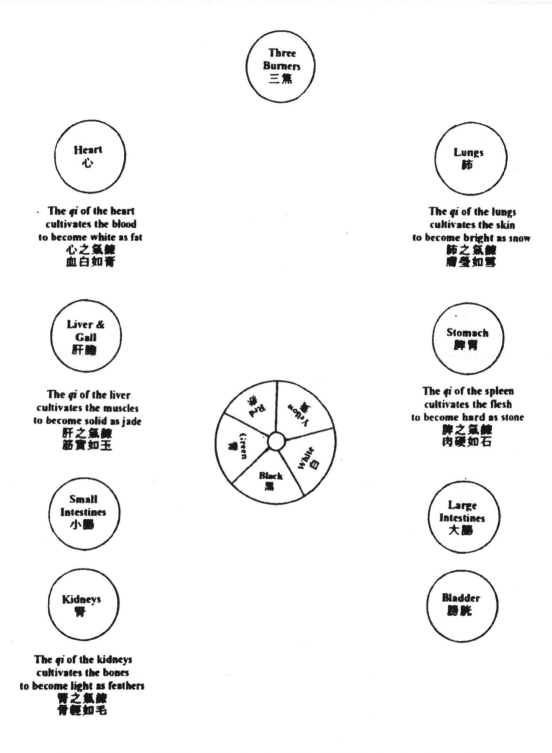

Figure 8. Diagram of the Five Qi Meeting the Origin and Refining Form into Greater Yang

[5a] Through alchemy, the Five Qi naturally meet the Origin. Refine your form and substitute the bones.

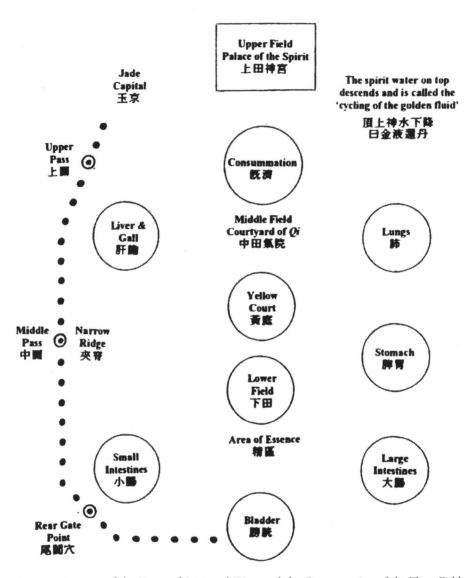

Figure 9. Diagram of the Union of Spirit and Water and the Consummation of the Three Fields

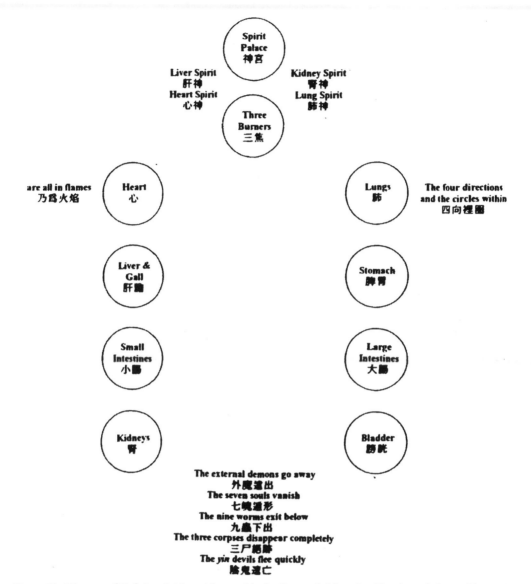

Figure 10. Diagram of Refining Spirit to Merge with the Dao and Advancing Fire through Inner Observation

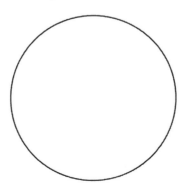

Figure 11. Diagram of Transcending the Mundane to Enter the Sacred and Casting Off the Husk to Become an Immortal

Diagram and Instructions on Coupling the Dragon and Tiger and Inverting the Five Phases

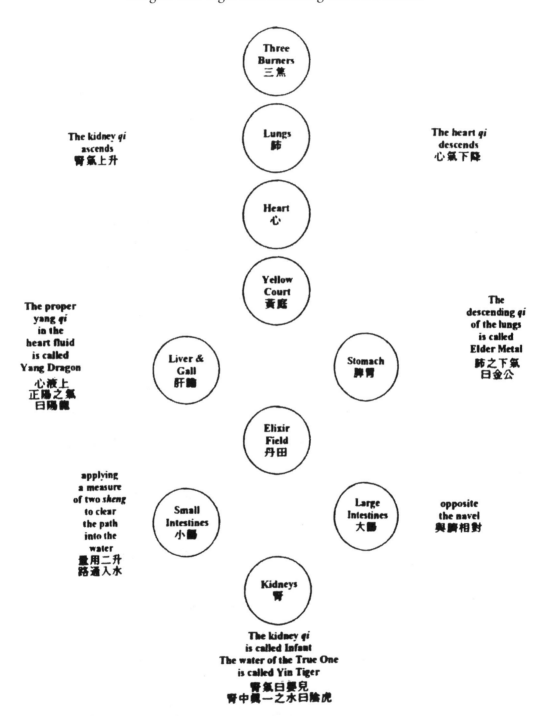

Three Burners
三焦

Lungs
肺

Heart
心

Yellow Court
黃庭

Liver & Gall
肝膽

Stomach
脾胃

Elixir Field
丹田

Small Intestines
小腸

Large Intestines
大腸

Kidneys
腎

The kidney *qi* ascends
腎氣上升

The heart *qi* descends
心氣下降

The proper yang *qi* in the heart fluid is called Yang Dragon
心液上正陽之氣曰陽龍

The descending *qi* of the lungs is called Elder Metal
肺之下氣曰金公

applying a measure of two *sheng* to clear the path into the water
量用二升路通入水

opposite the navel
與臍相對

The kidney *qi* is called Infant
The water of the True One is called Yin Tiger
腎氣曰嬰兒
腎中眞一之水曰陰虎

Figure 12. Diagram on Coupling the Dragon and Tiger and Inverting the Five Phases

[6a] Perfected Changchun instructed,[25] "The dragon is the qi of aligned yang above the heart *ye*-fluids. Regulate it so that it does not ascend and depart. If it meets the qi of the kidneys, they will unite naturally. The tiger is the water of perfect unity in the kidney qi. Regulate it so that it does not descend and leave. If it meets the *ye*-fluids of the heart, they will unite naturally. When the dragon and tiger commingle, you will obtain a kernel that resembles a millet grain in form. This method is called 'coupling the dragon and tiger.' Through this, you will encounter the medicinal ingredient.

"In the method of gathering the medicine, many people take the double-hour of *zi* [11 p.m.–1 a.m.] as the time when the qi of the kidneys issues forth. The double-hour of *wu* [11 a.m.–1 p.m.] is the time when the *ye*-fluids of the heart descend in practice. If there is nothing to impede this, it will succeed. **[6b]** If something does [impede this], it will fail. [Many people] do not understand how to pattern themselves on the wondrousness of Qian-heaven and Kun-earth.[26] When the qi of the kidneys rises, it is the time of *zi*. When the *ye*-fluids of the heart descend, it is the time of *wu*. It is also acceptable not to follow the time schedules. But in the methods of initial practice, you should close your eyes and internally gaze upon the Central Palace. Server your ties to anxiety, forget your concerns, and darken the heart-mind. Allow the mouth to become filled with the *jin*-fluids, without spitting them out or swallowing them down. When the right moment arrives, drink them.

"Considering the matter of a dose,[27] there is a different oral instruction, but I do not dare to write it down. Control your body slightly[28] and do not stand up. Cross your legs, extend the torso, and sit in an aligned position. Sit cross-legged,[29] not in the usual way. With the left hand, hold and [gently] lift the genitals. With the right hand, cover the Gate of Life. The navel. Block the doorway.[30] The mouth. Open the Gate of Heaven.[31] The nose, which is the Gate of the Mysterious Female. You must sever your ties to

---

25. Reading the subject "Perfected Changchun" as implied in the phrase *jueyue*, which could also be translated as "the instructions say." This pattern also appears in the *Jinguan yusuo jue*, attributed to Wang Chongyang. For a complete annotated translation of the latter see Komjathy 2007a.

26. The trigrams Qian-heaven ☰ and Kun-earth ☷, respectively. The former consists of three yang-lines and represents pure yang ("heaven"), while the latter consists of three yin-lines and represents pure yin ("earth"). In this pairing, yin has positive connotations. The trigrams may refer to the cosmos or to specific dimensions of human being, including head/abdomen and spirit/qi.

27. *Daogui* refers to a measurement in laboratory alchemy. For example, the phrase appears in chapter 38 of the fourth-century *Cantong qi* (Token for the Kinship of the Three; DZ 999; DZ 1004; trl. Wu and Davis 1932; Zhou 1988): "The color turns to purple, and one naturally completes the reverted elixir. Powdered and formed into a pill, the dose (*daogui*) leads to divinization (*shen*)." In internal alchemy, a dose relates to the formation of an internal elixir. See section 2.11a further on.

28. Reading *lianshen* for *hanshen*.

29. *Jiafu*, also appearing as *panzuo*, refers to the full-lotus posture.

30. An allusion to chapters 52 and 56 of the fourth-century BCE *Daode jing*. The various passages on "doors" and "gates" are frequently interpreted by Daoists as references to the senses.

31. An allusion to chapters 6 and 10 of the fourth-century BCE *Daode jing*.

everything. Afterward, [allow] the qi to come in through the nose. 'Coming in' refers to inhalation, breath, yin, and water. Simply allow the breath to enter in a fine and soft way. There is no sound as it enters the nose. Use the intent to gently guide [the qi] to enter the Central Palace until it reaches Tailbone Gate.[32] This means filling and opening the Pond of Primordial Chaos, and opening the Cavity of the Primordial. Once the qi reaches its utmost point, direct it through the Three Passes, along Narrow Ridge, to enter the nose. Gently release it. [7a] 'Releasing' refers to exhalation, dispersal, yang, and fire. Simply allow the breath to exit in a fine and soft way. There is no sound. Listening to the qi naturally exiting, do not allow your awareness to leave the Central Palace. Awareness refers to innate nature, spirit, perfect earth, and the Yellow Matron. However, the qi entering in through the breath reaches the Central Palace, where it joins and mixes with the original yang and perfect qi. A scripture says, 'Receive the limitless qi of heaven and earth, and extend the limited body [endowed by] your father and mother. This is heaven and earth uniting their power!'[33] Guide the two qi of water and fire to ascend and descend to meet each other. This is the same as the rising and sinking of heaven and earth. Entice the perfect qi in the kidneys. Lead and the tiger. [Entice] the Wood ye-fluids in the heart. Mercury and the dragon. They commingle and unite in the Central Palace. This is called the Five Phases becoming complete and united into a single family. They are naturally luxuriant and flourishing. A scripture says, 'Qi enters the navel as breath. Spirit enters qi to become the embryo. When the embryo and breath unite, it is called the Great Monad containing Perfection.'[34] This is called the 'copulation of the dragon and tiger.' It is the medicinal ingredient. As soon as the medicine is gathered, [tend to it] like a mother with an embryo. It feels as though something is in the Central Palace. This refers to something round and vigorous. You should employ the fire-talisman in decoction to ensure that the medicinal ingredient does not dissipate."

[7b] When practicing the aforementioned technique, you will initially feel a dry sensation in your mouth, which results in heart palpitations.[35] Next, there will be a sensation of tastelessness. It is like [the experience of] an imbecile who tastes soup but has difficulty describing it. This is the union of qi, and is thus called "copulation." Practice one coupling every day. You will obtain a substance whose shape resembles a grain of millet. Return it to the center of the Yellow Court. Naturally you will be able to increase your longevity and extend the years. If you use the firing times to refine it, it will become sufficient after three hundred days. It will naturally coalesce. Its form resembles a crossbow pellet, while its color is the same as a jujube. This is called the "internal elixir." It is like a dragon with a pearl—when a dragon has a pearl, it can take flight. When people have the internal elixir, they naturally have perpetual life and do not die.[36]

---

32. The Tailbone Gate (weilü) is the first of the Three Passes (sanguan) and is associated with the coccyx. See the appendix 1, Quanzhen Technical Glossary.

33. Source unknown.

34. Source unknown.

35. Xinchong, which literally means "heart in-flooding."

The oral instructions say,

> "Yin contains yang and yang contains yin;
> Redouble your inquiry into yin and yang.
> Students who do not understand mysterious and subtle principle
> Are wasting their time and deceiving themselves."

The Meaning of the Instructions on the Firing Times for Coupling the Dragon and Tiger and Inverting the Five Phases

[8a] Perfected Shi Huayang has said,[37] "The kidneys are water. The qi produced from water is called 'perfect fire.' The water of perfect unity stored in fire is called the 'yin tiger.' The heart is fire. The *ye*-fluids produced from fire are called 'perfect water.' The qi of aligned yang hidden in water is called the 'yang dragon.' Thus, the dragon and tiger do not refer to symbols of the liver and lungs, but represent the perfect yin and perfect yang of the heart and kidneys. For mixing these two substances together so that they become one, you must apply your intent during the double-hour of *zi*. They will coalesce naturally (Note: You must know that during the winter solstice you do not sit during *zi*). The form [of the elixir] resembles the size of a millet grain. Each day of practice results in a single grain [being formed]. Buddhists call this *śarīra*,[38] while Daoists refer to it as the 'mysterious pearl.' Each day that you increase the perfect qi by a certain length, your lifespan will be extended countless times. After three hundred days, the qi congeals and the elixir coalesces. Its form resembles a crossbow pellet, while its color is the same as a jujube. Through this, you yourself can have perpetual life and not die."[39]

The instructions say,

> "In the technique of inverting the Fives Phases,
> The dragon emerges from inside of fire.

---

36. *Changsheng busi.* A classical Daoist precedent appears in chapter 33 of the fourth-century BCE *Daode jing*: "To die but not to perish is longevity" (*si er buwang zhe shou*). In later Daoist movements, the phrase refers to longevity or immortality.

37. Adopting the pseudonym of the famous Tang poet, our Shi Jianwu (Huayang [Flourishing Yang]; fl. late tenth c.?) was a Daoist recluse who lived in the Xishan (Western Mountain) area of Nanchang in Jiangxi Province. He is the author of the *Xishan ji* (DZ 246), which possibly dates to the tenth century. See Schipper and Verellen 2004, 804–5, 1273–74.

38. *Sheli. Śarīra* refers to Buddhist relics or post-cremation remains. They often have miraculous qualities and are taken to be evidence of the deceased person's enlightenment.

39. These instructions correspond to a variety of passages in the *Xishan ji* (DZ 246), including 4.1a, 4.2ab, 4.4ab, 4.9b. Cf. *Chuandao ji*, DZ 263, 15.1a–4b.

When the Five Phases do not follow each other,
The tiger becomes produced from water.
The yang tiger originally emerges from the palace of Li-fire;
The yin tiger is again produced from the position of Kan-water.
When these two substances join, they become the root of the Dao;
Everywhere practice is fulfilled and one obtains the elixir."

Diagram and Instructions on the Firing Times of the Celestial Cycle and Inverting the Five Phases

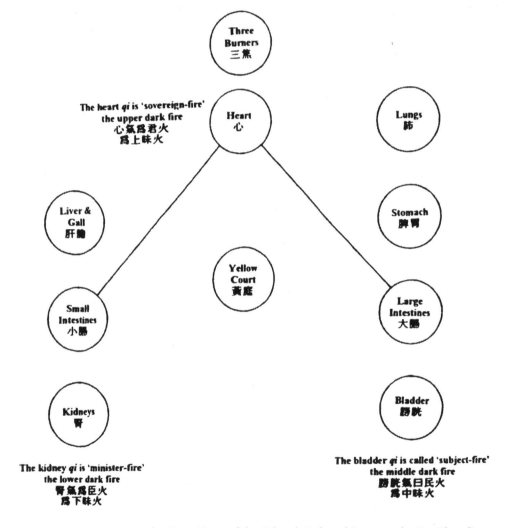

Figure 13. Diagram on the Firing Times of the Celestial Cycle and Inverting the Five Phases[40]

---

40. The Chinese text simply reads "Diagram of the Firing Times." I have amended the title to parallel those appearing in the *Dadan zhizhi* as a whole.

[9a] In the practice times for activating fire, "fire" refers to the heart, spirit, innate nature, Li-fire, the sun, and intent. Before gathering the medicine, when the two qi ascend and descend, how can one establish the medicinal ingredient and [practice] circulation without using awareness to guard the Central Palace? Although sages hide in the dark, they return to the square earth. The Central Palace. This is accomplished through the sun. Greater Yang is fire. The double-hours of *xu* [5 p.m.–7 p.m.] and *zi* require attention. Considering the exit and entry of spirit and innate nature, there are no set times. No one knows that this is the case. As soon as the two qi ascend and descend, gather the medicine. This is the time to intensify the activation of fire in the Central Palace. The "Diagram of Firing Times" says, "When according with the external years, months, days, and times, reside in the Center." A scripture says, "The Dipper handle revolves the Celestial Cycle, which is gathered in human beings." It also says, "If you use the firing exercises for three thousand days, the wondrous application will [come to fruition] in one undetermined moment." This is exactly it. The Central Palace is opposite the Palace of Zi.[41] This means that a single yang is naturally produced. A scripture says, "The roundness of the moon is preserved in the oral instructions. The double-hour of *zi* is wondrous in the mind-transmission. The two qi are like two halves of the moon. When the two half-moons join together, they become a completely round moon. When intent reaches the Central Palace, it is the double-hour of *zi*." When the Fu-return ䷗ hexagram[42] moves and reaches triple yang, the two sections of the bladder, water and metal, reach the navel and become warm. **[9b]** This is in response to the Tai-peace ䷊ hexagram[43] of heaven and earth.

For attaining this, you should only seek to arrest [mundane desires] and not allow even a single defilement to emerge. Become free of excessive thinking. Then the dragon and tiger will copulate. Gradually the *yangqi* ascends, eventually filling the entire body with a warm sensation. This corresponds to the Qian-heaven ䷀ hexagram.[44] When the medicine is completely full, it is like wind, rain, and waves sweeping and rolling. Bubbling up and boiling over, the medicine becomes hot. It transforms into the gold *ye*-fluids, which resemble a cold spring flowing downward naturally. This corresponds to the Gou-meeting ䷫ hexagram.[45] It gradually cools until it reduces [the heat]. This corresponds to the Pi-standstill ䷋ hexagram.[46] Through the fire in the elixir field, the qi gradually becomes subtle. This corresponds to the Bo-flayed

---

41. The Palace of Zi is most often associated with the perineum or the coccyx, with *zi* being the first of the twelve terrestrial branches (*dizhi*). If the Central Palace refers to the lower elixir field, then the Palace of Zi, "opposite the Central Palace," designates Mingmen (Gate of Life), the area between the kidneys.

42. Hexagram 24 (Fu) of the *Yijing*, comprised of five yin-lines above one yang-line. It symbolizes the emergence and initial growth of yang.

43. Hexagram 11 (Tai) of the *Yijing*, comprised of three yin-lines above three yang-lines. It symbolizes the equilibrium of yin and yang, with yang in ascendancy.

44. Hexagram 1 (Qian) of the *Yijing*, comprised of six yang-lines. It symbolizes pure yang and the completion of yang.

45. Hexagram 44 (Gou) of the *Yijing*, comprised of five yang-lines above one yin-line. It symbolizes the emergence and initial growth of yin.

46. Hexagram 12 (Pi) of the *Yijing*, comprised of three yang-lines above three yin-lines. It symbolizes the equilibrium of yin and yang, with yin in ascendancy.

☶☷ hexagram.[47] [The whole process] is one sequence of the Celestial Cycle. This method is called the "Firing Times of the Celestial Cycle."

When practicing this technique, slightly contract the body,[48] gently drawing in the abdomen while holding the breath for several counts. Quietly circulate the qi of the heart until it descends to reach the elixir field. Then breathe lightly through the nose in such a way as to be stored. Practice this without agitation, and simply allow your intent to constantly remain in the Central Palace.

Intent is the child of spirit; spirit is the mother of qi. When spirit directs qi, qi will circulate naturally through the Three Passes, moving from the Tailbone Gate cavity to enter Narrow Ridge, directly ascending to the Celestial Pass of the Windlass cavity. Located behind the brain. **[10a]** It enters Kunlun, and then once again descends to the elixir field. This circulation occurs continuously. The aligned qi of the northern direction The kidney qi is the Waterwheel. This is what we refer to as the "Waterwheel not daring to cease its movement";[49] the circulation enters the summit of Kunlun. The Central Palace is the pivot.[50] Intention. When you stimulate the pivot, the Celestial Pass responds. This is what we refer to as the "secret action of the spirit pivot."

The instructions say,

> "Spirit enters qi to become the embryo.
> Qi enters the navel to become breath."

When you practice the above technique according to the schedule, the qi will gather in the abdomen and will become warm naturally. If you are using this to repair deficiencies and replenish qi, apply four *liang* of fire during the three months of spring,[51] six *liang* of fire during the three months of summer, eight *liang* of fire during the three months of autumn, and two *liang* during the three months of winter. If you are using this to refine the dragon and tiger so that they copulate, apply five *liang* of fire during the first one hundred days, specifically from the double-hour of *you* to the double-hour of *hai*. **[10b]** Apply ten *liang* of fire during the second one hundred days, specifically from the double-hour of *shen* [3 p.m.–5 p.m.] to the double-hour of *hai* [9 p.m.–11 p.m.]. Apply fifteen *liang* of fire during the third one hundred days, specifically from the double-hour of *wu* [11 a.m.– 1 p.m.] to the double-hour of *hai*. Three hundred days of firing is sufficient for the elixir to coalesce and for the qi of pure yang to be produced. When holding the breath, count prayer beads. One hundred beads equal one *zhu*, and twenty-four *zhu* equal one *liang*. Count beads to measure the increase and decrease of the amount of time used.

---

47. Hexagram 23 (Bo) of the *Yijing*, comprised of one yang-line above five yin-lines. It symbolizes the fullness of yin just before it becomes pure or complete yin, which is expressed in Hexagram 2, Kun-earth ☷☷.

48. Again reading *lianshen* for *hanshen*.

49. The Waterwheel (*heche*) refers to circulating qi through the Three Passes into the head (Mount Kunlun). A concise description appears in the *Chuandao ji*, DZ 263, 15.19b–23b.

50. The "pivot" or "trigger" (*ji*) is the still point, the center of silence, from which all activity originates. According to chapter 18, "Ultimate Joy," of the *Zhuangzi*, "The myriad beings emerge from the pivot and enter into the pivot." The sixth-century *Yinfu jing* explains, "The human heart-mind is the pivot" (DZ 31, 1a).

51. *Liang* is an ancient Chinese weight measurement for object mass and monetary objects, often translated as "ounce" or "tael."

The oral instructions say,

> "Drawing in the abdomen when circulating the heart [qi] is fire;
> Gathering fluids when inhaling begins to complete the elixir.
> Students who do not fully understand mysterious and subtle principle
> Are wasting their time and spending their allotted life-span in vain."

At the beginning, do not count. The fire will reach the crucial point after half a year. On the first day of the first month, count the fire in the location of Fire [the heart].

The Meaning of the Instructions for the Firing Times of the Celestial Cycle and Inverting the Five Phases

Perfected Shi Huayang said, "The heart is the ruler of the five yang, while the kidneys are the ruler of the five yin. [11a] The five yin ascend and become water. The five yang descend and become fire. When practicing during the time of Qian-heaven,[52] having the qi descend from the heart to enter the elixir field is called 'advancing fire.' If you are using this for repairing deficiencies and replenishing qi, constantly practice the numerics of application. Through an entire year, you can grasp ten years of qi to repair ten years worth of deficiency. If practicing during the time of the Earth Door,[53] employ the technique of the dragon and tiger copulating. The perfect yin and perfect yang of the heart and kidneys coalesce to become something like the size of a millet grain. It descends and returns to the Yellow Court. Calculate the degree and amount, and apply the firing times. Three hundred days is sufficient. This is called refining the yang fire inside of yin. You should maintain it for an entire day."[54]

The previous technique does not employ the coupling of the dragon and tiger to increase or decrease the firing times. It is a comfortable and common method. If you use the dragon and tiger coupling [method], practicing in concert with the former technique, it involves refining the elixir through the fire of extraction and addition. For five *liang*, refine vital essence to become mercury. For ten *liang*, refine mercury to become cinnabar sand. For fifteen *liang*, refine cinnabar sand to become the elixir. The fire time of three hundred days is not erroneous. [11b] The elixir forms naturally, and the qi of pure yang is produced. Internally refining the five yin-organs is called "refining qi and completing spirit." Externally refining the four limbs is called "refining form and ingesting qi." If you do not refine the five yin-organs or the four limbs, but simply complete the elixir, you can still gain perpetual life. Applying the refinement of form is called "terrestrial immortality." Here both body and form become wondrous. Applying the refinement of qi is called "spirit immortality." Here one abandons the husk and transcends the mundane.

---

52. In *neidan* practice, Qian-heaven may refer to the head or the heart. The time of Qian-heaven usually corresponds to the terrestrial branch of *wu* (11 a.m.–1 p.m.).

53. In *neidan* practice, the Earth Door may refer to the perineum or the lower elixir field. The time of the Earth Door usually corresponds to the terrestrial branch of *zi* (11 p.m.–1 a.m.).

54. As far as my reading goes, there are no corresponding passages in the *Xishan ji* (DZ 246).

Perfected Changchun said,[55] "When refining the substances, do not interact with the yin-ghosts in their flourishing. When cooking the elixir, do not allow the fire dragon to fly away. The beautiful woman and talented child are in the prime of their lives. When flowers fall and dusk sets in, collection and assembly is difficult. Do not avoid the master's feelings becoming interrupted. When the time arrives, you must firmly close the Yang Pass." Not practicing according to the firing times and not engaging in internal refinement are methods of lesser completion. Through them, one can gain peace, joy, and longevity. When the Three Passes behind the back are connected, we refer to this as the reversion of the Three Fields. When the Five Phases in the Central Palace are circulated and applied, we refer to this as the inversion of the Five Phases. You gradually reach intermediate completion, the way of perpetual life and undying. Then we may speak of spirit immortals who traverse the earth. If you transmit this to unworthy people, the transgression will extend to nine generations. Be careful! Take care!

Diagram and Instructions on the Reversion of the Three Fields and Flying the Gold Essence behind the Elbows[56]

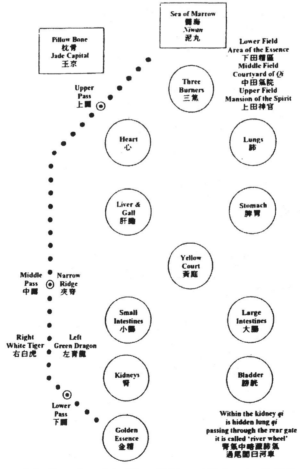

Figure 14. Diagram of the Reversion of the Three Fields and Flying the Gold Essence behind the Elbows

---

55. Again reading Qiu Changchun as the implied speaker. This amendment is added from this point forward.

56. Amending the title to include "instructions" (*jue*).

[12a] This method is called "Flying the Gold Essence behind the Elbows."[57] The primary technique is practiced after the double-hour of *zi* and before the double-hour of *wu*. When the qi is generated, loosen your robes and practice aligned sitting.[58] Seal the fists[59] and preserve spirit. First preserve [spirit] and then ascend [qi]. Direct the qi to ascend and then lie on your back.[60] Extending the chest outward and lying on your back opens the middle pass. Sitting with a stable base and lifting the head opens the upper pass. Ascend the qi and then store it in the lower waist area. From the abdominal area, gradually straighten the body and stand up. Then extend the chest and lie on your back. This opens the lower pass. Afterward, the qi becomes warm and gathers below the upper pass. [12b] Then you can straighten the body and stand up. By practicing aligned sitting for one sequence, the Three Passes become opened. This replenishes the brain marrow. Spontaneously, the complexion becomes rosy, the bones vigorous, the flesh pure, and the body lightened. We refer to this as "reversing agedness and returning to youthfulness." It is a method for "perpetual life without dying." When the young practice this, they will not age; when the aged practice this, they will regain their youth.

The oral instructions say,

"The 'gold essence behind the elbows' is ordered like a sequence of joints.
By keeping the body in a supine position, you may open the Three Passes.
For students who can awaken to mysterious and wondrous principle,
The reversal of agedness and return to youthfulness is not difficult."

The Meaning of the Instructions on the Reversion of the
Three Fields and Flying the Gold Essence behind the Elbows

Perfected Shi Huayang said, "At the double-hour of *zi*, allow the qi of the lung essence to gather in the kidneys. This is called the 'gold essence.' The gold essence consists of the unseparated gold water, the qi of the lungs and kidneys mixed together and made one. [13a] When you practice this technique, [the gold essence] circulates from the lower pass of Tailbone Gate to the middle pass of Narrow Ridge. From Narrow Ridge, it ascends to the upper pass of Jade Capital. After you open these passes

---

57. In the context of *neidan* instructions, "behind the elbows" may mean a number of things. First, it frequently refers to "up one's sleeve," in the sense of being esoteric and secret. Second, it may designate methods in which the back of the body is primary.

58. "Aligned sitting" (*zhengzuo*; Jpn.: *seiza*), or "upright sitting," is usually practiced by kneeling and sitting on the heels. In the case of the *Dadan zhizhi*, it is difficult to determine whether *zhengzuo* refers to that posture or is used synonymously for the full-lotus posture, which is mentioned in section 1.6b.

59. "Seal the fists" (*wogu*), which literally means "grasp firmly," is an allusion to chapter 55 of the *Daode jing*. In alchemical practice, it refers to a specific sacred hand gesture (Skt.: *mudrā*; Chin.: *shouyin*), wherein the tips of the thumbs touch the inside base of the associated ring-fingers and the other fingers fold over the thumbs.

60. This section seems to assume a specific Daoyin ("guided stretching") technique.

consecutively, employing one sequence through the Three Passes, [the gold essence] directly enters Niwan. This not only repairs deficiencies in the brain, but also extends one's lifespan and increases longevity, reversing agedness and returning youthfulness. It also extracts the qi of the kidneys without harming the Yellow Court. However, one must descend the fire to refine that area, so that the pure *yangqi* is produced.

"The elderly deteriorate with age. If prior to that time one has already practiced some methods, but only gained lesser accomplishment and moderate cultivation, it is not enough to practice the present method. In order to reverse agedness and return to youthfulness, a hundred days will not be sufficient to make the complexion rosy, the bones vigorous, the qi robust, and the body lightened. If the three procedures of copulating the dragon and tiger, the Celestial Cycle, and the firing times are practiced in conjunction, this is extracting and adding lead and mercury.[61] Gradually, one's lifespan is extended and longevity increases.

"The method of extraction and addition resembles the process of 'gathering the medicine and moving fire.' The yin-demons[62] as disturbances cause perverse thoughts. One should be concerned about controlling them. You must not allow the kidney qi to move downward and leak out. **[13b]** We refer to this as a danger. You should then practice extracting lead.[63] Sending out qi is lead, which is the qi of the kidneys. Then add mercury. Drawing in qi is mercury, which is the qi in the heart. If you draw in qi to reach the Central Palace, retain it there. Then send it out, using your awareness to guide it through Tailbone Gate. Whether standing up or lying on your back, extract it from the kidneys. Direct the qi from Tailbone Gate to the paired passes of Narrow Ridge. It then ascends directly to Celestial Pass and enters Kunlun. Prevent the dragon from fleeing upward or the tiger from escaping downward. Perverse thoughts then cease. If the qi has not yet awoken and begun circulating, lie down and practice extraction once again. Directly guide the qi to pass through [the passes]. This is called 'flying the gold essence behind the elbows.'"[64]

The initial stages of practice require strong determination. After a long time, it becomes very easy.

Perfected Changchun said,

> "Wearing a flower petal from the Toad Palace on the top of the head,[65]
> In the morning, wander to Peng[lai] Island; in the evening, return home.

---

61. This phrase more often appears as "extracting lead" (*choutian*) and "adding mercury" (*tianhong*). The tenth-century *Chuandao ji* (DZ 263, j. 14–16; trl. Wong 2000) contains a chapter entitled "Qianhong" (Lead and Mercury) and "Choutian" (Extracting and Adding).

62. In early Quanzhen, the yin-demons (*yinmo*) refer to mundane dreams, hallucinations, fantasies, and other dissipating mental states. See section 2.5a–8a.

63. Reading *chouqian* ("extracting lead") for *choutian* ("extraction and addition"), in order to create parallelism with the following sentence.

64. It is difficult to determine where these various quotations end. I have not found corresponding passages in the *Xishan ji* (DZ 246), though there is some parallel content in section 1.9b–10a, 5.6a–8b.

65. As *neidan* employs the symbol of the toad (also rabbit) in the moon and raven in the sun, the Toad Palace would refer to the moon (yin) and its symbolic associations. One interpretation involves the extraction of the yang-line (perfect qi) from the trigram Kan-water ☵ (the kidneys) so it ascends to the head region.

Gain the ability to ride the horse of Qian-heaven and mount the
    dragon chariot,
Let loose the ox of Kun-earth and take the reins of the tiger cart."

[14a] He also said,

> "Beneath the Jade Capital Mountain, a young sheep plays;
> Beside the Gold Water River, a stone tiger sleeps.
> From among the lilies, a pair of butterflies flits about;
> Going around in circles, they fly to the Chu imperial palace."

Generally speaking, high is based on low, and deep depends on shallow.[66] If one solely practices the copulation of dragon and tiger, one will only repair deficiencies, increase qi, move the blood, and have a radiant complexion. If one solely practices the firing schedule, one can only nourish the muscles and flesh as well as strengthen the sinews and bones. If one solely practices the Method of Flying the Gold Essence, one will only reverse agedness and return to youthfulness as well as invigorate the bones and lighten the body. However, if one can practice these three instructions together, that would be most beneficial. Now, when the dragon and tiger copulate, a thing like a millet grain returns to the center of the Yellow Court. If one does not apply the firing schedule, one will not be able to refine it and make it coalesce. Then, the firing schedule of the Celestial Cycle only results in empty qi gathering in the elixir field. One will not be able to attain the mysterious pearl from the copulation of the dragon and tiger or keep it settled. [14b] Both of these two methods are necessary. The second uses the "behind the elbows" [method] to extract qi from the kidneys to enter the brain. This does not complete the yang within yin. The former harms the elixir of pure yang. This is the mystery of mysteries, the wonder of wonders.[67]

After a hundred days, the sweet *jin*-fluids are produced in the mouth, and the body gives off a divine radiance. The bones become strengthened and the complexion becomes radiant. The skin becomes pure and the abdomen becomes warm. After two hundred days, one gradually becomes disgusted with and abandons eating meat and the strong-smelling vegetables. One continually smells extraordinary fragrances and one walks as though flying. One's dreams naturally decrease. After three hundred days, one stops eating and drinking. One is able to endure cold and heat. Saliva, sweat, and tears disappear. Sickness and difficulties also end. Abiding within stillness, one comes to hear the sound of distant music. Within a darkened chamber, one gradually sees the appearance of red lights. If you see these visions, do not become anxious. They are lesser experiential verifications. Practice this with utmost sincerity, and divine extraordinariness will manifest.

---

66. An allusion to chapter 2 of the fourth-century BCE *Daode jing*.

67. An allusion to chapter 1 of the fourth-century BCE *Daode jing*.

Diagram and Instructions on the Reversion of the Three Fields and the Reverted Elixir of the Gold *Ye*-fluids

[15a] The lungs are the Flower Canopy. The throat is the Storied Tower. The mouth is the Jade Pond and the Dui-lake Door.[68] The nose is the Celestial Gate and the Celestial Pillar. The area between the eyebrows is the Jade Hall. The forehead is the Celestial Hall. The crown of the head is the Celestial Palace. The ears are the Paired City Gates.

The kidney qi leads to the liver qi. The liver qi leads to the spleen qi. The spleen qi leads to the lung qi. The lung qi leads to the heart qi. The heart qi leads to the spleen qi. The spleen qi leads to the kidney qi.[69] This is the revolution of the Five Phases and is called the lesser reverted elixir. From the upper elixir field, [the qi] enters the middle elixir field. From the middle elixir field, it enters the lower elixir

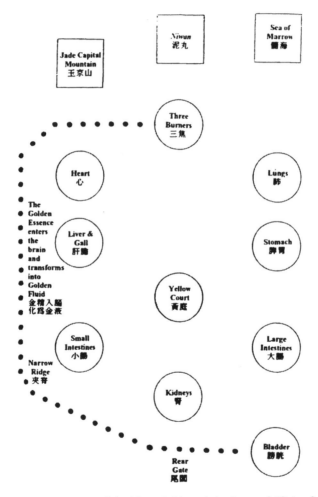

Figure 15. Diagram of the Reversion of the Three Fields and the Reverted Elixir of the Gold *Ye*-fluids

---

68. Dui-lake ☱ is one of the eight trigrams and consists of one yin-line over two yang-lines.

69. Thus, the order is as follows: kidneys (KI; water)—liver (LV; wood)—spleen (SP; earth)—lungs (LU; metal)—heart (HT; fire)—spleen (SP; earth)—kidneys (KI; water). This order deviates from the more conventional sequences of production (wood, fire, earth, metal, water) and control (wood, earth, water, fire, metal).

field. This is the reversion of the Three Fields and is called the greater reverted elixir. **[15b]** In this method for the reverted elixir of the gold *ye*-fluids, you must practice aligned sitting by making the whole body upright. Keep the ears sealed by not allowing anything to pass through them. The tongue rests against the upper palate. The pure and delicious fluids are produced. Do not rinse the mouth, but swallow them down.

The previous technique of flying the gold essence behind the elbows involves a sequential opening. Open the Three Passes one by one until the gold essence enters the brain. This repairs the marrow and increases qi. Then the complexion becomes radiant and the bones are strengthened. The skin becomes softened and the body is lightened. When following the hours and quarter-hours, simply practice balanced sitting by making the body upright. Do not stand up or lie down. You will naturally realize the perfect qi entering the brain. Quickly use the palms of the hands to tightly seal the ears. The kidney qi naturally enters the brain and transforms into the gold *ye*-fluids. They descend like rain-soaked dust. Each day, apply fire in one *liang*. Be careful of applying too much or too little fire. If there is too much fire qi, headaches will result. If there is too little fire qi, the gold essence will not fly forth. You must practice addition and subtraction [properly]. If firing is done too vigorously, **[16a]** the whole body heats up. In this case, do not advance the fire again. Be careful of the fire becoming inflamed and scorching the head and eyes. Here the great yang becomes injurious. The mouth and tongue may be scorched and damaged. This will certainly harm the medicinal ingredients. One must decrease the breathing and allow the intent to leave the Central Palace. Let the fire follow its own nature. No injury should occur.

If you do not want external concerns or perverse thoughts, you must use "cleansing and bathing." Move the fire to reach the two locations of metal and wood. Whether it is time to fly or not to fly, to proceed or not to proceed, it is most important to rectify your thoughts through guarding and restraining. Do not allow even a single thought to arise. If thoughts arise, they are "dust and dirt." Dust is yin, and here yin is demonic. When one is entangled with demons, the Three Passes are closed and disconnected. It is essential to dispel thoughts. As soon as thoughts are rectified, the two qi become unified naturally, coalescing as the gold elixir. A teacher has said, "Wash away the dust and dirt." The Dao says, "Bathe the gold elixir." The *Wuzhen pian* (Treatise on Awakening to Perfection) explains,[70] "At the onset of *xingde*,[71] the medicine assists it. This is the time to bathe the gold elixir." **[16b]** In the second month, when the three yin and three yang warm up, flowers and plants open up. Suddenly they are destroyed by cold, wind, and rain, and are unable to bear fruit. This means that there is *xing* within *de*. It is like being obstructed by yin-demons when practicing exercises. In the eighth month, when the three yin and three yang cool down, the myriad things gradually die off. Then, when the weather warms up, flowers and plants come back to life and bloom again. This means that there is *de* within *xing*. We refer to this as "guarding alignment and extinguishing thoughts." One realizes the harmony of yang. Cleansing and bathing in order to protect against danger involves subtle application through extracting and addition.

---

70. The eleventh-century *Wuzhen pian* (DZ 263, j. 26–30; DZ 1017, j. 18; trl. Cleary 1987), by Zhang Boduan (984–1028), a text which became central in internal alchemy circles from the late medieval period onward.

71. Lit., "punishment and virtue." The meaning is unclear, but the context suggests that *xing* involves harmful influences and patterns of decay, while *de* involves beneficial influences and patterns of flourishing.

The oral instructions say,

"When the Waterwheel revolves to reach Mount Kunlun;
You must firmly seal the Paired City Gates.[72]
The striking of thunder and lightning, a thunderclap;
Quickly gather the sweet rain to shower Qian-heaven and Kun-earth."

The Meaning of the Instructions on the Reversion of the Three Fields and the Reverted Elixir of the Gold *Ye*-fluids

[17a] Master Shi Huayang said, "When practiced individually, the Copulation of the Dragon and Tiger, the Firing Schedule of the Celestial Cycle, and Flying the Gold Essence behind the Elbows lead to peace, joy, and long life for two to three hundred years. This does not go beyond the revolution and inversion of the Five Phases. Here the exercises of production and completion are employed. These exercises are different than gathering and refining unified qi. This reverted elixir of the gold *ye*-fluids not only repairs the brain and increases marrow, but also extracts lead to supplement mercury. One gradually acquires the accomplishment of regained youthfulness. When the brain and marrow become full, you must employ methods to regulate them. The Spirit Water descends from the upper palate: it is clear, cool, sweet, and delicious. It again descends from the lungs to enter the Yellow Court. This is called the 'reverted elixir of the gold *ye*-fluids.' It is similar to suppressing the two qi of deficient yang from the elixir, in order to transform the cinnabar sand into gold. This is called the 'gold elixir.' A grain of gold elixir is enough to confer longevity and to live as long as heaven and earth. Thus, we refer to this as 'middle completion.' People should not set aside the previous exercises, but should only seek the reverted elixir of the gold *ye*-fluids. If you do not employ methods to obtain it, the Spirit Water will not descend. [17b] Even if one gains accomplishment by forcing water to descend from the head, it will not have a sweet and delicious flavor. Rather, it causes the human brain to become deficient and many diseases develop. This is of no benefit to anyone."[73]

Signs of Response When Practicing Exercises[74]

At first there will be a gradual feeling in the elixir field of the Yellow Court that is harmonizing and warming. The perfect qi ascends and your ears hear the sound of wind and rain. Your head gradually becomes filled with whistling sounds of gold

---

72. The ears.

73. Corresponding passage in the *Xishan ji* (DZ 246) unidentified.

74. Cf. the final section of the *Chuandao ji* (DZ 263, 16.27a–30b; Wong 2000, 143–48), which is titled "Lun zhengyan" (On Experiential Confirmation). It informs the aspiring adept that specific training regimens may result in specific types of experiences. See also the relevant three sections of the *Neidan jiyao* (Collected Essentials of Internal Alchemy; DZ 1258), namely, "Jindan zhengyan" (Experiential Confirmation of the Gold Elixir; 2.9a–13a), "Lun baguan jie" (Divisions of the Eight Passes; 3.10b–12a), "Lun liutong jue" (Instructions on the Six Pervasions; 3.12a–14a) (Eskildsen 2001, 149; 2004, 104, 120). On "signs of proof" in early Quanzhen see Eskildsen 2001; 2004, 95–114, 115–38.

and jade. Inside the gate of the jaws, known as the Celestial Pool, the gold *ye*-fluids well up and flow downward like a cool spring. Some of these fluids flow into the face, while others flow into the brain. Some form into pearl-like dew, while others enter the mouth through the upper gums. Its flavor is sweet and refreshing.

After a long time, your head fills with the sound of lutes, zithers, and bamboo chimes. There will also be the sounds of cranes calling, gibbons crying, and cicadas buzzing. These various sounds of suchness are really indescribable.

However, when you begin your practice, you may hear the noise of loud thunder in your dreams. **[18a]** This is the perfect qi thrusting through the head's yang-bone and penetrating the Nine Palaces. When spirit enters the chamber, it will soon ascend upward, and you may, naturally, become frightened. Sometimes, when meditating with eyes closed, a single large being may jump up and frighten you. However, if you get up and open your eyes, you will see that nothing is there. This is because your yang-spirit is not yet mature.[75] It is important not to become frightened or give rise to thoughts. After a long time, this spirit will mature and there will be no more [images or fear]. [Your yang-spirit] will be [simultaneously] hidden and manifest, and its transformations will be limitless. You will know what it is to act without effort. You will be free from attachments to anything seen or heard. Simply listen to suchness. If you become attached to appearances, these are only illusions.

Perfected Changchun said,

> "A wonderful nectar descends from heaven;
> Numinous medicines are produced and everlasting.
> When drinking wine, one must take a hundred cups;
> When wandering east and west, one must follow one's own course.
> In the beginning, the Spirit Water emerges from an elevated source;
> In an instant, it issues forth in the Yellow Court."

Diagram and Instructions on the Five Qi Meeting the Origin and Refining Form into Greater Yang

[18b] This relates to a method of middle completion, for extending life and not dying. This method may not be transmitted to relatives such as fathers and sons. If you lightly disseminate it and allow distant relatives to look at it, you will meet with calamities and grave retribution. Be careful about this!

---

75. As recorded by Yin Zhiping, "One evening in a dreamscape I [Qiu Changchun] saw Master [Chongyang] with a child about one hundred days old seated on his knee. When I woke up, there was an awakening in my heart-mind. I knew that my Dao-nature was still underdeveloped. Half a year later, I again beheld a dreamscape similar to the first one. Now the child was two years old. I woke up and awakened to the fact that my Dao-nature was gradually growing. Later I realized that I was free of perverse thoughts. One year later, I had the same dream, but the child was now three or four years old and was able to walk and stand by himself. After this, I no longer encountered [the vision]. Then I knew that I had received divine guidance and that I now had the ability to stand on my own" (*Qinghe yulu*, DZ 1310, 4.5a–5b).

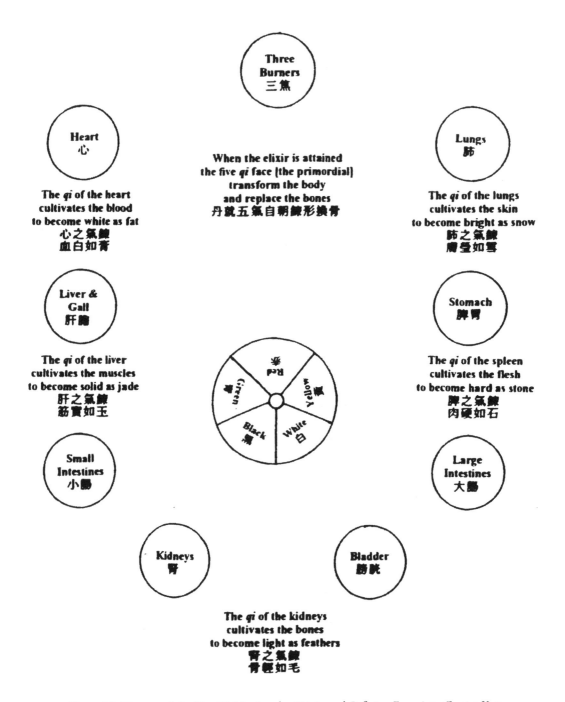

Figure 16. Diagram of the Five Qi Meeting the Origin and Refining Form into Greater Yang

This method is called "refining form into greater yang." The foundational method is used during winter solstice[76] when the *yangqi* is produced. **[19a]** It is also fine to practice it during each of the four seasons.[77] Straighten the body and practice aligned sitting in a motionless position. Close your eyes and forget thoughts. Silently circulate the heart fire and the maternal qi. Naturally allow the qi to fill the four limbs. Do not concern yourself with the personal body. Through the nostrils, your breathing becomes subtle and fine. It is as though it exists, but using it involves no movement.

In the previous [instructions], the "four seasons" include spare time to practice at one's convenience. Straighten the body and do not move. From the center of the elixir, the Five Qi arise unceasingly from within. Practice aligned sitting and do not lean. From the center of the elixir, the Five Qi unceasingly issue forth in every direction. The perfect qi of the kidneys refines the bones. The body becomes as light as a feather, and one is able to mount the wind and ride the mists. The perfect qi of the lungs refines the sinews. They become strong like jade, and one is able to move like a swift horse. The perfect qi of the heart refines the blood. It becomes pure like ointment, and one is able to permanently endure cold and heat. The perfect qi of the lungs refines the skin. It becomes lustrous like snow, and one is able to exchange the bones and change the form. The perfect qi of the spleen refines the flesh. It becomes as hard as stone, and one is able to transform the qi to resemble gold. As soon as the elixir is complete, **[19b]** the Five Qi meet perfection. Qi gathers and does not scatter. After this, employ the previous method and circulate [the qi]. Internally, it is transmitted to the five yin-organs; externally, it circulates to the four limbs. The Five Qi refine form. They coalesce and do not decay. This is called "form and spirit being mutually wondrous." They will last as long as heaven.

The oral instructions say,

> "When the elixir naturally meets the Five Qi,
> The qi becomes perfect and then can manifest as original spirit.
> Those who refine form and exchange bones are not ordinary people;
> They are human beings with perpetual life beyond thinghood."

The Meaning of the Instructions on the Five Qi Meeting the Origin and Refining Form into Greater Yang

Perfected Changchun said, "The reverted elixir of the gold *ye*-fluids transforms into gold. The pure *yangqi* is produced within this. This means that there is qi within qi. Through it, earthbound spirit immortals can live as long as heaven and earth. From ancient times to today, those who would ascend to perfection have repeatedly moved the qi of pure yang to enter the four limbs. **[20a]** This is called 'refining

---

76. Corresponding to the terrestrial branch of *zi* (11 p.m.–1 a.m.).

77. In addition to actual solar cycles, the "four seasons" often correspond to the terrestrial branches of *mao* (5 a.m.–7 a.m.; spring equinox), *wu* (11 a.m.–1 p.m.; summer solstice), *you* (5 p.m.–7 p.m.; autumn equinox); and *zi* (11 p.m.–1 a.m.; winter solstice).

form into greater yang.' When you transform the qi naturally, form and spirit are mutually wondrous. Follow the Five Qi, and then exchange the bones and change your appearance. You will be able to endure cold and heat. What in the past was a disposition toward decline is refined into a proper and correct one. What in the past was a withering appearance is refined into a rosy and fresh one. How can this simply be about reversing agedness and returning to youthfulness? It also relates to the body becoming light and the bones becoming strong. One rides the wind and ascends [to the heavens]; one mounts the mists and travels [through the distant realms]. One is referred to as 'a flying immortal of the Southern Palace' or 'a winged guest among the world of dust.' Although one has not yet cast off the husk and ascended to immortality, one can still soar and mount [the heavens] and abide in a state of independence. Among terrestrial immortals, this is a higher class; among celestial immortals, it is a lower rank.[78] Because of the Five Qi in the elixir field, one refines the body. On the outer reaches, this relates to the four limbs. The exercises for refining form are not inferior."

Perfected Changchun said,

"When the five horses are not disturbed, the gold water settles;
When the dragon is constantly guided, fiery clouds fly forth.
One can wander throughout the world in half a day of work;
Without dissipation, one can mount a phoenix and ride the dragon.
When the Five Qi are not disturbed, the elixir is obtained;
[20b] Outside the unitary yang, fire lightly flies forth."

Diagram and Instructions on the Union of Spirit and Qi and the Consummation of the Three Fields[79]

This is a method of middle completion, leading to perpetual life without dying. From the center of the head, the Spirit Water descends to the elixir field, while the perfect qi ascends. This is called "consummation."

---

78. There are various lists of ranks of immortals. One of the earliest classifications of immortals appears in Ge Hong's (Baopuzi [Master Embracing Simplicity]; 283–343) *Baopuzi neipian* (Inner Chapters of Master Embracing Simplicity; DZ 1185; trl. Ware 1966): "Superior adepts who rise up in their bodies and ascend to the Void are called celestial immortals. Mid-level adepts who wander among renowned mountains are called terrestrial immortals. Lesser adepts who first die and then slough off (*xiansi houshui*) are called corpse-liberated immortals (*shijie xian*)" (2.11a). The tenth-century *Chuandao ji* has the following: "The immortals have five ranks, including ghost immortal, human immortal, terrestrial immortal, and spirit immortal. The celestial immortal is beyond rank. All of these are immortals" (DZ 263, 14.2b). The *Chuandao ji* in turn describes the various characteristics of these immortals (see Wong 2000, 23–30). The twelfth-century *Jinguan yusuo jue* (DZ 1156; trl. Komjathy 2007a) lists ghost immortal, terrestrial immortal, sword immortal, spirit immortal, and celestial immortal (13a). The late thirteenth-century *Zhenxian yulu* (Discourse Record of Perfected Immortals; DZ 1256) contains the following information: "Patriarch Ma [Danyang] said, 'The immortals have four ranks, including ghost immortal, human immortal, terrestrial immortal, and spirit immortal'" (2.12a).

79. At the beginning of the text, this diagram is identified as the "Diagram of the Union of Spirit and Water and the Consummation of the Three Fields."

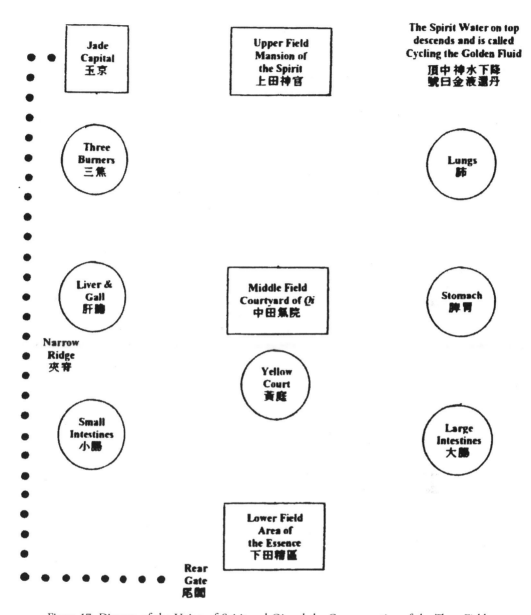

Figure 17. Diagram of the Union of Spirit and Qi and the Consummation of the Three Fields

Make one cycle through the Three Passes to enter the brain. This is called "flying the gold essence behind the elbows."

[21a] This method is called the "consummation of water and fire." The fundamental method is practiced during the yang hours[80] and middle quarter-hours. Practice level

---

80. Each of the twelve double-hours has a yin or yang association. The "yang hours" are every other hour beginning with *zi* (11 p.m.–1 a.m.) and ending with *xu* (7 p.m.–9 p.m.).

sitting and straighten the torso. Make one cycle through the Three Passes. Seal the ears, while the Spirit Water descends. Straighten the torso and draw in the abdomen. Guide a long inhalation through the nose. Silently circulate the fire of the heart to ascend.

As outlined earlier, during the time of Zhen-thunder ☳ and Gen-mountain ☶,[81] make one cycle through the Three Passes. The gold essence enters the brain to replenish it to sufficiency. The face becomes ruddy, and the skin becomes as pure as ointment. After the body becomes light, one can make a cycle through the Three Passes. When the gold essence enters the head, tightly seal the two ears. When you do not allow the kidney qi to manifest, it then enters the Celestial Palace. Through the transformative process, the gold essence descends. It is like rain-soaked dust. From the upper palate, the refreshing and delicious Spirit Water fills the mouth. If you swallow it down to the Yellow Court, it is called the "reverted elixir of the gold ye-fluids." At this time, when the sweet and delicious water descends from the upper palate, swallow it. Straighten the torso and draw in the abdomen. Silently circulate the fire of heart and subtly guide the perfect qi to ascend from the elixir field. [21b] Then exhale through the nose while raising the perfect qi to fill the four limbs. When the water from above and the fire from below meet beneath the Storied Tower, it is called "consummation."

The oral instructions say,

"When the Spirit Water in the head enters the Central Spring,
The perfect yang inside the elixir returns to the upper field.
Water and fire joining together is called "consummation";
They ascend from inside the court to enter the Great Network Heaven."[82]

The Meaning of the Instructions on the Union of Spirit and Qi and the Consummation of the Three Fields

Perfected Changchun said, "The consummation of Earth corresponds to pottery; pottery can last a thousand years. The consummation of Wood corresponds to ashes; ashes can last a hundred years. Those who long for perpetual life cannot ignore the method of consummation. It is practiced in conjunction with refining form through the reverted elixir. Reverting the elixir through the gold ye-fluids involves transforming the elixir to become gold. Refining form into greater yang involves [transforming] form to become like jade. When the reverted elixir has not yet been fully reverted, [22a] and the moment for form to be refined has arisen, let the water ascend and the fire descend. They meet beneath the Storied Tower. This is called the 'moment of consummation.' You must employ the Tai-peace ䷊ hexagram, composed of earth and heaven, after the hour of zi. Each time there is grain shaped like gold millet. Kernel after kernel returns to the Yellow Court. Each kernel produces a ray of gold

---

81. These trigrams are associated with the seasonal nodes of Spring Begins and Winter Begins, respectively. In standard sources on *neidan*, they do not have double-hour correspondences.

82. Daluo tian is usually identified as the celestial abode of the Jade Emperor. It is below the three purity heavens. At other times, it refers to the highest realms of the Daoist heavens. The contemporary Quanzhen liturgy, *Xuanmen gongke*, contains a variety of sections on this sacred realm.

light. When circulated and released beyond the body, the gold radiance can fill an entire room. How can this only be about perpetual life without dying? It is about the moment to seek casting off the husk and ascending to immortality."

Perfected Changchun said,

"The two luminaries are cast to become seven precious palaces;
A channel flows and circulates to enter as a wonderful nectar.
Water and fire come together and become merged;
Then the trigrams transform to become the Tai-peace hexagram.
Yin and yang ascend and descend, eventually merging together;
Water and fire join together and enter the lower field.
When consummation is uninhibited, the perfect qi is sufficient;
A grain of the gold elixir lasts for a billion years."

The previous techniques of reverting the elixir of the gold *ye*-fluids, refining form into greater yang, and the consummation of the Three Fields are methods for attaining perpetual life and not dying. [22b] Thus, they are called methods of middle completion. You must attain the anticipated results with the methods of lesser completion by practicing them continuously and concurrently. Practice them without errors, and you will quickly attain confirmation. If people do not practice the methods of lesser completion, but rather directly desire the middle completion, endeavoring to attain perpetual life without dying, not only will the results be slow in coming, but time and effort will also be wasted. One may practice reverting the elixir, but the Spirit Water will not descend. One may practice refining form, but the elixir fire will not ascend. One may practice consummation, but the water and fire will not join together. Those who slander the spirit immortals, falsely saying that "undying" is absurd, do not realize that they have gone too far.

If people can join the dragon and tiger together to become vital essence, apply the firing schedule sufficiently to become the elixir, employ the gold essence to replenish any brain deficiencies, direct the reverted elixir to become the gold elixir, apply the elixir fire to refine the perfect body, and simultaneously practice the methods of consummation, the benefits will be unsurpassable. [23a] If you are not practicing the six methods concurrently, you should quickly seek to decoct the elixir, the qi of pure yang. This involves refining qi to become spirit. Quickly seek the perfect numen from qi. This involves refining spirit to merge with the Dao. Under these conditions, reverting the elixir of the gold *ye*-fluids, refining form into greater yang, and the consummation of the Three Fields should not be practiced. Among the highest Perfected from ancient times to the present, these three instructions have been secretly transmitted throughout the endless *kalpas*. The methods of middle completion, which include reverting the elixir, refining form, and consummation, involve maintaining the body while residing in the world. Without the gold elixir, one cannot extend one's years. Without refining form, one cannot exchange the bones. Without consummation, one cannot become undying. Moreover, because there are no ill-looking Perfected and decaying spirit immortals are few, and because one can change form but retain a mundane appearance and engage in consummation but retain mortal bones, the future abandonment of the husk to depart [from the world] and the transcendence of spirit will also be delayed.

After reverting the elixir, refining form, and consummation, and following a hundred days, the four appearances manifest at the center of stillness. Through inner observation they circulate everywhere, while the Five Qi mix together. **[23b]** After two hundred days, one can see the gold flower and the body is encircled by radiant light. Azure qi emerges from the head, while purple mist fills the chamber. After three hundred days, the divine numen knows about past and future events. The perfect qi can dry out the external mercury. The body becomes so light that one can walk on wind and mist. The bones become so strong that one can live as long as heaven and earth. If you see these various phenomena, do not be startled. They are lesser signs of proof. Be resolute and sincere when practicing these methods. The divine anomalies that occur are beyond any expectation.

Diagram and Instructions on the Five Qi Meeting the Origin and Refining Spirit to Enter the Summit[83]

[2.1a] This is a method of greater completion, which involves casting off the husk and ascending to immortality. If it is discussed with inferior people, there will surely be obstruction and calamity. It is best to be attentive when speaking.

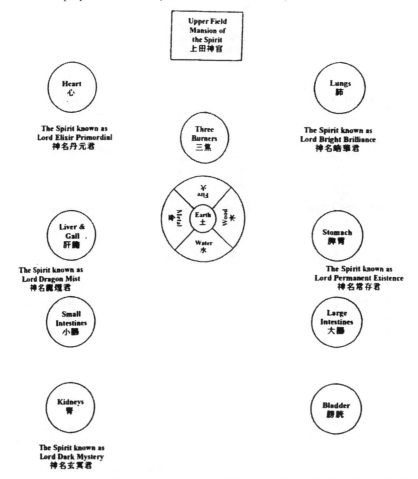

Figure 18. Diagram of the Five Qi Meeting the Origin and Refining Spirit to Enter the Summit

83. This diagram is not listed at the beginning of the text, which has led some readers to identify eight, rather than nine stages of alchemical transformation.

[1b] This method is called "refining qi to become spirit." The fundamental method is practiced during the double-hours of *zi* [11 p.m.–1 a.m.], *wu* [11 a.m.–1 p.m.], *mao* [5 a.m.–7 a.m.], and *you* [5 p.m.–7 p.m.]. On the *jia* and *yi* days,[84] refine the liver. On the *bing* and *ding* days,[85] refine the heart. On the *geng* and *xin* days,[86] refine the lungs. On the *ren* and *gui* days,[87] refine the kidneys. The spleen is not engaged. Store the refined qi in the four yin-organs. On the *wu* and *ji* days,[88] do not practice. Such are the days for refining the five yin-organs. On the *jia* and *yi* days, practice at the hour of *mao*. On the *bing* and *ding* days, practice at the hour of *wu*. On the *geng* and *xin* days, practice at the hour of *you*. On the *ren* and *gui* days, practice at the hour of *zi*. Such are the hours for refining the five yin-organs.

When practicing the aforementioned method at the corresponding times, practice quiet sitting in a darkened room. Burn a stick of incense and tap the teeth twenty-four times. Align the body and sit in a balanced position. [Practice] inner observation of the yin-organs being refined. Breathe through the nose in a subtle and fine [manner], so that it is preserved. When stillness reaches its apex, qi is generated. When qi reaches its apex, spirit manifests. As though dreaming, as though awake, in the midst of obscurity spirit and qi ascend. In this method, do not be confused about the days and hours, as spirit accords with these days. **[2a]** You must have the perfect qi accord with the times in its circulation. You must investigate the days and examine the hours when cultivating it. In one hundred days, qi becomes abundant and spirit manifests. [This indicates] that you will soon ascend to immortality, without stopping at [the state of] perpetual life without dying.

The oral instructions say,

"Accord with the days and follow the times without error;
When the five spirits gather together,[89] the Waterwheel is activated.
In the midst of stillness, after the perfect appearances meet the Origin,
One should still fear the yin-demons creating confusion and perversion."

The Meaning of the Diagram of the Five Qi Meeting the Origin and Refining Spirit to Enter the Summit

Perfected Huayang said, "Using the qi of pure yang in the elixir, refine the liver according to the corresponding days and times. Within twenty-four days, the azure qi appears; within twenty-four days, the yang-spirit manifests. Qi is the substance of spirit; spirit is the ruler of qi. Refine the heart, kidneys, liver, and lungs in this way. **[2b]** The spirit of the spleen and qi of the spleen follow the aligned qi of the four periods, ascending together. Practice inner observation in the midst of stillness. Notice that there are mountains and rivers inside the pot. The appearance of such things completes form. Through two forms of *samādhi*, one may discern the embryo. Guard against the

---

84. The first and second days of the Chinese ten-day week, which is based on the celestial stems.

85. The third and fourth days.

86. The seventh and eighth days.

87. The ninth and tenth days.

88. The first and sixth days, here associated with the spleen, the center, and stillness.

89. The spirits, or numinous qi, of the five yin-organs.

yin-ghosts, external demons, Seven Po,[90] and Three Death-bringers[91] from dispersing celestial perfection by confusing the yang-spirit and inhibiting it from ascending to the Celestial Palace. Thus, there is the method of initiating fire through inner observation. By extending through refining qi, the qi assembles and becomes spirit. Do not make any mistakes regarding the timing. Naturally, qi appears and spirit manifests. The perfect qi of the five directions join together and manifest in their original colors. The yang-spirit of the Five Qi manifests as the perfect form. It ascends and enters the inner courtyard of the Celestial Palace. This is the moment when spirit unites with the Dao.[92]

"If people practice the firing schedule amply for three hundred days, without refining the reverted elixir, refining form, or practicing consummation, but directly practice this method by utilizing the qi of pure yang in the elixir, then following the days in response to original qi in circulation and refining the five yin-organs is indeed a shortcut. This is called "grasping accomplishment by setting aside the methods." [3a] If people wish to reside in the mundane world and to attain perpetual life without dying, they should employ [the methods of] reverting the elixir of the gold *ye*-fluids, refining form into greater yang, and the consummation of the Three Fields."

Perfected Changchun said,

"The purple vapors of the Three Islands envelop the phoenix colors;
The red sun in the Nine Heavens refines the dragon essence."

The *Zhonghuang jing* (Scripture of the Central Yellow) says,[93] "The liver and birth correspond to the eastern direction; the color is green. Refine it, and the azure qi will emanate through the body. The kidneys and water correspond to the northern direction; the color is black. Refine them at the proper times, and the black qi will manifest in the body. When the pure *yangqi* fills the five yin-organs, spirit ascends in its original color to enter the Celestial Palace."

---

90. The Seven Po (*qipo*) are the seven corporeal souls. In the eleventh-century encyclopedia *Yunji qiqian* (Seven Tablets from a Cloudy Satchel; DZ 1032), they are identified as follows: (1) Shigou (Corpse Dog), (2) Fushi (Concealed Arrow), (3) Queyin (Sparrow Yin), (4) Tunzei (Seizing Thief), (5) Feidu (Negative Poison); (6) Chuhui (Oppressive Impurity), and (7) Choufei (Putrid Lungs) (54.7ab). Visual representations appear in the ninth-century *Chu sanshi jiuchong jing* (Scripture on Expelling the Three Death-bringers and Nine Worms; DZ 871, 3a). According to that text, "The Seven Po consist of yin and deviant qi. They are ghosts. They can make people into walking corpses, causing them to be stingy and greedy, jealous and full of envy. They give people bad dreams and make them clench their teeth. They command the mouth to say 'right' when the heart-mind thinks 'wrong.' In addition, they cause people to lose their vital essence in sexual passion and become dissipated by hankering after luxury and ease. Through them, people completely lose their purity and simplicity" (2a).

91. The Three Death-bringers (*sanshi*), alternatively rendered as Three Corpses and sometimes appearing as Three Worms (*sanchong*), are conventionally understood as three "biospiritual parasites" residing in the human body. They reside in the three elixir fields, namely, located in the abdominal, heart, and head regions. The ninth-century *Chu sanshi jiuchong jing* (Scripture on Expelling the Three Death-bringers and Nine Worms; DZ 871, 7a–8a) contains illustrations of the Three Death-bringers, wherein they are identified as follows: Peng Ju (upper), Peng Zhi (middle), and Peng Jiao (lower) (also DZ 817). Thus, they are sometimes referred to as the "Three Pengs" (*sanpeng*). Other texts, such as the *Sanchong zhongjing* (Central Scripture on the Three Death-bringers; *Yunji qiqian*, DZ 1032, 81.15b–17a), provide alternative names: Qinggu (Blue Decrepitude; upper), Baigu (White Hag; middle), and Xueshi (Bloody Corpse; lower) (also DZ 303, 4a). Other relevant information appears in the eleventh-century encyclopedia *Yunji qiqian* (Seven Tablets from a Cloudy Satchel; DZ 1032, 81–83) and the ninth-century *Zhonghuang jing* (Scripture on the Center Yellow; DZ 817, 7a–8a; also *Yunji qiqian*, DZ 1032, 13). Traditionally speaking, the Three Death-bringers want to free themselves by either accelerating the death of the body through diseases or shortening the life span through reporting a person's faults to the celestial bureaucracy. Various malevolent intentions and activities are ascribed to the Three Death-bringers. The upper death-bringer or worm creates sensual desire and causes madness; the middle death-bringer generates greed for wealth and causes moodiness; and the lower death-bringer stimulates desire for elegant clothes, alcohol, and sex.

92. Corresponding passage in the *Xishan ji* (DZ 246) unidentified.

93. Section 2.3b–6a of the ninth-century *Taiqing zhonghuang zhenjing* (DZ 817).

Diagram and Instructions on Initiating the Fire through Inner Observation and Refining Spirit to Merge with the Dao[94]

This is a method of greater completion, through which one can transcend the mundane and enter the sacred. Moving the pure *yangqi* in the elixir to enter the four limbs is called "burning the body."[95] Moving it into the five yin-organs is called "refining spirit." Sending it out of the body is called "taming the demons." Having it enter the summit is called "casting off the husk."

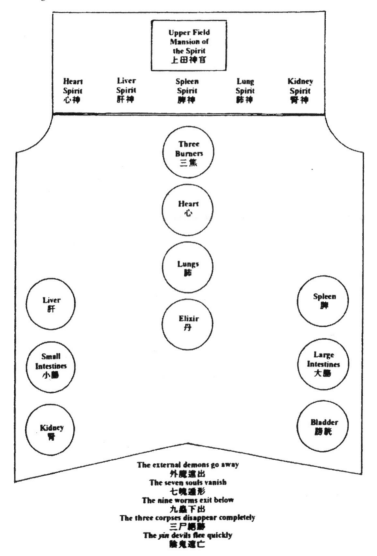

Figure 19. Diagram of Initiating Fire through Inner Observation and Refining Spirit to Merge with the Dao

94. At the beginning of the text, this diagram is identified as the "Diagram of Refining Spirit to Merge with the Dao and Advancing Fire through Inner Observation."

95. In the present context, "burning the body" (*fenshen*) clearly does not mean the Hindu and Buddhist ascetic practice of self-immolation or auto-cremation. See Benn 1998; 2007. As this section and section 2.5a indicate, the phrase refers to activating the *yangqi* in the body, which results in an internal heat filling the body. This parallels the meaning of the Indian Tantric and Yoga concept of *tapas* in certain practice contexts. See, e.g., Kaelber 1979; 1989.

[3b] These instructions are called "initiating the fire through inner observation." Fundamentally speaking, it does not have a fixed time schedule. Practice it every day when you have time. If thoughts arise, control them through practice. Practice quiet sitting each day. Spirit becomes known through inward attentiveness. Unify awareness and do not become dissipated. Constantly arrange the body in aligned sitting. Silently observe the five yin-organs. You should only want to separate real from unreal. Do not allow the yin-demons to usurp perfection.

This method of inner observation simply involves aligning the body in quiet sitting. One moves the qi of pure yang in the elixir. **[4a]** By internally observing the five yin-organs, qi adheres to spirit to ascend and enter the center of the head. By externally refining the four limbs, qi floods the gold radiance to manifest externally as a spirit body. Not long afterward, spirit merges with the Dao, casting off the husk and ascending to immortality. Guard against the yin-ghosts, external demons, Seven Po, and Three Death-bringers from assuming unreal forms. Such conditions disperse celestial perfection and confuse the yang-spirit. One is then unable to merge with the Dao. Therefore, you should not make distinctions between day and night, but constantly accord with qi circulation. During the double-hour of *mao*, observe the liver: the liver qi appears azure. During the double-hour of *wu*, observe the heart: the heart qi appears red. During the double-hour of *you*, observe the lungs: the lung qi appears white. During the hour of *zi*, observe the kidneys: the kidney qi appears black. When the five-colored qi manifests, the perfect landscape appears in the pot. It is not the same as the mundane world. The dignified majesty of its carriages and horses surpasses that of kings. If you do not abandon initiating fire to ascend through the body, real and unreal will naturally become separated.

The oral instructions say,

> **[4b]** "The dignified majesty of banners and flags is the same everywhere;
> Internally observe the forms and appearances that fill the pot.
> Shimmering lights repeatedly arise to ignite the body's fire;
> The resounding music of reeds and pipes enters the upper palace."

The Meaning of the Instructions on Initiating the Fire through Inner Observation and Refining Spirit to Merge with the Dao

Perfected Changchun said, "Refining qi is easy, but initiating fire is difficult. Silently circulate the qi of pure yang in the elixir according to the appropriate days and hours in order to refine the five yin-organs. The qi is perfected and appears naturally. Spirit is perfected and manifests naturally. They become mutually illuminated, ascending to enter the Celestial Palace. Guard against the yin-ghosts and external demons from usurping the real with the unreal. At this time, qi follows spirit in ascending, and spirit adheres to qi in rising from the middle field to enter the upper field. The yin-ghosts want humans to age quickly, while the external demons do not want people to be at peace. They vainly produce ranks [of illusory phenomena] and falsely give rise to fleeting attractions. They also overwhelm the yang-spirit by mixing together with it. What is a real appearance? What is a false form? These become mixed in confusion and difficult to separate. With the music of reeds and pipes all around, carriages and horses proceed. [5a] If you want to distinguish [real from unreal], nothing is better than urgently initiating the perfect fire in the elixir.

"The first stage is called 'burning the body.' The second is called 'taming the demons.' The third is called 'expelling the Three Death-bringers.' The fourth is called 'banishing the Seven Po.' The fifth is called 'gathering the yang-spirit.' Practicing inner observation within stillness, one naturally becomes clear and bright. As a flaming brilliance within the fire, one beholds humans and things mixed together. After a while, what begins to sing and play music is your very own yang-spirit. What weeps and departs are the yin-ghosts in the body. After some time, the fire stops. Inside the pot, things become clear and still, and accomplishment is incomparable. Guard against the ten demons from returning. In combination with the yin-ghosts and external demons, they create mischief and karmic influences by confusing the yang-spirit. When practicing inner observation, you should be able to distinguish them."

The Ten Demon Lords[96]

Sometimes there may be the hearing of the music of reeds and pipes, looking at fleeting attractions, tasting sweet flavors, or smelling strange fragrances. Your thoughts and emotions become excited and engaged, while your awareness and qi become extended. If you see them, do not engage them; you must recognize that they are the Demon of the Six Desires. [5b] This is the first [demon lord].

Sometimes there may be the ripples of a gentle wind, the comfort of warm sunlight, heavy rains from swift thunder, a lightning-flash within thunderstorms, the resonant sounds of music and singing, or the sounds of weeping and sorrow. If you see them, do not engage them; you must recognize that they are the Demon of the Seven Emotions. This is the second.

Sometimes there may be precious pavilions with magnificent towers, elegant chambers with fragrant orchids, kingfisher-green curtains with pearl strands, sculptured walls with high eaves, a whole area with jeweled treasures, or halls filled with gold and jade. If you see them, do not engage them; you must recognize that they are the Demon of Wealth. This is the third.

Sometimes there may be the activity of generals and ministers, the exercise of authority throughout the eight directions, the brilliant appearance of chariots and clothing, banners and pennants of vested envoys, the gathering of aristocratic and official ranks, or court books and tablets numerous enough to fill a bed. If you see them, do not engage them; you must recognize that they are the Demon of Nobility. This is the fourth.

---

96. Cf. *Chuandao ji* (DZ 263, 16.22b–26b; Wong 2000, 135–41), which is titled "Lun monan" (On Demonic Obstacles).

[6a] Sometimes there may be children afflicted with sickness and disease, parents passing away, brothers separated from each other, wife and child divided, kindred facing adversities, or clans suffering from calamities. If you see them, do not engage them; you must recognize that they are the Demon of Affection and Selfish Love. This is the fifth.

Sometimes there may be losing one's life in a burning cauldron, falling off an elevated peak, being punished or executed, getting poisoned to death, or encountering deviances that are difficult to avoid, or being chased and gouged by violent animals. If you see them, do not engage them; you must recognize that they are the Demon of Calamities and Difficulties. This is the sixth.

Sometimes there may be infantryman and cavalry amassing, weapons and swords shining like frost, spears and axes raised together, bows and crossbows drawn, contention arising with the intention to injure, or courageousness and agility difficult to measure. If you see them, do not engage them; you must recognize that they are the Demon of Violence and War. This is the seventh.

Sometimes there may be [the appearance of] the Three Purities[97] and Jade Emperor,[98] the enthroned kings of the ten earth-prisons, the four sages and nine luminaries,[99] or the Five Thearchs[100] and Three Officials.[101] **[6b]** They have banners and emblems majestically arrayed, soaring back and forth across the sky. If you see them, do not engage them; you must recognize that they are the Demon of Sages and Worthies. This is the eighth.

Sometimes there may be immortal women and jade maidens arrayed in rows. With music and song filling the air, they dance face-to-face in colorful costumes. Joined together in pairs of red sleeves, they vie for the opportunity to offer wine in gold chalices. If you see them, do not engage them; you must recognize that they are the Demon of Tavern Pleasures. This is the ninth.

Sometimes there may be a bevy of beauties with charming looks and rich adornments. Entertaining among elegant terraces throughout the evening, their smooth bodies are scantily clad. Leaning close and trembling seductively, they vie to couple with you. If you see them, do not engage them; you must recognize that they are the Demon of Feminine Charms. This is the tenth.

Generally speaking, adepts committed to clarity and emptiness, who have enjoyed silence and solitude for a long time, may unexpectedly encounter troubling phenomena. They may occasionally think that the perfect realm follows the same pattern, so that they do not abandon the mundane body. This is to become

---

97. The Sanqing (Three Purities) represent the three primordial ethers of the cosmos. They include Celestial Worthy of Original Beginning, who resides in the Jade Clarity Heaven; Celestial Worthy of Numinous Treasure, who resides in the Highest Clarity Heaven; and Celestial Worthy of the Dao and Inner Power (Lord Lao), who resides in the Great Clarity Heaven.

98. The cosmocrat or high god of differentiated existence.

99. The gods of the nine stars of the Northern Dipper.

100. The divine rulers of the five directions. Often associated with the Five Marchmounts.

101. The celestial officials in charge of heaven, earth, and water.

trapped in the "shadowy thoroughfare." [7a] Such people merely become earthbound immortals; they are unable to transcend the mundane and enter the sacred.

Take these people appearing before our eyes. Do not concern yourself with the phenomenal world. Then you can approach the Dao and gradually realize complete accomplishment. For students practicing inner observation, do not use the pure *yangqi* in the elixir to refine the five yin-organs. The perfected spirit of the Five Qi manifests the five colors. Throughout the ten [directions], reeds and pipes sound together, while arrayed banners are raised in unison. At this time, the yin-ghosts and external demons may distract the heart-mind with various images, which become mixed together and enter the Celestial Palace. Quickly initiate the fire to ascend through the body. The two armies within the fire naturally dissipate the sounds of mourning; they disappear throughout the four areas. Songs and music fill the air, subtle and mysterious in the elevated mountains. Eventually the fire ceases. A refreshing coolness in the midst the stillness, mountains and streams are beautiful. Through inner observation, heaven and earth become clear and bright. This is the perfect landscape within the pot.

It is not acceptable to think that the situation is resolved, as the Ten Demons may arrive sequentially quite soon. At this time, it may seem that you are dreaming even though you are not. It may seem that you are drunk even though you are not. The perfect numen of the five spirits has already entered the Celestial Palace.[102] The Four Elements[103] of the central region direct the heart-mind to become stabilized and aligned. In the midst of the dim and indistinct, [7b] do not mistake the wicked for the virtuous or the deviant for the aligned. If you do not stop the causes, you will not be able to abandon the mundane body. Moreover, you may be set adrift in perversion. Perhaps the demon of madness or the demon of recklessness will result in [the efforts to] complete spirit and qi being futile. Divine insight will be insufficient. How regrettable! Thus, the realm of demons has been discussed herein.

Activate the fire to ascend through the body without being satisfied with a few times. Constantly practice inner observation day and night until the fire becomes active. Between heaven and earth, there is no exception. Looking up, you only see heaven. Looking down, you only see earth. Looking in the four [directions], you see that everything is empty. When you are in stillness, you will hear the sound of music. Suddenly there will be extraordinary fragrances. At this time, there will be experiential confirmation, which is incomparable to the previous signs.[104] Your limbs and body will resemble those of a dragon in flight. This is the moment when the

---

102. Here one finds an interesting distinction between the numen (*ling*) and spirit (*shen*). In the present context, the spirits of the yin-organs designate the distinct and individual energetic presences of the corresponding corporeal locations, while the numen is the divine being or yang-spirit in which the Five Qi have become unified and integrated.

103. Derived from traditional Indian cosmology via Buddhism, the Four Elements (*sida*) conventionally designate earth, water, fire, and air (or wind). In this passage they seem to designate the heart (fire), vital essence (water), qi (air), and the body (earth). See *Ershisi jue*, DZ 1158, 3ab. Another possible reading is the four central directions.

104. Section 1.17b–18a.

spirit immortal casts off the husk. A red radiance surrounds the area where one is sitting. It is shaped like a lotus flower. The whole body is filled with the perfect qi. Its color resembles a golden radiance. The perfect qi of the Five Phases combine to become vital essence, qi, and spirit. The extraordinary treasures of the Three Powers combine to become the Dao in its own suchness. Gather spirit so that it reenters the Yellow Court. **[8a]** You will forever attain the state of perpetual life without dying. Wherever you go, the yin-spirit will manifest itself. It can ride the wind and walk on the clouds. Returning to the realm of dust, it is free from hunger and thirst, cold and heat. If you want to once again ascend the spirit, in order to reenter the Celestial Palace, train the spirit to abandon the husk. This is called the "Perfected casting off the husk." After a hundred days in the mountains, one generates the jade and casts off the husk. After a hundred days among the rivers, one generates the jade and casts off the husk. In the end, the perfected body emerges. This is called "spirit immortality." One returns to the Three Islands and no longer resides in the world of wind-blown dust.

Considering what is referred to as "casting off the husk to ascend to immortality," there are five instructions that are discussed as follows.

Diagram and Instructions on Casting Off the Husk to Ascend to Immortality and Transcending the Mundane to Enter the Sacred[105]

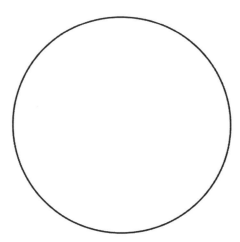

Figure 20. Diagram of Casting Off the Husk to Ascend to Immortality and Transcending the Mundane to Enter the Sacred

---

105. At the beginning of the text, this diagram is identified as the "Diagram of Transcending the Mundane to Enter the Sacred and Casting Off the Husk to Become an Immortal."

[8b] This method is called "refining form to unite with the Dao" and "casting off the husk to ascend to immortality." The fundamental method does not involve set times, but it clearly requires five methods. Master [Liu] Haichan[106] rode a crane to soar through the Celestial Gate.[107] In stillness, take perfect innate nature to be like a crane; it soars through the Celestial Gate. Naturally, there is the body-beyond-the-body.[108]

Patriarch Wang [Chongyang], the twelfth Perfected of Xishan (Western Mountain),[109] said, "If a blossoming tree emerges in the midst of stillness, you can view the blossoming tree without losing original nature." Once it emerges naturally, it may divide into multiple forms outside the body. The Yellow Emperor emerged out of stillness on a fire dragon. Riding the dragon of transformative fire, naturally he had the body-beyond-the-body. It is called the "Dharma Body of Clarity and Purity."[110]

Both Zhong and Lü,[111] the two Perfected, emerged from stillness using the red tower. They climbed up the three-tiered red tower, ascending level by level until they reached the end and leaped beyond it. They cast off their husks naturally.

Through this practice of refining spirit to unite with the Dao, of casting off the husk to ascend to immortality, accomplishment is reached naturally. For Buddhists, this involves entering *samādhi* in order to attain transformation through meditation.[112] For Daoists, this

---

106. Liu Cao (Haichan [Oceanic Toad]; fl. 940–1030?) is most often identified as a disciple of Chen Tuan (Xiyi [Infinitesimal Subtlety]; ca. 920–989) and a principal figure in the dissemination of *neidan* techniques during the Song dynasty. He was later recognized as a patriarch in the lineages of Quanzhen and the so-called Nanzong (Southern School) of internal alchemy. He appears as one of the Five Patriarchs of Quanzhen in the *Jinlian ji* (DZ 173) and *Jinlian xiangzhuan* (DZ 174).

107. The classical Daoist location for the Celestial Gate or Gate of Heaven (*tianmen*) is chapter 10 of the fourth-century BCE *Daode jing*. In Daoist cultivational contexts, it may refer to the nose, Yintang (Seal Hall; "third-eye"), or Baihui (Hundred Meetings; the crown-point).

108. *Shenwai shen.*

109. The Xishan (Western Mountain) lineage has yet to receive a comprehensive study. At the present time, it seems that earlier eremitic communities eventually coalesced into a Xishan *neidan* lineage, which was associated with the Zhong-Lü textual tradition and the geographical location of Xishan (near Nanchang, Jiangxi). Here the Tang literati Shi Jianwu stands out as an early recluse who practiced longevity techniques at Xishan. There are a number of extant works in the Ming-dynasty Daoist Canon associated with this Shi Jianwu as well as the pseudonymous Jin-Song author who wrote the *Xishan ji* (DZ 246; cf. DZ 126). Apart from its association with the famous Tang literati Shi Jianwu, Xishan as a geographical location is perhaps best known in Daoist history as the residence of Xu Xun (a.k.a. Xu Sun; Xu Jingyang; d. 292/374), the mythical founder of the Jingming (Pure Brightness) Daoist ritual tradition. See Boltz 1987, 70–78; Skar 2000; Schipper and Verellen 2004, 1115–27, 1284–85. Cf. *Xishan lu* (Record of Western Mountain; DZ 448).

110. The Dharma Body (*fashen*) is one of the Three Bodies (Skt.: *trikāya*; Chin.: *sanshen*) of a Buddha. These are the Dharmakāya, Sambhogakāya, and Nirmāṇakāya, that is, the dharma-body, bliss-body, and transformation-body. These correspond to (1) the body of a Buddha in its essential nature; (2) the body of a Buddha received for his own use and enjoyment; and (3) the body of a Buddha by which he can appear in any form. See Soothill and Hodous 1995 [1937], 77–78; Ding 1939, 302; Xingyun 1989, 555. In early Quanzhen, the Dharma Body is synonymous with the yang-spirit (*yangshen*) and body-beyond-the-body (*shenwai shen*) formed through internal alchemy practice. For example, according to the *Jinguan yusuo jue*, "If someone can fully comprehend these Three Transmissions, then he will transcend the Three Realms. The Three Realms are the realm of desire, the realm of form, and the realm of formlessness. The heart-mind, innate nature, and intention manifest as the Three Bodies. These are the Dharma Body of Clarity and Stillness, the Bliss Body of Enlightened Fullness, and the Transformation Body of Samādhi. These three each have a spirit of manifest traces" (DZ 1156, 12ab; trl. Komjathy 2007a). Similarly, the *Chongyang lijiao shiwu lun* explains, "The Dharma Body is a representation of formlessness. It is neither emptiness nor existence, has neither after nor before. It is neither low nor high, neither long nor short" (DZ 1233, 5b; translated here in chapter 3).

111. Zhongli Quan (second c. CE?) and Lü Dongbin (b. 798?), both of whom were recognized as patriarchs in Quanzhen Daoism.

112. To die.

involves entering stillness in order to send out the yin-spirit. **[9a]** Both, however, become ghosts of the clear Void; they do not become immortals of pure yang. Murky, unclear, and without manifestation, they accomplish nothing in the end. How can students commit such mistakes? They do not know [the alchemical process]. After refining vital essence to become the elixir, the pure *yangqi* is generated. After refining qi to become spirit, the perfect numen of spirit immortality transcends the mundane and enters the sacred. One casts off the husk and ascends to immortality. This is referred to as "transcendence through casting off." Throughout the endless generations, the methods for becoming a spirit immortal have not changed.

The oral instructions say,

> "To complete the work, you must come out of the Spirit Capital;
> The mundane concerns of the inner courtyard must not bind you.
> Obtain the instructions of the Five Immortals[113] for transcendence
>   through casting off;
> Refine and complete the immortal form and get out of the dust and
>   dirt."

The Meaning of the Instructions on Casting Off the Husk to Ascend to Immortality and Transcending the Mundane to Enter the Sacred

The Perfected said, "Considering adepts cultivating perfection who have practiced to the point of refining qi and completing form, they no longer want perpetual life in the world. **[9b]** They should quickly practice inner observation in order to refine spirit to unite with the Dao. Subjugate the demons until they dissipate. Refine spirit until spirit assembles. Being anxious and unwilling to sever ties to [the mundane world] is the reason why one cannot cast off the mundane husk. This is because one resides in the shadowy thoroughfare, so that one can only become an earthbound immortal. Generally speaking, one has anxiety because one has a body;[114] if one did not have a family, one would not have entanglements. From ancient times to the present, there has been a common saying: 'Through hard work, accomplishment reaches nonaction; strive to ensure that the craving-based self does not emerge.' Thus, casting off the husk to ascend to immortality involves refining spirit to emerge from the summit and transcending the mundane to become an immortal.

"People of the world are not adept at cultivation and refinement; they just want to cast off the husk and complete the way of immortality [without practicing]. How mistaken! You must sit in a darkened room and practice quiet sitting. Sever ties

---

113. Here the Five Immortals may refer to the Five Patriarchs of Quanzhen, namely, Donghua dijun (Sovereign Lord of Eastern Florescence), Zhongli Quan, Lü Dongbin, Liu Haichan, and Wang Chongyang. See *Jinlian ji*, DZ 173. Cf. *Jinlian xiangzhuan*, DZ 174.

114. An allusion to chapter 13 of the *Daode jing*.

to anxiety and forget thinking. The external landscape does not enter; the internal landscape does not manifest. With a body like withered wood and a heart-mind like dead ashes,[115] spiritual recognition is inwardly guarded, while unified intention is not dissipated. In concentration, there may emerge a spirit of yin numinosity. It is dark, obscure, and without manifestation. It is not an immortal of pure yang. Even though it can emerge from the husk, it is very difficult.

"From ancient times to the present, the highest Perfected have transmitted methods for casting off the husk. It certainly is not a problem. [10a] Practice naturally results in the inner elixir becoming complete, the pure *yangqi* being generated, and the original numinous spirit becoming manifest. When recognized through inner observation, one can cast off the husk and attain transcendence. When practiced in the correct sequence, one naturally transforms the fire dragon, so that it emerges from the summit. There is a body beyond the body, which is an appearance beyond the extraordinary. In the beginning, practice step one and then step two. Then move to stages three through five. Move from one stage to another without mistakes or carelessness. Afterwards, deposit the husk within mountains and streams, and forever become a companion of Penglai. This is 'casting off the husk,' and it completely rests in the experiential confirmation of the previous exercises. When practiced in order without mistakes, you naturally attain spirit immortality, ascending as a spirit through the top of the head.

"So, the highest Perfected bestowed these various methods for letting out that which has entered in. This is probably because students had received training for a long time by exerting effort. They practiced exercises day and night without success. When spirit gathers through inner observation, they might encounter the demon realm and become lost in deviant ways. That would render any further work as well as previous efforts useless. Thus, no effort to discuss these demons has been spared. Another concern is that students practice inner observation so that demons disperse and spirit assembles, eventually entering the Celestial Palace. [10b] Myriad types of vexing appearances may appear and be mistaken for the immortal realms. If they do not avoid them, they will once again have to go through the instructions for casting off the husk. Casting off the husk is not difficult. It will occur naturally when the work is complete. Thus, the instructions mention the 'blossoming tree' and 'black canopy' to signify the original body summoning spirit into the husk. There is also the 'crane breaking through' and the 'dragon leaping' to signify the ascending yang-spirit directing spirit to exit the body, to cast off the husk and ascend to immortality. From ancient times to the present, there were those among the highest Perfected who carelessly transmitted the instructions, failing to keep them secret. Their ancestors up to nine generations forever suffer in the Earth Prisons. For adepts cultivating perfection who want to bring their practice to completion through self-ascension, they cannot but practice in this way. From ancient times to the present, students have been vigilant and careful.

---

115. "Heart-mind of dead ashes" (*sihui xin*) and "body of withered wood" (*gaomu xing*) derive from chapter 2 of the *Zhuangzi*. See also chapter 23.

"The secret of the gold elixir resides in innate nature and life-destiny alone. Innate nature relates to heaven; it is constantly hidden in the head. Life-destiny relates to earth; it is constantly hidden in the navel. The head is the root of innate nature, while the navel is the stem of life-destiny. One root and one stem—these are the origin and ancestor of heaven and earth. The Yellow Court is below the navel. [11a] When the court is constantly guarded in the head and navel, it is called 'three layers.' The *Huangting jing* (Scripture on the Yellow Court) says, 'Through three repetitions, the zither heart sends the immortal embryo dancing.'[116] Here the zither obtains its harmony. Moreover, when human beings are born, the embryo coalesces in the navel, becoming connected with and welcomed into the Heart Palace of the mother. When cut off from the navel, it is called the 'stem.' The stem is the stem of life-destiny, while the root is the root of innate nature. However, because [Daoists] are concerned about dissipation and leakage, there are thousands and thousands of names, and many tens of thousands of formulas. The innate nature in the head is the lead, tiger, water, gold, sun, intention, Kan-water, Kun-earth, the stem *wu*, Maiden, and Jade Pass. Life-destiny in the navel is the mercury, dragon, fire, root, moon, corporeal soul, Li-fire, Qian-heaven, the stem *ji*, Child, and Gold Terrace. The head is the land of *wu*,[117] while the navel is the land of *ji*.[118] These two 'lands' make up the character *gui*.[119] This is what venerable immortal Lü [Dongbin] referred to as the 'dose.' This simply refers to the two elements of innate nature and life-destiny. [11b] A thousand scriptures and ten thousand discourses—there is only this."[120]

Practicing Methods

Each day, dawn to dusk is daytime, while dusk to the baleful moments of the five night-watches is nighttime.[121] Do not restrict your walking, standing, sitting, or lying down. Rather, during the daytime, practice the way of the life-stem in the navel. During the nighttime, practice the way of the nature-root in the summit gate. Do not distinguish between morning and evening or hungry and satiated. You must constantly practice these methods. After one hundred days, the elixir will coalesce. After three hundred days, the

---

116. Section 1a of the fourth-century CE *Huangting neijing jing* (DZ 331).

117. The fifth of the celestial stems, associated with Earth and yang.

118. The sixth of the celestial stems, associated with Earth and yin. The stem-combination of *wuji* refers to Earth and the center. It sometimes appears as *ertu*.

119. The author is playing on visual elements of the character *gui* ("a pinch"), which is composed of two *tu* ("earth") characters. That is, the elixir consists of the unification of innate nature and life-destiny, of the psychospiritual and biophysiological dimensions of oneself. Complete psychosomatic transformation occurs.

120. Cf. *Danyang yulu*, DZ 1057, 8a. The main body of the *Dadan zhizhi* ends here. This passage concludes the discussion of the ninth and final alchemical method. I have indicated that the subsequent sections may be addendums by using a smaller font. The text in turn becomes much more astronomical in content.

121. The "five night-watches" (*wugeng*) refer to the five periods of darkness. There were specific Quanzhen training regimens undertaken during these times, which I have referred to as "*wugeng* training." See Goossaert 2000; Komjathy 2007b, 175–79.

elixir medicine will become complete. After three years, the immortal embryo will be formed. Then the yang-spirit will enter and exit through the summit gate. It will come and go without any obstruction. This is what we refer to as the subtlety of the perfect elixir.

Practice

Considering practicing the life-stem during daytime, simply rub your hands together until they become warm. Place them over the navel circle, [12a] and use your awareness to concentrate on it. Simply keep watch on the navel circle without thinking or visualization. You simply want to make it still and concentrated. You will feel the Spirit Water descending to the navel and the perfect water becoming roused. From the elixir field below the navel, it leaps up to gather in the summit gate straight away. Allow things to happen naturally, and remain unconcerned about keeping track. Simply concentrate your awareness and keep watch on the navel circle. If you want to rest or stop, do not restrain yourself. After a while, the elixir field will seem as though it is on fire. Your vitality will be expansive and flourishing. The divine wondrousness is difficult to describe.

Considering practicing the nature-root during the nighttime, simply touch the tongue against the upper palate. Gradually close the two openings of the throat. Use your awareness to concentrate on them. Simply keep watch on the summit gate without thinking or visualization. You simply want to make it still and concentrated. You will feel the perfect fire surging upward from below. It leaps up to enter the summit gate straight away. If you want to rest or stop, do not restrain yourself. After a while, you will gradually hear what seem like the distant sounds of immortal music in your head. Perfect fragrances will issue from your nose. The divine wondrousness is difficult to describe. These are the secret instructions on the gold elixir; [12b] they do not go beyond this.

Instructions on Meditation Exercises

Through one inhalation, the original essence will come to ascend;
Through two exhalations, the Mysterious Female will open the summit gate.
Sometimes people do not recognize the perfect dragon and tiger,
But surmise that they are contained in the elixir field.

The Mysterious Decree

From the year, select the month. From the month, select the day. From the day, select the hour. Beware of the Wei-perilous Constellation,[122] and activate the fire on the last lunar day. Beware of the Dou-dipper Constellation,[123] and apply the fire on the first lunar day.

---

122. The Wei constellation (*weixiu*) is the twelfth of the twenty-eight lunar mansions of Chinese astronomy. It roughly corresponds to the Western constellation of Aquarius.

123. The Dou constellation (*douxiu*) is the eighth of the twenty-eight lunar mansions of Chinese astronomy. It roughly corresponds to the Western constellation of Sagittarius.

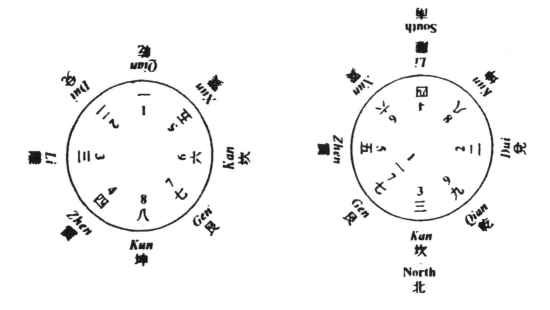

Figure 21. Diagram of Prior Heaven   Figure 22. Diagram of Later Heaven

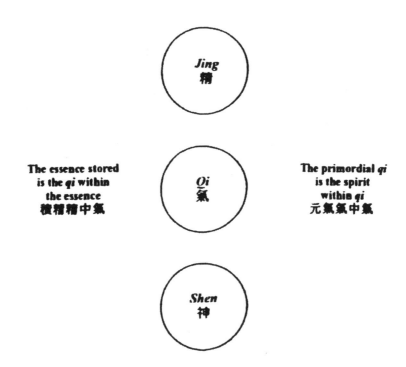

The essence stored is the qi within the essence 積精精中氣

The primordial qi is the spirit within qi 元氣氣中氣

Figure 23. Diagram of the Three Treasures

[13b] When yang begins to move, it is the double-hour *zi*. This is the time when the Dipper Handle turns, so it is the time of perfect *zi*. According to another method, in terms of the *zi* period during the ninth month and the number of *zi* periods that have passed, the ninth month as a *zi* period is the correct one. At this time, the two nasal openings contain qi. In terms of the Gold Duke and Maiden, they are the corridors for assisting Kan-water and Li-fire. When Frost Descends occurs in the middle of the ninth month, Winter Begins will occur in the eleventh month.[124]

The Wondrous Decree

Every month, constantly increase during the double-hour *xu*;
Every hour, observe the broken army.[125]
The Celestial Handle gains another position;
The living luminosity does not extend to human beings.

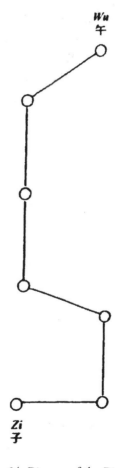

Figure 24. Diagram of the Dipper

---

124. These are two of the twenty-four seasonal periods.

125. Meaning unclear.

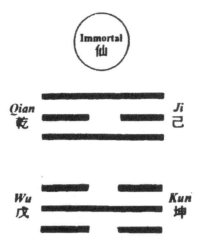

Figure 25. Diagrams of the Li-fire and Kan-water Trigrams

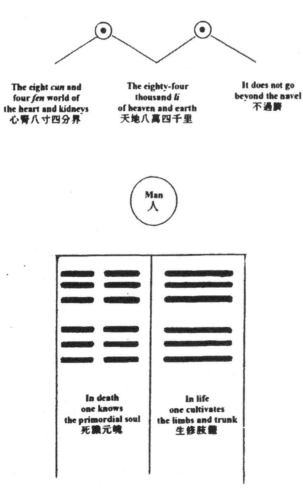

Figure 26. Diagrams of the Kun-earth and Qian-heaven Hexagrams

[14b] The Mysterious Pass is one *cun* and three *fen* inside the navel. The original qi of the father and mother is called the tripod vessel. The two kidneys are the tripod legs. When the firing schedule proceeds, the heart-mind begins its work. This is activating fire. The tiger and dragon copulate. The medicine ingredients are the dose. The bellows of Xun-wind rouses and expands the Flower Chamber.[126] This is advancing fire through extraction and addition. Beware of the dangers of mundane concerns during the double-hours of *mao* and *you*. Prior Heaven corresponds to the double-hour of *chou*. Later Heaven corresponds to the hours of foundational life and extending life.

The divine transformation of casting off the embryo involves employing one's own body and original life-destiny in order to attain perpetual life by calculating the four seasons. In this method, one year is a single Celestial Cycle, and one day is also a single Celestial Cycle. One day includes day and night, in which one employs the double-hours of *zi* to *wu*. The hours of life are called the hours of extending life. One must beware of dangers. Altogether, there are seven time-periods. It takes five hundred and sixty time-periods to make one duration. [There are moments of] mild nourishing and pure bathing, of birth through destruction as well as savage warfare. **[15a]** Casting off the embryo occurs within these periods. You must be careful. Do not divulge this.

The Saying of the Twelfth Perfected of Xishan[127]

When ordinary people try to speak about the Celestial Pivot,[128]
It can only be reckless speech because they are unable to know this.
Sentient beings in the mundane world will not have clear apprehension
Unless they meet Perfected who will explain what the Dao is and is not.

---

126. Also referred to as the Flower Canopy (*huagai*), here the Flower Chamber most likely refers to the lungs. The context suggests a breathing technique involving intentional inhalation and exhalation.

127. Based on the lineage configuration in section 2.8b, this would be Wang Chongyang.

128. In a Quanzhen context, the Celestial Pivot or Pivot of Heaven (*tianji*) usually refers to the heart-mind. See *Yinfu jing*, DZ 31, 1a.

Chapter Five

Scripture Study

Daoist scriptures exerted a formative influence on the early Quanzhen adepts and religious community. The most influential texts include the fourth-century BCE *Daode jing* (Scripture on the Dao and Inner Power), fourth- to second-century BCE *Nanhua zhenjing* (Perfect Scripture of Nanhua [Southern Florescence]; a.k.a. *Zhuangzi*), sixth-century CE *Yinfu jing* (Scripture on the Hidden Talisman; DZ 31), eighth-century *Qingjing jing* (Scripture on Clarity and Stillness; DZ 620), tenth-century *Chuandao ji* (Anthology of Transmitting the Dao; 263, j. 14–16) as well as other Zhong-Lü texts, and early twelfth-century *Jin zhenren yulu* (Discourse Record of Perfected Jin; DZ 1056). Certain Buddhist scriptures, especially the third-century CE *Xinjing* (Heart Sūtra; T. 250–57) and *Jingang jing* (Vajracchedikā Sūtra; Diamond Sūtra; T. 235–37, 273, 2734), which may date to the second century CE, also received a place of veneration.

Figure 27. Traditional Chinese Page of the Received Text of the *Qingjing jing* (DZ 620)

Here a few words are in order concerning the designation of "scripture." "Scripture" translates the traditional Chinese and Daoist designation of *jing*, which is often rendered as "classic" in the case of Confucianism and "sutra" in the case of Buddhism. There are many types of Daoist literature, including literary anthologies (*ji*), commentaries (*zhu*), discourse records (*yulu*), discourses (*lun*), hagiographies (*zhuan*), precepts (*jie/lü*), pure regulations (*qinggui*), scriptures (*jing*), treatises (*pian*), and so forth (see introduction herein). Generally speaking, among these, *jing* receive the most veneration. Historically speaking, *jing* are sacred texts written in classical Chinese using calligraphy, and most often transmitted in manuscripts. From a Daoist perspective, they are inspired or revealed. They are usually anonymous or attributed to divine beings such as Laojun (Lord Lao) or Yuanshi tianzun (Celestial Worthy of Original Beginning). Thus, for many Daoists, Daoist scriptures are not simply human compositions or material texts. They are manifestations of the Dao in the world, and they contain and express the numinous presence of the Dao. Most Daoist scripture study and extant Daoist commentaries, in turn, focus on *jing*.

Formal scripture study (*jingxue*) was a central practice of the early Quanzhen community and remained so throughout the various periods when the monastic order flourished. This is also the case in contemporary Quanzhen monastic communities, with the *Daode jing*, *Qingjing jing*, and *Yinfu jing* being primary.[1] Among the early Quanzhen adepts, we find a variety of perspectives on the importance of scripture study. For example, in an oft-quoted poem, Wang Chongyang explains,

> [To practice spiritual refinement] you must fully understand the three hundred characters
> of the *Yinfu jing* and read up on the five thousand words of the *Daode jing*. (*Quanzhen
> ji*, DZ 1153, 13.7b–8a)

On a broader level, Wang Chongyang gives the following advice on reading, understanding, and applying Daoist texts:

> The way to study texts is not to strive after literary merit, and thereby confuse your eyes.
> Instead, you must extract the meaning as it harmonizes with the heart-mind. Abandon
> texts after you have extracted their meaning and grasped their principle. Abandon principle
> after you have realized the fundamental ground. After you realize the fundamental
> ground, then attend to it until it completely enters the heart-mind. (*Chongyang lijiao
> shiwu lun*, DZ 1233, 1b–2a)

For Wang, and this view is clearly representative of the early Quanzhen adepts as a whole, the aspiring adept must reflect on the place of scripture study in his or her own life and practice. The relevance of scripture study is relative to the individual practitioner, and such relevance is based on his or her affinities and commitments. Reading and study (and translation) may support Daoist practice, or they may become a distraction. In a Quanzhen context, the point of reading and study is to deepen practice. One endeavors to apply a given text's insights to one's daily life. Scripture study thus is

---

1. This is so much the case that these texts are included in a modern list of "five scriptures" (*wujing*) and "four books" (*sishu*) of Daoism, which are canonical designations adopted from Confucianism. With respect to internal cultivation, the former include the *Daode jing*, *Huangting jing*, *Yinfu jing*, *Qingjing jing*, and *Longhu jing*, while the latter refer to the *Cantong qi*, *Wuzhen pian*, *Sanhuang yujue*, and *Qinghua miwen*. Min and Li 1994, 945.

not only an intellectual exercise; it is also a spiritual one.[2] According to Wang, one must focus on the transformational experience and influence of reading Daoist scriptures. Here there is a complex interplay among study, practice, and experience. Study without practice and experience may lead to a lack of discernment concerning relevance; practice and experience without study may lead to various forms of self-delusion. From a Daoist perspective, this is because scriptures (*jing*) are, etymologically and theologically speaking, threads and watercourses that form and re-form networks of connection.[3] As one of the external Three Treasures (*wai sanbao*) of the Dao, scriptures, and teachers, they connect the Daoist adherent to both the unnamable mystery that is the Dao and the Daoist tradition, the community of adepts that preceded one, as a historical and energetic continuum. It is that community and tradition that may correct mistaken views and egoistic distortions.

Other members of the early Quanzhen community also commented on the relative importance of scripture study. Two statements from Ma Danyang will help to qualify any definitive statements about Quanzhen views on reading Daoist texts.[4] On one occasion, Ma confronted his disciple Wang Yizhong (see chapter 2) on the potential detrimental effects of excessive reading:

> "Now, the Dao wants to form a contract with the heart-mind. If you can attain such a condition through literature, when is it time to awaken? Therefore, in terms of awakening to the Dao, [reading] the *Nanhua* is delusion becoming even more deluded." (DZ 1057, 3b)[5]

This is not an authoritarian statement on either the *Zhuangzi* in particular or scripture study in general. It is a context-specific admonition for a Quanzhen adept who had become overly engaged in and attached to reading. In the same text but in a different context, Ma comments,

> "When studying the Dao, you should not read scriptures and books extensively. This confuses consciousness and obstructs Daoist training. If [you want to read], Heshang gong's commentary on the *Daode jing* and Master Jinling's commentary on the *Yinfu jing* [are best]. When you read these two texts, there will be no obstruction." (Ibid., 10a)

So, it is not scripture study per se that is the problem from Ma Danyang's perspective; rather, it is *excessive* and consumptive reading that becomes a hindrance to spiritual training. The Quanzhen practitioner is not to read for mere enjoyment or entertainment; the point of scripture study is to clarify one's understanding and to deepen one's practice. Ma also emphasizes the importance of discernment when choosing which texts to study and apply.

---

2. Cf. the Benedictine and Carthusian Catholic practice of *lectio divina* ("sacred reading").

3. The character *jing* 經 consists of the *mi* 糸 ("silk") radical and *jing* 巠 ("underground stream"). The latter is generally taken to be a phonetic, meaning that it indicates pronunciation. However, a further etymological reading might suggest that the *jing* phonetic is also a meaning-carrier.

4. For some additional references see *Jin zhenren yulu*, DZ 1056, 2a, 3b; *Jinyu ji*, DZ 1149, 1.7b–8a, 2.19b, 5.2a; *Shenguang can*, DZ 1150, 18a, 19a; *Quanzhen ji*, DZ 1153, 10.20b, 21a; *Jinguan yusuo jue*, DZ 1156, 3a, 3b, 4a, 5a, 13a, 16a, 19b; *Ershisi jue*, DZ 1158, 4ab; *Ganshui lu*, DZ 973, 1.8a. See also the hagiographies translated in chapter 6.

5. See also *Jianwu ji*, DZ 1142, 2.32b.

Quanzhen scripture study involved both informal reading and more formal discipline, namely, the composition of commentaries. Like the work of literary and scholarly translation ("carrying over"), commentarial annotation involves close reading, deep reflection, and careful analysis. It also requires daring, dedication, and inspiration. Many of the early Quanzhen adepts wrote commentaries. The present chapter includes two commentaries by first-generation adepts and one by a later adherent.

The first selection is a translation of the *Taishang laojun shuo chang qingjing jing songzhu* (Recitational Commentary on the *Taishang laojun shuo chang qingjing jing*; DZ 974; abbr. *Qingjing jing zhu*), which was brushed by Liu Tongwei (Moran [Silent Suchness]; d. 1196). Liu Tongwei was Wang Chongyang's first formal Shandong disciple, who subsequent to his conversion joined the eremitic community of Liujiang in Shaanxi. His commentary focuses on the eighth-century *Taishang laojun shuo chang qingjing jing* (Scripture on Constant Clarity and Stillness as Revealed by the Great High Lord Lao; DZ 620; abbr. *Qingjing jing*),[6] which is part of a family of texts that I have elsewhere referred to as "Clarity-and-Stillness Literature" (Komjathy 2008, Handbook 7). It represents a continuation of Daoist adaptations and transformations of the Buddhist *Heart Sūtra*, which began with the seventh-century *Shengxuan huming jing* (Scripture on Protecting Life-Destiny and Ascending to the Mysterious; DZ 19) (see Kohn 1998, 64–69; Kohn and Kirkland 2000; Schipper and Verellen 2004, 562).[7] Believed to have been revealed by Laojun (Lord Lao), the deified Laozi, the *Qingjing jing* is an anonymous work of uncertain provenance, but the text exerted a seminal influence on various Daoist movements and lineages from the Tang dynasty (618–907) onward. It was especially revered in self-cultivation lineages, *neidan* circles, and of course Quanzhen.[8] With respect to the *Qingjing jing zhu*, the primary text of the commentary parallels that of the standard edition (DZ 620), with some variants (cf. DZ 758) and lacking the epilogue (DZ 620, 2b–3a), some of which is spuriously attributed to Ge Xuan (164–244; see also DZ 111). Liu Tongwei provides a cosmological and praxis-based reading. He stays close to the actual content of the *Qingjing jing*, although he often provides more of a poetic paraphrase than explanatory commentary. Liu emphasizes purification of consciousness and alchemical self-transformation. Beyond cryptic allusions to earlier Daoist scriptures, there are no clearly datable internal textual elements, and the text is not mentioned in Liu Tongwei's hagiography (*Zhongnan neizhuan*, DZ 955, 1.4a–5b; see chap. 6). Nonetheless, the *Qingjing jing zhu* is especially important because it is the only extant work attributed to Liu Tongwei.

Of the first-generation Quanzhen adherents, Liu Chuxuan (Changsheng [Perpetual Life]; 1147–1203) was by far the most committed to scripture study and exegesis. As Pierre Marsone has pointed out (2001, 104), Liu Changsheng emphasized the reading and application of Daoist scriptures as well as Buddhist and Confucian texts. He refers to these works with various names, including "alchemical texts" (*danshu*), "Daoist scriptures" (*daojing*), "ancient works" (*gushu*), "immortal texts" (*xianshu*), "doctrinal records" (*jiaodian*), "perfect scriptures" (*zhenjing*), and "sacred scriptures" (*shengjing*).[9] As

---

6. For some translations see Wong 1992; Kohn 1993, 25–29; Komjathy 2008a, Handbook 4. Note that the entry in *A Historical Companion to the Daozang* identifies the *Qingjing jing* with the questionable categorization of "Lingbao scripture."

7. Although there is an unmistakable debt to the Mahayana Buddhist doctrine of *śūnyatā*, the emptiness of separate existence and phenomenal appearances, the *Qingjing jing* also draws much of its content from a classical Daoist emphasis on "clarity and stillness" (*qingjing*). See, e.g., chapters 15, 16, 37, 39, 45, and 57 of the *Daode jing*.

8. There are a number of extant commentaries written from various Daoist perspectives. See Schipper and Verellen 2004, 332–33 (DZ 759), 728–30 (DZ 755–760).

9. *Xianle ji*, DZ 1141, 2.5a, 2.5b, 2.6a, 2.10b, 2.15b, 3.3b, 3.5b, 3.11b, 3.12b. Marsone 2001, 104, n. 34.

expressed in the fifth of his "Ten Admonitions" (*Xianle ji*, DZ 1141, 2.18ab; trl. here in chap. 3), "Do not, without relying on the scriptural teachings, talk about the Dao or universal principle." From Liu Changsheng's perspective, Quanzhen views must be rooted in textual study and scriptural precedents. In addition to the *Daode jing*, *Huangting jing*, *Qingjing jing*, and *Yinfu jing*, Liu also advocates a relaxed (*xian*; *wushi*) reading of the *Zhuangzi* and *Liezi*[10] and connects reading with playing the zither (*qin*)[11] (Marsone 2001, 104). Liu Changsheng, in turn, wrote commentaries on the *Daode jing* (lost), *Huangting neijing jing* (DZ 401; cf. DZ 331), and *Yinfu jing* (DZ 122; cf. DZ 31) (see *Jinlian ji*, DZ 173, 4.6b).[12]

In the second selection in this chapter, I have translated his *Huangdi yinfu jing zhu* (Commentary on the *Huangdi yinfu jing*; DZ 122; abbr. *Yinfu jing zhu*). The *Yinfu jing* (Scripture on the Hidden Talisman) is an anonymous sixth-century text of uncertain provenance, which is associated with the mythical Huangdi (Yellow Thearch / Emperor).[13] Historically speaking, the text has often been attributed to Li Quan (fl. 713–741), a moderately successful official and military expert under the Tang dynasty (618–907) (see DZ 108; DZ 110). However, this association is untenable, as is the theory of a military origin and interpretation of the text (see Rand 1979; Reiter 1984b). Like the *Qingjing jing*, the *Yinfu jing* has been and continues to be considered seminally important in self-cultivation lineages, *neidan* circles, and Quanzhen.[14] Liu's commentary is preceded by a preface (1191) by Fan Yi (fl. 1185), who was the superintendent of schools in Ninghai (Shandong) and who wrote many prefaces to early Quanzhen works (see DZ 1153; DZ 1154; DZ 1160). Contrasting Liu's commentary with earlier ones, Fan comments,

> With his expansive aptitude and learning, he connects old and new. His heart-mind wanders between the Dao and virtue. Thus, with broad-minded thinking he investigates what is essential, searching out the mysterious and making inquiries into the hidden. He puts it all into a clear commentary and explanation. Providing simple understanding, he makes it easy to know and easy to practice. It is thus beneficial for all later generations. It truly can be called an application of the heart-mind that is full of compassion and kindness for others.

The primary text of the commentary, in turn, follows that of the shorter version (approx. 300 characters) over the longer one (approx. 400 characters) (see DZ 110, preface, 1b); it thus lacks the final hundred or so characters of the received text (DZ 31, 2ab). Liu Changsheng's commentary is quite complex. Generally speaking, Liu emphasizes Quanzhen ascetic commitments and alchemical practice. With respect to the latter, the *Yinfu jing zhu* contains references to technical *neidan* theories

---

10. See, e.g., *Xianle ji*, DZ 1141, 2.2a, 2.3a, 5.9a.

11. See, e.g., *Xianle ji*, DZ 1141, 4.3a, 4.3b, 4.8a, 4.9a. Cf. *Chongyang lijiao shiwu lun*, DZ 1233, 4a.

12. Unfortunately, Liu's exegesis on the *Huangting jing* is more a poetic paraphrase than an explanatory commentary. Some insights into Liu's interpretations of the *Daode jing* may be gleaned from reading his *Yinfu jing zhu* and the *Changsheng yulu* (DZ 1058).

13. For some translations of the *Yinfu jing* see Rand 1979; Cleary 1991, 220–22; Komjathy 2008a, Handbook 7.

14. There are a large number of commentaries from a variety of Daoist perspectives. See Reiter 1984b; Schipper and Verellen 2004, 321–22 (DZ 108, 112, 311), 691–700 (DZ 109–111, 113–127). Interestingly, Zhu Xi (1130–1200), the famous systematizer of Neo-Confucianism, also wrote a commentary on the *Yinfu jing*.

and methods, which parallel other Quanzhen works, including the *Jinguan yusuo jue* (DZ 1156; trl. Komjathy 2007a) and *Dadan zhizhi* (DZ 244; trl. here in chap. 4). Liu also focuses on Daoist cosmology and Buddhist-inspired maps of consciousness. The commentary is outstanding for its close reading and clear explanations of the *Yinfu jing*, with Liu frequently explicating the technical language of the primary text. In certain instances, Liu's reading mirrors the commentary (DZ 121) by Tang Chun (Jinling daoren [Daoist of Nanjing]; eleventh c. CE?), which exerted some influence on early Quanzhen (see *Jin zhenren yulu*, DZ 1056, 2a; *Quanzhen ji*, DZ 1153, 10.20b; *Danyang yulu*, DZ 1057, 10a). Especially fascinating is Liu Changsheng's discussion of the "Nine Cavities" (*jiuqiao*; 6ab) and "spirit pervasion" (*shentong*; 11ab). In these passages, he suggests that "immortal anatomy" is different from that of ordinary people, and that it is possible for Quanzhen adepts to attain a state of mystical participation wherein the numinous presence of the Dao circulates through the whole of existence. In addition to frequent allusions to the *Daode jing*, Liu references Heshang gong's commentary on the *Daode jing* (5b), *Diamond Sūtra* (7b), and *Qingjing jing* (10a).

The third and final translated text originates in a completely different historical moment and possibly even a non-Quanzhen context. This selection focuses on the *Qingtian ge zhushi* (Commentary on the "Qingtian ge"; DZ 137) by Wang Jie (Daoyuan [Dao's Source]; Hunran [Primordial Suchness]; fl. 1331–1380) (Schipper and Verellen 2004, 1279; Pregadio 2008, 1012–13). Wang Jie lived toward the end of the Yuan dynasty (1279–1368) and the beginning of the Ming dynasty (1368–1644), a time when Quanzhen was already a monastic order with national distribution and when the order was being eclipsed by Zhengyi (Orthodox Unity) as the dominant Daoist tradition (see, e.g., De Bruyn 2000). There are no known extant biographies of Wang Jie; rather, biographical details derive from his own writings and a preface (1392) to the *Huanzhen ji* (DZ 1074) by Zhang Yuchu (1361–1410), the forty-third Celestial Master.[15] For present purposes, his potential connection with Quanzhen is most pertinent. Born near Nanchang, Jiangxi, Wang Jie trained with Cai Zhiyi (Baochan [Precious Toad]; fl. 1290–1360) (*Yingchanzi yulu*, DZ 1060, colophon) and possibly with Chen Zhixu (Shangyang [Upper Yang]; 1290–ca. 1350), who was from Ji'an, Jiangxi. The former was a disciple of Li Daochun (Yingchan [Shimmering Toad]; fl. 1288–1306), who is often identified as a member of both Nanzong (Southern School; via Bai Yuchan [1134–1229]) and Quanzhen (a.k.a. Beizong [Northern School]) and who indirectly influenced Wang Jie (see *Santian yisui*, DZ 250; *Yingchanzi yulu*, DZ 1060).[16] Chen Zhixu traced his lineage to Ma Danyang via Zhao Youqin (fl. 1329) (*Jindan dayao liexian zhi*, DZ 1069) and established a Quanzhen sublineage, the Jindan xianpai (Immortal Lineage of the Gold Elixir), associated with Ma Danyang (*Jindan dayao xianpai*, DZ 1070). Preliminary study of Wang Jie's various writings also indicates parallels with the work of Li Daochun and Chen Zhixu (see Schipper and Verellen 2004, 723–24, 1175; also Boltz 1987, 183–84). All of this is complicated by the relative neglect of Yuan and Ming Quanzhen;[17] future studies of Wang Jie's other works may clarify the place of the *Qingtian ge zhu* in his overall corpus.

---

15. Wang Jie wrote three commentaries, two independent compositions, and one collaborative work. These include the *Shengxuan huming jing zhu* (DZ 100), *Yinfu jing zhu* (DZ 126), and *Ruyao jing zhu* (DZ 135); *Huanzhen ji* (DZ 1074) and *Daoxuan pian* (DZ 1075); as well as the *Santian yisui* (DZ 250). See Schipper and Verellen 2004.

16. Li Daochun is the author of the highly influential *Zhonghe ji* (DZ 249; trl. Cleary 1989a). There has been an ongoing debate about his lineage affiliation, and I leave it to scholars with greater expertise than me to resolve the issue.

17. That is, of course, apart from Qiu Changchun's famous meeting with Chinggis Qan (Genghis Khan; ca. 1162–1227; r. 1206–1227) and the subsequent edicts of Qubilai Qan (Khubilai Khan; Emperor Shizu; 1215–1294; r. 1260–1294).

In any case, the aforementioned historical details point to Wang Jie's connection with "post-unification Quanzhen," specifically after the reunification of China under the Yuan (1279) when various southern lineages became incorporated into the Quanzhen monastic order and associated lay communities (see Schipper and Verellen 2004, 1129–30). Wang's *Qingtian ge zhu* is especially significant because it is the only extant commentary on an early Quanzhen work and because it reveals the way in which Quanzhen literature was read in later *neidan* communities. It specifically focuses on the "Qingtian ge" (Song of the Clear Sky; trl. here in chap. 1), a poem by Qiu Changchun that is contained in the *Panxi ji* (Anthology of Panxi, DZ 1159, 3.1ab). As documented in his preface, Wang Jie believes that the thirty-two lines of the original poem parallel the thirty-two heavens mentioned in the *Duren jing* (Scripture on Salvation; DZ 1). Wang in turn envisions the poem as divisible into three sections: the first twelve on innate nature; the second twelve on life-destiny; and the final eight on the fusion of innate nature and life-destiny. Wang Jie's commentary provides fairly straightforward cosmological and alchemical interpretations mixed with Buddhist existential views and a Chan-inspired approach to the purification of consciousness. With respect to datable internal elements, Wang cites the *Yijing* (2a), *Daode jing* (2b), *Mengzi* (2b), *Jingang jing* (3a), "Zhongyong" chapter of *Liji* (3a), and *Duren jing* (3b, 5b). Wang also mentions Yin Xi (2b–3a), Yan Hui (3b), and Master Liaozhen (5a).

With respect to the larger historical contours of Quanzhen, commentarial literature comprises a major portion of the overall literary tradition. A more comprehensive anthology might include other works from various historical periods. Considering the first-generation Quanzhen adherents, beyond the aforementioned commentary on the *Huangting jing* by Liu Changsheng, Hao Guangning's commentary on the *Caotong qi* (*Taigu ji*, DZ 1161, 1.1a–8b) and *Yijing* (ibid., 2.1a–3.13b) deserve study. There are no extant exegetical works from the second-generation, but the hagiographies provide evidence for a variety of lost commentaries (see Goossaert 1997, 424–35). Beyond the commentaries of Wang Jie, some noteworthy late medieval and late imperial works include Li Daochun's commentary on the *Qingjing jing* (DZ 755); He Daoquan's (Wugou [Free-from-Stain]; 1319?–1399) *Daode jing songzhu* (Detailed Commentary on the *Daode jing*), which is extant in a Ming-dynasty manuscript housed in the National Library of China; as well as Liu Yiming's (Wuyuan [Awakening to the Origin]; 1734–1821) various commentaries contained in his *Daoshu shier zhong* (Twelve Daoist Texts; see ZW 245, 253, 255, 259, 266; trl. Cleary 1991). Interestingly, Ren Farong (b. 1936), the former abbot of Louguan tai (Lookout Tower Monastery; Zhouzhi, Shaanxi) and current president of the Chinese Daoist Association, has written commentaries on the *Daode jing*, *Cantong qi*, and *Yinfu jing*.

Next to none of Quanzhen commentarial literature has been translated to date, which is also true of Daoist exegeses more generally. As mentioned, Thomas Cleary (1986a; 1991) has published a general-audience translation of selections from Liu Yiming's *Daoshu shier zhong*, including his commentary on the *Yinfu jing* and *Yijing*. More recently, Peter Acker published a translation of Liu Changsheng's *Yinfu jing zhu* (2006). I prepared my own translation of that work before finding Acker's rendering.[18] I have examined his translation and found some significant differences in our

---

18. Note that Acker does not translate Fan Yi's preface. Although Acker's translation is sound and his discussion of Liu Changsheng's life is accurate, caution must be exercised with respect to his overall understanding of early Quanzhen. The book contains some mischaracterizations and some inaccuracies. For example, Acker claims, "Wang Chongyang, the founder of *Quanzhen*-Daoism, never used the term *Quanzhen* in his own writing." This is simply false, as a close reading of the poems contained in the *Quanzhen ji* reveals. See Komjathy 2007a, 9–17. Cf. Hachiya 1992, 15.

interpretations. Interestingly, though, we both adopted a similar annotation method, which relies on Liu's discussion of various technical terms in his *Changsheng yulu* (DZ 1058).[19]

Commentary on the *Qingjing jing*[20]

Liu Tongwei, Master Moran

Preface

Now, when the source is clear and the current is still, you can collect the crashing waves of the ocean of phenomenal appearances. When the foundation is stable and the root is deep, you can embrace the circulation of the qi of pure yang. Through fullness and emptiness, through expiration and inspiration, the Six Pairings[21] make their revolutions. Heaven and earth are the origin of benefit and harm; yin and yang are the essential force behind the pivotal movements.

As a human being, offer your body to heaven and earth and simply take clarity and stillness as the return to suchness. Mingle your qi with yin and yang, so that every change pervades the transformations of perfect constancy. As for clarity, disturb it and it will not become turbid. As for stillness, settle it and it will not move.

Heaven attains unified clarity; earth attains unified serenity; and humans attain unified numinosity: All of this is unified spirit. The source of numinosity is completely penetrated; the sacred Dao circulates and becomes pervasive. Become silent, free from agitation; accord with transformations, free from fixed locations. Resonate with things and follow open pervasion: Where is the end of generation and development?

Heaven and earth have such constancy that clarity and stillness are limitless. When men and women lack a constant heart-mind, obscuration and delusion gain a foothold. Who, then, can respond to turbidity with cessation? Still it so that it gradually becomes clear. Then, in the end you will have attainment.

Thus, the Great High [Lord Lao][22] favored us with his great compassion, extending constant clarity and stillness, establishing the teachings and guiding ordinary [people], supporting the aligned and sustaining our lineage. Attending to the conversion of the masses through returning to the Source,[23] he caused them to embody perfection and embrace the One.[24]

---

19. The *Changsheng yulu* contains entries on the following paired terms: *fa* and *kong*, *zhi* and *jian*, *shan* and *e*, *xian* and *yu*, *sheng* and *si*, *gui* and *jian*, *gao* and *xia*, *le* and *ku*, *qing* and *zhuo*, *xian* and *yin*, *da* and *xiao*, *xu* and *shi*, *xian* and *mang*, *qu* and *lai*, *ping* and *chang*, *xi* and *you*, *de* and *shi*, *fu* and *huo*, *she* and *qu*, *zhong* and *bian*, *zhu* and *li*, *ren* and *wo*, *bian* and *na*, *sun* and *yi*, *chang* and *duan*, *qiao* and *zhuo*, *hui* and *zan*, *wang* and *tan*, *dao* and *su*, *fei* and *shi*, *si* and *shi*, *miao* and *wei*, *fang* and *yuan*, *ying* and *bian*, *qing* and *wu*, *ji* and *lü*, *qin* and *shu*, *yuan* and *jin*, *xing* and *zhu*, *wei* and *zhong*.

20. *Taishang laojun shuo chang qingjing jing songzhu*, DZ 974.

21. The Six Pairings (*liuhe*) usually refer to the four cardinal points as well as the zenith (up) and nadir (down) of the universe.

22. Laojun (Lord Lao) is the deified Laozi, a pseudo-historical figure and attributed author of the *Daode jing*. See, for example, Seidel 1969; Kohn 1999.

23. *Guigen*. An allusion to chapter 16 of the *Daode jing*: "Returning to the Source is called stillness; this means returning to life-destiny. Returning to life-destiny is called constancy; knowing constancy is called illumination."

24. *Baoyi*. An allusion to chapter 10 of the *Daode jing*: "Carrying the ethereal and corporeal souls, embracing the One, can you be without separation?" The phrase, in the more common form of *shouyi*, became a general name for Daoist meditation in the organized religious tradition. See Kohn 1989.

If you want to embody and become attuned with the mysterious Origin, refine spirit and merge with the Dao. Through winged transformation, become a flying immortal. Don't make any mistakes!

This was done so that those who believe and accept [the teachings] will embody and orient themselves with the essence of the divine law. Everyone should accord with this. If every person takes clarity and stillness as the rectification of the world,[25] then there will be a thousand Perfected and ten thousand sages. No one should depart from this!

Commentary[26]

The five stages of the Grand Inception[27] precede everything; there the Dao of emptiness and nonbeing is naturally so.[28] Chaos Prime[29] comes to regulate the ancestral alignment. In subtle embodiment, he joins the ancestral mystery. He spreads the teachings and illuminates the highest reaches [of the cosmos]. He knows constancy and bestows proper understanding. In accordance with the virtue of clarity and stillness,[30] he investigates it all, transforming it into the scripture and its chapters.

Lord Lao spoke: The great Dao is without form.[31] It brings forth and nurtures heaven and earth.

The great Dao is hidden in form, its perfect essence commingled with darkened obscurity. The two forces[32] divide as its first sign; the single, unified qi circulates without ceasing. Its support and sustenance are truly immeasurable; its generation and completion nourish what is lower. Like a kiln or mold, it has the ability to fashion things. Wriggling like worms, it completely contains the numinous.

---

25. An allusion to chapter 45 of the *Daode jing*. See also chapters 15, 16, and 57.

26. The commentary is arranged in eight five-character lines, and could thus be rendered as poetic stanzas. For readability, I have compromised on presenting the text in prose paragraphs. The first section is a commentary on the title of the text: *Scripture on Constant Clarity and Stillness as Revealed by the Great High Lord Lao*.

27. Taichu (Grand Inception) refers to a specific moment in cosmogonic emanation. In the Daoist tradition, it relates to the initial moment of differentiation emerging from primordial undifferentiation and to original qi before the formation of heaven and earth. According to chapter 12 the *Zhuangzi*, "In the Great Beginning [Grand Inception], there was nonbeing; there was no being, no name. Out of it arose One; there was One, but it had no form. Things got hold of it and came to life, and it was called Virtue. Before things had forms, they had their allotments; these were of many kinds, but not cut off from one another, and they were called fates. Out of the flow and flux, things were born, and as they grew they developed distinctive shapes; these were called forms. The forms and bodies held within them spirits, each with its own characteristics and limitations, and this was called the inborn nature" (Watson 1968, 131–32; also 43, 82–83, 192; *Daode jing*, chaps. 42, 52). See also chapter 3 of the *Huainanzi*; Major 1993.

28. "So of itself" translates *ziran*, which also appears as "suchness," "naturalness," "spontaneity," and "being-so-of-itself."

29. Hunyuan (Chaos Prime) may refer to the state of primordial undifferentiation, but is usually employed as an honorific name for Laozi. For an occurrence in Quanzhen, see *Jinlian xiangzhuan*, DZ 174, 11a.

30. "Virtue" translates *de*, which also appears as "inner power." While *de* may mean moral or ethical activity, it has a larger sense of being pervaded by the numinous presence of the Dao. Virtuous behavior is an expression or manifestation of that inner condition.

31. This line echoes chapters 4, 14, 21, 35, and 41 of the *Daode jing*.

32. The "two forces" (*eryi*) are heaven/yang and earth/yin.

The great Dao is without feelings. It regulates the course of the sun and moon.[33]

The sun and moon revolve in emptiness; bright and luminous, they extend everywhere. Attaining heaven, they can shine for a long time; **[1b]** their beauty can pervade everything. Being and substance are covered by their radiant warmth; free from feelings, they commingle with apparent manifestations.[34] Yin and yang constantly embody the Dao; they never cease moving in great Nonbeing.

The great Dao is without name. It raises and nourishes the ten thousand beings.[35]

The wondrous Dao is truly difficult to name—it embraces and contains the life of the ten thousand beings. When it circulates, it fills the meridians of the earth,[36] going along with its endowment of celestial clarity. It breathes the glistening perfection during ebb and flow; it harmonizes with great transformations and completions. In perfect pervasion, it returns to the state of unified embodiment. Here high and low are equal and identical.

I do not know its name; forced to name it, I call it Dao.[37]

The Dao is formless and free from residual traces;[38] difficult to name, its center rests in Primordial Chaos. Not yet sprouting forth as heaven, earth, and the sun, how can it become rain, clouds, and wind? Chiseled and broken, it forms embryos, patterns, and omens; it infuses and manifests as beings, images, and visions. Thus, it unfolds as the transformative process, the power of which is established through the limitlessness of the Dao.

Within the Dao, there is clarity and turbidity.[39] *Within the Dao, there is movement and stillness.*

[2a] Clarity and turbidity are the qi of yin and yang; they circulate and flow by ascending and descending. Suchness is completed through influences and transformations; in the end,

---

33. This line parallels chapter 5 of the *Daode jing*: "Heaven and earth are not humane; they regard the myriad beings as straw dogs. The sage is not humane; he regards the people as straw dogs." See also section 1b of Liu Changsheng's commentary on the *Yinfu jing* translated later in this chapter.

34. The stars.

35. These lines echo chapters 1, 32, 34, 37, and 41 of the *Daode jing*.

36. "Meridians" translates *mai*. Here Liu suggests that there are circulation networks (of fluids, qi, etc.) throughout the earth.

37. This line develops the description of the Dao in chapter 25 of the *Daode jing*: "It [Dao] may be considered the mother of the world. I do not know its name (*ming*), but call it (*zi*) 'Dao.' Forced to name it (*ming*), I call it 'great.'" The use of *ming* and *zi* is interesting, as *ming* designates the name given to one at birth, while *zi* is a later nickname.

38. "Residual traces" translates *ji*. It refers to the realm of differentiated beings and phenomenal appearances. As a Daoist technical term, the distinction between the Dao and its traces was especially emphasized within the early medieval school of Xuanxue (Profound Learning). On Xuanxue see Rudolf Wagner's various publications.

39. In the *Changsheng yulu*, Liu Changsheng, the master-brother of Liu Tongwei, discusses the paired terms of "clarity" (*qing*) and "turbidity" (*zhuo*). According to Liu, "Clarity refers to celestial clarity (*tianqing*), which manifests in the myriad forms. If the heart-mind is clear, it manifests as a guiding numinosity (*chenling*)" (DZ 1058, 7a). And, "Turbidity refers to the delusion of the mundane world. When such delusion distorts one's thinking, one becomes perverse and turbid" (ibid., 7b).

it merges with complete pervasion.[40] The ten thousand categories are joined in its nourishing presence; the Three Primes are matched in its unifying sameness. With Qian-heaven and Kun-earth[41] joined in exalted stability,[42] everything gathers together in the emptiness of unified perfection.

Heaven is clarity and earth is turbidity. Heaven is movement and earth is stillness. The male is clarity and the female is turbidity. The male is movement and the female is stillness.[43]

During the originating differentiation, the two powers divided; human beings, the most numinous, reached exalted veneration. The Three Powers were arranged in the cosmic spheres; the two presences became concentrated as Qian-heaven and Kun-earth. All things come to contain the perfect qi; the Primordial Origin manifests through phenomena. The firm and yielding support and employ each other. Embodying the Dao, who is able to remain?

Descending from the beginning, flowing toward the end, the ten thousand beings are born.

Descending from the Source, the ten thousand beings pervade the substance of perfection; returning to the Origin, they can see the causes of the branches.[44] In spring, they rise and spread flourishing abundance; **[2b]** in autumn, they preside over withering decrease. The Great Ultimate produces forms and transformations; Pure Harmony creates all things anew. The pivotal mechanism extends great circulation;[45] the controlling power allows spirit to become efficacious.

Clarity is the source of turbidity. Movement is the root of stillness.

Clarity and stillness regulate the dark and deep remoteness; who can fully understand this? Observe emptiness and expel the myriad phenomena; sever ties to appearances and become realized in your heart-mind. The moon of wisdom flows through the elixir galaxy; the clouds of compassion cover the verdant peaks. In deep serenity, spirit remains unmoving; according with beings, it manifests as the sound of knowing.

---

40. "Complete pervasion" (*yuantong*) refers to spiritual realization and mystical union.

41. The trigrams Qian-heaven ☰ and Kun-earth ☷, respectively. The former consists of three yang-lines and represents pure yang ("heaven"), while the latter consists of three yin-lines and represents pure yin ("earth"). In this pairing, yin has positive connotations. The trigrams may refer to the cosmos or to specific dimensions of human being, including head/abdomen and spirit/qi.

42. "Stability" translates *ding* (Skt.: *samādhi*). It refers to deep concentration, stabilized stillness, yogic stasis, and mystical absorption.

43. Here "male" and "female" refer to yang and yin, to "masculine" qualities/tendencies and "feminine" qualities/tendencies. They do not designate men and women.

44. Here "branches" refer to phenomenal appearances and karmic patterns.

45. "Pivotal mechanism" translates *shuji*. The "pivot" or "trigger" is the still point, the center of silence, from which all activity originates. According to chapter 18, "Ultimate Joy," of the *Zhuangzi*, "The myriad beings emerge from the pivot and enter into the pivot." The sixth-century *Yinfu jing* explains, "The human heart-mind is the pivot" (DZ 31, 1a). Astronomically speaking, Daoists often identify it as the Dipper handle. Anthropologically speaking, it usually corresponds to the heart-mind.

If you can be constantly clear and still, heaven and earth completely return.

When humans awaken, clarity and stillness are constant; the source of knowing is a subtle and sacred pivot. Since the Grand Inception, it is free from taint or obstruction; complete serenity hides the radiant brilliance. Darkened silence stores the sandy world; mysterious obscurity reaches to Purple Tenuity.[46] After the Three Primes ascend and descend, heaven and earth completely return.

The human spirit is fond of clarity, but the heart-mind disturbs it. The human heart-mind is fond of stillness, but desires meddle with it.

[3a] The heart-mind is the storehouse of the numen; if spirit perches in stillness, it can become calm. Greed, anger, and ignorance are easy to act through;[47] morality, concentration, and wisdom are difficult to follow.[48] If you deeply long for the alignment within alignment, firmly establish yourself in the seclusion within seclusion. Never giving rise to the Six Desires, the world of the divine law will naturally broaden.

If you can constantly banish desires, then the heart-mind will become still naturally. If you can constantly settle the heart-mind, then the spirit will become clear naturally.

Banish the various emotions and desires; cleanse the heart-mind through wondrous and penetrating observation. Merge with perfection and cease seeing things as things; return to serenity and abandon every sort of distraction. The distant waters are connected by celestial stillness; the elevated mountains are sustained by the lunar coldness. Completely integrated, you pervade insight and wisdom; in your inner cauldron, there is a golden pill.

Abiding in suchness, the Six Desires do not arise, and the Three Poisons are dispersed and destroyed.

Rectify your thoughts without partiality or fraction; penetrate emptiness and harmonize with suchness. The defilements of the Six Desires suddenly become stilled; [3b] the disease of the Three Poisons inevitably becomes healed. The wondrous Dao transcends emptiness and the *kalpa*s;[49] the complete spirit penetrates the highest heavens. In places of darkness and mysteriousness, the Mysterious Female naturally becomes continuous.[50]

---

46. Ziwei (Purple Tenuity), which sometimes appears as Ziwei yuan (Ziwei Court), is associated with the Northern Polestar and its corresponding emperor. It often designates the sacred realm and stellar abode of Beidi (Emperor of the North). For some insights see Little 2000, 143, 244.

47. The Three Poisons (*sandu*) mentioned in the next section.

48. These correspond to the Buddhist technical terms of *śīla*, *samādhi*, and *prajñā*.

49. Associated with space and time, *kalpa* is a Sanskrit technical term utilized in Hinduism and Buddhism. Often translated as "aeon," *kalpa* refers to enormous time periods and cosmological cycles.

50. The Mysterious Female (*xuanpin*) is a Daoist technical term that first appears in chapter 6 of the *Daode jing*: "The Valley Spirit does not die; it is called the Mysterious Female. The gateway to the Mysterious Female is the root of heaven and earth." In Daoist contexts, it frequently designates original spirit (*yuanshen*) housed in the Zuqiao (Ancestral Cavity), the center of the head.

Whoever cannot accomplish this has not yet settled the heart-mind; desires have not yet been banished.

On the road of delusion, one loses family and village, and every karmic influence conceals and encloses radiance. When the heart-mind drifts like this, it is easy to be agitated; when mental projections stew, they are difficult to forget. When desires taint you, how can you banish them? When perversion corrupts you, its revolutions cause recklessness. Turn your face toward the place of awakening within the head; revert your illumination to gaze upon the ruler of emptiness.[51]

If you can abolish desires, internally observing the heart-mind,[52] you see that in actuality there is no heart-mind.

When you realize the dissipation that comes from the various defilements, you clearly behold the opening of divine perception.[53] Then sights and sounds will not be able to disrupt you; knowledge and perception settle and necessarily become latent. When spirit becomes still, the thousand vexations are destroyed;[54] when the heart-mind becomes empty, the ten thousand worries are extinguished. A clear wind blows through the Jade Door,[55] and an amazing sound spontaneously emerges.

[4a] *Externally observing form, you see that in actuality there is no form.*

Observe that there is no [real] appearance in the various appearances, and each and every form is rooted in Nonbeing. It contains the perfect world of the divine law; it embodies and is merged with the great Void. When the clouds are still, the moon illuminates the dew; when you delve deeply into practice, sights become correctly arranged. This luminosity of *prajñā* manifests as a clear sign[56]—where is there to search for extinction and erasure?

---

51. As a Daoist practice, "reverting illumination" (*fanzhao*), also translated as "turning back the radiance," involves joining the combined radiance (*ming*) of the left eye (the sun; *ri*) and right eye (the moon; *yue*) at Yintang (Seal Hall; the "third-eye"). The gaze is then directed toward the center of the head, where it activates the divine light that fills and illumines the entire body, the inner landscape.

52. Inner observation (*neiguan*) refers to as specific form of Daoist meditation. See *Neiguan jing*, DZ 641; Kohn 1989. In terms of the practice in late medieval internal alchemy, see *Chuandao ji*, DZ 263, 16.16a–22b. Illustrated instructions appear in the *Dadan zhizhi*, DZ 244, 2.3a–5a (translated here in chapter 4).

53. *Daoyan*, here translated as "divine perception," literally means "Dao-vision."

54. "Vexation" (Chin.: *fannao*; Skt.: *kleśa*) is a Buddhist technical term that designates impurities of consciousness. It refers to pain, affliction, distress, worry, trouble, or whatever causes such conditions. In Chinese Buddhism, *fannao* refers to delusions generated by desire and ignorance that disturb the mind. There are both basic and derivative forms of vexation. See *Jinguan yusuo jue*, DZ 1156, 1a, 2b, 4b, 10b, 15a (trl. Komjathy 2007a).

55. The Jade Door (*yuhu*) may refer to the ears or the occiput, with the latter frequently designated as Yujing (Jade Capital) or Yuzhen (Jade Pillow).

56. *Prajñā* is a Buddhist technical term related to spiritual insight and wisdom into the true nature of existence, namely, suffering (based in desire), impermanence, and no-self.

Remotely observing things, you see that in actuality there are no things. When you awaken to these three, only then do you gain a glimpse into emptiness.

In silent illumination, observe the various things—how can their countless numens be different? Joined with Perfection, they cannot be perceived; severed from their traces, none can be seen as real. In deep realization, I observe my old self in the hall. In remote detachment, the Origin lies beyond every phenomenal appearance. Mysterious and again more mysterious,[57] the mystery keeps flowing; throughout the eight boundaries,[58] you can go along in open vastness.

Using emptiness to observe emptiness, you see that emptiness is not empty.[59]

Extend your insight to the world of perfect emptiness; in seclusion, observe the unification of Being and Nonbeing. Commingled and fused, unified with the great vastness, **[4b]** in deep serenity, embody emptiness and Nonbeing. Cavernous luminosity sounds through the constant silence; through complete pervasion, innate nature is self-so. Within the center, both internally and externally, you are free from dependency and return to the original beginning.

When even emptiness does not exist, you see that no-thingness is indeed no-thing.

When you completely realize a heart-mind of no-thingness, the nonbeing of Nonbeing is truly without beings. Why exhaust yourself with expelling chaotic imaginings? Why concern yourself with disputes over refined and coarse? When karmic connections are stilled, emptiness bestows insight; returning to Perfection ensures that you will not regress. *Prajñā* disperses and quiets every delusion; who would dare to force it into names and patterns?

Without even the nonexistence of no-thingness, there is only clear and constant silence.

The myriad phenomenal appearances originally come from emptiness; the nonexistence of no-thingness joins with sacred accomplishment. In deep immersion, there is no inside and no outside; in serene abiding, east and west are obliterated. With heart-mind and projections both forgotten, the square and round[60] are one in level sameness. In darkened obscurity, one leaps into the transformative process;[61] free from thinghood, everything is completely pervaded.

---

57. An allusion to chapter 1 of the *Daode jing*.

58. The "eight boundaries" (*baji*) include the four cardinal directions and the intermediate directions (NW, NE, SW, and SE).

59. This line and the following one are difficult to translate. The original Chinese reads as follows: *Guan kong yi kong, kong wusuo kong; suo kong ji wu, wuwu yi wu.*

60. The "square" (*fang*) and "round" (*yuan*) refer to earth and heaven, respectively.

61. "Transformative process" translates *zaohua*, which is sometimes problematically translated as "creation" or "Creator." Such translations distort the foundational Daoist cosmogony that is characterized by the Dao's impersonal and spontaneous unfolding through emanation, through a movement from primordial undifferentiation to differentiation.

[5a] *When silence is no longer silence, how can desires come forth? When desires do not come forth, this is perfect stillness.*

When partial serenity still works with substance, you must root out the causes of desire. Only when unreal karmic influences have been stopped will you find perfect stillness naturally renewed. Merged with the *dharma* of birthlessness, you realize a spring that has no nightfall. Solitary, you leap beyond heaven and earth, going along with awareness in calm relaxation.

Perfect stillness resonates with things. Perfect constancy realizes innate nature. Constantly resonating, constantly still, there is constant clarity, constant stillness.

Unified stability is realized in perfect constancy; spirit radiance is beyond measure. Illumination extends to the chambers of the Three Poisons, reaching and penetrating the Hall of the Five Luminosities.[62] As the precious moon shines on the dew of emptiness, the clouds of delusion are dispersed and their traces destroyed. The clear wind spreads out as a dispersive cessation; resonating through things, it goes along with their expansions.

When clarity and stillness are like this, you gradually enter the perfect Dao.[63] When you enter the perfect Dao, this is called "realizing the Dao."

Within the vast *kalpa*, you guard perfect completion; there is no obscuration and no illumination. The Valley Spirit constantly abides in silence;[64] **[5b]** the ocean of phenomenal appearances quiets and becomes clear. Rectify your thoughts and orient yourself toward the path to Perfection. Purify your heart-mind and gain access to the road to the Wondrous. Forever separated from the bonds of life and death, throughout the Three Realms you move along with the expanding movements.

Although we call this "realizing the Dao," in truth there is nothing to attain.

Realize silence and put an end to every sound and trace; in deep pervasion, reach the secret depths of principle. Once the serenity of perfect emptiness is attained, the origin of substance and appearance needs no cultivation. Drink and eat according to the established

---

62. Reference to the Hall of the Five Luminosities (*wuming tang*) echoes section 1a of the seventh-century *Shengxuan huming jing* (Scripture on Protecting Life-destiny and Ascending to the Mysterious; DZ 19), an earlier Daoist adaptation of the *Heart Sutra* and precursor to the *Qingjing jing*. In that text, it refers to the Daoist sacred realm of Lingbao tianzun (Celestial Worthy of Numinous Treasure). The Five Luminosities may refer to the five planets associated with the Five Phases and the five yin-organs by extension. With respect to the latter, the location correlates to either the lower or upper elixir field.

63. *Ru zhendao*, which I have translated as "enter the Way of Perfection" in my translation of the *Chongyang lijiao shiwu lun*. See chapter 3.

64. The Valley Spirit (*gushen*) is a Daoist technical term that first appears in chapter 6 of the *Daode jing*: "The Valley Spirit does not die; it is called the Mysterious Female. The gateway to the Mysterious Female is the root of heaven and earth." In Daoist contexts, Valley Spirit frequently designates original spirit (*yuanshen*) housed in the Zuqiao (Ancestral Cavity), the center of the head.

limits; the majestic guidelines allow you to be free. In open clarity, expel discrimination and deliberation; rest in calm stillness and guard what is perfectly complete.

Having the ability to transform all life, this is called "realizing the Dao." As for one who can awaken to this, that one is able to transmit the sacred Dao.

Acting through experiential understanding[65] transforms all existence; forget everything, every type of pursuit. Suddenly you reach the fruit of nondissipation;[66] serenity allows you to gain fundamental freedom. By following and extending calmness, you can act; the currents of karmic cause and effect have already been severed. In the blink of an eye, everything becomes released; the sacred Dao is revealed and transmitted.

[6a] *Lord Lao spoke: The superior adept does not compete; the inferior adept is fond of competing.*[67]

Why doesn't the superior adept compete? Through constant dedication, he maintains a firm aspiration. Perched in Perfection, constantly relaxed and at ease, he nourishes plainness[68] and hides himself in the dark mystery. Looking up, he observes the celestial principles; he fully pervades and penetrates the abyss of the Dao. He sighs deeply that many are not yet enlightened. Quarreling about phenomenal appearances, they obscure the heart-mind's field.

The highest virtue is not virtuous; the lowest virtue clings to virtue.[69] *All clinging and attachments have nothing to do with the Dao and virtue.*

The transforming influence of virtue does not seek reward; grace is vast and naturally tends toward sympathy. Hidden radiance is stored in the great vessel; enlightened nature shines forth steadily. In silent unification, you become elevated and remote; in deep pervasion, you reach the vastness of the Dao. How is this like the attachments of ignorant followers? Making distinctions, they force us to talk about "powers."

Sentient beings do not realize the perfect Dao because they have deviant heart-minds.

Many sentient beings turn their backs to the Dao, contrarily pursuing external things. When chaotic imaginings follow from such modes of being, **[6b]** the perfect numen is obscured and obstructed. The originally manifest is free from deficiency or scarcity—how false is it

---

65. *Weizheng.*

66. *Wulou guo. Wulou,* here translated technically as "nondissipation," literally means "without leakage" or "without outflows." The phrase refers to a condition wherein the adept has sealed himself or herself off from every possible source of dissipation. "Fruit" indicates an accomplishment, the beneficial result of Daoist practice. See *Jinguan yusuo jue,* DZ 1156, 4a, 6ab (trl. Komjathy 2007a).

67. These lines echo chapters 3, 8, 22, 41, 66, 68, 73, and 81 of the *Daode jing.*

68. "Nourish plainness" (*yangsu*) echoes chapter 19 of the *Daode jing*: "Appear plain and embrace simplicity; decrease personal interest and lessen desires."

69. An allusion to chapter 38 of the *Daode jing*: "The highest virtue (*shangde*) is not virtuous; therefore it is virtue. The lowest virtue never loses virtuousness; therefore it lacks virtue." The point is that, from a Daoist perspective, true *de* is beyond external expression or recognition. It involves inner cultivation and attainment.

to force practice and cultivation? Suddenly one brushes away the clouds of delusion, and the silver moon illuminates the Jade Tower.[70]

When the heart-mind is deviant, then spirit becomes startled. When spirit is startled, there is attachment to the ten thousand beings. When there is attachment to the various beings, then coveting and searching are born. When coveting and searching are born, then there are troubles and vexations.

When affairs involve scheming, chaos and error are produced; when perfection becomes perverted, activities agitate spirit. All such heart-minds are engulfed by affections and desires; attached to things, they give rise to greed and anger. Constantly kindling the fire of ignorance,[71] they enhance and increase vexations and defilements. Because of such karmic causes, they receive retribution, sinking ever deeper into the six paths of reincarnation.[72]

Troubles, vexations, deviations, and illusions cause grief and suffering for body and heart-mind. Then one meets with turbidity and defilements,

By foolishly giving rise to anger and desire, greed and ignorance produce karmic veils. Grief and sorrow grow into entanglements and fetters, and vexations hold one tightly bound. Acting like this, people deviate from the perfect Dao.[73] As a consequence, they get nothing but karmic transgressions. [7a] But if one can revert the radiance and turn back luminosity, one will awaken to the mystery within the wondrous.

Currents and waves, life and death. Continually drowning in the ocean of suffering, one is perpetually lost to the perfect Dao.

As karmic patterns of vexations increase thinking, how will one ever awaken the heart-mind? Confused and obscured, one encounters suffering and defilements; disturbed and annoyed, one can only sink and groan. Wasted and dying, there is no rest or cessation; vacant yet alive, the effects reach the present moment. As a result, the perfect Dao is lost, and nothing but dreams and fantasies invade one.

As for the Dao of perfect constancy, one who awakens to it will naturally realize it. Realizing and awakening to the Dao, one will have constancy in clarity and stillness.

If human beings pervade heaven and earth, the qi of the Dao will be completely preserved.[74] Deeply storing the root, one gains a firm support; one lets go of the corporeal soul and

---

70. Jade Tower (*yulou*) may refer to the Seal Hall (*yintang*; "third-eye") or a mystical cranial location.

71. "Ignorance" translates *wuming*, which corresponds to the Buddhist technical term of *avidyā*. It refers to ignorance concerning the true nature of existence, namely, impermanence. In this sense, it is ignorance understood as the state of being unenlightened. See also *Jinguan yusuo jue*, DZ 1156, 1a, 2b, 4b, and 10b (trl. Komjathy 20007a).

72. The "six paths [of reincarnation]" (*liudao*) include god, demigod, human, animal, hungry ghost, and hell-dweller.

73. Or "perfect path" or "path to Perfection."

74. "Qi of the Dao" (*daoqi*) is the numinous presence or sacred manifestation of the Dao. From a Daoist perspective, *daoqi* stands in contrast to ordinary qi and has a very specific quality, which is developed through Daoist practice and mystical realization. This view continues to be maintained in contemporary Quanzhen as expressed in the liturgical text of the *Xuanmen gongke*.

calms the ethereal soul. To attain awakening to the path of long life, one must open the gate of eternal perception. Find complete perfection and let spirit transform naturally; this superior method allows the ruler to be venerated.[75]

Commentary on the *Yinfu jing*[76]

Liu Chuxuan, Master Changsheng

Preface by Fan Yi

The *Yinfu zhenjing* (Perfect Scripture on the Hidden Talisman) consists of a little over three hundred characters. Its language is simple, and its meaning is elevated. Its writing is profound, and its issues are clearly elucidated. Considering the pivot of heaven and earth and of life and death, the principle of creative transformation of yin and yang, as well as subtle application and perfect accomplishment, each is contained in its pages.

In the past, Xuanyuan, the famed Huangdi (Yellow Thearch),[77] in leisure from the myriad obligations, abiding in deep silence, and wandering through the Void, obtained this perfect scripture. Later, he went to the Kongtong mountains to ask Tianzhen huangren (Sovereign Lord of Celestial Perfection) and Master Guangcheng (Expansive Completion) about it. Receiving their perfect assistance, he diligently practiced it. One day, he mounted a fiery dragon at Dinghu (Tripod Lake) and ascended to heaven.[78] These writings were accordingly transmitted to the world.

With their help, later adepts, who are cultivating immortality and longing for the Dao, can silently recognize the mysterious pivot and profoundly advance through the various doorways and boundaries. Time and again, adepts gain elevated attainments and have far-reaching results. They traverse the [divine] realms and ascend to the Void. By practicing nonaction, they are free from excess and multiplicity.

Over a period of several thousand years, not more than one or two people have written commentaries or explanations that are clearly worded. The majority are overly wordy and contain false discussions. They are filled with odd influences and crooked explanations. So, the perfect source has produced no dew. This situation has caused students to become imperiled among manifold

---

75. Here "ruler" (*wang*; lit., "king") refers to spirit, which is associated with the heart and considered the ruler of the body.

76. *Huangdi yinfu jing zhu*, DZ 122.

77. Huangdi, the Yellow Thearch / Yellow Emperor, is a legendary, prehistoric ruler of ancient China. He is most often associated with the creation of Chinese culture and civilization in general. In later Chinese and Daoist history, he has a variety of other associations, including longevity techniques and alchemical practices. He also becomes a member of the Daoist pantheon and thus has the ability to bestow revelations. His "biography" appears in chapter 1 of the Early Han (206 BCE–8 CE) *Shiji* (Records of the Historian), where he is identified as Gongsun Xuanyuan and said to have ruled from 2,497–2,398 BCE. Huangdi of course also occupies a major position in the *Huangdi neijing* (Yellow Thearch's Inner Classics) family of texts. See Unschuld 2003; Komjathy 2008a, Handbook 3.

78. This account incorporates details from chapter 11 of the *Zhuangzi*, wherein Huangdi meets Master Guangcheng in the Kongtong mountains (near present-day Pingjing, Gansu) (see Watson 1968, 118–20). See also the entry on Guangchengzi in the *Shenxian zhuan*; Campany 2002, 159–61. Interestingly, the same story is referenced in Eihei Dōgen's (1200–1253) "Mountains and Rivers Sūtra" (see Tanahashi 1985, 106).

precipices, reaching old age while laboring without accomplishment. The more they investigate the scripture, the more confused they become. Abandoning their quest halfway and unable to sort its threads, they point at this immortal scripture as empty words. This is deeply regrettable.

Fortunately, [in his commentary] Perfected Liu Changsheng of the divine mountains teaches the divine law and directs our abilities. With his expansive aptitude and learning, he connects old and new. His heart-mind wanders among the Dao and virtue. Thus, with broad-minded thinking he investigates what is essential, searching out the mysterious and making inquiries into the hidden. He puts it all into a clear commentary and explanation. Providing simple understanding, he makes it easy to know and easy to practice.[79] It is thus beneficial for all later generations. It truly can be called an application of the heart-mind that is full of compassion and kindness for others.

As we guarded perfect life-destiny together in Jinan [Shandong], I am happy to write this preface for him. I hope that it will be distributed broadly throughout the four directions and that it will become a guide for students. As students carefully read and reflect upon these writings, they can overcome doubt and resolve confusion. Becoming free from mundane entanglements, they will find direct principles and perfect explorations. They may remain carefree in the realm of chaotic vastness.

Written on the sixteenth day of the second month, xinhai year of the Mingchang reign period [1191] by Fan Yi, school superintendent of Ninghai

Upper Section: Extensive Way of Spirit Immortality and Embracing the One[80]

Observe the Way of Heaven,[81] attend to the activities of heaven,[82] and that is all.

"Observation"[83] refers to the five kinds of vision being completely illuminated.[84] They are celestial vision, wisdom vision, dharma vision, Dao vision, and spirit vision. When the

---

79. This is an allusion to chapter 70 of the *Daode jing*: "My words are easy to know and easy to practice, but no one in the world knows or practices them."

80. The Daoist classical location for "embracing the One" (*baoyi*) is chapter 10 of the *Daode jing*. See also chapters 16, 19, 22, 28, 32, 42, 52 of the *Daode jing* and chapters 9, 17, 19, and 24 of the "Neiye" (Inward Training) chapter of the *Guanzi* (trl. Roth 1999). For a general discussion of "guarding the One" (*shouyi*) as a technical term for Daoist meditation see Kohn 1989.

81. In terms of the "Way of Heaven," it is interesting that chapter 13 of the *Zhuangzi* is titled "Tiandao." See also chapters 9, 47, 73, 77, 79, and 81 of the *Daode jing*.

82. An alternative translation for *tianxing*, here rendered as "activities of heaven," would be "celestial phases." The latter refers to the Five Phases (*wuxing*) of traditional Chinese cosmology. In either case, this section advocates following the cosmological cycles and seasonal changes.

83. "Observation" translates *guan*, which is often used in a Daoist technical sense related to Buddhist insight or mindfulness meditation (Pali: *vipassanā*; Skt.: *vipaśyanā*). See Kohn 1989.

84. "Five kinds of vision" (Chin.: *wuyan*; Skt.: *pañca cakṣūmsi*; lit., "five eyes") is a Buddhist technical term that usually refers to the following: (1) The vision of those who have a material body (human), (2) The vision of celestial beings in the world of form (*deva*), (3) The vision of wisdom by which Theravada adherents observe the thought of impermanence or emptiness (Theravada), (4) The vision of *dharma* by which bodhisattvas perceive all teachings in order to lead all beings to enlightenment (Mahayana), and (5) Buddha-vision or omniscience. See Soothill and Hodous 1995 (1937), 123; Ding 1939, 554; Xingyun 1989, 1151. For a Quanzhen source, see *Jinguan yusuo jue*, DZ 1156, 4a (trl. Komjathy 2007a).

five radiances are luminous and penetrating,[85] the five aggregates return to emptiness.[86] One perceives the Way of Heaven. Within heaven, there is yet another heaven beyond the heavens; it resides above the earth. It is the heaven of pure qi, extending to a height of eighty-four thousand miles. This is elevated heaven. Every human body receives the unified qi of heaven; this qi may be abundant or deficient. When infused and harmonious, it brings forth worthies and sages. When rebellious and dispersed, it sinks to create the lowly and ghosts.

"The Dao" refers to that which is beyond heaven, earth, and the ten thousand things; it is the embodiment of empty Nonbeing. **[1b]** In the human body, you can catch a glimpse of its various appearances by means of an empty heart-mind. Then you may attain the state where innate nature and the Dao merge together.

"Attending" refers to guarding perfection and not being false, awakening to alignment and not being deviant.

"Heaven" refers to the heaven that produces the ten thousand things. Heaven produces the ten thousand things; it produces and completes them without restraining or taking hold of them.[87] It also supports the myriad peoples of the ten directions[88] and Three Realms without expecting recognition or recompense. It only wants every sentient being to completely realize the principles of the Way of Heaven and become enlightened. It wants human beings among the myriad affairs to be free of both aversion and attachment, like the evenness of heaven. Humans have emotions, but if they can awaken to the emotionlessness of heaven,[89] they will receive the grace of heaven.[90] If they do not follow the principles of heaven, they will become confused, turbid, perverse, deviant, and vulgar. Various diseases will befall them, and they will die before fulfilling their natural life span. They will sink into the Earth Prisons. After suffering reaches its limits, they will fall into lower forms of life and lose this human body.

However, if you follow the Way of Heaven and are constant in your virtuousness, then qi will be harmonious. If you are constantly clear, you will illuminate innate nature. If you

---

85. Reference to the "five radiances" (*wuguang*) is somewhat idiosyncratic. Based on the present context, it may refer to the activation of the five types of vision. However, other associations are possible, including the spirits of the five yin-organs or the five primary planets.

86. The five aggregates (Skt.: *skandha*) derive from Buddhism and refer to form, sensation, perception, psychic dispositions, and consciousness. They relate to the three characteristics of existence, namely, suffering, impermanence, and "no-self" (Pali: *anatta*; Skt.: *anatman*). In keeping with a foundational Buddhist worldview, careful investigation of one's "self" reveals that it is an illusion. Each aggregate is, in turn, impermanent, and the notion of a separate self (including "soul" or egoistic identity) is one of the primary sources of suffering.

87. This line echoes chapters 10 and 51 of the *Daode jing*.

88. The "ten directions" (*shifang*) refer to the four cardinal directions, the four intermediate directions, as well as up and down.

89. An allusion to chapter 5 of the *Daode jing*: "Heaven and earth are not humane (*ren*); they regard the ten thousand things as straw dogs. The sage is not humane; he regards the people as straw dogs." In the *Changsheng yulu* (DZ 1058, 26b–27a), Liu discusses "emotions" (*qing*), which appears with the paired term "thinghood" (*xing*). According to Liu, "Emotionality is distortion (*qu*; lit., 'crooked'). One's Dao-nature (*daoxing*) is emotionless, but the self (*shen*) seems to have emotions. If you regulate this, your Dao-nature will have emotions, but it will seem as though the self is emotionless" (26b). Liu goes on to explain how freedom from excessive and inappropriate emotionality leads to a state of nondissipation (*wulou*), of energetic and spiritual integrity.

constantly forget emotions, you will protect life-destiny. If you are constantly without flaws, you will understand the Dao. **[2a]** If you constantly refrain from offending the celestial order, you will be free of transgressions. Do not cultivate worldly rewards, but embrace the Dao and complete its perfect rewards. Then you will not be obstructed by side gates and lesser methods.[91] You must immediately understand nonaction and the myriad *dharmas*. In this way, the Three Realms will no longer constrain you.

Heaven has Five Thieves; one who perceives this prospers.[92]

With respect to "heaven having Five Thieves," heaven does not have [actual] thieves. This line does not refer to the thieves and bandits of the world; it also is not about the Six Thieves of human life. But what then are these thieves?

Heaven has the aligned qi of the five directions. Within the human body this is the mother of spirit.[93] Within the twelve time periods of the Celestial Cycle,[94] it is naturally extracted and added[95] throughout the circulating and revolving. In its utmost subtlety, which is inexhaustible, we refer to it as "Nonbeing." Its center contains heaven and earth, which send forth yin and yang. Their flourishing qi produces the myriad things.

Human beings eat the five grains to nourish their form. If they consist of unclean dregs, humans will sink into water and fire. When the essences of the five grains are stored inside the human body, they are protected and become life-destiny. **[2b]** When life-destiny obtains innate nature, one can live for a long time; when innate nature obtains life-destiny, one has extended longevity. Life-destiny is the black tortoise of the northern ocean.[96] If Elder Ding[97] constantly protects it, one will complete form.

The "Five Thieves" relate to perfect yang. When the perfect yang of heaven beholds perfect yin, the Five Thieves steal the treasure from the northern ocean. One who treasures it will prosper; it is as though the myriad beings have been stolen from humans.

---

90. Here I have chosen the problematic term "grace" to translate *en*, which can mean "benefit" or "blessing." "Grace" gives the sense that some divine or sacred process is involved, including an inward sense of support and energetic aliveness that transcends the boundaries of separate identity. See also section 15a later.

91. Doctrinally speaking, "side gates" (*bangmen*) refers to minor schools, specifically those characterized by dubious views. See also section 7b.

92. The Five Thieves usually refer to the five senses and the corresponding dissipation related to the five yin-organs. According to *Yinfu jing zhu* (Commentary on the *Yinfu jing*; DZ 121) by Tang Chun (eleventh c. CE?), which was recommended by Ma Danyang (DZ 1057, 20b), "The five thieves of heaven are [the Five Phases] of Wood, Water, Metal, Earth, and Fire" (1.3b).

93. For parallel passages see *Cunshen lianqi ming*, DZ 834, 1a; *Yinfu jing zhu*, DZ 121, 1.1b; *Jin zhenren yulu*, DZ 1056, 2a; *Quanzhen ji*, DZ 1153, 10.20b.

94. The "twelve periods of the Celestial Cycle" refer to the twelve double-hours, associated with the twelve terrestrial-branches. In internal alchemy, they are sometimes used to map out divisions of the Celestial Cycle (Microcosmic Orbit), that is, locations along the Governing and Conception vessels.

95. "Extracted and added" translates *choutian*, which often appear in *neidan* literature as "extracting lead" (*chouqian*) and "adding mercury" (*tianhong*). See my translation of the *Dadan zhizhi* in chapter 4.

96. Associated with the Water phase, the kidneys, and vital essence.

97. *Dingweng* ("Elder Ding") is an alternate version of *dinggong*. In internal alchemy practice, it frequently refers to the "firing times" (*huohou*). Ding is also the fourth celestial-stem and corresponds to the Fire phase. In the present context, Elder Ding would thus refer to consciousness and spirit.

The Five Thieves are in the heart-mind. They extend to and even affect heaven. The canopy of space and time is in your hands. Myriad transformations arise from your body.

"The Five Thieves residing in the heart-mind" relates to the Five Phases being inverted.[98] If they are in the heart-mind, the perfect water will ascend. If they are rebellious,[99] the cavities[100] of the heart-mind will not be pervaded.[101] Then the water of the kidneys moves downward; this is the road to death. People of the mundane world do not comprehend the way of the sages. Ordinary human beings who do not follow the Dao are all like this. Those who awoke to the Dao in ancient times, adepts with rare fluency, were extraordinarily different. However, people of the mundane world are attached to what they see, [3a] making distinctions between high and low.

But what is aligned can appear deviant, and what is deviant often detracts from the aligned.[102] When I contemplate deviant methods and teachings, it is like the luminescence of fireflies. But the correct Dao resembles the radiance of the sun and moon. Even when the night is dark, its subtle radiance is still present. When one focuses on the radiance of the sun and moon illuminating the ten directions and Three Realms, how can one pay attention to the luminescence of fireflies?

When sages attend to and take hold of the cosmos, yin and yang transform and become pervaded. Earth and heaven unite as the Tai-peace ䷊ hexagram.[103]

The "myriad transformations arising from your body" refers to the myriad transformations completing one's form. Among the myriad beings, human beings are the most venerable and the most precious. Take hold of the transformative process, and internally cultivate the body-beyond-the-body.[104] This is called "attaining the Dao." Pervade the myriad transformations, and externally assist beings by having compassion for sentient life. Awaken them from the worldly dreams and deceptions of the gold cangue, jade fetters, stone sparks, and wind-blown lamps.[105] Keep turbidity and perversion at a distance, and draw close to clarity and virtue.

---

98. "Inversion" (*diandao*) is a *neidan* term related to alchemical transformation. See my translation of the *Dadan zhizhi* in chapter 4. On the most basic level, it involves a movement back to primordial undifferentiation, from a Later Heaven (*houtian*) condition to a Prior Heaven (*xiantian*) condition.

99. "Rebellious" translates *ni*, which literally means "to go against." In the case of qi circulation, it usually indicates a disruptive or harmful pattern (cf. *zheng*). At times, *ni* may have a positive connotation and mean "to flow in reverse," as in the case of vital essence being stored and directed upward. However, in the present context *ni* has negative connotations. Cf. Acker 2006, 82, n. 28.

100. "Cavities" renders *qiao*, which means "openings" or "holes." In Daoism, it has the technical sense of the Seven Cavities and Nine Cavities. See appendix 1, Quanzhen Technical Glossary.

101. "Pervasion" translates *tong*, which may also be understood as connectedness or thoroughness. In a Quanzhen context, it relates to "spirit pervasion" (*shentong*). See sections 6ab and 11ab.

102. "Deviant" translates *xie*, while "aligned" renders *zheng*.

103. Hexagram 11 (Tai) of the *Yijing*, comprised of three yin-lines above three yang-lines. It symbolizes the equilibrium of yin and yang, with yang in ascendancy.

104. Body-beyond-the-body (*shenwai shen*) refers to the yang-spirit formed through alchemical practice and transformation. See chapter 4.

105. Deriving from Buddhism, these are symbolic references for the mundane world and phenomenal appearances, which are some of the sources of human suffering. In Quanzhen, the "gold cangue" (*jinjia*) and "jade fetters" (*yuniu*) are used to identify one's spouse and family as well as the corresponding emotional attachments. For example, in the *Xianle ji*, Liu Changsheng explains, "Women and children are the gold cangue; sentiments of love are the jade fetters" (DZ 1141, 4.12b). See Goossaert 2001, 124.

Externally resonate with the Way of Humanity; internally follow the perfect guidance of the Great High [Lord Lao] and the Patriarch-Buddha. The myriad *dharmas* will return to unity.[106] One may be in the midst of the chaotic world, but innate nature is like a lotus flower emerging from water. **[3b]** We refer to this as "completing inner power."[107] Once this is accomplished, you reside among the immortals and gain luminous penetration of the myriad transformations.

The innate nature of heaven is humanity. The human heart-mind is the pivot.[108] *Establishing the Way of Heaven enables the stabilization of humanity.*

The celestial nature of every human being has [the capacity to be] good or perverse,[109] great or petty. It longs for cultural refinement over military activity, for the Dao over ordinariness, for dignity over debasement, for loftiness over lowliness.[110] From ancient times to the present, the innate nature of human beings [has sought] to cast forth the [immortal] embryo and exchange the husk, to change the bones and transform form.[111] Like ants going out on their circuit, it has not ceased even for a moment.

The pivot of every human heart-mind daily and constantly goes through myriad transformations. [There are moments of] ingenuity and awkwardness, alignment and perversion, as well as profundity and shallowness. [There are moments of] kindness and cruelty, loyalty and contrariness, broad-mindedness and narrow-mindedness, greatness and smallness, clarity and turbidity, worthiness and rudeness, love and hate, as well as correctness and falsity.[112] If you examine this pivot of the heart-mind, you will know the innate nature of humans.

With respect to "establishing the Way of Heaven," those who are ignorant[113] about this way do not know that the grace of heaven is extensive. Spring is warm, and summer is hot; autumn is cool, and winter is cold. In each of these four seasons, there is a transformative influence. It produces and completes the myriad beings. Its assistance extends to the human world.

---

106. Here *dharmas* (Chin.: *fa*) refer to phenomenal appearances.

107. See also section 5ab of Liu Tongwei's commentary on the *Qingjing jing* translated earlier.

108. *Ji*, here rendered as "pivot," technically refers to a trigger. Liu Changsheng provides the following explanation in his *Changsheng yulu*: "The pivot is wisdom (*hui*). If people who lack the Dao employ wisdom, then they injure others to create ease for themselves. We refer to this as 'thievery.' If people who have the Dao employ wisdom, then they injure themselves to create ease for others. We refer to this as 'auspicious'" (DZ 1058, 27b).

109. As presented in the *Changsheng yulu*, "Goodness (*shan*) refers to the square becoming rounded and the crooked becoming straight. One responds to things and accords with people. Not giving rise to the myriad perversions is called true goodness" (DZ 1058, 2b). And, "Perversity (*e*) refers to human beings who are degenerate. Such people do not accord with heaven, and heaven does not accord with such people" (ibid., 2b–3a).

110. All of these terms appear as entries in the *Changsheng yulu* (DZ 1058).

111. These phrases usually refer to alchemical transformation, in which they of course have a positive connotation. It is also possible to read them negatively; in that case, the phrases would refer to the cycle of reincarnation. The initial reference to "innate nature" supports the former interpretation, while the subsequent reference to "ants on their circuit" supports the latter reading. For insights into the alchemical practice see my translation of the *Dadan zhizhi* in chapter 4.

112. Most of these terms appear as entries in the *Changsheng yulu* (DZ 1058).

113. See section 15b below where the *Yinfu jing* discusses the qualities of ignorant people.

The wealthy have fine clothes and excellent food; [4a] the impoverished have coarse food and tattered garments.[114] Each is so according to what suits him. The Dao produces beings and things. Its simplicity breaks apart in order to become these vessels.[115] It adorns the human realm like flower blossoms and fine tapestries. Everyone delights in its beauty.

In terms of "The Way of Heaven enabling the stabilization of humanity," the worthy[116] understand the principles of the Way of Heaven and secretly practice this way. They do not speak about it, but they are adept [at practicing it].[117] They resonate with steady inner power, but they do not let people know. They extend their blessings, but they do not expect compensation. If people can accord with this and practice the Way of Heaven, then their inner power, through stabilization, will assist human beings. They should inwardly cherish the wisdom that pervades [the universe].

Human beings long for all of the myriad transformations to become illuminated, and all of the myriad *dharmas* to be pervaded. They long for all of the myriad beings to be free from self-interest, and for all of the myriad defilements not to infect them. With innate nature pervaded by life-destiny, life-destiny becomes pervaded by heaven. With heaven pervaded by the Dao, the Dao becomes pervaded by its own suchness. Internally complete the Dao and externally complete inner power. This is called "worthiness" and "sageness."

When heaven manifests killing power, [it moves the stars and shifts the constellations. When earth manifests killing power,] dragons and snakes emerge from the ground.[118] *When humans manifest killing power, heaven and earth are overturned.*

[4b] "Heaven manifesting killing power" refers to the fact that when heat reaches its limit, it transforms into cold. Cold transforms to become the winds of Metal.[119] Metal transforms into the qi of the north.[120] Then the various plants and trees wither and decay. Dragons curl up in the expansive ocean, while snakes hibernate in deep holes. At winter solstice,

---

114. The early Quanzhen adepts generally emphasized the ideal of voluntary poverty, which often included begging. As expressed in the *Changsheng yulu*, "Considering the accomplished in ancient times who wanted to distance themselves from the dreams and mirages of the world, in outer appearance they looked like fools. The Ruist [Confucian] Yan Hui [embraced] pure poverty and [only owned] a rice bowl and drinking gourd. The Buddhist Śākyamuni begged for food and gathered one bowl from seven households. The Daoist Lü Chunyang [Lü Dongbin] practiced nonaction. He lived like a quail and ate like a fledgling" (DZ 1058, 3b). Similarly, a discourse record associated with Liu attributes the following statement to him: "The Great High [Lord Lao] said, 'If you can beg for food, you are my disciple.' There is benefit in begging" (*Zhenxian yulu*, DZ 1256, 1.10a). See also *Danyang yulu*, DZ 1057, 10b–11a. On "pure poverty" in early Quanzhen see Eskildsen 2004, 40–41.

115. An allusion to chapter 28 of the *Daode jing*. See also chaps. 15, 19, 32, 37, and 57. *Pu*, "simplicity" or the "uncarved block" (D. C. Lau), refers to the Dao's primordial undifferentiation and original purity as well as to the Daoist adept's innate nature, which is a manifestation of the Dao.

116. Here the understanding and practice of the "worthy" (*xianzhe*) stands in contrast to the previous commentary on the unknowing of the "ignorant" (*yuzhe*).

117. An allusion to chapters 56 and 70 of the *Daode jing*.

118. Liu Changsheng's version of the *Yinfu jing* conflates the first and second line of the received text.

119. This refers to the Metal phase, which is associated with autumn and west in Chinese correlative cosmology.

120. "Qi of the north" translates *shuoqi*, with *shuo* sometimes used to designate the new moon or the first lunar month. In the present context, the meaning of *shuo* makes sense because Metal produces Water in the production cycle.

a single yang is born;[121] it gradually gives rise to a harmonizing qi. When it reaches the vernal equinox, the myriad things produce sprouts. Dragons and snakes then emerge from their hibernation in the ground.

"Humans manifesting killing power" refers to human nature having the numinous radiance of pure yang. Every human heart-mind has a place that loves and desires the myriad things of the world. This is the residence of the fire of craving. Through affectionate love and the Seven Emotions, it contends for reputation and wrangles over personal profit. Such a heart-mind is deluded by alcohol, sex, wealth, and anger,[122] and covers itself over with every kind of pleasure and selfish love. There is no way to fulfill its demands. Thought after thought, in desire and emotionality, one becomes associated with yin qualities.

When innate nature manifests as yin, in the lower [regions] the gold tortoise in the Ocean of the Kidneys dissipates. In the upper [regions], the jade mercury of the Storied Tower disperses. The ethereal soul becomes confused, and the corporeal soul scatters.[123] Perfect innate nature no longer has a ruler. Yin prospers on the outside, while yang diminishes on the inside. One follows things in their dying and sinks down to the realm of ghosts.

[5a] If human beings can suddenly illuminate the utmost Dao, they may completely realize and discern the being of myriad things. We refer to this as "yang killing yin." Innate nature becomes like a luminous moon, while the heart-mind is clear like heaven. There are no clouds for ten thousand miles. The radiance manifests naturally, majestically extending through the myriad appearances.

"Humans manifesting killing power" refers to completely expelling the various yin elements. Naturally, the ethereal soul becomes clear and the corporeal soul becomes still. Yin and yang are inverted.

"Heaven and earth being overturned" refers to production and completion in the transformative process. When the three elixirs coalesce,[124] you may leave behind the covering of heaven and earth. Casting off form, you will manifest the perfected body-beyond-the-body.

---

121. Winter solstice is the apex of yin, after which yang begins to grow. Summer solstice is the apex of yang, after which yin begins to grow. As expressed by Liu Changsheng in the *Changsheng yulu*, "On the summer solstice, yin is born. On the winter solstice, yang is born" (DZ 1058, 4a).

122. The Four Hindrances (*sihai*) of early Quanzhen. See my translation of Wang Chongyang's poems in chapter 1. For a discussion see Komjathy 2007a, 98–113.

123. "Ethereal soul" translates *hun*, which also appears in Western literature as "cloud soul"; "corporeal soul" translates *po*, which also appears in Western literature as "white soul." On the most basic level, the ethereal soul is yang and associated with the liver and spiritual faculties; the corporeal soul is yin and associated with the lungs and emotionality. From a traditional Chinese perspective, after death, the *hun* ascends to the heavens, may become an ancestor, and eventually dissipates into the cosmos; the *po* descends into the earth, may become a ghost, and eventually decomposes with the flesh and bones. In Daoism, these sometimes appear as the Three Hun and Seven Po. See, e.g., the ninth-century *Chu sanshi jiuchong jing* (Scripture on Expelling the Three Death-bringers and Nine Worms; DZ 871).

124. The three elixirs (*sandan*) are most likely synonymous with the Three Treasures (*sanbao*), namely, vital essence, qi, and spirit.

When heaven and humanity join and manifest, the ten thousand transformations have a stable base.

"Heaven and humanity" refers to human nature being pervaded by heaven. If heaven and humanity join and manifest, then the heart-mind is completed through thinghood. When people completely comprehend the worldly dream of the human realm, they may understand the enduring concerns of flourishing and decay, esteem and disgrace, development and ruin, calamity and prosperity, despair and joy, life and death, as well as past and present.[125] When humans fully penetrate the celestial principles, they will have true flourishing and be free of decay. They will have true esteem and be free of disgrace. They will have true development and be free from ruin. **[5b]** They will have true prosperity and be free from calamity. They will enjoy true joyfulness and be free from despair. They will have true life and be free from death. They will understand the constancy of the Dao.[126]

With the constancy of the Dao, one pervades the myriad transformations and stabilizes the foundation of innate nature. Utmost innate nature pervades the boundaries. There is no thinghood among the myriad transformations, and one naturally attains myriad pervasions. It is like the highest goodness,[127] wherein the square is rounded and the crooked is straightened.[128] The myriad tributaries are clear and connected through the Jiang, He [Huang], Huai, and Ji rivers.[129] When they enter the great ocean, they become mixed together and completed, returning to oneness. We refer to this as "deep pervasion."

There are ingenious and dull natures—they can be subdued and concealed.[130]

Considering human beings who awoke to the Dao in ancient times, their inner natures were virtuous and ingenious. They employed skillful means[131] out of compassion for human beings. Externally, they seemed perverse and dull. In this way, they could be subdued and concealed. Internally, their radiance was hidden and unmanifest. As Heshang gong (Master

---

125. Many of these terms appear as entries in the *Changsheng yulu* (DZ 1058).

126. With respect to the "constancy of the Dao" (*daochang*), the *Changsheng yulu* contains entries on "Dao" and "constancy." Of particular note, Liu Changsheng explains, "Constancy refers to the Dao. If one constantly accords with the Dao, one rescues the numinous from the human. If one constantly accords with qi, one rescues form from thinghood" (11b–12a). The term's association with the Dao of course alludes to chapter 1 of the *Daode jing*: "The Dao that can be spoken is not the constant Dao." See also chapters 16, 28, 32, 37, and 55.

127. An allusion to chapter 8 of the *Daode jing*: "The highest goodness is like water. Water is good at benefiting the ten thousand beings because it has no need to compete with them. It resides in the places that people avoid. Therefore, it is close to the Dao."

128. This description parallels the entry on "goodness" (*shan*) in the *Changsheng yulu* cited earlier.

129. Here the names of these various Chinese rivers most likely refer to vital fluids in the body.

130. The *Changsheng yulu* contains entries on "ingenious" (*qiao*) and "dull" (*zhuo*) (DZ 1058, 19b–20b), but they are interpreted in a manner diametrically opposed to the one presented here.

131. "Skillful means" translates *fangbian* (Skt.: *upaya*), which is a Buddhist technical term. It refers to a method wherein teachings are adapted to the cognitive abilities and soteriological requirements of the listener.

Dwelling-by-the-River) said, "It is like beautiful jade contained in stone, and like a luminous pearl held in an oyster."[132]

Considering differences among animals, there are ingenious parrots with the ability to speak, but iron cages restrain and imprison them. There are dull pigeons that only coo, but they roost among myriad tree branches. **[6a]** Therefore, in the mundane world false ingenuity produces many calamities, while true dullness produces clear blessings.

Thus, heaven does not speak,[133] and it is naturally transformative and pervasive. Heaven is without feelings, and it naturally does not age. If humans want to understand the Way of Heaven, they should forget language and then thoroughly investigate the subtlety of the transformative process. They should forget emotionality, and understand the demeanor of antiquity. Considering what humans desire, if there is too much ingenuity, there will also be many errors. If there are many emotions, there will also be many difficulties. Forget the world and sever your ties to emotionality. Embrace the essentials of enjoying the Dao and protecting life-destiny.

The aberrations of the Nine Cavities are in the Three Essentials; they can be aroused or stilled.

The "Nine Cavities" refer to the yang pathways of the nine pervasions. The reason why they are not yet connected is because of the aberrant hindrances of the nine yin [influences]. The square inch of the heart-mind is empty. Inside [this emptiness] there is numinous luminosity. The heart-mind of a superior person has nine cavities. That of an average person has seven. That of an inferior person has five. If a person's heart-mind has no cavities, we refer to them as ignorant. **[6b]** Aberrant yin [influences] produce turbidity in one's innate nature. However, when the splendor of yang descends, spirit becomes clear.

With respect to "in the Three Essentials," the radiance of heaven includes the sun, moon, and stars; the treasures of the earth include gold, jade, and gems; and the pervasions of the Dao include lead, mercury, and perfection.

In terms of "being aroused or stilled," when heaven is active, the Three Radiances become luminous; when the earth is still, the Three Treasures are connected; when the Wondrous is illuminated, the Three Numinosities coalesce.

"Arousal," or "movement," refers to movement in forms.

"Stillness" refers to stillness in innate nature.

Consider the worthies and recluses of antiquity. When mixed up with the mundane world, they maintained an unagitated heart-mind. When residing in the mountains, they

---

132. The *Laozi zhangju* (Chapter-and-Verse Commentary on the *Laozi*; a.k.a. *Daode zhenjing zhu* [Commentary on the Perfect Scripture on the Dao and Inner Power]; DZ 682). Cf. *Danyang yulu*, DZ 1057, 10a; translated earlier. The quotation parallels Heshang gong's commentary on line 1 of chapter 1 of the *Daode jing* (DZ 682, 1.1a).

133. In the entry on "activity" (*xing*) in the *Changsheng yulu*, Liu comments, "Activity refers to the Great High [Lord Lao] acting through the Way of Heaven. Heaven and earth do not speak, but they secretly bestow grace to bring forth the myriad beings. The Great High does not speak, but he secretly bestows his virtue to bring about myriad benefits. Heaven and earth do not speak, but grace and goodness respond to each other" (DZ 1058, 29b).

did not display stillness through their form. When you illuminate being, you find stillness within the movement of being. When you pervade Nonbeing, you find a rumbling within the stillness of Nonbeing. If both movement and stillness are forgotten, you realize the constant subtlety of the Dao.[134]

When fire arises in wood, calamity manifests with certain destruction. When treachery arises in the country, time moves with certain destruction. Those who know this practice cultivation and refinement; we call such people sages.

Fire gives rise to the human heart-mind. Each day it is a constant presence wherever one goes. If you do not allow the perversions of myriad changes in Wood to occur, [7a] then you [will discover] innate nature.[135] If one's thinking is not illuminated, then there is Fire that destroys the innate nature of Wood.

Considering "calamities manifesting with certain destruction," when one abandons the auspicious, misfortune occurs. When one squanders blessings, calamities occur.

"Destruction" refers to killing perfection.

Concerning "treachery arising in the country," the scripture of the Most High [Lord Lao] says, "One who does not govern the country through knowledge is a blessing for the country. One who does govern the country through knowledge is a thief of the country."[136] When sycophants and deceptive people arise in the country, difficulty befalls the entire people no matter what. When "time moves," there will inevitably be dispersal and destruction. The ignorant are unaware of principle and bring chaos to the world; they invariably meet with the laws of punishment. If you do not govern the country through knowledge, and you govern all-under-heaven without concerns, Great Peace [will arrive] and the people will have peace.

"Those who know this practicing cultivation and refinement" does not refer to refinement by heating the five metals and eight minerals [external alchemy]. Rather, it involves cultivating innate nature and life-destiny so that one may fully penetrate principle and pervade the Mysterious. The Three Teachings refer to this as "awakening to the Dao."[137]

If you can constantly help beings and have compassion for the world, you may know the grace of heaven, which is referred to as "amassing virtue." It is through Huangdi's (Yellow Thearch's) awakening to the Dao that we have the *Yinfu jing* [7b]. During the Zhou dynasty, King Jinlun awakened as the Buddha, and so we have the *Jingang jing* (Diamond

---

134. An allusion to the final lines of chapter 1 of the *Daode jing*.

135. The meaning of these lines is unclear and open to a variety of interpretations. In the system of Five Phase correspondences, Wood is associated with the liver, ethereal soul, humaneness (yang emotion), and anger (yin emotion), while Fire is associated with the heart, spirit, ritual propriety (yang emotion), and hatred (yin). Wood in turn produces Fire, and Fire can overact on Wood. Adding the association of innate nature with Wood in internal alchemy, it seems that Liu is suggesting that innate nature cannot be obscured by ordinary mind, habitual tendencies, and harmful emotionality.

136. An allusion to chapter 65 of the *Daode jing*, although Liu Changsheng reverses the lines of the received text: "One who governs the country through knowledge is a thief of the country; one who does not govern the country through knowledge is a blessing of the country."

137. The Three Teachings (*sanjiao*) are Buddhism, Confucianism, and Daoism.

Sūtra).[138] After he attained Buddhahood, he was called Śākyamuni Buddha. The thirty-two [sections] of the *Jingang jing* discuss the essentials of his teachings. One should abandon egoistic appearance, human appearance, sentient appearance, and abiding appearance.[139] Without these four appearances, the heart-mind becomes elevated and free from the myriad errors. Like a sky without clouds, innate nature resembles the shining moon. Self-manifest and perfectly luminous, this is aligned innate nature.

"Innate nature" is like the root of a tree. The "body" is like the form of human beings. The "myriad methods" are like the branches and leaves of a tree.[140] According to the *Yinfu jing*, the tendencies of the transformative process are like flower blossoms and sprouting seeds.

When worldly people study the Dao, it is said that they are unable to completely pervade its principle.[141] Each one makes distinctions in trying to grasp the root, branches, and leaves, as well as the flower blossoms and sprouting seeds. Each one considers himself right and everyone else wrong. This is because their heart-minds still have not yet abandoned the four appearances. We refer to this as "side gates."

Middle Section: Extensive Method for Enriching the Country and Pacifying the People

[8a] *Heaven gives life; heaven takes life away—this is the principle of the Dao. Heaven and earth steal from the myriad things; the myriad things steal from humanity; humanity steals from the myriad things. When the Three Thieves are correctly ordered, the Three Powers are then at peace.*

"Heaven giving life and heaven taking life away" refers to the fact that in spring it becomes warm with a harmonizing qi. Heaven produces this in the myriad things. At the beginning of autumn, it is deep within metal and the wind moves. The myriad things wither and decay.[142] This is heaven taking away life. Birth and death are the principles of the Dao. Heaven is without emotionality and abides in suchness.

With respect to "heaven and earth stealing from the myriad things," heaven and earth have four seasons; their alterations pervade the transformative process. They produce and

---

138. The *Jingang jing* (Vajracchedikā Sūtra; Diamond Sūtra; T. 235–37, 273, 2734) is part of the Perfection of Wisdom (*prajñā-pāramitā*) family of texts (see Conze 1973; 1975) and related to the seventh-century *Xinjing* (Heart Sūtra; T.250–57) (see Nattier 1992). For a recent translation see Red Pine 2001. The *Diamond Sūtra* is mentioned in the *Quanzhen ji*, DZ 1153, 1.12b, 3.6b; *Ershisi jue*, DZ 1158, 4a.

139. Derived from Buddhism, the "four appearances" (*sixiang*), also translated as "four perceptions," are discussed in chapter 3 of the *Diamond Sutra*.

140. Cf. *Chongyang lijiao shiwu lun*, DZ 1233, 5b.

141. Cf. ibid., 6a.

142. Cf. section 4b.

complete the myriad things. The flourishing qi of heaven and earth as well as yin and yang is stored in the myriad things. The myriad things are what steal this flourishing qi.

Considering "the myriad things stealing from humanity," human beings are what steal the vital essence of the myriad things and snatch the flourishing qi of heaven and earth. This is destroyed by desires and thoughts. But with clarity and stillness protected, you may guard life-destiny.

In terms of "humanity stealing from the myriad things," **[8b]** humans are what desire the variegated appearances of the myriad things. Their eyes observe the five colors; their ears listen to the five sounds; and their tongues taste the five flavors.[143] They become intoxicated and fattened by rank flesh. They lose themselves in perversity, give rise to depravity, and squander their life-destiny. When pleasure reaches its limit, grief appears. [However], if humans abandon the mundane world and awaken, they may become free of emotionality and then external things will no longer be able to steal from them.

As for "the Three Thieves being correctly ordered," that which can steal the infinite, utmost treasure completes form through the transformative process. Even the myriad types of pearls and gems of the mundane world can hardly serve as a reward for such attainment.

Considering "the Three Powers being at peace," one once again accords with the Three Sages,[144] whose teachings are illuminated in the Three Vehicles.[145] One mysteriously awakens to the Three Sovereigns[146] and adeptly circulates the Three Radiances, inverting and extending the Three Carts[147] and tilling and harvesting the Three Fields. Through the Three Fires[148] of the Celestial Cycle, the Three Elixirs coalesce in the furnace. Spirit manifests as the Three Yang, and one ascends to the Three Heavens.[149] One becomes perfected and will not decay; one will live and not be destroyed. Completely fulfilling the Dao through thinghood, the Perfected and the Dao become the same substance. Then there is peace.

---

143. An allusion to chapter 12 of the *Daode jing*.

144. Kongzi (Master Kong; "Confucius"), Laozi, and Śākyamuni Buddha,

145. In Buddhism, the Three Vehicles refer to Theravada, Mahayana, and Vajrayana. Here they are synonymous with the Three Teachings.

146. The Three Sovereigns (Sanhuang), or Three August Ones, refer to the China's mythological emperors of Fu Xi, associated with the invention of writing and fishing; Shennong (Divine Farmer), associated with the invention of agriculture and herbology; and Huangdi (Yellow Emperor), associated with the establishment of Chinese (Han) culture more generally.

147. The Three Carts (*sanche*) represent a Daoist transformation of the Three Carts mentioned in chapter 3 of the *Lotus Sūtra*. They are mentioned in the famous Parable of the Burning House (see Watson 1993, 56–79), and are usually associated with the Three Vehicles of Buddhism, namely, that of the hearer or obedient disciple, that of enlightenment for oneself, and that of the bodhisattva. In internal alchemy practice, the Three Carts most often refer to the passageways through the Three Passes, located approximately at the coccyx, mid-spine, and occiput. They have the following correspondences: (1) Ram Cart, located at Tailbone Gate (*weilü*; GV–1), (2) Deer Cart, located at Narrow Ridge (*jiaji*; GV–6), and (3) Ox Cart, located at Jade Pillow (*yuzhen*; GV–17). See *Jinguan yusuo jue*, DZ 1156, 7b–8a (trl. Komjathy 2007a).

148. The Three Fires (*sanhuo*) are usually identified as the ruler-fire (*zhuhuo*), minister-fire (*chenhuo*), and subject-fire (*minhuo*), which are also rendered as ruling fire, subject fire, and common fire. See *Jinguan yusuo jue*, DZ 1156, 9b (trl. Komjathy 2007a); *Dadan zhizhi*, DZ 244, 1.3b, translated here in chapter 4.

149. The Three Heavens are Yuqing (Jade Clarity; highest), Shangqing (Highest Clarity; middle), and Taiqing (Great Clarity; lowest).

Therefore it is said, "Eat at the appropriate times, and the hundred bones will be regulated. Move in accordance with the pivot, and the myriad transformations will be at peace." **[9a]** *People know the spiritual as spiritual, but they do not know the nonspiritual as spiritual.*

In terms of "eating at the appropriate times," when one is hungry and encounters delicious food, one does not crave it. When one has to eat coarse food, one does not disdain it. Do not kill living beings or eat rank flesh. Such activity truly does not cultivate vegetarian abstinence and pure simplicity.[150]

It is simply this: when you are hungry, do not discuss whether the food is coarse or refined. When you are tired, sleep. When you are unencumbered, sing. When you are joyful, hum. If you want to sit, sit. If you want to sleep, sleep. If you want to stand, stand. If you want to walk, walk.[151] Let go of the Four Elements,[152] be free of constraint, and become independent. Then "the hundred bones will be regulated." When responding to the myriad appearances during the twelve double-hours, you should only want the perfect heart-mind to be constantly deep.

In terms of "movement," do not allow movement to occur in the heart-mind. Internally manifest the precious radiance; respond to the movement of things with form.

With respect to the "pivot," sages, worthies, and superior persons consider it to be wisdom. Generals consider it to be strategy. Common people consider it to be a mechanism. Lesser people consider it to be the husk.

In emptiness, sages are wise concerning the depth of great principle, but people of the mundane world are not capable of completely understanding this principle. **[9b]** [The former] cherish subtle wisdom, and their speech resonates with the constant pivot. They listen to those who are honest, and follow those who are virtuous. They are openly transformed through the myriad pervasions. After sudden awakening, the Dao emerges in serenity and stillness.

"People knowing the spiritual as spiritual"[153] refers to people of the mundane world who only know earthly prayers and yin-spirits as spiritual. They take wooden engravings and clay-fabricated gods as spiritual. Such ignorant people have no understanding. In their everyday activities, they commit their share of transgressions. Heaven then issues their share of calamities. They kill and injure pigs and goats as well as amply burn [paper] money and [paper] horses as their prayers. When they are sick, they seek peace [from the gods]. When they have calamities, they seek good fortune [from the gods].

---

150. This line could be alternatively rendered as "do not tend to vegetarian abstinence and pure simplicity." Under that reading, the adept should remain unconcerned about various dietary prohibitions.

151. Cf. *Quanzhen ji*, DZ 1153, 10.21a; *Danyang yulu*, DZ 1057, 7a, which are translated here in chapter 2.

152. Literally meaning the "four greats" (*sida*), these are the Four Elements of Indian and Buddhist cosmology, namely, earth, water, fire, and wind (or air). For some appearances in early Quanzhen literature see *Jin zhenren yulu*, DZ 1056, 2a; *Ershisi jue*, DZ 1158, 3ab; *Dadan zhizhi*, DZ 244, 2.7a. Cf. chapter 25 of the *Daode jing*, where *sida* refers to the Dao, heaven, earth, and the king.

153. "Spiritual" in the sense of being "of spirit" or divine.

With respect to "not knowing the nonspiritual as spiritual," they do not know that above the heavens each of the superior spirits of yang and the Dao are arrayed in their set positions. They secretly examine the virtuous and perverse among human beings. If people of the mundane world commit virtuous deeds for three years, without interruption for a thousand days, blessings will descend. If worldly people commit perverse deeds for a thousand days, without interruption for three years, calamities will descend.

Worldly people do not know that what is most numinous and most pervaded within the myriad things is their very own self. **[10a]** Original spirit has a radiant luminosity that pervades heaven and penetrates the earth. Worthies and sages of ancient times were those who awakened to Dao and cultivated perfection, abandoned the mundane and entered the sacred.[154]

A Buddha arrived in the Western Paradise twenty-eight generations ago. Before he became a Buddha through practice, he had been every [type] of sentient being. He made the six sense organs clear and pure and the five types of vision perfectly luminous. He annihilated the four appearances. Then he was called "Buddha" (Awakened One).

"Buddhahood" is the innate nature of human beings; "innate nature" refers to spirit. Innate nature *is* spirit; spirit *is* innate nature. These are simply different names. For Buddhists, when innate nature abandons the four appearances, it is called "Buddhahood." For Daoists, when spirit forgets the four appearances, it is called "immortality."

The sun and moon have calculations; large and small have limitations. Sacred accomplishment is born there; spirit illumination emerges there.

"The sun and moon having calculations" refers to the fact that [following] summer solstice the sixty quarter-hours of daylight gradually decrease, and a single yin is born. [Following] winter solstice the forty quarter-hours gradually increase, and a single yang is born. During the double-hour of *mao* [5–7 a.m.], the sun rises in the eastern ocean; during the double-hour of *you* [5–7 p.m.], the sun sets in the western mountains.

According to the *Qingjing jing* (Scripture on Clarity and Stillness), "The great Dao is without feelings. It regulates the course of the sun and moon."[155] **[10b]** Here the "sun" refers to circulating the radiance of wisdom, decreasing and increasing according to the [appropriate] calculations. The "moon" refers to the life-destiny of human beings. At the age of sixteen, boys are complete in the perfect gold of two and eight.[156] If they do not become awakened [to the state of] emotionlessness, they will lose one *liang* [ounce] every three years. When they reach eight and eight,[157] the sixty-four hexagrams are completely exhausted. Then the ocean of the kidneys is desiccated and exhausted.

---

154. On "abandoning the mundane and entering the sacred" as the culmination of alchemical practice see *Dadan zhizhi*, DZ 244, 2.8b–11b, which is translated here in chapter 4.

155. Section 1a of the eighth-century CE *Qingjing jing* (DZ 620).

156. According to classical Chinese medicine, vital essence is full at the age of sixteen for men and fourteen for women. See chapter 1 of the *Huangdi neijing suwen* (Yellow Thearch's Inner Classic: Basic Questions); Komjathy 2008a, Handbook 3.

157. According to classical Chinese medicine, the vital essence of ordinary men is exhausted at the age of sixty-four. See chapter 1 of the *Huangdi neijing suwen*.

If you have too many desires, you will become exhausted before the Wei[ji]-pre-completion ䷿ hexagram[158] and die prematurely. However, if you reduce your desires, you will increase your life span and attain extended longevity. If you wax and wane, you will die. If you become whole, without deficiencies, you will live.

With respect to "large and small having limitations," "large" refers to the Dao. The Dao's greatness embraces and contains heaven and earth. "Small" refers to the imperceptible. We may discuss the subtlety of the imperceptible as what can enter into the smallest spaces. When circulating, heaven and earth cannot limit it. When applied, ghosts and spirits cannot perceive it. Naturally, it becomes concentrated in the square inch.

"Sacred accomplishment being born there" refers to the Way of Heaven. Grace is produced from the greatness of heaven—it assists human beings in nourishing form. Accomplishment is produced from the sacredness of the Dao—it aids human beings in cultivating perfection.

With regard to "spirit illumination emerging there," [11a] spirit, when hidden, wanders through the Three Bureaus;[159] when manifest, it pervades the eight boundaries.

If you steal the pivot [of the universe], nothing under heaven can see you, no one can know you. When superior people attain this, they become stable and discerning. When inferior people attain this, they are irreverent toward life-destiny.

"Stealing the pivot" refers to the pivot of the myriad things. The myriad things are what steal the qi of heaven and earth.

Considering "nothing under heaven being able to see you," grace is produced from the greatness of heaven.

"No one being able to know this" refers to ignorant people who only know how to nourish their own bodies; they do not know that it is heaven that bestows grace and nourishes the various people. In spring there is planting, while in autumn there is harvesting. In summer there is blossoming, while in winter there is storing. These respond to the seasonal changes of frost, snow, rain, and dew. They bring nourishment and flourishing through the myriad transformations. For those who know this celestial grace, their innate natures will be pervasive and their luminosity will be penetrating.

With respect to "superior people attaining this to become stable and discerning," when discernment pervades the Dao, heaven and earth are also pervaded. When heaven and earth are pervaded, the myriad transformations are also pervaded. When the myriad transformations are pervaded, there is spirit pervasion. With spirit pervasion, one may resonate with the pivot through the myriad transformations. Embracing the One without separation,[160] [11b] one may silently nourish perfection and return to simplicity.[161]

---

158. Hexagram 64 (Weiji) of the *Yijing*, which consists of Li-fire ☲ over Kan-water ☵.

159. The Three Bureaus (*sanguan*) refer to heaven, earth, and water (or humanity).

160. An allusion to chapter 10 of the *Daode jing*.

161. An allusion to chapter 28 of the *Daode jing*. See also chapters 16 and 19.

Regarding "lesser people attaining this and being irreverent toward life-destiny," when lesser people attain this, they will insult and deceive heaven and earth. They do not have reverence for the worthies and sages, and they do not honor the laws of the country. Lacking humaneness and righteousness, they empower themselves and weaken others. They bring injury to things and harm human beings. When their transgressions reach the extreme, heaven brings retribution. Superior people respect innate nature, attaining pervasion of worthiness and sagehood. Lesser people are irreverent toward life-destiny, losing [their chance] by descending into nonhuman forms of life.

Lower Section: Extensive Technique for Strengthening the Troops and Preparing for Battle

The blind are adept at hearing; the deaf are adept at seeing. Sever your ties to the single source of selfishness by mobilizing the army ten times. Practice the Three Reversals day and night by mobilizing the army ten thousand times.

With respect to "the blind being adept at hearing," the eyes of human beings are the perceptual windows of the five yin-organs. When penetrated by [external] influences, people gaze at external things. However, just as paper-screens and rustic winds are separated from each other, the blind are unable to see external things. If external appearances do not enter into the center, there is a perfect, clear echo within the Void. **[12a]** One becomes adept at listening to the sound of the soundless.

Considering "the deaf being adept at seeing," if annoyances of the mundane world reach the ears, it is as though one is deaf. When the Dao's intonations[162] reach one's ears, one listens. However, if there is perverse speech, it is as though one is deaf. When one uses correct principles to select what is virtuous, the cavities of the ears become pervaded. Like a chisel penetrating through a wall to the outside, the radiance enters into the center. One perceives the being that lacks thinghood. Then one understands the subtlety of the vague and indistinct.[163]

"Severing ties to the single source of selfishness" refers to forgetting greed and becoming clear and unaffected. Put an end to selfishness and injurious acquisitiveness. There is too much injury and not enough kindness [in the world].

"Mobilizing the army ten times" refers to reaching the silent illumination that has tenfold accomplishment. By giving benefit to beings and caring for humans, one will have tenfold blessings.

In "practicing the Three Reversals day and night," the first reversal involves bestowing benefit from the upper prime: qi descends and becomes clear. The second reversal involves

---

162. "Dao's intonations" translates *daonian*, which might be rendered more conventionally as "thoughts of the Dao." However, *nian* may mean "remember" and "chant." I take the phrase to mean a deeper calling that resonates through the adept's being.

163. "Subtlety of the vague and indistinct" (*huanghu zhi miao*) alludes to a variety of chapters in the *Daode jing*, including chapters 1, 14, and 21.

pardoning transgressions in the middle prime: spirit is rarified and becomes numinous. The third reversal involves releasing distress and having life-destiny pervaded in the lower prime: yin is transformed into yang.

"Mobilizing the army ten thousand times" refers to the prosperity and adversity of worldly people in relation to things and commodities. **[12b]** With these come ten thousand sufferings and a thousand distresses. How much more so for those who are selfish—it is difficult to take hold of a onefold profit.

Awaken to the Dao and cultivate perfection; complete your own innate nature and life-destiny. Attain inexhaustible blessings and longevity. Reside among the precious places of the palaces of the immortals. Receive riches and honors above the heavens. This is ten thousand times better than the fortune and profit that ordinary people seek. You will be able to transform the oceans into mulberry groves and live forever in a country without night. How could such perfect joy only accrue a ten-thousand-fold benefit?

The heart-mind is born from things; the heart-mind dies from things. The pivot [of the heart-mind] is in the eyes.

Considering "the heart-mind being born from things," it manifests in [a realm] beyond thinghood.

Concerning "the heart-mind dying from things," when it dies,[164] it becomes pervaded by numinous things.

The world chases after "life," and innate nature consequently becomes wedded to the road to death. But if one completely penetrates the Dao and guards the [required] dying, spirit wanders along the road of life.[165] The Dao, ordinary life, and the road to death are different and mutually opposed.

With respect to "the pivot residing beyond the eyes,"[166] when the eyes look at things, the heart-mind moves as the pivot. Injury follows selfishness; **[13a]** contention follows greed. When the eye of wisdom perceives numinous things, one illuminates the pivot of heaven. By knowing the essential subtlety of the Dao, one puts an end to things and self. The pivot of ordinariness brings benefit to oneself and injury to others. The pivot of the Dao brings injury to oneself and benefit to others.

---

164. With positive connotations, reference to the "dead heart-mind" (*sixin*) echoes chapter 2 of the *Zhuangzi*, where the Daoist Nanguo Ziqi (Adept Variegated Darkness of South Wall) is described in meditative absorption: "He sat leaning on his armrest, staring up at the sky and breathing—vacant and far away, as though he'd lost his companion. Yancheng Ziyou (Adept Meandering of Completed Complexion), who was standing by his side in attendance, said, 'What is this? Can you really make the body like a withered tree and the mind like dead ashes? The man leaning on the armrest now is not the one who leaned on it before!'" (adapted from Watson 1968, 36).

165. Taking "dying" to be a necessary condition of the heart-mind in relation to excess emotional and intellectual activity. As Ma Danyang explains, "When the heart-mind is stable, emotions are forgotten. When the body is empty, qi circulates. When the heart-mind dies, spirit lives. When yang flourishes, yin dissipates. These are the principles of suchness" (*Danyang yulu*, DZ 1057, 5b; translated here in chapter 2).

166. Liu Changsheng adds *wai* ("beyond") to the line from the *Yinfu jing*.

Heaven is without kindness, but great kindness is born from this. With swift thunder and strong wind, all beings become active.

"Heaven being without kindness" refers to [heaven] extending qi and producing things, but not possessing them.[167]

"Great kindness being born from this" refers to the myriad things growing and developing. If the myriad things did not obtain the qi of heaven and earth, they would not be able to complete form within the transformative process. Thus, kindness is born from the greatness of heaven. It seems as though heaven is without kindness because it does not expect any recompense. [In contrast,] human kindness and assistance look at what others possess, expecting to receive a reward. Celestial kindness and human kindness are different. When "swift thunder" sounds, a pleasant rain descends; heaven and earth produce sprouts. When "strong wind" moves, floating clouds disperse; the sky is clear for ten thousand miles.

"All beings becoming active"[168] refers to becoming active and lodging the numinous, like an egg being warmed and transformed.[169] There is nothing that does not receive the unified qi of heaven when born. **[13b]** How much more is this the case for beings among the myriad things that are free from emotionality?

In utmost joy, innate nature is in balance; in utmost stillness, innate nature is pure.

Constantly enjoy the inexhaustibility of Dao-nature;[170] [constantly] discard the exhaustiveness of the corporeal world. I am free from pleasure, and so I am free from sorrow; ordinary people have likes, and so they have grief. Awakened in serenity and isolation, one attains it through perfect constancy. Deluded by sounds and appearances, one loses it through illusory dreams.

With respect to "in utmost stillness, innate nature being pure," when one attains utmost stillness, one completely exhausts thinghood. Innate nature is pure like a lotus blossom, which does not appear in water. Considering human beings who have completely penetrated the Dao, they may reside among the dust, but they are not tainted. They may abide among the desiring, but they are free of desire. If you polish the precious mirror, where is the obstruction in responding to the shapes and shadows of things?

There is a level where one has not yet penetrated the center or awakened to the luminous radiance of the Dao. If you can realize utmost stillness, casting aside being and dwelling in Nonbeing, weeding out fantasy and illusion and discerning the elevated from lowly, **[14a]** you will thoroughly realize the subtlety of the Dao. Then the world will seem like mere hemp.

---

167. An allusion to chapter 5 of the *Daode jing*.

168. Peter Acker (104, n. 121), modifying Christopher Rand, translates *chunran* as "simplicity." However, Liu Changsheng's commentary glosses this phrase as equivalent to *dong* ("to move").

169. Peter Acker (104, n. 122) takes this phrase to refer to the "four classes of beings" in Buddhism. My reading, in contrast, suggests a Daoist alchemical interpretation. This makes more sense in relation to the emphasis here on "lodging the numinous" (*sheling*).

170. *Daoxing*.

According to the *Daode jing* of the Great High [Lord Lao], "Virtuous speech is not beautiful, and beautiful speech is not virtuous."[171] The correct Dao and true speech are not beautiful. Perverse methods and false transmissions have much beauty. The intelligent in their concern for perceptible things love beauty; in this way they come to manifest perversity. They are not able to comprehend the great Dao.

Heaven is fundamentally private, but its application is ultimately open to all.

Heaven bestows its grace without allowing those below to know. This is "utmost privacy." Its production and development assists the human world. This is "utmost accessibility." When humans have the Dao, it is like jade hidden in stone. The carnal eyes of the worldly have not yet seen this treasure. You must urgently polish and refine [your innate nature], so that one day your accomplishment will be complete. Then you may manifest the body-beyond-the-body. Substance will be separated and completed in the great vessel.

Humans who are without the Dao are like worm-infested trees. The celestial eye has a gaze like the sun. You must apply axe and saw to prune the rotten and inessential. **[14b]** Immediately, the ethereal soul will take flight and the corporeal soul will disperse. Those with turbid natures forever sink into the gloomy underworld. Those who cultivate the Dao have compassion for the world: suffering is exhausted and sweetness arrives. If one creates perversity while asking for good fortune, myriad calamities will befall the body. One who accords with the decree of heaven, acts in opposition [to perversity]. One who goes against, acts in accordance.

Considering the highest of superior persons, the worthy completely penetrate and have reverence for the Dao and inner power. Considering heaven's recompense, it was fundamentally private beforehand, but becomes ultimately open afterward.

Considering the lowest of inferior people, the ordinary vie for sex and wealth. Considering heaven's recompense, it was ultimately open to all in the beginning, but becomes fundamentally private in the end.

The regulation of all beings comes from qi.[172]

"The regulation of all beings" refers to the hundred kinds of animals with different qualities. There is a crimson phoenix in the southern mountain. When it pervades the light and clear qi, innate nature becomes numinous. It then ascends on wind and enters into Nine Empyreans.

As for "qi," if it is turbid, then it sinks to the earth. If it is clear, then it rises to heaven. This is because below is turbid, while above is clear.[173]

---

171. This line modifies chapter 81 of the *Daode jing*: "Sincere words are not beautiful; beautiful words are not sincere."

172. Or, "The regulation of birds rests with air."

173. An allusion to the beginning of chapter 3 of the *Huainanzi* (DZ 1184). See *Dadan zhizhi*, DZ 244, 1.1a, which is translated here in chapter 4.

The black tortoise inhales Qian-heaven ☰ in the northern ocean. It exhales the light and clear original qi through eight hundred and ten fathoms. Then there is the yang number of double nine. **[15a]** When the three sections[174] of animals are infused and harmonized, they join together with the original qi and there is no dissipation. Qi pervades spirit; spirit pervades the Dao; and the Dao pervades its own suchness.

Life is the root of death; death is the root of life. Grace is born from harm; harm is born from grace.[175]

Considering "life being the root of death," there is a predominance of those seeking "life" in the world. When personal profit becomes abundant, one harms the body. One enters the road to death.

As for "death being the root of life," those who embrace the Dao do not seek "life." When inner power becomes abundant, one completes the body. One enters the road of life.

In the daytime the deluded crave worldly treasures, while at night they dissipate their internal treasures. The awakened sit and forget the world. When sleeping and dreaming, they guard their internal perfection.

With respect to "grace being born from harm," the Seven Emotions have sympathy for falsity, while the Six Thieves secretly harm perfection.

With respect to "harm being born from grace," when harm arises, one gains wisdom. With its sword, one severs ties to selfish love and desire. Through grace, one completely penetrates the Dao and knows the kindness of heaven. **[15b]** Eating like a fledgling, humans are free of harm. Roosting like a quail, one's emotions are free of "kindness."[176]

Ignorant people consider the patterns and principles of heaven and earth sacred; I consider the patterns and principles of the seasons and beings wisdom.

"Ignorant people consider the patterns and principles of heaven and earth sacred." Ignorant people squander life-destiny, while calling out to heaven in their search for peace. They daily and constantly amass transgressions, while praying to the sages in their search for good fortune.

The worthy understand that if one protects life-destiny, one's own spirit will become numinous. When one is free of transgression, the Dao's blessings are extensive.

Heaven and earth send down calamities to people who are turbid and perverse. The sages and worthies bestow blessings to those who are clear and virtuous.

---

174. Here "three sections" translates *sancun*, which literally means "three inches." In the present context, it might also be rendered as "three divisions." As *fangcun* ("square inch") refers to the heart or lower elixir field, I take *sancun* to refer to the Three Fields and Three Treasures, namely, vital essence, qi, and spirit.

175. Again translating *en* problematically as "grace." It might also be rendered as "benefit" or "favor."

176. A possible allusion to chapter 12 of the *Zhuangzi*: "If you share your riches with other men, what troubles will you have? The true sage is a quail at rest, a little fledgling at its meal, a bird in flight who leaves no trail behind. When the world has the Way, he joins in the chorus with all other things" (Watson 1968, 130). See also *Changsheng yulu*, DZ 1058, 3b.

Sentient beings of the great earth universally create karma without reforming themselves. They pray to the sages and worthies for their myriad calamities and difficulties to be remitted.

If the men and women of this country have the aspiration to universally venerate the Perfected, without resorting to praying to heaven and earth, virtue and blessing will constantly arrive.

"I consider the patterns and principles of the seasons and beings wisdom." I use the twelve double-hours of the Celestial Cycle to investigate the transformations of the myriad things. The patterns are beautifully manifested in the myriad florescences.[177] The principles are luminously manifested in the myriad pervasions. Wisdom is thoroughly revealed in the myriad transformations. This occurs through suchness, clarity and stillness, and nonaction.

[16a] "Suchness" is the Dao. "Clarity" is heaven. "Stillness" is the earth. "Nonbeing" is innate nature and the Dao becoming embodied in sameness. "Action" is bestowing kindness without expecting recompense.

The transformative process of the myriad things and the transformative process of human beings are not different. Heaven and earth circulate qi, and things become pervaded and transformed.

Decoct lead in the jade cauldron, and refine mercury in the gold furnace. After seven reversions, you will pervade the numinous. After nine reversions, the elixir will coalesce.[178] Lodge the Maiden in the Palace of Li-fire, and the Child in the Door of Kan-water. When the turtle and snake coil around each other, the dragon and tiger roar in concert. The vermillion bird moves in front, while the Mysterious Warrior follows behind.[179] The Golden Duke guards *gengxin*,[180] while the Yellow Matron keeps company with *jiayi*.[181] The ocean is dredged for gold, while Mount Kun[lun] is mined for jade. The Yellow Sprouts develop, and the white snow emerges. The Jade Flower opens, while the Gold Lotus blossoms.[182] The Three Radiances are luminous, while the Seven Treasures are resplendent. At two and

---

177. *Wanhua*, which most likely refers to the beings of the manifest world.

178. The "seven reversions" (*qifan*) and "nine reversions" (*jiuhuan*) refer to various stages, vital substances/corporeal locations and methods associated with alchemical practice and transformation. Simply stated, "reversion" or "inversion" involves a movement from differentiation to nondifferentiation, from materiality to subtlety. In the case of early Quanzhen, see *Jinguan yusuo jue*, DZ 1156, 6b, 7a, 9a; *Dadan zhizhi*, DZ 244, 1.12a–17b.

179. The vermilion bird, associated with the Fire phase as well as the heart and spirit, is the emblem of the south; the Mysterious Warrior (snake-turtle), associated with the Water phase as well as the kidneys and vital essence, is the emblem of the north.

180. Consisting of the seventh and eighth celestial stems, *gengxin* is associated with the Metal phase, west, the lungs, tiger, corporeal soul, life-destiny, and qi.

181. Consisting of the first and second celestial stems, *jiayi* is associated with the Wood phase, east, the liver, dragon, ethereal soul, innate nature, and spirit.

182. According to Wang Chongyang's "Guidance for the Jade Flower Society" (translated here in chap. 2), "The Jade Flower is the ancestor of qi; the Gold Lotus is the ancestor of spirit." These were also the names of two of the five Shandong community associations, namely, the Yuhua hui (Association of Jade Flower; Dengzhou, Shandong) and Jinlian hui (Association of Gold Lotus; Ninghai, Shandong). Like Xuanfeng (Mysterious Movement), Jinlian (Gold Lotus) also became one of the alternate names for Quanzhen.

eight [16], one is free of deficiencies; at six and three [18], one is free of imperfections. Metal and wood are divided, while water and fire are conjoined.

[16b] Within the vague and indistinct, there is a hidden presence that is difficult to fathom. This is the application of the Dao.[183]

Commentary on the "Qingtian ge"[184]

Wang Jie, Master Hunran

Preface

The "Qingtian ge" (Song of the Clear Sky) was written by Perfected Qiu Changchun. As a song with flowing tones comprised of thirty-two lines, it parallels the thirty-two heavens mentioned in the *Duren jing* (Scripture of Salvation). This is the Dao as circulation and transformation. Each time I chant its tones, I enjoy its literary terseness and the directness and authenticity of its principles. It covers shortcuts to cultivating perfection and graduated steps for entering the Dao. The first twelve lines illuminate the foundations of cultivating innate nature. The middle twelve lines discuss the work of returning to life-destiny. The final eight lines describe the fusion of innate nature and life-destiny. This is the subtlety of spiritual transformation and casting off the embryo. When the ignorant look at worldly people, they only compose mournful writings while singing and dancing. In the end, they do not know that the principles of the ten matchings and nine harmonies are inside this.[185] From ancient times to the present, those with mettle have composed commentaries for the benefit of later generations. When the unpretentious examine their simplicity and begin to study, nearly all of them will receive a beneficial influence on awakening.

Commentary

The clear sky: nothing rises higher, floating clouds mere veil. Nonaction is the foundation of the great Dao. *Clouds rise up and come to screen the myriad constellations.* Effortful activity in anything is a mistake.

"Clear sky" refers to the innate nature of human beings. "Floating clouds" refers to their various thoughts. These two sentences provide an essential principle for humans engaging in cultivation and practice. Generally speaking, during the twelve double-hours, the heart-mind must be clear and pure, while thinking must be deep and natural. Then, not even

---

183. The received *Yinfu jing* (DZ 31) contains more text. Thus, there are two versions: the present one with roughly three hundred characters, and the received one with roughly four hundred characters. Cf. DZ 31, 2a–2b, which continues as follows: "People assume that being ignorant is sagely; I assume that not being ignorant is sagely."

184. *Qingtian ge zhushi*, DZ 137. Note that the preface has been excluded from the *Zhonghua daozang* (2004).

185. "Ten matchings and nine harmonies" appear to be an obscure reference to aspects of Daoist alchemical practice.

a single selfish thought will arise. One locates perfect innate nature within suchness, like a clear sky without the veil of clouds. However, if the heart-lord is unable to become the ruler, one reacts to the external world and becomes aroused by things. One follows thoughts caused by shifting appearances. When these manifest even more thoroughly, "clouds" arise and shade the myriad forms.

Yet even then the stars form a dense network, warding off all perversities; When innate nature is still, emotions withdraw. *Their radiant luminosity never shines on the Demon King.* When the heart-mind is active, spirit becomes exhausted.

[1b] This refers to unified innate nature being correctly positioned and the hundred deviations naturally returning to alignment. Then, within the heaven and earth of the body, the myriad vapors become a single vapor, and the myriad spirits become a single spirit. Naturally, the heart-lord is totally stabilized and wards off the hundred deviations. If hatred cannot disrupt and desire cannot obstruct, then banished emotions will not return. Suffering demons are caused to assist one. Thus, my "bright radiance does not manifest," so that "perverse demons prosper."

When I first opened empty space, heaven and earth were clear—Renounce the self and return to ritual propriety. *Ten thousand doors, a thousand gateways, I just sang of Great Peace.* The world returns to humaneness.

This refers to adepts who have attained the Dao. They bring to light the original condition of the living body, which is free from any concerns. It is only when one is like this that clarity and stillness maintain perfection. When one constantly resembles a young child,[186] innate nature is naturally empty and life-destiny is naturally strong. [2a] Then, pervading the Four Elements of the body and the eighty-four thousand pores, blood and qi circulate. There is no place that does not flourish. The Kun-earth ䷁ hexagram of the *Yijing* (Classic of Changes) says, "The yellow center is pervaded by principle; its correct position is within the body. It flourishes in the four limbs, and is splendid within the center." How is this not "heaven and earth being clear" and "the ten thousand doors being regulated"?

And then there was a moment when a single black cloud appeared, Hatred does not disrupt and desires do not obstruct. *And each of the Nine Cavities and hundred bones lacked serenity.* Water and Fire are not regulated.

This refers to humans having perverse thoughts and places of agitation. It is like the arisal of black clouds. At that time, if one urgently wants to become realized, it is best to turn back the radiance and to revert luminosity.[187] This is possible by nourishing a peaceful

---

186. The Daoist classical location for a child as the Daoist ideal is chapter 55 of the *Daode jing*.

187. On "reverting illumination" and "turning back the radiance" see section 3b of Liu Changsheng's commentary on the *Yinfu jing*.

heart-mind. If one lacks restraint and does not take precautions, the Four Gates of the eyes, ears, nose, and tongue accordingly cause dissipation, while the covering form becomes their servant. Then the sky of innate nature becomes shrouded and blocked by black clouds; the ocean of suffering becomes agitated and upset by lewd desires. [2b] In this way, the Nine Cavities and hundred bones of the body lack serenity. The *Daode jing* (Scripture on the Dao and Inner Power) says, "Open the gates; attend to affairs. To the end of life, there will be no relief."[188] According to the Chan school, "Do not fear perverse thoughts arising; simply fear awakening too late."[189] Mengzi (Master Meng) has said, "One may lose a chicken or dog and know where to find them. But to lose control of the heart-mind and not know where to find it—how pitiful!"[190] Such students are unable to avoid mistakes.

When this occurred, I spread the teachings, making wisdom a strong current; As soon as spirit emerges, gather its arrival. *It extended through the Three Realms and ten directions as a great whirlwind.* Purify the heart-mind and cleanse yourself of anxieties.

This section admonishes students about the heart-mind, which constantly desires to reside in the hollow of the breast. Sometimes it is agitated, while at other times it is still. If it remains unshakable in its purity, it cannot be disrupted by the myriad causal influences. If you encounter various forms and appearances, you must disrupt and extinguish the heart's aspirations. Be on guard for agitated thoughts. Perfected Yin Xi said, [3a] "Now, considering the arisal of things, I respond to them with innate nature; I will not respond with the heart-mind."[191] The *Jingang jing* (Diamond Sūtra) also says, "You must not linger in form and give rise to a heart-mind. You must not linger among sound, smell, taste, touch, and phenomena and give rise to a heart-mind. You must be free of that which lingers and gives rise to a heart-mind. In this way, you can restrain the heart-mind."[192] Kongzi (Master Kong) said, "The superior person is simple in his position and his activities. He is unwilling to go beyond this."[193] These expressions teach people about the heart-lord. If it can rule correctly, wisdom naturally becomes completely pervasive. Then the Three Treasures within oneself are embodied as substance, and the ten directions become pacified. There is nothing that can separate or obstruct you.

---

188. Chapter 52 of the *Daode jing*.

189. Source unknown.

190. Section 11 of part 1 of book 6, titled "Gaozi" (Master Gao), of the *Mengzi* (Book of Master Meng). See Lau 1984, 236–37.

191. Yin Xi is the mythological Guardian of the Pass who allegedly received the *Daode jing* from the pseudo-historical Laozi. He is identified as the author of the *Wenshi zhenjing* (Perfect Scripture of Master Wenshi; DZ 667). The quotation comes from section 1.15a.

192. Section 10 of the *Diamond Sūtra*. See Red Pine 2001, 8–9. On the *Diamond Sutra* see section 7b of Liu Changsheng's commentary on the *Yinfu jing*.

193. This line derives from the "Zhongyong" (Doctrine of the Mean) chapter of the *Liji* (Book of Rites).

When clouds disperse in emptiness, substance becomes naturally perfect; Unified perfection is constantly preserved. *It spontaneously manifests as a florescence in lineage after lineage.* It pervades self and Dao.

These lines relate to the previous ones and speak about the Three Realms and ten directions. When they become naturally clear and pure, not even a single thought arises. **[3b]** Then my perfect innate nature is constantly preserved, so that its wondrousness pervades my body. The stars and moon manifest a radiant luminosity. This then is the way of sitting-in-forgetfulness[194] of the inner landscape.[195] It is similar to when the *Duren jing* (Scripture of Salvation) says, "Everything in the heavens returns to its [correct] position."[196] It is also like Master Yan who was often empty of right [and wrong].[197]

So even now, below the moon, the square earth sustains the piping flutes—When the *gui*-water emerges, you must quickly gather it.[198] *A single sound, one brilliant note, it guards flourishing contentment.* The returning wind mixes [it] together.

This relates to the following lines and relates to cultivating the art of life-destiny. "Below the moon" refers to winter solstice and the double-hour of *zi* in the body.[199] A single yang begins to move at the time when water emerges. At this time, urgently set to work on gathering it. Then use spirit [to direct] exhaling the breath. The breath then returns to the apertures. Internally blow out the sound; externally close the doors.[200] Harmonize with the [twelve] pitches, and mix together the hundred spirits. This then plays the flute without holes in my own body.[201] It issues a sound that is resonant and clear. Its vibrations are splendid and marvelous. **[4a]** If you do not encounter a true master, the oral instructions will be impossible to know.

---

194. "Sitting-in-forgetfulness" (*zuowang*) is a form of Daoist quietistic meditation first mentioned in chapter 6 of the *Zhuangzi*. During the Tang dynasty (618–907), the practice became systematized by Sima Chengzhen (646–735) in his *Zuowang lun* (Discourse on Sitting-in-Forgetfulness; DZ 1036; trl. Kohn 1987).

195. "Inner landscape" (*neijing*), also appearing as "inner luminosities" (*neijing*), refers to the body. It is clearly described in the third-century *Huangting jing* (Scripture on the Yellow Court; DZ 331; 332), and a corresponding practice appears in the eighth-century *Neiguan jing* (Scripture on Inner Observation; DZ 641). For a recent discussion see Komjathy 2008b; 2009.

196. The *Duren jing* (DZ 1), the received text of which dates to after the early twelfth century. Passage unidentified.

197. Yan Hui (Ziyuan; 514–483 BCE), a senior disciple of Kongzi ("Confucius"). For related passages in the *Lunyu* see V.26, VI.3, VII.11, IX.11, IX.21, XI.3, XI.7–11, XI.23, XII.1, XV.11. See Lau 1992 (1983). Yan Hui also appears in the exchanges on "fasting of the heart-mind" and "sitting-in-forgetfulness" in chapters 4 and 6 of the *Zhuangzi*.

198. *Gui* is the tenth celestial stem, which is associated with the Water phase. In terms of human sexual development, *gui*-water refers to the vital essence, specifically the appearance of menstrual blood in women and semen in men.

199. *Zi* (11 p.m.–1 a.m.), which conventionally corresponds to the gallbladder. However, in internal alchemy practice, it refers to winter solstice, the kidneys, and vital essence.

200. Possibly a literal admonition to seclude oneself, but more likely a symbolic reference to sealing the senses. In a Daoist context, the phrase "close the doors" (*bi qi men*) first appears in chapters 52 and 56 of the *Daode jing*.

201. On the "flute without holes" (*wukong zhi di*) see section 7a further on.

It startles and awakens the jade lad of the eastern direction; From the storehouse of water, seek the Mysterious. *He staggers and then mounts a white stag like a starry steed.* Take hold of Kan-water to go and fill Li-fire.

"Startles and awakens" refers to distillation. It rises up from below. "East" refers to the Wood of *jia*[202] giving rise to Fire in the position of [the branch] *yin*.[203] "Jade lad" refers to circulating awareness and letting spirit fly. "Staggers" refers to reversal and revolution. "White stag" refers to refining vital essence to become pure qi. This is the basic summary of these lines. Now, when it is time to enter the chamber to form the elixir, the lord of innate nature rules the interior and circulates intention. When it sinks into the storehouse of water, distillation occurs. Maintain the central root. As soon as the yang-fire gradually burns brightly, raise the fire to turn around at the upper pass. From *yin*, it arrives at *si*,[204] and then flows to the Earth of *wu*.[205] Directly advance the yang-fire and restrict the movement of the gold essence. It directly penetrates Three Passes, ascending to enter the Southern Palace. This repairs the yin inside of Li-fire **[4b]** to become the Qian-heaven image. It should be like the suddenness of flickering points of light.

Retiring and retreating, the sound is not like ordinary music—Leave being and enter Nonbeing. *It is neither the music of lithophones, nor that of horns.* This is the representation of the unrepresentable.

"Retiring and retreating" refers to gradual suspension from above to below. "Not being like ordinary music" refers to the six yang-lines assembled in the Qian-heaven ☰ hexagram. This is the embodiment of yang being without end or limitations. A single yin emerges below five yang.[206] Following this according to the previous one, there should be gradual suspension. From *wu* to *hai*,[207] take *ji*-earth[208] to withdraw the hidden talisman. Beneath the Gold Portal,[209] the Flowery Pond and Magpie Bridge produce copious amounts of fluids.[210] They enter the Vermilion Palace through the Storied Tower.[211] Directly guide them

---

202. *Jia* is the first celestial stem. It is associated with Wood and the eastern direction.

203. *Yin* is the third terrestrial branch. When the terrestrial branches are applied as a map to the Celestial Cycle (Microcosmic Orbit), *yin* roughly correlates to Mingmen (Gate of Life), which is located between the kidneys. The implication here is that one places the intent on this energetic location.

204. *Si* is the sixth terrestrial branch. Following the Celestial Cycle, it correlates to Yuzhen (Jade Pillow), which is the occiput.

205. *Wu* is the eleventh terrestrial branch. Following the Celestial Cycle, it correlates to Qihai (Ocean of Qi), which is the lower elixir field.

206. This refers to the Gou-meeting ䷫ hexagram, which is Hexagram 44 of the *Yijing*.

207. *Wu* is the seventh terrestrial branch, while *hai* is the twelfth. In the previous interpretation, these would refer to the crown point and pubic bone, respectively. However, the context suggests that the corresponding time periods (11 a.m.–1 p.m.; 9 p.m.–11 p.m.) may be implied.

208. "*Ji*-earth" (*jitu*) usually refers to the lower elixir field, with *ji*, the sixth celestial stem, associated with the Earth phase.

209. Gold Portal (*jinque*) is a mystical cranial location.

210. In the present context, the Flowery Pond (*huachi*) refers to the mouth, while Magpie Bridge (*queqiao*) refers to the tongue.

211. The Storied Tower (*zhonglou*) is an esoteric name for the throat, while Vermilion Palace (*jianggong*) refers to the heart region.

to be stored in the Earth Cauldron of the Palace of Kun-earth.[212] This produces a luminous pearl that resembles a full moon that is perfectly round. It can be compared to "neither lithophones nor horns."

[5a] *When there are three feet of cloud chimes and twelve cords of lute,* The three blossoms gather in the tripod. *Throughout the course of kalpas, Chaos Prime was cut up.* The Five Qi meet the Origin.[213]

Like the previous lines, this speaks about the meaning of "not being like ordinary music." Thus it says, "three feet of cloud chimes," which means that three kinds of superior music return to the cauldron. Wondrously joined, they coalesce in perfection. Through the art of a single instance, you recover the transformative process of twelve months of one year. This is what the alchemical classics mean by bursting through the year to the month, through the month to the day, and through the day to the hours. Within the hours, one may only use two periods to circulate the talismanic fire of the Celestial Cycle. Gather the medicine to enter the chamber. By practicing internal work, joined through smelting and refinement, you will bind and complete the sacred embryo. Then we may speak about "Chaos Prime being cut up" inside the years and successive *kalpas*. The *Duren jing* says, "When the center regulates the Five Qi, one can gather the hundred spirits. Through ten revolutions, one returns to numinosity, and the myriad qi unite into immortality." Master Liaozhen (Realizing Perfection) said, "The three kinds of superior music are vital essence, qi and spirit. [5b] Naturally, the child and mother form mutually beneficial relationships."[214] The returning currents join together and revert to a perfected embodiment. Through the art of refinement, you become renewed with each passing day.

Jade resonates and chimes ring to sever vulgar songs; The sky is free from the veil of clouds. *Clear and light, penetrating everywhere, the sound passes through every mind.* The Four Qi are clear and bright.[215]

Like the previous lines, this emphasizes the meaning of "Chaos Prime being cut up." Thus it speaks about "jade resonating and chimes ringing." Then you may realize the accomplishment of perfect fire becoming refined. You will cast off the stagnant impurity of old age and decay. In this way, you will attain harmony of spirit and harmony of qi. It is like a pure commingling of dance and music. Accordingly, you also become separated from the lewdness of Zheng-like music.[216] Awakening to the central earth within this very body,

---

212. The lower elixir field.

213. The "Five Qi meeting the Origin" refers to combining the qi of the five yin-organs in the lower elixir field. For instructions see sections 1.18b–20b of the *Dadan zhizhi*, which is translated here in chapter 4. See also *Chongyang lijiao shiwu lun*, DZ 1233, 4b, which is translated here in chapter 3.

214. Most likey a reference to Zhao Wuxuan (Liaozhen [Realizing Perfection]; 1149–1211).

215. The Four Qi refer to the qi of the four seasons, four directions, and sometimes four yin-organs (with the spleen excluded).

216. Located in present-day Kaifeng, Henan, Zheng was a feudal state under the Eastern Zhou dynasty (722–221 BCE). It was established in 806 BCE and annexed to Han in 375 BCE. In traditional Chinese culture, the state of Zheng is associated with vulgar music.

everything is made into green jade. There is no other color [to cloud it]. Naturally, the whole is thoroughly connected, and it penetrates into the human heart-mind. The *Duren jing* says, "Through the perfection of gold, purity becomes refined. Through the sound of currents, clouds flourish. Through the sound of jade, it assembles qi. Through the currents of the numinous, it collects mist."[217] **[6a]** Is this not a true transmission about the art of a verifiable path? Can you recognize that it is amazing?

Through them I attained my first realization, with ghosts and spirits in support; Demons do not dare to offend. *Then I entered the earth and ascended to heaven, leaping beyond past and present.* They respond and transform through me.

This refers to the perfect completion of the alchemical path. When transformation occurs independently, the entire cosmos is in oneself. The myriad transformations return to the body. When you reach this position, yin and yang circulate from you; the Five Phases perform their duties through you; wind and rain are summoned by you; and thunder and lightning emerge through you. Thus, you manifest a superior body, which extends everywhere, even in the smallest particle. The superior body is housed in the inferior body; it can carry Mount Xumi on its back.[218] In this way, none of the ghosts and spirits can fathom the movements. You can naturally keep them in order so that they serve and protect you. Thus, "entering the earth and ascending to heaven" as well as "leaping beyond past and present" are within myself. My responsiveness and transformation are immeasurable.

Everywhere completely self-abiding, I am free from attachments and concerns. One is not covered by the snare of form. *My heart-mind has no cravings and no desire for fame, my body no defilement.* Inside and outside are both forgotten.

[6b] Like the previous lines, these discuss the meaning of "leaping beyond past and present." Thus it says, "Everywhere completely self-abiding." This means that only the Dao is oneself—one does not accord with mundane changes. One refrains from becoming involved in perverse concerns. Instead, every transformation comes from oneself. How could there be anything to retain or bind? Blessing and worthiness, prosperity and flourishing, completely arrive at this time. How could anything arise to upset this? How could the heart-mind ever again have "cravings and desire for fame" or the body have any "defilement"? Such is the road of life and aliveness. If it is not the eminent ability of a great master, how could he have transmitted this?

In seclusion, I sing a song about pure snow in the alchemical vessel. The Dao is great at the center of the Void. *Tranquil and harmonious, beyond the world, it is a tune of pure spring.* Leap beyond the Three Realms.

Here "singing" means that you yourself have attained perfect joy. Then the body has another alchemical vessel where a celestial luminosity emerges. There is the constant presence of pure

---

217. Passage unidentified.

218. Xumi is the Chinese transliteration of Mount Sumeru, the famous Buddhist mountain said to be the *axis mundi* (cosmic axis).

snow flying slowly through the sky. It is so clear and pure [7a] that not even the smallest defilement can enter. This is what the *Zhuangzi* refers to as "purity emerging in the empty chamber"[219] and "spirit illumination naturally arising."[220] Perfected Yin also said, "Through one instant of serene emotionality, you ascend to the great Dao."[221] This, then, relates to the nine harmonies and ten matchings. With unified qi as pure yang, you leap beyond the Three Realms. How is this not a tune of the rising spring?

This song of my lineage is completely spontaneous; Form and spirit are both wondrous. *It is produced by a flute without holes, a zither without strings.*[222] Through the Dao, one unites with perfection.

This speaks about the nine-times reverted elixir becoming complete. One casts off the embryo so that spirit transforms. This is the Dao as suchness. It is embodied by merging with the Void. It is not the form and appearance that can be looked upon. Thus Yuanshi tianzun (Celestial Worthy of Original Beginning) said,[223] "Looking, you do not see it. Listening, you cannot hear it. Separated from each and every boundary, I call it the wondrous Dao."[224] How can it then be that a flute really has holes and a zither has strings? Through these reports, you can subtly meet with [the teachings of] the ancients. [7b] This is what they referred to as Dao originally being without form. I also am without "I." You suddenly and directly leap beyond and pass over the iron cliffs and silver mountains.[225] If students can grasp this single sentence, they will make progress in their studies and complete this undertaking. How can you doubt this!

Attain startled awakening and float above the dream of life; Emptiness and Nonbeing are pure. *Throughout day and night, a clear sound fills the grotto-heaven.* Among a solitary mist, gold perfection emerges.

This section explains the subtle meaning of the whole poem from beginning to end. "Attain" refers to finding the perfect Dao. It forever confirms the unbreakable diamond body. "Startled awakening and floating above" refers to all phenomena in existence. They

---

219. This line appears in chapter 4 of the *Zhuangzi* where Kongzi and Yan Hui have their famous exchange on the fasting of the heart-mind (*xinzhai*): "You have heard of the knowledge that knows, but you have never heard of the knowledge that does not know. Look into that closed room, the empty chamber where brightness is born! Fortune and blessing gather where there is stillness. But if you do not keep still—this is what is called sitting but racing around. Let your ears and eyes communicate with what is inside, and put mind and knowledge on the outside. Then even gods and spirits will come to dwell, not to speak of men! This is the changing of the ten thousand things" (Watson 1968, 58).

220. I have not been able to locate the second line in the *Zhuangzi*. However, there is a similar line in the *Yinfu jing*. See section 10a of Liu Changsheng's commentary translated earlier.

221. Perfected Yin may refer to Yin Xi and thus the *Wenshi zhenjing* (DZ 667), or to Yin Zhiping and the *Qinghe yulu* (DZ 1310). However, I have not located any corresponding passages, so Perfected Yin may be a different Daoist altogether.

222. In internal alchemy practice, "playing the flute without holes" often refers to breathing between the heart and lower abdomen.

223. Celestial Worthy of Original Beginning is the highest of the Sanqing (Three Purities).

224. An allusion to chapter 14 of the *Daode jing*.

225. Meaning unclear.

are like a dream. Through this, one can immediately ascend to the limitless and wondrous Dao. Both day and night, the body constantly contains the sounds of immortal music—it fills the grotto-heaven. This also admonishes students of later times about allowing their merit and reputation to be covered by the world and having their brilliance surpass others. [8a] Without attaining the true transmission of the utmost Dao, what is most important will become empty and fleeting, and you will lose what is real. If you are only concerned about craving and delusion and do not wake up, you will float and drown in the dream of ephemeral life. Reincarnation will not have a fixed limit. How then can you become free of life and death? Get rid of this and ardently seek out a great person, whose sincerity is extended, whose counsel is penetrating, and whose discernment is liberating. As soon as one awakens, one returns to the fundamental. One directly leaps beyond the realm of formlessness. Orient yourself toward the great Dao and engage in cultivation. Internally preserve spirit and nourish qi. Externally mix with the ordinary and join with the dust.[226] This is residing in the world while being beyond the world. Then you may join the assemblies of immortals and buddhas. How could these be empty words!

---

226. An allusion to chapters 4 and 56 of the *Daode jing*: "Loosen the tangles and untie the knots; harmonize the radiance and unite with dust."

Chapter Six

Hagiographical Ideals

Hagiographies, or "accounts of saints," are religious texts aimed at documenting the lives of major personages and at inspiring other adherents or potential members of the tradition. The genre is perhaps most often associated with the lives of medieval Catholic saints.[1] Hagiographies frequently include tales of extraordinary qualities, uncommon feats, and miraculous occurrences. In this way, hagiography differs from a modern notion of "biography," or third-person accounts of an individual that aim at "accuracy" and "objectivity." At the same time, hagiography is not "fiction." The study and reading of hagiography requires that one reflect on the compiler's potential motivations and concerns, those of his or her religious community, the intended audience, as well as audience expectations and generic conventions (see Campany 2002, 98–100). Moreover, as Robert Campany has pointed out,

> To hagiography as a type of writing we can apply the tired but serviceable notion that it, like other religious representations, serves as both "model of" and "model for"; that is to say, it is both descriptive of and prescriptive for religious life. The hagiographies of any religious tradition are where its airy speculations, its abstract pronouncements, and its systematic prescriptions for life touch ground in particularity and assume the scale of the human. Precisely because hagiography intends to inspire belief, veneration, and perhaps emulation, its depictions of the contexts of religious life must be, for the most part, realistic, which is to say, recognizable and familiar to readers. We too easily forget to ponder the expectations of the readers for whom premodern hagiographies were written, whose mental and social landscape was part of what was portrayed in them. Because it announces itself as an account of the lives of real persons, hagiography must meet readers on that familiar landscape before attempting to move them to the horizon where it meets transcendence; it must give a recognizable model for life as readers know it, and cannot content itself only with giving models for the ideal religious life. (2002, 100–1)

On a general level, hagiography may be read as providing insights into not only the lived religiosity of a given person but also the social framework and religious concerns of his or her community. This, of course, requires some degree of historical contextualization in order to understand the *specific* religio-cultural moment. The relevant biographical details, imagined undertakings, and required characteristics may be modified to address new contexts and concerns. Hagiography may

---

1. Cf. Martyrology and Buddhist Jātaka ("Birth") stories.

also have a variety of functions: descriptive, commemorative, reverential, inspirational, prescriptive, and so forth.

In the Quanzhen hagiographies translated here, we find a mixture of reliable biographical and historical information combined with more "literary" and purely "hagiographical" dimensions, including recurring conventions and anticipated content. For example, after identifying the person by name and birthplace, most of the entries begin with general poetic descriptions of the given adept's personal qualities. These are clearly expressions of veneration, as the hagiography compilers never met most if any of the first-generation Quanzhen adherents. Similarly, different readers will greet the accounts of ascetic feats, miraculous deeds, and mystical experiences with varying degrees of acceptance and skepticism. Taken as a whole, the Quanzhen hagiographies related to the early community, which is the focus of the present selection, attempt to solidify lineage and establish parameters of religious affiliation. They are part of what Vincent Goossaert has referred to as "identity-building mechanisms" (Goossaert 2001, 112). Interestingly, a close reading of the early Quanzhen textual corpus (see Komjathy 2007a, 382–422) reveals stages of social integration as well as competing constructions of authority (see Marsone 2001). In its formative and incipient organized phases (ca. 1167–ca. 1184), the early Quanzhen religious movement consisted of semiautonomous ascetic and eremitic communities characterized by local and sometimes regional religious leaders. It seems that a sense of collective identity focused on a single national leader did not emerge until Qiu Changchun succeeded Ma Danyang as the third patriarch and initiated a transition toward monasticism. In some sense then, the early hagiographies are intended to communicate the following: "As Quanzhen Daoists, these are the individuals whom we identify as the source of our tradition. Their lives are important to us because we are their spiritual descendants; we endeavor to remember them through our own practice and commitments." From my perspective, the early hagiographies aim to establish and maintain tradition and to inspire members of the Quanzhen religious community. In contrast, beginning in the Yuan dynasty (1279–1368) and extending through the Qing dynasty (1644–1911), the so-called Seven Perfected became incorporated into the storylines of plays and fiction aimed at popular entertainment (see Hawkes 1981; Wong 1990; Goossaert 2001).

Arranged alphabetically and utilizing the given adept's Daoist name (e.g., Wang Chongyang rather than Wang Zhe), the hagiographical entries translated here focus on the first-generation adherents and originate in two hagiographical collections, namely, the *Jinlian zhengzong ji* (Record of the Orthodox Lineage of the Golden Lotus; DZ 173; 5 j.; abbr. *Jinlian ji*) and *Zhongnan shan Zuting xianzhen neizhuan* (Esoteric Biographies of Immortals and Perfected of the Ancestral Hall of the Zhongnan Mountains; DZ 955; 3 j.; abbr. *Zhongnan neizhuan*). The *Jinlian ji* is the oldest extant Quanzhen hagiography. As contained in its title, Jinlian (Gold Lotus), like Xuanfeng (Mysterious Movement) and Wuwei qingjing (Nonaction and Clear Stillness), was an alternate name for Quanzhen. Containing an authorial preface dated to 1241, the *Jinlian ji* was compiled by the Quanzhen monk Qin Zhian (Shuli [Useless Timber]; 1188–1244), partially based on earlier stele inscriptions and common Quanzhen lore. Qin was a third-generation Quanzhen adherent.[2] He was

---

2. For a hagiography of Qin Zhian see the Jin-dynasty literati Yuan Haowen's (1190–1257) "Tongzhenzi mijie ming" (Tomb Inscription of Master Tongzhen), as contained in the *Ganshui lu* (DZ 973, 7.24a–26b; Chen 1988, 486–87). This work mentions four other lost works by Qin: *Yanxia lu* (Record of Misty Vapors), *Yixian zhuan* (Biographies of the Immortals of Yi), *Wuxian zhuan* (Biographies of the Immortals of Wu), and *Linquan ji* (Anthology of Forests and Springs). See also *Daozang quejing mulu*, DZ 1430, 2.21a.

the disciple of Song Defang (Piyun [Wrapped-in-Clouds]; 1183–1247), who had studied under Liu Changsheng and Qiu Changchun.[3] Both Song Defang and Qin Zhian are remembered in Daoist history for their leadership in the compilation of the *Xuandu baozang* (Precious Canon of the Mysterious Metropolis), which was completed in 1244 at their editorial headquarters of Xuandu guan (Monastery of the Mysterious Metropolis) in Pingyang (Shanxi).[4] As mentioned, the *Jinlian ji* was completed in 1241, and thus dates to a moment when Quanzhen had been transformed into a monastic order with national distribution (see Goossaert 1997; 2001; also Zheng 1987; 1995). The approximate composition date was fourteen years after the death of Qiu Changchun, who was the last surviving member of the first-generation Quanzhen adepts, and during the transition of national monastic leadership from Yin Zhiping (Qinghe [Clear Harmony]; 1169–1251), Qiu's successor, to Li Zhichang (Zhenchang [Perfect Constancy]; 1193–1256). It is also three years before Qin Zhian's own death. As such, we might understand Qin's compilation as a work intended to document and preserve important details related to the early Quanzhen religious leaders, specifically before their direct disciples, the second-generation adepts, passed out of the world. The *Jinlian ji* is also clearly meant to codify lineage and educate members of the monastic order. As expressed in his preface, Qin Zhian places emphasis on the Daoist affiliation of Quanzhen, on the historical origin of the movement with Wang Chongyang and his transmission to his seven principal Shandong disciples, and on alchemical practice and transformation as primary. According to Qin, "Considering our doctrine (*jiao*), the wellspring (*yuan*) comes from Donghua; the outflowing (*liu*) from Chongyang; and the tributary (*pai*) from Changchun" (2b).[5]

In terms of structure and content, the text begins with entries on Donghua dijun (Sovereign Lord of Eastern Florescence; a.k.a. Wang Xuanfu) (1.1a–2b), Zhongli Quan (1.2b–5b), Lü Dongbin (1.5b–9a), and Liu Haichan (1.9a–11b).[6] This is followed by the hagiographies of Wang Zhe (Chongyang [Redoubled Yang]; 1113–1170) (2.1a–10a), He Dejin (Yuchan [Jade Toad]; d. 1170) (2.10a–12b), and Li Lingyang (Lingyang [Numinous Yang]; d. 1189) (2.12b–14a). He Dejin and Li Lingyang were members of the Daoist eremitic community of Liujiang (present-day Huxian, Shaanxi), where Wang Chongyang's second hermitage was located. The hagiographies disagree on whether these Daoist hermits were Wang's teachers, companions (*daoyou*), or students. Qin Zhian next provides entries on Wang's Shandong disciples, the so-called Seven Perfected (*qizhen*):[7] (1) Ma Yu (Danyang [Elixir Yang]; 1123–1184) (3.1a–13b); (2) Tan Chuduan (Changzhen [Perpetual Perfection]; 1123–1185) (4.1a–3a); (3) Liu Chuxuan (Changsheng [Perpetual Life]; 1147–1203)

---

3. A hagiography of Song Defang appears in section 3.20b–23b of the *Zhongnan neizhuan* (DZ 955). No independent works by Song survive, but the *Zhongnan neizhuan* mentions the lost *Lequan ji* (Anthology of Joyful Completion) (3.23b). See also Schipper and Verellen 2004, 1275; Pregadio 2008, 915–16.

4. This Jin-dynasty Daoist Canon was the only such project in history initiated and carried out by an individual Daoist sub-tradition without government sponsorship. The *Xuandu baozang* contained some 7,800 *juan* and was the largest Daoist Canon ever compiled (Liu 1973, 114–15; Loon 1984, 50–57; Boltz 1987, 6; Komjathy 2002b, 4–5; see also Goossaert 1997, 462–70).

5. Each of these terms contains the *shui* ("water") radical, with the connotation of flowing movement. The terms also are used to mean "source," "movement," and "lineage," respectively.

6. This group with the addition of Wang Chongyang is referred to as the Five Patriarchs (*wuzu*). However, in the *Jinlian xiangzhuan* (DZ 174; 1326), Laozi is added as the first Patriarch, while Wang Chongyang stands between the so-called Five Patriarchs and the Seven Perfected.

7. On the development of the notion of the Seven Perfected see Marsone 2001; 2010; also Hachiya 1998.

(4.3a–7a); (4) Qiu Chuji (Changchun [Perpetual Spring]; 1148–1227) (4.7a–14a); (5) Wang Chuyi (Yuyang [Jade Yang]; 1142–1217) (5.1a–6a); (6) Hao Datong (Taigu [Grand Antiquity]/Guangning [Expansive Serenity]; 1140–1213) (5.6a–9a); and (7) Sun Buer (Qingjing [Clear Stillness]; 1119–1183) (5.9a–11b). Each entry contains a descriptive text, an elegy (*zan*), and sometimes a concluding poem by a certain Zhang Shentong. Some sections also include poems that are contained in the extant literary anthologies.[8] I have, in turn, provided a complete translation of the text beginning with the entry on Wang Chongyang.

The second group of hagiographical entries derives from the *Zhongnan neizhuan*. The title of the work refers to the Zuting (Ancestral Hall) in the Zhongnan mountains (Liujiang [Huxian]; Shaanxi), the location of Wang Chongyang's second hermitage and where his body was interred in 1170; the monastery of Chongyang gong (Palace of Chongyang) was eventually established at the same location in honor of the founder. The *Zhongnan neizhuan* was compiled by the Quanzhen monk Li Daoqian (Hefu [Harmonious Beginning]; 1219–1296).[9] Li was a disciple of Yu Zhidao (Dongzhen [Cavernous Perfection]; 1166–1250),[10] the abbot of Chongyang gong who was eventually succeeded by Li (1277) after his death. Li is principally remembered in Quanzhen history as one of its greatest historiographers. In addition to the *Zhongnan neizhuan*, he compiled and edited the *Qizhen nianpu* (Chronological Accounts of the Seven Perfected; DZ 175; 1271) and the *Ganshui xianyuan lu* (Record of the Immortal Stream of Ganshui; DZ 973; 1288), with the latter being a collection of inscriptions that remains one of the principal sources for Quanzhen history. Li's cultural contributions are all the more impressive given the fact that, according to the postface of the *Ganshui lu* by his disciple Zhang Haogu, he collated all of the texts of the collection himself (10.32a–33a; Schipper and Verellen 2004, 1141). The *Zhongnan neizhuan* also contains a preface dated to 1284 by Wang Daoming (fl. 1285), the abbot of Yuxian gong (Palace for Encountering Immortals) in Ganhe, the location where Wang Chongyang reportedly had one of his mystical experiences. According to Wang Daoming's preface, "Considering individuals studying the Dao, they hide their traces among cliffs and valleys, guard themselves in overgrown thatched huts, and wear coarse clothes and keep their jade hidden" (1a).[11] Like the aforementioned Li Daoqian, Wang sees Quanzhen religious commitments as involving ascetic training and alchemical transformation. The point of the *Zhongnan neizhuan* is, in turn, "to ensure that later individuals understand their ancestral roots" (1b).

Working in the later part of the thirteenth century, Li Daoqian thus compiled the *Zhongnan neizhuan* about forty years later than the *Jinlian ji*, at a time of radical challenges to the Quanzhen monastic community. Specifically, its historical provenance locates it within the context of the

---

8. Note that Florian Reiter's entry in *A Historical Companion* (Schipper and Verellen 2004, 1135–36) claims that the text mentions honors bestowed by emperors of the Jurchen Jin and Yuan dynasties. This is only partially the case. More complete information may be found in the *Jinlian xiangzhuan* (DZ 174) and *Qizhen nianpu* (175).

9. For a hagiography of Li Daoqian see the "Xuanming wenjing tianle zhenren Ligong daoxing ming" (Inscription on the Daoist Activities of Master Li, Perfected Celestial Joy, Literary Brilliance, and Mysterious Illumination; 1306) by his disciple Song Bo. This inscription mentions a variety of lost works by Li, namely, the *Yunxi ji* (Anthology of Bamboo-lined Streams), *Yunxi bilu* (Written Record of Bamboo-lined Streams), and *Zhongnan shan ji* (Record of the Zhongnan Mountains). See Chen 1988, 713–15; Goossaert 1997, 431–32; 545–46; Pregadio 2008, 636–37.

10. A hagiography of Yu Zhidao appears in section 3.13a–20b of the *Zhongnan neizhuan* (DZ 955). One extant work by Yu is contained in the Ming-dynasty Daoist Canon, namely, the *Wuxuan pian* (Chapters on Awakening to the Mysterious; DZ 1046).

11. An allusion to chapter 70 of the *Daode jing*: "The sage wears coarse clothes and hides his jade within." Or more literally, "The sage wears hemp robes with his jade close to his breast."

Buddho-Daoist court debates of 1258 and 1281, the loss of which by the Daoist side resulted in a series of anti-Daoist edicts by Qubilai Qan (Khubilai Khan; Emperor Shizu; r. 1260–1294) of the Mongol-Yuan dynasty (1279–1368). This culminated in the burning and destruction of Daoist texts, textual collections, and printing blocks in 1281 (only the *Daode jing* was to be spared), under which much of the *Xuandu baozang* was lost.[12] As noted in *A Historical Companion to the Daozang* (Schipper and Verellen 2004, 1135), "Most of these [hagiographical and biographical] works appeared during the half century 1230–1280, when Quanzhen identity was being elaborated in a very competitive setting. In particular, Li Daoqian and Shi Zhijing [1202–1275] were active around the time of the famous Buddho-Taoist controversies of the 1250s, and [some of] their works might very well be in answer to them, although they do not show any prejudice against other religions." The *Zhongnan neizhuan* also provides evidence for the central importance of the Shaanxi communities in thirteenth-century Quanzhen monasticism.[13] It may be partially understood as a more inclusive, revisionist history that seeks to elevate the status of Quanzhen Daoists associated with Liujiang (Huxian), Zuting, Chongyang gong, and other Shaanxi monasteries and sacred sites. This might have included the additional motivation to gain greater national recognition.

The *Zhongnan neizhuan* contains thirty-seven hagiographies of first-, second-, and third-generation Quanzhen adherents associated with the Zhongnan mountains. It begins with He Dejin (Yuchan [Jade Toad]; d. 1170) and ends with Gao Daokuan (1195–1277). In terms of the first-generation adepts, it includes entries on He Dejin (Yuchan [Jade Toad]; d. 1170) (1.1a–2b), Li Lingyang (Lingyang [Numinous Yang]; d. 1189) (1.3a–4a), Liu Tongwei (Moran [Silent Suchness]; d. 1196) (1.4a–5b), Shi Chuhou (Dongyang [Cavernous Yang]; 1102–1174) (1.5b–7a), and Yan Chuchang (Changqing [Perpetual Clarity]; 1111–1183) (1.7a–8a). I have translated the hagiographies of Liu Tongwei, Shi Chuhou, and Yan Chuchang, as they are the earliest extant accounts of these largely forgotten figures. Liu Tongwei was Wang Chongyang's first Shandong disciple, who converted in Yecheng and then traveled west to join the eremitic community at Liujiang. Shi Chuhou and Yan Chuchang were Wang Chongyang's earliest disciples; they began their Daoist training under Wang in Liujiang before he moved to Shandong. We might thus recognize a Shaanxi lineage, with Liujiang as its community center, and a Shandong lineage, which included Yanxia dong (Cavern of Misty Vapors) in the Kunyu mountains and the five Shandong associations (*wuhui*), all of which were located in the eastern peninsula of Shandong.[14]

As documented in the translations here, and in contrast to conventional presentations centering on Wang Chongyang and the so-called Seven Perfected,[15] the early Quanzhen eremitic community

---

12. Scholarly opinion differs on the overall effects of these edicts on the Quanzhen order.

13. The study of late Song-Jin and Yuan dynasty Quanzhen monasticism is only just beginning. See Zheng 1987; 1995; Goossaert 1997; 2001.

14. In this respect, some reservations must be exercised with respect to the claim that "Quanzhen lore is centered on lineages, not on places" (Schipper and Verellen 2004, 1135).

15. The so-called Seven Perfected eventually became associated with seven distinct lineages (*qipai*): (1) Huashan (Mount Hua) with Hao; (2) Longmen (Dragon Gate) with Qiu; (3) Nanwu (Southern Emptiness) with Tan; (4) Qingjing (Clarity and Stillness) with Sun; (5) Suishan (Mount Sui) with Liu; (6) Yushan (Mount Yu) with Ma; and (7) Yushan (Mount Yu) with Wang. Ma's associated lineage sometimes appears as Yuxian (Meeting Immortals). It seems that this standardization occurred in the late imperial period. The associated seven one-hundred-character lineage poems (*paishi*) are contained in the modern Quanzhen liturgy (*gongke*). In the modern world, the Longmen lineage is most prominent, but I have also met Quanzhen monastics in mainland China who self-identify as Huashan and Qingjing.

thus consisted of thirteen elite Daoist practitioners.[16] As mentioned, in contrast to the hagiographies that are organized along different lines, often privileging Wang Chongyang, Ma Danyang, and Qiu Changchun, my translations are arranged alphabetically and primarily according to the given adherent's Daoist name (in parentheses):

Table 3. Hagiographies of the Early Quanzhen Community

Name	Position
Hao Datong 郝大通 (Taigu 太古 [Grand Antiquity]/ Guangning 廣寧 [Expansive Serenity]; 1140–1213)	Shandong disciple
He Dejin 和德瑾 (Yuchan玉蟾 [Jade Toad]; d. 1170)	Shaanxi ascetic and community elder
Li Lingyang 李靈陽 (Lingyang 靈陽 [Numinous Yang]; d. 1189)	Shaanxi ascetic and community elder
Liu Chuxuan 劉處玄 (Changsheng 長生 [Perpetual Life]; 1147–1203)	Shandong disciple
Liu Tongwei 劉通微 (Moran 默然 [Silent Suchness]; d. 1196)	First Shandong disciple, then member of Shaanxi community
Ma Yu 馬鈺 (Danyang 丹陽 [Elixir Yang]; 1123–1184)	Senior Shandong disciple and second Patriarch
Qiu Chuji 丘處機 (Changchun 長春 [Perpetual Spring]; 1148–1227)	Youngest Shandong disciple and third Patriarch
Shi Chuhou 史處厚 (Dongyang 洞陽 [Cavernous Yang]; 1102–1174)	Shaanxi disciple
Sun Buer 孫不二 (Qingjing 清靜 [Clear Stillness]; 1119–1183)	Senior female Shandong disciple
Tan Chuduan 譚處端 (Changzhen 長真 [Perpetual Perfection]; 1123–1185)	Shandong disciple
Wang Zhe 王嚞 (Chongyang 重陽 [Redoubled Yang]; 1113–1170)	Founder and first Patriarch
Wang Chuyi 王處一 (Yuyang 玉陽 [Jade Yang]; 1142–1217)	Shandong disciple
Yan Chuchang 嚴處常 (Changqing 長清 [Perpetual Clarity]; 1111–1183)	Shaanxi disciple

16. There would be fourteen if one included Zhou Deqing (Xuanjing [Mysterious Stillness]; fl. 1122–1170), Wang Yuyang's widowed mother. See his hagiography later in this chapter.

The hagiographies principally portray these individuals as dedicated to solitary ascetic training. Another distinctive characteristic of the *Jinlian ji* and *Zhongnan neizhuan* is that they center on each individual's relationship to Wang Chongyang and personal life; they provide little information on the interactions among the various first-generation adherents. A few technical remarks are also in order. Generally speaking, each individual has multiple names: surname (*xing*); given name (*ming*), which is also referred to as taboo name (*hui*); personal name (*zi*), also translated as "style-name" or "sobriquet"; secondary personal name (*hao*); religious name (*faming*); and Daoist name (*daohao*). For present purposes, the latter two are most important, as they locate the given adept within the Quanzhen movement and as part of Wang Chongyang's lineage.[17] In the notes I have also included references to other extant hagiographies, other known names of the given adept, as well as other attributed and lost works.

A more thorough study of the lives of the early Quanzhen adepts and of the history of Quanzhen Daoism would have to consider other related works (see Boltz 1987, 56–59, 64–68, 123–24, 159–60; Schipper and Verellen 2004, 1134–42; Komjathy 2007a, 414–22). This would include attention to discrepancies, additions, and embellishments in the various accounts. In this respect, the Ming-dynasty Daoist Canon contains records (*lu/ji*) related to Qiu Changchun's meeting with Chinggis Qan (Genghis Khan; ca. 1162–1227; r. 1206–1227), namely, the *Xuanfeng qinghui lu* (Record of Celebrated Meetings of the Mysterious Movement; DZ 176; abbr. *Xuanfeng lu*) and *Changchun zhenren xiyou ji* (Record of Perfected Changchun's Westward Travels; DZ 1429; abbr. *Xiyou ji*). There are also a variety of relevant "extra-canonical" texts (see de Rachewiltz 1962; Reiter 1990b; Katz 2001; Schipper and Verellen 2004, 1134–35). Additional biographical and historical information may be gleaned by consulting the prefaces and colophons of the literary anthologies and the rare introductory comments to specific poems. A profitable study of the Shaanxi community could be undertaken through the analysis of the entire *Zhongnan neizhuan*.

No readily available translations of Quanzhen hagiographies have been published to date.[18] Florian Reiter (1997) has published an English translation of Liu Changsheng's hagiography contained in the *Lishi tongjian xubian* (DZ 297, 2.5a–10a). Selections from Liu's various hagiographies are also translated in Acker's study of Liu's *Yinfu jing zhu* (2006, 33–41). Paulino Belamide has included selections of Qiu Changchun's biography from the *Yuanshi* (History of the Yuan Dynasty) in his dissertation (2002, 174–75). Arthur Waley (1931) has published a translation of the *Xiyou ji* (DZ 1429), which also includes selections from the *Xuanfeng lu* (DZ 176) (21–25). Also noteworthy in this respect is Vincent Goossaert's comprehensive study of Quanzhen social history, which catalogues and utilizes the various inscriptions. It is to be hoped that this research will eventually appear in print. In the translations that follow, I have included images from the early fourteenth-century *Jinlian*

---

17. On the development of the Quanzhen name system see Goossaert 1997, 136–46; 2001, 129–32; Marsone 2001, 101–2. The observant reader will note that in its early expression under Wang Chongyang, many of the first-generation adherents received religious names beginning with *chu* ("abiding") and Daoist names beginning with *chang* ("perpetual").

18. For a general-audience translation of a popular Ming-dynasty novel on Wang Chongyang and the so-called Seven Perfected see Eva Wong's *Seven Taoist Masters* (1990). Readers should note, however, that the work is largely ahistorical and far removed from the actual lifetimes of the early Quanzhen adherents. It is not a Quanzhen text, here defined as a work written by a Quanzhen adherent and within a Quanzhen religious context (see Komjathy 2007a). The novel is perhaps best read as the way in which some members of Chinese culture, and perhaps some Daoists, remembered the cultural and religious legacy of Quanzhen.

xiangzhuan (Illustrated Biographies of the Golden Lotus; DZ 174); there is no way to know who brushed them and whether or not they are accurate portraitures. There are no extant depictions of He Dejin, Li Lingyang, Liu Tongwei, Shi Chuhou, and Yan Chuchang.

Hao Guangning[19]

Figure 28. Hao Guangning

The master had the taboo name Lin, and the Daoist name Tianran (Quiet Suchness). He gave himself the name Daoist Taigu (Grand Antiquity).[20] His family was from Ninghai,[21] and members of each generation had been roaming officials who sought administrative positions.

The master was the younger second cousin of the Grand Master for Court Precedence.[22] He took care of his mother with the greatest filial piety. His natural disposition was luxuriant and abundant. He had no desire for the glory of official service, and his understanding of the art of divination was deep. The works of Huangdi (Yellow Thearch),[23] Laozi (Master Lao), Zhuangzi (Master Zhuang), and Liezi (Master Lie) were never far from his reach. Whenever he found himself among the seclusion of places with forests and springs, he would wander around in every direction, forgetting to return for an entire day.

---

19. The hagiography of Hao Datong (1140–1213) from *Jinlian ji*, DZ 173, 5.6a–9a. The illustration comes from the *Jinlian xiangzhuan*, DZ 174. Other hagiographical accounts of Hao Guangning's life include the following in chronological order: (1) "Guangning Tongxuan Taigu zhenren Hao zongshi daoxing bei" (1286) by Xu Yan (d. 1301) (*Ganshui lu*, DZ 973, 2.18a–24b; Chen 1988, 672–74); (2) *Lishi tongjian xubian* (post-1294) by Zhao Daoyi (fl. 1294–1307) (DZ 297, 3.6a–8a); (3) *Jinlian xiangzhuan* (1326) by Liu Zhixuan (fl. 1326) (DZ 174, 39a–41a); and (4) *Jindan liexian zhi* (ca. 1331) by Chen Zhixu (fl. 1270–1350) (DZ 1069, 6ab). For some relevant secondary sources on Hao's life see Reiter 1981; Hachiya 1998; Marsone 2001, 106–7; 2010.

20. Hao's original given name was Sheng. His other Daoist names include Datong (Great Pervasion) and Guangning (Expansive Serenity).

21. Present-day Muping, located in the northeastern part of the Shandong peninsula near Yantai.

22. *Chaolie dafu.* This is a Jin-dynasty prestige title for officials of the rank 5b2. Hucker 1985, 330.

23. In the context of early Quanzhen, the *Huangdi yinfu jing* (DZ 31) is most likely the text associated with Huangdi. See chapter 5 in this volume. There are also various longevity (*yangsheng*) and alchemical texts with similar mythological associations.

In autumn of the *dinghai* year of the Dading reign period [1167],[24] he was securing a livelihood by divining in the city when a number of scholar-officials gathered in a circle and sat down. Wang Chongyang was the last one to arrive. He sat down facing backward. Master Hao spoke saying, "Why don't you turn your head around?" **[6b]** Chongyang replied, "My only fear is that you are unwilling to turn your head around." Somewhat taken aback, Master Hao hurriedly stood up and made the appropriate ceremonial gestures. He invited Master Chongyang to go to another place and have a leisurely conversation. Questions and answers went back and forth as though throwing stones into water. Master Hao offered a poem that read as follows:

> The gentlemen sitting with me enjoy discussions of grand antiquity;
> However, they do not clearly understand the road of the vague and obscure.
> This morning I was able to encounter the song of a virtuoso—
> I humbly hope that the master will bestow some jade verses.

Wang Chongyang composed a poem in response:

> This speech longs for Master Hao to penetrate the highest antiquity;
> This speech discusses the heart-mind on the road to spirit immortality.[25]
> Standing among the kingfisher-green mist, I welcome the arrival of this moment—
> Day after day I long for your verses composed of clarity and stillness.

Master Hao read through it and understood its meaning. After this he went home.

In the third month of the following *wuzi* year [1168], he traveled alone to Yanxia dong (Cavern of Misty Vapors) in the Kunyu mountains.[26] He offered incense and expressed his reverence to Wang Chongyang. He committed himself to sweeping and cleaning duty. Wang Chongyang then gave him the religious name of Datong (Great Pervasion) and the Daoist name of Guangningzi (Master Expansive Serenity).[27] Together with Qiu, Liu, Tan, and Ma, Master Hao served Wang Chongyang. After living this way for seven months, Wang Chongyang directed the disciples to return to Ninghai. **[7a]** Only Master Qiu stayed at his side. It was not several days later when Wang Chongyang ordered Master Qiu to go and summon Master Hao. After he arrived [at Yanxia dong], Wang addressed him saying, "I have a hemp-cloth patched cassock that I have cut the sleeves off of. I want to exchange [what is on our] backs and give it to you. When passing the winter you can mend the sleeves yourself." Master Hao offered his respects and accepted it. Generally speaking, this resembles a method of bestowing garments from antiquity.[28]

---

24. The Dading reign period (1161–1189) of the Jin emperor Shizong (1123–1189; r. 1161–1189). In terms of the early history of the Quanzhen movement, and as indicated in the hagiographies, this period is probably the most pivotal one.

25. *Shenxian*, also translated as "divine transcendence." My preferred choice of "spirit immortal" suggests that immortality, or postmortem existence requires the formation of a yang-spirit, as documented in previous chapters. "Divine transcendence" is a more problematic translation because it suggests some state beyond the human, beyond embodiment, and beyond the world.

26. The Kunyu mountains are located near Yantai and Weihai in eastern Shandong.

27. Some of the other hagiographies mentioned earlier suggest that Hao received his Daoist names from an unidentified "divine being" (*shenren*) in 1172.

28. That is, taking an oath and establishing a formal relationship.

After this, Wang Chongyang went south to Bianliang,[29] while Master Hao traveled around Hebei. In the *yiwei* year [1175], he was begging for alms in Wozhou[30] when he suddenly awakened to secret teachings of Wang Chongyang. The dispensation was expansive. Master Hao accordingly went to live on a bridge,[31] where he remained silent and practiced quiet meditation. If hunger or thirst came, he remained unmoved. If extreme heat or cold arrived, he remained unchanging. If people brought provisions as offerings, he would eat. If they did not come, he would refrain from eating. Even if there were people who attempted to insult or ridicule him, he did not become angry. His aspiration was to forget his form. He practiced like this for three years. The people called him "Master Speechless."[32]

One evening, the sky was dark and gloomy. There happened to be a drunkard passing by. He kicked the master under the bridge. Master Hao remained silent and did not come out for seven days. **[7b]** People did not know what had happened; they thought that he had left.

One day, it just so happened that a traveling official was passing by on horseback. The horse reared up in fear. The official whipped his horse, but he still would not advance [over the bridge]. He fell off the horse. He then addressed his attendants saying, "There must be something strange under this bridge. If this were not the case, why did my horse rise up in fear?" He then ordered his attendants to go take a look. There they found a Daoist sitting calmly. When they questioned him, he did not speak. With his hand he wrote on the ground: "I have not eaten for seven days." When the local people heard this, they vied to offer food to him. They burned incense and made petitions, asking him to come out. However, Hao simply waved his hand and did not respond. He just stayed under the bridge practicing meditation for another three years. Water and fire became inverted, and yin and yang became harmonized. He completed the accomplishment of the ninefold reversion.

Then, in a state of pure joy, he stood up. He picked up his staff and sandals and began traveling north. He lingered about in Zhengding.[33] As he wandered around, those who sought help from him were countless in number. He established many [Daoist] palaces and monasteries. He ascended the halls and urged people to transform themselves. The Mysterious Movement[34] became brilliant and flourishing because of this. In the poem "Wu Nanke" (Awakening from Nanke's Dream),[35] he addressed the people as follows:

> Master Chongyang of Difei,
> Immortal Taigu of Kunyu,
> **[8a]** We formed a covenant before we were born.

---

29. Bianliang corresponds to present-day Kaifeng, Henan, which is located in the northeastern part of Henan near Zhengzhou. While on his way back to Shaanxi, Wang Chongyang died in Bianliang.

30. Wozhou (a.k.a. Zhaozhou) is located southeast of Shijiazhuang in the central western part of Hebei.

31. The famous Zhaozhou Bridge. Constructed at the beginning of the Sui dynasty (581–618), Zhaozhou Bridge is the world's oldest open-spandrel stone segmental arch bridge. It provides passage over the Xiao River.

32. Buyu xiansheng.

33. Present-day Zhengding, Hebei.

34. Xuanfeng, literally meaning "mysterious winds." It may also be rendered as "mysterious currents" and "mysterious movement." In combination with Jinlian (Gold Lotus), Xuanfeng is an alternate name for the Quanzhen movement.

35. A reference to the "Dream of Nanke," in which a certain Chun Yufen dreams of being appointed as head magistrate of Nanke. He eventually fails in battle, his army defeated, his body wounded, and his beautiful wife killed. He then wakes up to find that it was a useless dream about an imaginary place. Cf. *Taigu ji*, DZ 1161, 4.2b; translated in chapter 1 herein. This parallels the famous "Yellow Millet Dream" of Lü Dongbin.

We assumed our dwelling in the mundane world,
And flew down from the Daluo (Grand Network) Heaven.[36]
Together we opened up the teachings of the Mysterious Origin;
Whether moving or hiding, we ordained those with karmic connections.
How could there not be awakening when springs flow together?
After we parted and met again,
We formed another oath to last a thousand years.

From the Mingchang era [1190–1196] onward,[37] Master Hao returned to the eastern provinces. There he built other monasteries and ordained many disciples. Three years beforehand he directed workmen to dig an underground palace and to line it with tiles. About once every day he would go to lie down and rest in there. He told them the following: "Be prepared by the thirtieth day during the month of the La festival."[38] It was like this for three years. His Dharma body was healthy and strong. Then he addressed his disciples saying, "Masters and Perfected have a covenant with Penglai; I will return there." After he finished speaking, he lay down and returned to perfection. This occurred exactly on the thirtieth day during the month of the La festival.

His springs and autumns amounted to eighty-four. Throughout his whole life, he composed songs and odes. He thoroughly explained the matter of inverting dragon and tiger. He used the hexagrams and their commentaries to calculate the timing of ascent and descent. [These songs and odes were compiled under] the title *Taigu ji* (Anthology of Taigu; DZ 1161), which circulates widely in the world.[39]

I offer this elegy for him:

[8b] Considering Daoist Guangning,
He deeply investigated the images [of the *Yijing*].
Despising mundane attitudes and behavior, he immediately abandoned his wife and child.[40]
He longed for the mysterious currents and joyfully received hairpin and cap.[41]
He went into seclusion at Yanxia dong;
He paid his respects at the foot of Master Chongyang's mat.
He passed through many stages of practice,
And resorted to various methods.
He made a flourishing display of the essential blossoms of grand antiquity.

---

36. The Daluo Heaven is usually identified as the highest heaven of early medieval Daoism, located above the Three Heavens of Jade Clarity, Highest Clarity, and Great Clarity. In a more contemporary context, it is often understood as located below the Three Heavens and as the celestial abode of the Jade Emperor.

37. The Mingchang reign period (1190–1195) of the Jin emperor Zhangzong (r. 1190–1208).

38. The La festival is the winter sacrifice, held three days after the winter solstice. Thus, the La month corresponds to the twelfth month of the Chinese lunar calendar.

39. There are a variety of lost works attributed to Hao Guangning, including the *Kunyu wenji* (Prose Anthology of Kunyu) (*Taigu ji*, DZ 1161, preface, 1b), *Sanjiao ruyi lun* (Discourse on the Three Teachings in the *Yijing*) (ibid., 5a), *Shijiao zhiyan* (Direct Instruction to Reveal the Teachings) (ibid.; *Jinlian xiangzhuan*, DZ 174, 41a), *Xinjing jie* (Explanation of the *Xinjing*) (ibid.), and *Jiuku jing jie* (Explanation of the *Jiuku jing*) (ibid.). Goossaert 1997, 426–27.

40. Note that the main body of the hagiography does not mention Hao's marriage or family.

41. The hair-pinning and capping ceremony that indicates ordination. See chapter 7 herein.

He completely ingested the bone marrow of Complete Perfection.
He investigated tortoise and snake until they coalesced together.
He circulated dragon and tiger so that they coiled around each other.
In the town of Ninghai, he secretly received a wondrous transmission of garments;
Beneath the Wozhou bridge, he dedicated himself to practicing exercises for refining qi.
He observed the body-beyond-the-body;
He pacified the mouth inside the mouth.
The Three Pengs were destroyed, and water and fire became inverted.[42]
The Four Vapors circulated, and lead and mercury became harmonized.
Spontaneously, the nine-times reverted elixir was completed.
The Three Blossoms became fully formed and joined together.
He completely attended to the ancient oath of Penghu;[43]
He divined the exact time of the La month.
If he had not been a person who lodged his traces among people,
While his mind penetrated beyond images,
How could such things have been done?

Zhang Shentong wrote the following poem:[44]

> Whether residing in the city or living in mountains, he adhered to suchness;
> In stillness, he became completely united with the mystery inside the *Yijing*.
> So today he reclines in an intoxicated state above Penglai,
> Where all of the ancient ones commune with the immortal Taigu.

He Dejin[45]

The master had the given name Dejin (Virtuous Brilliance).[46] He was originally from Ganquan County in Qinzhou.[47]

---

42. The Three Pengs (*sanpeng*) refer to the Three Death-bringers (*sanshi*). See chapter 4 and appendix 1, Quanzhen Technical Glossary.

43. Penglai, the eastern island of immortality.

44. Adept unidentified.

45. The hagiography of He Dejin (d. 1170) from *Jinlian ji*, DZ 173, 2.10a–12b. Other hagiographical accounts appear in the *Lishi tongjian xubian*, DZ 297, 3.8a–8b; *Zhongnan neizhuan*, DZ 955, 1.1a–2b.

46. He's Daoist name is Yuchan (Jade Toad). This name may indicate a lineage connection with Liu Cao (Haichan [Oceanic Toad]; fl. 940–1030?), who is often identified as a disciple of Chen Tuan (Xiyi [Infinitesimal Subtlety]; d. 989). He's name also parallels that of the famous Daoist *neidan* master Bai Yuchan (1134–1229), who was a disciple of Chen Nan (d. 1213) and a member of so-called Nanzong (Southern School). The character *chan*, which refers to the three-legged toad believed to live in the moon, became a lineage identifier via Liu Haichan and Bai Yuchan.

47. Ganquan is located directly north of Xi'an and south of Yan'an in Shaanxi. It is close to Yan'an. Qin, an ancient Chinese state, is often used to designate Shaanxi. In this way, it parallels the use of Qi-Lu for Shandong. In the present context, Qiuzhou refers to a western division of Shaanxi during the Jurchen Jin.

In talent and ability, he was lofty and exceptional. His capacities were truly surpassing. Mysteriously endowed, he could shine through dense mist; wondrously equipped, he could disperse the clouds. His physique was vigorous.

Even more, he applied himself at brush and ink. In the beginning he hid himself among scribal clerks, but he was naturally pure in intention and had a calm nonattachment about him. Taking the Dao as his center, **[10b]** he would not accept wealth that came from disreputable means. He also never failed to seek out and consult recluses and the guests of disengagement.

One day it just so happened that he was relaxing and free from extraneous involvements. He met a Daoist and joined him at a banquet to discuss the Mysterious. At the end of the evening Master Yuchan still was not tired, and he decided that this was because it was a meeting without obstruction.[48]

On a different day the Daoist arrived carrying an owl in his arms. He entered from outside and addressed Adept He: "This is a strange animal. While its eyes are large, it lacks the ability to recognize humans." The master did not understand, but simply offered a polite response.

About a month passed, and Master Yuchan was unaware that the Daoist had been infected with a foul illness. None of the various physicians could cure it. After several days Master Yuchan was informed that the Daoist had died. Thereupon he prepared a funeral, purchased the coffins and buried him.

After several weeks, an old woman unexpectedly knocked at the master's gate and called out: "In the past you were notified here of the death of a Daoist; he was my son. How can I bear this old age, when our two lives were joined like a whirlwind? Now I have no support, and I am unable to secure food and clothing. Tell me what am I to do?" Master Yuchan had compassion for her and gave her precious metals and fabric for clothing. The old woman replied, "I want to go to the cemetery and see the coffin. I want to see my son. **[11a]** Then, at the end of my life, I will have no regrets." She begged the master four times, and ritual propriety in the end prevailed. The master ordered the coffin to be opened, but he couldn't see any bones. There was only the precious metals and cloth that he had given to the old woman. He returned to seek her out, but she was nowhere to be found.

Adept He sighed saying, "The transformations of spirit pervasion are extraordinary like this. If he was not an immortal or divine being, what could he have been? Because of this, I will make the appropriate response, abandon mundane karmic connections, and withdraw to live in the forests. I will cultivate and refine vital essence and my heart-mind, and merge with the Dao in Perfection."

[Around this time] he had heard that Patriarch Chongyang was in the Zhongnan mountains and that he had deeply realized the techniques of nine-times reverted refinement. He then went to join him. They lived together in the Zuting (Ancestral Hall).[49] With each passing day, he progressed [in realizing] the Mysterious and Wondrous. His qi gradually became infused and harmonized, and the ground of his heart-mind became expansive and pervaded. He gained the illumination of initial realization.[50]

---

48. An allusion to the two famous passages on Daoist friendship in chapter 6 of the *Zhuangzi*. The first reads as follows: "Master Si, Master Yu, Master Li, and Master Lai were talking together: 'Who can look on nonbeing as his head, on life as his back, and on death as his rump? Who knows that life and death, existence and annihilation, are all a single body? I will be his friend!' The four men looked at each other and smiled. There was no obstruction in their heart-minds and so they became friends" (adapted from Watson 1968, 83–84).

49. Zuting is an honorific designation for Liujiang (present-day Huxian, Shaanxi) after the interment of Wang Chongyang's body there. Liujiang was the site of Wang Chongyang's second hermitage and of an eremitic community, of which He Dejin and Li Lingyang were members.

50. *Xianjian zhi ming.*

He had prior knowledge of the forthcoming arrival of Qiu, Liu, Tan, and Ma.[51] At that time he and Li Lingyang were lodging in a bakery where they were collecting alms from various areas. They directed the leader of the lay supporters as follows: "Today four immortal guests will arrive. They are known as Qiu, Liu, Tan, and Ma. Wait for them here." They then returned to [Liujiang].

[11b] After some time, the four Daoists did indeed arrive. The leader of the lay supporters addressed them saying, "Are you not Qiu, Liu, Tan, and Ma?" The four men looked at each other and laughed saying, "How did you know this?" He responded, "The two elders He and Li were already here collecting alms." The four sighed and said, "Perfected and extraordinary beings."

After they finished eating, they departed. When [the six Daoists] met each other, they were happy. It was such joy that it seemed as though they were old friends.

Three years before he was going to achieve ascension, as a premonition he commissioned an artist to paint the image of a Perfected with a tiger in front of him. Then he went into a deep trance as though asleep. Nobody could wake him.

On the nineteenth day of the second month in the *gengyin* year of the Dading reign period [1170],[52] Adept He summoned Adept Ma, our virtuous religious leader, saying, "I, an inferior adept, have received your great kindness, but I lack the means to repay you. If you ever find yourself in difficulty, please offer incense and quietly chant my name. I will come to assist you." On that very day, the weather was clear and agreeable—the clouds were variegated and the sunlight was brilliant. In the eastern neighborhoods and western lodgings we could smell a strange fragrance. At that time Master Yuchan went to his grass-thatched hut and lay down with his arm as a pillow. [12a] Silently, he left the world of things and returned to Perfection. Thus he had foreknowledge that his time of return [death] would occur in the *gengyin* year.

After Master Yuchan attained ascension, there was a certain Zhang Lintong who had been suffering from a chronic illness for a long time. None of the host of physicians was able to cure it. It became so serious that he was on the verge of death. One night he dreamt that he met a man, who told him about a specific medicinal formula that would cure him. Zhang asked his name, and the man said "Adept He." When Zhang woke up, he used the recommended remedy. The illness was indeed completely cured. He was content because he saw that the master's spirit was undying and continued to exist.

I offer this elegy for him:

How amazing!
Humans are difficult to transform;
The Dao is difficult to understand.
Because Master Yuchan longed for the invisible and inaudible,[53]
He was single-mindedly focused on the mysterious and wondrous.
The Dao brought forth gateways to transformation and interchanges for him, yet he did
　　not awaken.
A thousand methods and ten thousand means enticed him, and yet he did not awaken.

---

51. The hagiography leaps from 1167, the time of Wang Chongyang's departure, to 1170, the time of Wang's death when four of his Shandong disciples returned to Shaanxi.

52. The Dading reign period (1161–1189) of the Jin emperor Shizong (1123–1189; r. 1161–1189).

53. Xiyi, which refers to a medicinal ingredient related to immortality as well as to one of the Daoist names of Chen Tuan (d. 989).

An owl's eyes alarmed him, and yet he did not awaken.

There was a foul disease to respond to, and yet he did not awaken.

There was corpse-liberation when he opened the coffin, and yet he did not awaken.

There was an old woman who came to visit, and yet he did not awaken.

[12b] Then, opening the coffin and seeing no bones,

And losing the old woman,

He later realized such are the resonating influences of sages.

He was startled and finally awakened.

He received the [Daoist] hairpin and cap, and began refining and investigating innate
  nature and life-destiny.

He offered obeisance to Master Chongyang and received clear direction and instruction.

He realized the Nine Reversions and refined himself until completely accomplished.

He had foreknowledge of the arrival of the four guests,

And he knew to leave behind the cakes.

He commissioned the painting three years [prior to his ascension],

And was able to determine his own time of return [death].

Afterward, he was able to ascend to emptiness and pace the Void.

He sent out his spirit to enter dreams.

We may refer to these things as the Dao not abandoning humans.

In truth, a spark of redoubled yang lays bare the instructions on the reverted elixir,

And an old woman completely reveals the karmic connections of former lives.[54]

Laughing as one mounts tigers to depart,

The wind circulates and one merges with the purple golden lotus.

Li Lingyang[55]

The master's given name has been forgotten. His Daoist name was Lingyang (Numinous Yang).[56] He was originally from Jingzhao in the Zhongnan mountains.[57]

[13a] He sank into deep serenity and lessened his speaking. His discernment transcended the mundane world. In his studies and inquiries, he demonstrated extensive knowledge. In discernment and consideration, he was magnanimous and profound. He attended to the Dao and virtue in his own heart-mind, severing his thinking from personal profit and reputation. With sincere motivations, he longed for and eventually obtained a meeting with Perfected Chongyang, who secretly bestowed the currents of Perfection.[58] Master Lingyang immediately nullified mundane thoughts. By inverting Kan-water and Li-fire, he refined and transformed himself throughout morning and evening.

54. "Former lives" translates *sushi*.

55. The hagiography of Li Lingyang (d. 1189) from *Jinlian ji*, DZ 173, 2.12b–14a. Other hagiographical accounts appear in the *Lishi tongjian xubian*, DZ 297, 3.8b–9b; *Zhongnan neizhuan*, DZ 955, 1.3a–4a.

56. Wang Chong**yang**'s Daoist name is usually interpreted to indicate a lineage connection with Zhongli Quan (Zheng**yang**) and Lü Dongbin (Chun**yang**). However, it is noteworthy that Li Ling**yang**'s name also connects him with the founder of Quanzhen.

57. Jingzhao is located near Xi'an, Shaanxi.

58. Other Quanzhen hagiographies suggest that He Dejin and Li Lingyang were Wang Chongyang's "companions of the Way" (*daoyou*) and "master-brothers" (*shixiong*).

He frequently met with Adept He [Dejin], Master Yuchan, [to discuss how] to care for humans and assist beings, to diminish selfishness and benefit others, to increase and gather hidden merit, and to secretly merge with the great transformation.

Perfected Chongyang has a poem that reads,

> Exchanging transmissions with Adept He and Adept Li,
> From the beginning three people had the same aspirations.

In the second month of the *wushen* year of the Dading reign period [1188], Emperor Shizong[59] issued a summons to Adept Qiu, Master Changchun, to go to the imperial palace.[60] When Master Changchun was about to leave to see the emperor, he addressed Master Lingyang saying, "Liujiang has a close karmic connection [to our lineage], having been established by the Patriarch [Wang Chongyang].[61] This cannot be considered lightly. It would be good if you serve as the head priest."

Master Lingyang responded, "Next year in early spring, the vernal radiance[62] will return accompanied by cranes. These mountain wilds alone will attend to me in my mourning." No one understood what he meant.

[13b] In the second month of the subsequent *jiyou* year [1189], Master Lingyang, free from any sign of illness, abruptly purified himself [in preparation for ascension]. A disciple urgently addressed him, saying, "The master's physical body is pure and healthy. In addition, you do not eat grains. What are you doing?" Master Lingyang replied, "Do not have any doubts. I am just waiting for the chief mourner."

At this time, Master Changchun had just obtained imperial permission to return to the old mountain. He passed through Qin [Shaanxi] and crossed into the market town. He rested there and did not travel farther. Master Lingyang sent his disciples to welcome him, at which point Master Changchun hurriedly departed [for Liujiang]. Just as he reached the hermitage, Master Lingyang harmoniously transformed to become the happiness of Zhou's butterfly[63] and return [to the Source]. Beneficial clouds blew over the land; auspicious vapors coalesced in the sky; azure phoenixes appeared together; and a white crane soared forth. Not one of the various magistrates and officials failed to show his respect or grief. Thereupon Master Changchun directed the disciples to take the inner and outer coffins and bury them. This occurred on the first day of the third month of the *jiyou* year.

I offer this elegy for him:

---

59. The Jin emperor Shizong (1123–1189; r. 1161–1189).

60. During the years of 1153 to 1214, the Jin capital was located in Zhongdu (Central Capital; Yanjing/Beijing). Following this period (1214–1233), the court moved to Kaifeng, Henan.

61. Liujiang (present-day Huxian, Shaanxi) was the site of the Wang Chongyang's second hermitage.

62. *Chunguang* is most likely a play on Qiu Changchun's name, which means "perpetual spring."

63. An allusion to the "butterfly dream" (*diemeng*) of Zhuang Zhou, appearing in chapter 2 of the *Zhuangzi*: "Once Zhuang Zhou dreamt he was a butterfly, a butterfly flitting and fluttering around, happy with himself and doing as he pleased. He didn't know he was Zhuang Zhou. Suddenly he woke up and there he was, solid and unmistakable Zhuang Zhou. But he didn't know if he was Zhuang Zhou who had dreamt he was a butterfly, or a butterfly dreaming he was Zhuang Zhou. Between Zhuang Zhou and a butterfly there must be some distinction! This is called the Transformation of Things" (adapted from Watson 1968, 49). In the present context, this allusion suggests Li Lingyang has merged with the Dao's transformative process.

Within the world,
There cannot be two *dao*s,
And sages do not have two heart-minds.
[14a] Thus, Adept Wang, Adept He, and Adept Li
Transmitted secret instructions to each other.
Together, they refined the reverted cinnabar.
The cinnabar cassia of Zhongnan became fragrant,
And the Gold Lotus of the seaside flourished.
Accordingly, among the disciples and ranks of the Quanzhen lineage
They are considered the Three Patriarchs.[64]
Reverence and religious offerings are thus given to them.
But how can one be content with this!

There is a poem that reads,

> Two hands join together to guide the revolutions of sun and moon;
> Bright and brilliant, the illumination breaks open ten thousand blossoms.
> On the point of hesitating to lighten his allotted responsibility,
> He straightaway waited for Changchun to become the master.

Liu Changsheng[65]

Figure 29. Liu Changsheng

---

64. This represents an alternative lineage construction to the more standard one focusing on the so-called Five Patriarchs (*wuzu*). Here He Dejin, Li Lingyang, and Wang Chongyang are identified as the Three Patriarchs (*sanzu*), which appears to reflect influence from the Shaanxi Quanzhen community.

65. The hagiography of Liu Chuxuan (1147–1203) from *Jinlian ji*, DZ 173, 4.3a–7a. The illustration comes from the *Jinlian xiangzhuan* (DZ 174). Other hagiographical accounts of Liu Changsheng's life include the following in chronological order: (1) "Changsheng zhenren Liu zongshi daoxing bei" (ca. 1230) by Qin Zhi'an (1188–1244) (*Ganshui lu*, DZ 973, 2.1a–5a; Chen 1988, 469–70); (2) *Lishi tongjian xubian* (post-1294) by Zhao Daoyi (fl. 1294–1307) (DZ 297, 2.5a–10a); (3) *Jinlian xiangzhuan* (dat. 1326) by Liu Zhixuan (fl. 1326) (DZ 174, 29b–31b); and (4) *Jindan liexian zhi* (ca. 1331) by Chen Zhixu (fl. 1270–1350) (DZ 1069, 4b–5a). For some relevant secondary sources on Liu's life see Reiter 1997, 444–54; Hachiya 1998; Marsone 2001, 104; 2010; and Acker 2006, 33–41.

Perfected Changsheng was from Donglai.[66]

He was a member of an esteemed family of the Maojin clan, a talented descendant of the renowned Han imperial house.[67] **[3b]** Bold and strong were his arrayed pinions; refined and dignified was his elevated spirit. Lakes and oceans could not contain his relaxed manner; stars and constellations could not overshadow his lofty brilliance. His ancestors and father were from Wuguan.[68] They were proficient in hidden virtue and enjoyed extending favors. They had compassion for the cold and hungry and were kind to the orphaned and helpless. They donated fertile fields measuring more than eighteen *qing*[69] to extend imperial prosperity to numerous monasteries. In this way, they constantly helped to establish foundations for future generations to be prosperous. During the Taiping xingguo period of the Song dynasty,[70] the imperial household honored their filial piety and righteousness by conferring testimonials of merit to the family. They were also excused from taxes and conscripted labor. Their radiant luminosity pervaded the prefecture. Heaven does not turn its back on the benevolent. From the red mists and cinnabar radiances, Heaven selected the finest and brightest of its immortal material [Liu Changsheng] to bestow its auspiciousness on Yecheng.[71]

Because [from youth] he already excelled [ordinary people], Master Liu diligently served his widowed mother and became renowned for his filial commitment. He vowed never to marry or to become a government official. He detested ornamentation and was repulsed by extravagance. In clarity and stillness, he guarded himself. He kept himself vague and obscure, as though muddle-headed. When he regarded worldly things, nothing could disrupt the sincerity in his bosom. He frequently wanted to take leave of his old mountain home in order to meet extraordinary people, but his mother would put on a look of displeasure and forbid him to go.

[4a] In spring of the *jichou* year of the Dading reign period [1169],[72] he unexpectedly discovered two odes hidden in the wall of a neighbor's residence where no human being could have reached. The black brushstrokes were still fresh, but the odes did not contain the name of the author. The final lines read,

> Wuguan is a place for perfected immortals to nourish innate nature;
> There must be a person of perpetual life beyond dying here.

Master Liu was pleased with the concentrated vigor of the brushwork. He wondered if it was the composition of a divine being, but he was unable to decide what he believed.

---

66. Donglai is located on the far western edge of the Shandong peninsula. Liu had the following Daoist names: Chuxuan (Abiding Mystery), Tongmiao (Pervasive Subtlety), and Changsheng (Perpetual Life).

67. *Maojin* is an esoteric reference to the Liu family. The right-hand side of the character *liu* consists of *mao* above *jin*. *Maojin* in turn refers to the imperial house of the Han dynasty.

68. I have not been able to locate this Wuguan on historical maps of Song-Jin China. Based on context (see section 5b further on), it seems that Wuguan was located near Laizhou, Shandong.

69. One *qing* equals approximately one hundred *mou*, with one *mou* equaling about 240 square paces. Thus, one *qing* is about fifteen English acres.

70. This was one of the reign periods, dating from 976 to 983, of the Northern Song emperor Taizong (939–997; r. 976–997).

71. Yecheng most likely refers to Yexian, which was located near Laizhou during the Jurchen Jin dynasty. Laizhou is on the western edge of the eastern peninsula of Shandong.

72. The Dading reign period (1161–1189) of the Jin emperor Shizong (1123–1189; r. 1161–1189).

In the ninth month of that same year, the frost was cold and the dew was clear. Patriarch Chongyang, wearing sandals and carrying his staff, was traveling west with the eminent three immortals Qiu, Tan, and Ma. They traversed along the ocean and among its islands; they passed through mountains and cities. Master Liu heard about this and made every effort to hasten after them. After he caught up, he burned incense, took an oath, and greeted them. Patriarch Chongyang turned his head around and laughed, saying, "There are dark marks between walls—do you know what I am talking about?" The three disciples looked at each other and laughed in jest. Just then Master Liu was startled by the realization that the ode had appeared through the transformations wrought by the spirit pervasion [of Wang Chongyang]. He thereupon committed it to memory and reflected on it with sincerity; he etched it on his bones and vowed to dedicate his life to [the patriarch]. He carried his armrest, staff, cap, and pitcher. [4b] As an attendant, he obeyed orders and was committed to regulating himself, whether through life or death. Patriarch Chongyang appreciated his diligence and attentiveness, and admired his commitment and devotion. He recognized that Master Liu's spiritual allotment was not like the multitude. Then he sighed, saying, "The moon through the pines; snow on the bamboos—they do not collect the yellow dust." He then bestowed a poem that read,

> When one finishes fishing and returns home, one encounters the great sea-turtle;
> You have personally realized that your allotment is among the arrayed immortals.
> Birds sing to each other in the willow trees because they understand your aspirations—
> To cleanse and expel the crashing waves measuring some ten thousand *zhang* in height.

Following his earlier selection of a meaningful phrase for the wall, Patriarch Chongyang gave new names to Master Liu. His religious name was Changsheng (Perpetual Life); his taboo name was Chuxuan (Abiding Mystery); and his personal name was Tongmiao (Pervasive Subtlety). This was the year before Master Liu turned twenty years old.

At that time, the reputation of Qiu, Liu, Tan, and Ma extended into the nine wildernesses and eight borders. They traveled [with Patriarch Chongyang] to Bianliang.[73] They lodged at Yimen, begging for alms and refining form. They kept their family and given names a secret [so that people did not know who they were]. In the morning they offered their respects [to Patriarch Chongyang], and in the evening they requested instruction. They practiced as though set on fire and meditated as though being cooked alive. The Patriarch carefully and thoroughly taught them about the mysterious pivot; he gave them repeated injunctions and transmitted the alchemical classics. He swept away the clouds of doubt and melted the icicles of delusion. Having completely bestowed [his insights on] the four images and Five Phases, Patriarch Chongyang then left behind the material realm and separated from humans [5a] in order to withdraw into the heavens. This is what we refer to as attaining affiliation and departing to Peng[lai] and Ying[zhou].

The four disciples then gathered the immortal's bones as compensation for his vast compassion. They paid their respects at Xianyang,[74] passing through Huayin [on the way].[75] They settled in

---

73. Bianliang corresponds to present-day Kaifeng, Henan, which is located in the northeastern part of Henan near Zhengzhou. While on his way back to Shaanxi, Wang Chongyang died in Bianliang.

74. Xianyang is located slightly northwest of Xi'an, Shaanxi. It was Wang Chongyang's birthplace.

75. Huayin is located about one hundred kilometers east of Xi'an. It is the closest major town to Huashan (Mount Hua), the Western Marchmount.

Liujiang,[76] which was a desolate place filled with thickets and the Patriarch's old thatched hut. The aspirations of each of the four disciples were different—Master Liu decided to go into seclusion in Luojing.[77] He refined innate nature while among the chaos of the mundane world; he nourished simplicity while among the disorder of the entangling marketplaces. The sounds of musical instruments were not sufficient to disrupt his harmony; beautiful women and prostitutes were not sufficient to disturb his vital essence. The ashes of his heart-mind became increasingly cold; the wood of his body did not put forth new growth.[78] When people offered food to him, he would eat. When they did not, he never showed even the slightest sign of indignation. When people asked him questions, he responded with hand [gestures]. When he was alone, he spent the whole day in simplicity and purity. The power of his meditative absorption was fully complete; his celestial light emitted radiance.

Then he went to live as a wandering ascetic among the banks of Yunxi.[79] His disciples dug a cavern chamber for him in the rocky cliffs. Suddenly, they encountered a cold spring in an ancient well, which was cool and fresh. The rest of his company was startled by the well's strangeness. Master Liu laughed and commented **[5b]**, "Within less than a few more feet, there are two more wells. This is a place where I cultivated and practiced during a previous life." When they chiseled it out, such was indeed the case. Even up to the present day, the cavern palace goes by the name Sanquan (Three Springs).

In the *bingshen* year [1175], Master Liu once again returned to Wuguan in order to pay his respects to his mother. They were overjoyed to see each other. He chose a plot of land at the northern foot of Mount Taiji (Great Stability), and erected the ancestral hall of Lingxu guan (Monastery of Numinous Emptiness). With his own hands, he planted a cypress tree—it was iridescent green when completely grown. After he had lived there for a short while, some villagers falsely accused Master Liu of killing someone. He did not deny the charges and allowed himself to be bound.[80] He sat in prison, like a bound wild dog, for close to a hundred days. When Patriarch Chunyang[81] heard the jade clepsydra, he mounted an iridescent green unicorn, descended through the blue mists, and entered the darkened prison. He appeared behind Master Liu's wooden prisoner-collar and entrusted his care to the city. After Patriarch Chunyang taught him to practice literary composition, the actual murderer came forward and confessed his guilt. Master Liu was excused from punishment and bondage. After he got out of jail, the quality of his brushwork and ink was surpassing: it had the form of dragons and snakes taking flight and ascending.

In the *wushen* year of the Dading reign period [1188], Master Liu conducted a *jiao*-offering ritual in Changyang.[82] Variegated clouds gathered around the altar; white cranes danced in the

---

76. Liujiang is located in present-day Huxian, Shaanxi, which is about fifty kilometers southwest of Xi'an. It is fairly close to the famous Daoist monastery of Louguan tai (Zhouzhi, Shaanxi). It was the site of Wang Chongyang's second hermitage and of an eremitic community, of which He Dejin and Li Lingyang were members. After the interment of Wang Chongyang's body there, Liujiang became identified as the Zuting (Ancestral Hall) of Quanzhen.

77. Luojing refers to Luoyang, located in the northwestern part of Henan.

78. "Heart-mind of dead ashes" (*sihui xin*) and "body of withered wood" (*gaomu xing*) derive from chapter 2 of the *Zhuangzi*. See also chapter 23.

79. Near Luoyang, Henan, Yunxi refers to the location of Tan Changzhen's meditation hut, namely, Yunxi an (Hermitage of Cloudy Ravines). It seems that Tan and Liu Changsheng lived as members of a Quanzhen eremitic community at this place. See Tan's hagiography later in this chapter. It is also noteworthy that Sun Buer lived in Luoyang.

80. This corresponds to the practice of "patience under insult" (Skt.: *kṣāti*), which is one of the Six Perfections (Skt.: *pāramitā*) of Mahāyāna Buddhism, namely, generosity, morality, patience, diligence, meditation, and insight.

81. Lü Dongbin.

82. Changyang most likely corresponds to Weihai, but it may also refer to Yantai, both of which are on the eastern peninsula of Shandong.

courtyard. [6a] During autumn of that same year, there was a drought. Master Liu once again offered prayers for rain with deep sincerity. When he ascended to the altar, there were no clouds to be seen in any of the four directions. He commented, "Rain will arrive in the morning during the convergence of the hours of *si* [9 a.m.–11 a.m.] and *wu* [11 a.m.–1 p.m.]. We should have sweet water pouring down as though [the sky] is turned upside down." His prediction came true, like shadows responding to form, like echo responding to sound.

Later, in Dongzhou,[83] he performed another *jiao*-offering before an altar where he was the only master functioning as head officiant. There inevitably was an auspicious wind, quiet and still. He gathered the donations of mulberry paper and silk [bank notes] and ascended [to the altar]. The corresponding response seemed divine. Even to the present day, stone engravings of the associated prefectures recording these events still exist.

In the third year of the Cheng'an reign period [1198],[84] Emperor Zhangzong heard that Master Liu's way was as valuable as rare gems and precious metals. The emperor then sent officials to inquire after him. They came in a crane-board carriage with rush-muffled wheels upon which the emperor had pressed his imperial seal. The emperor treated Master Liu like an honored guest, conferring the name Xiuzhen [guan] (Monastery for Cultivating Perfection) to his monastery.[85] Officials and scholars, with their formal dress of silk robes and cords, visited the monastery constantly; there was never a moment when the area outside the door was not filled with shoes.

In the third month of the following year, Master Liu begged [the emperor to allow him] to return to his old mountain home. The emperor did not presume to treat him like a vassal. He bestowed an imperial plaque upon Lingxu guan, bringing the radiance of his favor on the master's ancestral hall.

Then, during the auspicious day of the sixth day of the second month, in mid-spring of the *guihai* year [1203], he beat the drums and summoned the monastic community. [6b] Master Liu declared that [it was time for him] to move to a distant and secluded park. He closed his eyes, rested his head on his left arm, and instantly returned to Perfection. There was an auspicious radiance and enshrouding mists, blessed vapors of every imaginable type.

Master Liu left behind the following writings: the *Xianle ji* (Anthology of Immortal Bliss), *Taixu ji* (Anthology of Great Emptiness), *Panyang ji* (Anthology of Coiled Yang), *Tongchen ji* (Anthology on Merging with the Dust), *Anxian ji* (Anthology of Serene Seclusion), and *Xiuzhen ji* (Anthology of Cultivating Perfection).[86] He also wrote commentaries on the *Daode jing* (Scripture on the Dao and Inner Power), *Yinfu jing* (Scripture on the Hidden Talisman), and *Huangting jing* (Scripture on the Yellow Court).[87] He mysteriously traversed the hiding-places of principle, and completely accessed sacredness and Perfection. His commentaries are sufficient to provide a model for ten thousand generations.

---

83. Dongzhou refers to the central-eastern part of Shandong.

84. The Cheng'an reign period (1196–1200) of the Jin emperor Zhangzong (1168–1208; r. 1190–1208).

85. I have not been able to identify the location of Xiuzhen guan, but it may have been built in the Jin capital of Zhongdu (Beijing).

86. I have added *ji* to the titles. Of these works, only the *Xianle ji* (DZ 1141) survives. In addition to the lost works listed here, the *Lishi tongjian xubian* (DZ 297, 2.9b–10a) identifies the following titles: *Dacheng ji* (Anthology of Great Completion), *Datong ji* (Anthology of Grand Sameness), and *Shenguang ji* (Anthology of Spirit Radiance). There are also two extant discourse records attributed to Liu: *Changsheng yulu* (DZ 1058) and "Changsheng Liu zhenren yulu," as contained in *Zhenxian yulu* (DZ 1256, 1.10b–12a).

87. Liu's commentary on the *Daode jing* is no longer extant. The Ming-dynasty Daoist Canon contains his *Huangting neijing zhu* (DZ 401) and *Yinfu jing zhu* (DZ 122). For a translation of the latter see chapter 5 herein; also Acker 2006.

I offer this elegy for him:

> The venerable immortal Changsheng
> Advanced conversion according to the circumstances.
> He ingested empty Nonbeing
> And exhaled suchness.
> He ascended the purple clouds and descended to wander among ocean shores.
> After gaining a meeting through the mathematical shifts of *jia* and *zi*,
> He joined Perfected Chongyang because of the karma of numerous *kalpa*s.
> He traversed the hundred passes,
> Passed through the nine springs,
> Drove away the four animals,
> And tilled the Three Fields.
> He sat near the city well of Luoyang,
> And chiseled the grotto-heaven of Yunxi.
> He smelted white snow to complete the elixir powder;
> He decocted the mysterious mist, which was smokeless.
> His resounding name spread in reports to Fengzhou (Phoenix Prefecture);
> His radiant florescence was illuminated through Jinlian (Gold Lotus).
> He built the noble residence that is Lingxu guan;
> [7a] He offered his respect to the emperor at the imperial court.
> He returned to his former residence in Donglai;
> Later his bones and flesh became completely transformed.
> > He wandered to rest among the eight springs.

Zhang Shentong wrote the following poem:

> He practiced deep seclusion in Penglai to realize celestial perfection;
> His spark of numinous illumination was distant from dust.
> In exalted sleep among eastern winds, after departing to return [to the Dao],
> He barred the lock in numinous emptiness, as spring came to jade halls.

Liu Tongwei[88]

The master had the surname Liu, taboo name Tongwei (Pervasive Subtlety), [religious] name Ledao (Enjoying Dao), and Daoist name Moran (Silent Suchness). He was originally from Yecheng in Donglai.[89] Over the generations, his family had become esteemed in the village, so his life was free and easy, free from obstructions. When still a young man, having not yet gone through the capping ceremony, he flew falcons, walked dogs, took joy in cock-fighting, and confusedly wandered in the threshing-floor of wine and women.

---

88. The hagiography of Liu Tongwei (d. 1196) from the *Zhongnan neizhuan*, DZ 955, 1.4a–5b.

89. Yecheng most likely refers to Yexian, which was located near Laizhou during the Jurchen Jin dynasty. Laizhou is on the western edge of the eastern peninsula of Shandong.

One day he became infected with a strange illness. Quite some time passed, and still he did not get better. In a dream he entered the realms of the immortals. Afterward he returned to balance and health.

After awakening to the principle of death and transformation, he focused his heart-mind on the Dao. In summer of the *dinghai* year of the Dading reign period [1167],[90] **[4b]** Patriarch Chongyang was traveling to the sea. While on the road he passed by Yecheng and caught a glimpse of Master Moran; he saw that his spirit and disposition were vigorous and surpassing. He had the presence of shifting clouds and rising vapors. After talking with him for a while, he realized that it was karmic influence that brought them together, like the halves of a talisman [being reunited]. Patriarch Chongyang then transmitted secret decrees on cultivating perfection and gave him his religious appellation and Daoist name.

After Master Moran obtained the seal, he abandoned his family and relatives. Departing with his walking stick, he eventually entered the pass.[91] He built a grass-thatched hut near Gangu in the Zhongnan mountains.[92] Humming amid the winds and whistling beneath the moon, he rinsed his mouth with rocks and pillowed his head on streams. He released his cares and dwelt beyond the world of dust.

In spring of the *gengyan* year [1170], the four masters Qiu, Liu, Tan, and Ma came west. When the master met with them, they were all deeply happy. They repaired the hermitage in Liujiang[93] and lived there together. Then the four masters returned to Bianliang[94] in order to retrieve the Patriarch's husk of immortality, which they buried on the side of the hermitage. Master Moran lived in a thatched hut near the grave mound for three years. After this, he traveled north to Languan.[95]

Inside he completed the Dao's wondrousness, while outside he responded to the karmic connections of the world. For people who lifted their robes to request the teachings, he was always there and never a day passed when his mat was empty. Afterward, he established a monastery to assist people, and the Mysterious Movement[96] stirred strongly in Xishan (Western Mountain).[97] His excellent work became widely known, **[5a]** so that his reputation eventually reached the imperial capital.

At the beginning of the Mingchang reign period [ca. 1190],[98] he was summoned to the imperial court. The emperor asked him about the matter of the nine reversions and seven inversions. The master responded, "What an honor for this lowly mountain and forest rustic. Under these steps,

90. The Dading reign period (1161–1189) of the Jin emperor Shizong (1123–1189; r. 1161–1189).

91. With regard to Liu's westward travel, Guanzhong designates Hangu Pass, which is located near Lingbao, Henan. This is the western edge of Henan on the border of Shaanxi, directly east of Xi'an.

92. Gangu is located in the western part of Shaanxi, northwest of Xi'an. It is just west of Baoji.

93. Liujiang is located in present-day Huxian, Shaanxi, which is about fifty kilometers southwest of Xi'an. It is fairly close to the famous Daoist monastery of Louguan tai (Zhouzhi, Shaanxi). It was the site of Wang Chongyang's second hermitage and of an eremitic community, of which He Dejin and Li Lingyang were members. After the interment of Wang Chongyang's body there, Liujiang became identified as the Zuting (Ancestral Hall) of Quanzhen.

94. Bianliang corresponds to present-day Kaifeng, Henan, which is located in the northeastern part of Henan near Zhengzhou. While on his way back to Shaanxi, Wang Chongyang died in Bianliang.

95. Location unknown. It may correspond to present-day Lanao, which is south of Xi'an. However, this would contradict the direction in which the text suggests Liu traveled.

96. Along with Jinlian (Gold Lotus), Xuanfeng (Mysterious Movement) is an alternate name for Quanzhen.

97. Xishan usually refers to the mountain by that name near Nanchang, Jiangxi. However, there is no evidence that Liu Tongwei went farther south than Shaanxi Province. This is even less likely given the fact that Jiangxi was part of Song territory. There is also an area by this name near Baoji, Shaanxi, which is located in the western part of the province.

98. The Mingchang reign period (1190–1195) of the Jin emperor Zhangzong (r. 1190–1208). The central capital was in present-day Beijing.

there are ninety-five positions. The ruler who nourishes the people within the four oceans ought not to concern himself with this matter. However, you may respond by taking the clarity and stillness and nonaction of Huang-Lao as the essentials for cultivating self and governing the country."

The emperor was greatly pleased. He issued an imperial order to the public officers to designate Tianchang guan (Monastery of Celestial Perpetuity) as a Daoist temple in perpetuity.[99] He also ordered a new hall to be opened in order to practice the Dao and so that it could be filled with those outside the tradition who needed instruction on the Three Teachings and Nine Lineages.[100]

Shortly after receiving this decree, Master Moran returned to the mountains. He sent a letter to the imperial household in appreciation of the emperor's act. He then took flight to the area of Qi-Lu,[101] arriving at Niejia village in Shanghe County in Daizhou.[102] There he addressed his disciples saying, "I have returned to rest in this place." Thereupon he built a reed-thatched shelter and lived there. One day, he lit incense and offered obeisance to the sages. He gathered the community together and encouraged them with a discourse on cultivating perfection. He concluded saying, "The masters and Perfected have issued a summons with the boundless winds. Now I must return [die]."

[5b] Not long thereafter, his false [form] was transformed. This occurred on the fifteenth day of the second month in the first year of the Cheng'an reign period [1196], on the day of the Prime festival. Throughout his life he composed *shi*-poetry and *ci*-lyrics, which, according to a catalogue, were circulated in the world as the *Quandao ji* (Anthology of the Complete Way).[103] Today the great buildings of Chaoyuan gong (Palace for Attending the Origin) have been established in the place where he became an immortal.[104]

Ma Danyang[105]

Figure 30. Ma Danyang

---

99. Tianchang guan was the earlier name of present-day Baiyun guan (White Cloud Monastery) in Beijing. See Marsone 1999. "Daoist temple in perpetuity" (*yongshou daoyuan*) may be a specific institutional designation within the imperial sanctioned monastic system.

100. The Three Teachings (*sanjiao*) refer to Buddhism, Confucianism, and Daoism. The meaning of Nine Lineages (*jiuliu*) may refer to nine "schools" in the Warring States period (480–222 BCE). See Min and Li 1994, 50–51.

101. Shandong.

102. Shanghe is located north of Jinan, Shandong.

103. This work is lost. We do have the *Qingjing jing zhu* (DZ 974), a translation of which appears in chapter 5.

104. The most famous early Quanzhen monastery named Chaoyuan gong was located in Kaifeng, Henan. Based on the present context, our Chaoyuan gong would have been near Jinan, Shandong.

105. The hagiography of Ma Yu (1123–1184) from the *Jinlian ji*, DZ 173, 3.1a–13b. The illustration comes from the *Jinlian xiangzhuan* (DZ 174). Other hagiographical accounts of Ma Danyang's life include the following in chronological order:

The master was from Ninghai.[106] He had the Daoist name Danyang (Elixir Yang). His ancestral taboo name was Jue, and his style-name was Huasou.[107]

He thoroughly investigated the Five Classics[108] and was honest and dignified in his personhood. His speech was free from stale or stock answers.

In former days, he traded silk fabrics in a neighboring town. One evening when he was resting in a tavern, he saw a poor woman in deep grief weeping silently. He heard someone say, "She is a virtuous woman. Her husband died at a young age, and she vowed not to remarry. She has taken care of her father-in-law and mother-in-law in a filially dutiful manner. Unfortunately, they have both perished. She lacks the means to bury them, so she intends to offer herself in exchange for the cost of the coffin." The master had a serious look about him and said, "Even when people of our neighboring village become sick, we must help them. If someone in our village dies and we do not help them, we lack filial piety and righteousness." He thereupon gathered two measures of double-bound silk and donated them for the burial. **[1b]** He did not try to reveal his name, but simply departed quickly to his former lodging place.

On that very evening the master's property was stolen by bandits. He did not tell anyone. Instead, he remained unaffected and returned home. When his wife asked what happened,[109] he made excuses about selling things on credit.

After six months had passed, the thieves had divided the loot into uneven amounts. [One of the thieves] came to Master Ma to confess and expose [his accomplices]. The master said, "Your gains are plentiful. Taken together, they implicate you in more than one incident. Such a reckless undertaking will lead to investigation. Your booty measures almost a hundred feet. When recklessness reaches its extreme, punishment will occur. It is not good to be like this. It would be better to take two *liang* of silver. This should appease your anger at the booty not being equal." The man responded by thanking him and left.[110]

At that time, the harvest was scarce. There was rice being dried in a courtyard, and a local village woman stole it. The master went out and secretly observed this. However, he once again hid himself and avoided her. He simply allowed her to take the rice.

---

(1) "Danyang zhenren Magong dengzhen ji" (1185) (*Ganshui lu*, DZ 973, 1.14a–18a; Chen 1988, 433); (2) "Quanzhen dier dai Danyang baoyi wuwei zhenren Ma zongshi daoxing bei" (1283) by Wang Liyong (ca. 1231–ca. 1307) (*Ganshui lu*, DZ 973, 1.18a–27b; Chen 1988, 638–41); (3) *Lishi tongjian xubian* (post-1294) by Zhao Daoyi (fl. 1294–1307) (DZ 297, 1.12a–22a); (4) *Jinlian xiangzhuan* (dat. 1326) by Liu Zhixuan (fl. 1326) (DZ 174, 23b–26b); and (5) *Jindan liexian zhi* (ca. 1331) by Chen Zhixu (fl. 1270–1350) (DZ 1069, 3b–4a). For some relevant secondary sources on Ma's life see Hachiya 1992; Marsone 2001, 103; 2010.

106. Present-day Muping, located in the northeastern part of the Shandong peninsula near Yantai.

107. Ma Danyang's original given name was Congyi. Additional names include Xuanbao and Xuanfu.

108. The Five Classics that formed the textual foundation of classical Confucianism; they include the *Shujing* (Classic of History), *Shijing* (Classic of Poetry), *Yijing* (Classic of Changes), *Liji* (Record of Rites) and other ritual compendia, as well as *Chunqiu* (Spring and Autumn Annals).

109. Sun Buer.

110. The meaning of this section is somewhat obscure. My translation/interpretation suggests that Ma Danyang advises the thief to be content with a small amount of stolen goods. That is, rather than harbor resentment, report his accomplices, and receive punishment, the thief is advised to accept things as they are. While the reader might question Ma's virtue, the paragraph seems to urge one to recognize Ma's nonattachment to material possessions.

His father's taboo name was Shiyang and his personal name was Xixian.[111] His appearance was eminent and dignified. His comportment was solemn and magnanimous. He had five children. He selected the characters for humaneness, righteousness, ritual propriety, wisdom, and honesty[112] for the children's given names, and their secondary given names contained "constancy." Master Ma's estate was extremely wealthy, so the people referred to it as "Ma's half province." **[2a]** Three of the family's sons and nephews were selected as *jinshi* candidates,[113] so there is a Hall of Residual Good Fortune. It is also now known as the Subdivision of the Descended Immortal.

In the *xinhai* year [1131] there were frequent famines. On a clear morning in the eighth month, there was a visitor who frantically threw a woven silk padded garment on the desk as he passed by the door suddenly, and then disappeared. Nobody knew where he went. When the gentleman [Ma Shiyang], wanting to store it in his cloth box, lifted it, it was very heavy. When he opened it up to look inside, the luster of gold pierced his eyes. When weighed, it was two *yi* in weight.[114]

After ten days passed, the visitor returned. [Ma Shiyang] thereupon presented the gold to him. The guest thanked him, saying, "I am immortal Lü.[115] My home is in the village of Yougu (Dark Valley). Collecting ceramics is my occupation. I had acquired two *yi* of gold, and was about to sell it in the market. A tax collector pursued me and I was close to being punished. I entrusted it to you in order to avoid this. I want to give half of it to you in appreciation for your favor."

Ma Shiyang responded, "Precious metals gained through illicit means, I fear, will bring misfortune." Thus he declined, and did not receive it.

Immortal Lü said, "The master has the currents of the yellow direction.[116] At another time, a spirit immortal shall emerge from among your descendants."

After this, the Elder Ma frequently visited the people of Yougu to inquire about whether or not Immortal Lü was around. **[2b]** Everyone would say, "From former times to today, there has been no Lü family [in these parts]. Ma Shiyang suspected that he was a divine being."

The master's mother had a piece of green jade that was stolen by a family servant. The servant fled. Everyone said that if they immediately chased after her, she would be caught. Ma Shiyang did not ask a single question [about the matter]. After this his wealth and property increased even more, and he lived to be sixty-four.

---

111. The translation endeavor becomes more challenging here because of how much information is supplied on Ma Shiyang, Ma Danyang's father. That is, the chronology and organization are somewhat perplexing. This is the case with many hagiographies, as they often incorporated material from many sources. The present section also stands in contrast to most of the hagiographies, which do not contain much information on the given adherent's family. It may be that Ma Danyang's high stature as the second Quanzhen Patriarch and successor of Wang Chongyang led to more attentiveness toward his family history. As documented in various Quanzhen sources, Ma was also a member of the Ninghai cultural elite, so information may have been more readily available. Note his associations with Fan Mingshu, a wealthy landowner and aristocrat, and Fan Yi, the superintendent of schools in Ninghai.

112. The five classical Confucian virtues.

113. *Jinshi* ("presented scholar") is the highest degree of the imperial examination system.

114. *Yi* is a Chinese weight measurement for coins, equivalent to twenty *liang* ("taels").

115. The famous immortal Lü Dongbin (Chunyang [Purified Yang]; b. 798 CE?), who was identified as one of the so-called Five Patriarchs of Quanzhen. See *Jinlian ji*, DZ 173; *Jinlian xiangzhuan*, DZ 174.

116. Honesty.

Master Ma Danyang was the second son [of Ma Shiyang].[117] His taboo name was Congyi and his personal name was Yifu. He was born on the twentieth day of the fifth month of the *guimao* year [1123] at midnight. His mother, a member of the Tang family, dreamt that she visited Magu (Hemp Maiden) and received a kernel of elixir. She swallowed it, and then gave birth. [Baby Ma Danyang's] body had the color of fire, which dissipated only after seven days. He gripped both his fists for one hundred days, and finally let go. When he was a child, he constantly recited words pertaining to ascending upon clouds and mounting upon cranes. In his dreams, he frequently ascended to the heavens with a Daoist priest.

It's amazing that, [as a young man], he took care of feeding more than forty people.[118] After the people finished eating, he would lick the remaining kernels of food while he gathered up the eating vessels.[119] He also only wore old garments.

In former times, the Daoist Li Wumeng (Li the Dreamless)[120] refined the great elixir among the Kunyu mountains; he engaged in this work three years without completion. [3a] He said, "When a spirit immortal descends to supervise, the elixir will be complete." One day, Master Ma and various other eminent ministers were wandering around at leisure. When they reached the furnace, they found that the elixir had been reverted and completed. Master Wumeng saw this and was amazed. He addressed Master Ma, saying, "Your forehead has three mountains. Your hands hang down to your knees. Truly, you have the material to become a great immortal."

Thereupon he composed an ode that read,

> Your body and physicality are eminent and dignified;
> Your face is round and your ears elongated;
> Your eyebrows are orderly and your eyes refined;
> Your nose is straight and your mouth square.
> You have all of the distinguishing marks [of a holy person];
> Your head emits divine radiance.
> When Yifu receives this record,
> He becomes a fellow traveler among Peng Village.
> This elixir has now become complete—
> Thanks to your inner power, sir,
> You shall hereby receive acclaim.

His dignity and familial loyalty are elegantly expressed in these words of Master Wumeng.

Sun Zhongxian regarded Wumeng's words as beautiful, and thus gave his daughter to [Master Ma] as a wife.[121] She gave birth to three sons, who were named Yanzhen, Yanrui, and Yangui.

Master Ma had a reputation for being filial and dutiful. From the beginning he was endowed with intelligence. He deeply investigated the classics and histories. He enjoyed playing with children.

---

117. Here the hagiography returns to Ma Danyang.

118. It is unclear if the "forty-plus mouths" here refers to relatives or the poor.

119. That is, Ma Danyang refrained from eating in order to feed others.

120. Adept unidentified.

121. Sun Buer, the only female member of the so-called Seven Perfected. A translation of her hagiography appears later in this chapter.

He treated wealth lightly and righteousness seriously. If he lent money and someone was unable to repay the loan, he simply burned the contract.

In the second year of the Dading reign period [1162], there was a locust plague and a great famine. **[3b]** A certain Liu Jin, who was a tenant farmer, had stolen and killed the plough oxen [for food]. He was in the process of killing all of them. The master hastily came and saw him. He said, "This year's grain has not yet risen, and [the village] is impoverished in food provisions. I was about to distribute aid and relief. Yet, you fail to recognize these oxen as the foundation of agriculture, and contrarily put these innocent [oxen] to death. This is unbearable to me."

Master Ma then made Liu Jin walk about carrying the hide and horns on his back. Thereupon both old and young cried out in grief. Someone made the following pronouncement: "Now the legal statutes are stern and clear. From now on the rules on transgressions and punishments will cause fathers and sons to no longer see each other." The master did not speak.

He then went to Jingge yuan (Temple of the Scriptural Pavilion) and donated the five ox hides. Master Ma directed Liu Jin to face the Three Treasures and to confess his transgression of killing the oxen in order to atone for his guilt. The people of that time sang, "In ancient times, they lauded Chen Shi;[122] today we talk about Yifu."

There was a certain ignorant youth who had three hundred strings of cash, with which he was going to buy thin gauze robes. In this way, each side would be taken advantage of and deceived. Master Ma then offered half of a thousand cash. The youth was angered by this small generosity and abruptly spit on him.

Just then Guo Fengxin scolded and drove [the youth] away. Someone said, "There is spit on your face; wipe and dry it off." **[4a]** Master Ma replied, "To wipe it off would constitute resisting his anger. I will let it dry by itself."[123]

Master Ma addressed his acquaintance, saying, "Last night I dreamt about two people wearing coarse black woolen [criminal] clothes. The person on the inside wore simple, patched robes and a pair of shoulder shackles. That man was weeping and pleading: 'The living members of my clan number ten times ten thousand, with many being recognized among the ranks of dukes and rulers.' With these deceptive words, the man quickly fled and ran into the southern alley. I followed him, and saw him enter the butcher shop of Liu Qing. He turned his head around, and he saw an ode on the wall:

> 'In the *jihai* year [1119], we were ten times ten thousand;
> In the *xinsi* year [1161],[124] the great majority had already been killed.
> Within our gates, it seems as though there is no compassion or favor;
> Generation after generation, the axle-head repeatedly tears asunder.'

"When I awoke from this dream, I heard the sound of a pig being slaughtered. I opened the curtains and saw two pigs bound together. There was one with white streaks on his two shoulders. At this very moment, people live between awakening and dreaming during the *jihai* year, which is

---

122. Chen Shi (104–187) was a famous scholar-official of the Later Han dynasty. It is unclear why he is invoked here.

123. An expression of *kṣānti*, or "patience under insult." This is one of the Six Perfections of Mahāyāna Buddhism.

124. Forty-two years later.

the year of the pig. Master Liu was born during the [previous] *xinsi* year [1101], which is the same year that I wrote the ode on the wall."

The butcher's heart was so thoroughly hardened in feeling that he was still unable to be inspired toward transformation. That night he had a dream during which two cranes flew around and then landed in his vegetable garden. [4b] He accordingly established a Daoist temple and summoned the Daoist Lu to be the head priest.[125]

In autumn of the *dinghai* year [1167], Master Ma traveled with Gao Jucai of Liaoyang[126] to Yuxian ting (Pavilion for Encountering Immortals) on Fan Mingshu's estate.[127] There they got drunk and began composing impromptu poetry. His final line read, "In the midst of drunkenness, there is a tranquil person who provides support." No one could discern his meaning. On the first day after Middle Prime,[128] Perfected Chongyang arrived in Dongmu[129] from the Zhongnan mountains. He passed by and entered Yuxian ting. Master Ma addressed him: "Where did you come from?" Perfected Chongyang replied, "The road was several thousand miles long; I specifically came to help drunkards." Everyone felt that his words were strange. Master Ma asked another question: "What is the meaning of *dao*?" Perfected Chongyang replied, "When I was not yet born from father and mother, the Five Phases had no place to reside." As they conversed together on the mysterious, they had not realized that wind had begun blowing. In accordance with ritual propriety, they invited Perfected Chongyang to return with them and stay in the family hall.

When his wife, whose maiden name was Fuchun,[130] opened the curtains and saw Perfected Chongyang, she addressed Master Ma, saying, "I noticed that Master Wang's face resembles an open lotus flower. His eyes are as beautiful as opaque jade. His voice is like a finely crafted bell, and his speech resembles a gushing spring. [5a] Eminent and dignified, he has the manner and qualities of aligned yang. We should treat him with deep respect and reverence." They accordingly treated him with the reverence appropriate for a spiritual teacher.

Perfected Chongyang addressed Master Ma, saying, "I wish to lock myself in a hut for a hundred days and fast."[131] Master Ma accepted this, and they built a meditation enclosure. Even if the four types of wind and snow arrived, the water in the ink-stone did not freeze. Outside seekers of poetry came and went like woven threads. With a flourish of ink-brush, he would cycle through paper, so that as soon as he began composing a *fu*-rhapsody it was completed. Wang Chongyang constantly sent out his yang-spirit to come and sit inside the pavilion. Master Ma would then send people away and offer his respect to it. Simultaneously, Perfected Chongyang was inside his hermitage majestically practicing silent meditation.[132]

---

125. Adept unknown.

126. Liaoyang is located in the central part of Liaoning Province, south of Shenyang.

127. Located in present-day Muping, Shandong. Today there is a defunct temple named Leigong miao (Temple of the Thunder Duke) at this site, which includes a variety of late imperial steles. Author's field observations.

128. A reference to the Three Primes (*sanyuan*) as calendrical dates and cosmological moments: (1) Upper Prime (*shangyuan*; fifteenth day of second lunar month); Middle Prime (*zhongyuan*; fifteenth day of the seventh lunar month); and Lower Prime (*xiayuan*; fifteenth day of the tenth lunar month).

129. Near Yantai on the eastern peninsula of Shandong.

130. Sun Buer.

131. This corresponds to the early Quanzhen practice of meditation enclosure (*huandu*). See Goossaert 1997, 171–219; 1999; Komjathy 2007a, 157–66.

132. *Mozuo.*

Beginning in the first month of winter, Perfected Chongyang auspiciously bestowed a single poem, directing Master Ma to join him [in ascetic practice]. Again and again he presented a slice of pear for Master Ma to eat. Every fifth day, he would send taro and chestnuts, each split into six pieces. On the eleventh day, he presented a pear split in two and directed the husband and wife [Ma and Sun] to eat them. After this, every time ten days passed, he added one section. On the thirtieth day, he divided it into three sections, and into four sections on the fortieth day. It continued like this until he had divided it into ten sections on the hundredth day.[133] This matched the odd and even numerical divisions of heaven and earth.

[5b] Master Ma gradually awakened[134] to its true principle, and he accordingly divorced his wife. He then received hairpin and cap.[135] Then he went to beg for alms in order to humble himself.[136] Perfected Chongyang was satisfied.

One day Perfected Chongyang said, "Master Ma is destroying a Daoist." Master Ma responded, "How, master, do you know this?" Perfected Chongyang explained, "Last night you dreamt about drinking alcohol, which forces me to discuss the matter." Master Ma responded, "I become happy when I drink, especially when I drink a lot. Perfected beings in earlier times knew this."

They then went into the Kunyu mountains to live in Yanxia dong (Cavern of Misty Vapors).[137] Master Ma suddenly got a headache. It arose so quickly that it was like his head was being torn open. Some people said, "Master Ma may not live to see another day." Perfected Chongyang said, "Even at a range of over three thousand *li*, I have resolutely transformed such people. Why do you say that he will die?" Wang Chongyang then magically infused[138] some water and gave it to [Master Ma]; as soon as he drank it, he was healed.

In autumn of the ninth year of the Dading reign period [1169],[139] Perfected Chongyang directed four of his senior disciples to travel west with him. In Dengzhou,[140] Geshilie,[141] the local prefect, formally waited for them to arrive so that he could pay his respects to the master. He asked him, "Where will our next meeting take place?" Perfected Chongyang responded, "Exactly in Liangyuan."[142]

---

133. This is the famous "dividing pears" episode, during which Wang Chongyang urged Ma Danyang and Sun Buer to divorce. *Fenli* ("dividing a pear") is a pun on the parallel *fenli* ("to divorce"). For relevant poems see *Fenli shihua ji*, DZ 1155.

134. This phrase is also found in Ma Danyang's literary anthology titled *Jianwu ji*, DZ 1142.

135. An initiation ritual during which one becomes a formal disciple and member of the Daoist religious community. One's hair is bound in a topknot with the hairpin. See chapter 7 herein.

136. *Jiangxin*, which literally means "descend the heart-mind." Interestingly, discourse 8 of the *Chongyang lijiao shiwu lun*, translated here in chapter 3, is titled "Jiangxin."

137. The Kunyu mountains are located on the eastern peninsula of Shandong, southeast of Yantai and southwest of Weihai. Today it is home to a small Quanzhen monastic community with a number of steles from various historical periods. Author's field observations. Relevant materials relating to the history of Kunyu shan and Quanzhen Daoism may be found in Shandong sheng Wendeng shi zhengxie 2005.

138. "Magically infused" here translates *zhou*. That character may also be rendered as "incantation" or "invocation." The more conventional "spell" is problematic in terms of its modern connotation.

139. The Dading reign period (1161–1189) of the Jin emperor Shizong (1123–1189; r. 1161–1189).

140. During the Jurchen Jin dynasty, Dengzhou corresponded to the central northern part of the eastern peninsula of Shandong. As a city, it corresponded to Penglai.

141. Geshilie Zhizhong. A.k.a. Hu Shahu (d. 1213), who was a high-ranking Jurchen military leader who eventually led forces against the invading Mongol army in 1211.

142. Liangyuan is an alternate name for Bianliang, which corresponds to present-day Kaifeng, Henan.

Later, when Perfected Chongyang became an immortal[143] in Yimen, Geshilie had been transferred to the position of assistant regent of Nanjing.[144] **[6a]** He accordingly became the chief mourner for Perfected Chongyang.

After Perfected Chongyang became an immortal, Master Ma guided the other disciples to enter Jingzhao.[145] Begging for alms, they acquired cash that amounted to several thousand. They also took a mutual oath to continue traveling east in order to retrieve the golden bones of Perfected Chongyang and to reinter them in the Zhongnan mountains.

Master Ma combed his hair and formed it into three topknots. He lost his mind for six years, practicing silent meditation in a meditation enclosure. Considering the three topknots, the character in Perfected Chongyang's taboo name [*zhe*] consists of three *ji* ("auspicious") characters. In this way, Master Ma expressed his reverence by wearing such a hairstyle.

Master Ma's determination was like iron and stone; he would practice even if the ground was frozen. For thirteen years, rival political theories unfurled and exchanged positions of supremacy. All the while, Master Ma never wore thin silk robes, and he never touched money. At night, he slept out in the open air. When the people expressed pity for his suffering bitter cold, he would respond, "No one should be surprised that I have been uncovered for three winters; I was seeking the spark inside my own elixir field."[146]

One day he addressed a disciple named Lai Lingyu,[147] saying, "How do the people inside the pass refer to those living in tattered garments and strongly cultivating principle?" The disciple responded, "They refer to them as *chaixi* ('diminished and cleansed')." Master Ma said, "For years, members of our community in the east have been deeply oppressed and broken. I should also become one of the diminished and cleansed."

[6b] Not even half of a month had passed when a high official issued an imperial decree that commanded every Daoist to return to his birthplace. Master Ma accordingly returned to [Shandong] through the pass.[148]

Master Qiu Changchun was then living in Longshan.[149] One day he addressed Li Dasheng,[150] saying, "My district is in the east. Even though an imperial decree has been issued, I am unwilling to leave through the pass [go east]. If I leave, the currents of our teachings within Qin [Shaanxi]

---

143. *Yuhua*, which literally means "winged transformation," is a common phrase used by Daoists to refer to the "death" of a Daoist.

144. This is the "Southern Capital" of the Jurchen Jin dynasty, which corresponds to present-day Kaifeng, not to the modern city of Nanjing in Jiangsu.

145. Jingzhao is located near of Xi'an, Shaanxi.

146. For poems that derive from this moment see *Jianwu ji*, DZ 1142, 2.21b, 2.22ab. A translation of the former appears here in chapter 1.

147. Lai Lingyu, whose hagiography appears in section 1.11b–12a of the *Zhongnan neizhuan* (DZ 955). His name also appears in the preface to the *Quanzhen ji* (DZ 1153), and he is mentioned in the *Danyang yulu*, which is translated here in chapter 2.

148. This occurred in the fourth lunar month of 1182 following the imperial edict of 1181 by Jurchen-Jin Emperor Shizong (1123–1189; r. 1161–1189) requiring that all Daoists return to their hometowns. See *Lishi tongjian xubian*, DZ 297, 1.18b–19a; *Ganshui lu*, DZ 973, 1.22b–23b.

149. Longshan is located in the far northwest part of Shaanxi.

150. Li Dasheng was a contemporary and master-brother of Cao Zhen (d. 1207), Lai Lingyu, and Liu Zhenyi (Langran [Clear Suchness]; d. 1206). See *Zhongnan neizhuan*, DZ 955, 2.1ab. His hagiography appears in the *Zhongnan neizhuan*, DZ 955, 1.14b–16a. Li was a native of Huating, which was located northwest of Xi'an during the Jurchen Jin dynasty.

that are sweeping the land will cease to exist." He then descended from the mountains. Inside the province, both officials and people demanded that he conform to the decree. In response, he went back into the mountains and lived there.

At the same time, Master Ma himself was traveling through the pass, with the goal of reaching his hometown. His hanging tufts had already turned white. He sang and danced along the road. When he entered [Shandong], it was like meeting a phoenix or auspicious star. He strained to be the first to see it, and was happy when he did. He then returned to his country village.

There he again saw the butcher Liu Qing, and instructed him, saying, "In former days, I wrote that ode on the wall. Without realizing it, some twenty years have passed. When I count the days from the moment that you slaughtered the three pigs, I estimate that it has been some ten thousand days. That's enough. Moreover, you are now eighty-three years old; [7a] your clan has expanded and your family is notable. According to our principles, you should stop killing." Mister Liu then understood. He in turn chose a specific day and arranged a personal fast. He selected a stone vessel from outside the outer walls and lit a fire in it.

That same day, Master Ma went to Jinlian tang (Gold Lotus Hall),[151] where he saw six people in deep despair. They were not able to provide support.

He went to a nearby well and drank: the water was refreshing like a sweet spring. A local prefect had named it Lingye (Numinous Fluid). He had a pavilion built there and erected a stele, which made the spring known throughout the four directions.

In the fifth month of the *renyin* year [1182], there was a great draught in Dongmu, and the best crops became dry and useless. People everywhere prayed to the mountains and streams, but not a single one had any effect. Through repeated ritual overtures, officials at the provincial and prefectural levels asked Master Ma to help, so that everyone might receive the necessary moisture. Master Ma lit a single stick of his renowned incense, and this was sufficient to bring nourishing rain.

In the seventh month of autumn, a local prefect sponsored a great *jiao*-offering ritual at Chaoyuan guan (Monastery for Attending the Origin).[152] For successive days, it was cloudy and rainy. Both Daoists and ordinary people became afraid. They worried that the weather would ruin the altar site. Master Ma said, "Don't worry. Today the weather will certainly clear." It happened just as he said. At Middle Prime, he burned a petition. Five clouds enveloped the area, while Luan-birds and cranes began assembling. Such was the response to his request.

[7b] In the second month of winter, he traveled to Dengzhou where Master Han, a Buddhist disciple, had lit incense and was offering prayers: "Our households have wells of suffering. May there be at least a modest bestowal of the Dharma's power, so that all may regain the taste [of happiness]." Master Ma then made an incantation for him, asking that the flavor [of their lives] would be immediately transformed into sweetness like cake and honey.

In the evening, the rains came. Master Ma accordingly went to stay in Master Han's dwelling-place. He wrote in a playful manner:

> Outside the gates, the hissing rain falls;
> The heavens bequeath this, not humans.
> Rulers and ministers think they can do it
> By smashing the heads of Daoists.

---

151. Jinlian hui in Ninghai (Muping), Shandong.

152. Based on the previous hagiography of Liu Tongwei, this Chaoyuan guan most likely was located north of Jinan, Shandong.

No one could discern his meaning. After a little while, they had Kangchan ask Master Ma about the Dao. They suddenly saw roof tiles falling so that there was a hole in ceiling: it looked like the [character] "head" in the center. Everyone became startled as they recognized the final sentence.

After the *jiao*-offering rite had been performed on the Double Nine day, the gates of heaven[153] opened on the southeast; auspicious clouds gathered near moon's edge. Every single one of the local prefects and district people expressed their reverence.

On the eighth day of the second month, Master Ma advised the people of Langye[154] village in Dongmu to set fire to fishing nets,[155] so that the winds would return and the snow would become regular.[156] They suddenly beheld a storied tower on a kingfisher-green mound. This strange occurrence terrified the people. Then a mirage appeared in Nanyang.

[8a] On the thirteenth day of the fourth month in the *guimao* year [1183], Master Ma traveled to Zhiyang[157] to serve as the head officiant for a *jiao*-offering. The wind and rain were great. All of the people wailed and prayed that the sky might clear. Master Ma tapped his teeth and closed his eyes in prayer. At that very moment, the clouds dispersed and the sun came out.

On the fifteenth day, between the double-hours of *shen* [3 p.m.–5 p.m.] and *wei* [5 p.m.–7 p.m.], a dragon tail appeared in the southeast. As it moved across [the sky], it did not disappear. At night, variegated clouds entwined the moon.

On the twenty-eighth day of the fourth month, Master Ma again visited Zhiyang. A mirage appeared from morning until night.

When Master Ma arrived at Huiguang an (Hermitage of Returning Radiance), Ma Congshi[158] was overjoyed and naturally wanted to burn a thousand-plus stacks of paper offerings. He accordingly had the people make ornaments and assemble fishing nets, which were burned. A mirage appeared again. Its appearance resembled the form of dragon chariots and crane carriages.

There was also a mirage that pervaded the outer walls and encircled the trees. The people assembled fishing nets and burned them. Suddenly they saw clouds assembling and shifting sideways among the islands of mulberry fields. Mists and radiances were clear and indistinct. It seemed as though they were under the supervision of spirit armies arrayed with armor and horses.

Master Ma lived in a meditation enclosure at Huating.[159] [8b] Nearby there was a red apple tree[160] with rotten branches and a rotten core. He was planning on cutting it down and using it for firewood. Sometime near the initial ninth day of the fourth month,[161] he was washing the tree

153. The sky.

154. Langye is located on the southern coast of the Shandong peninsula, south of Qingdao and north of Rizhao.

155. Or, "boat ropes."

156. This is most likely a local Shandong folk tradition intended to ensure protection and safety as well as celebrate important events. It is mentioned throughout the hagiographies.

157. Location unidentified, but possibly near Yantai. All of the places in this section of the hagiography were most likely in the eastern peninsula of Shandong.

158. Person unidentified.

159. As Ma was living near his hometown of Ninghai (Muping) at this time, Huating (Flower Pavilion) must have been a local district or Ma's name for his residence. Based on the context, it cannot have been the place by that name northwest of Xi'an, Shaanxi, that is, unless these stories derive from the time before Ma returned to Shandong (ca. 1173–1181). See also *Danyang yulu*, DZ 1057, 3b–4a, which is translated in chapter 2 herein.

160. The eastern peninsula of Shandong Province is famous for its apples.

161. A numeric preceded by *chu* ("initial") is the traditional Chinese way of indicating the "first day" in a series. For example, *chujiu* means the ninth day of the month. After the "initial tenth day" (*chushi*), the numbering shifts to the more conventional format.

with water. Suddenly his disciple Yao Xuan[162] appeared holding the lineage record of Perfected Chunyang. Master Ma then realized that [Yao] had been born on the fourteenth day of the fourth month underneath the red apple tree. Master Ma joyfully commented: "I was born on the twentieth day of the fifth month; when that day arrives, the red apple tree will again burst forth and produce leaf-buds." He then wrote an ode:

> Thirty-six above the heavens,
> And thirty-six below the earth.
> When the heavens and earth enter the precious jar,
> Seventy-two periods of five days are sufficient.

Master Li bowed his head and requested that Master Ma explain the ode. Master Ma laughed and responded, "It's a riddle. At a future time, you will naturally understand it."

At night on the seventeenth day of the fifth month, Master Li dreamt that the red apple tree produced two leaves to the north and south. In the morning, he looked at it and saw that the buds were visible. On the morning of Master Ma's blessed birthday, the green leaves were completely open. At that moment, he explained the ode, saying,

> "Four times nine is thirty-six days,
> So the heavens and earth together make seventy-two days.
> **[9a]** When the energetic moment is fulfilled,
> It changes the rotten into the flourishing.
> How can there be any difficulty?"

Near Quanzhen an (Hermitage of Complete Perfection),[163] there were two strands of transplanted bamboo and a pine tree. In the fourth month, their branches and leaves became withered and yellow. A Companion of the Way[164] named Master Cui addressed Master Ma, "Will the pine tree and bamboo ever flourish again?" In a state of delight, Master Ma composed the following couplets of poetry:

> The gateway to the Daoist community is called perpetual life;
> It is our sincere wish that what is dry and rotten be transformed from its old form.
> We constantly direct the various stems to be perpetually young and vibrant;
> We have never directed a single leaf not to bloom or flourish.

He also wrote the following:

> I connect with the method of living in order to lead beings back to life;
> The manifest qi and physical forms shift positions and exchange shapes.

---

162. Yao Xuan (fl. 1170–1183) was a second-generation Quanzhen disciple, a contemporary and master-brother of Cao Zhen (d. 1207), Lai Lingyu, and Liu Zhenyi (Langran [Clear Suchness]; d. 1206). His hagiography appears in the *Zhongnan neizhuan*, DZ 955, 1.8a–9b.

163. Most likely the former hermitage of Wang Chongyang, located in Ninghai (Muping). A small Quanzhen eremitic community was established there after Wang's departure from Shandong.

164. "Companions of the Way," or Daoist friends, translates *daoyou*. See discourse 6 of the *Chongyang lijiao shiwu lun* translated here in chapter 3.

> Outside the window, there is not only the vigor of superior persons;
> In front of the hut, there is also the vibrancy of accomplished adepts.
> In accordance, I wash my face so that it is purified with water;
> In less than ten days, I extract an unfolding leaf from the center.

On the third day of the sixth month while dwelling in Jinyu an (Hermitage of Gold and Jade),[165] Master Ma planted six small pine trees. Everyone bowed their heads, saying, "The pine tree and bamboo of the Hermitage of Complete Perfection are again flourishing and prosperous. How is it that only the small pine trees of the Hermitage of Gold and Jade are haggard and care-worn?" [9b] Master Ma then extended his perfect qi three times to infuse them. He wrote the following three poems about the event:[166]

> In the sixth month, I planted six pine trees in front of my hermitage;
> Then I reverted to being wind-mannered Ma [Crazy Ma].
> Extending my qi three times, there is no need for additional power;
> Returning to life through six vows, there is great accomplishment.

He also wrote,

> At that time, the pine tree became nourished through several prostrations;
> Secluded from Companions of the Way, I train this Crazy Ma.
> I am saying the six trees did not revive on their own;
> People say Mister Triple Topknots has perfect accomplishment.[167]

And

> On the initial third day of the six month, I planted a small pine tree;
> Six trees changed color when they encountered the supporting wind [me].
> In my prayer for flourishing, I borrowed the qi of Redoubled Yang;
> Responding to my efforts, people recount the accomplishments of Mister Triple Topknot.

The pine trees did not change back [to their former state], and their branches easily put forth leaves. Their azure and iridescent green colors were so admirable that the local people accordingly engraved Master Ma's poems on a nearby rock formation.

In the past, Lü Chunyang produced a pill of medicine, and he wrote a poem about reviving a rotten poplar tree in Longxing si (Temple of the Flourishing Dragon) of Laizhou.[168] The poem still exists in our own time; it reads,

---

165. Ma's Shandong hermitage, which was most likely located in Huangxian, Shandong.

166. These three poems are also contained in the *Jinyu ji*, DZ 1149, 1.23ab.

167. Here the three topknots refer to Ma Danyang as well as the teachings of Wang Chongyang that he transmits. See the hagiography of Ma Danyang earlier in the chapter.

168. Laizhou is located on the western edge of the eastern peninsula of Shandong.

With my long cotton sleeves, I move out from east of the river;
At night, I lodge in a shrine to the earth-spirit, located among former courts.
During the day, I travel through the city tracking the traces of sages,
And learning how to pass a thousand winters from an ancient poplar tree.

[10a] In a similar vein, today Master Ma has written three poems about reviving the six pine trees of Zhiyang. Both former and later sages thus return to a single consideration.

The impoverished officials of Zhiyang gathered together and were complaining about their physical pain and suffering. Master Ma had them drink some infused water. As soon as they had finished drinking, they felt as though they were flying.[169]

There was an accomplished person from Luanwu[170] who had been suffering for a long time from rheumatism. A hundred herbal remedies had no effect. Master Ma infused a piece of fruit and had him swallow it. After one day he was totally healed.

One morning Master Ma suddenly began singing and dancing in a state of self-amusement. He was extraordinarily happy. His disciples suddenly announced, "On the last lunar day of the twelfth month of the *renyin* year [1182], Immortal Maiden Sun,[171] with her forearm for a pillow, abandoned the world in Henan at the age of sixty-four years old." Master Ma said, "Last night she mounted the variegated clouds and, accompanied by immortal music, returned east above the ocean. I myself saw it. The reason why I am singing and dancing is because of this.[172] I knew it before it happened."

In the ninth month of that same year, Master Ma served as head priest to perform a *jiao*-offering rite for an orphaned soul at Qiyu an (Hermitage of Joined Encounter) in the Kunyu mountains. Blessed clouds, brilliant and dazzling, assembled. Luan-birds and cranes came and went in such large numbers that they could not be counted.

[10b] Master Ma traveled east to Wenshan[173] in order to oversee the building of Qibao an (Hermitage of the Seven Treasures). They dug a well about nine-feet deep and still did not reach a spring. A large rock obstructed further digging. Master Ma offered the following announcement: "We must drill through the rock so that the well is twenty-nine feet deep; then a sweet spring will naturally respond with a clear sound." He accordingly directed a workman to drill until he reached the depth of one *zhang*[174] and eight feet. A cold spring gushed forth.

---

169. That is, the pain of physical movement was gone.

170. Location unknown.

171. Sun Buer, Ma's former wife and the only female member of the so-called Seven Perfected.

172. This recalls the famous story of the death of Zhuang Zhou's wife. As documented in chapter 18 of the *Zhuangzi*, "When Huizi went to convey his condolences, he found Zhuangzi sitting with his legs sprawled out, pounding on a tub and singing. 'You lived with her, she brought up your children and grew old,' said Huizi. 'It should be enough simply not to weep at her death. But pounding on a tub and singing—this is going too far, isn't it?' Zhuangzi said, 'You're wrong. When she first died, do you think I didn't grieve like anyone else? But I looked back to her beginning and the time before she was born. Not only the time before she was born, but the time before she had a body. Not only the time before she had a body, but the time before she had a spirit. In the midst of the jumble of wonder and mystery a change took place and she had a spirit. Another change and she had a body. Another change and she was born. Now there's been another change and she's dead. It's just like the progression of the four seasons, spring, summer, fall, winter. Now she's going to lie down peacefully in a vast room. If I were to follow after her bawling and sobbing, it would show that I don't understand anything about fate. So I stopped'" (adapted from Watson 1968, 191–92).

173. Location unidentified.

174. Technically about ten feet or three meters. Like Chinese measurements in general, there tends to be communal, regional, and historical variation.

One day at Qibao an, an ox cart was moving large beams. The road was dangerously steep. The cart driver tripped and stumbled on the wheel ruts. The wheel rolled over his chest. While this was happening, the man chanted the name Danyang, and he emerged without injury.

In the third month of the *renyin* year, Master Ma was resting at Wuchao in Jinan prefecture. Old and young people only wished to show their reverence and respect; those who vied to enter through the gates numbered several thousand. They were so numerous that the door-leafs were torn from the gate. Master Ma stood there in a dignified manner, and not even a single person was injured.

In the second month of winter, two transplanted cypress trees, which had been planted near Qibao an and which measured several *xin*[175] in height, had gradually become dry and withered. Master Ma used his perfect qi to blow on them; he also washed them with water. Within the space of ten days they were kingfisher green in color, just as they had been at the beginning.

[11a] On the Lower Prime day,[176] Master Ma went to Wenshan to perform a *jiao*-offering. There were dark clouds and rain on successive days. Everyone was upset at this. Master Ma heard a voice from the Void speak: "Perfected Chongyang has arrived." This amazing occurrence was also heard by the two attendants at Master Ma's side.

At the *wu* hour [3 p.m.–5 p.m.] on the sixteenth day, Nimanggu Wujie, the district magistrate, looked up and saw a celestial manifestation. He beheld an immortal wearing an azure kerchief and long white robe. The immortal was sitting on a green lotus flower on the back of a white tortoise. The giant tortoise was swaying its tail back and forth. The immortal looked to be about a hundred years old. Nimanggu said, "It was Master Wang [Chongyang] as depicted in the illustrated book." He quickly prepared to burn incense, and every single person expressed their reverence. He suddenly saw the Perfected shift his body so that he was lying on his side. Then he departed toward the southeast. Master Ma recorded this event in a *ci*-lyric composed to the tune "Manting fang" (Fragrance Filling the Courtyard), which the local people had engraved on a rock formation.

Laiyang requested that Master Ma travel to Youxian guan (Monastery of Wandering Immortals) in order to discuss the performance of a *jiao*-offering. In the middle of the twelfth month, Master Ma announced, "Later on, three forms will appear." On the twenty-second day, at the hour of *chen* (7 a.m.–9 a.m.) when Perfected Chongyang had first descended into the world [was born], Master Ma advanced to know the dance of "Guichao huan" (Joy of the Return Visit). [11b] He looked up and beheld Perfected Master Chongyang and Master He,[177] his master-uncle, hovering in the midst of emptiness and only barely perceptible. Master Ma said, "With an eminent and dignified manner, it is time for me to depart to return [to the Dao]; I will quickly become a living immortal." He also said, "It is appropriate to go to an eminent place; I will strive to return as though shaking my sleeves."

He addressed his disciple Liu Zhenyi,[178] saying, "Each of you wants to become an immortal. How could this be easy if you meet demons and difficulties.[179] Be cautious; don't give up or be remiss. Be attentive to the point that you surpass attentiveness. Then you will attain it. You have received these words from me; don't forget them." He accordingly lay down with his head facing

---

175. About eight feet or two meters.

176. Lower Prime (*xiayuan*) refers to the fifteenth day of the tenth lunar month.

177. He Dejin (Yuchan [Jade Toad]; d. 1170). See his hagiography earlier in the chapter.

178. Liu Zhenyi (Langran [Clear Suchness]; d. 1206) (DZ 1153, preface, 3b). His hagiography appears in section 1.13a–14b of the *Zhongnan neizhuan* (DZ 955). See also *Danyang yulu*, DZ 1058, 4b, which is translated here in chapter 2.

179. See section 2.5a–8a of the *Dadan zhizhi* (DZ 244), translated here in chapter 4.

east and addressed the community: "When I open my eyes, I see; when I close my eyes, I see. Primordial perception does not require eyes. When realized spontaneously in the heart-mind, there is nothing that is not perceived." Then he conversed and laughed with his disciples. At the second drum-sounding,[180] strong wind and rain arrived. There was a single thunderclap. Master Ma, with his forearm for a pillow, took flight.

After this, Guo Fuzhong, the local alcohol tax collector, heard a knock on his gate and became deeply anxious. We went out to take a look. It was Master Ma. He invited him to come in and talk. Master Ma asked for some paper and wrote the following ode:

> [12a] The years of my life amount to sixty-one;
> In the world, no one now recognizes me.
> A single thunderclap on this level earth—
> How amazing to follow the wind and arise.

They talked to each other for a good long time, and then Master Ma hastily departed from him.

Among the local people there was a certain metalsmith named Liu. On that same night he beheld light like a bright torch coming through a crack in his room. He went to look at the light and saw a strip of paper. Using a bamboo pole to get it down, he found a four-line poem on the paper. It read,

> Within the gathering of three *yang*, practice and accomplishment are complete;
> Riding the wind on ethereal horses, I myself have become an immortal.
> I urge you to commit yourself [to cultivating] the dragon and tiger;
> Then you will naturally have this endowment and ascend to the heavens.

Master Ma's taboo name appeared at the end of the poem. Liu hastily cast it into the fire and burned it. It filled his house with a fragrance like sandalwood. After a few moments someone made the following announcement: "Last night Master Ma became an immortal." They then realized that it was Master Ma's yang-spirit that Guo Fuzhong and Liu the metalworker had seen. For seven days, his spirit-form majestically appeared everywhere, even though his body had been buried at Youxian guan.

At its initial founding, Donghua an (Hermitage of Eastern Florescence)[181] contained several dozens of pine trees. All of their branches and leaves turned white. [12b] Master Ma said, "The whiteness of these pines is simply myself." On the eighteenth day of the first month of the *jiachen* year [1184], between the hours of *si* [9 a.m.–11 a.m.] and *wu* [11 a.m.–1 p.m.], a certain *jinshi* graduate named Liu Shaozu and others saw Luan-birds and cranes flying back and forth in the sky. The clouds and vapors changed and transformed. Perfected Chongyang, attired in a cloud-cap and vermillion robes, and Master Danyang, wearing three topknots and plain white robes, appeared amid the clouds. After a short while, they were gone.

In the evening on the twelfth day of the fifth month, Master Ma suddenly appeared to northwest of Yingxian qiao (Bridge of Responsive Immortals).[182] An immortal lad served as his

---

180. The hour of *hai* (9 p.m.–11 p.m.).

181. Location unknown.

182. Location unknown.

attendant. After a short while, cold clouds enveloped the area. At that time, Yu Xin[183] and others, some twenty-one in number, beheld this occurrence.

After Master Ma had been buried, the local people constantly suspected that disciples from Shaanxi wanted to steal his immortal bones and take them away. On the twenty-fourth day of the first month of the *yisi* year [1185], Mister Liu, the county magistrate, had the coffin exhumed and inspected it. The body's physical form appeared as though it was still alive. The limbs were soft and pliant. They then combed the corpse's hair and changed its clothes. When people in the surrounding areas heard about this, they vied to pay their respects. There was never a break in the lines of arriving carriage wheels and horse hooves. In the ninth month, they reburied it, but this time they used a stone coffin.

[13a] His various literary anthologies include the *Fenli shihua ji* (Anthology of Ten Conversions through Dividing Pears), *Jianwu ji* (Anthology on Gradual Awakening), *Jingwei ji* (Anthology of Pure Tenuity), *Zhaiwei ji* (Anthology of Gathered Tenuity), *Sanbao ji* (Anthology of the Three Treasures), *Xinghua ji* (Anthology on Practice and Transformation), and *Jinyu ji* (Anthology of Gold and Jade), among others.[184] These have been handed down as models for the world. Sampling the meaning of his literary compositions, they connect the Three Teachings and gather the Five Phases together. They toast the present and harmonize with the past; they speak of things and instruct people. They contain mysterious conversations and wondrous principles. Reading them, it seems as though the Island of Penglai is right before our eyes. They reveal the sword of wisdom and the knife of insight. By following them, the Three Death-bringers are expelled from the body. By conforming to them, one returns to goodness and becomes distant from transgression. If you can awaken through them, you will enter the sacred and transcend the mundane. How could this be considered minor assistance!

I offer this elegy for him:

> When he first encountered Perfected Chongyang,
> He understood the nine reversions
> Through ten gestures of divided pears,
> He secretly transmitted the shifting alterations.
> Through six times of bestowing taro,
> Yet another subtle mechanism opened.
> He pervaded the unified qi that predates our birth;
> He focused on the place before the Five Phases appeared.
> This led him to open the Jade Door
> And to pass through the Gold Gate.
> A brilliant sun and moon dwell within the pot;
> Assembling clouds and mists are contained in the tripod.

---

183. Person unidentified.

184. The following titles are still extant: *Jianwu ji* (DZ 1142), *Jinyu ji* (DZ 1149), *Shenguang can* (DZ 1150), and *Fenli shiwu ji* (DZ 1155). The latter contains poems by both Wang Chongyang and Ma. There are also various discourse records associated with Ma Danyang, namely, (1) *Danyang yulu* (DZ 1057); (2) *Danyang zhiyan* (DZ 1234); (3) Untitled opening section of the *Zhenxian yulu* (DZ 1256, 1.1a–2a); and (4) "Danyang zhiyan" in the *Qunxian yaoyu zuanji* (DZ 1257, 2.15a–16a). See chapter 2 herein. Other hagiographies list the following lost works: *Chengdao ji* (Anthology of Completing the Dao) (*Jinlian xiangzhuan*, DZ 174, 26b) and *Yuancheng ji* (Anthology of Perfect Completion) (ibid., 26b; *Lishi tongjian xubian*, DZ 297, 1.23a). Goossaert 1997, 425.

Grasping his walking sandals, he abandoned the "half-province" estate;

On the top of his head, he formed his hair into three topknots.

For several tens of years, he slept among snow and frost;

[13b] He wandered for several ten thousand *li*, traversing mountains and fording streams.

Among the seven petals of the Gold Lotus, he was most advanced in understanding;

Considering the secret instructions in five sections,[185] he alone transmitted them.

With that single sounding of a thunderclap,

He did not turn his back on the agreement of red mists.

Through the karma of ten thousand *kalpa*s,

He once again returned to the wandering of blue skies.

He began handing down the Way of Complete Perfection,

Issuing and directing those within the Mysterious Doctrine.

Zhang Shentong wrote the following poem:

Among the literati of the seaside, he was a premier scholar;

In the past, Perfected Chongyang once supported him while drunk.

Among those cultivating perfection in the past and present,

No one compares to Master Ma in practice and attainment.

Qiu Changchun[186]

Figure 31. Qiu Changchun

---

185. See the hagiography of Wang Chongyang further on.

186. The hagiography of Qiu Chuji (1148–1227) from the *Jinlian ji*, DZ 173, 4.7a–14a. The illustration comes from the *Jinlian xiangzhuan* (DZ 174). Other hagiographical accounts of Qiu Changchun's life include the following in chronological order: (1) "Changchun zhenren benxing bei" (1228) by Chen Shike (fl. 1228) (*Ganshui lu*, DZ 973, 2.5a–11a; Chen 1988, 456–58); (2) *Lishi tongjian xubian* (post-1294) by Zhao Daoyi (fl. 1294–1307) (DZ 297, 2.10a–22a); (3) *Jinlian xiangzhuan* (dat. 1326) by Liu Zhixuan (fl. 1326) (DZ 174, 32a–36a); and (4) *Jindan liexian zhi* (ca. 1331) by Chen Zhixu (fl. 1270–1350) (DZ 1069, 5a–5b). Largely due to his meeting with Chinggis Qan, Qiu Changchun has received the most scholarly attention. For some relevant secondary sources on Qiu's life and place in Quanzhen Daoism see Yao 1986; Wong 1988; Reiter 1993; Hachiya 1998; Zhao 1999; Katz 2001; Marsone 2001, 105; 2010; Belamide 2002. For a chronology of Qiu's early life and religious activities see Yao 1959b.

Master Qiu had the taboo name Chuji [Abiding Pivot] and the personal name Tongmi (Pervasive Secret). His religious name was Changchun (Perpetual Spring).[187] His worldly home was Qixia.[188]

He was part of an extremely renowned clan. He was intelligent and exerted great effort to learn things. He was highly capable and elevated in talent. His eyebrows were relaxed and broad. He committed himself to carefully examining the essential and refined. Considering his virtuous appearance, people would say that his features exhibited tortoise patterns[189] and that he certainly would become an emperor, king, or master. When he was still young, before he went through the capping ceremony, he became very interested in the Mysterious Movement [Daoism]. If conversations did not focus on perpetual life and relevant considerations, he would not speak. If discussions did not include riding Luan-birds and mounting phoenixes [immortality], he would not participate.

In spring of the *dinghai* year of the Dading reign period [1167],[190] **[7b]** he heard that Master Chongyang was living in Yanxia dong (Cavern of Misty Vapors) in the Kunyu mountains.[191] He exerted effort, at times even slipping and stumbling, to get there. He lifted his robes and requested to receive the teachings. As soon as Master Chongyang saw him, he had great affection for him. They talked with each other until late in the evening. They were united by the mysterious pivot. Master Chongyang in turn conferred a poem that read,

> Fish with finely textured golden scales play in the flowing blue;
> Chasing after fragrant cakes, they end up swallowing a hook.
> Here in retirement, you have received the silk thread cloth—
> Drag your tail and enter Penglai, forever free and independent.[192]

Master Qiu bowed and respectfully received it.

Throughout morning and evening, he served as an assistant to Master Chongyang. He willingly accepted work that involved sweeping and cleaning. He went east with Master Chongyang amid the ocean and mountains; they wandered south to Bianliang.[193] After long months and years of training, Master Qiu's aspirations and qi were full and firm. He assisted Master Chongyang in transmitting the Dao; they were closer than as though being attached by glue and varnish. By wondrously supporting the Mysterious Gate, many people began to become illuminated.[194]

---

187. Qiu's original name is unknown.

188. Qixia is located in the central western part of the eastern peninsula of Shandong. It is southwest of Yantai.

189. Tortoises are traditionally associated with divination (prognostication) and longevity. The present description suggests auspicious marks concerning Qiu's "fate."

190. The Dading reign period (1161–1189) of the Jin emperor Shizong (1123–1189; r. 1161–1189).

191. The Kunyu mountains are located in the eastern peninsula of Shandong, southeast of Yantai and southwest of Weihai. They were the site of Yanxia dong (Cavern of Misty Vapors), where Wang Chongyang trained his Shandong disciples.

192. Possibly an allusion to chapter 17 the *Zhuangzi*: "Once, when Zhuangzi was fishing in the Pu River, the king of Chu sent two officials to go and announce to him: 'I would like to trouble you with the administration of my realm.' Zhuangzi held on to the fishing pole and, without turning his head, said, 'I have heard that there is a sacred tortoise in Chu that has been dead for three thousand years. The king keeps it wrapped in cloth and boxed, and stores it in the ancestral temple. Now would this tortoise rather be dead and have its bones left behind and honored? Or would it rather be alive and dragging its tail in the mud?' 'It would rather be alive and dragging its tail in the mud,' said the two officials. Zhuangzi said, 'Go away! I'll drag my tail in the mud!'" (adapted from Watson 1968, 187–88).

193. Bianliang corresponds to present-day Kaifeng, Henan, which is located in the northeastern part of Henan near Zhengzhou.

194. Or, "he became more and more illuminated."

One day, the Patriarch-master [Wang Chongyang] announced that he had a covenant with Penghu; he abandoned things and left people, and then entered the heavens. After a great burial ceremony, Master Qiu traveled west to Fengxiang.[195] He begged for alms in Panxi.[196] In the place where his ancestors went fishing, he fought the demon of sleep and expelled his various thoughts.

For about seven years, he forced himself to remain in seclusion. He wore a rain-cloak of leaves and bamboo rain-hat, **[8a]** regardless of whether it was hot or cold. People thus called him Master Rain-cloak. Among the wondrous, he united with empty Nonbeing; within principle, he pervaded mysterious obscurity. He once again returned to Liujiang,[197] which was the site of the first master's old hermitage. Because of his strong connection, he was unable to leave.

In the second month of the *wushen* year of the Dading reign period [1188], Emperor Shizong heard about Master Qiu's reputation. He sent an envoy with a summons requesting his presence at the imperial court; it was bestowed with deep sincerity. It stated that the emperor was waiting to issue an imperial edict [granting Master Qiu control of] Tianchang guan (Monastery of Celestial Perpetuity).[198]

At a later time, he received an imperial request to serve as the head officiant for a Wanchun jiao (Offering for Endless Longevity).

During the new moon of the fourth month, an imperial decree was issued that appointed him abbot of Quanzhen tang (Hall of Complete Perfection);[199] it once again had a seal-script heading with the emperor's signature.

On the first day of the fifth month, Master Qiu was summoned for an audience at Changsong dao (Island of Perpetual Pine).

In autumn, on the tenth day of seventh month, he was again summoned. The emperor requested for Master Qiu to expound on the principle of heaven and humanity and to illuminate the ancestor of the Dao and inner power. If this were done, he would be deeply content and highly pleased.

Master Qiu responded by sending an offering of the "Yaotai diyi ceng" (On the First Floor of the Turquoise Terrace), which reads,

> Precious substances circulate and dragons fly among the four oceans
> When numerous immortals descend and leave their traces.
> There are myriad opportunities and leisure increases.
> If one accords with the Three Numinosities
> And does not move armed banner guards,
> One can stretch out among jade towers and gold halls.

---

195. During the Jurchen Jin dynasty, Fengxiang was located slightly northeast of Baoji, in the northwestern part of Shaanxi.

196. Panxi is a small tributary of the Wei River, located just southeast of Baoji, Shaanxi. It is most well known in Quanzhen as the location of Qiu Changchun's first hermitage.

197. Liujiang is located in present-day Huxian, Shaanxi, which is about fifty kilometers southwest of Xi'an. It is fairly close to the famous Daoist monastery of Louguan tai (Zhouzhi, Shaanxi). It was the site of Wang Chongyang's second hermitage and of an eremitic community, of which He Dejin and Li Lingyang were members. After the interment of Wang Chongyang's body there, Liujiang became identified as the Zuting (Ancestral Hall) of Quanzhen.

198. Tianchang guan was the earlier name of present-day Baiyun guan (White Cloud Monastery) in Beijing. See Marsone 1999.

199. Location undetermined.

[8b] Among moon-gazing terraces and breezy cottages overlooking ponds,
In tranquil inactivity,
Floating and drifting on variegated boats—
Oars sing among the cool bamboo and Pingqi play.
Even when earlier kings interrupted their work,
Great Peace was still difficult to meet,
And the Dao was difficult to encounter.
Extending the protection of heaven,
The distant wilds have sent in tribute
So that the Mysterious Doctrine may relieve confusion.
Sit at court and extend your listening,
Leisurely associating with Master Chisong (Red Pine)[200]
And conversing with Master Xiyi (Infinitesimal Subtlety).[201]
Exerting your utmost effort,
After a short interval among humans,
Return to the emptiness beyond the heavens.
With the great joy of highest perception,
Return to speak in the evening.

At dawn of the next day, the main envoy presented a dish of peaches. Master Qiu had not consumed tea or fruit for over ten years. Because the envoy's sagely kindness was so generous, Master Qiu forced himself to eat one piece.

In the middle of autumn, he received an imperial decree while returning to the mountains. It conferred one hundred thousand strings of cash. After it was displayed, he declined.

In the second month of the *jiyou* year [1189], crane-riding, he left Yantai.[202] When he arrived at the pass to Shaanxi, he suddenly received news that the emperor [Shizong] had died. Master Qiu sighed and said, "How pitiful, the great matter of life and death. It would take ten thousand carriages to carry his honor; his beneficial influence was the size of the four oceans. And yet, he was not able to live to one hundred years. Who else is like him?"

[9a] Then, without hesitation, he accordingly had the determination to go west. He passed through Hangu Pass[203] and traversed the Zhongnan mountains. He adapted himself to the opening and transformation, so that the Mysterious Movement might benefit.

When the reign title changed to Mingchang,[204] he returned east toward the seacoast and went into seclusion in Qixia, where he had the altar eaves repaired.

From then until the *wuchen* year [1208], the worldly status of the Dao expanded and flourished. Master Qiu's reputation filled the four directions, and the emperor came to admire him. He issued

---

200. A famous Daoist immortal, often associated with health and longevity practice.

201. Chen Tuan (Xiyi [Infinitesimal Subtlety]; d. 989).

202. Yantai is located in the central northern part of the eastern peninsula of Shandong.

203. Hangu Pass is located in Lingbao, Henan. It is most famous in Daoist history as the mythological site where Laozi transmitted the *Daode jing* to Yin Xi.

204. The Mingchang reign period (1190–1195) of the Jin emperor Zhangzong (r. 1190–1208).

an imperial edict conferring the Taixu guan (Monastery of Great Emptiness).[205] He also added a gift of the *Xuandu baozang* (Precious Canon of the Mysterious Capital),[206] which consisted of over six thousand *juan*. It was permanently housed at the monastery. He began residing there shortly afterward.

Armored troops began filling the area north of the river. Both Song and Jin envoys brought imperial summons and came to pay their respects. At the same time, the Mongols, dwelling in the north, sent the envoy Liu Zhonglu to present an imperial summons. Everyone felt that Master Qiu should move south. In this way, the idea of revering the Dao would become deeply established in the south. If they remained in the north, people felt that a major massacre would occur. They repeatedly talked about this without any resolution. Master Qiu did not speak, but rather selected disciples who were willing to travel with him. They amounted to eighteen people.[207] He accepted the summons and traveled west with Liu Zhonglu.

[**9b**] After passing through various overgrown and wild places, they arrived at Dexing prefecture[208] and stayed in Longyang guan (Monastery of Dragon Radiance). There he sent a poem to his various friends in Yanjing, which read,

> Through ten years of military arson fires, tens of thousands of people grieved;
> Among a hundred thousand, not one or two survived.
> Last year I was fortunate to receive a merciful imperial summons;
> This spring I must commit to braving the cold and travel.
> I did not shrink from the northern mountain passes, three thousand *li* high,
> Because I repeatedly remembered the two hundred counties of Shandong.
> The impoverished were hastily executed, with the dying all around.
> From early on, I have taught the importance of life to relieve grief.

He passed by white bones throughout the country, through dark winds and heavy snow. The cold entered his bones and marrow, and the road was filled with danger and hardships. He had prepared himself for such experiences.

He then wrote a long essay to an ancient tune in order to record his travel impressions:

> On a path east of the golden mountains and west of shadowed mountains,
> A thousand peaks and ten thousand ravines frame the deep creek.
> Near the creekside, scattered rocks are sleeping on the road;
> From ancient times to the present, it was not permitted for carriages and horses to enter.
> In previous years, armed troops gathered strength under two emperors;

---

205. Taixu guan is located in Qixia, Shandong. It was partially rebuilt, renovated, and repopulated by Quanzhen Daoists in 2005. Author's field observations.

206. The Jin-dynasty *Daozang* (Daoist Canon) completed in 1191 under the reign of Emperor Zhangzong (r. 1190–1208).

207. The *Xiyou ji* (DZ 1429, 1.1b) mentions nineteen, but in the appendix (5b–6a) to the same text only eighteen names are given. Judith Boltz notes that section 1.22b of the same text informs the reader that one disciple, a certain Zhao Jiugu (a.k.a. Zhao Daojian; Xujing [Empty Stillness]; 1163–1221), died *en route* (Boltz 1987, 315, n. 421). However, Zhao is listed as one of the eighteen disciples, so the identity of the nineteenth, if there were nineteen, remains unknown.

208. Location unidentified.

They fixed the roads and made bridges to connect the creek waters.
This year I have expressed the desire to travel west;
The noise of carriages and horses is heard passing by here.
Among silvery mountains and iron walls piled in a hundred thousand layers;
[10a] They compete and wrangle to brag about purity and bravery.
Each day we go out to look down at the vast and cold ocean environs—
The moon illuminates above and connects with the River of Heaven.
The celestial pines are straight like brushes and reeds;
Their lush vegetation's movement extends to over a hundred feet in height.
Among ten thousand densely entwining green branches,
A solitary bird holds back its song among the sky's silence.
Through narrow paths and foreign passes, we press on in the grand travel;
Compared to this, our great plan seems very common.
Paired draught carts go up and down, suffering under the effort;
Among the hundred mounted horsemen in front and back, many become startled.
Celestial ponds and oceans reside above the mountain peaks;
For a hundred *li* mirroring the sky, they hold myriad appearances.
Tying up carriages and tethering horses, we descend the western mountains.
The area beneath forty-eight bridges measures ten thousand *zhang*.
South of the river and north of the ocean, mountains are endless;
Through a thousand changes, ten thousand transformations, the pattern remains the same.
Even though it seems that this mountain is a great and unique hindrance,
Boulders will fall and steep hillsides will be overcome through our spiritual accomplishment.
The time of our arrival will occur during the eighth or ninth month;
We have already ascended half of the mountains, all snow-covered.
The grasses and trees in front of the mountains are warm like spring;
The clothing and quilts behind the mountains are cold like iron.

They traveled west for several thousand *li*. [10b] During their travels, they saw mountain forms and river conditions, strange people and extraordinary things. Many of these were completely different from the Central Kingdom.

At this time, Emperor Chengjisi[209] was protecting the outer edges of the kingdom; he had not yet crossed the borders. The envoy Liu Zhonglu accordingly introduced Master Qiu in an imperial audience. The emperor addressed him, saying, "You have never before responded to the summons from other kingdoms. But now you have traveled a vast distance of ten thousand *li* and come here. We are greatly pleased by this." Master Qiu responded, "Among the mountain wilds, I reverently received your summons and its arrival was celestial. It was not by human power that this has been done." The emperor invited Master Qiu to dine with him. After they finished eating, he inquired, "The Perfected has arrived from a great distance; does he have the medicine of perpetual life, which may help me?" Master Qiu responded, "I only have the way of protecting life; I don't have the medicine of perpetual life."

---

209. Chinggis Qan (Genghis Khan; ca. 1162–1227; r. 1206–1227).

The emperor was very fond of Master Qiu's honesty and authenticity; each day he accordingly summoned Master Qiu to audience. During these times, Master Qiu admonished him to decrease violence and killing and to extinguish desire and anger. The instructions before and after these amount to several thousands of words. At that time, Yelü Jinqing[210] was serving as vice-chancellor, and he made a record of their conversations in the *Xuanfeng qinghui lu* (Record of Celebrated Meetings of the Mysterious Movement).[211] The emperor received the instructions with sincerity and tried to apply them. [11a] He asked Zhenhai[212] the following question: "How should one refer to a Perfected?" Zhenhai respectfully replied, "If he is someone deserving of respect, we should call him 'father-master'; if he is a Perfected, we should call him 'spirit immortal.'"[213] Thereafter, in keeping with Zhenhai's advice, he referred to Master Qiu as "spirit immortal."

In spring of the *guiwei* year [1223], Master Qiu reverently received an imperial edict requesting that he return to Yanjing escorted by several thousand armored horsemen. It also ordered that Tianchang guan be renamed Changchun gong (Palace of Changchun) and that Baiyun guan (White Cloud Monastery) be renovated. These two were joined into a single monastery. The northern palace on Wansui shan (Mountain of Ten Thousand Years) near Taiye chi (Pond of Great Waters) was also conferred; its name was changed to Wan'an gong (Palace of Ten Thousand Serenities). The edict also decreed that all monastics and virtuous people throughout the realm would be under Master Qiu's direction. This was decreed through the gift of a golden tiger tally. It was thus appropriate for him to undertake the task, and a large number of people received the imperial orders.

Master Qiu then served as abbot of Changchun gong and engaged in the great undertaking of teaching and conversion. The Way of Complete Perfection became closely entwined and grew dramatically. Master Qiu served as the head officiant at the *jiao*-offering altar. When he prayed for wind and rain, they would arrive at the appointed time without fail, like shadow and echo. Among a thousand gateways and ten thousand windows, there was no one who did not turn to observe it.

[11b] At that time, Master Qiu was often free and uninvolved. Generally speaking, after the afternoon meal, he frequently went with several horsemen to Wan'an gong. He delighted in the nourishing beauty of mountains and creeks; he enjoyed the evening mists among animals and fish. He would go out at daybreak, and would return toward dusk.

On the twenty-third day of the sixth month of the *dinghai* year [1227], Master Qiu did not go out because of a slight illness. Between the hours of *si* [9 a.m.–11 a.m.] and *wu* [11 a.m.–1 p.m.], the people announced that great thunder and rain had occurred. The southern bank of Taiye pond broke off, and the waters moved into the eastern lake. The sound was heard for several tens of *li*. All of the sea tortoises and freshwater turtles left. The pond accordingly dried up. The mountain cliff near its northern mouth spontaneously collapsed. When Master Qiu heard this, he laughed and said, "The mountain cliff is destroyed and the pond dried up; I will prepare to join them."

On the initial fourth day of the seventh month, Master Qiu addressed his disciples: "In the past, Master Danyang offered a record to you that read, 'After I perish, there will be a great

---

210. Jinqing is the personal name of Yelü Chucai (1190–1244).

211. The *Xuanfeng lu* (DZ 176; partially translated in Waley 1931, 21–25) is attributed to the Yila Chucai (Yelü Chucai), who also wrote the *Xiyou lu*. See de Rachewiltz 1962. Cf. The *Xiyou ji* (DZ 1429) by Li Zhichang (Zhenchang [Perfected Constancy]; 1193–1256). The latter text has been translated by Arthur Waley (1931).

212. Zhenhai's Mongolian name was Cingqai; he was one of Chinggis Qan's military advisors.

213. *Shifu* and *shenxian*, respectively.

flourishing of our tradition. It will be disseminated throughout the four directions so that they join together as a Daoist village. This will occur when the time is appropriate. The abbots of every large temple and monastery will receive an imperial edict that mentions each of their names. As is the normal case, officials wearing imperial tallies will ride out and give notification. **[12a]** When merit becomes complete and reputation becomes fulfilled, it will be time to return and resign.' Each and every one of Master Danyang's words has proven true, and I will now return without any remaining remorse or regrets."

Then in the manifest silence,[214] at the first quarter-hour after noon on the ninth day, he ascended to Baoxuan tang (Hall of Precious Mystery) and left behind the following ode:

> Life and death, dawn and dusk—they are exactly the same;
> Empty bubbles float up and burst apart, while the water is perpetually at ease.
> Among the manifest place of subtle radiance, I leap over raven and rabbit;[215]
> Within the opening moment of mysterious limit, I enclose oceans and mountains.
> I attend to affairs within the eight expanses as though close at hand;
> I encourage the myriad beings as though controlling the motive power.
> With this wild message and descending brush, I complete the dust;
> I send my message to contemporaries who reside among false rumors.

After this, Master Qiu returned to Baoguang tang (Hall of Contained Radiance), and joyfully embraced the transformation of the butterfly.[216] At that time, there were azure Luan-birds and white cranes flying all around. Auspicious vapors flooded the area, and immortal music enveloped the locale. He ascended into emptiness and was gone. Of the various officials and literati, there was no one who did not express their reverence. They buried his coffin near Chushun tang (Hall of Abiding Prosperity) at Baiyun guan.

After three years, they opened the coffin to change the clothes. **[12b]** The body's hands and feet were like soft padding; the facial color and appearance resembled those of the living.

Master Qiu left behind a variety of writings, including songs and poetry, miscellaneous reflections, written documents, essays, direct instructions, and discourse records. They have the following titles: *Panxi ji* (Anthology of Panxi), *Mingdao ji* (Anthology of Singing the Dao), and *Xiyou ji* (Record of Westward Travels).[217] They contain several thousand poems and have been circulated throughout the world.

Master Xuefeng[218] wrote the following elegy:

> Qian-heaven and Kun-earth form the hall's rooms;
> The sun and moon serve as luminous candles.

---

214. That is, "dying." Reading *shiji* for *shiji*. The former is often used as a respectful expression for the death of a Buddhist.

215. The raven corresponds to the sun (yin within yang) and the rabbit to the moon (yang within yin).

216. *Diehua*, "butterfly's transformation," alludes to chapter 2 of the *Zhuangzi*. See note 63 in this chapter.

217. Of these titles, the *Panxi ji* (DZ 1159) and *Xiyou ji* (DZ 1429) are still extant, although the latter was written by Li Zhichang, one of Qiu's senior disciples. The *Xiyou ji*, like the *Xuanfeng lu* (DZ 176), contains various teachings attributed to Qiu. There are also two other extant works attributed to Qiu: *Dadan zhizhi* (DZ 244), which is translated in chapter 4 herein, and "Changchun Qiu zhenren ji Xizhou daoyou shu" (DZ 1256; 1.12a–19a), which is translated in Belamide 2002, 178–84.

218. Adept unidentified.

Among the layered mists, a venerable immortal
Looks up and down from the central lunar lodging.
Responding to the masses, he converses about the celestial—
His communications blow through icicles and jade.[219]
He opens the pivot of mystery and subtlety;
He secretly accepts offerings among his vast prosperity.
Through refinement, his spirit becomes pure—
Spirit radiance shines forth from his eyes.
Rising to stand, his body becomes light—
Clear currents give rise to strength and sufficiency.
Whether or not the great Dao flourishes,
It reaches and resides in the heart-mind and thought.
Whether or not the golden elixir is complete,
White clouds fill the cliffs and valleys.

I offer the following elegy:

In the past, I traveled to Yantai
And saw three people conversing about venerable immortal Qiu's accomplishment and virtue.
The first person said,
"For seven years, he practiced with strong determination among the waters and banks of
     Panxi;
[13a] For several years, he passed his time like a stream at Baoxuan tang.
He refined the foundation of the golden elixir and great medicine;
He tended to the tree of the flaming date and joined pear.
Sending out spirit and entering dreams,
He circulated across earth and then returned to the heavens.
Such is his greatest accomplishment and virtue."
The second person responded,
"This is not the case.
He oversaw the renovation of temples and the building of monasteries;
He transmitted the teachings in order to rescue people.
He opened the lotus of the seven petals of Complete Perfection
And planted a tree of the three blossoms of formlessness.
In ordaining people,[220] he converted half of the country;
In discoursing on the Dao and inner power, he traveled throughout the world.
There was no one who did not drink from Twofold Mystery;
Everything was completely soaked in utmost transformation.
Such is his greatest accomplishment and virtue."
The third person replied,

---

219. Vernacular for "father-in-law" and "son-in-law."
220. Literally, "received hairpin and cap."

"Considering what you two masters have said,
You have only noticed his lesser merit, not his greatness.
You have realized the coarse, but have not identified the refined.
You have merely grasped a handful of Taishan (Mount Tai)
And collected a leaf from the forests of Deng.
I, on the other hand, consider when the Mongolian crack-troops came south—
After watering their horses, [13b] they put forth effort to cross the Yellow River;
After unleashing their arrows, they aimed to bring ruin to the Western Marchmount
　　[Huashan].
They set fire without distinguishing between jade and stone;
Both the worthy and foolish were slaughtered equally.
Corpses piled up like mountains, seemingly reaching the Dipper.
Blood gushed forth like oceans, seemingly covering the sky.
Their fearsomeness was like thunder;
Their mercilessness was like a tiger.
Fortunately for us, venerable immortal Qiu Changchun responded to the summons;
As soon as the emperor saw him, his face became clear like the sky.
After another imperial audience, the celestial decree gradually returned.
The emperor decreed that those who followed his orders would not be punished.
He promised that the surrendering cities would avoid death;
He forgave the people and granted pardons;
He released prisoners so that they would become peaceful and virtuous.
Within the four hundred regions, half the people lived peacefully.
Throughout an area of several ten thousand *li*, people received the benefit.
This is what we refer to as extending one's arm to support mountains of broken peaks,
As laying one's body horizontally to protect rivers and stream banks.
Master Qiu salvaged life and numinosity from within the tripod and cauldron;
He took hold of innate nature and life-destiny from below the knife and saw.
The numbers saved went beyond hundreds, thousands, or even millions—
Taking into account the capital and frontiers, the numbers are inestimable.
Such was his hidden merit.
It completely pervaded the celestial decree;
[14a] It was so strong that it extended to the cerulean mists
Like a brilliant sun in its ascent.
Compared to this, what is the use of the nine-times reverted cinnabar sand
Or the seven-times inverted jade *ye*-fluids?"

Zhang Shentong also wrote a commemorative poem:

> Engaging in refinement at Panxi, he refined the nine-times reverted sand;
> He took the elegant chapters of the *Daode jing* as the highest expression.
> When the time of Three Islands arrived, he responded and departed;
> At that moment, Luan-birds and cranes sang among layered mists.

Shi Chuhou[221]

The master was from an old and esteemed family of Liquan in Qianzhou.[222] He had the surname Shi and given name Gongmi.

When still a youth with hanging tufts of hair, his heart-mind longed to attain the Dao. In the *renwu* year of the Dading reign period [1162],[223] he heard that Patriarch Chongyang had met an immortal,[224] had received secret instructions and was nourishing the Dao in the Zhongnan mountains. At that time, Adept Shi went to request to take the religious oath, which he was accordingly granted. He was trained in the Quanzhen study of innate nature and life-destiny. After this instruction, he received the [religious] name Chuhou (Abiding Authenticity) and the Daoist name Dongyang (Cavernous Yang). From then on, he begged for his food and refined his heart-mind, wandering around Hu village in the Zhongnan mountains.[225]

In spring of the *dinghai* year, the seventh year [of the Dading reign period] [1167], Patriarch Chongyang was preparing to travel eastward to the sea. He directed Master Dongyang to serve him on his travels, but the master excused himself from this duty on account of his mother's advanced age. [6a] He did not dare to travel so far away. Patriarch Chongyang accordingly painted a Daoist with three topknots residing among the clouds. Beside him, there was a pine and a crane.[226] He gave it to Master Dongyang, saying, "Attend to the secret that is stored here; this is the talisman of unification that was given in earlier times."

Later, in spring of the *gengyan* year [1170], Patriarch Chongyang became an immortal in Bianliang,[227] and Patriarch Danyang led his three Daoist companions to enter the pass. They arrived at Kongxian an (Hermitage of Immortal Kong) in Chang'an. Master Shi went out on the road to welcome them. This was the time when Patriarch Danyang first began wearing his hair in three topknots.[228] Master Dongyang remembered the day when Patriarch Chongyang transmitted the painting, and he had great admiration for that extraordinary event.

The four masters told him about the beginning and development [of the teachings] on the coast [in Shandong], and the event of the Patriarch's ascension to immortality in Bianliang. He had handed on the seal to them so that it could be transmitted further. The master was deeply happy. Then with the four masters he repaired the hermitage in Liujiang and lived there. Patriarch Danyang frequently instructed them with poetry and lyrics, time and again encouraging and supporting them. Whether in activity or leisure, he was competent and diligent and full of the great Wondrousness.

Afterward, Master Dongyang returned to Liquan, harmonizing his radiance and amusing himself in the world. He was unrestrained by ritual propriety or laws. When people referred to him as Shi Fengzi (Lunatic Shi), he shouted at them. He frequently sang and danced in the marketplace,

---

221. The hagiography of Shi Chuhou (1102–1174) from the *Zhongnan neizhuan*, DZ 955, 1.5b–7a.

222. During the Jurchen Jin dynasty, Liquan was located slightly northwest of Xi'an, Shaanxi.

223. The Dading reign period (1161–1189) of the Jin emperor Shizong (1123–1189; r. 1161–1189).

224. It is unclear in this text whether Wang met one or more than one immortal.

225. Hu village most likely refers to Huxian, which is about fifty kilometers southwest of Xi'an.

226. These are symbols of longevity and immortality.

227. Present-day Kaifeng, Henan.

228. As a symbol of his lineage connection with Wang Chongyang, whose name Zhe consists of three *ji* ("auspicious") characters. "Zhe" could thus be interpreted as "Threefold Auspiciousness." In appearance, Ma Danyang's three topknots resemble and symbolically represent the character "Zhe."

[6b] only saying that he would soon return to Peng Village. None of the ordinary people understood his meaning. It was like this for three days, after which he went to his hermitage and suddenly [cast off] the cicada shell. This was the fifteenth day of the six month of the *jiawu* year [1174].

The local officials and magistrates did not offer their respects to him, and he was initially buried in Liquan. However, the following year Patriarch Danyang had him moved and reburied in the immortal grave-mounds of Liujiang. When they opened the inner coffin, they saw that the color of his face still resembled that of the living.

Patriarch Danyang composed an elegy in four-character lines that reads,

> Master Shi gained a meeting,
> Gained a meeting with Chongyang.
> Chongyang gave him the transmission,
> Gave him the transmission of the Mysterious Yellow.[229]
> Through the Mysterious Yellow, he reached utmost principle,
> Utmost principle that was not forgotten.
> Internally, he practiced cultivation and refinement;
> Externally, he severed ties to hot and cold.
> The water and fire were then completed,
> And the sun and moon joined their radiance.
> The dragon hummed in the position of Li-fire;
> The tiger roared in the chamber of Kan-water.
> Wood and Metal became divided,
> And the maiden and women formed a circle and square.
> With a dose swallowed as a glistening drink,
> He himself knew its taste and fragrance.
> With the divine elixir correctly coalesced,
> A dazzling radiance and flourishing yang.
> The wind's immortals arrived to liberate him,
> Manifesting a wonderful blessing.
> He sang and danced for three days,
> Taking leave from urban roads and wards.
> He simply said he was returning,
> Hastening to leap into Peng Village.
> **[7a]** He once gain entered his hermitage
> To quickly meditate and then disappeared.
> The one who observes clouds collecting
> Realizes situations and principle as extraordinary.
> The unified numen, perfect innate nature,
> Moves among the ranks of arrayed immortals.

Concerning the master's allotment of the Dao, you yourself can discern it based on reading the words of this elegy. He enjoyed seventy-three years of life.

---

229. Alchemy.

In the *guihai* year of the Zhongtong reign period [1263],[230] people once again visited the grave-mounds of the immortals [Liujiang]. When they opened the tomb and looked within, almost one hundred years later, the master's bones still had not separated or scattered. They had the color of gold and the concentration of stone. I am one of those who saw this. How extraordinary!

Sun Buer[231]

Figure 32. Sun Buer

Immortal lady Sun was the daughter of Sun Zhongyi.[232] Her worldly home was Ninghai.[233] Before she was born, her mother had a dream in which seven cranes were dancing inside her chamber. After a while, six cranes flew away, but one solitary crane entered her bosom. When she awoke, she realized that she was pregnant. Later on she gave birth to this girl.

Master Sun's nature was extremely intelligent and wise. While still living in the women's chambers, she followed the rules with attentiveness and veneration. She studied and became proficient with brush and ink and became very skilled at recitation.

She eventually married Master Ma [Danyang] and gave birth to three children, all of whom she taught how to be just and righteous.

In winter of the *dinghai* year of the Dading reign period [1167],[234] Master Chongyang arrived from the Zhongnan mountains. Ma Xuanfu began treating him with deep respect,[235] **[9b]** but immortal lady Sun did not yet believe in him. She then locked Master Chongyang in his hermitage

---

230. The Zhongtong reign period (1260–1263) of the Yuan emperor Qubilai Qan (Khubilai Khan; Emperor Shizu; r. 1260–1294).

231. The hagiography of Sun Buer (1119–1183) from the *Jinlian ji*, DZ 173, 5.9a–11b. The illustration comes from the *Jinlian xiangzhuan* (DZ 174). Other hagiographical accounts of Sun Buer's life include the following in chronological order: (1) *Lishi tongjian houji* (post-1294) by Zhao Daoyi (fl. 1294–1307) (DZ 298, 6.15b–19a); (2) *Jinlian xiangzhuan* (dat. 1326) by Liu Zhixuan (fl. 1326) (DZ 174, 39b–41a); and (3) *Jindan liexian zhi* (ca. 1331) by Chen Zhixu (fl. 1270–1350) (DZ 1069, 6b–7a). For some relevant secondary sources on Sun's life see Hachiya 1998; Despeux and Kohn 2003, 140–49.

232. Sun Buer's original given name was Fuchun. In Daoist literature, she is also sometimes referred to as Sun Yuanzhen or Sun Xiangu (Immortal Maiden Sun).

233. Present-day Muping, located slightly southeast of Yantai, Shandong.

234. The Dading reign period (1161–1189) of the Jin emperor Shizong (1123–1189; r. 1161–1189).

235. Xuanfu, sometimes appearing as Yifu, was the original given name of Ma Danyang.

for more than one hundred days, without offering food or drink.[236] She occasionally opened the door to see how he was doing. His facial complexion was even better than usual. At this point, she began to have faith and express respect for him.

Master Chongyang would send out his spirit and enter their dreams, resorting to all kinds of shifting appearances. He tried to frighten them with visions of the Earth Prisons and to entice them with thoughts of the Celestial Hall. After ten occasions of dividing pears and six moments of offering taro, Xuanfu accordingly became his disciple and entered the Dao. However, even after that immortal maiden Sun's feelings of affections were not yet extinguished. She had not yet made her decision. After waiting for a year, she began separating from her sons. She donned a bamboo cap and cotton robe, and was summoned to Jinlian tang (Hall of the Gold Lotus) in her home prefecture,[237] where she offered her respects to Master Chongyang and received ordination. Master Chongyang gave the following poem to her:

> Over these years, I made ten attempts to convert you through divided pears;
> I matched auspicious times with the heavens in their original suchness.
> At that time you were unwilling to separate from your family;
> You simply waited patiently for the right time to coalesce the golden lotus.

Master Chongyang then conferred the religious name Buer (Nondual)[238] and the Daoist name Qingjing sanren (Recluse Clear Stillness). Master Sun also received celestial talismans and secret instructions in cloud-seal script.

Master Chongyang then went south to Bianliang[239] and abandoned his husk there. **[10a]** Master Qiu, Liu, Tan, and Ma gathered his immortal bones and returned to the Zhongnan mountains to bury them. When immortal maiden Sun heard this, she began wandering west. She passed through the clouds and crossed over the moon. She lay down in the snow and slept in the frost. She ruined her facial appearance without any sense of grief.[240]

In spring of the *renchen* year [1172], she went to Jingzhao[241] and visited Penglai zhai (Residence of Penglai), where she met Ma Danyang. There he transmitted a wondrous decree on the *Cantong qi* (Token for the Kinship of the Three),[242] so that she could pass through the cavity of principle. Master Ma then conferred a poem titled "Lian dansha" (Refining Cinnabar Sand), which reads,

---

236. This section has an important discrepancy, as other hagiographies suggest that Wang Chongyang locked himself in Quanzhen an (Hermitage of Complete Perfection) in order to practice meditation enclosure. This account may be read generously as Sun Buer testing Wang Chongyang's authenticity or negatively as an attempt on Sun's part to kill Wang. There is a hint of misogynistic discourse here. For some basic insights into the historical inclusion and exclusion of Sun Buer in the so-called Seven Perfected see Marsone 2001.

237. The Jinlian hui in Ninghai.

238. Literally, "not two." Thus, Buer could be read as "Without Second," in the sense of being unmatched in excellence.

239. Present-day Kaifeng, Henan.

240. Unlike later hagiographies and fictional accounts, which suggest that Sun threw boiling oil on her face in order to intentionally disfigure herself (see Wong 1990), the present work appears to suggest that the disfigurement was a byproduct of committed and sustained Daoist practice. Nonetheless, Sun was unconcerned about her physical appearance and conventional notions of "beauty." I leave it to the reader to determine if physical beauty is incompatible with spiritual realization.

241. During the Jurchen Jin dynasty, Jingzhao was basically synonymous with Xi'an, Shaanxi.

242. The *Cantong qi* (DZ 999 and DZ 1004) is a terse and highly symbolic discussion of external alchemy, which became influential in later internal alchemy traditions.

I offer this poem to Lady Fuchun
That she may abandon the desire to follow me—
Today we are no longer husband or wife.
Each must engage in self-cultivation and complete perfection according to her own situation.
Abandon the three defilements and refine qi, but do not teach the coarse.
Whether high or low, there is a sense of relaxation;
It is continuous and subtle, as though simultaneously existent and nonexistent.
Within each person there is a numinous purity—
If we harmonize ourselves through its influence,
We will be able to journey to the immortal capital.

Immortal maiden Sun received the poem with gratitude, at which point they parted company and went in opposite directions. They lived in solitary places and refined their heart-minds while in meditation enclosure. After seven years, Master Sun's Three Fields were reverted and the hundred cavities were completely connected and circulating.

She accordingly left the enclosure and traveled east, eventually arriving in Luoyang.[243] **[10b]** There she urged people to convert according to their own inclinations, and she ordained many people.

One day she wrote a lyric to the tune "Bu suanzi" (Casting Lots), which reads,

> When you seal the fists and loosen your robes,
> The Water and Fire will immediately commingle and merge.
> The misty vapors of the myriad districts manifest below the ocean;
> With a single strike, the Three Passes become penetrated.
> Immortal bliss continually expands
> As you constantly drink the delicious wine.
> The wondrous medicine is completely beyond time limits;
> The nine-times reverted cinnabar sand becomes complete.[244]

After completing this, she made the following declaration to her disciples: "Masters and Perfected have a covenant; each must journey to the Turquoise Pond when the moment of immortality arrives." She then bathed and changed her robes. Afterward she addressed her attendants: "Is it early or late in the day?" They responded, "It's noon." She accordingly took the full lotus posture, practiced upright meditation, and calmly accepted the moment.[245] Her complexion still appeared as though she was living, and a fragrant wind filled the room. Auspicious vapors enveloped the area, and descended to spread across the outlying wilds. They did not disperse for an entire day. This occurred on the twenty-ninth day of the twelfth month in the *renyin* year [1182].

---

243. Luoyang is located in the northwestern part of Henan. According to the *Lishi tongjian houji*, Sun moved to Luoyang in 1179, where she possibly trained with a female Daoist recluse from Henan named Feng Xiangu (Immortal Maiden Feng; fl. 1145–1179). It appears that Feng lived in an "upper cave" (*shangdong*) and had Sun live in the lower one. Sun practiced and taught there until her death in 1182.

244. See the relevant translations in chapter 1 herein.

245. That is, "died."

At that time, Master Danyang was living in a meditation enclosure in Ninghai. He looked up and saw immortal lady Sun mounted on five-colored auspicious clouds, which shifted back and forth as she sat suspended in the sky. **[11a]** She laughed and said, "I am the first to return to Penglang!" When Master Danyang heard this, he threw off his clothes and began dancing. The event led him to write the "Zuixian ling" (Order of the Drunken Immortal).[246]

I offer this elegy for her:

> The reputation of Buer is lofty—
> She guarded the One until her accomplishment was great.
> She was a descendant of the Fuchun clan
> And was born into the Zhongyi family.
> She married Ma Danyang whose talent was surpassing;
> She planted offspring in the half province of Ninghai.
> She severed her affections and eventually separated from her three sons—
> She embraced the mysterious and offered her respects to Chongyang.
> She ruined her radiant complexion and went west toward Zhongnan;
> She covered herself in wind and frost and left the eastern oceanside.
> Living in a meditation enclosure for seven years,
> She refined and completed the nine-times reverted cinnabar sand.
> Through the perfect explanation of a single sentence,
> She passed through the Three Passes and the upright path.
> Through six occasions of receiving taro
> And ten attempts at conversion through divided pears,
> She tended to karmic connections beyond the present epoch;
> She reverted the transformative process within the pot.
> She nourished the immortal embryo and her heart-mind wandered in the vast expanse;
> She abandoned the mundane husk and her body entered into Penglai.
> How great!
> How amazing!
> **[11b]** She formed one petal of the Gold Lotus;
> She became a ranked immortal among the Seven Perfected.

---

246. There are no surviving independent collections of Sun Buer's writings. The only reliably attributed poems are contained in the mid-fourteenth-century *Minghe yuyin* (DZ 1100), which have been translated here in chapter 1. There are also various later, spuriously attributed works. Most of these date to the Ming (1368–1644) and Qing (1644–1911) dynasties, during which time female alchemy (*nüdan*) became more systematized and Sun Buer was elevated to the position of matriarch. Relevant texts include the *Sun Buer yuanjun fayu* (Dharma Sayings of Primordial Goddess Sun Buer; JY 212; ZW 370) and *Sun Buer yuanjun chuanshu dandao bishu* (Secret Writings on the Way of the Elixir Transmitted by Primordial Goddess Sun Buer; JY 213; ZW 371) (see Boltz 1987, 155–56; Despeux 1990, 170, 292–301; Yao 2000, 578; Despeux and Kohn 2003, 212–14, 241–43). Later poems attributed to Sun appear in various collections, including the *Sun Buer nüdan shi zhu* (Commentary on Sun Buer's Poetry on Female Alchemy; Chen 1934), *Nüdan hebian* (Collected Works on Female Alchemy; Tao 1989, 1–188), and *Nü jindan fayao* (Essential Methods of the Gold Elixir for Women; JH 48) (see Despeux 1990, 170, 291–302; 2000; Despeux and Kohn 2003, 206, 212–14). Sections of this text and the *Sun Buer yuanjun gongfu cidi* (Practices and Stages of Sun Buer; Tao 1989, 282–88) have been translated in Thomas Cleary's *Immortal Sisters: Secret Teachings of Taoist Women* (1989b). Readers should note, however, that none of these works were actually composed by Sun Buer. The most that can be said is that some of the works claim to be inspired or revealed by Sun.

Zhang Shentong wrote the following poem in memory of her:

> She wiped off face-powder and the obscurity of dual faces;
> For ten years she exerted herself tending the Yellow Sprouts.
> With accomplishment complete, she mounted an azure Luan-bird;
> She became the seventh petal of the Gold Lotus.

Tan Changzhen[247]

Figure 33. Tan Changzhen

The master had the taboo name Yu. His personal name was Boyu. His surname was Tan, and his worldly home was Ninghai.[248]

He was a generous and loyal person. His degree of distinction and discernment was extraordinary. Filial piety and righteousness had been maintained within his family, so that they became deeply respected among the local villages.

In winter of the *dinghai* year of the Dading reign period [1167],[249] he suffered from vertigo and paralysis. He was so thoroughly bound up that it could not released. He had numerous acupuncture and herbal treatments, but they had no effect.

He heard that Master Chongyang had arrived from the Zhongnan mountains and was living in a hut on the propriety of Lord Ma Xuanfu.[250] Supported by his walking stick, Master Tan went to visit Master Chongyang. He was seeking a method to heal his condition.

Master Tan peered through the unlined doorway and saw that Master Chongyang was securely guarded within. In the evening, Master Tan tapped on the door. Before he had even finished, the

---

247. The hagiography of Tan Chuduan (1123–1185) from the *Jinlian ji*, DZ 173, 4.1a–3a. The illustration comes from the *Jinlian xiangzhuan* (DZ 174). Other hagiographical accounts of Tan Changzhen's life include the following in chronological order: (1) "Changzhenzi Tan zhenren xianji beiming" (*Ganshui lu*, DZ 973, 1.27b–31b; Chen 1988, 454–55); (2) *Lishi tongjian xubian* (post-1294) by Zhao Daoyi (fl. 1294–1307) (DZ 297, 2.1a–5a); (3) *Jinlian xiangzhuan* (1326) by Liu Zhixuan (fl. 1326) (DZ 174, 27a–29a); (4) *Jindan liexian zhi* (ca. 1331) by Chen Zhixu (fl. 1270–1350) (DZ 1069, 4ab). For some additional information on Tan Chuduan see Reiter 1996; Hachiya 1998; Marsone 2001; 2010.

248. Tan had the religious name Chuduan (Abiding Decency) and the Daoist name Changzhen (Perpetual Perfection). He also had the additional name of Tongzheng (Pervasive Alignment).

249. The Dading reign period (1161–1189) of the Jin emperor Shizong (1123–1189; r. 1161–1189).

250. Ma Danyang.

door suddenly opened on its own. Master Chongyang was extremely happy; he believed that it was a meeting of immortal karma. Master Chongyang then invited him to share his sleeping quarters. **[1b]** They talked about how they had a close relationship because of a former meeting.[251]

When they awoke that morning, Master Tan's old illness was suddenly healed. His four limbs were light and vigorous. He walked around and it felt like he was flying. Then he knew that Master Chongyang was an extraordinary being.

He instantly renounced his material possessions as though they were heaps of dung. He requested to serve as Master Chongyang's assistant, saying that he would not cease until the end of his life.

Master Chongyang then gave him the religious name Chuduan (Abiding Decency), the personal name Tongzheng (Pervasive Alignment), and the additional religious name Changzhen (Perpetual Perfection). He also conferred the following poem:

> Leap beyond yin and yang to the pass of creative transformation;
> Unify your heart-mind with the Dao so that you never return.
> The root of clarity and emptiness is the road to perfected immortality;
> Simply strive to dwell in serenity and nourish your internal condition.

Master Tan then received Master Chongyang's instructions: Destroy self and other; sever ties to worry and anxiety; put on the azure kerchief; and wear thin cotton clothing.

In the *wuzi* year of the Dading reign period [1168], he took leave from family and relatives, abandoned village and township, and followed the Patriarch-master [Chongyang] as an attendant. They wandered south to Bianliang.[252] In the morning, Master Tan received counsel; in the evening, he asked questions. He obtained many mysterious decrees.

After three years, the Patriarch-master ascended into the clouds and gained an audience with the Origin. Then Master Tan and the other disciples carried his immortal bones west and returned to Liujiang.[253] They buried them with the appropriate ritual propriety.

[2a] Later on, he hid his traces among the Yi and Luo rivers,[254] where he harmonized his spirit and refined his qi. Even if he found himself among mundane happenings and imperial affairs or brothels and taverns, his heart-mind was like earth and wood.[255] He never experienced any agitating thought. Even if he found himself among yellow gold measuring ten thousand *liang*, he never became entangled in it. He accordingly drifted and floated at leisure, eventually arriving at Chaoyuan gong (Palace for Attending the Origin) in Shuinan.[256] This was the place where Master Langran (Clear Suchness) refined the elixir,[257] so Master Tan loved it and did not leave.

---

251. Previous incarnation.

252. Present-day Kaifeng, Henan. The timeline here seems slightly off, as the other hagiographies have Wang Chongyang and his four disciples going to Bianliang in 1170, that is, the year of Wang's death.

253. Present-day Huxian, Shaanxi.

254. Shaanxi and Henan, respectively.

255. Stable and unconcerned.

256. Shuinan most likely refers to the area below the Wei and Yellow rivers. The present Chaoyuan gong would thus have been in Henan Province, probably in Luoyang.

257. Master Langran is probably the Daoist alchemist Liu Xiyue (924–ca. 1008). Liu lived in Tongxuan guan (Luoyang), which was renamed Jizhen guan in posthumous honor of him. See *Taixuan Langranzi jindao shi* (DZ 271); Schipper and Verellen 2004, 931.

From that point on, large numbers of disciples gathered there. They quickly received large amounts of alms. While begging, they passed by an old Buddhist monastery, where a Chan master was living and collecting offerings of food and money. When he saw them, the Chan master was greatly angered and punched Master Tan in order to drive him away. The blow broke two of Master Tan's teeth, which mixed together with blood and were swallowed into his stomach. Everyone around the two men wanted him to strike back. However, Master Tan simply laughed and bowed his head; there was not the slightest amount of agitation in his heart-mind. Because of this event, Master Tan's reputation became well known throughout Jingluo.[258]

In the evening, Master Tan enjoyed writing the two characters *gui* 龜 ("turtle") and *she* 蛇 ("snake"). He practiced continually. They marvelously conveyed his spirit and had the quality of flying and ascending transformation. Many sincere adepts who revered the Dao collected his calligraphy because they regarded it as a rare treasure. [2b] Later on, there was a calamitous fire in the prefecture that burned down a hundred homes. However, all of the houses of those who had collected his characters were spared.

One day, he addressed his disciples, saying, "Perfected Chongyang and I have a covenant with Penglai; now I will leave." As soon as he finished speaking, auspicious clouds in five colors encircled the edges of the courtyard, while azure Luan-birds and white cranes soared to and fro. Then, with his head to the east and his face toward the south, he used his forearm for a pillow and cast off his bones. This happened on the first day of the fourth month.

The songs and hymns that he left as a model for the world amount to around several hundred. They are collected in an anthology called *Shuiyun ji* (Anthology of Waters and Clouds).[259] They deeply illuminate lead and mercury and the way of tracing the Source. May they be extensively practiced in the world.

I offer this elegy for him:

The venerable immortal Changzhen,
A noble adept from Ninghai,
Became a fellow student of Mister Three Topknots.[260]
He bowed to Chongyang and received the covenant.
One evening, before the pure conversation had finished,
His illness of several years was suddenly healed.
He rejected a thousand gold pieces without consideration;
He gave away a hundred robes while content in his own poverty.
[3a] Refining his qi and harmonizing his spirit,
He wandered for several years below the Luo River.
He returned to the root and reverted to life-destiny,
But did not go back to Shandong for half his life.

---

258. If Jingluo is a specific place, I have not been able to locate it. In a broader sense, it refers to the imperial capital on the Luo River; under this reading, it corresponds to the provinces of Shaanxi and Henan.

259. The *Shuiyun ji* (DZ 1160) is still extant. There is also one attributed discourse record: "Changzhen Tan xiansheng shi menren yulu" as contained in the *Zhenxian yulu* (DZ 1256, 1.9b–10b); cf. *Shuiyun ji*, DZ 1160, 1.20b–21a.

260. Ma Danyang.

He guarded against a hundred oddities by hiding his form.
Writing the two characters for turtle and snake,
He maintained the two rites through his own effort,
Working on the nine reversions of dragon and tiger.
He directly met the fragrance of cinnabar and cassia
And encountered the brilliance of the Gold Lotus.
In the *Anthology of Water and Clouds* he commented on lead and mercury;
Among the mists and smoke, he became a traveler of Penglang.
If not for his flesh and bones taking flight together,
And his form and spirit joined in mutual wondrousness,
How else could he have become like this?

Zhang Shentong wrote the following poem:

> With wind and fire in his chest, he was committed like iron and stone;
> Upright, dedicated, and heroically strong, he inwardly returned the radiance.
> Among the warm springs of Luoyang, his spirit wandered about;
> It was as though he was the turtle and snake guarding the northern direction.

Wang Chongyang[261]

Figure 34. Wang Chongyang

---

261. The hagiography of Wang Zhe (1113–1170) from the *Jinlian ji*, DZ 173, 2.1a–10a. The illustration comes from the *Jinlian xiangzhuan* (DZ 174). Other hagiographical accounts of Wang Chongyang's life include the following in chronological order: (1) "Zhongnan shan shenxian Chongyangzi Wang zhenren Quanzhen jiaozu bei" (1225) by Wanyan Shu (1172–1232) (*Ganshui lu*, DZ 973, 1.2b–10a; Chen 1988, 450–54); (2) "Zhongnan shan Chongyang zushi xianji ji" (1232) by Liu Zuqian (ca. 1175–1232) (*Ganshui lu*, DZ 973, 1.10b–14a; Chen 1988, 460–62); (3) *Lishi tongjian xubian* (post-1294) by Zhao Daoyi (fl. 1294–1307) (DZ 297, 1.1a–11b); (4) *Jinlian xiangzhuan* (dat. 1326) by Liu Zhixuan (fl. 1326) (DZ 174, 18a–23a); *Jindan liexian zhi* (ca. 1331) by Chen Zhixu (fl. 1270–1350) (DZ 1069, 2b–3a). For some relevant secondary sources on Wang Chongyang's life see Hachiya 1992; Reiter 1994; Marsone 2001, 97–101; 2010.

The master had the taboo name Zhongfu and the given name Yunqing.[262] He was from one of the most renowned families of Xianyang.[263]

At the time, Liujiang[264] was a remote place filled with water and bamboo, mist and vapors. He began building a country villa there, which was finished according to his plan.

Regarding his character, his constitution was strong and robust, while his manner was honest and flexible. His eyes were bigger than his mouth, and his beard hung down to his stomach. His voice was like a bell, and his complexion had the appearance of jade. Like a clear wind, he was airy and graceful. Like a purple vapor, he was present and abundant. One could make out the marks of lakes and oceans in him. He had the strength of two people, and his talent was beyond the norm.

In earlier years, he focused on the classics and histories. In later years, he studied military pursuits. At this time he was uselessly placed among mounds and torches, having been given an official position in spring. However, because he held his own opinions, he was dismissed. Next, he tried a military career, but could advance no further than a foot soldier.

When he reached forty-seven years old, **[1b]** he sighed deeply and said, "At forty Kongzi [Confucius] was free from doubts, while at the same age Mengzi [Mencius] had a heart-mind without agitation. I have already passed that age, but even with all my trying I can only consume rank flesh and peck at rotting meat. Distorting my divine qualities and hankering after precious metals, is this not the depth of great ignorance?"

Following this, he resigned from office, got rid of his seal, and abandoned his wife and children. He brushed off the dust of the external world from his clothing. He restrained himself from wild license and let himself loose in the vastness. This occurred in the *jimao* year of the Zhenglong reign period [1159],[265] when he was forty-eight years old.

On a bridge in Ganhe[266] he passed by a butcher's door. He was fond of coarse roots and wanted to get one to chew on. There happened to be two Daoists in this place,[267] and each one was unrolling a white mat. Unexpectedly and suddenly, they came [toward Patriarch Chongyang] from the south. They had the manner of misty vapors, and the essence and spirit of the Milky Way. By observing their eyebrows, he could see that they generally looked like the same type of person.

The master, unaware of the apprehension rising up in him, hastened to enter. He lowered his head and prostrated himself in front of them. Speaking together with a language that was beyond this world, they cleansed and purified his defilements. They separated fat from bone and cut out every delusion. It was like a drunkard becoming sober, like a mute finding his voice. They secretly transmitted the perfect instructions. Then they gave him the given name Zhe (Wise),[268] personal

---

262. Wang Zhe also had the following names: Zhiming (Wisdom Illuminated; personal name), Dewei (Virtuous Majesty; personal name), Shixiong (Hero of a Generation; personal name), and Chongyang (Redoubled Yang; Daoist name).

263. Xianyang is located just northwest of Xi'an, Shaanxi.

264. Liujiang is located in present-day Huxian, Shaanxi, which is about fifty kilometers southwest of Xi'an.

265. The Zhenglong reign period (1156–1160) of the Jin emperor Wanyan Liang (a.k.a. Hailing wang; r. 1149–1160). The date for these events is often given as the first year of the Dading reign period (1161) of the Jurchen-Jin emperor Shizong (1123–1189; r. 1161–1189).

266. During the Jurchen Jin dynasty, Ganhe was located slightly northwest of Liujiang (Huxian), Shaaanxi.

267. Other hagiographies identify these Daoists as "immortals" (*xianren*), "perfected" (*zhenren*), "divine beings" (*shenren*), or "extraordinary beings" (*yiren*). Some also claim that they were the famous immortals Zhongli Quan (Zhengyang [Aligned Yang]; second c. CE?) and Lü Dongbin (Chunyang [Pure Yang]; b. 798?), with the former sometimes said to have been born in Xianyang, Shaanxi. For a skeptical analysis see Marsone 2001, 98–100, 103. For a more sympathetic account see Komjathy 2007a.

268. This character consists of three *ji* ("auspicious") characters, which is significant in the later tradition. For example, when Ma Danyang binds his hair into three topknots, it is taken as a symbolic representation of Wang Chongyang's name.

name Zhiming (Knowing Illumination), and religious name Chongyang (Redoubled Yang). **[2a]** When this was completed, they pointed toward the east and said, "Why don't you look over there?" When the master turned his head to look, the Daoists said, "What do you see?" Patriarch Chongyang responded, "I see a seven-petaled golden lotus bearing seeds." The Daoists laughed and said, "How can it stop there and be completed? There will be a ten-thousand-petaled jade lotus that becomes fragrant."

When they finished speaking, the master suddenly became disoriented. After this, he became disheartened and disconsolate. He begged for his food in the marketplaces using shallow baskets and broken gourds. He slept on ice and snow. He has a poem that reads,

> At forty-eight years, I obtained my first encounter—
> With the oral instructions transmitted, there was accomplishment.
> A seed of the golden elixir, its appearance incomparable—
> Above the mountains of the Jade Capital, it manifests its deep redness.

The next year, in the *gengchen* year [1160], he found himself lodging together with a Daoist. During the month, the Daoist addressed him saying, "I live among the great mountains of the northwest. In that place, there are people who take joy in deep conversation, especially on the essential meaning of the *Yinfu jing* (Scripture on the Hidden Talisman) and *Daode jing* (Scripture on the Dao and Inner Power).[269] I have heard that in the past you yourself liked these two scriptures. Why don't we go together so that we might experience and observe the situation ourselves?" The master was unsure about this and had not yet decided. **[2b]** The Daoist suddenly stood up. Taking hold of his staff, he mounted the wind and departed. The master went around trying to find him, but there was no news or sign of him. He was startled as though something had been lost.

During mid-autumn, he passed through Liquan County,[270] where he again met the Daoist. He hastened to greet him and offer his obeisance. Filled with joy, they invited each other to enter a tavern. They drank together, during which the master asked where he was from. The Daoist responded, "In the eternal joy of mats and cliffs is where I live." The master also asked his age. The Daoist responded, "I have seen twenty-two springs and autumns." Then the master asked his clan. The Daoist remained silent and would not speak. The Daoist then asked for a brush and some ink in order to write secret instructions in five sections.[271] After writing them, he read them with great care. He then allowed the master to read them several times. Master Chongyang eventually realized their wondrous principles. The Daoist cautioned him saying, "The pivot of heaven[272] cannot be dispersed lightly." Then he commanded him to throw them into the fire. After this, the Daoist said, "Quickly go to the eastern ocean. Among its Qius, Lius, and Tans, there is a superior Ma.[273] You can catch him." After he finished speaking, he disappeared.

269. On these texts in early Quanzhen see chapter 5 in this volume.

270. Liquan is located slightly northwest of Xianyang, Shaanxi.

271. *Miyu wupian.* Cf. the late, "extra-canonical" *Wupian lingwen* (JY 202; ZW 866).

272. "Pivot of heaven" translates *tianji*, which echoes various sections of the sixth-century *Yinfu jing*. See chapter 5 in this volume.

273. These names anticipate Wang Chongyang's later Shandong disciples, with the reference to *ma* playing with the meaning of "horse." This sentence also confirms the reader's suspicion that Ma Danyang receives a place of privilege in the *Jinlian ji*, as the length and details of his hagiographical entry indicate.

The first instruction said, "Leap over this land of Qin [Shaanxi]. Drift and travel through Chang'an. Sell the elixir in the marketplaces and towns, **[3a]** or hide your traces in the mountains and forests. Then, after several years like this, you will be able to perceive living beings with open eyes—they eventually end up as lower ghosts, inhuman and wayward. Today I have met you, my disciple. Why don't you immediately abandon the ocean of the mundane? Courageously awaken from the insubstantial clamor. Enjoy eating vapor in front of the blue ridges, and continue to refine your qi below the pine-covered peaks. Intercede in the transformative process, and invert yin and yang. Make the arrayed lunar lodgings resplendent in the nine cauldrons. Collect the ten thousand transformations inside the single pot. After a thousand dawns of accomplishment being fulfilled, your name will be suspended in the immortal metropolis. After three years of diligent work, you will forever ward off negative influences through the ten thousand *kalpas*. I am afraid that if you undertake this too late, your body will sink beneath the springs."

The second instruction said, "Do not delight in the insubstantial clamor like holding a jug of alcohol; restrain yourself each day in the marketplace. When the dragon and tiger become agitated,[274] cast icy waves toward them; when the sound of water comes down, the blue dust disperses. As soon as you awaken to the appearances of mundane life, allow your thoughts to go forth without any set plan! One morning, the nine-times reverted divine elixir will appear, and we will go to Penglai together."

The third instruction said, "When the snake and dragon are refined in the pavilion of the beacon fire, **[3b]** the fierce tiger is caught and corralled in the vital essence of Water. Through strong determination, do not speak and recklessly discuss the Dao, chaotically concerning yourself with rival theories about affairs and emotions."

The fourth instruction said, "Lead is the medicine of mercury; mercury is the vital essence of lead. If you recognize lead and mercury, innate nature will abide and life-destiny will settle."

The fifth instruction said, "When nine reversions are completed, you will enter Nanjing (Southern Capital). Through deep familiarity, you will go to Peng[lai] and Ying[zhou]."

Master Chongyang accordingly returned to Liujiang. He built a hermitage with a beamed roof; he attached a board that read "Huo siren mu" (Tomb for Reviving the Dead).[275] He also placed a paper banner above the tomb's entrance, upon which he wrote "Wang Haifeng lingwei" (Tomb Marker of Lunatic Wang). He wrote the following poem:

> Wang Zhe, the living dead man, has lost his mind;
> Water and clouds recognize this and ridicule him.
> He goes by the Daoist name of Master Chongyang;
> Whether ridiculed or praised, he lies buried in the earth.

When travelers arrived, they did not forget to show their affection; they would walk over to the hanging tomb marker.

On a different day, he found a jug of alcohol placed on the road. A Daoist called out to him: "Haifeng, Haifeng, will you have a drink?" Master Chongyang agreed, and they drank together

---

274. Internal sexual movement.

275. Or, "Tomb of the Living Dead."

until the jug was empty. [4a] The Daoist then had him take the empty jug and fill it with water from the Gan River.[276] The Daoist commanded him to drink. The water tasted amazing—it was the drink of Perfected and immortals. The Daoist then declared, "I am Master Haichan."[277] As soon as he finished speaking, he suddenly disappeared. From that moment on, Master Chongyang ceased drinking alcohol. He only drank water.

Still, he constantly seemed drunk and would recite the "Yu meiren" (On the Excellent): "Haifeng drinks water in inestimable quantities. Because of this, he pervades the mysterious and wondrous. Clothed in white hemp robes and capped with a cotton azure kerchief, he enjoys the style and manner of the Perfected; he delights in his own vitality. There's no need to look for illumination in front of a mirror; in each and every situation the heart-mind is realized. Within this dream, distinguish and peer through the dream-encased self. Then, being carefree, you will completely understand the person who stands above the shore-banks."

Suddenly one day he set fire to his hermitage. His neighbors arrived and exerted effort to extinguish the fire. Master Chongyang simply remained unconcerned and danced about. The people asked the reason. He responded, "After three years, I found that this person has become cultivated." He then wrote the following poem:

> With my thatched hut set ablaze, the great affair is finished;
> There assuredly are those who will withdraw and commit to cultivation.
> [4b] It will be best to act alertly and develop courage and fervor;
> This is what will inspire study and attainment, causing my movement to flow.[278]

On the twenty-sixth day of the fourth month of the seventh year of the Dading reign period [1167],[279] he began traveling east. He passed through Xianyang and drew a map on a strip of cloth. He became a three-topknotted Daoist. Azure pines were densely arrayed; white clouds gathered around; and immortal cranes danced about. Such was his departure from influence of dust.

When we investigate the histories on wind-carried immortals, they happily honor him as follows: "The way that you waited for me the other day may be compared to someone who takes hold of a horse and arrives [like the wind]."

Master Chongyang also passed through Luoyang,[280] during which time he visited Shangqing gong (Palace of Highest Clarity). He affixed a poem on the wall that read,

> The currents of Qiu, Tan, and Wang take hold of Ma and Liu;
> On the peak of the Kunyu mountains, we will strike and create a jade globe.

---

276. Gan River is a southern tributary of the Wei River, located just southwest of Xi'an, Shaanxi.

277. Liu Cao (Haichan [Oceanic Toad]; fl. 940–1030?) is most often identified as a disciple of Chen Tuan (Xiyi [Infinitesimal Subtlety]; d. 989) and a principal figure in the dissemination of *neidan* techniques during the Song dynasty. He was later recognized as a patriarch in the lineages of Quanzhen and the so-called Nanzong (Southern School) of internal alchemy. He appears as one of the Five Patriarchs of Quanzhen in the *Jinlian ji* (DZ 173) and *Jinlian xiangzhuan* (DZ 174).

278. It is difficult to convey the literariness of this section. The entry plays with the character *feng* (lit., "wind") throughout. The meaning alternates among currents, fashion, lunacy, movement, qi, and actual wind.

279. The Dading reign period (1161–1189) of the Jin emperor Shizong (1123–1189; r. 1161–1189).

280. Luoyang is located in the southwest corner of Henan.

> You must send it to the inside of the encompassing ocean;
> Hold on to it for three thousand and eight hundred calculations.

While in Donghai and Weizhou,[281] he met Perfected Xiao,[282] who had too much of the airs of immortal currents and Daoist bones.[283] Master Chongyang had a deep desire to strike him. Instead, they strolled about for several days, talking with each other without agreement. Master Chongyang offered him a piece of writing about leaping over mountains and streams: "The Perfected is already awakened; among the four oceans, your reputation is the first to arrive. This is only because there is a sound to hear. You still remain separated from the mysterious, primordial, and wondrous Dao. **[5a]** How pitiful that immortal bones will descend and take on the form of ghosts. One aspect is decay; another is old age. It is pointless to consider the aspect that becomes realized. How can one come to know the mysterious and wondrous if one firmly clings to pride in body and mind? You pass the days as if deaf and blind. You disperse yourself without recognizing the cinnabar sand and the furnace. If you find a way to take hold of two substances, you will coalesce and complete the elixir inside the tripod. If you swallow it down, you will attain perpetual life. Seize this with your own hands to return to Peng[lai] Island!" Perfected Xiao read it, but in the end he was unable to realize its wondrous decree. He simply nodded in assent and that was all.[284]

Patriarch-Master Chongyang accordingly went east to the seaside. He wandered around for several years, during which time he admonished and induced people to transform themselves.[285] He eventually gained the loyalty of Qiu, Liu, Tan, Ma, Hao, Sun, and Wang, who became the seven petals of the Gold Lotus. They collectively converted the three prefectures and founded the five associations: Pingdeng hui (Association of Equal Rank), Jinlian hui (Association of Gold Lotus), Yuhua hui (Association of Jade Flower), Sanguang hui (Association of Three Radiances), and Qibao hui (Association of Seven Treasures).[286] Their temple-boards read as follows: "We take equal rank to be the ancestor of the Dao and inner power, as the source of clarity and purity. It is the root of the Gold Lotus and Jade Flower; it is the ancestor of the Three Radiances and Seven Treasures. **[5b]** It provides universal assistance to sentient beings, so that each and every one leaps beyond the mundane. Silvery flames fill the eight boundaries; variegated mists envelop and fill the ten directions. Every person endeavors to produce the Yellow Sprouts; everyone avoids wandering among dark thoroughfares. The Jade Flower is the ancestor of qi, and the Gold Lotus is the ancestor of spirit. When qi and spirit coalesce, we refer to this as 'spirit immortality.'"[287]

---

281. During the Jurchen Jin dynasty, Weizhou was located in the southwest corner of Hebei.

282. Perfected Xiao refers to Xiao Daoxi (a.k.a. Han Daoxi; 1157–?), the second patriarch of the Taiyi (Great Unity) movement. Kubo 1967, 116–18; Hachiya 1992, 75–76. On the Taiyi movement see Yao 1980, 27–33; Goossaert 1997, 40–43. Based on the fact that Xiao Daoxi would have been ten years old at this time, this meeting is most likely a later accretion, indicating a moment when Quanzhen incorporated members and elements from the Taiyi and Dadao movements. I take the sentence to mean that Xiao was pretending to be a realized being. One could also read the sentence in a more positive light as "a disproportionate share" of divine endowments.

283. *Xianfeng daogu*.

284. Note the polemical and sectarian characteristics of this section.

285. Or "converted people."

286. Established in Laizhou, Ninghai, Dengzhou, Fushan, and Wendeng, respectively.

287. See also "Yuhua she shu" (Guidance for the Jade Flower Society; *Quanzhen ji*, DZ 1153, 10.20b–21a), which is translated here in chapter 2.

One day, Master Chongyang directed Qiu, Liu, Tan, and Ma to travel south with him to Bianjing.[288] It had been several years since Master Chongyang lodged somewhere at leisure. During this time, he guided the illumination of many people. This caused him to write the "Zhuzhang ge" (Song of the Bamboo Staff), which reads as follows:

> Leaning on a single elongated staff, my name remains undisplayed;
> Joint by joint, moment by moment, a brilliant radiance is clearly arrayed.
> How powerful this empty heart-mind, aligned and ordered!
> Inside everything is a numinous elixir medicine.
> Neither agitated nor moving, I am naturally clear and expansive;
> When responding to things, I follow the pivot and act appropriately.
> Above the ocean, I engage in solitary inquiry, knowing that companions will arrive.
> I determine who is fit to become a follower and supporter.
> Last night in a dream I saw numerous young dragons gathered together;
> There were four dragons among them who were able to leap and dance.
> With a single staff extension,
> My foot moves one pace.
> The top of my head is interspersed with silvery strands;
> [6a] With hoary eyebrows and dew-filled eyes, my vitality quickens.
> Issuing forth a numinous pearl, my radiance flashes brilliantly;
> The luminous flame inspires everyone to become joyous.
> White clouds are unable to bear the brilliance of red mists.

After he wrote this poem, he addressed his disciples, saying, "At a former time, I received a secret instruction from a perfected master. It said, 'When the nine reversions are complete, you will enter the Southern Capital. You will know friendship, and then wander to the islands of Peng and Ying.' Now I will join with its covenant."

His disciples were deeply alarmed. They begged for him to leave behind teachings for the world. The Patriarch-master said, "Three years ago I wrote this on a wall: 'Master Chongyang of Difei[289] is also called Wang Haifeng (Lunatic Wang). His arrival follows the sun and moon. His departure relies on east and west. He has become a companion of clouds and water; he has become the associate of emptiness and nonbeing. When the unified numen and perfect nature reside, there is no more joining with the masses.'"

He also wrote the following poem:

> Haifeng, Haifeng, old age and illness issue forth—
> Your lifespan will not exceed fifty-eight years.
> When the two masters decide to arrive,
> Unified numen and perfect nature are purified.

---

288. Bianliang, present-day Kaifeng, Henan.

289. Difei is an alternate name for the Zhongnan mountains, located about seventy kilometers southwest of Xi'an, Shaanxi.

He also addressed the community: "After I return [to the Source], don't allow your grief to overwhelm you." After he finished speaking, he cast off his husk. **[6b]** Master Danyang did not realize that tears were flowing down his face. He was deeply grieved. The people admonished him, saying, "It isn't right to ignore the words of the immortal master." Master Danyang responded, "In entering the Dao, I still lack any attainment. My master has abandoned me, and I don't know what to do."

Before he had even finished speaking, Master Chongyang suddenly opened his eyes and spoke: "Why do you have this deep vexation? In the past, I obtained the secret instructions in five sections at Ganhe. Today I transmit them to you." Master Danyang bowed again and then knelt down to receive them.

Master Chongyang then addressed Master Tan: "I place each of your innate natures and life-destinies in the hands of Danyang." He accordingly composed poems about the kinship beyond thinghood:

> A nephew, two sons and one mountain rustic—
> We are joined together as five adepts with a single aspiration.
> Six luminosities meet as regularly as the moon meets the sky's edge;
> Seven vitalities come together like a wind over the ocean.
> Within perfect wondrousness, we pick out the hidden Wonder;
> Above the clear sky, we find our way in the empty Void.
> East, west, north, and south form a complete circuit—
> When you reach this complete understanding,[290] you pervade every place.

He also wrote,

> One younger brother, one nephew, and two children—
> We are connected to each other as five adepts engaging in cultivation.
> **[7a]** Bound together to become perfected kin beyond thinghood,
> We abandon the unreal composite corpse residing among humans.
> The encircling seeds develop in the realm of clear purity;
> The extending transmission offers a branch of purple numinosity.
> On the mountain peak, I leap out of the gathering of numinous flowers—
> I find my way to Penglai to become the first to offer respects to the masters.

After he finished composing this poem, he immediately returned to Perfection. Amazing fragrances enveloped the area; auspicious vapors filled the place. White cranes flew through the sky, while azure Luan-birds wandered over the earth. Immortal rituals were imperceptibly held on the lofty boundaries of the clouds. Literati and officials expressed their respect and reverence. It was like they were mourning for their own deceased mothers. There was no one who did not lament his passing: truly his extraordinary presence is gone forever.

They thereupon prepared his coffins, death garments, and shroud, and performed the requisite ceremonies and buried him. This occurred on the initial fourth day of the first month in the *gengyin* year of the Dading reign period [1170].

---

290. Literally, "squared knowing."

After he ascended into the distance, Master Chongyang discussed the mysterious and inspired goodness in the heart of an old man beneath the Junyi Bridge.[291] At the side of the brook near Liujiang, he provided medicine that healed the illness of Master Zhang. He was also seen dancing near Kunming pool and singing among places in the Zhongnan mountains. These various signs indicate that he was not, in fact, dead.

[7b] His four disciples Qiu, Liu, Tan, and Ma traveled west together to Chang'an. There they met Master Shi Feng,[292] who presented a picture of pines and cranes to them. Master Shi Feng laughed and said, "When this was made for me, I compared it with [Perfected Chongyang's] original. It exactly matches this picture. Comparing the two images, there is not a single discrepancy." They then traveled through the Zhongnan mountains and went to Liujiang, where they served as the resident leaders of the ancestral hermitage. They repaired and renovated it close to its original condition. They then went back to Liangyuan [Bianliang] in order to collect Master Chongyang's immortal bones. When they opened the coffin to inspect the body, they found that its appearance and spirit still had the quality of being alive. The four disciples then collected the bones and began traveling west. When they reached the road, they were about to pay the fees, but they were turned back by an attendant named Lü, who said, "A Daoist already came and settled the account." The disciples tried as hard as they could to go after him, but in the end they were unable to find him. When they inquired about his appearance, they realized that it was the Transformation Body of the Patriarch-master.

After they arrived in the Zhongnan mountains, they divined an appropriate place and reburied the remains.[293] They initially wandered outside of Wangxian men (Gate for Gazing on Immortals) in Dengzhou.[294] They encountered a minister on a painted bridge, who addressed them as follows: "In former times, why was this bridge destroyed?" No one could discern his meaning.

[8a] Later on they found a record that said Master He, a local prefect, hated the bridge's extremely dangerous steepness. He accordingly destroyed its sloped ravine and made it level by installing brickwork. Today the bridge is called Yuxian qiao (Bridge for Encountering Immortals).[295] That's what the meeting was about.

Following this, a *jiao*-offering ritual was performed in Wendeng among clouds of five colors.[296] They saw a huge white tortoise with a lotus flower on its back. Patriarch-master Chongyang was sitting in meditation on the lotus stamen. After a little while, he lay down on his side and disappeared. The local magistrate Nilong Kuqin was one of those who witnessed this event. Afterward, he lit incense and offered obeisance. He ordered artists to draw realistic depictions. All of the people of the three prefectures vied to gain a glimpse of the renderings.

---

291. The Junyi Bridge was located near Liujiang (Huxian), Shaanxi.

292. Most likely Shi Chuhou. According to his hagiography, the picture of pines and cranes was painted by Wang Chongyang.

293. Traditionally identified as Huxian, Shaanxi, where Chongyang gong (Palace of Redoubled Yang) was established. This was the location of the Liujiang eremitic community, where Wang practiced before going to Shandong.

294. I have been unable to locate Dengzhou on historical maps of Shaanxi. However, based on the context and other historical details, it must have been near Xi'an.

295. Original location unknown. In contemporary China, a bridge by this name is contained in the compound of Baxian gong (Palace of Eight Immortals; Xi'an, Shaanxi). Author's field observations.

296. Wendeng is located in the northeast part of the eastern peninsula of Shandong.

Master Danyang heard about this and wrote a lyric to the tune "Manting fang" (Fragrance Filling the Courtyard) to commemorate the events:

> In the ancient prefecture of Dengzhou,
> Beyond the Wangxian Gate,
> On a painted bridge carriages and horses find it difficult to pass.
> The sacred traces of Chongyang
> Respond to the people by manifesting a lineage influence.[297]
> Preparing to discuss "why the bridge was ruined,"
> We find a record:
> Master He, the local magistrate, felt that the gorge was dangerous;
> He commanded the people to demolish it
> And mandated that workman commence their work.
> In Wendeng, Master Chongyang appeared two times:
> On a lotus flower on a white tortoise
> And practicing seated meditation amid emptiness.
> This caused the chief magistrate to kneel to the ground
> [8b] And gain a glimpse of Master Chongyang's perfected form.
> He suddenly observed Master Chongyang turn and lie down on his side—
> As auspicious clouds floated about,
> He once again returned to the immortal palaces.
> When divided illumination appears,
> And the red and azure colors extend into the distance,
> Each and every place expresses its reverence.
> We refer to this as dying but not perishing.
> It is fitting indeed that he is the ancestor of the Seven Perfected.

Instances of his spirit transformations are inestimable and unable to be recounted. Among the eastern ocean and in western Qin he admonished and converted both Daoists and ordinary people. His songs of varying lengths amount to more than a thousand. They are collected in the early and later versions of *Quanzhen ji* (Anthology of Complete Perfection) and *Yunzhong lü* (Record among the Clouds).[298] They clearly explain lead and mercury as well as Kan-water and Li-fire. They have been handed down to the world. In addition, he wrote poems to the Daoist community in Dengzhou, which included nineteen supporting illustrations.

One piece of his writing reads as follows:

---

297. *Jiafeng.*

298. Of these works, the *Quanzhen ji* (DZ 1153) is still extant. Other extant literary anthologies include the *Jiaohua ji* (DZ 1154) and the *Fenli shihua ji* (DZ 1155), which contain poems by Ma Danyang as well. There are also a variety of attributed works, including the *Chongyang zhenren jinguan yusuo jue* (DZ 1156; trl. Komjathy 2007a), *Chongyang zhenren shou Danyang ershisi jue* (DZ 1157), *Chongyang lijiao shiwu lun* (DZ 1233), "Chongyang zushi xiuxian liaoxing bijue" (DZ 1056, 4b–6b), and "Da Ma shifu shisi wen" (DZ 1056, 6b–8b). Of these, I believe that the *Ershisi jue* and the latter two texts contained in the *Jin zhenren yulu* are definitely spurious. The hagiographies also list the following lost works: *Taoguang ji* (Anthology of Hidden Radiance) (*Jinlian xiangzhuan*, DZ 174, 22b; *Lishi tongjian xubian*, DZ 297, 1.11a) and *Hao lixiang* (On the Joy of Abandoning Villages) (*Fenli shihua ji*, preface, 2a). Goossaert 1997, 424.

I bow my head in reverence:
Circulating through the four seasons,
I am able to retain a youthful appearance.
The Three Teachings are clearly distinguished
And I work to release the suffering of ordinary life.
The various adepts realize unified awakening by regular cultivation;
The nine reversions are completed by directing the sun.
[9a] I ascend to immortality as the eight gates open,
While perpetual spring becomes my constant companion.
I dare to strive after the Wondrous;
I attend to joining with the Mysterious.
Then I write rustic stanzas
And later express them in illustrations.[299]

[9b] He also wrote the following poem:

By knowing constant unification, the Dao becomes familiar;
By striving to realize the Mysterious, one joins with it.
Awaken to principle without forgetting the instructions of the Three Teachings;
Complete Perfection by striving to attain spring within the four seasons.
Nourish and complete original qi until it becomes completely full;
Coalesce and form numinous spirit so that there is no dissipation.
Nineteen brilliant radiances follow from my personal vows;
I dare to invite my companions to delight in celestial perfection.

I offer this elegy in memory of him:

After the Patriarch-master abandoned the mundane world,
He gained four encounters with Perfected and immortals.
With a single taste of water from the Gan River,
He received secret instructions in five sections.
When nineteen leaves were contained by the Cassia tree,
Ten thousand branches ceased being separate from the Gold Lotus.
A precious mirror held high
Illuminated the landscape within the pot for Tan and Ma.
The divine pearl shining forth alone
Revealed the karma beyond *kalpa*s for Qiu and Liu.
Who knows that the lineage influence of Taigu
Can be relied on for protection and hidden guidance?
Who can maintain the memory of Yuyang
And trust in his name of Zhuyang for the secret transmission?

---

299. This section is followed by a circular poem that I have not translated.

[10a] Reverently holding up hooks and poles,
A great master was brought forth as the ocean of Moran.
Later returning to the drifting boats,
A recluse wandered around as the wellspring of Qingjing.
He became the director of the source of great teachings;
He opened the beginning of the gateway of Complete Perfection.
When his accomplishment was complete and his name enduring,
He mounted Luan-birds and cranes and ascended into the clear heavens.

Zhang Shentong wrote the following poem:

> He took leave of the cavern-heaven in the Zhongnan mountains;
> He went toward the eastern ocean to guide the various immortals.
> He solely focused on entering the sacred and transcending the mundane;
> He planted and brought forth the seven-petaled lotus of yellow gold.

Wang Yuyang[300]

Figure 35. Wang Yuyang

The master had the taboo name Chuyi (Abiding Unity). His Daoist name was Master Yuyang (Jade Yang). His surname was Wang,[301] and his worldly home was Dongmu in Ninghai.[302]

When still young, he lost his father, and accordingly took care of his mother with utmost filial piety. His physical appearance was eminent and strong. As a young boy, he was not confused by trivial

300. The hagiography of Wang Chuyi (1142–1217) from the *Jinlian ji*, DZ 173, 5.1a–6a. The illustration comes from the *Jinlian xiangzhuan* (DZ 174). Other hagiographical accounts of Wang Yuyang's life include the following in chronological order: (1) *Tixuan zhenren xianyi lu* (thirteenth c.) (DZ 594); (2) "Yuyang tixuan guangdu zhenren Wang zongshi daoxing beiming" (1307) by Yao Sui (1238–1313) (*Ganshui lu*, DZ 973, 2.13a; Chen 1988, 718–20); (3) *Lishi tongjian xubian* (post-1294) by Zhao Daoyi (fl. 1294–1307) (DZ 297, 3.1a–5b); (4) *Jinlian xiangzhuan* (dat. 1326) by Liu Zhixuan (fl. 1326) (DZ 174, 36b–39a); and (5) *Jindan liexian zhi* (ca. 1331) by Chen Zhixu (fl. 1270–1350) (DZ 1069, 5b–6a). For some relevant secondary sources see Hachiya 1998; Marsone 2001, 105–6; 2010.

301. Wang Chuyi's original name is unknown. He also had the honorific name of Tixuan (Embodying Mystery).

302. Present-day Muping, Shandong, located southeast of Yangtai on Shandong's eastern peninsula.

pursuits. Instead, he delighted in chanting the transcendental language of clouds and mists. At the age of seven, he encountered our founder Donghua [dijun] (Sovereign Lord of Eastern Florescence),[303] from whom he received instructions on the enduring matter of perpetual life.

At fourteen, while climbing mountains, he saw an old man sitting on a great rock, who called to Master Wang to come up. Thereupon he rubbed his head and addressed him: "In the future you will certainly become celebrated by the imperial court; at that time, you will become a great Patriarch-teacher of the Mysterious Gate." After he finished speaking, he got up and left with staff in hand. **[1b]** Master Wang went after him, unwilling to separate. Master Wang inquired, "Master, who are you?" He replied, "I am the ruler of Xuanting gong (Palace of the Mysterious Court)." Master Wang turned his head to search for him, but the old man was nowhere to be found. After this event, he would only discuss far-reaching matters. He refrained from mixing together with the mundane world. In his activities, he ceased engaging in any kind of unrestrained and reckless behavior.

In spring of the second month of [the *dinghai* year of] the Dading reign period [1167],[304] he had a day of leisure and traveled to a banquet being held at the Yuxian ting (Pavilion for Encountering Immortals) on Fan Mingshu's estate. He saw Patriarch-master Chongyang of the Zhongnan mountains there. After observing that Master Wang's body frame was truly uncommon, the Patriarch-master said, "Are you willing to become my disciple?" Master Wang replied, "Such is my vow; I dare not simply pledge my life." From that point on, he served as his assistant.[305] He formed deep and uninterrupted friendships with Master Qiu, Liu, Tan, and Ma.

He repeatedly requested to learn each and every one of the secret instructions of cultivating perfection. The Patriarch-master sighed and made the following proclamation: "Yunguang dong (Cavern of Clouds and Radiance) at Tiecha shan (Seeking Iron Mountain) in Wendeng[306] is where you will ascend to Perfection. You can live and prosper there, remaining free from laxity. At a future time, I will confer religious names to you." Master Wang respectfully received these instructions and returned to the mountain, **[2a]** going into seclusion in the cavern.

During the fourth month of that year, the Patriarch-master was traveling to Longquan.[307] He had borrowed Fan Mingshu's umbrella so as to protect himself from the sun. Master Qiu, Liu, Tan, and Ma went on ahead. The Patriarch-master had taken up the rear and was about a half-mile behind them. Suddenly he threw the umbrella into the sky. It floated up and drifted toward the northwest, flying who knows where. Master Qiu and Liu were startled by it. They quickly ran back and asked what had happened. They said, "It is floating away as though rising and falling on a great wind. We didn't know what was happening."

It was like this from early morning to late afternoon. At that time, it descended and crashed down in front of Yunguang dong. When Master Wang struck and broke its handle, inside it contained

---

303. Quanzhen hagiographies claim that Donghua dijun, whose supposed original name was Wang Xuanfu, transmitted the Dao to Zhongli Quan in the Zhongnan mountains. He is identified as the first and second patriarch of Quanzhen in the *Jinlian ji* (DZ 173, 1.1a–2b) and *Jinlian xiangzhuan* (DZ 174, 13a–14a), respectively.

304. The Dading reign period (1161–1189) of the Jin emperor Shizong (1123–1189; r. 1161–1189).

305. According to the *Jinlian xiangzhuan* (DZ 174, 36b–37a), Wang Yuyang's widowed mother, whose maiden name was Zhou, also became a disciple of Wang Chongyang in the Kunyu mountains. She received the personal name Deqing (Virtuous Clarity) and the religious name Xuanjing (Mysterious Stillness). This would have made her the second senior female member of the early Quanzhen religious community.

306. Wendeng is located in the far eastern part of Shandong's eastern peninsula.

307. Location unidentified.

his Daoist name, Zhuyangzi (Master Enveloping Yang), and his personal name, Chuyi (Abiding Unity). The character in his Daoist name is pronounced *zhu*, in the sense of "bamboo." Previous writings and poetry do not have this character, so it was probably created by the Patriarch-master. The character contains seven *ren* ("person") elements, which correspond to the seven petals of the Gold Lotus. This great covenant was formed when the thrown umbrella arrived at Yunguang dong after traveling over two hundred *li*.

Some days after Master Wang received it, he came to express his gratitude to the Patriarch-master. The Patriarch-master conferred the following poem:

> The principles and undertaking of cultivation and practice were recorded through
>   recitation;[308]
> [2b] We simply want the illumination within stillness to reside in the heart-mind.
> When the realm of the eyes does not arise, the dragon naturally resides;
> When the gates of the nose are not closed, the tiger constantly abides.
> When the root of the tongue renounces flavors, the spirit of the heart-mind is lively;
> When the inside of the ears discards sounds, the water of the kidneys is pure.
> The blended infusion of south and north return to a unified place;
> The commingling marriage of east and west destroys the Three Pengs.
> When wood and metal are bound together, one abides in relaxation;
> When Child and Maiden accord with each other, one practices in freedom.
> After the golden elixir coalesces, send it out through the top of the head;
> After the Five Radiances are emitted and penetrating, variegated clouds envelop.

Master Wang Yuyang bowed and received the poem.

After this, he wandered between Deng and Ning.[309] At night, he would return to the entrance of Yunguang dong. There he stood alone, leaning slightly to one side, lifting the opposite leg and standing on his other foot. He maintained this practice for nine years. In the morning, he would face east toward the ocean and refrain from sleep. The people called him "Master Iron Leg."[310]

Perfected Qiu composed the following tribute for him:

> For nine summers he stood welcoming the sunlight;
> For three winters he slept embracing the snow.
> He practiced this refinement of form for nine years,
> Eventually entering the great Wondrousness.
> Practicing inversion, practicing reversion,
> Sometimes he sang and sometimes danced.
> He sent out his spirit to enter dreams
> To assist others and benefit sentient beings.

---

308. Reading *dingning* for *dingning*.

309. Dengzhou and Ninghai, or the central and eastern part of Shandong's eastern peninsula, respectively.

310. *Tiejiao xiansheng.*

[3a] In the *wushen* year of the Dading reign period [1188], Emperor Shizong[311] heard that the value of his way was extremely high. He sent out an envoy with gifts to invite Master Wang to court, which he accepted. A Buddhist disciple became envious and jealous. He offered many bribes to the central officials and said that Master Wang was not a perfected immortal. He urged them to poison his alcohol in order to test him. The emperor agreed to this test, and had three cups offered to him. Master Wang drank every last drop. However, he suffered no ill effects, and in the end he was unable to be harmed. The emperor was amazed and grateful. He gave him a gold cap and ritual robe as well as a comfortable carriage with a team of four horses. The emperor also issued an imperial decree to renovate Quanzhen tang (Hall of Complete Perfection) so that Master Wang could live there. The decree had a seal-script heading with the emperor's signature.

On the fifth day after Qingming (Clear Brightness) in the *jiyou* year [1189], an imperial decree was issued that allowed him to return to his former mountain. The emperor once again offered a gift to him, this time consisting of vast amounts of golden brocade material. After receiving it, Master Wang departed.

In autumn of the eighth month of the third year of the Cheng'an reign period [1198], Emperor Zhangzong[312] issued a decree to seek Master Wang from seclusion. It summoned him to court, where the emperor would hold court in a side-hall. Master Wang responded like flowing water, and the emperor was extremely pleased. He conferred the title of Tixuan dashi (Great Master Embodying Mystery) and ordered for Xiuzhen guan (Monastery of Cultivating Perfection) to be built so that Master Wang could live there.[313]

In the *renxu* year of the Taihe reign period [1202], [3b] Master Wang was directed to go to Taiqing gong (Palace of Great Clarity) in Bozhou[314] and to serve as the head officiant for a Universal Benefit Offering.[315] Ten thousand cranes flew to and fro, and the Great High [Lord Lao] manifested in the clouds: His complexion was reddish brown like the sun. Master Wang wrote the following poem:

> A sage responds to the proclamation by emerging from the cavern-heaven;
> The extensive doctrine of the Golden Gate is a blessing beyond limits.
> Among clouds and seas of the east, Master Yuyang finds his dwelling-place;
> This special granting of sovereign grace represents the fourth proclamation.

After this, Master Wang returned to Yunguang dong, where he ordained thousands of Daoist priests.

In Dongmu, there was a mentally retarded man[316] of the Hao family. He served the master with deep sincerity. One day, he was suddenly affected by a perverse wind. A hundred physicians were unable to cure the illness, and the man was unable to move. Master Wang had compassion

---

311. The Jin emperor Shizong (1123–1189; r. 1161–1189).

312. The Jin emperor Zhangzong (1168–1208; r. 1190–1208).

313. Based on the fact that the Jin capital was Zhongdu (Beijing) during Zhangzong's reign, it seems likely that our Xiuzhen guan was located there.

314. Bozhou is located in the northwestern part of modern Anhui. During the Jurchen Jin, it was close to the southwest border of Shandong.

315. *Putian jiao*, that is, a Daoist *jiao*-offering rite for the benefit of the entire country.

316. Literally, "Tardy metal" (*chijin*), which suggests a correlative association with the Metal phase.

for him. He directed the people to boil fifteen tails of black fish, so that they could be made into pastry-rolls and fed to the man. As soon as he filled up on them, he was able to walk around as though flying. The entire area was amazed by this, and many people endeavored to follow and convert to the teachings.

One day Master Wang was begging for alms in Fushan County in Dengzhou. There he found out that Hermit Pan had died and was about to be buried. He covered Hermit Pan's ears with his hands, and shouted at the terrestrial officers to let him be. **[4a]** At that very moment, Hermit Pan sat up and began drinking and talking like himself. Many of his disciples presented offerings to Master Wang as a gesture of gratitude. He smiled slightly, shook his sleeves, and then left.

When Master Wang was staying in Ninghai, two cruel followers wanted to injure him. Each one grasped his staff and invited the master to drink with them. After he was drunk, they beat him up. Before they had finished drinking, they began fighting with each other. One man had a heart attack and died. When the other one saw this, he became frightened. He was certain that he would be implicated in this and have no way to escape. Master Wang let out a great laugh and said, "The Eastern Marchmont will not take him."[317] At that very moment, the dead man revived. The other man's various anxieties were accordingly relieved.

One day Master Wang traveled to Jiyang County,[318] where reports of his reputation were numerous. At the third drum-sounding, Master Wang moistened his brush and arranged writing paper. He wrote the two characters *zeiren* 賊人 ("thief"). He repeatedly ground ink on the whetstone so that the sound *zei* ("thief") was formed. Everyone went outside the gates, and they saw several people holding military weapons. They were startled and wanted to escape, but no one knew where to go because there was a large stone in front of Shengshui dong (Cavern of Sacred Waters). It extended out for what was several *zhang* or more. To try and traverse the incline was too terrifying. **[4b]** They discussed how to get out, and decided to hammer and chisel through the stone. After several days of striking and chipping away at it, their work amounted to a hundred pieces, but not even one inch had been gained. Master Wang laughed and went over to the stone. He hit the stone with three hammer-strikes. A sound like thunder issued forth, and the stone immediately fell. Purple mist covered and filled the cliffs and valleys for three days before dispersing.

The *bingwu* year of the Dading reign period [1186] was the time when Perfected Chongyang sent down his traces and when Perfected Danyang flew his bones.[319] Master Wang went to Langye Village.[320] He urged the local boatmen to completely burn their fishnets. In response to his request, an oceanic mirage appeared in the southeast. It consisted of storied pagodas and kingfisher-green mounds, cowry towers and pearl palaces. The vision startled people in several prefectures. This was the source of Jie Dongbo's rhymed essay in one chapter, although much of this writing has not survived: "Through prayers to the dragons, rains arrive. A boiled chicken once again comes back. Leaking cups gush wine, and withered posts produce branches." I am unable to recall any more.

On the twenty-third day of the fourth month in the *dingchou* year of the Zhenyou reign period [1217],[321] five-colored clouds spontaneously appeared in the southeast. Two azure-robed celestial lads

---

317. "Eastern Marchmount" refers to Taishan (Mount Tai), which is located in Tai'an, Shandong, south of Jinan. In Chinese folk beliefs, it is believed to house the underworld.

318. Jiyang is located slightly northeast of Jinan, Shandong.

319. The chronological sequence has been broken here. We are now in an earlier historical moment.

320. Langye is located on the southern coast of the Shandong peninsula, south of Qingdao and north of Rizhao.

321. The Zhenyou reign period (1213–1216) of the Jin emperor Xuanzong (r. 1213–1223).

descended holding a summons. Banners and pennants covered the sky. Everyone looked up and was filled deep respect. Master Wang made an announcement to his disciples: [5a] "Before the third day, all of the various sages will arrive." As soon as he finished speaking, he lit incense and offered his respect to the ten directions. He picked up a brush and wrote an ode:

> I skip among the transformative process of Qian-heaven and Kun-earth;
> My spirit radiance is luminous and bright throughout the multifarious heavens.
> Whirling to and fro on mounted cranes, I leap beyond the Three Realms;
> I joyfully receive the golden books and the Jade Thearch's proclamation.

He then dropped the brush and lay down. He immediately returned to Perfection. An auspicious radiance filled the mountains and valleys; a blessed emanation covered the river sources. It was several days before it dispersed. Considered as a whole, his collected poetry amounts to more than a thousand poems. They are collected in the *Qingzhen ji* (Anthology of Clear Perfection) and *Yunguang ji* (Anthology of Clouds and Radiance), which have circulated throughout the world.[322]

I offer this elegy for him:

> He refined his vital essence into jade yang;
> He sheathed his radiance in sacred water.
> In the handle of a bamboo umbrella,
> He found the hidden transmission of names.
> Beneath Tiecha mountain,
> He dedicated himself to many years of practice.
> For three winters, he embraced snow and slept peacefully;
> For nine summers, he welcomed sunlight and stood firmly.
> He was then able to merge south with north and return to Oneness.
> He wedded east with west and destroyed the Three Pengs.[323]
> He secured encounters with the transmissions of immortals and sages;
> He accepted the summons of emperors and rulers four times.
> [5b] He drank the poison wine, and his radiant complexion remained unaffected.
> He burned fishnets, and the oceanic mirage filled the horizon.
> Master Pan had already died,
> But with the sound of three yells he was revived.
> For those who were retarded, old, or paralyzed,
> He offered a single meal and they were well again.
> Young children emerged from the incense burner;
> Elderly lords became manifest among cloud blessings.
> After his hands took hold of the iron weight,
> A large rock was heard in the falling torrent.
> After his mouth transmitted the jade instructions,
> The various mountains appeared as shifting peaks.

322. Of these works, only the *Yunguang ji* (DZ 1152) is extant.
323. The Three Pengs are the Three Death-bringers.

Above the rootless post, branches and leaves came alive;
Within the bottomless pot, the wine dregs did not leak out.
Cranes descended and repeatedly danced in front of the altar.
The boiled chicken cried again from the scaffold.
The thief took the military weapons and ran away;
The cruel followers took his staff and were driven away.
He leaped beyond the transformative process of Qian and Kun;
He revolved the moving power of the sun and moon.
On a mat among his disciples,
He ordained thousands and hundreds in our community.
Peacefully living with skillful dexterity,
He transmitted the thirty-six arrangements.
Thus he could receive a proclamation from the Jade Thearch,
[6a] And go to the Association of the Gold Lotus.

Zhang Shentong wrote the following poem:

With lofty fame, he received proclamations from emperors and rulers;
In response, he obtained golden books and was offered the name Tixuan.
With the Dao and inner power, he completed spirit transformation;
At the foot of Tiecha mountain, waters flowed in response.

Yan Chuchang[324]

The master had the surname Yan, [religious] name Chuchang (Abiding Constancy), and Daoist name Changqing (Perpetual Clarity). He was originally from Liyang County in Jingzhao.[325] He was also a relative by marriage of Patriarch Chongyang.

When young, he studied the Confucian tradition, but his aspirations were directed at clear emptiness. Because his parents were involved with the imperial court, he was unable to follow the lofty path beyond mundane concerns. He thus became a judicial magistrate in the county, administering to affairs with consideration and compassion.

One day when returning home in the evening, he happened to pick up a book that was lying in the road. [7b] Its title read *Yuling shengshu* (Sacred Book of the Jade Numen), and it noted that whoever obtained it would become an immortal. After this, he lit incense and took the following oath: "I am twenty-nine years old today; I vow that in the year when I am without delusion [40] I will purify my body and enter the Dao." After he completed this vow, he poured alcohol into a libation bowl. Suddenly there was a sound, hidden and mysterious, that seemed like thunder. All of his family members thought that this was strange.

---

324. The hagiography of Yan Chuchang (1111–1183) from the *Zhongnan neizhuan*, DZ 955, 1.7a–8a.
325. During the Jurchen Jin dynasty, Liyang was located slightly northeast of Xi'an, Shaanxi.

After twelve years had passed and both of his parents had died, he suddenly was taken ill with an eye problem. Every attempt to cure it only made it worse. Master Changqing silently admonished himself saying, "In the past I found that sacred book and vowed that I would become a renunciant at forty. Now that time has passed. When this illness is finally cured, I will immediately follow the Dao." Shortly afterward, his eyes became clear and bright like before.

Master Changqing accordingly went to Liujiang[326] in the Zhongnan mountains. He visited Patriarch Chongyang and expressed his longing to receive the teachings and to become his disciple. This occurred in the *guiwei* year of the Dading reign period [1163].

Master Changqing then entered Mengyun[327] and set his aspirations toward the Dao. After several years the Patriarch conferred the subtle decree to him.

In summer of the *dinghai* year, the seventh year [of the Dading reign period] [1167],[328] the Patriarch began traveling east. Master Changqing then traveled to Quanshi in the Zhongnan mountains.[329] He lived there, nourishing his spirit until it became flourishing and expansive.

In spring of the tenth year [1170], the four masters Qiu, Liu, Tan, and Ma entered the pass [Shaanxi], **[8a]** and Yan Chuchang met Patriarch Danyang and again received instruction. Patriarch Danyang bestowed it with a willow branch and a lyric that read,

> The tiger, the dragon, united in a sleeping place—
> Stir them to join and make a circuit.
> One exhalation, one inhalation, united in the Celestial Cycle—
> Revolve them through the Three Fields.
> The wheat, the hemp, connected by a single thread—
> Spiral them into an auspicious smoke.
> One arrival, one departure, united by returning to the Origin—
> Produce the immortal embryo.

The master offered his obeisance, and then realized that he was free from doubts and obstruction. He lived at the Zuting (Ancestral Hall)[330] for another ten years or so, forming a contract with the Dao through perfect constancy.

On the eighth day of the fourth month of the *guimao* year, the twenty-third year of Dading [1183], the master lit incense and took leave of the community. He passed away without any sickness. He had experienced seventy-three springs and autumns.

---

326. Present-day Huxian, Shaanxi.

327. Location unidentified, but Mengyun must have been in the central part of Shaanxi.

328. The Dading reign period (1161–1189) of the Jin emperor Shizong (1123–1189; r. 1161–1189).

329. Based on context, Quanshi would have been located southwest of Xi'an, near Liujiang, Shaanxi.

330. Liujiang, Shaanxi, the site of Wang Chongyang's second hermitage and of the eremitic community of which He Dejin and Li Lingyang were members.

Chapter Seven

Monastic Life

With the texts translated in this section, we move into a completely different set of historical contexts and Daoist concerns than most of the earlier selections, that is, the early Quanzhen textual corpus associated with Wang Chongyang and his first-generation disciples (see Komjathy 2007a, 382–422). These texts date to the expansive and resurgent historical phases of Quanzhen, as expressed in my earlier periodization (ibid., 33–36; see also the introduction herein). They document a moment when Quanzhen was an organized monastic system. In my categorization schema, they are monastic manuals aimed at establishing and maintaining Quanzhen monastic models and communal harmony (see Schipper and Verellen 2004, 1167–69). Like the seventh-century *Fengdao kejie* (Rules and Precepts for Worshipping the Dao; DZ 1125; DH 39; see Kohn 1997; 2004a; Reiter 1998), the earliest extant Daoist monastic manual, I leave it to readers to reflect on and scholars to research the extent to which these texts are descriptive or prescriptive. That is, the potentially idealized or utopian vision expressed deserves consideration. To what degree did contemporaneous monastics and monastic communities embrace, apply, and embody them?

The first text translated here is the *Quanzhen qinggui* (Pure Regulations of Complete Perfection; DZ 1235) by Lu Daohe (Tongxuan [Pervading Mystery]; fl. 1280–1360?). The "pure regulations" (*qinggui*) of the title refers to monastic guidelines.[1] This text is the earliest extant Quanzhen monastic manual, though the specific provenance and motivating force behind its compilation are somewhat obscure. The Ming-dynasty Daoist Canon edition only gives a single vague clue regarding the compiler, Lu Daohe: his birthplace or residence is identified as Yaojiang (present-day Yuyang, Zhejiang). However, we do not know when and by whom he was ordained into the Quanzhen monastic order. The specific date of the text, its intended audience, as well as its degree of acceptance and application in the larger Quanzhen monastic order are also unclear. With respect to dating, Vincent Goossaert has pointed out that articles 11 and 13 are found in section 9.13b–15b of the *Minghe yuyin* (Lingering Overtones of the Calling Crane; DZ 1400; 1347) and in its extra-canonical version, the *Quanzhen zongyan fangwai xuanyan* (Mysterious Words from the Realm of Ancestral Perceptions of Quanzhen) (1997, 269, 440; see also Boltz 1987, 188–90; Schipper and Verellen 2004, 1150–52). In the *Minghe yuyin*, article 11 of the *Quanzhen qinggui* is attributed to Perfected Zhao, which refers to the second-generation monk Zhao Wuxuan and parallels our text; article 13 is attributed to Perfected Feng, an attribution not included in the *Quanzhen qinggui*. There are two important Quanzhen masters with the surname

---

1. It appears that the *Quanzhen qinggui* was at least partially modeled on the early twelfth-century *Chanyuan qinggui* (Pure Regulations for Chan Monasteries; T. 2025, 48.1157c–1158b), commonly misidentified as the *Baizhang qinggui* (Pure Rules of Baizhang). On the latter text see Cleary 1978; Foulk 1987; 1993; 2004; Yifa 2002. A profitable comparative study of the two texts could be undertaken.

Feng, namely, Feng Zhiheng (1180–1254) and Feng Changquan (fl. 1232). If these sections of the *Minghe yuyin* derive from the *Quanzhen qinggui*, then our text would date to the late thirteenth or early fourteenth century. A later date is supported by the fact that Wang Chongyang is identified as *dijun* ("sovereign lord"), an honorific title bestowed by Emperor Wuzong in 1310. In any case, we have a relatively clear composition date, roughly between the time of Qubilai Qan's proscription (1281) and the Yuan Emperor Wuzong's subsequent recognition of the early Quanzhen religious leaders. These details might support reading Lu's work as an attempt to ensure the preservation of the inner world, the lived religiosity and communal experience, of the Quanzhen monastic institution. Based on content, one can surmise that it is meant to be a prescriptive model for late medieval Quanzhen monastic life. The text provides some glimpses into the informing concerns, communal organization, and institutional structures of earlier Quanzhen monasticism. The *Quanzhen qinggui* consists of thirteen primary divisions:

Table 4. Section Divisions of the *Quanzhen qinggui*

1. Rules for Guiding Novices (1a–2b)	9. Hymn of the Bowl-chamber (9a–11b)
2. The Hair-pinning Ceremony (2b–3b)	10. List of Prohibitions of Sovereign Lord Chongyang (11b–13a)[2]
3. Traveling to Visit Masters (3b–4b)	11. Text on Entering the Hall by Master Liaozhen (13ab)
4. Order of Seniority in the Meditation Hall (4b–5a)	12. List of Regulations of Perfected Changchun (13b–15a)
5. Regulations for Bowl-clepsydra Meditation (5ab)	13. Letter from the Enlightened Master to His Family (15a–16a)
6. Standards of the Patriarch (5b–6a)	
7. Three Conditions under Which You May Not Stand Up (6a–7a)	
8. Substance and Function of Complete Perfection (7a–9a)	

The text thus emphasizes the importance of the following: discernment concerning who is admitted into the monastic order; novices' spiritual direction under community elders; monastic structures (hierarchal ordering based on seniority) and protocol, including rules; as well as meditation-based training, including bowl-clepsydra retreats (discussed later). The *Quanzhen qinggui* also provides an outline of a standard, daily monastic schedule:

> 3 a.m.–5 a.m.: Wake-up
> 5 a.m.–7 a.m.: Morning meal
> 7 a.m.–9 a.m.: Group meditation
> 9 a.m.–11 a.m.: Individual meditation
> 11 a.m.–1 p.m.: Noon meal
> 1 p.m.–3 p.m.: Group meditation
> 3 p.m.–5 p.m.: Individual meditation
> 5 p.m.–7 p.m.: Formal lecture or interviews
> 7 p.m.–9 p.m.: Group meditation and tea
> 9 p.m.–11 p.m.: Individual meditation
> 11 p.m.–1 a.m.: Scripture recitation
> 1 a.m.–3 a.m.: Personal time
> (Cf. Yifa 2002, 39; Welch 1967, 427)

---

2. As mentioned, this section could have been included in chapter 3 on daily practice, especially on "daily external practice," which refers to ethical reflection and activity.

Taken as a whole, the *Quanzhen qinggui* thus provides a fairly comprehensive model of Quanzhen monastic life, though the degree to which it is representative of daily life in late medieval Daoist monasteries deserves more research.

The second selection is a translation of the anonymous *Quanzhen zuobo jiefa* (Practical Methods for the Sinking Bowl-clepsydra from Complete Perfection; DZ 1229). The fact that the text is anonymous and lacks any other datable internal dimensions (e.g., personal names, places, etc.) makes its historical provenance impossible to determine. This is especially lamentable as the author and his community clearly had a sophisticated understanding of astronomy and cosmology, applied mathematics, fluid mechanics, as well as metallurgical engineering. Based on parallel concerns with the *Quanzhen qinggui* and its clear monastic context, the *Quanzhen zuobo jiefa* most likely dates to the middle of the Yuan dynasty (1279–1368), a time when Quanzhen had returned to a position of imperial favor. In terms of content, the text has the following sections:

Table 5. Section Divisions of the *Quanzhen zuobo jiefa*

1. Preliminary Remarks (1ab)	5. Method of Adding and Subtracting Coins (3ab)
2. Method of Making the Containers (1b–2a)	6. Method for Establishing the Rising and Setting
3. Method of Water-flow (2ab)	of the Sun (3b)
4. Method of Making the Tally (2b)	7. Chart of Perfected Ninefold Yang (4a)

As the title indicates, the *Quanzhen zuobo jiefa* is a technical manual on the production and utilization of a bowl-clepsydra as a timing device for Quanzhen meditation. *Zuobo*, literally meaning "sitting bowl" or "sitting with the bowl," refers to both the object itself and the corresponding practice.[3] The former is a sinking bowl-clepsydra (water-clock). This clepsydra, which stands in contrast to other types (see Needham et al. 1959, 313–29; Hua 1991; also Goossaert 1997, 223–25; Mori 2003), was a small copper bowl with a hole drilled in the bottom. The smaller bowl was placed in a larger one filled with water. The smaller bowl would slowly fill with water and sink to the bottom of the larger one, a process that took roughly six double-hours to complete (2ab). The *Quanzhen zuobo jiefa* thus divides the day into two primary periods (*du*): from *mao* (5 a.m.–7 a.m.; dawn) to *you* (5 p.m. and 7 p.m.; dusk), and from *you* to *mao* (section 2ab). The bowl-clepsydra was the central focus of the Quanzhen hundred-day winter meditation retreat, also referred to as *zuobo*, which began on the first day of the tenth lunar month, extended through the winter solstice and the lunar new year, and ended ten days into the first month, which roughly corresponds to the beginning of spring (see *Quanzhen qinggui*, DZ 1235, 5ab; also 9a–11b). With respect to method, it seems that individual monastics may have practiced different techniques, both quietistic and alchemical, suited to their specific spiritual needs and level (*Quanzhen qinggui*, DZ 1235, 6ab), but stillness and emptiness-based meditation was the primary collective method (ibid., 9b). The Quanzhen winter

3. The Quanzhen practice of bowl-clepsydra meditation has yet to receive scholarly attention, except in the form of passing comments. Important information appears in Vincent Goossaert's dissertation (1997, 220–58). However, that account must be used with some caution, as the author uses materials from a wide variety of historical periods as though contemporaneous. Beyond the present translations, important primary sources include the late Yuan-dynasty "Botang ji" (Record of the Clepsydra Hall), as appearing in the extra-canonical *Quanzhen zongyan fangwai xuanyan* (trl. in Goossaert 1997, 237–40), and sections 5.3b–4a and 5.30a–36b of the early Ming-dynasty (1368–1644) *Tianhuang zhidao taiqing yuce* (Jade Registers of Great Clarity on the Utmost Way of the Celestial Sovereign; DZ 1483; abbr. *Taiqing yuce*). Quanzhen collective meditation centering on the bowl-clepsydra may have continued into the Qing dynasty (1644–1911), though the matter is open to debate. For some insights into the latter see Esposito 2005; 2009; Goossaert 2007, 148, 155, 159–60.

retreat took place in the clepsydra-hall (*botang*) and was facilitated by the clepsydra-master (*bozhu*). The clepsydra-hall was either a separate residence for itinerant monks and employed for communal meditation or a meditation hall specifically modified for the winter retreat. Based on our Quanzhen texts and roughly contemporaneous sources, we may, following Goossaert (1997, 227; cf. Welch 1967, 49), reconstruct the layout as follows:[4]

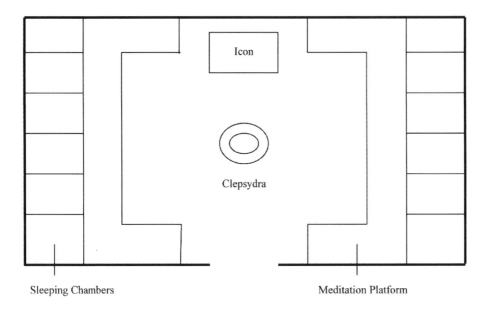

Figure 36. Approximation of a Late Medieval Quanzhen Clepsydra-hall

The *Quanzhen zuobo jiefa* also provides important technical details concerning the use of the bowl-clepsydra. It advises practitioners to account for the waxing and waning of sunlight by adjusting the weight of the bowl-clepsydra; this was done by subtracting and adding coins as follows (lunar month / morning coins / evening coins): first/11/9; second/10/10; third/9/11; fourth/1/19; fifth/0/20; sixth/1/19; seventh/9/11; eighth/10/10; ninth/11/9; tenth/11/9; eleventh/20/0; twelfth/19/1.[5] This is especially interesting because it reveals a distinctive Daoist view of time. Here "time" is not the colossal hoax of clocks and calendars; it is a flexible and transformative cycle marked by seasonal and energetic shifts. The text also maps the directions of sunrise and sunset (3b) and provides a chart of the lunar and solar phases (4a). The chart is framed by the opening lines of the sixth-century *Yinfu jing* (Scripture on the Hidden Talisman; DZ 31), which here refer to seasonal and cosmological attunement: "Observe the Way of Heaven; attend to the activities of heaven." This diagram generally

---

4. Sometimes the order of seniority and corresponding monastic hall positions follow the twelve terrestrial branches, beginning with *zi* and ending with *hai*. Cf. the institutionalization of meditation enclosure as the enclosure-hall (*huantang*) (Goossaert 1997, 253–58).

5. These can be mapped with rough twenty-four seasonal node correspondences, beginning with Spring Begins (approx. February 5) and ending with Great Cold (approx. January 21). Among these the Eight Nodes, the beginning of the seasons, solstices, and equinoxes are most important.

depicts the moon phases from the new moon on the first day of the month, through the full moon on the fifteenth, and ending with final moment of the waning crescent on the thirtieth day.[6] This primary diagrammatic level is supplemented by the solar cycles mapped according to twelve hexagrams from the *Yijing*.

Table 6. Cosmological Cycles Utilized in the *Quanzhen zuobo jiefa*

Day 3: Zi 子: Fu-return ䷗: eleventh month: Heavy Snow & Winter Solstice	Day 18: Wu 午: Gou-meeting ䷫: fifth month: Bearded Grain & Summer Solstice
Day 5: Chou 丑: Lin-descent ䷒: twelfth month: Slight Cold & Great Cold	Day 20: Wei 未: Dun-concealed ䷠: sixth month: Slight Heat & Great Heat
Day 8: Yin 寅: Tai-peace ䷊: first month: Spring Begins & Rain Water	Day 23: Shen 申: Pi-standstill ䷋: seventh month: Autumn Begins & Limit of Heat
Day 10: Mao 卯: Dazhuang-great form ䷡: second month: Excited Insects & Spring Equinox	Day 25: You 酉: Guan-observation ䷓: eighth month: Pure Dew & Autumn Equinox
Day 13: Chen 辰: Guai-certainty ䷪: third month: Clear Brightness & Grain Rain	Day 28: Xu 戌: Bo-flayed ䷖: ninth month: Cold Dew & Frost Descends
Day 15: Si 巳: Qian-heaven ䷀ : fourth month: Summer Begins & Slight Fullness	Day 30: Hai 亥: Kun-earth ䷁: tenth month: Winter Begins and Slight Snow

Beyond these highly technical aspects, we should also recognize the poetic and symbolic dimensions of the bowl-clepsydra as object and in practice (see *Quanzhen qinggui*, DZ 1235, 9a–11b). On the most basic level, the character *bo* 鉢 consists of *jin* 金 ("metal") and *ben* 本 ("root"), which includes *mu* 木 ("wood").[7] As an alchemical symbol, this character represents the joining of Metal (white tiger) and Wood (azure dragon), corresponding to the unification of qi and spirit through alchemical transformation. Similarly, the sinking of the bowl corresponds to concentrating on the lower elixir field so that qi becomes stored. Just as the water of the larger container is displaced, so too the adept's qi circulates through the body's organ-meridian networks. Just as the smaller container fills with water and sinks to the bottom of the larger one, so too qi sinks into and becomes stored in the lower elixir field as the body's energetic center (see chapter 4 herein). One returns to the Root through alchemical forging and refinement.

The final translated text is the *Chuzhen jie* (Precepts of Initial Perfection; JY 292; ZW 404), which dates from a later period of Quanzhen history, namely, the early Qing dynasty (1644–1911). While this work could be categorized as a precept text, and thus have been included in chapter 3 in terms of ethical guidelines, it is more accurately understood as a late imperial Daoist monastic manual. The *Chuzhen jie* was compiled, partially from earlier Daoist sources, by Wang Changyue (Kunyang [Paradisiacal Yang]; 1594?–1680). Wang was a native of Lu'an, Shanxi, and the son of a local Daoist family. His original name was Wang Ping. In his youth, he traveled extensively, eventually

6. There are eight primary lunar phases: new moon, waxing crescent (right-side illumined), first quarter, waxing gibbous, full moon, waning gibbous (right-side darkened), third quarter, and waning crescent. The new moon and full moon are especially significant moments in Daoist practice.

7. The variant character *bo* 缽 consists of *fou* 缶 ("jar"; earthenware pottery) and *ben* 本. The former, which would have an Earth-phase association, might be taken as a symbol for the center, the lower elixir field, and stillness.

meeting Zhao Fuyang (fl. 1600–1640), the sixth Longmen (Dragon Gate) Patriarch and heir of the Longmen Discipline (Vinaya) Masters (*lüshi*) line. According to his own autobiographical account in the preface (1656) to the *Chuzhen jie*, Wang met Zhao on Jiugong shan (Nine Palaces Mountain; near Wuhan, Hubei) in 1628 (cf. Esposito 2001, 193). Zhao ordained Wang and bestowed the Longmen lineage name (*paiming*) of Changyue (Constant Moon). Wang continued to live as an itinerant monk (*yunyou*), training at various monasteries for the next decade or so. He eventually emerged as a major monastic leader, becoming appointed as abbot of Baiyun guan (White Cloud Monastery; Beijing) in 1655 and commencing the public ordination of novices in 1656. Although the Longmen lineage of Quanzhen is most often traced to Qiu Chuji (Changchun [Perpetual Spring]; 1148–1227) and his supposed lineage-successor Zhao Xujing (Daojian [Resolute-in-the-Way]; 1163–1221), the official, "orthodox" Longmen lineage was codified by Wang Changyue and his successors.[8] While abbot of Baiyun guan in the late 1600s, Wang systematized the formal Longmen ordination system and monastic regulations into three levels:

Table 7. Longmen Ordination Ranks as Systematized by Wang Changyue

Ordination Rank	Precept Text	Ritual Vestment
Wondrous Practice / Initial Perfection	*Chuzhen jie*	Devotion Robe of Initial Perfection
Wondrous Virtue / Medium Ultimate	*Zhongji jie*	Pure Robe of Lightened Dust
Wondrous Dao / Celestial Immortality	*Tianxian jie*	Mist Robe of Celestial Immortality

The first level, open to both monastics and laypeople, centered on the Five Precepts and Ten Precepts of Initial Perfection; the second level consisted of the Three Hundred Precepts of Medium Ultimate; and the third level was less clearly defined, but included the Ten Virtues of Celestial Immortality and the Twenty-seven Virtuous Activities of Celestial Immortality (see Kohn 2004b, 112–13; Komjathy 2008a, Handbook 5). According to official Longmen accounts, Wang Changyue compiled, or at least disseminated, the three corresponding monastic manuals, the *Chuzhen jie* (Precepts of Initial Perfection; JY 292; ZW 404),[9] *Zhongji jie* (Precepts of Medium Ultimate; JY 293; ZW 405), and *Tianxian jie* (Precepts of Celestial Immortality; JY 291; ZW 403),[10] as guidebooks for Quanzhen monastic life (see Min 1990, 86–116; Goossaert 2007, 150–53).[11] They evidence a late imperial

---

8. Academic attempts to distinguish historical fact from legend with respect to late imperial Daoism, particularly the Long-men lineage, are only just beginning. Most of this work has been done by Japanese scholars and by the late Monica Esposito (1962–2011), former director of the Daozang Jiyao Project. For some important qualifications see Esposito 1993; 2000; 2001; 2004; 2005; 2009.

9. According to Wang Changyue, the *Precepts of Initial Perfection* "teach you how to control the form-body (*seshen*) without allowing it to move incorrectly or to act rashly"; the Precepts of Medium Ultimate "teach you how to subdue the illusory-mind (*huanxin*) without allowing delusions or wild thoughts to arise"; and the Precepts of Celestial Immortality "teach you how to free perfect awareness (*zhenyi*) without being bound by attachments" (*Biyuan tanjing*, ZW 330, 2.1ab, 10.180; Esposito 2001, 196).

10. Recent revisionist scholarship challenges the attribution of the *Tianxian jie* to Wang Changyue. It seems, rather, that the text may have been the product of spirit-writing attributed to the immortal Liu Shouyuan and linked with the spirit-writing altar of Jiang Yupu (Yuanting [Origin Court]; 1755–1819), one of the principal editors of the *Daozang jiyao* (Collected Essentials of the Daoist Canon). See Mori 2005. I am grateful to the late Monica Esposito for clarifying this matter and for providing references to the relevant scholarship.

11. There are two other important extant works associated with Wang Changyue: the *Longmen xinfa* (Central Teachings of Dragon Gate; ZW 201) and its slightly divergent counterpart, the *Biyuan tanjing* (Platform Sutra of the Jade Garden; ZW 330). Interestingly, it also seems that Wang compiled a history of Quanzhen transmission titled *Bojian* (Examination of the Bowl; possibly lost).

Longmen monastic hierarchy, with the ethical requirements, expectations, and types of adherence becoming increasingly strict as individuals progressed through the levels of Daoist commitment and participation.

Returning to the text translated here, the *Chuzhen jie*, which Wang may have first completed in 1656 while abbot of Baiyun guan, consists of the following sections:

Table 8. Section Divisions of the *Chuzhen jie*

1. Preface (1a–2b)	9. Monastic Attire and Paraphernalia (20ab)
2. Precepts of Initial Perfection (8a–10a)	10. Conduct Guidelines of the Mysterious Gate
3. General Outline of the Practice and Observance of	for Observing the Precepts (21a–27b)
Precepts (10–11b)	11. Rules for Disciples Serving the Master
4. Essential Rules for Practicing the Precepts (12a–14a)	(28a–29b)
5. Basic Guidance for the Three Masters (14ab)	12. Forty-six Precepts Regarding Ritual Vestments
6. Rules for the Three Robes (14b–15a)	(30a–31b)
7. Rules of Repentance after Transgressing the	13. Nine Precepts for Female Perfected (32a–32b)
Statutes (15ab)	14. *Gathas* Transmitted by Precept Master
8. Invocations for Daily Activities (16a–19b)	Kunyang (33a–34a)

The main body of the text begins with Wang Changyue emphasizing that Quanzhen adepts must take refuge in the Three Treasures (8ab) and be familiar with the Five Precepts of Lord Lao and the *Taishang ganying pian* (Great High Lord Lao's Treatise on Action and Response; DZ 1167) (8b–9a) before receiving the Ten Precepts of Initial Perfection (9ab). In the fourth section, Wang discusses ordination levels and corresponding requirements for the La winter festival and hundred-day winter bowl-clepsydra retreat (see Goossaert 1997, 245–47). He also covers specific implements and monastic paraphernalia (rope-bed, robes, bowl, staff, discipline stick, pitcher, certificate pouch, fragrance hanger, and toothbrush) as well as the appropriate ritual decorum for their care and use. The fifth section identifies the three primary monastic positions in relation to novices, namely, ordination master (*chuanshi/lüshi*), confirmation master (*zhengshi*), and discipline master (*jianshi*).[12] In terms of the larger monastic administration, we should add the abbot (*fangzhang*), prior (*jianyuan*), provost (*dujian*), meditation master (*jingshi*), and liturgical master (*jingshi*). Next, Wang covers the three ritual vestments, which correspond to the three Longmen ordination ranks. Illustrations of these and other monastic paraphernalia appear in section 20ab. It is also noteworthy that the *Chuzhen jie* contains invocations for daily activities, such as waking, dressing, washing, offering incense, eating, bathing, and going to sleep. Wang Changyue clearly had a strong affinity for and commitment to precept study and application. He saw this form of Daoist religious practice as centrally important. According to Wang, the precepts (*jie*) represent the "staff for subduing demons," "talisman for protecting life-destiny," "ladder for ascending the heavens," and "lamp for illuminating the Way" (*Biyuan tanjing*, ZW 330, 1.19b, 10.168). "Maintain the precepts (*chijie*) in your heart-mind as though holding something in your hand. Once you let go of something, it becomes lost. Similarly, once the precepts in your heart-mind are abandoned, they become broken" (ibid., 1.22b, 10.169). The precepts in turn relate to the perfect heart-mind (*zhenxin*), as they enable one "to ascend to immortality and realize the Dao" (ibid., 1.6a, 10.161; Esposito 2001, 194). The centrality of ethics and virtue in Wang Changyue's monastic system and in the Longmen lineage is confirmed by the

---

12. This may be compared with both medieval monastic positions (see Kohn 2003, 2004) and modern ones (see Goossaert 2007, especially 332–34). On the Buddhist side, see Welch 1967, 36–42, 49, 421–25; Buswell 1993; Yifa 2002.

fact that it centers on three precept manuals. In fact, modern Quanzhen monastics often refer to Longmen as the "Vinaya lineage" (*lüjia*/*lüpai*),[13] and the *Chuzhen jie*, *Zhongji jie*, and *Tianxian jie* remain the centerpiece of that lineage. The *Chuzhen jie* is the beginning of the system.

A word is also in order concerning extant editions of the *Chuzhen jie*. In terms of the present anthology, the *Chuzhen jie* is the only text not contained in the Ming-dynasty Daoist Canon (see Schipper and Verellen 2004), which is used for the "standard, received editions" of pre-Qing Daoist texts. The *Chuzhen jie* is found in "extra-canonical" collections such as the *Daozang jiyao* (Collected Essentials of the Daoist Canon; abbr. JY) and *Zangwai daoshu* (Daoist Texts Outside the Canon; abbr. ZW) (see Komjathy 2002). I have also utilized a manuscript edition, which I collected at Qingyang gong (Azure Ram Palace; Chengdu, Sichuan) during fieldwork in 2003. Qingyang gong possesses the block-plates of the Erxian an (Hermitage of the Two Immortals) edition of the *Daozang jiyao* (1906),[14] from which my own manuscript derives. In addition to printing complete sets of the collection, Qingyang gong also circulates independent editions of various Daoist texts. During my visits to Quanzhen monastic communities throughout the years, I have collected Daoist manuscripts, with the *Chuzhen jie* being one of them. In the translation here, I provide page numbers to the text as contained in the *Zangwai daoshu*, so that interested readers may readily access the original Chinese text. My Qingyang gong manuscript contains Wang Changyue's preface, which is absent from the ZW version.

Little research has been done on Daoist monasticism in general and Quanzhen monasticism in particular.[15] There are a variety of valuable Quanzhen monastic manuals that deserve future study and translation. Some important texts include the aforementioned *Longmen xinfa*, compiled by Wang Changyue's disciples as a record of his oral teachings, as well as the early nineteenth-century *Qinggui xuanmiao* (Pure Regulations, Mysterious and Wondrous; ZW 361), as appearing in the *Gu Shuyin lou cangshu* (Collected Texts from the Ancient Pavilion of Hidden Books) by the eleventh Longmen Patriarch Min Yide (Lanyun [Lazy Cloud]; 1758–1836) (see Esposito 2001, 199–221). Moving into the contemporary period, there is also the *Daojiao yifan* (Daoist Religious Models; 1990) by Min Zhiting (Yuxi [Jade Rivulet]; 1924–2004), the former president of the Chinese Daoist Association. This work includes selections from the three Longmen precept texts attributed to Wang Changyue, and has wide circulation throughout mainland Chinese Quanzhen monastic communities.

In terms of previous publications and studies, Akizuki Kan'ei (1958) published a study of the "Prohibitions of Sovereign Lord Chongyang," appearing as article 10 of the *Quanzhen qinggui* (DZ 1235, 11b–13a). Vincent Goossaert's dissertation includes a complete French translation of

---

13. This phrase has been used frequently by contemporary Quanzhen monastics during my ethnographic fieldwork, specifically during conversations with Laoshan and Huashan monks. I have been engaging in participant-observation of contemporary Daoist monastic life since 1998. Of particular note, I lived as a visiting monk at Laoshan and Huashan during spring of 2006.

14. Compared to the Ming-dynasty Daoist Canon, very little work has been done on the extra-canonical Daoist collections. This makes research difficult because biographical and historical details are scarce. Even the most rudimentary work is yet to be done. For information on the *Daozang jiyao* see the online Daozang Jiyao Project (www.daozangjiyao.org), which was under the direction of the late Monica Esposito. There are various modern reprints of the *Daozang jiyao* in circulation in mainland China. My initial inspection has revealed a great deal of divergence in terms of contents and organization.

15. For some insights into early medieval Daoist monasticism see Kohn 1997; 2003a; 2004a; Reiter 1998. The most comprehensive study of early Quanzhen monasticism is Vincent Goossaert's dissertation (1997; see also Zheng 1995), and one hopes that it will eventually be revised and published. Some important work on late imperial and early modern Quanzhen has also appeared in print. See Hackmann 1920; 1931; Yoshioka 1979; Esposito 1993; 2000; 2001; 2004; Goossaert 2004; 2007; Liu 2004a; 2004b; Komjathy 2008b; 2009. On contemporary Chinese Quanzhen monasticism see Herrou 2005.

the *Quanzhen qinggui* (1997, 269–86). Heinrich Hackmann (1864–1935), a German minister, theologian, and Protestant missionary, published a partial translation (sections 8a–13b) of the *Chuzhen jie* (1920; see also Hackmann 1931), which is one of the earliest Western-language studies of Daoist monasticism. Hackmann's work is especially significant because in 1911 he spent three months living in Taiqing gong (Palace of Great Clarity) at Laoshan (Mount Lao; near Qingdao, Shandong), where he observed daily monastic life and collected twenty-eight Daoist texts (see Strachotta 1997; Kohn 2003b). Livia Kohn included a partial translation (sections 8a–14a) of the *Chuzhen jie* in her *Cosmos and Community* (2004b, 253–63), which is based on the Laoshan manuscript collected by Hackmann. Kohn's work also contains a translation of a Longmen ordination certificate (*jiedie*) of a certain Liu Yuxi (ibid., 87; cf. Goossaert 1997, 129–33, 162–68; 2007, 55–57, 102–4), which appears at the beginning of Hackmann's manuscript version of the *Chuzhen jie*. The electronic supplement to *Cosmos and Community* includes a select translation of the *Zhongji jie*, and Kohn's research also identifies corresponding passages in earlier precept manuals.

Pure Regulations of Complete Perfection[16]

Edited by Lu Daohe, Master Tongxuan

Rules for Guiding Novices

Generally speaking, novices of initial perfection who have become renunciants must seek an interview with an illuminated teacher.[17] After making the necessary prostrations and gestures of veneration, the renunciant should listen to his teacher's counsel. With time, one will certainly become an accomplished person.

Upon receiving the disciple, the teacher must first inquire about his level of spiritual realization and moral foundation. He also must investigate whether his ancestors and his family are virtuous as well as try to discern the degree of his own aptitude. Then and only then should the teacher accept him as a disciple.[18]

As his first action, the aspirant must take off his ordinary [garments], exchanging his clothes for the currents of immortality and vapors of the Dao.[19] At this point, the teachings and instructions that follow will necessarily be different.

---

16. *Quanzhen qinggui*, DZ 1235.

17. "Renunciants" is my liberal rendering of *chujia*, which literally means "to leave the family." In early Quanzhen *chujia* referred to embracing an ascetic way of life, while in the monastic order it means to become a monk or nun. Cf. Discourse 1 of the *Chongyang lijiao shiwu lun* (DZ 1233) translated in chapter 3 herein.

18. I have utilized masculine pronouns for convenience. The reader should keep in mind that the Quanzhen monastic order includes both ordained monks and nuns. According to Vincent Goossaert, by the late thirteenth century there were some four thousand Quanzhen sacred sites and twenty thousand monastics (Goossaert 2001, 114–18), with possibly one-third or roughly six thousand being nuns (ibid., 118). See also Despeux and Kohn 2003, 140–74.

19. *Xianfeng daoqi*.

The Great High [Lord Lao] said, "Constantly knowing the regulations is called mysterious virtue. [Through this] one can become the norm of the world."[20] Regulations[21] refer to ritualized patterns, exemplars, models, and guidelines. Such regulations originate in antiquity, but have come to flourish in the [monastery] halls of today.

[1b] An illuminated teacher who has accepted disciples teaches and instructs them initially concerning effort. Afterward, he has them study nonaction. Excelling disciples of such an eminent community who consistently practice will make progress. [In contrast,] there are teachers who lack spiritual realization and are deluded. They may accept disciples, but they completely lack comprehension. They teach their students about nonaction [first]. Such is ignorance becoming even more ignorant, delusion becoming even more deluded! In life, they contravene the religious community. In death, they enter Hanchi (Frigid Pond).[22] As recompense for the debt of their [deficient] instruction, they are reincarnated for endless *kalpa*s.

Adepts who have the aspiration become affiliated with an illuminated teacher. In the morning they receive guidance, while in the evening they engage in ritual activity. They put what they hear into practice. They study the scriptures and classics. With reverence, they hold to the pure regulations. From morning to evening, they offer incense and light candles in respectful gratitude to the heavens and earth. They prostrate themselves before the sages and worthies, as well as serve their teachers and elders. They become accomplished throughout their various activities. They concentrate body and heart-mind by aligning the body and practicing quiet sitting.[23] They do not give rise to impure thoughts. Keeping the spinal column erect, [with the legs crossed in front of the body,] the right foot is placed underneath and the hands are joined in tranquil silence. The heart-mind remains unconcerned with the external, and the eyes remain closed. Sit for one to two watches. Such is the liturgical service.[24]

One sleeps during the five night-watches.[25]

Before the hour of the alarm bell,[26] it is only fitting that one wakes up early. [2a] One should wash one's face, comb one's hair, put on one's robes, and wait on the others. Everyone begins assembling at the main hall when the first bell sounds. The novices[27] enter the hall and assemble in ranked array on the inside [row]. At the second bell sounding, the elders assemble at the main hall and stand in ranked array on the outside [row]. At the end of third bell sounding, the abbot

20. A synthesis of chapters 65 and 45 of the *Daode jing*. The latter explains, "Clarity and stillness are the rectification of the world." See also chapters 37, 39, 57, and 78.

21. "Regulations" translates *shi*, which generally refers to "forms," "patterns," and "models."

22. A cold Earth Prison, or postmortem underworld.

23. "Quiet sitting" translates *jingzuo*, which also appears as "tranquil sitting" or "stillness meditation." The standard practice parallels "silent illumination" (*mozhao*) in Caodong Chan (Soto Zen). Emphasis is placed on stillness and emptiness.

24. "Liturgical service" translates *gongke*. The contemporary version involves communal recitation focusing on important personages, deities, sacred realms, Daoist scriptures, atonement (*chanhui*), and universal benefit (*pudu*). For a basic study see Kim 2006.

25. The five night-watches (*wugeng*) are the five periods of darkness and correspond to five terrestrial branches, namely, the double-hours of *xu* (7 p.m.–9 p.m.), *hai* (9 p.m.–11 p.m.), *zi* (11 p.m.–1 a.m.), *chou* (1 a.m.–3 a.m.), and *yin* (3 a.m.–5 a.m.). For some insights on *wugeng* training in early Quanzhen see Goossaert 2000; Komjathy 2007a, 175–79.

26. "Hour of the alarm bell" translates *kaijing shi*, which in the present context announced the beginning of the monastic day.

27. "Novices" translates *tongzi*, which literally means "youths" and "juniors" by extension.

enters the main hall and takes his place at the center of the gathering.[28] When the chanting of the scriptures is completed, the novices are the first to exit, [again] chanting as they walk together. When they arrive at the front of the hall, everyone again assembles in rows at the main hall. With the chanting of the scriptures complete, the abbot takes his seat. The novices then engage in full-body prostrations, after which they give a grand salutation with a loud voice. Following this, the entire assembly takes its seats, and tea is distributed. When the bowls are empty, the assembly disperses.

The novices once again enter their teachers' chambers. After prostrating themselves and making a salutation, they receive their teachers' directions. Sometimes this involves studying scriptures and the teachings, while at other times one must sweep the temple grounds. For each, there are tasks to complete.

When one encounters an elder, one joins the hands in front of the heart and [shows one's respect by] bending the body forward while the hands encircle in front. Then, one stands off to the side in order to allow the elder to pass. Afterward, one may again return to one's original position.

When one encounters a visitor, one should first bow to them, **[2b]** and then inform one's master and prepare tea. One serves the master first, and the visitor next. Joining the hands together, one stands in attendance. [After they finish their tea], one first collects the visitor's bowl, and then the master's bowl. If the guest gets up, one must go ahead to open the door and to draw the curtains. The visitor and the master exit, and one follows behind.

If one accompanies the master on an outing, one may not sit down with him. Joining the hands together, one stands in attendance. Each time someone enters or leaves, one bows to the members of the community. When a gift is presented, one must bow in gratitude and thank them.[29]

You may not act as you please or engage in deceptive conversation. You must clear out various thoughts, and constantly practice compassion and moral goodness. Remember the Dao and contemplate perfection. Your walking must be conscious and slow. Your speaking must be moderate and subdued. Endeavor to lessen suffering and difficulty, and be a beneficial presence. In addition, allow your heart-mind to be expansive and magnanimous. Embody loving kindness, flexibility, and harmony. Help all beings, and work for the benefit of humans. Amass merit and accumulate good deeds. Act in accordance with these practices and restraints, and the Dao will not be distant!

The Hair-pinning Ceremony[30]

When abandoning the mundane and committing oneself to the hair-pinning ceremony, one will first arrange one's hairpin, hat, and various Daoist ritual implements on the table of the patriarch. **[3a]** With the entire community sitting in a circle, the ordinand offers obeisance to his parents. He then

28. "Abbot" translates *zhuren*, which literally means "lord," "master," or "host." Later sections of the text identify various other monastic functionaries, such as the "bowl-master" (*zhubo*; 5a). As the *zhuren* takes the central position in the hall, it seems likely that the term refers to the most prominent member of the monastic community, namely, the abbot. It might also refer to the monastic "superior" or "prior," who would be one rank below the abbot in ecclesiastical rank. See section 4a.

29. This section is highly ceremonial and ritualistic. There is a repetition of Chinese terms for respect, the reverential tone of which is difficult to convey.

30. Literally, "sequence for binding the hair [topknot] with a hairpin." This is a Daoist ordination ritual during which one formally enters the religious community or monastic order through having one's hair bound into a topknot with a hairpin.

changes his clothes, socks, shoes, and other vestments. Kneeling before the Patriarch, the initiation master combs his hair, [forms a topknot], and inserts the hairpin. The community assembles in the main hall and begins chanting the scriptures and invoking the sages. Standing in front of the incense table, [the initiation master] displays and recites the announcement poem.[31] [The ordinand] bows three times, offers incense, and then steps back and makes another six prostrations. When the invocation is completed, one enters the Hall of the Perfected Official and chants the scriptures. One walks in front of the Patriarch, expressing one's veneration according to the earlier precedent. When the scripture chanting is completed, the community members again take their seats. The incense and lamps are arranged for a ritual before the master. The ordinand comes forward and bows before the master. He makes three prostrations, offers incense, and again offers obeisance. He extends his hands and [prepares] to receive the announcement poem. Kneeling before the master, the announcement is displayed, at which point he receives it and reads it. He has now been given the transmission of the Dao from the master. He shows his veneration by once again bowing three times.

When these prostrations are completed, the ordinand offers incense at the incense table and exits behind the elders. The community members exit in a single-file line. Each one in turn offers incense just as the one before him had done. When this respectful activity is completed, the ordinand enters the refectory where he shows his veneration to the patriarch [3b] and offers incense while bowing three times. Standing on both sides of the ordinand, the community members offer incense and prostrate themselves six times. Then everyone is invited to eat. When the meal is completed, everyone rises from their seats, accompanying any visitors to the door so that they may return home. They again walk through the kitchen and thank the staff.

There are certain things that one must practice through daily application. Practice skillful means in every situation, so that suffering may end and others may gain benefit. Remain humble and dispense with rumination. Revere your teachers and value your friends. Never give rise to mundane emotions, and constantly examine your own transgressions. In this way, innate nature will arise and direct the heart-mind. Request counsel from your elders, and reverently uphold the pure regulations.

Traveling to Visit Masters

When traveling to various regions to visit eminent masters, one must make sure that one has all the necessary Daoist supplies. When initially entering a temple compound, one looks in the western portico to see if it contains the phrase "rest your shoulders" or "lodge your crane." If you find such a place, you may rest. If you plan to rest for a long time, you should place an eave on the ground.

If you pass by, make sure that you pay attention to what is above and below. Lean on the wall, and try to hold onto your overcoat with your hands joined together.

If the caretaker of the guesthouse[32] comes out [4a], it is important for you to put on your overcoat and bow your head as is appropriate for guest-host relations. If he makes inquiries concerning

---

31. "Announcement poem" translates *ci*. It may have one of two meanings. First, it may simply refer to the ordination certificate. Second, it may correspond to lineage poems, in the sense of poetry transmitted to or written for the ordinand by his master. This would diverge from the more standardized use of lineage poems (*paishi*) as the source of ordination names. For example, the seven hundred-character poems associated with the lineages of Seven Perfected are contained at the end of the modern Quanzhen liturgy (*gongke*).

32. "Caretaker" translates *binzhu*. In the present context, the *binzhu* is in charge of sleeping-quarters, guest rooms, and the corresponding registers.

which regions you visited as well as the names of the monasteries and masters, you should respond [in the form of] place, region, and name. After this exchange, you may request to enter. If you are spending the night, you must leave all of your personal effects in your backpack with the exception of bedding.

When your bedding is laid out, wash your feet and change your vestments. Then you may again seek out the prefect[33] and respectfully address him as follows: "Venerable master in charge of this guesthouse, please accept my humble gestures of respect. May there be auspiciousness in everything you do. For a long time I have heard that there are hidden immortals, and I have come specifically to gaze upon your venerable visage. You have welcomed me with great kindness. I have laid out my bedding in this locale and set out my bowl, but I am undeserving of this highest honor. I offer my respect."

When you gain an audience with the superior,[34] respectfully address him as follows: "Perfected steward of this locale, please accept my humble gestures of respect. May there be auspiciousness in everything you do. For a long time I have heard that currents of the Dao are vast and expansive, and I have come specifically to sit at your feet and to gaze upon your venerable visage. You have welcomed me with great kindness. I have laid out my bedding in this locale and set out my bowl, but I am undeserving of this highest honor. I offer my respect."

If you are invited to stay, after the tea is finished stand up to take leave and thank the superior saying, "Just now I have disrespected your residence and your kindness has become my distress. [4b] My humble sentiments are submerged in the height of my embarrassment. I offer my respect." After you complete these expressions of veneration, return to your place. The superior may respond, "These mountain gates [monastery] have been blessed with the descent and abiding of your crane. Our attendance of you has been deficient. We are not worthy . . ." He may also rise from his seat and initiate the following exchange: "These temple gates [monastery] are deeply serene; our cookery is meager. We dare to hope that eminent adepts will tether their cranes here for a long time and assist the emergence of the Dao's manifestations. With deep yearning we hope that you will remain unfettered and free from difficulties, and that you will receive the utmost grace. We offer our respect."

Order of Seniority in the Meditation Hall

When joining the monastic community, one must first spend three nights [in the monastery]. Afterward, the community members may invite you to "enter the storeroom." They will examine your documents to determine in which place and during which year, month, and day you were accepted by your master and received the Dao. They will register you in the monastery's registry.[35] Next, they will assign you a community rank.[36] In that case, upon consulting of the registry, which is arranged in order according to given name and surname, each person can determine his rank and know his position in relation to the position of others. In this way, one may observe the order of seniority and show the appropriate senior-junior relationship when practicing together. [5a] Through this, one may follow this order when

---

33. "Prefect" translates *zhike*. This title appears to be synonymous with the "caretaker."

34. "Superior" translates *zhu*.

35. "Monastery registry" renders *qingce*.

36. "Community rank" translates *dan*.

entering the temple or meditation hall. One must also follow these guidelines in every activity, whether walking, standing, sitting, or sleeping. One should maintain the divisions between elder and younger and put these into practice. If each and every one maintains the order of seniority, there will not be any transgressions in superior-inferior relationships. In following the order within the monastery, one should act in accordance with senior-junior relationships that pertain to life outside the monastery.

Regulations for Bowl-clepsydra Meditation

The bowl-clepsydra meditation[37] commences on the first day of the tenth month when the entire monastic community gathers together. It extends through winter solstice and the lunar new year until ten days into the first month. After one hundred days, [the retreat] is completed.

Concerning those who enter the meditation hall, each is asked about his anxieties and longings. The truth is that each and every one must figure certain things out for himself. The issue of life and death is profound. Everything is impermanent and quickly dissipates. Such alterations in the end develop one's insight. [Concerning these matters] reverently ask for instructions from the eminent masters and follow their guidance.

The bowl-clepsydra meditation involves [periods of] movement and stillness.[38] During the periods of movement, it is acceptable to engage in ordinary or leisurely activity. During the periods of stillness, it is not like this.

If there are those who have fallen asleep, are nodding off, or shifting their bodies, the bowl-master first walks around on watch with the discipline stick.[39] **[5b]** He suspends the stick over the body of the adept who has fallen asleep. Then he strikes [the adept's shoulders] three times and withdraws. Afterward, [the offender] attentively takes hold of the discipline stick, quietly gets up from his position, and begins inspecting the others. He is replaced in turn by the next offender. As long as the bowl-clepsydra meditation has not yet ended, the bell has not yet sounded, and the "stillness" placard has not yet been substituted,[40] one may not enter or leave, speak, or move without a reason. Anyone who does not abide by these regulations will be disciplined.

---

37. "Bowl-clepsydra meditation" is my inelegant translation of *zuobo*. As documented in the *Quanzhen zuobo jiefa* (DZ 1229), which is translated in this chapter, this was a bowl with a small hole in the bottom used as a time-measurement device for communal meditation sessions. The bowl was placed in water and its sinking measured the desired training period. Thus, *zuobo* could refer to the actual object and be translated as "sitting bowl," or it could refer to the corresponding practice and be translated as "clepsydra meditation." In either case, it is important to keep in mind that this is a bowl-type clepsydra, a fact that has informed my translation. As this section indicates, bowl-clepsydra meditation was a communal meditation retreat practiced from roughly the beginning of winter through the beginning of spring (by traditional Chinese reckoning). In this way, it parallels the winter Zen meditation retreat (Jpn.: *ango*; also *sesshin*), which is in turn modeled on the traditional India rain retreat (Pali: *vasso*; Skt.: *varsah*). Note the different seasonal and cosmological concerns. In the Indian case, the retreat corresponds to the monsoon season; in the Chinese case, it moves through the apex of yin and the growth of yang (winter solstice) and the lunar new year (a moment of both completion and new beginnings), and culminates with the increasing ascendancy of yang in the beginning of spring. The latter is associated with the first node of the Wood phase and symbolizes new life.

38. That is, walking and seated meditation practice.

39. "Bowl-master" translates *zhubo*, while "discipline stick" renders *pai*. The latter corresponds to the "wake-up stick" (Jpn.: *keisaku*; *kyosaku*) in Zen Buddhism. The discipline stick is a thin, elongated, and flat stick used to hit inattentive monastics on the shoulders during communal meditation. More often than not, it is not a form of punishment; rather, it is seen as an act of compassion aimed at assisting awakening. This reading is supported by the identification of the patrolling monk with the disciplined monk and the subsequent exchange of positions.

40. It seems that there was a "stillness placard" (*jingpai*) and a "movement placard" (*dongpai*) that were hung respectively when meditation commenced and ended.

If there is someone who disregards the previously mentioned issues, the bowl-assistant[41] initiates the required action and the bowl-master disciplines the offender. At the first infraction, one must clean the meditation hall. At the next infraction, one must serve tea. At the third infraction, one is expelled from the meditation hall. If someone repeats such behavior, one must apply the pure regulations.

Standards of the Patriarch

A day of twelve cycles of the bowl-clepsydra corresponds to the twelve double-hours;[42] three involve stillness and nine are unregulated. These divisions correspond to the Three Primes and to the Nine Vapors.[43] They also correspond to the Three Reversions and to the Nine Reversals.[44]

[6a] Each day begins at the fifth night-watch. At the hour of *yin* [3 a.m.–5 a.m.], upon hearing the sound of the wake-up clackers,[45] each adept washes his face and rinses his mouth in preparation for an audience with the Perfected and for offering obeisance to the sages.[46] At the hour of *mao* [5 a.m.–7 a.m.], one partakes in the morning meal. At the hour of *chen* [7 a.m.–9 a.m.], there is group meditation.[47] At the hour of *si* [9 a.m.–11 a.m.], the stillness-bell is struck three times. Everyone practices quiet sitting [individually] in accordance with the methods appropriate to his own accomplishment.[48] At the hour of *wu* [11 a.m.–1 p.m.], one goes to the refectory [for the noon meal]. At the hour of *wei* [1 p.m.–3 p.m.], there is group meditation. At the hour of *shen* [3 p.m.–5 p.m.], one enters stillness [in private practice] as before. At the hour of *you* [5 p.m.–7 p.m.], there is the evening gathering.[49] At the hour of *xu* [7 p.m.–9 p.m.], there is group meditation and tea is served. At the hour of *hai* [9 p.m.–11 p.m.], one enters stillness individually as before in accordance with the method appropriate to one's own accomplishment. At the hour of *zi* [11 p.m.–1 a.m.], one chants the religious discourses or the poems[50] for combating the demon of sleep.[51] The

---

41. "Bowl-assistant" translates *fubo*.

42. The twelve double-hours correspond to the twelve terrestrial branches.

43. The Three Primes (*sanyuan*) may refer to the Three Purities (*sanqing*), Three Heavens (*santian*), or the Three Treasures (*sanbao*). The Nine Vapors (*jiuqi*) is a less common Daoist technical term, though it clearly refers to some cosmological dimension.

44. The Three Reversions (*sanfan*) and Nine Reversals (*jiuhuan*) refer to aspects of alchemical training and accomplishment. See the translation of the *Dadan zhizhi* (DZ 244) in chapter 4 of the present volume.

45. "Clackers" translates *ban*. Contextually speaking, its material characteristics are unclear. However, they most likely parallel the same implements utilized in Zen Buddhism. They are two square pieces of wood that are hit together.

46. Here incense offerings and prostrations are made to the icons and statuary on the central altar.

47. Yao (1980a, 91; 2000, 589) translates *hunzuo* (lit., "mixed sitting") as "group meditation," while Goossaert (1997, 274) translates it as "méditation non stricte." While both are viable, the overall context suggests that this is a compulsory, communal meditation period. The other double-hours reserved for meditation would be a personal or voluntary training period. In either case, there are three periods of communal meditation and three periods of private, individual practice.

48. This line indicates that different monastics were practicing different meditation techniques. Based on extant texts, it is unclear if a stage-based system was utilized. The texts suggest that Quanzhen monastics practiced quietistic meditation (*jingzuo*) as well as internal alchemy (*neidan*).

49. "Evening gathering" (*wancan*) may refer to "evening interviews" with the meditation master or one's own teacher (Jpn.: *dokusan*), a formal lecture, or a religious ceremony.

50. The specific texts utilized are unclear. One would assume that the *Daode jing*, *Qingjing jing*, and *Yinfu jing* occupied a central position.

51. Here "demon of sleep" (*shuimo*) refers to sleep as such. In other Quanzhen contexts, it is used synonymously with "yin-ghosts" (*yingui*), which refer to dreamtime phantasms and fantasies that may lead to dissipation. This is especially dangerous for monks who may have involuntary, nocturnal emissions.

bowl-master is the first to begin. Each text is recited three times and no more. At the hour of *chou* [1 a.m.–3 a.m.], the gathering is dismissed, and each monk can do as he pleases. The bowl-assistant holds the position of the bowl. [In recognition of the fact that] he has not rested for a long time, each person expresses gratitude to him.

Three Conditions under Which You May Not Stand Up

[6b] Now, the interdiction not to stand up concerns the entire monastic community and permanent monks. Supposing that there is an attendant of the monastic hall who is responding to guest invitations, entertaining guests, or attending to visitors, it is not permissible for other community members to move, as this will disrupt the order of the monastic hall.

First, when practicing meditation, do not stand up. Purify the celestial heart-mind, and regulate the breath with the original harmony. From the end to the beginning, through the silent revolving of the Mysterious Pivot, the physical form should be like the great Void—do not sway, do not move. When entering and leaving, each person maintains a sincere heart-mind. Then quiet sitting follows the prescribed method and ritual procedure.

Second, when chanting the scriptures, do not stand up. When the heart-mind is active, each person should maintain a disposition of reverence and ceremonial dignity. Harmonize your voice by circulating qi. The heart-mind, thought, and intent are released. The ears listen, and the eyes observe. Voice and sound are mutually harmonized, and the recitation continues. Walking in a single-file line, each monk follows the other when entering and leaving. Each person takes refuge [in the Dao] and chants the scriptures according to the prescribed method.

Third, when eating, do not stand up. Remember the Dao and contemplate Perfection. The heart-mind is clear and thinking is stilled. Spirit is stabilized and qi is harmonized. [7a] Serenely and silently offer thanks [for the meal]. Extend your bowl without making a sound, and enter the meditation hall without speaking. Following the others according to junior or senior standing, each person maintains a reverential presence and sits and eats according to the prescribed method.

Substance and Function of Complete Perfection

The patriarchs established the teachings, and the immortals and sages liberated humans. They opened the pathway of the Greater Vehicle [Daoism] and established the watchtower of myriad wonders.

They enable us to return to the Origin and attend to principle, to rectify the disorder of our heart-minds by means of Complete Perfection. [They enable us] to maintain a steadfast heart-mind through clarity and stillness, to attend to complete innate nature through simplicity and humility. They profoundly understood the short duration [of human life] and attained joyfulness like a perpetual spring.[52] This is because they were unconcerned with personal benefit and fame and because they were unattached to the affairs of the mundane world. By illuminating the great substance, their heart-minds attained the purity of gold and the luster of jade. By nourishing the

---

52. Here "perpetual spring" (*changchun*) invokes the Daoist name of Qiu Chuji (1148–1227), the third Quanzhen Patriarch.

original pivot, their aspirations attained the firmness of stone and the purity of ice. They aided human beings and benefited all beings, embracing unified principle so that all would be pervaded. They refined themselves and returned to the Origin, gathering all virtue and attaining completeness. They took responsibility [for rectifying] the narrow-mindedness of their followers and culled adepts who had experienced the perfect pivot. They refrained from argumentation and from contention, from arrogance and from discussing right and wrong. **[7b]** Living in seclusion in a temple, and residing among a group in a residential monastery, they did not pay attention to the faults and transgressions of others. Instead, they cleared out the tendency toward domination and self-conceit. Once the heart-mind is cleansed of defilements, one adapts oneself to the circumstances. Once open joyfulness is extended, kindness and goodness extend to everyone.

In the morning and evening when going to the refectory, one must join one's hands together, maintain a sincere heart-mind, and sit in silence. At dawn and at dusk, one participates in [the liturgical service for] the sages. One must be attentive to one's joined hands, slow steps, and be filled with devotion. When one stands in a higher position, one's deportment is reverential and serious. When one occupies a lower rank, one's comportment is unconstrained and casual. One must go to secretly touch the pivot of Perfection and reverentially merge with the essence of the Mysterious. One honors one's master with utmost respect and genuine gratitude. Inquire about the Dao with pure sincerity and devout expressions. Comprehend the myriad principles so that you may return to the Origin; one attains unification with Perfection and then there is subtle application. Clearly opening divine perception,[53] in serenity one's silent illumination extends to wondrous tenuity.[54] Clearly penetrating the celestial heart-mind, in resonance one's inverted observation extends to numinous emanation.

If you go against the rules and put on appearances, your transgressions will be derided. With a humble disposition, one should interact with one's companions with deference. Deny yourself and quietly treat others with kindness. When studying religious texts or explaining scriptural writings, you must thoroughly investigate their numinous origins. **[8a]** You must not engage in empty or disrespectful conversations about them. [The aim is] to go beyond the thoughts of the sage's heart-mind and to penetrate the origin of your own innate nature. When your understanding becomes clear, you may abandon study.[55] When your pervasion becomes complete, you begin to enjoy nonaction. When the heart-mind conforms to innate nature, you gaze into suchness. Authentically joyful in nondifferentiation, qi is infused and flooded with spirit. Silent and solitary, one's physical structure merges with the great Void. Like the calmness and clarity of water, one becomes flexible and fluid. Like the indistinctness and ethereality of clouds, one becomes uninhibited and expansive.

As a matter of course, one desires to penetrate the Dao and become self-realized, to become complete in authentic practice and perfect accomplishment. In disciplining one's impulses, one avoids falling into prejudice and perversion. By abiding in what is real, one realizes the return to balance and alignment. By getting rid of one's own faults, one may have constant joy, peace, and harmony. If you do not have self-conceit, who can compete and contend with you? When the emotions are

---

53. Literally, "eyes of the Dao" or "Dao-vision" (*daoyan*), which is one of the potential numinous abilities that arises as a byproduct of Daoist religious practice.

54. "Silent illumination" (*mozhao*) is one of the standard names for Caodong Chan (Soto Zen) meditation.

55. Cf. Discourse 3 of the *Chongyang lijiao shiwu lun* translated in chapter 3 in this volume.

extinguished, the heart-mind becomes corralled. When the dust is clarified, defilements become purified. In your everyday activities, do not make decisions solely in terms of personal concerns; when considering what should be done, you must constantly abide by the general welfare.

The person who shows deceit or indolence squanders his virtue and makes his faults visible; the person who shows jealousy or dishonesty damages his body and loses his life.[56] The person who follows sensual enticements and delights in success is mediocre **[8b]**; the person who avoids distinctions between self and other and rests in the Center is sagely. In this way, one's profound insight becomes increasingly [manifest through] hidden virtue; one's standing as a Perfected becomes secretly [manifest through] concealed accomplishment. You must constantly preserve the qi of the Dao,[57] and avoid mundane influences. When the precepts are upheld with refined dignity, you sever ties to the four errors[58] and [develop] the eight forms of consciousness.[59] When your effort is continuously intense, you attain the nine reversions and six pervasions.[60] When unconstrained in desire, you become conditioned by the appearances of perverse demons; when craving the necessities of life, you fall among hungry ghosts. Constantly meditate in silence, and wisdom will become bright; do not allow emotions to come forth, and delusion will be left behind. When intention is fixed in equanimity, the heart-mind becomes joyous in stable consistency. Looking at phenomena, one divorces oneself from the obscuration of attachments and personal preferences. Responding to circumstances, one works on behalf of the community with dedication.

It is necessary that your comportment conforms to the needs of the moment and that you not speak and act before fully understanding [the situation]. Your partial views, lapses [of judgment], and transgressions must be rectified as soon as possible. If the heart-mind is contorted, then one encounters conflict in every circumstance. If innate nature is stable, then one gains the confidence of every person. When reckless and arrogant,[61] innate nature invariably becomes insensitive. Through flattery, contempt, and deceit, one's life-destiny and thoughts diminish prosperity. The highest adept consolidates his qi by nourishing [himself]; elevated in luminosity, he is humble and disciplines himself. Do not dishonor the purity and high-standing of the teachings; **[9a]** do not incur the

---

56. This corresponds to article 5 of the punishments of Wang Chongyang in section 12a.

57. *Daoqi*.

58. "Four errors" translates *sifei*; I have not been able to locate a corresponding set of referents.

59. "Eight forms of consciousness" renders *bashi*, literally, "eight recognitions." These are the eight Buddhist *parijñāna* or kinds of consciousness. They include sight, hearing, smell, taste, touch, intellect, discrimination, and storehouse-consciousness. See Soothill and Hodous 1995 [1937], 40; Ding 1939, 149, 2858; Xingyun 1989, 316.

60. As a Buddhist technical term the "six pervasions" (*liutong*), *abhijñā* or *sad-abhijñā*, are the six "supernatural" or universal powers (Skt.: *siddhi*) acquired by a Buddha. They include "magical" powers such as the ability to go anywhere at will (teleportation and multilocality) and to transform oneself or objects at will; the ability to see anything at any distance (clairvoyance); the ability to hear anything at any distance (clairaudience); the ability to know others' thoughts (telepathy); (5) the ability to know the former lives of oneself and others; and the ability to destroy all negative passions. See Soothill and Hodous 1995 [1937], 138; Ding 1939, 649; Xingyun 1989, 1290, 1292. The "Lun liutong jue" (Instructions on the Six Pervasions; *Neidan jiyao*, DZ 1258, 3.12a–14a; Eskildsen 2004, 230, n. 15), a Yuan dynasty internal alchemy text, identifies them as follows: (1) Pervasion of Heart-mind Conditions, involving the ability to experience unified nature as distinct from the ordinary body; (2) Pervasion of Spirit Conditions, involving the ability to know things beyond ordinary perception; (3) Pervasion of Celestial Vision, involving the ability to perceive internal landscapes within the body; (4) Pervasion of Celestial Hearing, involving the ability to hear the subtle communications of spirits and humans; (5) Pervasion of Past Occurrences, involving the ability to understand the karmic causes and effects relating to the Three Worlds of desire, form, and formlessness; and (6) Pervasion of the Heart-minds of Others, involving the ability to manifest the body-beyond-the-body.

61. This corresponds to article 6 of the punishments of Wang Chongyang, which appear in section 12a.

shame of being punished for violating the monastic regulations! You must have reverence for this body that you have inherited; in all situations it is most appropriate to be careful and considerate. Unite vital essence and spirit so that they are firmly guarded. Conserve original qi so that it is not lost.[62] When this body experiences the Gold Lotus,[63] it will result in your ascent to the jade regions. In unification, one wanders carefree at the commencement of the mysterious origin.[64] In totality, one enjoys the primordial state before the appearance of Di.[65] Ah, the roundness of heaven and squareness of earth conform to our regulations. The numinosity of our innate nature and abundance of our life-destiny are merged with golden immortality.

Hymn of the Bowl-chamber

The Way of Complete Perfection is the ocean; the heart-mind of immortal sagehood is the well-spring. At the center is the luminous Great Ultimate;[66] on the inside is the hidden gourd-heaven. Your expansive mind pervades the Center, which resembles a numinous abyss that surges forth. The center of the bowl penetrates the base,[67] causing the Spirit Water to ascend as saliva. If elevated luminosity abides, one must face the Sovereign at the center of Emptiness. If highest adeptness resides,[68] one must remain pliable when according with the Source. If you rest within the ripples, the heart-mind comes to resemble clear blue water. If you are still among the wind-blown waves, innate nature takes on the structure of the Gold Lotus. Unified aspiration is silent and unaffected. The three minds are purified and free from agitation.[69] **[9b]** If the water does not overflow, one is calm to the point of absorption. If you are tranquil, you can be complete.

This is bowl-clepsydra meditation for practicing concentration, of entering the chamber to cultivate accomplishment. Find the center within emptiness, and the grotto will be penetrated. Act in accordance with this real location in order to attain complete pervasion. Join heaven and earth within the half-*sheng* vessel.[70] Hide away your emotions and innate nature within the bowl-chamber. Fuse the ancestral qi of the mysterious origin. Rouse the perfect currents of the Grand Kalpa.

> When the myriad *dharma*s are fully penetrated,
> [There is] tranquility within the Scarlet Tower.

---

62. Reading *shi* ("to lose") for *xian* ("the first").

63. Gold Lotus (*jinlian*) may refer to enlightenment or the culmination of alchemical transformation.

64. An allusion to chapter 1 of the *Zhuangzi*.

65. An allusion to chapter 4 of the *Daode jing*. Di, also appearing as Shangdi (Supreme Thearch), was the high god of the Shang dynasty, who sat at the apex of the Shang pantheon. The implication of the passage in the *Daode jing* is *not* that gods do not exist; rather, every individuated deity emerged at a later cosmogonic moment. The Dao as Source and primordial undifferentiation is primary.

66. Great Ultimate translates *taiji*, literally, "great ridgepole." It refers to yin-yang interaction, and thus to the source of all differentiated existence.

67. The author is moving back and forth between the dual meanings of *xin* as "heart-mind" and "center."

68. An allusion to chapter 8 of the *Daode jing*. See also chapters 15, 41, 65, and 68.

69. "Three minds" (*sanxin*) is a technical Buddhist term that designates consciousness of past, present, and future. As a Daoist technical term, it may also designate the "three centers," the three elixir fields.

70. Half-*sheng* vessel is a symbolic name for the lower elixir field.

> When every defilement is completely purified,
> [There is] clarity within the Numinous Palace.[71]

Cloud-companions [Daoist adepts] are unified in their heart-minds and respect difference. Mist-companions are harmonized in their aspirations and embrace sameness. Generally speaking, you must pacify your thoughts and purify your heart-mind, revert your emotions and return to your innate nature. In your activities, it is essential that your serenity is constant; in your eating and drinking, you must refrain from excess. When the uncontrolled heart-mind is extinguished, there is the silent illumination of original spirit. When the perfect breath is regulated, there is melded infusion of wisdom and life-destiny. When entering meditation, contain your radiance in darkened silence by means of an empty heart-mind. When widening stillness, return to perception through gradual consideration and emerge from concentration. If the demons of sleep suddenly have arrived, those who are not awake nod their heads and sway their bodies. **[10a]** If veils of confusion unexpectedly have come, those who lack understanding open their mouths and disperse their qi. The person on patrol with the goal of preventing [these conditions] presents the discipline stick and rectifies [the situation]. [The person receiving rectification] must reply with humility and flexibility, refrain from confusing himself and become strengthened [in his commitment].

Fundamentally, for the maintenance and conservation of life, you must not give rise to disputation among self and others. It is urgent and appropriate that you abandon obscuration and dissipation, and that you investigate vital essence and spirit. Respect for yourself begins with offering obeisance to the immortal sages and turning your head to show your gratitude for [their] determination and humaneness. Live in joy and appreciation; do not give rise to anger and hatred. A calm exhilaration naturally arises in your heart-mind; an amazing youthfulness joyously arises within the gourd. To deny yourself and reward virtue is truly [the comportment of] a superior adept. To strengthen resentment and respond to disdain is truly [the comportment of] a lesser person. Do not be self-conceited, hollow, or deceptive; reduce your faults and nourish simplicity and genuineness.

Carefully examine and maintain the regulations of the sages and the principles of the bowl of the patriarchs. When gold returns to the Origin,[72] you have the foundation of the bowl; when emotions return to innate nature, you have the principle of the bowl. The Primordial Chaos of the bowl resembles the Origin of Qian-heaven; the emptiness of the Center resembles the Great Beginning.[73] The variegated net is concentrated at the center; the transformative process is completed on the inside. Accordingly, when there is dissipation, you will not awaken, but rather sink [into the ocean of suffering]; **[10b]** accordingly, when there is not even the slightest leakage, you instantly rise above [such a condition]. When the ice becomes clear, awakening returns to the Source; when the bowl bobs up and down, illumination returns to oneself. On the whole, one understands being by means of Nonbeing, falsity by means of truth, and substance by means of emptiness.

---

71. Here Scarlet Tower (*jiangque*) and Numinous Palace (*linggong*) refer to the heart-mind, especially to the psychosomatic center of the heart.

72. This line invokes the graphic composition of the character *bo*, which consists of *jin* ("gold") and *ben* ("source"/"root"). The character also occurs with the *fou* ("pottery") radical. The first version also designates the begging-bowl of Buddhist mendicants.

73. Grand Beginning (*taishi*) is a cosmogonic designation that refers to the earliest beginnings of the Dao's spontaneous, impersonal unfolding as emanating transformative process.

To cut and polish [the mind-mirror], follow the example of the master and your companions [in the Dao]; to develop comprehension, exert strong effort. Discover the illumination at the beginning before your parents gave birth to you;[74] constantly revert the luminosity[75] at the commencement before your body and heart-mind began to toil. In responding to sincere and aspiring adepts, be humble and respectful; in responding to unexceptional and reckless companions, be flexible but accordingly keep your distance. Master Hu, among round windows with jar-like shapes, was truly joyful in his limitlessness;[76] Master Yan, among empty baskets and gourds, was completely joyful in his boundlessness.[77] Model yourself on the sages and immortals [who meditated] in darkened quietude and secret residence; emulate the Perfected [who resided] in meditation enclosures by means of abyss-like abiding. Attain this in calm stillness, enjoy this in quiet suchness, and investigate this in the bowl-chamber. Living in great monasteries with their arrayed rows or among enlightened individuals residing together is truly a rare opportunity and exceptional chance.

> Refining perfection in the empty Void,
> Everyone becomes joyous in original expansiveness.
> Producing purity in the empty chamber,
> Everyone becomes calm in great simplicity.

The end is realized in the beginning;[78] **[11a]** the morning culminates in the evening. It is not a matter of interrupting the abundance of the moment, but of simply being complete in every activity. Completely detached in the highest wisdom, the heart-mind [attains] expansive clarity and graceful ease [like] white clouds. Completely vexed in the lowest ignorance, innate nature [attains] grasping obscuration and deluded concealment [like] black fog. Devote two time-periods to nourish the divine numen continuously and secretly. Devote one hundred days to congeal the concentrated qi calmly and constantly. In the morning and evening, leisurely stretch out. Your nourishment should be grafted to the seasons, and your garments should be able to withstand the cold. If you are excessive in your work, then your internal organs will lose their guiding principles. If you regulate your rest, then spirit and qi will be constantly calm. Being earnest in your aspirations is essential to your cultivation. You must also do away with sleep and forget food. Remaining constant in silent illumination, polish and refine the contented heart-mind. Returning to perfect observation, put forth effort in your renunciation of

74. This is a famous Chan *gong'an* (Jpn.: *kōan*), or enigmatic saying, which more frequently appears as "the face before your birth" or "original face" (*benlai mianmu*).

75. In Daoist internal cultivation, *fanzhao*, "reverting the luminosity" or "turning back the radiance," involves directing the gaze inward in order to illuminate the inner landscape.

76. The text identifies him as Hugong. The present reference suggests that our author has a personage from the *Zhuangzi* in mind. Huzi (Gourd Master) appears as the teacher of Liezi (Master Lie) in chapter 7 of the *Zhuangzi*. See Watson 1968, 94–97. The present section combines this story with other references to "meditation enclosure" (*huandu*) in chapters 23 and 28 of the *Zhuangzi*. See Watson 1968, 248–49, 315–16. A hagiography of a certain Hugong, which does not contain the present details, also appears in the *Shenxian zhuan*. See Campany 2002, 161–64. As Campany points out, it seems that these figures are unrelated.

77. Yanzi refers to Yan Hui (Ziyuan; 514–483 BCE), a senior disciple of Kongzi ("Confucius"). For relevant passages in the *Lunyu* see V.26, VI.3, VII.11, IX.11, IX.21, XI.3, XI.7–11, XI.23, XII.1, XV.11. See Lau 1992 [1983]. Yan Hui and Kongzi also appear as mouthpieces for the Daoist practice of "fasting the heart-mind" (*xinzhai*) and "sitting-in-forgetfulness" (*zuowang*) in chapters 4 and 6 of the *Zhuangzi*. Cf. *Changsheng yulu*, DZ 1058, 3b.

78. An inversion of chapter 64 of the *Daode jing*: "Be as careful at the end as at the beginning."

self. Nourish qi and spirit until they become unified and stabilized; innate nature and life-destiny naturally complete each other. Unite the Three Powers into a single sequence; this is the wondrous portal of Nondifferentiation. [Obtain] the Six Pervasions and Four Penetrations;[79] here is the expanse of the great Void. This is what establishes the substance of donations and merits as well as the place accorded to the master in the monastery. Gradually transcend disorder and deception, and [you will attain] eternal joy and true happiness. Alas! Escape from the illusory world of life and death and leap beyond the heaven and earth of the transformative process [manifest universe]. Frolic in Prior Heaven and [11b] wander carefree in the immense cosmos. Be unaffected in Nondifferentiation and take joy in the perfect Origin. You become unconstrained in the state of Complete Perfection and highly accomplished. Eminent, you alone are established among the venerated predecessors. Then you reside within the Mysterious Gate, offering reverence to the teachings. Desiring to leap beyond the shores of the Dao, rely on the raft of compassion.

List of Prohibitions of Sovereign Lord Chongyang, Master of the Teachings

Now then, the principle of the Dao is beyond the darkened indistinctness of the Great Ultimate. How can this be easily perceived? Consequently, those in the world who seek it are many, while those who awaken to it are few. Within the Dao of emptiness and nonaction, Qian-heaven and Kun-earth are the qi of flood-like suchness. When yin and yang flourish, they produce things and forms through [interactive] movement. But how can one bear the diversity of the present and the distance of the past? How can you become disciplined in your solitary practice and personal lot? In movement and rest, one's comportment and ceremonial behavior must not go against [the prohibitions]. For this, occupy a beneficial place and personally build a hall for honoring the sages. There you can gather devout companions from throughout the country and form a community of virtuous associates from every direction. It is for this reason that the teachings and regulations have been established: [12a] in hopes that derision may be inspected [and rectified].

1. Those who offend civil laws will be expelled from the order.

2. Those who steal valuables or property and disrespect superiors and elders will have their robes and bowls burned, in addition to being expelled.

3. Those who speak falsely, causing disturbances in the monastic hall and trouble in the community, will be flogged with a bamboo switch, in addition to being expelled.

4. Those who drink alcohol, indulge in sex, seek wealth, lose their temper,[80] or eat strong-smelling vegetables[81] will be expelled.

---

79. Four Penetrations translates *sida*. Under one reading, it refers to knowledge of past, present, and future events and sacred domains.

80. The Four Hindrances (*sihai*).

81. The five strong-smelling vegetables (*wuhun; wuxin*), which are five substances in the onion family. They are usually identified as garlic, onions, chives, shallots, and leeks. These are claimed to excite the senses and activate sexual energy. The prohibition and corresponding avoidance would thus support a monastic way of life.

5. Those who are villainous, treacherous, indolent, crafty, jealous, or deceitful will be expelled.

6. Those who are insubordinate, arrogant, and do not act cooperatively with others will undergo [compulsory] fasting.

7. Those who engage in highfalutin talk and brag, and those who are impatient with their work will [be made to] burn incense.

8. Those who speak about strange occurrences and joke, and those who leave the temple gates without [good] reason will [be made to add] oil [to the lamps]. **[12b]**

9. Those who do not concentrate on their work, and those who are villainous, treacherous, indolent, or lazy will [be made to serve] tea.

10. Those who commit minor offenses will undergo [compulsory] prostrations.[82]

May these regulations be honored and distributed so that everyone may understand them. Always follow this guideline: "When three people walk together, I will certainly find my teacher among them."[83] When one lives in a chamber in the company of sparrows, working with zeal and converting [people] through oral instruction, in accordance with our models, then laws are not able to surpass the highest goodness and firmness is not able to outmatch the utmost softness. "A sage who examines himself three times may be called great."[84]

It is fortunate to meet an enlightened master and to become acquainted with the sacred teachings. Without teachings and practice, how can you become fully adept? [These regulations] are clearly displayed [when the monks] gather in the meditation hall; examine yourself even more and do not transgress them. After receiving these prohibitions and precepts, it is not permissible for men and women to live together or to give free rein to passions and inclinations.

If you constantly penetrate your fears, the offerings of religious benefactors will be difficult to exhaust. If you neglect this for a single instant, you will regret it and will not be able [to pass the test of] the "passage in the Void."[85] By being attentive to cultivation, each person will attain the heart-mind of the Dao that is firm and stable. [In contrast], the undisciplined risks completely ruining his previous efforts. **[13a]** Reflect on this list in detail.

---

82. Something must have been rotten in Denmark. The fact that these rules emphasize increasing strictness and harsh punishments seems to indicate that there was laxity and corruption in the monastic order or that the monastic authorities were trying to tighten the reins on certain social undesirables who had found their way into Quanzhen monastic communities. The latter is a common function of large-scale monasticism, that is, to lodge and feed those who lack education, who come from lower socioeconomic backgrounds, or who have physical or mental disabilities. Compare these monastic rules with the classical Daoist emphasis on humans' innate goodness and rejection of legalistic approaches to existence (e.g., *Daode jing* chaps. 57 and 75) and Wang Chongyang's direct requirements of ascetic commitments for adherence.

83. *Lunyu* (Analects), Book 7. The passage in question reads as follows: "Even when walking in the company of two other people, I am bound to be able to learn from them. The good points of the one I copy; the bad points of the other I correct in myself" (adapted from Lau 1992 [1983], 63).

84. *Lunyu* (Analects), Book 1: "Every day I examine myself on three counts. In what I have undertaken on another's behalf, have I failed to do my best? In my dealings with my friends, have I failed to be trustworthy in what I say? Have I failed to practice repeatedly what has been passed on to me?" (Lau 1992 [1983], 3).

85. According to Goossaert (1997, 283, n. 63), the "passage of the Void" (*xudu*), which also appears as *xudu guan*, is a ceremony within which the novice expresses his total commitment to maintain Daoist religious training, to renounce mundane concerns and distractions, and to remain a member of the monastic order.

Text on Entering the Hall by Master Liaozhen[86]

Since the Sage Ancestor of the Mysterious Origin[87] revealed the gateway to all wonders and the teachings of Complete Perfection of the Great Dao in order to transform all beings, [we have seen the flowering of] the Seven Petals of the Gold Lotus of Chongyang[88] within the Paradise of the Turquoise Pond and the Myriad Leaves of the Jade Flower of Changchun within the Paradise of the Garden of Joy.[89] Nevertheless, although these branches at their tips are different, ultimately the diverse leaves return to the root. Hence, although these tributaries[90] in their currents are diverse, invariably the various streams return to the ocean. Wherever one finds the teachings, one gathers with cloud-companions from throughout the country. Anywhere one accumulates [positive] karma, one assembles mist-companions from the three mountains. Reed-thatched huts and grass-thatched shelters are restored and become beautiful temples and magnificent palaces.[91] Those who wear vestments stuffed with paper or woven with hemp are awarded with caps of the stars and pendants of the moon. We refer to such people as "those who are able to exalt the Dao."[92] By elucidating the regulations of the former sages, these Daoist methods naturally influence people and open the eyes of later generations.

In the Liaozhen tang (Hall of Realizing Perfection), **[13b]** there fundamentally is not even a trace of entanglement in the heart-mind; in the school [that unites] all practices, the community practices correctly and exerts strong effort. The most elevated person manifests compassion in every situation; the most humble person constantly maintains reverence and deference. The defiled heart-mind competes and quarrels and does not manifest our lineage as embodying the Mysterious. [In contrast,] those who guide one and all through divine perception take the life of our predecessor Danyang as their model. Those who in previous lives became immortals of transcendental realities are at the present time the inhabitants of our tradition. If you collectively cultivate the fruits of the Dao while residing in the world, you will leap beyond the mundane and take your place among the company of ranked immortals.

Future immortals who become renunciants must maintain introspection with clarity; eminent adepts who become separated from the dust must examine themselves with sincerity. If you attend to the broad discourses on the mysteries, this may yet again interfere with [the moment of] taking your place among the immortals. I bow my head before my fellow cloud-companions, and humbly offer my deep-felt concern.

---

86. A reference to Zhao Wuxuan (Liaozhen [Realizing Perfection]; 1149–1211). His hagiography appears in section 1.20a–21b of the *Zhongnan neizhuan* (DZ 955). Zhao was a second-generation adept, disciple of Ma Danyang, and contemporary of such Quanzhen luminaries as Yin Zhiping (Qinghe [Clear Harmony]; 1169–1251) and Song Defang (Piyun [Wrapped-in-Clouds]; 1183–1247). The present text also appears in section 9.13b–14a of the *Minghe yuyin* (DZ 1100) (Goossaert 1997, 283, n. 64). It is unclear why Zhao was considered so significant.

87. Laozi.

88. The seven petals of the Gold Lotus refer to Wang Chongyang's seven primary Shandong disciples, the so-called Seven Perfected.

89. The leaves of the Jade Flower refer to Qiu Changchun's disciples, specifically those who were ordained by him and who became the leaders of the Quanzhen monastic order.

90. "Tributaries" here translates *pai*, which also refers to lineages.

91. This line echoes Discourse 5 of the *Chongyang lijiao shiwu lun* (DZ 1255).

92. An allusion to Book 15 of the *Lunyu* (Analects): "It is Man [*sic*] who is capable of broadening the Way. It is not the Way that is capable of broadening the Way" (Lau 1992 [1983], 157).

List of Regulations of Perfected Changchun[93]

When residing in hermitages, you need to be clear, empty, imperturbable, immobile, and silent. Realizing innate nature[94] should be your substance, and nourishing life-destiny should be your function. Pliant suppleness is your constancy, and deferential responsiveness is your virtue. Compassionate sympathy is the foundation, and expedient means is the entry-point. **[14a]** Staying among the multitude, constantly maintain utmost humility. Residing in stillness, do not give rise to defiled emotions. In mundane undertakings, utilize the appropriate effort and do not exceed the necessary degree. With regard to clothing and consumption, do not be excessive and only take what is necessary. In planning provisions for a hermitage, do not amass surpluses. In taking care of the body and life necessities, do not be covetous. If the community possesses goods in surfeit, distribute them to other adepts who are impoverished or suffering. If others are lodged in and acting through karma, perform a *zhai*-purification ritual for communal benefit. Throughout the twelve time-periods, do not evidence any falsity and constantly seek to illuminate perfection. Whether sweeping away dust [from courtyards], drawing water, carrying firewood, or cooking food, always cleanse yourself of selfish desires and do not allow anger to rise in your heart-mind.

Each of you should reside in an individual chamber where you purify the heart-mind and attend to the Dao; each of you also has a place in the hierarchy and must carry out your specific duties. In interacting with others, regulate and refine perfect innate nature. Do not become attached to being useful or argue about right and wrong. Instead, commit yourself to maintaining humility and eliminating divisions between self and other. Forget sensory phenomena, abandon appearances and erudition, and become pure and free from desires. **[14b]** When observing followers of the Three Teachings, treat everyone the same, refraining from being disrespectful or rude. Do not leave the hermitage without justification. Keep your door shut from twilight until daybreak; from daybreak to evening, open your gates. When a donation is offered, receive it in an ordinary manner; if nothing is offered, do not be resentful.

Generally speaking, considering itinerant monks who spend three days [in a monastery], the most eminent are invited to take a place among the community. Those who lack determination are made to stay in other locations and then continue traveling. [In either case,] one verifies their ordination certificates[95] and examines their provenance in detail. If some things are not clear, and if you are afraid that there is something clandestine happening, the person who has counterfeit [documents] must not be allowed to secure any advantage. Ignorant Daoists and deceptive individuals are expelled

---

93. A reference to Qiu Chuji (Changchun [Perpetual Spring]; 1148–1227), the youngest of the first-generation adherents and the third patriarch of Quanzhen.

94. "Realizing innate nature" translates *jianxing* (Jpn.: *kenshō*). This is most often equivalent to an enlightenment experience. Cf. *satori*.

95. "Ordination certificate" translates *jiaose* (lit., "foot color"), which may also refer to one's rank or profession. For some information on early Quanzhen monastic ordination see Goossaert 1997, 129–33; also 136–47, 162–68. A translation of a Longmen ordination certificate, which was collected by Heinrich Hackmann at Laoshan (Mount Lao; near Qingdao, Shandong) in 1911, appears in Kohn 2004b, 87. Cf. Goossaert 2007, 55–57, 102–4. In a modern Quanzhen monastic context, *jiedie* ("precept document") indicates Longmen ordination, while *zhengming shu* ("certification document") is an official document, usually provided by the local Daoist association through the authority of the Bureau of Religious Affairs. On the sociopolitical and economic side, one must be aware of the increasing and troubling practice of selling ordination certificates to foreigners by some mainland Chinese monastics. This is most common among non-temple-based Daoists in Beijing, Hubei, and Sichuan as well as in the Wudang shan and Longhu shan environs.

from the hermitage for even the slightest suspicious remark or even the slightest dishonesty among the disciples. Those who pass their time in idle talk or slander must be reprimanded and expelled.

If there is someone who wants to join the hermitage and become a monk, you must not act irresponsibly when allowing him to join. Instead, you must first observe his penchant for the Dao and then perceive [the extent to which] he has awakened to the Dao. Next, [take note of] the morality of his family and **[15a]** finally the depth of his own virtue and behavior. Eminent adepts are accommodating, while ignorant adepts are dismissive. When attending to affairs within the hermitage, you should first consult the superintendent,[96] and then discuss things with the Daoist community gathered in the monastic hall. When choosing a superintendent among the monks, do not concern yourself with his length of service in the tradition or with his age, but rather give attention to the clarity of his heart-mind and his understanding of universal principle. Generally speaking, when converting to the Dao, you must not usurp the reputation of the master's lineage; you also must not be selfish in directing support for the hermitage. You deceive the community if you take the donations of benefactors and use them for selfish gain. Highest heaven keeps watch; it certainly does not punish lightly! It is for this reason that I have transmitted this list, which each person should become familiar with.

Letter from the Enlightened Master to His Family[97]

It is difficult to obtain a human body, difficult to be born in the central kingdom [China], and difficult to encounter the correct teachings [Daoism]. Completing these three conditions **[15b]** is the greatest of chances. How much more is this true for the numerous immortals, leaving the world at this moment, who prepare the ladder for ascending to heaven and the raft for saving people from suffering? When the mysterious pivot unfolds in silent disclosure, there is no choice but to respond. I completely understand the insubstantiality of time and suddenly realize the impermanence of the world. Every one of my thoughts pays homage to the mysterious currents of the ancient sages, and I endeavor during each moment to emulate the accomplished individuals who have returned to simplicity. I abandon the fiery pit[98] and enter the realm of clarity and purity; I reject mundane undertakings and forever abide in the place of unfettered independence.

Do not wait until you are old, because no one knows when death will arrive. As soon as I realized this, I became resolute in cutting through obstruction and rigidity and would not allow the teachings to become defiled or polluted. I corrected what was false with the truth and split them in half with a single knife strike. If you do not sever your ties to craving and anger, how can the field of the heart-mind become clear and still? You must separate yourself from passion and desire, and then your facility with the sacred teachings will become complete. If you do not realize the perfect heart-mind, in the end you will return to an illusory dream. Pull yourself out of the net of the passions and abandon the cage of the mundane. Then you may reach the immortal district of the Purple Palace, forever casting off the deviant conditioning of the red dust.

---

96. "Superintendent" translates *zhu'an*, literally, "hermitage director."

97. I take this section to be a "form letter" that may be adapted to the needs of a given adept. It appears to represent the final letter from an ordinand to his or her family upon entry into the monastic order.

98. *Saṃsāra*, or the mundane world of suffering.

My pilgrimage staff has floated carelessly in three thousand clouds and waters; **[16a]** my patchwork robe has visited the twelve grotto-heavens.[99] Within the gates of clarity and stillness, on the path of nonaction, the taste of the sacred teachings nourishes my body and I penetrate the depth of true joy. Immersed in quiet meditation in a thatched hall, I drink the pure wind and open the door of the Mysterious and Wondrous. Enclosed in secluded living in an earthen cabin, I appreciate the luminous moon and take hold of the marrow of yin and yang.

My wife, concubine, children, and grandchildren are like birds perched together for the night; gold, silver, pearls, and jade are like floating clouds passing before my eyes. This is because I have joyfully abandoned familial bonds in order to find the cavern prefectures [of the immortals]; the conjugal attachments have been broken forever, as spilt water cannot be gathered. Father, mother, wife, and sons follow their own paths. Henceforth, I regard you as strangers, and I become a guest in foreign lands. For those who have become monks and are free from insolence and indolence, as well as for those who still participate in family life but have the intention of escaping from their position, these are my vows. I respectfully submit this letter and humbly offer my deep-felt concern.

Practical Methods for the Sinking Bowl-clepsydra from Complete Perfection[100]

Anonymous

In antiquity, people noted how sunlight was displayed in caves and how shadows fell on walls. In this way, they calculated a year from winter solstice of one year to winter solstice of the following year.[101] What we call the correct reckoning of a solar revolution consists of one day and one night. This is generally approximated as one hundred quarter-hours. Each of the eight quarter-hours[102] has twenty divisions; this equals one double-hour. Only the hours of *yin* [3 a.m.–5 a.m.], *shen* [3 p.m.–5 p.m.], *si* [9 a.m.–11 a.m.], and *hai* [9 p.m.–11 p.m.] have nine quarter-hours. All of these, in sequential relationship to *zi* [11 p.m.–1 a.m.] and *wu* [11 a.m.–1 p.m.], fix day and night.[103]

Today, this is established through water leaking from a pot,[104] which is a different constant that does not conform to the ancient methods. One must regard this as a pivotal development. In the

---

99. The standardized list of the major grotto-heavens (*dongtian*) includes ten rather than twelve locations. They are Wangwu shan (Henan), Weiyu shan (Zhejiang), Xicheng shan (Shanxi), Qingcheng shan (Sichuan), Xixuan shan (Huashan; Shaanxi), Luofu shan (Guangdong), Chicheng shan (Zhejiang), Linwu shan (Jiangsu), Gouqu shan (Maoshan; Jiangsu), and Kuocang shan (Zhejiang) (Hahn 2000, 696).

100. *Quanzhen zuobo jiefa*, DZ 1229.

101. From a traditional Chinese and Daoist perspective, winter solstice is the apex of yin and contains the seed of yang. It is the moment when yang/sunlight begins its ascendancy, eventually culminating at summer solstice. In terms of an energetic worldview focusing on time measurement, it makes sense to begin with the winter solstice.

102. There are eight quarter-hours (*ke*) because each "hour" (*shi*) is a double-hour, consisting to two conventional Western hours.

103. *Zi* and *wu* correspond to winter solstice and summer solstice, respectively. That is, the Eight Nodes (beginning of the seasons, equinoxes, and solstices) of the annual solar and agricultural cycle also occur every day.

104. This is the sitting bowl-clepsydra (*zuobo*). Note that the character for "bowl" may appear with the "metal" radical or the "pottery" radical.

mechanical technique of every four drum-soundings[105] equaling one hour, one can see the ingenuity. When systems lack regulation, it only makes sense that hours and quarter-hours are imprecise and inaccurate. Then mistakes are made, and oversights have no end.

Today, we have embraced and developed the method of sequential water flow, through which water amasses for one year and then reaches completion. [This method] neither exhausts people's strength nor wastes their time and material prosperity. It is a wondrous application, mysterious and subtle, superior in its simplicity and ingenuity. Even if [water] goes out of the containers in excess of ten thousand miles, **[1b]** all of them can catch the movement through the corners of a large elongated table.

What we refer to as astronomical instruments for tracking celestial movements are all based on the sun. Moreover, if you carefully observe the superior person tending to such affairs, you notice that sometimes he utilizes a signal watch,[106] while at other times he utilizes a smoke seal.[107] Of course, if the incense is dry, then it is easy to burn; but if the incense is moist, its ember will be slowed. Similarly, if the skies are clear, then the solar watch can be accurate; but if it is cloudy and dark, it also cannot be checked. These three instruments are not methods with an ancient pedigree. If one instead follows the advancement [described here], things will be much less complicated. The essence of the instrument will pervade the Mysterious Tenuity. This is the wondrous within the Wondrous.[108]

Method of Making the Containers

For this method you need two copper[109] containers, a large one and a small one. The large one is for storing water. As long as its size is larger than the small one, that is sufficient. If it is not, use a porcelain container as a substitute for it. The small one must weigh five *liang*[110] and must be three *cun* and four *fen* in height.[111] The bottom surface should be four *cun* and seven *fen* in width. The top and bottom should [thus] be four [*cun*] when measured perpendicularly.

---

105. Reading *gu* ("drum") for *gu* ("blind"). Conventionally speaking, as a time measurement, "drum-soundings" or "watches" (*geng*) correspond to the double-hours. In the present context, the author suggests that there are four drum-soundings in each double-hour, which would mean that a drum-sounding occurs every two quarter-hours. In Western terms, this would equal a "half-hour."

106. The exact instrument indicated by "signal watch" (*biaobiao*), also appearing as "solar watch" (*ribiao*), is unclear. It would appear to have been something like a personal sundial, as the text indicates that it depends on clear skies and sunlight.

107. The specific instrument indicated by "smoke seal" (*yanzhuan*) is also unclear. The context suggests that it was an incense clock, through which time was measured by the burning of incense.

108. An allusion to chapter 1 of the *Daode jing*: "Mysterious and again more mysterious, the gateway to the Wondrous."

109. *Tong* may refer to copper or bronze. Copper is a pure metal, while bronze is a metal alloy consisting of copper and one or more other metals (e.g., silicon, lead, aluminum, zinc), usually with tin as the main additive. As bronze is more resistant to corrosion, it may have been the preferred metal. However, assuming that *tong* refers to copper, as my translation indicates, its use as material for the bowls probably developed for three principal reasons: first, it was readily available; second, it is easily worked and formed into the desired shaped, as copper is fairly ductile and malleable; and finally, it has a relatively high degree of resistance to corrosion, as the oxidized layer that occurs through the interaction of water and air stops further, bulk corrosion in copper. In either case, the specific metallurgical qualities of the container materials would be especially significant here, as they would alter the actual function of the vessel.

110. One *liang* roughly equals 1.7 ounces or 50 grams. The equivalences often change with the specific dynasty.

111. One *cun* roughly equals 1.3 inches or 3.3 centimeters. One *cun* contains ten *fen*.

When making these, do not be afraid about the measurements having slight discrepancies. [2a] You should take fifty Taiping (Great Peace) coins and use them as the weight measurement.[112]

After you have completed making these, drill one small hole in the base of the [small] container. It should be about the size of a needle eyelet. [When you place the small container so that] it floats on the surface of the [large] container, this causes the water to revert. The water from outside the hole moves backward and begins to move upward. Water enters into the small container. Use a tally to measure this. When the water reaches the double-hour of *zi* (11 p.m.–1 a.m.),[113] it shows *zi*. When it reaches the double-hour of *wu* (11 a.m.–1 p.m.), it shows *wu*. When it reaches a watch,[114] it shows one watch. All the other time periods may be calculated like this.

Method of Water-flow

Each day when the morning light begins to emerge, take the small container and place it on the surface of the water in the large container. When the sun begins to set, the small container fills with water. The small container sinks to the bottom of the water [in the large container], and this becomes a time measurement.

Then, retrieve the small container, dump the water out, and place it again on the surface of the water. It will become completely filled at dawn [of the following day], sinking to the bottom of the water as before. Dusk and dawn, then, are the two time periods.[115] We take the water's filling as a time interval, and this establishes day and night.

If there comes a time when the water stops flowing, you must clean and purify [the water and container] so that they are spotless. [2b] Do not allow dirt and sediment to clog the water hole. This will ensure that there is no obstruction.

Method of Making the Tally

You may use a tablet as well as a wooden or bamboo strip. Anything will work for making the tally, a divination lot or comb for example. Accordingly, it should have a certain length and height so that you can write the double-hours and quarter-hours on it. Use [the tally] to investigate the water, so that you may establish and verify the double-hours, branches, watches, and smaller divisions. A slip of bamboo is quite practical.

---

112. The specific Yuan-dynasty coin, including its important weight, is unidentified. The coin itself would have been the standard round coin with a square hole in the center. See Hartill 2005.

113. The first double-hour of the terrestrial branches, with the latter including the following: (1) *zi* (11 p.m.–1 a.m.); (2) *chou* (1 a.m.–3 a.m.); (3) *yin* (3 a.m.–5 a.m.); (4) *mao* (5 a.m.–7 a.m.); (5) *chen* (7 a.m.–9 a.m.); (6) *si* (9 a.m.–11 a.m.); (7) *wu* (11 a.m.–1 p.m.); (8) *wei* (1 p.m.–3 p.m.); (9) *shen* (3 p.m.–5 p.m.); (10) *you* (5 p.m.–7 p.m.); (11) *xu* (7 p.m.–9 p.m.); and (12) *hai* (9 p.m.–11 p.m.).

114. The watches usually refer to the five night-watches (*wugeng*), the periods of darkness. They include (1) *xu* (7 p.m.–9 p.m.), (2) *hai* (9 p.m.–11 p.m.), (3) *zi* (11 p.m.–1 a.m.), (4) *chou* (1 a.m.–3 a.m.), and (5) *yin* (3 a.m.–5 a.m.). In certain contexts, "watch" (*geng*) refers to periods of darkness, while "double-hour" (*shi*) refers to daylight hours.

115. This suggests that the clepsydra consists of two primary time divisions: from *mao* (5 a.m.–7 a.m.) to *you* (5 p.m.–7 p.m.), and from *you* to *mao*.

Generally speaking, the tally has thirty-four divisions. All of these are arranged along twelve sections, and each of these sections has two divisions and five smaller increments. As mentioned previously, only the double-hours of *yin*, *shen*, *si*, and *hai* have four additional divisions.[116] We refer to this as binding and determining the calculations through addition. To compensate for excessive time lengths and for specific years involves calculations based on reduction.

Today everyone makes the practical choice of using the same method, using the floating fish to indicate the relevant point.

Now, one year consists of twelve months. Just use twenty Taiping coins based on the moon cycles, adding and subtracting them accordingly. This allows one to keep [the water volume of] the small container in order.

Method for Adding and Subtracting

[3a] In the eleventh lunar month, use twenty Taiping coins in the morning, placing them in the base of the small container. In the evening, use an empty container. In the twelfth lunar month, use nineteen Taiping coins in the morning and one coin in the evening. From the beginning of the twelfth lunar month, once every seven days subtract one coin in the morning and add one coin in the evening. In the first lunar month, use eleven coins in the morning and nine in the evening. In the second lunar month, use ten coins in the morning and ten in the evening. In the third lunar month, use nine coins in the morning and eleven in the evening. From the beginning of this month, once every seven days subtract one coin in the morning and add one in the evening. In the fourth lunar month, use one coin in the morning and nineteen in the evening. In the fifth lunar month, use an empty container in the morning and twenty coins in the evening. In the sixth lunar month, use one coin in the morning and nineteen in the evening. From the beginning of this month, once every seven days add one coin in the morning and subtract one in the evening. [3b] In the seventh lunar month, use nine coins in the morning and eleven in the evening. In the eighth lunar month, use ten coins during both intervals. In the ninth lunar month, use eleven coins in the morning and nine in the evening. From the beginning of this month, once every seven days add one coin in the morning and subtract one in the evening. In the tenth lunar month, use eleven coins in the morning and nine in the evening.

Method for Establishing the Rising and Setting of the Sun

In the first and ninth month, the sun rises at *yi*[117] and sets at *geng*.[118] In the second and eighth month, it rises at Rabbit[119] and sets at Rooster.[120] In the third and seventh month, it rises at *jia*[121]

---

116. That is, one additional quarter-hour for each of these double-hours.

117. *Yi* is the second of the ten celestial stems and corresponds to the Wood phase, east, and Jupiter.

118. *Geng* is the seventh of the ten celestial stems and corresponds to the Metal phase, west, and Venus.

119. The Rabbit (*tu*) zodiac sign (Cancer), which corresponds to *mao*, the fourth of the twelve terrestrial branches. Rabbit is associated with the eastern direction.

120. The Rooster (*ji*) zodiac sign (Capricorn), which corresponds to *you*, the tenth of the twelve terrestrial branches. Rooster is associated with the western direction.

121. *Jia* is the first of the ten celestial stems and corresponds to the Wood phase, east, and Jupiter.

and sets at *xin*.[122] In the fourth and sixth month, it rises at *yin*[123] and sets at Dog.[124] In the fifth month, it rises at Gen-mountain[125] and sets at Qian-heaven.[126] In the second month of winter, it rises at Xun-wind[127] and sets at Kun-earth.[128] Although these are only ten of the twelve months, its rising at *chen*[129] and setting at *shen*[130] must be carefully investigated.

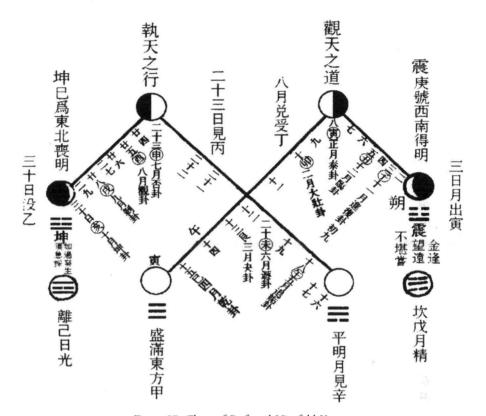

Figure 37. Chart of Perfected Ninefold Yang

122. *Xin* is the eighth of the ten celestial stems and corresponds to the Metal phase, west, and Venus.

123. *Yin* is the third of the twelve terrestrial branches and corresponds to the zodiac sign of Tiger (*hu*; Gemini). It is associated with east-northeast.

124. The Dog (*quan*) zodiac sign (Aquarius), which corresponds to *xu*, the eleventh of the twelve terrestrial branches. Dog is associated with west-northwest.

125. The Gen-mountain trigram, which corresponds to northeast.

126. The Qian-heaven trigram, which corresponds to northwest.

127. The Xun-wind trigram, which corresponds to southeast.

128. The Kun-earth trigram, which corresponds to southwest.

129. *Chen* is the fifth of the twelve terrestrial branches and corresponds to the zodiac sign of Dragon (*long*; Leo). It is associated with east-southeast.

130. *Shen* is the ninth of the twelve terrestrial branches and corresponds to the zodiac sign of Monkey (*hou*; Sagittarius). It is associated with west-southwest.

Precepts of Initial Perfection[131]

Wang Changyue, Master Kunyang

Preface

Concerning the numinous literature of dark obscurity, the great Dao and august emptiness, as well as the jade statutes of the pure metropolis, great Perfection and lofty sacredness, the myriad sages consider them precious and deserving of veneration. The myriad numens receive them with deep devotion. If you do not have gold bones and a jade name, you should not carelessly examine or receive them. The precepts express what is restricted and prohibited. They increase goodness and inhibit deviance. They restore perfection and dispel recklessness. This is what "precept" means.

In the past, Lord of the Dao of August Emptiness[132] considered the various sentient beings of the vast earth with sympathy. They were only concerned with personal profit and with pursuing fame and reputation. Consumed by greed, they wanted to take control of sounds and colors. They did not know the causes of calamity and good fortune. Because he himself had handed down punishments to many beings, he was moved by compassion to assist and rescue those drowning [in the ocean of *saṃsāra*]. He thus transmitted and disseminated the precepts, statutes, scriptures, and teachings. He began converting humans and the various heavens of the phenomenal worlds so that they would become beacons of wisdom for planting good fortune and cultivating beneficial karmic causes. He did this so that they would become vessels of compassion for ascending to Perfection and entering the Dao.

Generation after generation received them, and master after master transmitted them. Among the classified items of the *Daozang* (Daoist Canon), there are still some records. However, when the major disruption of the Qin [Shaanxi] fires occurred, eight or nine out of every ten Daoist scriptures containing precepts and statutes were destroyed. Thus, of the rules for maintaining order among the ranks of disciples, only one or two have been preserved. Consequently, before the present generation, the precepts and sacred teachings were practiced daily to the utmost. However, in our own day, those who have attained this transmission are only one or two in one hundred million people. Notwithstanding the myriad generations who did not reproduce them, the mysterious statutes still have not yet been lost. Today I have responded by collecting these elegant explanations of the various virtues. This is done so that the transformational benefit of the Mysterious Origin and the extensive clarity and stillness of the ancestors may become known. The moment when the Wondrous arrives resides in this single offering. It is my sincere hope that it will come to inhabit our own time. May it accordingly be announced that my reason for following this course is veneration and benefit.

In the first year of the [Chongzhen] era [1628],[133] I followed the cloud traces to Chu [Hubei] in order visit the community of Perfected Zhao Fuyang of Jiugong shan (Nine Palaces

---

131. *Chuzhen jie*, JY 292, ZW 404. I have based my translation primarily on a Qingyang gong manuscript that I acquired in 2003. This text derives from the Erxian an (Hermitage of the Two Immortals) edition of the *Daozang jiyao* (see n. 14). Section numbers refer to the *Zangwai daoshu* (ZW) edition, which does not contain Wang Changyue's preface. As mentioned, all catalogue numbers follow Komjathy 2002. I dedicate this translation to the memory of the late Monica Esposito (1962–2011; Kyoto University).

132. Xuhuang daojun.

133. The reign of the Chongzhen Emperor (1611–1644; r. 1627–1644), who was the last Ming emperor.

Mountain).[134] There I received the precepts and sacred teachings[135] and obtained guidance concerning what is essential.

Thus, I have not evaded the transgression against brazen and reckless [dissemination]. Today, I set forth the sacred teachings on this, the fifteenth day [full moon] of the third month of the *bingshen* year [1656].

At Baiyun guan (White Cloud Monastery), I have established the Ordination Platform[136] in order to transmit the precepts, bestow the bowl, and offer up prayers. Now, in hopes of expanding the glory and prosperity of the sages, masters, thearchs, and Dao, I offer my prayers for the emperor, officials, magistrates, and all people to have personal and familial blessings. May this continue my original vow to the former ancestors and highest sages to liberate the world. May this assist later adepts to advance and initiate the Dao's circulation as the currents of Perfection, free from disorder.

If you are among those who receive the precepts, you will definitely be able to discipline and encourage yourself. Your heart-mind will behold self and world as alterations of floating clouds. For this, it is essential to be diligent in your practice of the precepts. Take the precepts and statutes as the cultivation of what is urgent and fundamental. Resolve the great matter of life and death, and complete the perfect constancy of innate nature and life-destiny.

Supposing that you have the personal hardships of hunger, cold, wind, or heat, do not be lenient in your exercise of the precepts. Supposing that you have the fluctuations of life and death or disgrace and humiliation, do not fail to take hold of them with determination. In truth, the true ancestors increase merit and manifest power. Because of this, karmic bonds become like thawing ice. Because of this, accomplishment and merit increase daily.

If you yourself practice the precepts, you will become refined naturally and connect with the center of transformation. If you grasp even half a sentence of the statutes, you can appear and disappear inside of yin and yang, and the Celestial Hall and Earth Prisons will both become finished. Within the lineage of precept disciples, the sun, moon, stars, and constellations are all one's own heart-mind. In a life calibrated through its center, you may ride the luminosities and traverse the Void. There is no need to become esteemed. If the teachings spread, heaven prevails, ancestors are remembered, and the earth lasts. Then the silent darkness will support the imperial laws. Subsequently, one may return the merit for the benefit of all beings.

Written by Wang Changyue, Master Kunyang, the Daoist priest transmitting the precepts, high religious leader of Xijin [Shanxi], in the bingshen year, the thirteenth year of the Shunzhi reign period [1656].[137]

---

134. Zhao Fuyang (fl. 1600–1640) was the master-father (*shifu*) of Wang Changyue. Zhao Fuyang was the sixth Longmen Patriarch and heir of the Longmen Discipline (Vinaya) Masters (*lüshi*) line. According to Wang's autobiographical account here, Zhao ordained Wang and bestowed the lineage name (*paiming*) of Changyue (Constant Moon) on Mount Jiugong (near Wuhan, Hubei). Cf. Esposito 2001, 193.

135. "Precepts and sacred teachings" translates *jiefa*. This phrase could also be rendered as "method of the precepts."

136. In the contemporary monastic compound of Baiyun guan, the Ordination Platform (*jietan*), also translatable as "precept altar," is located in the back courtyard. See introduction herein. It is used for large-scale, public Longmen ordination and precept transmission.

137. The reign period of the Shunzhi Emperor (1638–1661; r. 1644–1661) of the Qing dynasty. This preface is followed by a variety of other prefaces, which due to length restrictions have been excluded from the present translation. The manuscript versions of the *Chuzhen jie* also include a Longmen ordination certificate. See Hackmann 1920, 146–47; 1931, 67; Kohn 2004b, 87.

Precepts of Initial Perfection

[8a] When first entering the gate of the sacred teachings of the orthodox lineage of the Highest [Lord Lao], regardless of whether you come from Daoist or ordinary background, you must honor and follow the highest gold rules and jade statutes as well as the various precept texts of the Three Caverns.[138] You must also present offerings to the statues of the worthies of the great Dao and send a formal petition to the various celestial lords requesting to become a member of the community. Then you must take the precepts of the Three Refuges:[139]

> First: I take refuge with my body in the highest great Dao of Nondifferentiation. (Note: Through this you may be forever liberated from the cycle of transmigration. Thus we refer to this as the Treasure of the Dao.)

> Second: I take refuge with my spirit in the venerable scriptures in thirty-six sections. (Note: Through this you are able to hear the orthodox sacred teachings. Thus we refer to this as the Treasure of the Scriptures.)

> [8b] Third: I take refuge with my life-destiny in the great masters of the sacred teachings residing among the Mysterious. (Note: Through this you will never fall into deviant views. We refer to this the Treasure of the Masters.)

The Celestial Worthy said: The precepts of the Three Refuges are the pivot of heaven and earth and form the root of spirit immortality. By developing and practicing them after your ordination, you establish the original condition of the heart-mind. As you circulate qi and contain the numinous, you join with Perfection and enter Principle. As you embrace the network and become part of the cosmic patterns, your form becomes boundless. Anyone observing the Three Refuges will be blessed with and enjoy the spirit illumination of heaven and earth. Your heart-mind will become full of wisdom, and your ears and eyes will become open and clear. The myriad beings will be reverent and respectful. Your six yang-organs[140] will be mutually resplendent. The host of Perfected will guard and protect you; the multitude of living beings will be like your parents. Throughout the many generations, you will be free from decline and always born in prosperous situations.

---

138. The Three Caverns (*sandong*) are the three primary divisions of the Daoist Canon, namely, Cavern Perfection (*dongzhen*), originally corresponding to the Shangqing (Highest Clarity) tradition; Cavern Mystery (*dongxuan*), originally corresponding to the Lingbao (Numinous Treasure) tradition; and (3) Cavern Spirit (*dongshen*), originally corresponding to the Sanhuang (Three Sovereigns) tradition. See Komjathy 2002.

139. The Three Refuges (*san guiyi*) or the external Three Treasures of the Dao, scriptures, and teachers.

140. The six yang-organs include gall bladder (Wood), small intestine (Fire), stomach (Earth), large intestine (Metal), urinary bladder (Water), and Triple Warmer. Paired with the Pericardium, and also referred to as the Triple Burner or Three Burners, on the most basic level the Triple Warmer (*sanjiao*) is not an "organ" per se, but rather represents three subtle regions of the body and related functions. In classical Chinese medicine, the Triple Warmer is three things simultaneously: one of the six yang-organs, a thoroughfare for original qi (*yuanqi*), and three divisions of the body. For its importance in Quanzhen Daoism and *neidan* training see Komjathy 2007a.

After taking the Three Refuges, you must receive the Five Precepts as revealed by the Great High Lord Lao.[141] These enable you to accumulate merit and return to the Source.[142]

1. Do not kill any living being.

2. Do not consume impure food or intoxicants.

3. Do not say "yes" and think "no."[143]

4. Do not steal.

5. Do not engage in perversion and depravity.[144]

Whoever observes the Five Precepts, making strong effort without lapses, will increase his reckoning and extend his lifespan. The celestial spirits will protect and assist you. You will be forever liberated from the sufferings of the five punishments, and generation after generation you will never forego human birth.

[9a] Once you have received the Five Precepts revealed by Lord Lao, which enable you to accumulate merit and return to the Source, each morning and evening offer incense and recite the highest perfect scriptures of the great thearchs of the Three Primes, Three Ranks, and Three Bureaus.[145] These protect the community, assist the people, extend life, and protect life-destiny. You should also begin to memorize the *Taishang ganying pian* (Great High Lord Lao's Treatise on Action and Response).[146] As you recite this text each day, examine and rectify your own body and heart-mind. Note whether or not you have committed any transgressions. With every sentence of your recitation of the scriptures and the *Ganying pian*, reflect and think to yourself: Can I properly receive this or not? Can I practice this or not? If you do this, you will be brave and committed in your efforts, and your words and practice will not deviate from each other.

If you do not violate the Three Refuges and are free from transgressions in your observance of the Five Precepts, then all deviant thoughts will dissipate completely after one hundred days of discipline and refinement. Your organs and vessels will be purified.

---

141. Although the so-called Five Precepts (*wujie*) originate in Buddhism, they were eventually adopted and transformed by Daoists, specifically by adding Five Phase (*wuxing*) correspondences. See, for example, the sixth-century *Taishang laojun jiejing*, DZ 784, 6a–15a; trl. Kohn 2004b, 147–50.

142. An allusion to chapter 16 of the *Daode jing*: "Returning to the Source is called stillness; this means returning to life-destiny. Returning to life-destiny is called constancy; knowing constancy is called illumination."

143. More literally, "do not have 'yes' in your mouth and 'no' in your heart-mind." More liberally translated, "do not lie."

144. These precepts and ethical commitments appear in more conventional lists as follows: Do not kill; do not take intoxicants; do not lie; do not steal; and do not engage in sexual misconduct. The latter has two senses. For laypeople, it usually refers to not engaging in adultery; for monastics, it includes actual celibacy as well as purity of mind regarding sensual desires. The precepts could be reformulated prescriptively, rather than proscriptively, as follows: Respect and support life; maintain purity of consciousness; maintain purity of speech; only take what is given; and maintain energetic integrity. Taken as a whole, they refer to thought, speech, and action. It should also be mentioned that purity of speech includes not engaging in gossip, backbiting, and the like.

145. The Three Primes (*sanyuan*) refer to the Three Purities (*sanqing*) and Three Heavens (*santian*). The Three Bureaus (*sanguan*) refer to the officials related to heaven, earth, and water, with water sometimes replaced by humanity.

146. The twelfth-century *Taishang ganying pian* (DZ 1167; abbr. *Ganying pian*), a popular morality book (*shanshu*) primarily composed by Li Changling (937–1008). For translations see Suzuki and Carus 1973 (1906); Wong 1994.

After this, you may receive the Ten Precepts of Initial Perfection as revealed by the Celestial Worthy of August Emptiness:[147]

1. Do not be disloyal, unfilial, inhumane, or dishonest. Always exhaust your allegiance to your lord and family and be sincere when relating to the myriad beings.

2. Do not secretly steal things, harbor hidden plots, or harm other beings in order to profit yourself. Always practice hidden virtue and widely aid the host of living beings.

3. Do not kill or harm anything that lives in order to satisfy your own appetites. Always act with compassion and kindness to all, even insects and worms. **[9b]**

4. Do not be debased or deviant, squander your perfection, or defile your numinous qi. Always guard perfection and integrity, and remain without deficiencies or transgressions.

5. Do not ruin others to create gain for yourself or leave your own flesh and bones. Always use the Dao to help other beings and make sure that the nine clan members all live in harmony.

6. Do not slander or defame the worthy and good or exhibit your talents and elevate yourself. Always praise the beauty and goodness of others and never be contentious about your own accomplishments and abilities.

7. Do not drink alcohol or eat meat in violation of the prohibitions. Always harmonize qi and innate nature, remaining attentive to clarity and emptiness.

8. Do not be greedy and acquisitive without ever being satisfied or accumulate wealth without giving some away. Always practice moderation in all things and show kindness and sympathy to the poor and destitute.

9. Do not have any relations or exchange with the unworthy or live among the confused and defiled. Always strive to control yourself, becoming perched and composed in clarity and emptiness.

10. Do not speak or laugh lightly or carelessly, increasing agitation and denigrating perfection. Always maintain seriousness and speak humble words, so that the Dao and inner power remain your primary concern.

Your reception of the Ten Precepts of Initial Perfection is already the first fruit of your work toward becoming a Perfected. If you then continue to make strong effort with courage and enthusiasm,

---

147. These ten precepts first occur in the early medieval *Chuzhen shijie wen* (DZ 180), also known as the *Xuhuang tianzun chuzhen shijie wen*. This earlier text dates from the late seventh century and is first mentioned in Zhang Wanfu's *Sandong zhongjie wen* (DZ 178). Its precepts are designated for those who have just made the decision to leave the family and pursue the Dao and contain both a prohibitive and prescriptive part. Before their inclusion into the Quanzhen rules, they are also found in *Yunji qiqian* 40.7a–8a. See Goossaert 1997, 509–18; Kohn 2004b, 253.

and observe and maintain the precepts in word and action without even the slightest transgression, you will soon be permitted to receive **[10a]** the Three Hundred Precepts of Medium Ultimate as revealed by the Great High Lord Lao.[148]

However, if you merely recite the rules with your mouth and go against them in your heart, or if you start out with diligence but become lazy and abandon them halfway, then we call this "knowing but still transgressing." This offense is mortally serious and can never be expiated; it will cause you to fall into perdition forever. Without aspirations for the Celestial Statutes of Nüqing,[149] even if the Great High [Lord Lao] were to emerge again, there would be no way to rescue you. Students of the Dao and adepts of immortality: consider this and take care!

General Outline of the Practice and Observance of Precepts

Whether you are a monastic or layperson, when you join the community of the four ranks[150] you will receive the precepts and sacred teachings. After this, you should stabilize your aspirations and focus your spirit, giving rise to strong determination and solidity. Like Mount Kunlun, this must be as though it cannot be moved or shaken; like a diamond, this must be as though it cannot be ground down or destroyed. Completely concentrate and unify the heart-mind and do not give rise to the various thoughts. If you practice every night, spirit illumination will arise and merge with your body. If you abstain from sensual pleasures every day, the ghostly qi[151] will not be able to enter your orifices.

When you do one beneficial act,[152] the heart-mind will be concentrated and spirit will be calm.[153] When you do ten beneficial acts, vital essence and spirit will be healthy and vigorous. When you do twenty beneficial acts, you will no longer experience sickness or disease. When you do thirty beneficial acts, all of your wishes will come true with ease. When you do forty beneficial acts, your disciples and family will blossom and flourish. When you do fifty beneficial acts, your sons and grandsons will grow numerous and prosperous. **[10b]** When you do sixty beneficial acts, you will be able to change difficulties into benefits. When you do seventy beneficial acts, spirit illumination will be supported and protected. When you do eighty beneficial acts, the earth will benefit and the people will be harmonious. When you do ninety beneficial acts, you will excel and triumph among

148. The *Zhongji jie* (JY 293; ZW 405), which is also attributed to Wang Changyue and corresponds to the second level of Longmen ordination. A translation of the Three Hundred Precepts of Medium Ultimate is contained in the electronic supplement to Livia Kohn's *Cosmos and Community* (2004b).

149. Most likely a reference to the fourth-century *Nüqing guilü* (DZ 790), here apparently referring to precept texts more generally. Sections of this text have been translated in the electronic supplement to Kohn's *Cosmos and Community* (2004b).

150. The four ranks usually refer to monks, nuns, laymen, and laywomen.

151. "Ghostly qi" translates *guiqi* and suggests harmful energetic influences related to external phenomena that generate sensual desire and emotional reactivity.

152. That is, engage in meritorious activities and good deeds that neutralize negative karma and produce positive karma.

153. This list is similar to the one contained in the fourth-century *Chisongzi zhongjie jing* (DZ 185, 4a–5b) and repeated in Du Guangting's *Yongcheng jixian lu* (DZ 783, 1.4a–5a). A translation of the former appears in Kohn 2004b, 154–67, while a partial translation and study of the latter has been published by Suzanne Cahill (2006).

others. When you do one hundred beneficial acts, the three qi will be harmonious in your body. When you do two hundred beneficial acts, your virtue will spread throughout the world. When you do three hundred beneficial acts, you will be reborn as a person of great wealth. When you do four hundred beneficial acts, you will be reborn as a person of high nobility. When you do five hundred beneficial acts, you will be reborn as a person of extended longevity. When you do six hundred beneficial acts, you will be reborn as a person of good fortune. When you do seven hundred beneficial acts, you will be reborn as a person of great loyalty. When you do eight hundred beneficial acts, you will be reborn as a person of great filial piety. When you do nine hundred beneficial acts, you will be reborn as a person of great wisdom. When you do one thousand beneficial acts, you will be reborn as a sage king or spirit immortal.

On the other hand, if you give in to emotions and follow sensual desires, [there will be difficulties]. When you commit one deviant act, your ethereal soul and dreams will not be peaceful. When you commit ten deviant acts, people will despise and reject you. When you commit twenty deviant acts, your body will suffer from many ailments and diseases. When you commit thirty deviant acts, your wishes will never be realized. When you commit forty deviant acts, you will experience bad luck, decline, and damage. When you commit fifty deviant acts, your family members will be separated and scattered. When you commit sixty deviant acts, you will encounter nothing but falsity, violation, and obstacles. When you commit seventy deviant acts, ghosts and demons will come to invade you. When you commit eighty deviant acts, water and fire will bring calamity and injury. When you commit ninety deviant acts, your future births will have a short life span. When you commit a hundred deviant acts, the celestial officers will come to capture and kill you.

Ultimately you should endeavor to maintain an unvarying heart-mind and practice the essential, secret, and wondrous methods. Never go against a single precept or transgress a single rule. Never allow yourself to become deviant in order to stay alive. Rather, hold fast to what is beneficial, even if it means dying. [11a] If you can be a precept disciple like this, you may be called a disciple of pure faith in the great Dao.[154] Then the ten thousand demons will support and guard you, and the various heavens will give you guidance and protection. In the end, the sovereign kings of the Four Heavens[155] will order the officers of the ten divisions to get into green carriages of flying clouds, float through the air, and descend to inspect and observe your wondrous practice. Even though your merit and deeds are not yet complete, the officers will still be compelled to return and enter your seed name into the numinous charts and ledgers of immortality.

Still, there may be those who are not in awe of the celestial entries and do not follow the precepts and statutes with diligence. They pretend to observe the rules and regulations, but in fact do not cultivate the parameters of perfection. They are accordingly subject to the punishments of the office of Nüqing,[156] which measures the weight of their transgressions and hands down appropriate deductions from their emoluments and life allotment. If there are too many [transgressions] to be taken care of in this way, the remainder will be visited upon their next life. From *kalpa* to *kalpa* it will continue in this way, and they will never be able to find release and liberation.

---

154. *Dadao qingxin dizi.*

155. The Four Heavens (*sitian*) are the heavens of the four primary cardinal directions.

156. Here Nüqing (Female Purity) refers to a divine being who plays a central role in the otherworldly offices that keep records on good and bad behavior. It thus roughly corresponds to an Earth Prison, or underworld.

Essential Rules for Practicing the Precepts

[12a] ITEM: A person who has received the *Tianxian jie* (Precepts of Celestial Immortality)[157] is called a Master of Wondrous Dao.[158]

A person who has received the *Zhongji jie* (Precepts of Medium Ultimate) is called a Master of Wondrous Virtue.[159]

A person who has received the *Chuzhen jie* (Precepts of Initial Perfection) is called a Master of Wondrous Practice.[160]

Those who have received the same precepts but at different times are called "same robes."[161]

Those who preside over them are called "earlier enlightened masters."[162]

At the time of the La [mid-winter] festival,[163] adepts are to observe the following practices.

Followers of the Precepts of Celestial Immortality must focus on the *Daode jing*. For one hundred days, you must practice devotions by bowing ten times to the ten directions[164] every day during the time of *yin* [3 a.m.–5 a.m.]. During the times of *zi* [11 p.m.–1 a.m.] and *wu* [11 a.m.–1 p.m.], practice quiet sitting and inner observation. Do not concern yourselves with human affairs but strive to cleanse and purify yourself of the three karmic factors.

Followers of the Precepts of Medium Ultimate must first offer obeisance at the feet of the discipline master[165] every day during the time of *si* [9 a.m.–11 a.m.]. After this, you should rise to bow in audience rites and recite the *Tianchan* (Celestial Repentance)[166] and the *Lingbao dachan* (Great Repentance of Numinous Treasure).[167] Maintain this for one hundred days. After each recitation, practice cessation and stillness.

Followers of the Precepts of Initial Perfection must first offer obeisance at the feet of the discipline master every day during the time of *si* [9 a.m.–11 a.m.]. After this, you should rise,

---

157. The *Tianxian jie* (JY 291; ZW 403), which is also attributed to Wang Changyue, corresponds to the third and highest level of Longmen ordination.

158. *Miaodao shi*. This is the third and highest Longmen ordination level, which is also referred to as Celestial Immortality (*tianxian*).

159. *Miaode shi*. This is the second and middle Longmen ordination level, which is also referred to as Medium Ultimate (*zhongji*).

160. *Miaoxing shi*. This is the first and lowest Longmen ordination level, which is also referred to as Initial Perfection (*chuzhen*).

161. *Tongyi*.

162. *Xianjue shi*.

163. The winter festival held three days after winter solstice.

164. The ten directions include the four cardinal directions, the four intermediary directions, as well as up and down.

165. "Discipline master" translates *lüshi*, or the monk responsible for adherence to the monastic rules.

166. Another name for the *Chaotian fachan* (Repentance for Attending to Heaven). See section 15b.

167. *Chan* may be translated as "repentance" or "litany," with the latter being a form of liturgical prayer involving petition. I have been unable to identify the specific texts related to this repentance/atonement practice (*chanhui*). One would assume that the corresponding texts are extant in the Baiyun guan collection, that is, the monastic archive controlled by the Chinese Daoist Association, which contains texts and material culture such as that catalogued in Stephen Little's *Taoism and the Arts of China* (2000). There are various texts in the Ming-dynasty Daoist Canon that could be abbreviated *Lingbao dachan*, with the *Taishang lingbao chaotian xiezui dacha* (DZ 189) being most likely. However, that is an enormous work, consisting of ten *juan*. In any case, the Daoist practice of *chanhui* involves atoning for past moral transgressions; rectifying physical, psychological and spiritual harm; purifying oneself of negative tendencies; and making petitions for such help and corresponding benefits. One specifically makes amends and asks for forgiveness, whether through actual activity or internal gestures.

bow, and recite the *Youzui fachan* (Repentance of the Divine Law for Pardoning Transgressions).[168] Maintain this for one hundred days. After each recitation, practice cessation and stillness.

These are the regulations to be observed at the beginning of the La festival. Anyone going against them will be punished by the agents of Nüqing.

In addition, for these one hundred days a prohibition against walking around is in effect. You cannot go outside to perform offerings, and you cannot go outside to recite scriptures. After the hundred days are over, the proscription on these activities is lifted.

Moreover, in every situation and interaction, you must be forbearing and withdrawing, benevolent and pliant. **[12b]** You should not discriminate and discuss right and wrong. Rather, whether rising or stopping, moving or resting, you should be attentive and careful. On every *wu* day,[169] you should also join with your fellow precept disciples and earlier enlightened masters. Make progress by attending to virtuous work or by discussing sacred scriptures such as the *Daode jing* (Scripture on the Dao and Inner Power), *Nanhua jing* (Scripture of Southern Florescence), *Wenshi zhenjing* (Perfect Scripture of Master Wenshi), *Tanzi* (Book of Master Tan), *Huangjing jing* (Scripture on the Yellow Court),[170] or any other Daoist text from our tradition. If you study even one scroll with full dedication, the supervising officers will increase your merit by tenfold. If you discuss even one scroll with clarity, the supervising officers will increase your merit by a hundredfold.

Generally speaking, those who have taken the precepts should focus on self-control and practice the highest wondrous and dignified observances. You must practice the highest wondrous observation and perception of the precepts. Then spirits will arrive independently to offer their support and protection, and the members of the four ranks will appear spontaneously to offer their respect. Thus, maintain an upright form and never incite distorted shadows. Then the shadows will rectify naturally. Maintain a harmonious sound and never become hindered by the rippling echoes. Then the echoes will return naturally.

ITEM: Regarding the rope-bed,[171] if you happen to be awake during the times of *zi* and *wu*, sit cross-legged[172] on the bed and practice quiet sitting. Your hands should not be straight or pointed. Your feet should not be extended or coiled up. Your mouth should not utter any sounds. Your eyes should not allow spirit to manifest. Your head should not hang forward, and your body should not be hunched over.

You must never sit or sleep on a brick-bed[173] of an ordinary household.

If people come to pay respects to you, there are three conditions under which you cannot get up:[174]

---

168. This may be the *Leiting yushu youzui fachan* (DZ 196).

169. The fifth of the ten-day week based on the ten celestial stems.

170. The *Nanhua zhenjing* is the *Zhuangzi* (Book of Master Zhuang; DZ 670); the *Wenshi zhenjing* (DZ 667) is also known as the *Guanyinzi* (Book of Master Pass-guardian Yin); the *Tanzi* is the *Huashu* (Book of Transformations; DZ 1044; cf. DZ 170); and the *Huangting jing* appears in two versions (DZ 331; DZ 332).

171. "Rope-bed" translates *shengchuang*.

172. *Panxi*. Full-lotus posture.

173. "Brick-bed" translates *chuangkang*.

174. Cf. *Quanzhen qinggui*, DZ 1235, 6b–7a, which is translated earlier in this chapter.

Do not get up if you are sitting in meditation.
Do not get up if you are reading scriptures.
Do not get up if you are eating.

Just observe them in deep concentration and receive their respects with an appropriate invocation. Wait until you have completed the activity, then get off the platform and return the greeting.

[13a] Before going to sleep, tap your teeth together and recite the following invocation: "May my spirit now perch in the darkened valley." Then interrupt thinking and forget language.

Do not be lax or reckless or go outside the community of monks. If you have to go out, travel and walk very carefully, stepping straight ahead without looking to the right or left. Do not extend your arms and legs hastily or hurriedly. Every time you go against this, the supervising officers will mark it down as one transgression.

ITEM: You should have one Cavern Robe, one Pure Robe, one Devotion Robe, as well as a Cap of the Numinous Diagram of the Five Peaks. You should also have a pure kerchief, a feathery skirt, and a pair of regulation straw sandals.[175] Since the locality, earth and various other gods as well as azure-robed divine youths watch over and protect these garments, do not lend them to others for use. Do not put them in an impure place, sell them, or mix them together with ordinary clothes. If they get old or torn, burn them on the ninth day of the ninth month[176] while facing northwest. Then take the ashes and scatter them into an eastward flowing stream, allowing them to be taken away by the currents.

If you follow these rules, your years will be extended, longevity will be increased, and your body will be completely free of demonic obstructions. If you go against them, your life will be beset by misfortune and injury, and the supervising officers will mark you up for ten transgressions.

ITEM: The bowl should have the shape of the eight trigrams.[177] Only the opening for the lid should be round. It should be kept in a special bowl bag and taken out only when it is time to eat. After finishing the [meal] invocation, [13b] gather qi and preserve spirit. Eat without opening your mouth too wide and without making any sounds. Use a spoon when appropriate. After you have finished eating, wash the bowl and return it to its bag. Every time you go against this, it will count as one transgression.[178]

ITEM: The staff[179] should be taken from a numinous mountain and made from a seven-notched bamboo that has been facing the sun. Make the upper and lower sections straight and smooth.

---

175. Cavern Robe (*dongyi*), Pure Robe (*jingyi*), Devotion Robe (*xinyi*), pure kerchief (*jingjin*), feathery skirt (*yuqun*), and straw sandals (*mangxie*) were the standard late imperial Longmen monastic attire. The three robes correspond to the highest, middle, and lowest ordination ranks, respectively. The Five Peak Cap (*wuyue guan*) was used and continues to be used in formal ritual, especially by head officiants. Descriptions and images appear in this chapter. For some preliminary insights into Daoist clothing see Wilson 1995; Kohn 2003a; 147–59; 2004a, 91–93.

176. Double-nine day (*chongyang jie*), which numerologically represents pure yang, completion, and heaven.

177. *Bo* is a begging or alms-bowl used by Buddhist itinerant and mendicant monastics. In the Longmen monastic context, the eight-trigram bowl (*bagua bo*) is a monk's personal bowl used for eating in the refectory.

178. Hackmann's (1920, 148–58) translation ends here, which is followed by a brief summary of the remaining sections.

179. *Zhang*.

Sweet bamboo is a good choice. Once cut and smoothed, inscribe it with the Seal of Primordial Beginning.[180] Whether walking, standing, sitting, or lying down, always keep it by your side. The staff is a vertical talisman of the Five Thearchs[181] that can be used for support and protection. If you encounter suffering and misfortune, use your staff to point at them. Hold onto it while chanting the Invocation of the Four Obscurities.[182]

ITEM: The discipline stick should be made from peach wood and be inscribed with talismans and seal script on all four sides.[183] Use it to eliminate inauspiciousness and when more recent disciples commit a transgression. If the violation is very serious, however, you must destroy the offender's bowl and burn his robe. For the worst transgressions, you must expel him from the order.[184] If he begs for leniency, use the discipline stick to mete out punishment in the measure of the transgression.

ITEM: Regarding the pitcher for pure water,[185] when you pour water into it, take care not to spill or lose any. Use a bag to cover it. When traveling far away, always carry it with you, so that you can wash your hands whenever it is convenient.

[14a] ITEM: The certificate pouch[186] should be sown into the seam of the precept robe. Then fill the inside of a kerchief with the precepts and statutes.

ITEM: The fragrance hanger[187] should be used to hang the three robes. First construct the basic frame from white sandalwood. Then hold it over the incense burner to give it fragrance.

ITEM: The toothbrush[188] should be made of coir palm. In addition, your comb, clothes chest, pillow, sitting mat, quilt, bed platform, and all other necessities must be kept clean and pure. Never let ordinary people use them, sit on them, or sleep on them.

All of the aforementioned items are taken and arranged on the basis of the *Daozang* (Daoist Canon). If students of later generations fail to venerate their traditional system, they risk becoming selfish and losing the wisdom [of earlier generations]. Anyone who changes or modifies these items

---

180. The corresponding image for the Seal of Primordial Beginning (*yuanshi zhang*) is unknown.

181. The Five Thearchs (*wudi*) are the divine emperors of the five directions.

182. The specific content of the Invocation of the Four Obscurities (*siming zhou*) is unknown. My Qingyang gong manuscript version identifies the invocation as the Invocation for Releasing Misfortunes (*jiehui zhou*).

183. The discipline stick (*jiechi*) corresponds to the "wake-up stick" (Jpn.: *keisaku/kyosaku*) in Zen Buddhism. The discipline stick is a thin, elongated, and flat stick used to hit inattentive monastics on the shoulders during communal meditation. In a late imperial monastic context, it seems to have become an instrument for punishment, which diverges from its original purpose. Cf. *Quanzhen qinggui*, DZ 1235, 5ab.

184. Cf. *Quanzhen qinggui*, DZ 1235, 11b–12b.

185. *Jingshui ping*.

186. *Dienang*.

187. *Xunlong*. Possibly more of a basket-like instrument.

188. *Yashua*.

is a transgressor within the order.[189] Going against the statutes will be punished; there will be no leniency.

Basic Guidance for the Three Masters

ITEM: The primary master who transmits the precepts[190] is the master of the great virtue of the highest ancestors who disseminates the teachings and initiates conversion. If one has not received the *Precepts of Celestial Immortality*, one may not transmit the precepts.

[14b] Each year, on the fifteenth day [full moon] of the first lunar month, the fifteenth day of the seventh lunar month, and the fifteenth day of the tenth lunar month, the master assembles the four ranks of the community. He opens the altar and transmits the precepts. After the precepts are received, they must be practiced and observed. The community practices bowl-clepsydra meditation for one hundred days.[191]

ITEM: The great master who confirms illumination[192] gives direction concerning the rules and regulations of conduct about the scriptures, repentances, teachings, and books. He trains and guides the precept disciples with regard to body and heart-mind, specifically in regulating and governing the Seven Emotions and Six Desires.

If one has not received the *Precepts of Medium Ultimate*, one may not hold this position.

ITEM: The great master who inspects the precepts[193] supervises and examines those who have received the precepts. He does not allow them to transgress the precepts or offend the statutes. If there is someone who is not compliant, he determines the severity of the offense. He uses the discipline stick to mete out punishment and repentance. If one has not received the *Precepts of Medium Ultimate*, one also may not hold this position.

Rules for the Three Robes

Those who have received the Ten Precepts of Initial Perfection, Three Precepts, Five Precepts, Eight Precepts, and Wondrous Precepts of Nine Perfected may wear the Devotion Robe of Initial Perfection. This outfit includes two hundred and forty folds, three terraces, ten pleats, a cloud belt with two ends, as well as a pure kerchief and straw sandals. If these disciples practice one thousand and two hundred beneficial deeds, they may receive the *Qingjing jing* (Scripture on Clarity and Stillness),

---

189. "Transgressor within the order" translates *jiaozhong zuiren*. Cf. "Thief of the teachings" (*xuedao*) derived from section 14b of the *Jinguan yusuo jue* (DZ 1156); trl. Komjathy 2007a.

190. *Chuanjie benshi.*

191. See my translation of the *Quanzhen zuobo jiefa* (DZ 1229) herein.

192. *Zhengming dashi.*

193. *Jianjie dashi.*

Datong jing (Scripture on Great Pervasion), and *Donggu jing* (Scripture of Cavernous Antiquity).[194] After receiving the precepts of the Perfected, if they truly practice them and completely observe them, they may then receive the Pure Precepts of Medium Ultimate, **[15a]** also known as the Precepts for Maintaining Body, Precepts of Wisdom, Precepts for Observing Self, or Precepts of the Wondrous Forest.[195]

This level of disciple may wear the Pure Robe of Lightened Dust. This may be made of simple, indigo cotton or pure silk. It also consists of three terraces, a cloud belt, pure kerchief, and straw sandals. If one practices two thousand and four hundred beneficial deeds, one may receive the Great Laws of the Jade Thearch and take the Earth Immortal Precepts. If one truly practices them and completely observes them, one may then receive the Wondrous Precepts of the Great Virtue of Celestial Immortals, and practice the One Hundred and Eighty Precepts or the Three Hundred Great Precepts.[196] After one practices three thousand and six hundred beneficial deeds, one may receive the *Daode zhenjing* (Perfect Scripture on the Dao and Virtue).

This level of disciple may wear the Mist Robe of Celestial Immortality.[197] For this, the collar should be straight, with open sleeves and unjoined seams. This robe also includes a mist girdle with cloud-style sides, the Cap of the Perfect Forms of the Five Peaks, and the Light Shoes of the Five Clouds. If one practices and completely observes this level, one will obtain the fruits of the Precepts of Celestial Immortality.

Rules of Repentance after Transgressing the Statutes

If you have received the precepts, and supposing that you have committed one transgression against them, on the *gengshen* day[198] you should offer respect before the Dao through formal ritual expression. Recite the *Youzui fachan* (Repentance for Forgiving Transgressions)[199] while making an offering of one vessel of pure water. You should then recite the *Qiuzu chanhui wen* (Writings for Announcing Transgressions to Patriarch Qiu).[200] After this, practice tranquil meditation for one month. If you have committed two transgressions, follow this same procedure.

---

194. The eighth-century *Taishang laojun shuo chang qingjing miaojing* (DZ 620), thirteenth-century *Taishang dongxuan lingbao tianzun datong jing* (DZ 327; cf. DZ 105), and the thirteenth-century *Yuanshi tianzun shuo taigu jing / Taishang chiwen donggu jing* (DZ 102; DZ 106; DZ 107). Li Daochun (Yingchan [Shimmering Toad]; fl. 1288–1306), a lineage descendant (second-generation) of Bai Yuchan (1134–1229), wrote commentaries on the latter two texts (DZ 105; DZ 107).

195. Among these titles, there is a corresponding text, namely, the sixth-century *Guanshen dajie* (DZ 1364). A translation appears in Kohn's *Cosmos and Community* (2004b, 202–26).

196. The One Hundred and Eighty Precepts most likely refers to the *Laojun yibai bashi jie* (DZ786, 4a–12b). For a translation see Hendrischke and Penny 1996; Kohn 2004b, 136–44.

197. The section further on refers to this robe as the Grotto Robe of Celestial Immortality.

198. The *gengshen* (Jpn.: *kōshin*) day is the fifty-seventh day of the sixty-day cycle. Traditionally speaking, this day was believed to be the moment when the Three Death-bringers ascend to heaven to report a person's transgressions and to receive celestial instructions for punishments, such as sickness, bad fortune, and early death.

199. See section 12a.

200. A text by this title appears toward the end of the evening section of the contemporary Quanzhen liturgy (*gongke*). See Kim 2006; Mori 2006.

If you have committed three transgressions, **[15b]** on the *jiazi* day[201] you should offer respect before the Dao through formal ritual expression. Recite the *Chaotian fachan* (Repentance for Attending to Heaven) and the *Lingbao dachan* (Great Repentance of Numinous Treasure)[202] while making an offering of three vessels of pure water. Practice tranquil meditation for three months.

However, if your offenses reach five to ten transgressions, yang will dissipate and yin will prosper. Ghosts will plague you, and spirits will despise you. You may not repent [and receive absolution].

Invocations for Daily Activities[203]

Invocation When Waking Up

[16a] May all sentient beings awaken from delusion and instantaneously gain clear understanding.

Invocation When Hearing the Bell Sound

May this great and rare sound enable awakening and the experience of perfection.

Invocation When Putting on Undergarments

May I transform deviance and return to goodness. In the ledgers, may the Three Radiances grant perpetual life, so that I may ride the luminosities and mount the clouds.

Invocation for Combing Hair

Above Niwan,[204] the precious essence of Xuanhua (Mysterious Flower).[205] To the left, a hidden sun; to the right, the moon's base.[206] May vital essence be refined through the six directions, so that the hundred spirits receive grace.

Invocation for Washing Hands and Face

[16b] May I wash away the dirt so that spirit expands. May I coalesce perfection without dissipation.

---

201. The *jiazi* day is the first day of the sixty-day cycle.

202. On these texts see section 12a.

203. In the original Chinese, these invocations are in the standard four-character pattern of recitation texts, that is, in a format that allows them to be easily remembered. They have a mnemonic quality.

204. A reference to Niwan gong (Palace of Nirvana), here corresponding to the crown-point.

205. Xuanhua is the name of the spirit of the hair.

206. In terms of the Daoist internal landscape, the left eye corresponds to the sun, while the right eye corresponds to the moon.

Invocation for Rinsing the Mouth

May Great Yang harmonize the qi, opening spring and giving life to the willows. In taking this single branch, may I be able to purify body and mouth. In studying the Dao and cultivating perfection, may I transcend the Three Realms.

Invocation for Fixing Hair and Cap

May all sentient beings' head and face be constant and upright, so that their faces manifest the myriad classes.

Invocation for Putting on Robes

May I arrange and tie these in a dignified demeanor, so that my clothing and upper garments express goodness and the sacred teachings.

Invocation for Putting on Socks and Shoes

May all sentient beings walk in perfection and truth, and move without ever leaving the Dao.

Invocation When Offering Incense

[17a] Constantly burning the incense of my heart-mind, may I attain great clarity and purity.

Invocation for Lighting the Lamps

May these lamps eliminate the heavy darkness, so that cavernous luminosity spreads through the ten directions.

Invocation When Having an Audience with the Three Precious Ones

May the great Hong, Cheng, and Ming protect my form and spirit.[207]

Invocation When Receiving People and Offering Respects

May the utmost Dao infuse and harmonize this meeting, forever expelling any defilements or negative karmic bonds.

---

207. These are esoteric, talismanic characters relating to the Sanqing (Three Purities). Hong refers to Yuanshi tianzun (Celestial Worthy of Original Beginning), Cheng to Lingbao tianzun (Celestial Worthy of Numinous Treasure), and Ming to Daode tianzun (Celestial Worthy of Dao and Virtue). They appear, for example, on the *Wulei lingpai* (Summoning Tablet of the Five Thunder Gods) used in contemporary Daoist ritual.

Invocation for Drinking Water

May this Spirit Water enter my belly, enabling the five yin-organs to become clear and luminous.

Invocation for Receiving Food into the Empty Bowl

[17b] The great Void is inexhaustible. May its perfect unity give rise to spirit.

Invocation for the Living

A single grain from the beneficial husk, a single drop from the clear spring—I cannot bear to eat these solely for my own nourishment. May they feed the ethereal souls of the departed. I receive this as an offering so that all may rely on the Dao's grace. Only the Dao, only the numinous, enables one to realize innate nature and have continual existence.

Invocation When Eating

May the vapors of the Five Stars, the essences of the Six Jia-spirits,[208] and the celestial granaries of the Three Perfected remain pure and prosperous, with continual surplus. May the Yellow Father [emperor] and innocent children [people] guard the central kingdom so that it is without disturbance.

Invocation When Finishing Eating

May the hundred grains enter my stomach, harmonizing spirit and qi. May they repair any deficiencies in my blood and fluids. The worms and perverse influences are destroyed and expelled. Living in perpetual life with heaven and earth, may I alight and ascend to the Jade Tower. By employing the Six Ding-spirits[209] as servants, may I receive protection from the numinous lads.

Invocation for Washing the Bowl

[18a] May I scour and expel every external taste and smell so that the aligned qi may be perpetually preserved.

Invocation for Storing the Bowl

May the single, unified qi of Chaos Prime penetrate the Abyss Source through my heel breathing.[210]

---

208. The Six Jia-spirits (*liujia*) refer to spirits associated with the stem-branch combinations of *jiazi, jiaxu, jiashen, jiawu, jiachen*, and *jiayan*.

209. The Six Ding-spirits (*liuding*) refer to the spirits associated with the stem-branch combinations of *dingmao, dingsi, dingwei, dingyou, dinghai*, and *dingchou*.

210. The classical location for "heel breathing" (*zhongxi*) is chapter 6 of the *Zhuangzi*: "Realized beings (*zhenren*) of ancient times slept without dreaming and woke without care; they ate without enjoyment and their breath came from deep inside. Realized beings breathe through their heels; the masses breathe through their throats." In later Daoist longevity practices, there is an actual method for breathing through the Yongquan (Bubbling Well) point, which is located in the center of the ball of the feet and corresponds to the first point on the kidney channel (KI-1).

342 / The Way of Complete Perfection

Invocation for Receiving Alms

May the radiant forest of the Seven Treasures come to shine in the elixir terrace.

Invocation for Receiving Robes and Objects

May the essence of the myriad things preserve the perfection of the Dao's qi.[211]

Invocation for Exiting the Monastic Hall

May the four directions be free from obstruction, so that I may enter the gateway to all wonders.[212]

Invocation for Carrying the Bowl

[18b] O imperial order inside the body. The Three Bureaus, Eight Luminosities, thirty-nine spirits, and sixteen thousand spirits who protect the body. *An ye ye ye lang san bo ye fu gu luo hu.*[213]

Invocation for Grasping the Pure Bottle

May the Great Mystery contain unity so that the myriad beings are free from entanglement.

Invocation for Applying Ashes

May I wash with ashes to expel the dirt,[214] applying the ashes as my foremost concern. May pollution depart and perfection arrive. By this, I purify my heart-mind and mouth. May this complete the Dao and liberate humans and enable heaven to extend and the earth to abide.

Invocation for Bathing

When heaven and earth are open and bright, the Four Elements become constant. May these mysterious waters cleanse every contamination and expel anything that lacks auspiciousness. May the two youths guard and protect me. May the seven numens bring calm serenity to this chamber. May the cloud fluids purify me, so that the myriad vapors become commingled and healthy. May inside and outside gain benefit and purity and protect this yellow-clad disciple.

---

211. *Daoqi.*

212. An allusion to the last line of chapter 1 of the *Daode jing.*

213. This is pseudo-Sanskrit. It is intended to be an esoteric invocation.

214. That is, using ashes to brush one's teeth. "Applying ashes" (*yonghui*) also invokes the earlier Daoist Tutan zhai (Mud and Soot Purification), which was a purification ritual for the remission of transgressions, both for the penitents and the larger community. See Lu Xiujing's (406–477) *Dongxuan lingbao wugan wen* (DZ 1278).

Invocation When Going to Sleep

[19a] May the jade maidens of Great Perfection attend to my perfection and protect my ethereal soul. May the gold lads of Three Palaces come to guard my Gate of Life.

Invocation for Sleeping and Dreaming[215]

May auspicious dreams come like pearls and jade. May nightmares be controlled like grass and shrubs.

Invocation When Examining the Sick

May wisdom illuminate the myriad numens through the nonaction of perfect innate nature.

Daily Avoidances

In the morning, do not speak about your dreams and sleep. In the afternoon, do not speak about death and punishment. In the evening, do not speak about ghosts and spirits. [20a]

Monastic Attire and Paraphernalia

| Grotto Robe of Celestial Immortality[216] | Pure Robe of Lightened Dust | Devotion Robe of Initial Perfection |

Figure 38. The Three Robes

---

215. This invocation consists of two five-character lines, thus deviating from the previous structure.

216. Section 15a identifies this robe as the Mist Robe of Celestial Immortality.

This robe has the Three Stars, a skirt with ten pleats, and two hundred and forty sections.

Front   Back

Figure 39. Pure Kerchief

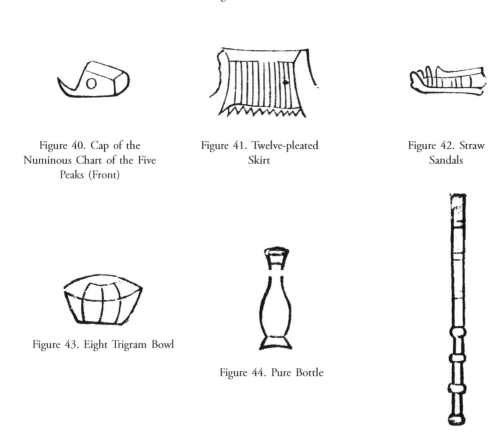

Figure 40. Cap of the   Figure 41. Twelve-pleated   Figure 42. Straw
Numinous Chart of the Five   Skirt   Sandals
Peaks (Front)

Figure 43. Eight Trigram Bowl

Figure 44. Pure Bottle

Figure 45. Seven-notched Staff

Conduct Guidelines of the Mysterious Gate for Observing the Precepts[217]

[21a] Now then, adepts who have not yet studied the precept books may not study the scriptures and the teachings. Those who are not yet experienced entering the Ordination Platform to study the *Precepts of Initial Perfection* may not advance to the next rank and receive the *Precepts of Medium*

---

217. Xuanmen (Mysterious Gate) refers to Daoism more generally and Quanzhen in particular.

Ultimate. Those who are only beginning to examine the precept books must offer incense and make the appropriate prostrations. They must not carelessly unroll and examine them. They must not allow ordinary people to steal a glance at the precept books. They must not covertly listen to the *dharma* talks of the perfected masters. Through formal ritual, they must chant the liturgy with reverential attentiveness and without a lack of decorum during the three prescribed times.

Those who have entered the bowl-clepsydra hall, cultivated and refined their body and heart-mind, as well as practiced and observed *Precepts of Medium Ultimate* for three years, may then receive the *Precepts of Celestial Immortality*. They must not disturb and defraud the conduct guidelines in order to seek veneration from people. They must not talk extensively about karmic fruits in order to gain donations from people. They must not, at inappropriate times, attempt to offer formal prostrations; during the times designated for sleep, they should remain with others. They must not disturb the altar or formal rituals, but instead constantly maintain their assigned position. In attending to the altar, offering incense, or filling the lamps, they must move with subtlety and never act in unrefined ways. When burning incense, use the following secret invocation:

> Through constant burning, may the incense of my heart-mind attain great clarity and purity.[218]

When lighting the lamps, use the following secret invocation:

> May these lamps eliminate the heavy darkness, so that cavernous luminosity spreads through the ten directions.[219]

You should not merely select and study scriptures with which you resonate. **[21b]** If you encounter unbearable poverty and difficulty, you should find peace in your life-destiny and comfort yourself; do not curse heaven and hate the earth. Do not discriminate between monastics and ordinary people; you should make offerings that produce blessings. Do not discuss the Dao and sacred teachings in contrast to non-Daoist teachings. Do not forcefully urge benefactors to donate wealth and material; you also should not enjoin wealthy friends and relatives to collect offerings. Do not increase wealth through profit-making. Do not falsely exaggerate karmic affairs in order to accumulate wealth for your own personal profit and use.

Conduct Guidelines for Entering and Exiting

Do not, without good reason, enter other Daoist temples and monasteries or Buddhist temples. Do not, without good reason, go to ordinary homes. If you do have some affair that requires entering an ordinary home, you should return as soon as it is finished; do not stay for more than the necessary

---

218. This corresponds to the Invocation for Offering Incense in section 16b–17a.

219. This corresponds to the Invocation for Lighting Lamps in section 17a.

220. Although *zashu* is often used in a technical, bibliographical sense as "miscellaneous writings" (i.e., books that contain writings from various "schools"), the meaning here suggests non-Daoist books or books that are confused and may confuse the Daoist adept. This intended meaning is clear based on the following passages where the text discusses *zahua* ("confused speech") and *zating* ("confused listening").

amount of time. Do not tell jokes or engage in unnecessary discussions with relatives, ordinary people, children, and so forth. Do not leave or store your robes and things at an ordinary home. Regardless of traveling far or near, or entering and exiting, do not lose your ritual decorum. It should be the same in every situation. If you do lose your decorum, do not make it worse by smiling or laughing.

Conduct Guidelines for Serving the Master

[22a] When you visit the master on the first and fifteenth of the lunar month [new and full moon], you must offer obeisance to him. When asking the master about the Dao and sacred teachings, you must bow. The only exceptions are when he is drinking and eating, sitting to develop merit, or studying the scriptures. If you want to stop bowing, you should only do so in accordance with the master's directive. If the master bows, you should not bow at the same time. If you are in front of the master, you should not receive people with prostrations. When serving the master while he is preaching about the Dao and the sacred teachings, if he becomes tired and concludes his teachings, you should respond by leaving.

Generally speaking, when entering and exiting, you should first consult the master. When having robes, caps, kerchiefs, and other things made, you should first consult the master. When undertaking various affairs, such as cloud-wandering, guarding the mountain, discussing virtue, developing beneficial relationships, and so forth, you should first consult the master. When responding to people's requests to borrow your personal effects, you should first consult the master; if he gives his permission, you may lend them. If you wish to borrow other people's personal effects, you should first consult the master; if he allows it, you may do it. If you want to study the scriptures and repentances, you should first consult the master. If people wish to donate things, you should first consult the master; if he grants his permission, you may receive them. If you want to donate something to someone, you should first consult the master; if he gives his permission, you may do it.

Generally speaking, when making requests of the master, and when he deliberates whether or not to grant his permission, you should make the necessary prostrations and then retire; you should not linger. If the master becomes ill, you should do your best to diagnose and mend it; do not be negligent. If the master directs you to wash his clothes, do not go inside [his chamber]. If the master directs you to empty his commode, do not reject it as unclean. [22b] If the master spits, you should immediately remove it. In the evening, when you are beneath the moonlight, you should not walk on or pass through the master's shadow. When the master instructs you about the precepts with sternness, do not talk back to him.

When people ask about your master's taboo names, respond with such and such former name, and such and such later name. When they ask about his religious name, respond by saying master such and such.

Conduct Guidelines for Looking and Listening

When examining the scriptures, you should sit in a formal manner and consider your level of recognition.

Do not rudely point at the sun and moon or rainbows and their aftereffects. Do not stare for a long time at the sun, moon, clouds, or Milky Way.

Do not look at books that come from outside the tradition. Do not read fiction, stories about unusual occurrences, or confused writings.[220]

When serving and sitting at the side of the master and attending to guests and visitors, look straight ahead; do not look up, down, or side-to-side. Do not stare at appearances that produce confusion, vexation, desire, or strange captivations.

When following the master to climb lofty peaks and gaze at distant locations, look at what the master looks at; do not look at other things. When following the master to enter and exit, do not look left or right; you should lower your head and gaze, and follow behind him.

When entering cities or marketplaces and encountering the various illusory affairs of sentient beings, do not take note of them with your eyes. When you return to the monastery, do not engage in exaggerated speech about the sights and sounds of the marketplace.

[23a] When taking books or letters to the master's friends, do not open and read them. When entering the chambers of the master's friends, do not seditiously pick up scriptures and records in order to rifle through and read them. When entering cities and marketplaces, do not turn your head around to look at women. You also should not stare at women or steal a listen to their conversations.

In general, you should not bend your ear to listen to things. Do not listen to licentious pleasures. Do not listen to jokes or confused speech. Do not listen to singing. Do not strain yourself in order to listen to people talking behind partitions and dividing-walls.

When the master recites the scriptures or lectures on the Dao, you should reverently stand up and listen with discernment; do not listen in a state of confusion.

Conduct Guidelines for Speaking

When entering the hall of sacred teachings[221] and serving the master's mat, do not speak loudly. You also should not cough loudly. Do not speak a lot. Do not speak about disease. Do not imitate the master's speech and secretly mock him. If the master does not address you, you should not speak. If the master has not yet finished speaking, you should not speak.

Do not speak about other people's transgressions and shortcomings. Do not speak about the domestic affairs of fellow adepts or ordinary people. Do not speak about imperial or political affairs. Do not speak about the affairs of women's quarters. Do not speak to matchmakers or watchmen.

[23b] Do not speak about the Dao and sacred teachings at inappropriate times. Do not speak with ladies in a low voice or with intimate language. Do not tell jokes or engage in lighthearted conversations with children and adolescents. Do not speak when drinking or eating. Do not speak when going to sleep. If you have friends or relatives come to visit, do not sit and talk for a long time in the hall of sacred teachings; you should go to the forest or near the water to sit and discuss their feelings.

When asking questions to resolve doubts or making inquiries about the Dao, you should offer obeisance and express your reverence. If someone asks the master a question, you should bow and express your reverence; you should not insist that you know something that he does not, and thus consider yourself to be correct. If someone has a question about domestic or common affairs, you must not bow; you should simply receive them and respond with what is correct.

---

221. "Hall of sacred teachings" translates *fatang*. This is the building where formal lectures are given.

When speaking with fellow adepts and ordinary people, do not discuss the techniques of stove and fire[222] as well as Yellow and White.[223] Do not speak about the methods of other schools. Do not speak about talismans, invocations, or magical arts. Do not complain about the wind or curse the rain. Do not speak about the lesser methods of subsidiary schools. Do not speak about positive or negative qualities of non-Daoist traditions.

Conduct Guidelines for Washing and Combing

When washing your face, rinsing your mouth, or spitting out water, you should get rid of the water in a slow and dignified manner. Do not gargle or spit by making loud sounds.

[24a] During the summer months, your washbasin should be covered so that living insects cannot [get in]. When discarding impure water, do not throw it on paths or the ground, but simply sprinkle it on the ground. You also should not throw it into the air, as it may splash people's clothes. Do not throw hot soup on the ground.

If your inner robes happen to have lice or mites, it is acceptable to wash them immediately; you may also first try to pick them out.

Concerning your hair, if your comb amasses a lot of hair, it is acceptable to burn the hair in a secluded and quiet place; do not place it inside your chamber or in the seam of a partition-wall.

In the hall of sacred teachings, in front of the statues of the gods, do not rinse your mouth, clean your teeth, or spit out water. You should do this in a secluded and quiet place. You also should not spit toward the north.

If you happen to have a sore, rash, or other skin problem, you should avoid contacting other people; you also should not wash your hands in a public basin. If you have a serious skin condition or the like, do not touch people's eyes.[224]

Conduct Guidelines for Drinking and Eating

Generally speaking, when the community gathers to eat, they should first express their reverence and offer worship. The entire community of sages and Perfected should arrange themselves in the proper manner, standing in the established order, and recite chapters from the numinous books. When this is finished, before taking their seats, they should send out [gratitude] to all sentient beings for the food contained on the serving dishes. Recite the following *gatha*:

> To each of you ghosts and spirits
> I now offer my gratitude
> From this food of the ten directions
> May every ghost and spirit benefit
> *An hong ling suo he*
> (Three times)

---

222. "Stove and fire" (*luhuo*) may refer to alchemy or mundane affairs. With respect to the latter, it relates to sexual practices or so-called bedroom arts (*fangzhong shu*), sometimes inaccurately referred to as "Daoist sexual yoga" in popular constructions of Daoism. Such practices most likely originated in medical and imperial court circles, rather than in Daoist communities. Note the fact that these Longmen monastics are technically celibate.

223. Yellow and White (*huangbai*) may refer to either external or internal alchemy as well as sex.

224. Here one notes a fairly sophisticated understanding of hygiene as well as infection and disease transmission.

Concerning food, you should not eat noodles made from the seven grains. **[24b]** Do not eat even a smidgen of steamed bread.[225] Do not eat even a pinch of reptiles or crustaceans. Your food should consist solely of vegetables, not of living beings.

When eating, recite this subtle invocation:

> May the vapors of the Five Stars,
> Essences of the Six Jia-spirits
> And celestial granaries of Three Perfected
> Remain pure and prosperous, with continual surplus.
> May the Yellow Father and innocent children
> Guard the central kingdom so that it is without disturbance.[226]

When drinking, recite this subtle invocation:

> May this Spirit Water enter my belly,
> Enabling the five yin-organs to become clear and luminous.[227]

When eating and drinking, do not tell jokes. Do not talk with food in your mouth. Do not discuss whether the food is good or bad. Do not scratch your head. Do not pick your teeth; if you must pick your teeth, cover your mouth with your sleeve. Do not eat with your mouth open and make sounds while you chew. Do not make faces with your mouth. Do not make sounds with your tongue. Do not lack humility and lust after food. Do not return food that you have partially eaten or tasted into the serving dishes. If there happen to be husks or shells in the food, you should remove and eat them; do not throw them on the ground. If there are insects or worms in your food, secretly remove them in an appropriate manner; do not make this known to other community members.

When you have finished eating, do not immediately leave your seat. When setting your bowl and chopsticks down, do not make a sound. Do not try to influence the eating [patterns] of other community members. Do not give undue attention to excellent flavors and generate craving for additional food.

When the entire community is gathering together to eat, do not be overly leisurely. **[25a]** You also should not be overly hurried. When lifting or setting down your chopsticks, do not do so before the master or elders. If the serving of the food has not yet begun, do not become vexed or worried; do not sign or call out in a loud voice. When it is time to drink and eat, do not lose your decorum. If you do, do not make it worse by laughing. When everyone has finished eating and drinking, and the chime is struck, the entire community stands up and files out together.

---

225. These prohibitions parallel the earlier Daoist practice of "abstention from grains" or "cereal avoidance" (*bigu; quegu*). In some cases, this practice involved eliminating grains from one's diet, while in other expressions, it required complete fasting. The motivation behind the practice involved the extermination of the Three Death-bringers (*sanshi*).

226. This repeats the Invocation When Eating in section 17b.

227. This repeats the Invocation for Drinking in section 17a.

Conduct Guidelines for Hearing the Divine Teachings

When hearing the sacred teachings, concentrate your own thinking and attend to your own body with strong determination. Do not give free rein to your mouth and ears. Young adepts who have received the *Precepts of Initial Perfection*, but who do not yet have a firm commitment to the Dao or the ability to practice unassisted, should observe the basic precepts. They should not prematurely receive the *Precepts of Medium Ultimate*. They should not form friendships with sons and brothers of ordinary backgrounds. They also should not make pacts with female Daoists or send letters back and forth with their sisters.

Conduct Guidelines for Walking

When entering the hall of sacred teachings, you should walk calmly and report [to the superior] in a dignified and composed manner. When people are examining the scriptures, do not walk in front of the table where the scriptures are. **[25b]** When people are engaging in ritual activity or prostrating themselves, do not walk in front of their heads. When entering the monastic compound, do not walk in the center; you should walk on the left or right side of the path. When walking behind the master, you follow behind him with your head and gaze lowered; do not look around. Do not stand on the side of the road for a long time talking with other people. Do not walk in a hurried manner. Do not flail your arms when you walk. Do not tell jokes or walk with young Daoists or ordinary people. Do not walk in front of, behind, or together with women. Do not walk in front of, behind, or together with people who are drunk or crazy. When following the master, if you happen to become separated and there is a set meeting time, do not be late. Generally speaking, when meeting officials, do not discuss what is superior and inferior; it is also acceptable to avoid the meeting.

For young adepts who are not yet established in practicing the precepts, they should not travel to distant places.[228] They must simply desire to meet a master and receive instruction about the Dao. They should choose worthy companions. They should not join with the unworthy or walk with rebels.

Conduct Guidelines for Standing Up

When standing up, do not push off on one foot while relying on a table or leaning against a wall. When serving the master, do not stand up facing him. You also should not stand in a higher position or far away. Stand behind the master. Do not rely on the master's seat to stand up. When you see the master stretching to stand up **[26a]** or guests standing up after the scriptures have been recited, you should take this as a moment that deserves your attention, like when someone is sick. When serving the master, if he directs you to sit then you should sit. If the master is receiving a question, you should stand up. The Confucian *Li[ji]* (Book of Rites) says, "When the superior person receives a question, he arranges himself and then stands up to respond."

Conduct Guidelines for Sitting and Sleeping

When reading and examining the scriptures and sacred books, do not sit with your legs spread out or in a squatting posture; you should light incense, straighten your garments, and sit in a dignified

---

228. Cf. Discourse 2 of the *Chongyang lijiao shiwu lun* translated in chapter 3 herein.

manner. You should not sit [in front of] the sacred images and statues. For your sitting method, rely upon what your master transmitted to you; practice quiet sitting and do not lose this opportunity. Do not sit facing your master or elders. Do not sit facing guests.

During the night, increase your time for meditation and decrease that for sleeping. Do not sit with women. Do not sit with female Daoists. If female Daoists arrive and ask about the Dao, retire as soon as you have finished giving your response; do not sit and entertain them for a long time.

Practice quiet sitting for about one hour; then read the scriptures or go to sleep. If you are meditating with other people, do not meditate directly across from each other. Do not meditate in a kneeling position, and do not join your arms on your knees.

It is best to sleep on your side.[229] When you wake up, extend your feet and then stretch. Do not sleep on your back. Do not sleep in the same room as your master. If you must stay in the same room, do not sleep in the same bed. If the master has not yet fallen asleep, make sure that you do not go to sleep first. [26b] If he is already asleep, do not talk.

Do not take off your undergarments when you sleep. Do not sleep in forbidden places. When getting ready to go to bed and extinguishing the fires in the eight rooms, you should find out whether or not those sharing your room have any of the eight desires.[230] Before you extinguish the fire, you should also find out whether or not they need to use a lantern.

During the time of Great Heat,[231] do not sleep on the ground. Do not sleep in damp places. Do not sleep in sunny places. Do not sleep on a full stomach. Do not sleep with a flame next to your pillow.

Do not carry dirty vessels in front of the hall of sacred teachings. When you wake up in the morning, use your left foot first to get out of bed.

Recite this invocation when going to sleep: May the jade maidens of Great Perfection attend to the Perfected and protect my ethereal soul. May the gold lads of Three Palaces come to guard my Gate of Life.[232]

Recite this invocation when waking up: May I assist all sentient beings to awaken from delusion and immediately gain clear understanding.[233]

Recite this invocation when getting out of bed: May I transform deviance and return to goodness. In the ledgers, may the Three Radiances grant me perpetual life, so that I may ride the luminosities and mount the clouds.[234]

---

229. The standard guideline is to sleep like a bow (*wo ru gong*). This involves sleeping on one's right side, usually with the legs slightly bent and with the right hand near the right ear and the left hand resting between the legs. This facilitates the blood returning to the liver, which purifies the blood during the night. It also enables the ethereal soul (*hun*), the yang-ghost associated with dreaming and postmortem existence as an ancestor, to return to its associated organ, the liver, in order to rest.

230. The specific meaning of the eight desires (*bayu*) is unclear, but the context suggests the desire to eat, drink, urinate, and so forth.

231. Great Heat (*dashu*) is the twelfth of the twenty-four seasonal nodes (*ershisi jie*) and the sixth of the summer nodes. It roughly corresponds to July 23.

232. This is the Invocation When Going to Sleep in section 18b–19a.

233. This corresponds to the Invocation When Waking Up in section 15b–16a.

234. This is the Invocation When Putting on Undergarments in section 16a above.

Conduct Guidelines for Labor

Generally speaking, when engaging in labor, you should not try to avoid difficult or taxing duties. Every day, you should have compassion for things that are unable to move; do not be uncontrolled and violent toward rice, grain, flour, dough, and so forth.

[27a] When washing vegetables, you should lightly rinse them three times. When drawing water, you should first wash your hands. When drawing water, you should also examine it to see if there are any insects in it; if there are no insects, strain it through a mesh filter and then use it. If it is a severe winter, do not filter water in the early morning; you should wait until the sun comes up.

When cooking, do not use rotten firewood for fuel. When preparing a meal, you should wash your hands three times; do not wash in a stream that is scummy or dirty.

When sweeping the ground, you should first sprinkle water in every direction within five feet. Then sweep it one time. Do not simply redistribute the dust. Do not sweep against the wind. Do not sweep dust and matter behind door-leafs.

Conduct Guidelines for Bathing

It is best to bathe on the first day of each lunar month; do not bathe if it is windy. Do not tie your hair in a topknot if it is still wet. Do not stroke your hair if you are unable to avoid being in front of people.

Do not bathe several times at once. Do not bathe, as is customary, for two days. When entering the bathhouse and taking off and putting on your robes, you should be calm, attentive, and alone.

When entering the water, you should first find an unoccupied place. Do not urinate in the water. Do not rudely or brashly splash other people with hot water. When entering the water, do not talk with other people. Do not bathe for a long time according to your own whims, thus preventing the next person from bathing.

[27b] If you have sores, rashes, or some other skin problem, you should bathe after everyone else; do not bathe first. If the water is cold and needs hot water added, follow the custom of shaking the rattle; do not shout or call out in a loud voice.

For bathing, it is best to use five-fragrance water, which consists of iris root, peach bark, cedar bark, and various other pure woods.[235] When bathing, if you are not yet dry, do not sit or lie down.

Recite this subtle invocation when bathing: When heaven and earth are openly respected, the Four Elements become constant. May these waters of the Mysterious cleanse every contamination and expel anything that lacks auspiciousness. May the two youths guard and protect me. May the seven numens bring calm serenity to this chamber. May the cloud fluids purify me, so that the myriad vapors become commingled and healthy. May inside and outside gain benefit and purity and protect this yellow-clad disciple.[236]

As written, if you do not attend to this detailed practice, in the end you will be exhausted and humiliated. You must form a covenant with great virtue; then you will understand the undertaking that has been described. If you do not go against this undertaking, developing it through complete

---

235. The specific substances require more research. The Chinese reads *baizhi*, *taopi*, and *bopi*.

236. This corresponds to the Invocation for Bathing in section 18b.

reverence, you will realize the extent of its vastness. So vast, how could it stop with every category of being before three thousand manifestations?

If you are able to remain committed to this undertaking, embodying and realizing it, you will transcend the various categories [of reincarnation] and pervade the Beginning. If you exert yourself with strong determination, in the end you will return to suchness.

Practice this fearlessly and resolutely. Free yourself of pleasure and carelessness. Then you will not only gain blessings as recompense; you will also undoubtedly enter the realms of the immortals, breaking the bounds of name and reputation. You will be protected by the divine king who oversees the precepts. You will embody and have direct experience of the boundless Dao.

Rules for Disciples Serving the Master[237]

[28a] Each month when disciples take leave of the masters and scriptures, they arrange caps and sashes, extend their audience tablets and bow with full prostrations. They should not expose their white robes.

Each night when disciples take leave of the masters and the scriptures, they should offer obeisance through prolonged bows. This should be done even for masters who are in some distant location.

Disciples should not praise the masters by making distinctions about who is the master of whom.[238]

When visiting the master, a disciple should not sit down without the proper ceremonies and based on his own sense. If the master directs him to sit down, then he may sit down.[239]

Disciples should not refer to their masters as Daoist priests;[240] everyone should say that they are masters of the tradition.[241]

Disciples should not transgress the taboo [against discussing] their master's reputation. If ordinary people ask, do not merely respond with talk about superior and inferior reputations.

Disciples should not be unceremonious toward the things that surround them; everything has a divine official in charge of prohibitions.

When disciples have an audience with the master, if they have committed transgressions, they should confess it from the deepest place and through prolonged bowing. Do not speak with the master about right and wrong or ugly and vile in front of other people.

When disciples speak with the master, they should not use a loud voice or excessive speech.

When disciples share a room with the master, they should not go to sleep first or wake up last.

When disciples eat with the master, they should not eat before the master.

When prostrating before the master, disciples should follow what has been received concerning superiors and inferiors. They should gather their kerchief and robes by extending their audience tablet. They should not take hold of their white robes.

---

237. These precepts follow those listed under the same section title in the *Sandong zhongjie wen* (DZ 178, 2b–4b). I am grateful to Monica Esposito for this reference.

238. Literally, praising this one as yours and that one as mine.

239. I have translated this section using the masculine pronoun, but female disciples are also implied.

240. *Daoshi*.

241. *Jiashi*.

When following the master in getting up, staying, walking or waiting, disciples should be modest, humble, and reverent. They should not, even for a moment, lose their reverential standing like officials who live at a distance of some two thousand stone-throws from their parents. **[28b]** Disciples should not consider themselves lofty and elevated, acting carelessly or slighting the master. Such a transgression is not minor; it has been written down in the *Mingzhen ke* (Rules of Illuminated Perfected).[242]

When sitting on the master's bed, disciples should follow the pattern of the master in terms of standing up, moving, walking, or waiting. Disciples should not unconcernedly continue to sit.

Disciples may not receive the sacred teachings and precepts before other novices of the same rank, senior adepts, or paternal cousins of the same surname.

For disciples who visit the master to receive the sacred teachings after they have had grandchildren, they must simply request this with humble, modest, and reverent language. They should also praise the master's reputation. They do not need to follow the preceding rule.

When disciples wear coarse hemp clothes[243] [in order to mourn a master's death] with his relatives, they should not serve as masters [for the funeral rite]. This is because once you have received the sacred teachings [from a master], your relationship has been confirmed before the Three Assemblies and Seven Patriarchs. Any approach as if you were a parent coming to inspect what descendants have received [from the deceased] would be a breach of the covenant.[244]

Disciples should not have hatred or envy toward the master; they also should not allow hatred to reside in their heart-minds. This admonishment is contained in the *Mingzhen jing*.

When having an audience with the master and asking about the Dao and the sacred teachings, disciples should arrange cap and sash and extend their audience tablets, showing their humility and earnestness to seek instruction. They should not be in a hurry.

When disciples join with masters in the first lunar month of the new year to examine [the condition of] the scriptures,[245] they should arrange caps and sashes, extend their audience tablets, and make three full prostrations using deep bows and tapping their heads against the ground. When they finish, they should offer obeisance one more time. Then, to complete this obligation, they should offer five additional prostrations. These do not have to be the same as the first ones. Understand each as an act of sincerity for the scriptures.

Disciples should not quarrel with the master or carelessly mock his ideas.

When serving the master, disciples should be continually respectful. **[29a]** They should not be insolent or without the appropriate ritual behavior. The *Mingzhen jing* admonishes one to be careful about this.

Disciples should not argue with the master about who possesses and who lacks accomplishment and reputation. They should maintain a disposition based in yielding and declining such things.

When having an audience with the master, disciples should simply inquire about what they have received. They should not discuss personal and mundane matters.

---

242. Most likely a reference to the fifth-century *Dongxuan lingbao changye zhi fu jiuyou yugui mingzhen ke* (DZ 1411).

243. *Sima*, the three-month mourning garment.

244. My translation here is more tentative than in other places.

245. Possibly airing out the scriptures, but the time of year would make this somewhat impractical.

When serving the master, if the master is returning from traveling, disciples should meet him on the road both far and near. They should respectfully receive him and welcome him. They should not simply sit in a formal manner and quietly wait for him to arrive.

When traveling with the master, disciples should not walk on or pass through the master's shadow. One must remain attentive to this!

When sitting with the master, disciples should not receive people by kneeling and offering obeisance. This is because there cannot be two positions of honor.

Disciples should not have secret plots, malicious purposes, or resentment toward the master.

If they must enter and leave and are planning to do something, disciples should first ask the master. They should decide on their own.

When serving the master, disciples should display kindness, affection, sincerity, and honesty. They should not be of two minds.

Disciples should not steal the master's implements from his satchel. Offending the master is forbidden by the precepts, rules, and statutes and must be punished.

Disciples should not rebel against the master. One must remain attentive to this! It also is written in the *Mingzhen jing*.

When staying in the same place as the master, disciples should not spit on the ground. One must remain attentive to this!

When serving as an attendant to the master, if the master is receiving guests, disciples should serve the master by standing on his left or right.

Disciples should not climb into the great seat and join with ordinary people without discrimination, pretending as though everyone is superior and there is no need for honor. One must remain attentive to this!

[29b] After receiving the master's sacred teachings and instructions, and when mysterious virtue has become complete, disciples then become a class of person with ancestors. Disciples should show their humility through bowing and recalling the original master. They should not forget his earlier kindness.

When disciples are serving the master, they should not unceremoniously sit on the master's bed. This place is monitored by a divine official in charge of prohibitions.

Forty-six Rules of Precepts Regarding Ritual Vestments[246]

[30a] 1. Unless attired in ritual vestments, do not ascend to the altar, practice meditation,[247] bow in prayer, make announcements or requests, confess transgressions, or seek grace.

2. Unless attired in ritual vestments, do not approach the scriptures and precepts, lecture or explain, recite or chant them.

---

246. These rules are the same as those found in the early eighth-century *Sandong fafu kejie wen* (Rules and Precepts Regarding Ritual Vestments, DZ 788), which was compiled by Zhang Wanfu (fl. 713). It is translated in the electronic supplement to Kohn's *Cosmos and Community* (2004b). A rendition of the first few pages is also found in Kohn 1993, 335–43.

247. *Rujing.* Kohn has "enter the oratory."

3. Unless attired in ritual vestments, a Daoist must not perform rites of purgation and precepts, accept other people's obeisance, eat or drink holy food.

4. Unless attired in ritual vestments, a Daoist must not pay obeisance to the venerable masters and priests of extensive virtue nor accept the obeisance of disciples.

5. Unless attired in ritual vestments, a Daoist must not enter or leave any dwellings, travel among people, or be seen by ordinary folk.

6. Unless attired in ritual vestments, a Daoist must not offer spells, prohibitions, talismans, indictments, petitions, memorials, memoranda, or announcements.

7. Unless attired in ritual vestments, a Daoist must not go to see the ruler of the country, his or her parents, or other people of the world.

8. When sleeping, resting, or relaxing, Daoists must take off all ritual vestments.

9. When bathing, washing, or cleaning themselves, Daoists must take off all ritual vestments.

10. When using the outhouse, Daoists must take off all ritual vestments.

11. When in danger of getting spattered by mud and rain, Daoists must take off all ritual vestments.

12. When making offerings to the venerable masters and parents, Daoists should not take off their ritual vestments.

13. When preparing and cultivating services for the merit and virtue of all beings, Daoists should not take off their ritual vestments.

14. When preparing and setting out purgation offerings, flowers and fruit, **[30b]** Daoists should not take off their ritual vestments.

15. When preparing seeds and plants, Daoists should not take off their ritual vestments.

16. When free from imprisonment and disease, Daoists should not take off their ritual vestments.

17. Unclean hands or feet must never be allowed to offend the ritual vestments.

18. Dirty vessels or other objects must never be allowed to offend the ritual vestments.

19. Soiled beds or mats must never be allowed to offend the ritual vestments.

20. Dusty carriages or sedan chairs must never be allowed to offend the ritual vestments.

21. The naked or exposed body must never be allowed to offend the ritual vestments.

22. Birds and beasts, insects and fish must never be allowed to offend the ritual vestments.

23. Foul breath and spittle must never be allowed to offend the ritual vestments.

24. People who are not fellow students or disciples must never be allowed to offend the ritual vestments.

25. When Daoists first wish to leave the family, they should prepare a set of vestments.

26. When Daoists get ready to receive the scriptures and precepts, they should prepare a set of vestments.

27. When Daoists visit the master to request scriptures, precepts, and registers, they should put on ritual vestments.

28. When Daoists visit the master to request a blessing or spell to dissolve all danger and suffering, they should put on ritual vestments.

29. Daoists must not use five colors in creating ritual vestments.

30. Daoists must not use nonritual materials in creating ritual vestments.

31. Daoists must not use damask or embroidery in creating ritual vestments.

32. Daoists must not use nonritual procedures in creating ritual vestments.

33. Daoists must not lend their ritual vestments to others. [31a]

34. Daoists must not cast off their ritual vestments at their convenience.

35. Daoists must not rest on their beds wearing ritual vestments.

36. Daoists must not sit or lie down on their ritual vestments.

37. Daoists must not wash their ritual vestments by trampling them with their feet or pounding them.

38. If worn and torn, ritual vestments should be burned for pure transformation.

39. Daoists should not own more than three sets of ritual vestments; extra robes should be given to others.

40. Ritual vestments may be worn out, excessive, or unsatisfactory; if not used, they should be given to others to wear.

41. Once the ritual vestments are complete, Daoists should offer incense and make an announcement to the Three Treasures. First offer the vestments up to the Three Treasures, then to the host of immortals, Perfected, and sages. Only after that are they fit to be worn.

42. Ritual vestments that have been close to the scriptures or statues must never be worn among ordinary people or in an unclean location.

43. Ritual vestments must be carefully washed, purified with incense, and kept in a special clothes chest, lest they be soiled and defiled. They should always be kept in a clean room.

44. Daoists must not wear ritual vestments to the five kinds of ordinary families.

45. Daoists must not take off their vestments and travel incognito among ordinary people.

46. In all sitting, rising, laying down, and resting, Daoists should always follow the rules and precepts.

Nine Precepts for Female Perfected[248]

[32a] 1. Be filial and respectful, soft and harmonious, careful in speech, and never jealous.

2. Be chaste and pure, controlled in body, and always separate from all foul activities.

3. Develop sympathy for all beings that have life, be compassionate and friendly, and never kill.

4. During rites and recitations, be diligent and circumspect, give up all eating of meat and drinking of alcohol.

5. In your garments be practical and simple, never favoring floweriness or ornaments.

6. Maintain an even and harmonious disposition, never giving rise to anger and afflictions.

7. Do not frequently go out to attend purgations and banquets.

8. Do not be cruel in your employment of servants and slaves.

9. Do not steal other people's things.

[32b] If female Daoists and female believers can practice and observe these Nine Precepts for Female Perfected without interruption, they will receive great benefit. They will not experience the suffering of the Earth Prisons. They will certainly be born in families of the ten virtues. They also will be able to make essential progress in their cultivation, to the point of completion. With the fruits of these precepts, female adepts will ascend to Zifu (Purple Palace) and take their places among the ranks of arrayed immortals.

Gathas Transmitted by Precept Master Kunyang

One: Maintaining Robes

[33a] The Great High [Lord Lao] handed down the precept robes—
Headdresses, hairpins, kerchiefs, and shoes were all regulated.
Sit up straight and remain aligned, and walk without haste;
Keep the body upright and dignified, with the eyes cast down.
When begging and going to offer services, avoid slippery stones;
When performing audience rituals, do not track in mud.
Do not fold up your robes in front of lamps or candles;
Make sure that wall nails are far away from the flames.

---

248. A French translation of these precepts appears in Despeux 1990, 147–55.

Two: Protecting the Bowl

The bowl is the ruler of the great sacred teachings of Complete Perfection;
The satchel is the storehouse of the protective covering of Brahmic vapors.[249]
When carrying it while traveling, guard against slipping or dropping it;
When lodging or taking your seat, do not hang it on a wall.
Do not recklessly lend it to your fellow disciples under any condition;
After you finish eating, wash and clean it, but do not be hurried.
Attend to this as though protecting your life-destiny;
Be careful with your cultivation and the Dao will naturally prosper.

Three: Taking Care of Shoes

[33b] Straw sandals must not be compared with ordinary shoes;
They visit sages, have audience with the Perfected, and enter the hall of sacred teachings.
If you use a close wrapping, put them straight into the pouch;
Do not allow mud or dirt to make its way into your robe bag.
When engaging in reverent prayer or pure announcements, take them off;
When walking on roads or traveling, use a different pair.
Do not recklessly pass through impure or muddy areas;
Avoid mending them with leather underneath, and do not make any mistakes.

Four: Storing Tablets and Documents

Precept scriptures and precept tablets should be respectfully stored in the body;
This cannot be compared to ordinary or other types of literature.
Innate nature and life-destiny are what connect the heart-mind to the essential and subtle;
Spirit immortals have their share, remembering and waiting for Perfection.
If dust or dirt has accumulated on a table, do not place them there;
Do not lightly and recklessly discuss them with your fellow companions.
Use a small sack made of cloth that can be worn at the waist;
Through wondrous practice, refined and majestic, you will move ghost and spirits.

Five: Having an Audience

When reverently visiting the superior, bow down in respect.
Know that you are a guest in a community with a lent position.
Do not try to pick up exchanges happening on the other side of partitions;
Do not spit in pure places or in the cloud hall.
Follow the community to the hall and diligently chant the liturgy;

---

249. "Brahmic vapors" refer to the purest and most divine form of qi in the cosmos.

When you meet people, respond with respectful words and speech.
Maintain a tranquil heart and concentrated qi, with a tone that is harmonious and slow;
[34a] Practice deep heel breathing and do not engage in casual exchanges.

Six: Maintaining Practice

The precepts are the first pass of Complete Perfection;
Receiving them is relatively easy, but maintaining them is difficult.
In relation to people, it is most important to lessen words and speech;
In meditation, be constant in the teachings, and calm your thinking and ideas.
Carry the bowl to beg for alms and melt away the time and seasons;
With the cloud traces and crane tracks, awakening becomes clear and remote.
Sink the heart-mind and become firm and fixed through prolonged practice;
Innate nature becomes stable and spirit coalesces, and you naturally return.

Appendix 1

Quanzhen Technical Glossary

aspirations for the Dao (*daozhi* 道志): Commitment to a Daoist religious path with the aim of merging with the Dao.

azure ox (*qingniu* 青牛): Vital essence, vital fluids or qi. May also refer to the lower elixir field (*dantian* 丹田). Sometimes used synonymously with "white ox" (*bainiu* 白牛).

Baiyun guan 白雲觀 (White Cloud Monastery): Contemporary monastic headquarters of Quanzhen and its Longmen lineage as well as of the Chinese Daoist Association. First built in the Tang dynasty (618–907) and reconstructed in 1167, its earlier name was Tianchang guan 天長觀 (Monastery of Celestial Perpetuity). Historically speaking, its control alternated between the Quanzhen order and the Zhengyi 正一 (Cheng-i; Orthodox Unity; a.k.a. Tianshi 天師 [T'ien-shih; Celestial Masters]) movement. Following his meeting with Chinggis Qan (Genghis Khan; ca. 1162–1227; r. 1206–1227) in 1222, Qiu Changchun was appointed abbot. It subsequently became the headquarters of the Longmen lineage during the Qing dynasty (1644–1911). In contemporary China, it houses the Daoist seminary (Daojiao xueyuan 道教學院) and oversees most of the formal Longmen ordination rituals.

black (*hei* 黑): Symbolic name for yin. Sometimes appears as black tiger (*heihu* 黑虎). Black is also the corresponding color of the kidneys.

body-beyond-the-body (*shenwai shen* 身外身): The transcendent spirit formed through alchemical practice. Also referred to as the immortal embryo (*xiantai* 仙胎), spark (*yidian* 一點), or yang-spirit (*yangshen* 陽神).

bowl-clepsydra (*zuobo* 坐鉢/坐缽): A water-clock used in Quanzhen monasteries as a time-measuring device. Refers to both the actual object ("sitting-bowl") and the corresponding practice ("meditation with the bowl-clepsydra"). Consists of a small bowl with a hole drilled in the bottom, which was placed in a larger one filled with water. Described in the *Quanzhen zuobo jiefa* (DZ 1229).

Burning House (*huoyuan* 火院): Symbolic name for *saṃsāra*, the apparently endless cycle of reincarnation characterized by suffering and determined by karma. Derived from the famous Parable of the Burning House in the *Lotus Sūtra*.

cauldron (*ding* 鼎): An alchemical vessel in external alchemy (*waidan* 外丹). Also translated as "tripod." In internal alchemy, the cauldron may refer to the Palace of Nirvana (center of head or crown-point), the heart region, the Yellow Court (*huangting* 黃庭), or the lower elixir field. The latter is the Ocean of Qi, which is "heated" through focused concentration. This alchemical term often appears paired with the furnace (*lu* 爐).

Celestial Cycle (*zhoutian* 周天): An internal alchemy practice in which one circulates qi through the Governing Vessel (perineum to upper lip) and the Conception Vessel (lower lip to perineum) in a continuous circuit. Also translated as Microcosmic Orbit. Celestial Cycle may also refer to creating energetic patterns of interaction between the heart (spirit) and kidneys (vital essence).

Celestial Pivot (*tianji* 天機): The center of the heavens, often identified as the Northern Dipper (Big Dipper). Sometimes associated with the human heart-mind. Also rendered as "trigger of heaven."

celestial stems (*tiangan* 天干): One of the major symbol systems used in Chinese cosmology and time-measurement. The ten celestial stems are as follows: (1) *jia* 甲 (yang); (2) *yi* 乙 (yin); (3) *bing* 丙 (yang); (4) *ding* 丁 (yin); (5) *wu* 戊 (yang); (6) *ji* 己 (yin); (7) *geng* 庚 (yang); (8) *xin* 辛 (yin); (9) *ren* 壬 (yang); (10) *gui* 癸 (yin). Traditionally speaking, the week is divided into ten days, beginning with *jia* and ending with *gui*. The celestial stems are combined to form Five Phase associations: (1) *jiayi* 甲乙: Wood: east; (2) *bingding* 丙丁: Fire: south; (3) *wuji* 戊己: Earth: center; (4) *gengxin* 庚辛: Metal: west; (5) *rengui* 壬癸: Water: north. Combined with the twelve terrestrial branches (*dizhi* 地支), the ten celestial stems are used to form the so-called sexagenary cycle, that is, designations for the sixty-year cycle.

Central Palace (*zhonggong* 中宮): The lower elixir field, heart, or center of the head.

Child (*ying'er* 嬰兒): Symbolic name for the kidneys and vital essence. The Child may also refer to the liver, ethereal soul (*hun* 魂), original qi (*yuanqi* 元氣), and perfect qi (*zhenqi* 真氣). Often paired with the Maiden (*chanü* 奼女).

Chinese Daoist Association (Zhongguo daojiao xiehui 中國道教協會): The officially recognized national, political organization overseeing all temples and monasteries in mainland China. Originated in the first national Daoist association, called the Daojiao hui 道教會, founded in 1912, and the first Zhongguo daojiao xiehui, which was founded in 1957. Part of the Chinese Communist bureaucracy, with most of its leaders being official members of the Chinese Communist Party. Its current president is Ren Farong 任法融 (b. 1936), former abbot of Louguan tai. Its vice-president is Zhang Jiyu 張繼禹 (b. 1962), the current Celestial Master associated with Longhu shan 龍虎山 (Dragon-Tiger Mountain; near Yingtan, Jiangxi).

crane (*he* 鶴): A symbol of longevity.

Crimson Dragon (*chilong* 赤龍): Symbolic name for the tongue.

currents of the Dao (*daofeng* 道風): The subtle, numinous presence of the Dao. Resembles the movements of an invisible and mysterious wind. Also referred to as the "qi of the Dao" (*daoqi* 道炁).

Daoist elder (*daozhang* 道長): Title of respect used by lineage-affiliated ordinands to address and identify each other. Literally, "elder of the Dao." Fellow members of the Daoist religious tradition. Sometimes used by laypeople to address Daoist priests and monastics.

Daoist priest (*daoshi* 道士): An initiated and ordained Daoist priest. Literally, "adept of the Dao." May refer to both monastics and ritual experts, and to both celibate (Quanzhen) and householder

(Zhengyi) priests. Although conventionally used functionally (i.e., priests who perform Daoist rituals), it may also be employed ontologically (i.e., for priests who are fully committed to and embody a Daoist religious path). Also used as a title of respect to address formal members of the Daoist tradition.

defilement (*chen* 塵): Psychological disruptions and spiritual impurities. Usually associated with external phenomena and sensory perception. *Chen* literally means "dust" or "dirt."

disposition of the Dao (*daoqing* 道情): A psychological condition wherein one is aligned with the Dao. Free of mundane concerns and emotionality.

dizi 弟子: A formal Daoist disciple with lineage-standing. Indicates a relationship with a specific master-father (*shifu* 師父).

double-hour (*shi* 時): Traditional Chinese division based on the twelve terrestrial branches (*dizhi* 地支). Also related to the five night-watches (*wugeng* 五更).

Dragon (*long* 龍): Sometimes appearing as "azure dragon" (*qinglong* 青龍), and thus associated with the Wood phase, the east, and the liver. Usually associated with spirit (*shen* 神) and paired with the Tiger (*hu* 虎).

Duke (*gong* 公): Symbolic name for the heart and spirit. Usually appears as Gold Duke (*jingong* 金公). Often paired with the Yellow Matron (*huangpo* 黃婆).

earth (*di* 地): The terrestrial landscape. Often symbolized as a square and depicted as a flat plane. In internal alchemy practice, earth may refer to the feet or the perineum. Also refers to the lower elixir field (naval region).

Earth (*tu* 土): Symbolic name for the lower elixir field, corresponding to the abdominal or naval region. As one of the Five Phases (*wuxing* 五行), Earth corresponds to the center, spleen, thought, honesty, and so forth. Used in the sense of perfect or true earth (*zhentu* 真土), it refers to stillness (*jing* 靜).

eight trigrams (*bagua* 八卦): Eight three-line diagrams that combine to generate the sixty-four hexagrams of the *Yijing* 易經 (Classic of Changes). Each trigram consists of one or more yang or unbroken lines (—) and one or more yin or broken lines (– –). The eight trigrams include (1) Qian-heaven (*qian* 乾) ☰, (2) Kun-earth (*kun* 坤) ☷, (3) Li-fire (*li* 離) ☲, (4) Kan-water (*kan* 坎) ☵, (5) Dui-lake (*dui* 兌) ☱, (6) Zhen-thunder (*zhen* 震) ☳, (7) Sun-wind (*sun* 巽) ☴, and (8) Gen-mountain (*gen* 艮) ☶. Among various symbolic associations, they have directional (Prior Heaven and Later Heaven) and anatomical correspondences: Qian/south/northwest/head; Kun/north/southwest/feet; Li/east/south/heart; Kan/west/north/kidneys; Dui/southeast/west/lungs; Zhen/northeast/east/liver; Sun/southwest/southeast/gall bladder; and Gen/northwest/northeast/urinary bladder.

elixir field (*dantian* 丹田): Storehouses of vital and subtle substances in the body. Most often refers to the Ocean of Qi (*qihai* 氣海), the lower abdominal region which stores qi. There are three elixir fields. In one system, they refer to Palace of Nirvana (*niwan gong* 泥丸宮; upper; center of head), Vermilion Palace (*jianggong* 絳宮; middle; heart region), and Ocean of Qi (*qihai* 氣海; lower; abdominal region). Alternatively, the Palace of Nirvana (upper), Ocean of Qi (middle), and Meeting of Yin (*huiyin* 會陰; lower; perineum). These correspond to the standard three stages of *neidan* practice, involving the transformation of vital essence to qi, qi to spirit, and spirit to emptiness.

Fire (*huo* 火): One of the Five Phases (*wuxing* 五行). Fire corresponds to summer, south, heart, spirit, respect, and so forth. Used in the sense of perfect or true fire (*zhenhuo* 真火), it refers to original spirit (*yuanshen* 元神). Also associated with the Li-fire ☲ trigram.

Five Associations (*wuhui* 五會): The five early Quanzhen Daoist associations in Shandong. Primarily established to create a communal gathering place for lay adherents and potential converts as well as to institute patronage patterns. They included Yuhua hui 玉華會 (Association of Jade Flower; Dengzhou), Qibao hui 七寶會 (Association of Seven Treasures; Wendeng), Jinlian hui 金蓮會 (Association of Gold Lotus; Ninghai), Sanguang hui 三光會 (Association of Three Radiances; Fushan), and Pingdeng hui 平等會 (Association of Equal Rank; Laizhou).

Five Centers (*wuxin* 五心): Five energetic points on the body. Refers to the crown-point, palms of hands, and soles of feet.

Five Marchmounts (*wuyue* 五嶽): The five sacred mountains of China, corresponding to the five directions, some of which are specifically associated with Daoism. They include Huashan 華山 (west; Shaanxi), Taishan 泰山 (east; Shandong), Hengshan 恒山 (north; Shanxi), Hengshan 衡山 (south; Hunan), and Songshan 嵩山 (center; Henan).

Five Patriarchs (*wuzu* 五祖): The five "founders" or lineage-ancestors of Quanzhen. In the mid thirteenth-century *Jinlian ji* 金蓮記 (Record of the Golden Lotus; DZ 173), they are identified as Donghua dijun 東華帝君 (Sovereign Lord of Eastern Florescence; a.k.a. Wang Xuanfu 王玄甫), Zhongli Quan 鍾離權 (Zhengyang 正陽 [Aligned Yang]; second c. CE?), Lü Dongbin 呂洞賓 (Chunyang 純陽 [Purified Yang]; b. 798?), Liu Cao 劉操 (Haichan 海蟾 [Oceanic Toad]; fl. 1031), and Wang Zhe 王嚞 (Chongyang 重陽 [Redoubled Yang]; 1113–1170). In the early fourteenth-century *Jinlian xiangzhuan* 金蓮像傳 (Illustrated Biographies of the Golden Lotus; DZ 174), Laozi is added as the first patriarch, while Wang Chongyang stands between the so-called Five Patriarchs and Seven Perfected.

Five Phases (*wuxing* 五行): The five energetic phases and corresponding substances of classical Chinese cosmology. Also translated as "Five Agents" and "Five Elements." Often referred to as correlative cosmology or systematic correspondence. The Five Phases include Wood, Fire, Earth, Metal, and Water.

Five Qi (*wuqi* 五氣): The qi of the five yin-organs, namely, liver, heart, spleen, lungs, and kidneys. Sometimes appears as Five Spirits (*wushen* 五神), which are the corresponding body-gods or energetic presences.

Five Thieves (*wuzei* 五賊): The five primary sense-organs and corresponding activities (eyes/looking, ears/listening, nose/smelling, mouth/tasting, and body/touching) as sources of dissipation.

Five Visions (*wuyan* 五眼): A Buddhist technical term that designates five types of perception related to five corresponding ontological conditions. They include (1) the vision of those who have a material body (human), (2) the vision of celestial beings in the world of form (*deva*), (3) the vision of wisdom by which Theravada adherents observe the thought of impermanence or emptiness (Theravada), (4) the vision of *dharma* by which bodhisattvas perceive all teachings in order to lead all beings to enlightenment (Mahāyāna), and (5) Buddha-vision or omniscience.

five yin-organs (*wuzang* 五藏/五臟): The five primary organs. They include liver (Wood), heart (Fire), spleen (Earth), lungs (Metal), and kidneys (Water).

Four Elements (*sida* 四大): The four elements of classical Indian and Buddhist cosmology, namely, Earth, Fire, Water, and Air/Wind.

Four Hindrances (*sihai* 四害): The four substances and states that lead to spiritual disorientation and dissipation. They are alcohol (*jiu* 酒), sex (*se* 色), wealth (*cai* 財), and anger (*nu* 怒).

fruits of the Dao (*daoguo* 道果): Stages of realization or attainments on the Daoist path. Some typical Daoist attainments are terrestrial immortality (*dixian* 地仙), flying immortality (*feixian* 飛仙), self-dependence (Chin.: *zizai* 自在; Skt.: *isvāra*), freedom-from-dissipation (Chin.: *wulou* 無漏; Skt.: *anāsrava*), and effortless activity (*wuwei* 無為). Some lists include being carefree (*xiaoyao* 逍遙). The fruits of the Dao also relate to numinous abilities (*shentong* 神通).

furnace (*lu* 爐): An alchemical vessel in external alchemy (*waidan* 外丹). Also translated as "stove." In internal alchemy, the furnace may refer to the heart or the lower elixir field. This alchemical term often appears paired with the cauldron (*ding* 鼎).

gold elixir (*jindan* 金丹): Symbolic name for the culmination of internal alchemy practice. Often described as a feeling of energetic fullness and warmth in the lower elixir field. Sometimes used synonymously with the body-beyond-the-body (*shenwai shen* 身外身) and the yang-spirit (*yangshen* 陽神). Also the name of a group of loosely connected late medieval movements, which are more commonly referred to as "internal alchemy" (*neidan* 內丹).

grotto-heaven (*dongtian* 洞天): Also rendered as "cavern-heavens," *dongtian* refers to specific Daoist sacred sites and terrestrial portals to the Dao. In the standardized list, there are ten major grotto-heavens and thirty-six minor ones. The earliest references date back to the fifth century, with standardized lists becoming increasingly prominent from the Tang dynasty (618–907) onward. The composition changes with shifts in Daoist geographical distribution. In the standard list, the ten major *dongtian* are as follows: Wangwu shan 王屋山 (Henan), Weiyu shan 委羽山 (Zhejiang), Xicheng shan 西城山 (Shanxi), Qingcheng shan 青城山 (Sichuan), Xixuan shan 西玄山 (Huashan) (Shaanxi), Luofu shan 羅浮山 (Guangdong), Chicheng shan 赤城山 (Zhejiang), Linwu shan 林屋山 (Lake Tai) (Jiangsu), Gouqu shan 句曲山 (Maoshan) (Jiangsu), and Kuocang shan 括蒼山 (Zhejiang). In internal alchemy practice, grotto-heaven may also refer to subtle locations in the body, especially the elixir fields.

heaven (*tian* 天): The sky or Daoist sacred realms, consisting of multiple heavens. Often symbolized by a circle and depicted as a canopy or dome. In internal alchemy practice, heaven may refer to the head or crown-point.

hermitage (*an* 庵/菴): A grass-thatched hut or reed-thatched shelter. The most famous early Quanzhen hut was the Quanzhen an 全真庵 (Hermitage of Complete Perfection), which was built by Wang Chongyang on Ma Danyang's property. The first section of the *Chongyang lijiao shiwu lun* is titled "Living in Hermitages." In later usage, *an* may designate a formal sacred site and be translated as "temple."

Huashan 華山 (Flower Mountain): The Western Marchmount, or sacred peak. Located near Huayin, Shaanxi, Huashan is characterized by elevated granite peaks. It is famous for its cave-hermitages and mountain recluses. According to Daoist tradition, it received its name because its peaks resemble a five-petaled lotus flower. In terms of the contemporary Quanzhen order, like most sacred sites and temples, its administration consists largely of members of the official Longmen lineage. On a symbolic level, it may refer to the lungs.

Huashan pai 華山派 (Mount Hua lineage): The Quanzhen lineage associated with Chen Tuan 陳摶 (Xiyi 希夷 [Infinitesimal Subtlety]; d. 989), Hao Datong 郝大通 (Guangning 廣寧 [Expansive Serenity]; 1140–1212), one of the first-generation Quanzhen adepts, and Huashan. Although its actual history is currently unclear, the Huashan lineage may have been formally established by Hao's disciple He Zhizhen 賀志貞 (1212–1299). The contemporary lineage emphasizes quietistic meditation, lineage-specific *neidan* techniques, and mountain contemplation.

innate nature (*xing* 性): One's original nature. Associated with original spirit (*yuanshen* 元神). Etymologically speaking, composed of "heart" (*xin* 心) and "to be born" (*sheng* 生). The heart-mind with which one was born. The Dao made manifest as one's consciousness. Often paired with "life-destiny" (*ming* 命).

internal alchemy (*neidan* 內丹): Designates a type of Daoist practice systematized during the late medieval period, specifically during the ninth and tenth centuries, and the corresponding movements. Literally meaning "inner pill," *neidan* incorporates dimensions of classical Daoist texts, correlative cosmology, *Yijing* lore, meditational and physical disciplines of nourishing life (*yangsheng* 養生), medical theory, Buddhist soteriology, and Confucian moral philosophy. It is a type of physiological alchemy that incorporates aspects of earlier laboratory or operative alchemy (*waidan* 外丹) as a symbol-system. Emphasis is placed on internal cultivation and transformation, a movement from ordinary human being to immortality/transcendence (*xian* 仙) and perfection (*zhen* 真). Involves the activation of a subtle, ethereal body within the body, the creation of a spirit capable of transcending dissolution and physical mortality. In its late medieval and Quanzhen expressions, *neidan* involves a stage-based training regimen grounded in complex techniques aimed at complete psychosomatic transformation.

Jade Flower (*yuhua* 玉華): Symbolic name for original qi. Also the name of one of the early Shandong associations, namely, Yuhua hui 玉華會 (Association of Jade Flower; Dengzhou).

Jade Lock (*yusuo* 玉鎖): Symbolic name for the locking mechanism of the jaw.

Jade Nectar (*yujiang* 玉漿): Symbolic name for fluids produced during internal alchemy training, specifically manifesting as clear and pure saliva. Also referred to as the Sweet Dew (*ganlu* 甘露) and White Snow (*baixue* 白雪).

Jade Pass (*yuguan* 玉關): Internal alchemy term that usually designates the upper pass (*shangguan* 上關), corresponding to the occiput. Used synonymously with Jade Capital (*yujing* 玉京) and Jade Pillow (*yuzhen* 玉枕).

Jade Pond (*yuchi* 玉池): The mouth as storehouse of the jade fluids (*yuye* 玉液). Alternatively referred to as the Celestial Pond (*tianchi* 天池).

Jinlian 金蓮: Gold Lotus. Alternate name for Quanzhen. Also the name of one of the early Shandong associations, namely, the Jinlian hui 金蓮會 (Association of Gold Lotus; Ninghai). In internal alchemy practice, refers to original spirit.

Kan-water ☵ (*kan* 坎): One of the eight trigrams derived from the *Yijing* 易經 (Classic of Changes). Consists of one yang-line inside of two yin-lines. In internal alchemy practice, symbolizes the vital essence and the kidneys. Paired with Li-fire, they exchange their middle lines to become Kun-earth and Qian-heaven, respectively. In that map, the middle line corresponds to qi in the kidneys.

Kun-earth ☷ (*kun* 坤): One of the eight trigrams derived from the *Yijing* 易經 (Classic of Changes). Consists of three yin-lines and corresponds to pure yin, here a positive condition. It may refer to the feet, the lower elixir field, or the perineum.

Kundao 坤道: Female Daoist ordinands. Literally means the "way of earth (women)." Used synonymously with *nüguan* 女冠 ("female cap"). May also designate women's Daoist practice, specifically female alchemy (*nüdan* 女丹).

Kunlun 崑崙: Mount Kunlun. Both a paradisiacal land of immortality and the body as locale of perfection. In the former sense, a western mountain overseen by Xiwangmu 西王母 (Queen Mother of the West), whose peaches of immortality come to fruition every thousand years or so. As a reference to the body, usually associated with a mystical cranial location, as well as with spirit and consciousness.

Kunyu shan 崑崳山: Mount Kunyu. Located on the Shandong eastern peninsula near Yantai and Weihai, this is the place where Wang Chongyang and his disciples established Yanxia dong 煙霞洞 (Cavern of Misty Vapors). This occurred in 1168, and Wang was accompanied by Ma Danyang, Qiu Changchun, Tan Changzhen, and Wang Yuyang. This was an intensive training period, during which Wang initiated a program of rigorous asceticism that included sleep deprivation, exposure to extreme heat and cold, scoldings, and beatings when their diligence faltered. Wang Chongyang also forced them to beg for alms in their hometowns.

Later Heaven (*houtian* 後天): Refers to postnatal influences and conditions. Also translated as "posterior heaven" and "deuterocosmic." Usually appears as *houtian qi* 後天氣, which is translated as "postnatal qi." Refers to sources of qi acquired after birth, specifically derived from food and breath. Contrasted with Prior Heaven (*xiantian* 先天).

lead (*qian* 鉛): Associated with original spirit (*yuanshen* 元神). Lead corresponds to innate nature, dragon, fire, and perfect yang. Usually paired with mercury (*hong* 汞).

leakage (*lou* 漏): Dissipation, especially the loss of vital essence and vitality through sensory engagement and sexual activity. Associated with the Buddhist technical term *āsrava*.

Li-fire ☲ (*li* 離): One of the eight trigrams derived from the *Yijing* 易經 (Classic of Changes). Consists of one yin-line inside of two yang-lines. In internal alchemy practice, symbolizes spirit and the heart. Paired with Kan-water, they exchange their middle lines to become Qian-heaven and Kun-earth, respectively. In that map, the middle line corresponds to fluids in the heart.

life-destiny (*ming* 命): One's foundational vitality and endowment from the Dao. Also translated as "fate." Associated with original qi (*yuanqi* 元氣). Life-destiny relates to one's core vitality and physicality, or corporeality more generally. Often paired with "innate nature" (*xing* 性).

lineage (*pai* 派): Master-disciple connections. Literally refers to a tributary. Poetically speaking, the Dao is the ocean, the Daoist tradition is the river leading one toward the Dao, and lineages are branches of that river with their own particular contours and pathways. Daoist lineages are most often associated with specific places, teachers, scriptures, and practices. In contemporary Quanzhen, there are ordination names derived from lineage-poems (*paishi* 派詩), as contained in the Quanzhen liturgy.

Liujiang 劉蔣: The site of Wang Chongyang's second hermitage and of a small Daoist eremitic community. Later renamed Zuting 祖庭 (Ancestral Hall) after Wang's death and interment there in 1170.

Longmen dong 龍門洞 (Dragon Gate Grotto): The place where Qiu Changchun engaged in intensive Daoist training at various times from 1181 to 1191. It is located near present-day Xinjichuan 新集川 and Longxian 隴縣, Shaanxi, and is the home to a small Quanzhen monastic community. It is considered the Zuting 祖庭 (Ancestral Hall) of the Longmen lineage.

Longmen pai 龍門派: Dragon Gate lineage. The Quanzhen lineage associated with Qiu Chuji 丘處機 (Changchun 長春 (Perpetual Spring); 1148–1227), but systematized by Wang Changyue 王常月 (Kunyang 崑陽 [Paradisiacal Yang]; 1594?–1680). The contemporary lineage places primary emphasis on precept study and application. It has the largest membership and its members hold most of the temple administrative and political positions throughout mainland China. In the modern world, there are nonmonastic Longmen organizations with only loose affiliations with the official lineage. The Longmen lineage exists, at least nominally, outside of mainland China in Australia, Canada, England, France, Hong Kong, Italy, Singapore, Taiwan, and the United States.

Louguan tai 樓觀臺: Lookout Tower Monastery. Mythologically speaking, the place where Laozi transmitted the *Daode jing* to Yin Xi, the Guardian of the Pass. Also the first Daoist monastery, established in the fifth century. Located in Zhouzhi, Shaanxi, Louguan tai remains an important Daoist sacred site. Currently controlled by Quanzhen.

Maiden (*chanü* 姹女): Symbolic name for the lungs or vital essence stored in the kidneys. The Maiden may also refer to the corporeal soul (*po* 魄) or original spirit (*yuanshen* 元神). Usually paired with the Child (*ying'er* 嬰兒).

Master-brother (*shi xiongdi* 師兄弟): Title of respect used to address or identify lineage-affiliated ordinands of the same generation (*dai* 代). This may include those ordained earlier ("elder brother"; *shixiong* 師兄) or later ("younger brother"; *shidi* 師弟) than one.

Master-father (*shifu* 師父): Title of respect used by lineage-affiliated ordinands to address and identify their master and teacher, specifically the person who initiated one.

Master-grandfather (*shiye* 師爺): Title of respect used by lineage-affiliated ordinands to address and identify their master's master, specifically the person who initiated one's master and transmitted the lineage that enabled one's ordination.

Master-uncle (*shi boshu* 師伯叔): Title of respect used by lineage-affiliated ordinands to address and identify ordinands of the same generation (*dai* 代) as their master, specifically those individuals who provide guidance for one's spiritual practice. This may include those ordained earlier ("elder uncle"; *shibo* 師伯) or later ("younger uncle"; *shishu* 師叔) than one's master.

Matron (*po* 婆): Symbolic name for the spleen and qi. Usually appears as Yellow Matron (*huangpo* 黃婆). Sometimes used as an alternative name for the Yellow Court (*huangting* 黃庭). Usually paired with the Gold Duke (*jingong* 金公), which is associated with the heart and spirit.

mercury (*hong* 汞): Associated with original qi (*yuanqi* 元氣). Mercury corresponds to life-destiny, tiger, water, and perfect yin. Usually paired with lead (*qian* 鉛).

meridians (*jing* 經 / *luo* 絡 / *mai* 脈): Subtle channels in the body through which qi circulates. Embedded in the larger organ-meridian networks. The standard system includes twelve primary meridians and eight extra channels. The latter, including the Governing, Conception, Belt, and Thrusting channels, are especially important in Daoist cultivation.

Metal (*jin* 金): As one of the Five Phases (*wuxing* 五行), Metal corresponds to the west, lungs, corporeal soul (*po* 魄), righteousness, and so forth. As "gold," the purest metal, symbolizes alchemical transformation.

Microcosmic Orbit. *See* Celestial Cycle.

monastery (*guan* 觀): A Daoist monastery. Literally meaning "observatory," it may also designate a temple. In Quanzhen contexts, a religious community adhering to a monastic way of life. In its contemporary expression, technically includes celibacy (no sex), sobriety (no intoxicants), and vegetarianism (no meat).

Mysterious Female (*xuanpin* 玄牝): Symbolic name for a variety of esoteric locations in the body. Originates in chapter 6 of the fourth-century BCE *Daode jing*. Most often refers to breath. May also designate the heart, kidneys, center of the head, original spirit, and so forth.

Mysterious Pass (*xuanguan* 玄關): Symbolic name for the location between the kidneys, the kidneys themselves, and the three elixir fields. Occasionally refers to the jaws.

Nine Cavities (*jiuqiao* 九竅): The nine entry-points to the body. The Seven Cavities (*qiqiao* 七竅), eyes, ears, nose, and mouth, plus the small intestine and large intestine, with the latter two terms suggesting the associated body openings of urethra and anus. Sometimes the former are referred to as the yin cavities (*yinqiao* 陰竅), while the latter are called the yang cavities (*yangqiao* 陽竅). The term appears in chapter 2 of the fourth- to second-century BCE *Zhuangzi* 莊子 (Book of Master Zhuang; DZ 670) and in section 1a of the sixth-century *Yinfu jing* 陰符經 (Scripture on the Hidden Talisman; DZ 31).

Nine Palaces (*jiugong* 九宮): Nine mystical cranial locations. In one list they include the Hall of Light (*mingtang* 明堂), Grotto Chamber (*dongfang* 洞房), Elixir Field (*dantian* 丹田), Flowing Pearl (*liuzhu* 流珠), Jade Thearch (*yudi* 玉帝), Celestial Court (*tianting* 天庭), Secret Perfection (*jizhen* 機真), Mysterious Elixir (*xuandan* 玄丹), and Great Sovereign (*taihuang gong* 太皇宮). Other lists mention the Ancestral Cavity (*zuqiao* 祖竅) and Mud-ball (Niwan 泥丸 [Nirvana]).

nonaction (*wuwei* 無爲): Effortless activity. Classical Daoist practice focusing on simplicity and minimalism. Living through necessity and beyond contrivance. Doing only what is essential.

nonleakage (*wulou* 無漏): Nondissipation. Literally meaning "without leakage," freedom from outflow. A state of energetic and physiological integrity, wherein one is sealed off from every possible source of dissipation (*lou* 漏; Skt.: *āsrava*).

ordination (*rudao* 入道; *rumen* 入門): The formal entry into a Daoist movement or lineage. Literally, "enter the Dao" or "enter the gate." Also referred to as *chuanshou* 傳授 or *shoudu* 授度. May involve public ordination ceremonies or private oral transmission. In Longmen, often referred to as *chuanjie* 傳戒 ("transmission of the precepts"), with the corresponding bestowal of the Longmen precept texts and ordination certificate (*jiedie* 戒牒). Historically speaking, there were various ordination systems with corresponding ranks. The late imperial Longmen standardization includes three ranks: (1) Wondrous Practice / Initial Perfection (lowest; *Chuzhen jie*); (2) Wondrous Virtue / Medium Ultimate (middle; *Zhongji jie*); and (3) Wondrous Dao / Celestial Immortality (highest; *Tianxian jie*).

ordination certificate (*dudie* 度牒): A document that confirms formal membership in the Daoist tradition. Usually a state-issued license and often available for purchase. In Longmen, with its emphasis on precepts, usually referred to as *jiedie* 戒牒 ("precept certificate"), which parallels the Zhengyi liturgical register (*lu* 籙). In contemporary mainland China, many Daoist monastics do not have formal ordination certificates. Rather, they are given identification cards, called *zhengming shu* 證明書, from the local Bureau of Religious Affairs and Daoist Association.

original qi (*yuanqi* 元氣): The qi bestowed by the cosmos. Sometimes used synonymously with "prenatal qi" (*xiantian qi* 先天氣), original qi refers to one's primal condition of energetic integration, beyond dissipation.

original yang (*yuanyang* 元陽): The pure numinous presence of the Dao contained in each being. Associated with innate nature, original spirit, the seed of immortality, and the immortal embryo.

palace (*gong* 宮): Technical designation for imperially recognized Daoist temples or monasteries. Only an emperor could confer the title *gong*.

Patriarch (*zuzong* 祖宗): In Quanzhen, refers to the leaders who were lineage-descendants of Wang Chongyang and then Qiu Changchun. The early succession is as follows: (1) Wang Chongyang; (2) Ma Danyang; (3) Qiu Changchun; (4) Yin Zhiping 尹志平 (Qinghe 清和; 1169–1251); (5) Li Zhichang 李志常 (Zhenchang 真常; 1193–1256); (6) Zhang Zhijing 張志敬 (Chengming 誠明; 1220–1270); (7) Wang Zhitan 王志坦 (1200–1272); and (8) Qi Zhicheng 祁志誠 (Dongming 洞明; 1219–1293). Sometimes Tan Changzhen is identified as the second Patriarch, and Liu Changsheng or Wang Yuyang is identified as the third. As an honorific title, Patriarch may also refer to the founder of specific lineages (e.g., Hao Guangning and Huashan).

Penglai 蓬萊: Penglai. Both a paradisiacal land of immortality and the body as locale of perfection. In the former sense, an eastern island paradise. As a reference to the body, usually associated with the lower elixir field.

perfect qi (*zhenqi* 真氣): A specific type of qi. Sometimes used synonymously with original and prenatal qi. Perfect qi may also designate the culmination of the qi production cycle in Chinese medicine or qi transmuted alchemically through *neidan* practice.

pine tree (*song* 松): A symbol of longevity.

pot (*hu* 壺): An alchemical vessel. In *neidan*, usually refers to the lower elixir field.

Prior Heaven (*xiantian* 先天): Refers to prenatal influences and conditions. Also translated as "anterior heaven" and "protocosmic." Usually appears as *xiantian qi* 先天氣, which is translated as "prenatal qi." Refers to sources of qi acquired before birth, specifically derived from one's ancestors and the cosmos.

qi of the Dao (*daoqi* 道炁): The numinous presence of the Dao. Manifested in Daoist lineages, scriptures, and realized adherents. The specific qi associated with the Dao in its primordial suchness and differentiation. Preserved and transmitted by the Daoist tradition.

Qian-heaven ☰ (*qian* 乾): One of the eight trigrams derived from the *Yijing* 易經 (Classic of Changes). Consists of three yang-lines and corresponds to pure yang. It may refer to the head and original spirit.

Quanzhen 全真: Complete Perfection. Alternatively translated as Complete Reality, Complete Realization, or Completion of Authenticity. The twelfth-century Daoist religious movement established by Wang Chongyang and its subsequent monastic order. Also refers to the culmination of Quanzhen training regimens. An ontological condition wherein one has attained complete alchemical transformation and immortality.

rabbit (*tu* 兔): Symbolic name for yang. Often appears as rabbit in the moon (*yuetu* 月兔), representing yang within yin. Usually paired with raven (*wu* 烏).

raven (*wu* 烏): Symbolic name for yin. Often appears as the raven in the sun (*riwu* 日烏), representing yin within yang. Usually paired with rabbit (*tu* 兔).

scripture (*jing* 經): A Daoist sacred text, technically referred to as *daojing* 道經. In other traditions, may be rendered as "classic" or *sūtra*. Historically speaking, Daoist scriptures are sacred texts written in classical Chinese using calligraphy, and most often transmitted in manuscripts. From a Daoist perspective, they are inspired or revealed. They are considered sacred emanations of the Dao and one of the external Three Treasures (*wai sanbao* 外三寶). Etymologically speaking, the character *jing* 經 is composed of *mi* 糸 ("silk") and *jing* 巠 ("well"). Threads and watercourses that form and re-form networks of connection. They connect the Daoist adherent to both the unnamable mystery that is the Dao and the Daoist tradition, the community of adepts that preceded one, as a historical and energetic continuum.

Seven Cavities (*qiqiao* 七竅): Seven sources of dissipation and disruption. Refers to the seven sensory openings in the human body, namely, eyes (2), ears (2), nose (2), and mouth (1). First mentioned in chapter 7 of the *Zhuangzi*. Also appears in the third-century *Huangting waijing jing* (DZ 332).

Seven Emotions (*qiqing* 七情): Seven harmful emotional states or patterns. Most often refers to pleasure (*xi* 喜), anger (*nu* 怒), worry (*you* 憂), thought (*si* 思), grief (*bei* 悲), fear (*kong* 恐), and fright (*jing* 驚).

Seven Perfected (*qizhen* 七真): Wang Chongyang's seven principal Shandong disciples. They are as follows: (1) Ma Yu 馬鈺 (Danyang 丹陽 [Elixir Yang]; 1123–1184), (2) Tan Chuduan 譚處端 (Changzhen 長真 [Perpetual Perfection]; 1123–1185), (3) Qiu Chuji 丘處機 (Changchun 長春 [Perpetual Spring]; 1148–1227), (4) Liu Chuxuan 劉處玄 (Changsheng 長生 [Perpetual Vitality]; 1147–1203), (5) Wang Chuyi 王處一 (Yuyang 玉陽 [Jade Yang]; 1142–1217), (6) Hao Datong 郝大通 (Guangning 廣寧 [Expansive Serenity]; 1140–1213), and (7) Sun Buer 孫不二 (Qingjing 清靜 [Clear Stillness]; 1119–1183). In later Quanzhen, there are seven lineages (*qipai* 七派) associated with these individuals: Huashan pai 華山派 with Hao, Longmen pai 龍門派 with Qiu, Nanwu pai 南無派 with Tan, Qingjing pai 清靜派 with Sun, Suishan pai 隨山派 with Liu, Yushan pai 遇山派 with Ma, and Yushan pai 崳山派 with Wang.

Seven Po (*qipo* 七魄): The seven corporeal souls or white-ghosts. In standardized medieval lists they are identified as follows: (1) Shigou 尸狗 (Corpse Dog), (2) Fushi 伏矢 (Concealed Arrow),

(3) Queyin 雀陰 (Sparrow Yin), (4) Tunzei 吞賊 (Seizing Thief), (5) Feidu 非毒 (Negative Poison); (6) Chuhui 除穢 (Oppressive Impurity), and (7) Choufei 臭肺 (Putrid Lungs). They exert negative and perverting influences on human beings. Sometimes understood to be actual malevolent entities; at other times interpreted as psychological influences and states.

Seven Treasures (*qibao* 七寶): Seven precious substances in the body. Vital essence (*jing* 精), blood (*xue* 血), subtle breath (*qi* 氣), marrow (*sui* 髓), the brain (*nao* 腦), kidneys (*shen* 腎), and heart (*xin* 心).

she 蛇: snake. Usually associated with qi, but sometimes refers to the heart and spirit. Often appears with the dragon (*long* 龍), which in this pairing relates to the kidneys and vital essence.

Six Desires (*liuyu* 六慾): Six harmful desires. Generated by the Six Roots (*liugen* 六根), namely the eyes, ears, nose, mouth, body, and mind or thinking. Appears in section 1b of the eighth-century *Qingjing jing* (Scripture on Clarity and Stillness; DZ 620). Alternatively referred to as the Six Thieves (*liuzei* 六賊).

Six Emotions (*liuqing* 六情): Six harmful emotional states or patterns. Usually identified as pleasure (*xi* 喜), anger (*nu* 怒), grief (*ai* 哀), happiness (*le* 樂), selfish love (*ai* 愛), and hatred (*wu* 惡).

Six Roots (*liugen* 六根): The six sense-organs and corresponding sensory activities. They are eyes/looking, ears/listening, nose/smelling, mouth/tasting, body/touching, and mind/thinking.

Six Thieves (*liuzei* 六賊): Six harmful sensory activities and corresponding desires. Associated with the Six Roots and Six Desires.

spark (*yidian* 一點): The seed of the divine. Often appears as "original yang" (*yuanyang* 元陽). The potential for mystical integration, numinous pervasion, and immortality actualized through religious training and *neidan* practice.

spirit pervasion (*shentong* 神通): A condition of mystical being wherein spirit becomes all-pervading and one becomes an embodiment of the Dao in its mysteriousness and numinosity. Alternatively rendered as "divine connection" or "sacred pervasion." Associated with the Buddhist technical term *siddhi*, numinous abilities or "supernatural"/"paranormal" powers. They include clairaudience, clairvoyance, knowledge of previous incarnations, self-directed reincarnation, and so forth.

square inch (*cunfang* 寸方): Symbolic name for the heart. Sometimes designates the lower elixir field.

Storied Tower (*zhonglou* 重樓): Symbolic name for the trachea. Also appears as Twelve-storied Tower (*shier zhonglou* 十二重樓).

stove (*lu* 爐). *See* furnace.

stove (*zao* 灶): An alchemical vessel. Used symbolically to refer to the lower elixir field.

suchness (*ziran* 自然): Being-so-of-itself. Literally, "self-so." Often translated as "spontaneity" or "naturalness." One's original state of cosmological integration. Being beyond contrivance, distortion, and fabrication. Often associated with the state of simplicity (*pu* 朴/樸), or the state of the "uncarved block." In the case of human beings, characterized by desirelessness (*wuyu* 無欲) and nonknowing (*wuzhi* 無知).

Sweet Dew (*ganlu* 甘露): Symbolic name for fluids produced during internal alchemy training, specifically manifesting as clear and pure saliva. Also referred to as the Jade Nectar (*yujiang* 玉漿) and White Snow (*baixue* 白雪).

Ten Demons (*shimo* 十魔): Ten malevolent entities, psychological states, or harmful behavior patterns. Also referred to as the Ten Demon Lords (*shi mojun* 十魔君), they are ten forms of temptation: (1) Demon of the Six Desires (*liuyu mo*六欲魔); (2) Demon of the Seven Emotions (*qiqing mo* 七情魔); (3) Demon of Wealth (*fumo*富魔); (4) Demon of Nobility (*guimo*貴魔); (5) Demon of Affection (*en'ai mo*恩愛魔); (6) Demon of Calamity (*zainan mo*災難魔); (7) Demon of Violence (*daobing mo*刀兵魔); (8) Demon of Sagely Excellence (*shengxian mo*聖賢魔); (9) Demon of Prostitute Pleasure (*zhile mo*妓樂魔); and (10) Demon of Women and Sex (*nüse mo*女色魔). Note that these focus on male Daoist practitioners.

terrestrial branches (*dizhi* 地支): One of the major symbol systems used in Chinese cosmology and time-measurement. Including the symbolic zodiac correspondences and their yin-yang associations, the twelve terrestrial branches are as follows: (1) *zi* 子 (rat/yang); (2) *chou* 丑 (ox/yin); (3) *yin* 寅 (tiger/yang); (4) *mao* 卯 (rabbit/yin); (5) *chen* 辰 (dragon/yang); (6) *si* 巳 (snake/yin); (7) *wu* 午 (horse/yang); (8) *wei* 未 (sheep/yin); (9) *shen* 申 (monkey/yang); (10) *you* 酉 (rooster/yin); (11) *xu* 戌 (dog/yang); and (12) *hai* 亥 (boar/yin). Also used to designate times of the day, which are associated with specific organs (*zangfu* 藏府): (1) *zi* (11 p.m.–1 a.m. / gall bladder); (2) *chou* (1 a.m.–3 a.m. / liver); (3) *yin* (3 a.m.–5 a.m. / lungs); (4) *mao* (5 a.m.–7 a.m. / large intestine); (5) *chen* (7 a.m.–9 a.m. / stomach); (6) *si* (9 a.m.–11 a.m. / spleen); (7) *wu* (11 a.m.–1 p.m. / heart); (8) *wei* (1 p.m.–3 p.m. / small intestine); (9) *shen* (3 p.m.–5 p.m. / bladder); (10) *you* (5 p.m.–7 p.m. / kidneys); (11) *xu* (7 p.m.–9 p.m. / pericardium); (12) *hai* (9 p.m.–11 p.m. / triple warmer). In internal alchemy (*neidan* 內丹), sometimes the correspondences are changed to the following: *zi* with Water/kidneys, *mao* with Wood/liver, *wu* with Fire/heart, and *you* with Metal/lungs. The terrestrial branches may also refer to energetic points along the body, beginning with the coccyx, moving up the back, around the crown-point, and down the front of the body: (1) *zi* (Huiyin 會陰 [Hundred Meetings]; CV-1), (2) *chou* (Weilü 尾閭 [Tailbone Gate]; GV-1), (3) *yin* (Mingmen 命門 [Gate of Life]; GV-4), (4) *mao* (Jiaji 夾脊 [Narrow Ridge]; GV-6), (5) *chen* (Zhiyang 至陽 [Utmost Yang]; GV-9; a.k.a. Difei 底肺 [Bottom of Lungs]), (6) *si* (Yuzhen 玉枕 [Jade Pillow]; GV-17), (7) *wu* (Baihui 百會 [Hundred Meetings]; GV-20), (8) *wei* (Mingtang 明堂 [Hall of Light]; GV-23), (9) *shen* (Yuhu 玉戶 [Jade Door]; CV-22; a.k.a. Tiantu 天突 [Celestial Chimney]), (10) *you* (Zigong 紫宮 [Purple Palace]; CV-19), (11) *xu* (Zhongting 中庭 [Central Court]; CV-16), and (12) *hai* (Qihai 氣海 [Ocean of Qi]; CV-6). Combined with the ten celestial stems (*tiangan* 天干), the twelve terrestrial branches are used to form the so-called sexegennial or sexagenary cycle, that is, designations for the sixty-year cycle.

Three Bodies (*sanshen* 三身): A Buddhist technical term (Skt.: *trikāya*). Refers to the threefold body or nature of a Buddha: the Dharmakāya (*zixing* 自性), Sambhogakāya (*shouyong* 受用), and Nirmānakāya (*bianhua* 變化), that is, the dharma-body (*fashen* 法身), bliss-body (*baoshen* 報身), and transformation-body (*huashen* 化身). These correspond to (1) the body of a Buddha in its essential nature; (2) the body of a Buddha received for his own use and enjoyment; and (3) the body of a Buddha by which he can appear in any form. There are various Daoist adaptations.

Three Carts (*sanche* 三車): The ox cart (*niuche* 牛車), deer cart (*luche* 鹿車), and ram cart (*yangche* 羊車). Borrowed from the famous Parable of the Burning House in the Buddhist *Lotus Sūtra* (chap.

3), in Buddhist usage they are synonymous with the Three Vehicles (*sansheng* 三乘), namely, that of the hearer or obedient disciple (Chin.: *shengwen* 聲聞; Skt.: Śrāvaka), that of the enlightenment for oneself (Chin.: *yuanjue* 緣覺; Skt.: Pratyeka-buddha), and that of the bodhisattva (Chin.: *pusa* 菩薩), or universal salvation. In internal alchemy (*neidan* 內丹) practice, the Three Carts most often refer to the passageways through the Three Passes (*sanguan* 三關), located approximately at the coccyx, mid-spine, and occiput. They have the following correspondences: (1) Yangche 羊車 (Ram Cart), located at Weilü 尾閭 (Tailbone Gate; GV-1), (2) Luche 鹿車 (Deer Cart), located at Jiaji 夾脊 (Narrow Ridge; GV-6), and (3) Niuche 牛車 (Ox Cart), located at Yuzhen 玉枕 (Jade Pillow; GV-17).

Three Death-bringers (*sanshi* 三尸): Three bio-spiritual parasites inhabiting the body. Alternatively rendered as Three Corpses and sometimes appearing as Three Worms (*sanchong* 三蟲). They reside in the three elixir fields (*san dantian* 三丹田), namely, Palace of Nirvana (*niwan gong* 泥丸宮; center of head), Vermilion Palace (*jianggong* 絳宮; heart region), and Ocean of Qi (*qihai* 氣海; lower abdomen). In standardized medieval lists they are identified as Peng Ju 彭琚 (upper), Peng Zhi 彭質 (middle), and Peng Jiao 彭矯 (lower). Thus, they are sometimes referred to as the "Three Pengs" (*sanpeng* 三彭). Alternative names include Qinggu 青古 (Blue Decrepitude; upper), Baigu 白姑 (White Hag; middle), and Xueshi 血尸 (Bloody Corpse; lower). They exert negative and perverting influences on human beings. In some systems, it is claimed that they ascend to the heavens on every *gengshen* 庚申 (fifty-seventh) day to report one's transgressions. Sometimes understood to be actual malevolent entities; at other times interpreted as psychological influences and states.

Three Defilements (*sanchen* 三塵): Three impurities of consciousness. Usually associated with external phenomena and sensory perception. May refer to the eyes, ears, and mouth. Possibly an alternate name for the Three Poisons (*sandu* 三毒).

Three Essentials (*sanyao* 三要): Usually refers to the eyes, ears, and mouth. Appears in the section 1a of the sixth-century *Yinfu jing* (DZ 31). Sometimes divided into the "internal Three Essentials" (*nei sanyao* 內三要) and "external Three Essentials" (*wai sanyao* 外三要). The former refers to vital essence (*jing* 精), subtle breath (*qi* 氣), and spirit (*shen* 神), and is thus an alternative name for the Three Treasures (*sanbao* 三寶). The latter refers to the eyes, ears, and mouth.

Three Fields (*santian* 三田): Three subtle locations in the body. Also appearing as three elixir fields (*san dantian* 三丹田). Most often refers to the Palace of Nirvana (*niwan gong* 泥丸宮; center of head), Vermilion Palace (*jianggong* 絳宮; heart region), and Ocean of Qi (*qihai* 氣海; abdominal region). Associated with the three basic stages of *neidan* practice and attainment: transforming vital essence to qi, qi to spirit, and spirit to emptiness.

Three Heavens (*santian* 三天): The three purity or clarity heavens. They are Taiqing 太清 (Great Clarity; lowest), Shangqing 上清 (Highest Clarity; middle), and Yuqing 玉清 (Jade Clarity; highest). Associated with the Three Purities (*sanqing* 三清).

Three Hun (*sanhun* 三魂): The three ethereal souls or cloud-ghosts. Associated with the liver, they are the yang and positive "souls." In standardized medieval lists they are identified as Shuangling 爽靈 (Lively Numen), Taiguang 台光 (Terrace Radiance), and Youjing 幽精 (Mysterious Essence). They are understood to be beneficial and enlivening spiritual presences in the body.

Three Islands (*sandao* 三島): Both paradisiacal lands of immortality and the body as locale of perfection. In the former sense, three eastern island paradises usually identified as Penglai 蓬萊, Fangzhang 方丈, and Yingzhou 瀛洲. Sometimes appears as the three islands of Penglai. As a technical *neidan* term, refers to the three elixir fields, with the head as the upper island, the heart as the middle island, and the kidneys as the lower island.

Three Numinosities (*sanling* 三靈): Possibly an alternate name for the Three Radiances or Three Purities. Also may refer to the three elixir fields.

Three Passes (*sanguan* 三關): Symbolic name for three locations along the spine, through which it is difficult to circulate qi. They are Tailbone Gate (*weilü* 尾閭; GV-1; the coccyx), Narrow Ridge (*jiaji* 夾脊; GV-6; mid-spine), and Jade Pillow (*yuzhen* 玉枕; GV-17; occiput). The latter is sometimes referred to as Jade Capital (*yujing* 玉京).

Three Pengs (*sanpeng* 三彭): Alternate name for the Three Death-bringers.

Three Poisons (*sandu* 三毒): Three harmful emotional states or sources of dissipation. In Buddhist technical usage, refers to greed (*tan* 貪), anger (*chen* 嗔), and ignorance (*chi* 痴). Sometimes refers to the body (*shen* 身), thinking (*yi* 意), and the mouth (*kou* 口). Also used synonymously with the Three Essentials (*sanyao* 三要), usually referring to eyes, ears, and mouth. Appears in section 1b of the eighth-century *Qingjing jing* (DZ 620).

Three Powers (*sancai* 三才): Heaven, earth, and humans. First appears in the *Yijing* and emphasized in the sixth-century *Yinfu jing* (DZ 31). Sometimes each primary power is associated with its own three powers: heaven (sun, moon, and stars), earth (the stems of *yi* 乙, *bing* 丙, and *ding* 丁), and humans (vital essence, qi, spirit).

Three Primes (*sanyuan* 三元): The Three Fields (*santian* 三田) or Three Purities (*sanqing* 三清).

Three Purities (*sanqing* 三清): The three primordial ethers of the cosmos anthropomorphized as old Chinese men. Sometimes identified as the "three high gods" of Quanzhen and contemporary Daoism. Some Daoists believe that they are deities with personal agency. Including their associated heavens they are as follows: Yuanshi tianzun 元始天尊 (Celestial Worthy of Original Beginning; highest) and Jade Clarity; Lingbao tianzun 靈寶天尊 (Celestial Worthy of Numinous Treasure; middle; on YSTZ's left) and Highest Clarity; and Daode tianzun 道德天尊 (Celestial Worthy of the Dao and Virtue; a.k.a. Lord Lao; lowest; on YSTZ's right) and Great Clarity. They also correspond to the external and internal Three Treasures: Dao/spirit, scriptures/qi, and masters / vital essence.

Three Radiances (*sanguang* 三光): Most often refers to the sun (*ri* 日), moon (*yue* 月), and stars (*xing* 星). May also designate vital essence (*jing* 精), subtle breath (*qi* 氣), and spirit (*shen* 神).

Three Realms (*sanjie* 三界): Three realms of existence and ontological conditions. Alternatively translated as Three Worlds. They are the realm of desire (*yujie* 欲界), the realm of form (*sejie* 色界), and the realm of formlessness (*wuse jie* 無色界).

Three Treasures (*sanbao* 三寶): Three precious substances in the body and in the Daoist religious community. The former are the "internal Three Treasures" (*nei sanbao* 內三寶) of vital essence, qi, and spirit. The latter are the "external Three Treasures" (*wai sanbao* 外三寶) of the Dao, scriptures, and masters/teachers.

Tiger (*hu* 虎): Tiger. Sometimes appearing as "white tiger" (*baihu* 白虎), and thus associated with the Metal phase, the west, and the lungs. Usually associated with qi and paired with the Dragon (*long* 龍).

transformative process (*zaohua* 造化). Also rendered as "creative transformation." Sometimes inaccurately translated as "Creator" or "creation." The cosmos as impersonal process, characterized by unending change. The Dao as manifested in the universe and nature.

tripod (*ding* 鼎). *See* cauldron.

turtle (*gui* 龜): A symbol of longevity.

Twelve Storied Tower (*shier zhonglou* 十二中樓): Symbolic name for the trachea.

Two Luminants (*erming* 二明): The sun and moon. In the human body, the left eye is the sun and the right eye is the moon.

vexation (*fannao* 煩惱): Pain, affliction, distress, worry, trouble, or whatever causes such conditions. *Fannao* is the Chinese translation of the Sanskrit *kleśa*. In Chinese Buddhism, *fannao* refers to delusions generated by desire and ignorance that disturb the mind. There are both basic and derivative forms of vexation. The six basic forms include covetousness (Chin.: *tan* 貪; Skt.: *rāga*), anger (Chin.: *chen* 嗔; Skt.: *pratigha*), ignorance (Chin.: *chi* 痴; Skt.: *mūdha*), arrogance (Chin.: *man* 慢; Skt.: *māna*), doubt (Chin.: *yi* 疑; Skt.: *vicikitsā*), and false views (Chin.: *jianwu* 見惡; Skt.: *dṛṣṭi*). One unifying concern is the poison of egotism.

Water (*shui* 水): One of the Five Phases (*wuxing* 五行). Water corresponds to winter, north, kidneys, vital essence, wisdom, and so forth. Used in the sense of perfect or true water (*zhenshui* 真水), it refers to original qi (*yuanqi* 元氣). Also associated with the Kan-water ☵ trigram.

Waterwheel (*heche* 河車): An internal alchemy practice in which one circulates qi through the Governing Vessel (perineum to upper lip) and the Conception Vessel (lower lip to perineum) in a continuous circuit. Alternatively referred to as the Celestial Cycle (*zhoutian* 周天; a.k.a. Microcosmic Orbit).

white (*bai* 白): Symbolic name for yang. Sometimes appears as white gold (*baijin* 白金). White is also the corresponding color of the lungs.

White Snow (*baixue* 白雪): Symbolic name for fluids produced during internal alchemy training, specifically manifesting as clear and pure saliva. Also referred to as the Jade Nectar (*yujiang* 玉漿) and Sweet Dew (*ganlu* 甘露).

Wood (*mu* 木): One of the Five Phases (*wuxing* 五行). Wood corresponds to spring, east, liver, ethereal soul (*hun* 魂), humaneness, and so forth.

white horse (*baima* 白馬): Symbolic name for vital essence. Used synonymously with white ox (*bainiu* 白牛). Sometimes refers to purified consciousness, to corralling the "horse-will" (*mayi* 馬意). Along with the "monkey-mind" (*yuanxin* 猿心), the latter refers to unrestrained desires and chaotic thinking.

Wudang pai 武當派: Wudang lineage. Modern Daoist lineage associated with Mount Wudang 武當 (near Shiyan, Hubei). At times associated with both the Quanzhen and Zhengyi movements.

Mythologically associated with Zhang Sanfeng 張三丰 (fl. fourteenth c.?) and the creation of the so-called "internal martial arts" (*neijia* 內家). Preliminary historical research indicates that the Wudang system of martial arts, which combines elements from Bagua zhang 八卦掌 (Eight Trigram Palm), Taiji quan 太極拳 (Yin-yang Boxing), and Xingyi quan 形意拳 (Form Intent Boxing), was not formed until the late nineteenth or early twentieth century. The Wudang lineage exists, at least nominally, outside of mainland China in Europe, Hong Kong, Taiwan, and the United States.

Wuwei qingjing 無爲清靜: Nonaction and Clear Stillness. An alternative name for the Quanzhen movement.

Xuanfeng 玄風: Mysterious Movement. An alternative name for the Quanzhen movement. Also translated as "mysterious winds" and "mysterious currents," in the sense of the numinous presence of the Dao manifesting in/as/through the world.

Yanxia dong 煙霞洞: Cavern of Misty Vapors. Located near Yantai and Weihai, this was the cave-hermitage in the Kunyu 崑崳 mountains where Wang Chongyang and some of his first-generation Shandong disciples trained during 1168. Today a small Quanzhen monastic community lives there, and the temple is currently being reconstructed.

yang-spirit (*yangshen* 陽神): The transcendent spirit formed through alchemical practice. Also referred to as the body-beyond-the-body (*shenwai shen* 身外身), immortal embryo (*xiantai* 仙胎), or spark (*yidian* 一點).

Yellow Court (*huangting* 黃庭): Symbolic name for the spleen or lower elixir field.

Yellow Sprouts (*huangya* 黃芽): Symbolic name for the numinous presence in the lower elixir field. Usually experienced as energetic fullness and warmth in *neidan* practice.

yin-ghosts (*yingui* 陰鬼): Dreamtime phantasms. They are the objects of sexual attraction that may lead to seminal emission in the case of male adepts, which is an acknowledged source of depletion in Daoism.

Zuting 祖庭: Ancestral Hall. In terms of early Quanzhen, refers to Chongyang gong 重陽宮 (Palace of Chongyang; present-day Huxian, Shaanxi), the location of the eremitic community of Liujiang 劉蔣 where Wang Chongyang engaged in religious praxis from 1163–1167 and where he was buried after his death in 1170. Considered the "ancestral hall" (*zuting* 祖庭) of the Quanzhen 全真 (Complete Perfection) movement. There are other *zuting* associated with Quanzhen in contemporary Longmen 龍門 (Dragon Gate). Louguan tai 樓觀臺 (Lookout Tower Monastery; Zhouzhi, Shaanxi) is considered the Ancestral Hall of Daoism, as it is where Laozi 老子 is believed to have transmitted the *Daode jing* 道德經 to Yin Xi 尹喜. Longmen dong 龍門洞 (Dragon Gate Grotto; near Longxian, Shaanxi) is considered the Ancestral Hall of Longmen, as it is where Qiu Changchun engaged in intensive training.

Appendix 2

Quanzhen Texts Translated in
The Way of Complete Perfection

Chinese Text	English Title	Catalogue #	Section Translated	Chapter
Chongyang lijiao shiwu lun 重陽立教十五論	Chongyang's Fifteen Discourses to Establish the Teachings	DZ 1233	Complete	3
Chuzhen jie 初真戒	Precepts of Initial Perfection	JY 292 / ZW 404	Complete	7
Dadan zhizhi 大丹直指	Direct Pointers to the Great Elixir	DZ 244	Complete	4
Danyang zhenren yulu 丹陽真人語錄	Discourse Record of Perfected Danyang	DZ 1057	Complete	2
Huangdi yinfu jing zhu 黃帝陰符經註	Commentary on the *Huangdi yinfu jing*	DZ 122	Complete	5
Jianwu ji 漸悟集	Anthology on Gradual Awakening	DZ 1142	2.9b–10a	1
Jin zhenren yulu 晉真人語錄	Discourse Record of Perfected Jin	DZ 1056	1a–4b	2
Jinlian zhengzong ji 金蓮正宗記	Record of the Orthodox Lineage of the Golden Lotus	DZ 173	2.1a–5.11b	6
Jinyu ji 金玉集	Anthology of Gold and Jade	DZ 1149	6.8b–9a, 10.19b–20a	1
Minghe yuyin 鳴鶴餘音	Lingering Overtones of the Calling Crane	DZ 1100	5.7a, 6.13a–17a	1
Panxi ji 磻溪集	Anthology from Panxi	DZ 1159	1.3ab, 4.13b–15a	1
Qingtian ge zhushi 青天歌註釋	Commentary on the "Qingtian ge"	DZ 137	Complete	5
Quanzhen ji 全真集	Anthology of Complete Perfection	DZ 1153	1.14a–16b, 1.18a–19a, 3.8b, 9.11b–12b	1
			10.20b–21a	2
Quanzhen qinggui 全真清規	Pure Regulations of Complete Perfection	DZ 1235	Complete	7
Quanzhen zuobo jiefa 全真坐鉢捷法	Practical Methods for the Sinking Bowl-clepsydra from Complete Perfection	DZ 1229	Complete	7
Taigu ji 太古集	Anthology of Taigu	DZ 1161	4.1a–8b	1
Taishang laojun shuo chang qingjing	Recitational Commentary on the *Taishang*			

jing songzhu 太上老君說常清靜經頌註 *laojun shuo chang qingjing jing*	DZ 974	Complete	5
Xianle ji 仙樂集 Anthology on Immortal Bliss	DZ 1141	2.1a–17a, 5.1a–20a	1
		2.18ab	3
Yunguang ji 雲光集 Anthology of Cloudlike Radiance	DZ 1152	3.19b, 3.20ab	1
Zhenxian zhizhi yulu 真仙直指語錄 Discourse Records and Direct Pointers of Perfected Immortals	DZ 1256	1.19a–22b	2
		1.8b–9b	3
Zhongnan shan Zuting xianzhen neizhuan 終南山祖庭仙真內傳 Esoteric Biographies of Immortals and Perfected of the Ancestral Hall of the Zhongnan Mountains	DZ 955	1.4a–5b, 1.5b–8a	6

Chinese Character Glossary

"Botang ji" 缽堂記
"Bu suanzi" 卜算子
"Changchun Qiu zhenren ji Xizhou daoyou shu" 長春丘真人寄西州道友書
"Chongzhen pian" 崇真篇
"Choutian" 抽添
"Chuzhen shijie" 初真十戒
"Danyang zhiyan" 丹陽直言
"Gaozi" 告子
"Guichao huan" 歸朝歡
"Hao Taigu zhenren yu[lu]" 郝太古真人語[錄]
"Huo siren mu" 活死人墓
"Jiaozhu Chongyang dijun zefa bang" 教主重陽蒂君責罰榜
"Jindan shi" 金丹詩
"Jindan zhengyan" 金丹證驗
"Lian dansha" 鍊丹砂
"Lun baguan jie" 論八關節
"Lun liutong jue" 論六通訣
"Lun monan" 論魔難
"Lun zhengyan" 論證驗
"Manting fang" 滿庭芳
"Qianhong" 鉛汞
"Qingtian ge" 青天歌
"Sanfa song" 三法頌
"Siqi diaoshen lun" 四氣調神論
"Tiandao" 天道
"Tongzhenzi mijie ming" 通真子慕碣銘
"Wang Haifeng lingwei" 王害風靈位
"Wu Nanke" 悟南柯
"Wuzhen ge" 悟真歌
"Xiaoyao you" 逍遙遊
"Xuanming wenjing tianle zhenren Ligong daoxing ming" 玄明文靖天樂真人李公道行銘
"Yaotai diyi ceng" 瑤臺第一層
"Yu meiren" 虞美人
"Yuhua she shu" 玉華社疏

383

"Zhongyong" 中庸
"Zhuzhang ge" 竹杖歌
"Zuixian ling" 醉仙令
an 庵/菴
ango 安居
Anle yuan 安樂園
Anxian ji 安閑集
bagua bo 八卦鉢
Bagua zhang 八卦掌
Bai Yuchan 白玉蟾
Baigu 白姑
Baihui 百會
Baiyun guan 白雲觀
Baizhang qinggui 百丈清規
baizhi 白芷
baji 八極
ban 板
banan 八難
bangmen 傍門
Baochan 寶蟾
Baoguang tang 葆光堂
Baopuzi 抱朴子
Baopuzi neipian 抱朴子內篇
Baoxuan tang 寶玄堂
baoyi 抱一
baoyi 抱元
bashi 八識
Baxian gong 八仙宮
bayu 八欲
Beidi 北帝
Beidou zhenjing 北斗真經
Beidou zhou 北斗咒
ben 本
benlai mianmu 本來面目
bi qi men 閉其門
bianhua 變化
Bianliang 汴梁
biaobiao 表標
bigu 辟穀
bin 賓
bing 丙
binzhu 賓主
Biyan lu 碧嚴錄
Biyuan tanjing 碧苑壇經

Bo 剝
bo 鉢
bo 鉢
Bojian 鉢鑑
bopi 柏皮
botang 鉢堂
Boyu 伯玉
Bozhou 亳州
bozhu 鉢主
Buer 不二
Buer yuanjun fayu 孫不二元君法語
Buliangyi 卜梁倚
buxiu 不修
buyu xiansheng 不語先生
Cai Zhiyi 蔡志頤
canghai sangtian 滄海桑田
cangtou 藏頭
cangtou chaizi 拆字藏頭
Cantong qi 參同契
Cao 曹
Cao Tian 曹填
Cao Zhen 曹瑱
chaixi 拆洗
chan 懺
Changchun gong 長春宮
Changchun yandao zhujiao zhenren 長春演道主教真人
Changchun zhenren xiyou ji 長春真人西遊記
Changchun 長春
Changmei 長眉
Changqing 長清
changsheng bulao 長生不老
changsheng busi 長生不死
Changsheng 長生
Changsong dao 長松島
Changwuzi 長梧子
Changyang 昌陽
Changyue 常月
Changzhen 長真
chanhui 懺悔
chanü 妊女
Chanyuan qinggui 禪院清規
chaolie dafu 朝列大夫
Chaotian fachan 朝天法懺
Chaoyuan gong 朝元宮

Chaoyuan guan 朝元觀
chen辰
Chen Mingbin 陳明霦
Chen Shi 陳寔
Chen Tuan 陳摶
Chen Yuan 陳垣
Chen Zhixu 陳致虛
Cheng'an 承安
Chengdao ji 成道集
Chengjisi 成吉思
chenhuo 臣火
chenling 臣靈
Chicheng shan 赤城山
chijie 持戒
chijin 遲金
Chisong 赤松
Chongxu 沖虛
Chongyang 重陽
Chongyang gong 重陽宮
Chongyang hui 重陽會
chongyang jie 重陽節
Chongyang lijiao shiwu lun 重陽立教十五論
Chongyang zhenren jinguan yusuo jue 重陽真人金關玉鎖訣
Chongyang zhenren shou Danyang ershisi jue 重陽真人授丹陽二十四訣
Chongzhen 崇禎
Chongzhen崇真
chou 丑
Choufei 臭肺
chouqian抽鉛
choutian 抽添
Chu sanshi jiuchong jing 除三尸九蟲經
Chuandao ji 傳道集
chuangkang 床炕
Chuanlu 傳盧
chuanshi 傳師
Chuchang 處常
Chuduan 處端
Chuhou處厚
Chuhui 除穢
chuiding 垂頂
chuiling 垂領
Chuji 處機
chujia 出家
Chun Yufen 淳于棼

chunguang 春光
chunran 蠢然
Chunyang 純陽
Chushun tang 處順堂
Chuxuan 處玄
Chuyi 處一
chuzhen 初真
Chuzhen jie 初真戒
Chuzhen shijie wen 初真十戒文
ci 詞
cipai 詞牌
Congyi 從義
cun 寸
Cunshen lianqi ming 存神鍊氣銘
Dacheng ji 大成集
Dadan zhizhi 大丹直指
dadao qingxin dizi 大道清信弟子
Dading 大定
Daizhou 埭州
dajue 大覺
Daluo tian 大羅天
Daluo 大羅
dan 單
danshu 丹書
Danyang 丹陽
Danyang zhenren yulu 丹陽真人語錄
Danyang zhiyan 丹陽直言
dao 道
daochang 道常
Daode jing songzhu 道德經頌註
Daode jing 道德經
Daode tianzun 道德天尊
Daode zhenjing zhu 道德真經註
Daofeng 道風
daogui 刀圭
daohao 道號
Daojia jinshi lue 道家金石略
Daojian 道堅
Daojiao hui 道教會
Daojiao yifan 道教儀範
daojing 道經
Daolu si 道錄司
daonian 道念
daoqi 道氣

daoqi 道炁
daoshi 道士
Daoshu shier zhong 道書十二種
Daoshu 道樞
Daoxian 道顯
daoxing 道性
Daoxuan pian 道玄篇
daoyan 道眼
Daoyin 導引
daoyou 道友
Daoyuan 道淵
Daozang 道藏
Daozang tiyao 道藏提要
Daozang xubian 道藏續編
dashu 大署
Datong ji 大同集
Datong jing 大通經
dawu 大悟
de 德
Deng 鄧
Deng Xiaoping 鄧小平
Dengzhou 鄧州
Deqing 德清
Dewei 德威
Dexing 德興
Di 帝
diandao 顛倒
diehua 蝶化
diemeng 蝶夢
dienang 牒囊
Difei 地肺
dijun 帝君
ding 丁
ding 定
dinggong 丁公
Dinghu 鼎湖
dingning 丁寧
dingweng 丁翁
dingxin 定心
dizhi 地支
dokusan 独參
donggong 動功
Donggu jing 洞古經
Donghai 東海

Donghua an 東華庵
Donghua dijun東華帝君
Donglai 東萊
Dongmu 東牟
dongpai 動牌
dongshen 洞神
*Dongxuan lingbao changye zhi fu jiuyou yugui mingzhen ke*洞玄靈寶長夜之府九幽玉匱明真科
Dongxuan lingbao wugan wen 洞玄靈寶五感文
dongxuan 洞玄
Dongyang 洞陽
dongyi 洞衣
Dongzhen 洞真
dongzhen 洞真
Dongzhou 東州
dou 斗
Doujing 斗經
douxiu 斗宿
du 度
duan 端
dudie度牒
dujian 都監
Duren jing 度人經
e 惡
Eihei Dōgen 永平道元
en 恩
ershisi jie 二十四節
ertu 二土
Erxian an 二仙庵
eryi 二儀
fa 法
faming 法名
Fan Mingshu 范明叔
Fan Yi 范懌
Fan Yuanxi 范圓曦
fang 方
fangbian 方便
fangcun 方寸
fangzhang 方丈
fangzhong shu 房中術
fannao 煩惱
fanzhao 返照
fashen法身
fatang 法堂
Feidu 非毒

fen 分
Feng 馮
Feng Bi 馮璧
Feng Changquan 馮長筌
Feng Xiangu 風仙姑
Feng Zhiheng 馮志亨
Fengdao kejie 奉道科戒
Fengdu 酆都
Fengxiang 鳳翔
Fenli shihua ji 分梨十化集
fenli 分梨
fenli 分離
fenshen 焚身
fou 缶
fu 復
fu 符
Fu Xi 伏羲
fubo 副鉢
Fuchun 富春
Fushan 福山
Fushi 伏矢
Gabyō 畫餅
Gan 甘
Gangu 甘谷
Ganhe 甘河
Ganquan 甘泉
Ganshui xianyuan lu 甘水仙源錄
Gao Daokuan 高道寬
Gao Jucai 高巨才
Gao Yuanming 高圓明
gaomu xing 槁木形
Gaoshang 高尚
ge 歌
Ge Hong 葛洪
Ge Xuan 葛玄
gen 根
Gen 艮
geng 庚
geng 更
gengjia 庚甲
gengshen 更申
gengxin 庚辛
Geshilie 紇石烈
Geshilie Zhizhong 紇石烈執中

Gong Daosheng 龔道昇

gong 功

gong'an 公案

gongke 功課

Gongmi 公密

Gongsun Xuanyuan 公孫軒轅

Gou 姤

Gouqu shan 句曲山

gu 瞽

gu 鼓

Gu Shuyin lou cangshu 古書隱樓藏書

guan 觀

guan kong yi kong, kong wusuo kong; suo kong ji wu, wuwu yi wu 空亦空空，空無所空；所空既無，無無亦無

Guangcheng 廣成

Guangchengzi 廣成子

Guangning 廣寧

Guangningzi 廣寧子

Guanshen dajie 觀身大戒

Guanyinzi 關尹子

guanzhong 關中

Guanzhong 關中

gugua 孤寡

gui 圭

gui 癸

gui 龜

guigen 歸根

guilu 鬼錄

guiqi 鬼氣

Guo Fengxin 郭奉信

Guo Fuzhong 郭復中

gushen 谷神

gushu 古書

hai 亥

Haichan 海蟾

haifeng 害風

Hailing wang 海陵王

Han 韓

Han Daoxi 韓道熙

Han Tao 韓淘

Hanchi 寒池

Hangu 函谷

hanshen 歛身

hao 號

Hao 豪
Hao Datong 郝大通
Hao Guangning 郝廣寧
Hao lixiang 好離鄉
Hao Taigu 郝太古
He 何
He Daoquan 何道全
He Dejin和德瑾
He Yuchan 和玉蟾
heche 河車
Hefu 和甫
hongmeng 鴻蒙
hong汞
hou 猴
houtian qi 後天氣
houtian 後天
hu 虎
Hu 鄂
Hu Shahu 胡沙虎
huachi 華池
huagai華蓋
huandu環堵
Huang Zutai 黃祖太
huangbai 黃白
Huangdi 黃帝
Huangdi neijing suwen 黃帝內徑素問
*Huangdi yinfu jing zhu*黃帝陰符經註
huanghu zhi miao 恍惚之妙
Huang-Lao 黃老
huangpo 黃婆
Huangting jing 黃庭經
Huangxian 黃縣
huantang 環堂
Huanzhen ji 還真集
Huashan 華山
Huashu 化書
Huasou 華叟
Huating 華亭
Huayang 華陽
Huayin 華陰
Hugong 壺公
hui 慧
hui諱
Huiguang an 回光庵

huiguo 悔過
Huizi 惠子
hun 昏
hun 魂
hunhun dundun 混混沌沌
hunhun momo 昏昏默默
Hunran 混然
Hunyuan 混元
hunzuo 混坐
Huo siren mu 活死人墓
huohou 火候
Huxian 戶縣
Huzi 壺子
ji 吉
ji 己
ji 機
ji 記
ji 跡
ji 集
ji 雞
jia 家
jia 甲
jiafeng 家風
jiafu 跏趺
jiaji 夾脊
Jiang Sheng 姜生
Jiang Xi 姜禧
jiangchan 講懺
jianggong 絳宮
jiangque 絳闕
jiangxin 降心
jianjie dashi 監戒大師
jianshi 監師
Jianwu ji 漸悟集
jianxing 見性
jianyuan 監院
jiao 教
jiao 醮
jiaodian 教典
jiaose 腳色
jiaozhong zuiren 教中罪人
jiashi 家師
jiayi 甲乙
jiazi 甲子

jie 戒
Jie Dongbo 借東坡
jiechi 戒尺
jiedie 戒牒
jiefa 戒法
jiehui zhou 解悔咒
jielü 戒律
jietan 戒壇
Jin Chongzhen 晉崇真
Jin Daocheng 晉道成
Jin zhenren yulu 晉真人語錄
jin 斤
jin 金
Jinan 濟南
Jindan xianpai 金丹仙派
jindan 金丹
jing 巠
jing 經
Jingang jing 金剛經
Jingde chuandeng lu 景德傳燈錄
Jingge yuan 經閣院
jinggong 靜功
jingjin 淨巾
Jingluo 京洛
Jingming 淨明
jingong 金公
jingpai 靜牌
jingshi 淨室
jingshi 經師
jingshi 靜師
jingshui ping 淨水瓶
Jinguan yusuo jue 金關玉鎖訣
Jingwei ji 精微集
jingxue 經學
jingyi 淨衣
Jingzhao 京兆
jingzuo 靜坐
jinhu 金戶
jinjia 金枷
Jinlian hui 金蓮會
Jinlian tang 金蓮堂
Jinlian xiangzhuan 金蓮像傳
Jinlian zhengzong ji 金蓮正宗記
Jinlian 金蓮

Jinling daoren 金陵道人
Jinlun 金輪
jinque 金闕
Jinshan 金山
Jinyu an 金玉庵
Jinyu ji 金玉集
jitu 己土
Jiugong shan 九宮山
jiuhuan 九還
Jiuke jing jie 救苦經解
jiuliu 九流
jiuqi 九氣
jiuqiao 九竅
jiuxing 九行
jiuxing 九星
Jiyang 濟陽
Jizhen guan 集真觀
Jue 覺
jue 訣
jueju 絕句
jueyue 訣曰
Junyi 濬儀
kaijing shi 開靜時
Kangchan 康禪
ke 刻
keisaku/kyosaku 警策
Kongtong 崆峒
Kongxian an 孔仙庵
Kongzi 孔子
koujue 口訣
Kun 坤
kundao 坤道
Kunming 昆明
Kunyang 崑陽
Kunyu shan 崑崙山
Kunyu wenji 崑崙文集
Kunyu 崑崙
Kuocang shan 括蒼山
La 臘
Lai Lingyu 來靈玉
Laizhou 萊州
Lanao 嵐皋
Langran 郎然
Languan 嵐管

Langye 瑯琊
Langyuan gong 閬苑宮
Lanyun 懶雲
Laojun yibai bashi jie 老君一百八十戒
Laojun 老君
Laoshan 嶗山
Laozi bashiyi hua tu 老子八十一化圖
Laozi zhangju 老子章句
Laozi 老子
Ledao 樂道
Leigong miao 雷公廟
Leiting yushu youzui fachan 雷霆玉樞宥罪法懺
Lequan ji 樂全集
Li Bai 李白
Li Changling 李昌齡
Li Daochun 李道純
Li Daoqian 李道謙
Li Dasheng 李大乘
Li Hefu 李和甫
Li Lingyang 李靈陽
Li Quan 李筌
Li Wumeng 李無夢
Li Yingchan 李瑩蟾
Li Zhenchang 李真常
Li Zhichang 李志常
liandu 煉度
liang 兩
Liangyuan 梁園
lianshen 斂身
Liaoyang 遼陽
Liaozhen tang 了真堂
Liaozhen 了真
libu 禮部
Liezi 列子
Liji 禮記
Lijiao shiwu lun 立教十五論
Lin 璘
ling 令
ling 鈴
ling 靈
Lingbao dachan 靈寶大懺
Lingbao tianzun 靈寶天尊
Lingbao 靈寶
linggong 靈宮

Lingxu guan 靈虛觀
Lingxu 靈虛
Lingyang 靈陽
Lingye 靈液
Lingyin 靈隱
Linquan ji 林泉集
Linwu shan 林屋山
Liquan 醴泉
Liu 劉
liu 流
Liu Biangong 劉卞功
Liu Cao 劉操
Liu Changsheng 劉長生
Liu Chengyin 劉誠印
Liu Chuanlu 柳傳盧
Liu Chuxuan 劉處玄
Liu Gaoshang 劉高尚
Liu Haichan 劉海蟬
Liu Huayang 柳華陽
Liu Jin 劉進
Liu Langran 劉郎然
Liu Moran 劉默然
Liu Qi 劉祁
Liu Qing 劉清
Liu Shaozu 劉紹祖
Liu Suyun 劉素雲
Liu Tongwei 劉通微
Liu Wuyuan 劉悟元
Liu Xiyue 劉希岳
Liu Yiming 劉一明
Liu Zhenyi 劉真一
Liu Zhonglu 劉仲祿
liudao 六道
liuding 六丁
liuhe 六合
liujia 六甲
Liujiang 劉蔣
liutong 六通
Liyang 櫟陽
long 龍
Longmen 龍門
Longmen dong 龍門洞
Longmen xinfa 龍門心法
Longquan 龍泉

Longshan 隴山
Longxian 隴縣
Longxing si 龍興寺
Longyang guan 龍陽觀
Louguan tai 樓觀臺
Louguan 樓觀
lu 錄
Lu 陸
Lu Daohe 陸道和
Lü Dongbin 呂洞賓
Lu Tongxuan 陸通玄
lü 律
Lü 旅
Lu'an 潞安
Luanwu 欒武
Lügong zhuan 呂公傳
luhuo 爐火
lüjia 律家
lun 論
Lunyu 論語
Luo 洛
Luofu shan 羅浮山
Luojing 洛京
Luoyang 洛陽
lüpai 律派
lüqi 驢契
lüshi 律師
lüshi 律詩
ma 馬
Ma Congshi 馬從仕
Ma Danyang 馬丹陽
Ma Gu 麻姑
Ma Xuanfu 馬宣甫
Ma Yu 馬鈺
Magu 麻姑
mai 脈
mangxie 芒鞋
mao 卯
maojin 卯金
Mengyun 蒙允
Mengzi 孟子
mi 糸
miao 妙
miaodao shi 妙道師

miaode shi 妙德師
miaoxing shi 妙行師
Min Lanyun 閔懶雲
Min Yide 閔一得
Min Yuxi 閔玉溪
Min Zhiting 閔智亭
ming 冥
ming 名
ming 命
ming 明
Mingchang 明昌
Mingdao ji 鳴道集
Minghe yuyin 鳴鶴餘音
Mingmen 命門
mingming yaoyao 冥冥杳杳
Mingzhen ke 明真科
minhuo 民火
miyu wupian 秘語五篇
mo 默
mojun 魔君
Moran 默然
mozhao 默照
mozuo 默坐
mu 木
Muping 牟平
Nanbo Zikui 南伯子葵
Nanhua jing 南華經
Nanhua zhenjing 南華真經
Nanjing 南京
Nanguo Ziqi 南郭子綦
Nanke 南柯
Nanshi 南時
Nanyang 南陽
Nanzong 南宗
Nei riyong jing 內日用經
nei riyong 內日用
Neidan jiyao 內丹集要
neidan 內丹
neiguan 內觀
Neijing tu 內經圖
neijing 內境
neijing 內景
ni 逆
Niejia 聶家

Nilong Kuqin 尼龍窟親
Nimanggu wujie 尼庞古武節
Ninghai 寧海
niwan gong 泥丸宮
niwan 泥丸
Nü jindan fayao 女金丹法要
Nüdan hebian 女丹合編
nüdan 女丹
nüguan 女冠
Nüqing guilü 女青鬼律
Nüqing 女青
Nüyu 女偊
pai 派
pai 牌
paiming 派名
paishi 派詩
Pan 潘
Panshan Qiyun Wang zhenren yulu 盤山棲雲王真人語錄
panxi 盤膝
Panxi 磻溪
Panxi ji 磻溪集
Panyang ji 盤陽集
panzuo 盤坐
Peng Ju 彭琚
Peng Zhi 彭質
Peng Zhizhong 彭致中
Penghu 蓬壺
Penglai 蓬萊
Penglai zhai 蓬萊宅
Pi 否
Pingdeng hui 平等會
Piyun 披雲
po 魄
pu 僕
pu 朴
pudu 普度
putian jiao 普天醮
qian 乾
qian 鉛
Qianzhou 乾州
qiao 巧
qiao 竅
Qibao an 七寶庵
Qibao hui 七寶會

qifan 七返

Qihai 氣海

Qi-Lu 齊魯

Qin Shuli 秦樗櫟

Qin Zhian 秦志安

qin 琴

qing 情

Qing'an Yingchanzi yulu 清庵瑩蟾語錄

qingce 青冊

Qingcheng shan 青城山

Qingfeng 清風

Qingfu 清甫

Qinggu 青古

qinggui 清規

Qinggui xuanmiao 清規玄妙

Qinghe 清和

Qinghe zhenren beiyou yulu 清和真人北遊語錄

qingjing 清靜

Qingjing jing 清靜經

Qingjing sanren 清靜散人

qingjing wuwei xiaoyao zizai buran buzhuo 清靜無爲逍遙自在不染不着

Qingshe 青社

Qingtian ge zhushi 青天歌註釋

Qingyang gong 青羊宮

Qingyun 輕雲

Qingzhen ji 清真集

Qinzhou 秦州

qipo 七魄

Qiu Changchun 丘長春

Qiu Chuji 丘處機

Qiuzu quanshu jieji 丘祖全書節輯

Qixia 栖霞

Qiyu an 契遇庵

Qiyun 棲雲

qizhen 七真

Qizhen dian 七真殿

Qizhen nianpu 七真年譜

Qizhen xianzhuan 七真仙傳

qu 曲

quan 犬

Quandao ji 全道集

Quanshi 泉石

Quanzhen 全真

Quanzhen an 全真庵

Quanzhen ji 全真集
Quanzhen qinggui 全真清規
Quanzhen tang 全真堂
Quanzhen yaodao 全真要道
Quanzhen zaowan tan gongke 全真早晚壇功課
Quanzhen zongyan fangwai xuanyan 全真宗眼方外玄言
Quanzhen zuobo jiefa 全真坐鉢捷法
quegu 卻穀
queqiao 鵲橋
Queyin 雀陰
Qunxian ji 群仙集
Qunxian yaoyu zuanji 群仙要語纂集
Ququezi 瞿鵲子
ren 人
Ren 仁
ren 仁
Ren 任
ren 壬
Ren Farong 任法融
Ren Shouyi 任守一
Renfeng 任風
Renfengzi 任風子
renxian 人仙
ri 日
ribiao 日表
riyong 日用
rouruo 柔弱
ru zhendao 入真道
rudao 入道
rujing 入靜
rumen 入門
Ruyao jing zhu 入藥鏡註
san 傘
san guiyi 三皈依
sanbao 三寶
Sanbao ji 三寶集
sancai 三才
sanche 三車
sanchong 三蟲
Sanchong zhongjing 三蟲中經
sancun 三寸
sandan 三丹
sandong 三洞
Sandong fafu kejie wen 三洞法服科戒文

Sandong zhongjie wen 三洞中戒文
sandu 三毒
sanfan 三返
sanguan 三官
sanguan 三關
Sanguang hui 三光會
Sanhuang 三皇
sanhuo 三火
sanjiao 三教
Sanjiao ruyi lun 三教入易論
sanming 三命
sanpeng 三彭
sanqi 三奇
Sanqing 三清
sanqing 三清
Sanquan 三泉
sanshen 三身
sanshi 三尸
Santian yisui 三天易髓
santian 三天
sanxin 三心
sanyao 三要
sanyuan 三元
seshen 色身
sesshin 接心/攝心
shan 善
Shandong daojiao zhi 山東道教志
shangde 上德
Shangdi 上帝
shangdong 上洞
Shanghe 商河
Shangqing 上清
Shangqing gong 上清宮
Shangqing taixuan jiuyang tu 上清太玄九陽圖
Shangyang 上陽
shangyuan 上元
shanshu 善書
Shao Yong 邵雍
she 蛇
sheli 舍利
sheling 舍靈
shen 申
shen 神
shen 身

Shen Qingyun 沈輕雲
Shen Yibing 沈一炳
sheng 升
Sheng 昇
shengchuang 繩床
shengjing 聖經
Shengshui dong 聖水洞
Shenguang ji 神光集
Shengxuan huming jing 昇玄護命經
Shengxuan huming jing zhu 昇玄護命經註
Shennong 神農
shenren 神人
shentong 神通
shenwai shen 身外身
Shenxian zhuan 神仙傳
shi 世
Shi 史
shi 失
shi 時
Shi Chuhou 史處厚
Shi Dongyang 史洞陽
Shi Feng 史風
Shi Fengzi 史風子
Shi Huayang 施華陽
Shi Jianwu 施肩吾
Shi Zhijing 石志經
shiba jie 十八戒
shi'e 十惡
shifang 十方
shifu 師父
Shigou 尸狗
shiji 示疾
shiji 示寂
Shijiao zhiyan 示教直言
shijie xian 尸解仙
shiquan 十勸
shishu 師叔
Shixiong 世雄
shixiong 師兄
Shiyang 師揚
shiye 師爺
Shizong 世宗
Shizu 世祖
Shōbōgenzō 正法眼藏

shouyi 守一
shouyin 手印
shu 術
shui 水
shuihuo水火
shuimo 睡魔
Shuinan 水南
Shuiyun ji 水雲集
shuji 樞機
Shuli 樗櫟
Shun 順
Shunzhi 順治
shuoqi 朔氣
si 巳
si er buwang zhe shou 死而不亡者壽
sida 四大
sida 四達
sifei 四非
sihai 四害
sihui xin死灰心
sima 緦麻
Sima Chengzhen 司馬承禎
siming zhou 四溟咒
sishi四時
sishu 四書
sitian 四天
sixiang 四相
sixin 死心
Song Bo 宋渤
Song Defang 宋德方
Song Piyun 宋披雲
sugu 宿骨
Suiji yinghua ji 隨機應化錄
Sun Buer 孫不二
*Sun Buer nüdan shi zhu*孫不二女丹詩註
*Sun Buer yuanjun chuanshu dandao bishu*孫不二元君傳述丹道秘書
Sun Buer yuanjun fayu 孫不二元君法語
Sun Buer yuanjun gongfu cidi 孫不二元君功夫次第
Sun Qingjing 孫清靜
Sun Simiao 孫思邈
Sun Xiangu 孫仙姑
Sun Yuanzhen 孫瑗禎
Sun Zhongyi 孫忠翊
sushi 宿世

Suyun 素雲
Tai 泰
Taichu 太初
Taigu 太古
Taigu daoren 太古道人
Taigu ji 太古集
Taiji 太基
taiji 太極
Taiji quan 太極拳
Taiping 太平
Taiping xingguo 太平興國
Taiqing 太清
Taiqing gong 太清宮
Taishan 太山
taishang 太上
Taishang chiwen donggu jing 太上赤文洞古經
Taishang dongxuan lingbao tianzun datong jing 太上洞玄靈寶天尊說大通經
太上洞玄靈寶天尊說大通經
Taishang ganying pian 太上感應篇
Taishang laojun jiejing 太上老君戒經
Taishang laojun nei riyong miaojing 太上老君內日用妙經
Taishang laojun shuo chang qingjing jing songzhu 太上老君說常清靜經頌註
Taishang laojun shuo chang qingjing miaojing 太上老君說常清靜妙經
Taishang laojun wai riyong miaojing 太上老君外日用妙經
Taishang lingbao chaotian xiezui dachan 太上靈寶朝天謝罪大懺
Taishang xuanling beidou benming yansheng zhenjing 太上玄靈北斗本命延生真經
taishi 太始
Taixu guan 太虛觀
Taixu ji 太虛集
Taiye chi 太液池
taiyi 太乙
Tan 譚
Tan Changzhen 譚長真
Tan Chuduan 譚處端
Tang Chun 唐淳
Tanzi 譚子
Tao Hongjing 陶弘景
Tao Qian 陶潛
Taoguang ji 韜光集
taopi 桃皮
Tianchan 天懺
Tianchang guan 天長觀
tiandao 天道
tiandi gen 天地根

tianhong 添汞
Tianhuang zhidao yuce 天皇至道太清玉冊
tianji 天機
tianmen 天門
tianqing 天清
Tianran 恬然
tianxian 天仙
Tianxin 天心
Tianxian jie 天仙戒
tianxing 天行
Tianzhen huangren 天真皇人
Tiecha shan 鐵槎山
tiejiao xiansheng 鐵腳先生
Tixuan dashi 體玄大師
tong 通
tong 銅
Tongchen ji 同塵集
Tongmi 通密
Tongmiao 通妙
Tongwei 通微
Tongxuan 通玄
Tongxuan guan 通玄觀 tongyi 同衣
Tongzheng 通正
tongzi 童子
tu 兔
Tunzei 吞賊
tutan zhai 塗炭齋
Wai riyong jing 外日用經
wai riyong 外日用
Wan'an gong 萬安宮
wancan 晚參
Wanchun jiao 萬春醮
wang 王
Wang 王
Wang Changyue 王常月
Wang Chongyang 王重陽
Wang Chuyi 王處一
Wang Cui 王粹
Wang Daoming 王道明
Wang Daoyuan 王道淵
Wang Haifeng 王害風
Wang Jie 王玠
Wang Ka 王卡
Wang Kunyang 王崑陽

Wang Lingyin 王靈隱
Wang Ping 王平
Wang Qiyun 王棲雲
Wang Xuanfu 王玄甫
Wang Yizhong 王頤中
Wang Yunqing 王允卿
Wang Yuyang 王玉陽
Wang Zhe 王嚞
Wang Zhijin 王志瑾
Wang Zhongfu 王中孚
Wangwu shan 王屋山
Wangxian men 望仙門
wanhua 萬華
Wansui shan 萬歲山
Wanyan Liang 完顏亮
Weihai 威海
Weiji 未濟
Wei-Jiang ji 葦江集
weilü 尾閭
weixiu 危宿
Weiyu shan 委羽山
weizheng 為證
Weizhou 衛州
Wendeng 文登
Wenshan 文山
Wenshi zhenjing 文始真經
wo ming zai wo, buzai tian 我命在我，不在天
wo ru gong 臥如弓
wogu 握固
Wozhou 沃州
wu 午
wu 戊
wu 無
Wu Chongxu 伍沖虛
Wu Shouyang 伍守陽
Wuchao 舞朝
Wudang shan 武當山
Wudang 武當
wudi 五帝
wugeng 五更
Wugou 無垢
wugu 五鼓
Wuguan 武官
wuguang 五光

wuhui 五會
wuhun 五葷
wujie 五戒
wujing 五經
wukong zhi di 無孔之笛
Wulei 五雷
Wulei lingpai 五雷令牌
Wu-Liu 伍柳
Wu-Liu xianzong 伍柳仙宗
wulou 無漏
wulou guo 無漏果
Wumen guan 無門關
wuming 無名
wuming tang 五明堂
Wupian lingwen 五篇靈文
wushi 無事
Wuwei qingjing 無爲清靜
wuwu 五五
Wuxian zhuan 麥仙傳
wuxin 五辛
wuxing 五行
Wuxuan pian 悟玄篇
wuyan 五眼
Wuyuan 悟元
wuyue guan 五嶽冠
Wuzhen pian 悟真篇
Wuzong 武宗
wuzu 五組
xian 先
xian 閑
xianfeng daogu 仙風道骨
xianfeng daoqi 仙風道氣
xiangu 仙骨
Xiangyan Zhixian 香嚴智閑
xianjian zhi ming 先見之明
xianjue shi 先覺師
Xianle ji 仙樂集
xianren 仙人
xianshu 仙書
xiansi houshui 先死後蛻
xiantian 先天
xiantian qi 先天氣
Xianyang 咸陽
xianzhe 賢者

Xiao 蕭
Xiao Daoxi 蕭道熙
xiaoyao 逍遙
xiayuan 下元
Xicheng shan 西城山
xie 泄
xie 邪
Xijin 西晉
xin 辛
xinchong 心沖
xing 姓
xing 性
xing 行
xingde 刑德
Xinghua ji 行化集
Xingyi quan 形意拳
xinhai 辛亥
Xinjichuan 新集川
Xinjing 心經
Xinjing jie 心經解
xinyi 信衣
xinyuan 心猿
xinzhai 心齋
Xishan 西山
Xishan ji 西山記
Xishan Xu zhenjun bashiwu hua lu 西山許真君八十五化錄
Xisheng jing 西昇經
xiuxing 修行
Xiuzhen guan 修真觀
Xiuzhen ji 修真集
Xiuzhen tu 修真圖
Xixian 希賢
Xixuan shan 西玄山
xiyi 希夷
Xiyi 希夷
Xiyou ji 西遊記
Xiyou lu 西遊錄
xu 戌
Xu Jingyang 許旌陽
Xu Xun 許遜
Xu zhenjun shangsheng zhuan 許真君上昇傳
Xuanbao 玄寶
Xuandu baozang 玄都寶藏
Xuandu guan 玄都觀

Xuanfeng 玄風
*Xuanfeng qinghui lu*玄風慶會錄
Xuanfeng qinghui tu 玄風慶會圖
Xuanfu 宣甫
Xuanhua 玄華
Xuanjiao da gong'an 玄教大公案
Xuanjing 玄靖
Xuanmen 玄門
Xuanmen risong zaowan gongke 玄門日誦早晚功課
xuanpin 玄牝
Xuanting gong 玄庭宮
Xuanxue 玄學
Xuanyuan 軒轅
Xuanzong 宣宗
xudu 虛度
xudu guan 虛度關
xuedao 學盜
Xuefeng 雪峰
Xueshi 血尸
Xuhuang daojun 虛皇道君
Xuhuang tianzun chuzhen shijie wen 虛皇天尊初真十戒文
Xujing虛静
Xumi 須彌
Xun 巽
xunlong 薰籠
Yan 嚴
Yan 顏
Yan Changqing 嚴長清
Yan Chuchang 嚴處常
Yan Hui 顏回
Yancheng Ziyou 顏成子游
yangshen陽神
yangsheng 養生
yangsu 養素
Yangui 延珪
Yanjing 燕京
Yanrui 延瑞
Yantai 煙臺
Yanxia dong 煙霞洞
Yanxia lu 煙霞錄
Yanzhen 延珍
yanzhuan 煙篆
Yanzi 顏子
yao 杳

Yao Xuan姚鉉
Yaochi dian 瑤池殿
Yaojiang 姚江
yashua 牙刷
ye 葉
Yecheng 掖城
yegen 業根
Yelü Chucai 耶律楚材
Yelü Jinqing 耶律晉卿
Yexian 掖縣
yi 乙
Yi 伊
yi 易
yi 鎰
Yifu 宜甫
Yijing 易經
Yila Chucai 移剌楚才
yima 意馬
Yimen夷門
yin 寅
Yin Qinghe 尹清和
Yin Xi 尹喜
Yin Zhiping 尹志平
yinde 陰德
Yinfu jing 陰符經
Yinfu jing zhu 陰符經註
Yingchan 瑩蟾
yinger 嬰兒
yingui 陰鬼
Yingxian qiao 應仙橋
yingyan 應驗
Yingzhou 瀛洲
yinmo 陰魔
Yinshan 陰山
Yintang印堂
yiren 異人
Yixian zhuan 繹仙傳
yonghui 用灰
Yongle gong 永樂宮
Yongquan 湧泉
yongshou daoyuan 永壽道院
you 酉
Yougu 幽谷
Youxian guan 遊仙觀

Youzui fachan 宥罪法懺
Yu 玉
Yu Daoxian 于道顯
Yu Dongzhen 余洞真
Yu Tongqing 于通清
Yu Xindeng 于信等
Yu Zhenguang 于真光
Yu Zhidao 于志道
Yu Zhidao 余志道
Yu Zhike 于志可
yuan 圓
yuan 源
Yuancheng ji 圓成集
Yuanming 圓明
yuanshen 元神
Yuanshi 元史
Yuanshi tianzun 元始天尊
Yuanshi tianzun shuo dedao liaoshen jing 元始天尊說得道了身經
Yuanshi tianzun shuo taigu jing 元始天尊說太古經
yuanshi zhang 元始章
yuantong 圓通
Yuanxuan xueyuan 圓玄學院
Yuchan 玉蟾
yue 月
yuhu 玉戶
yuhua 羽化
Yuhua hui 玉華會
Yujing 玉京
Yuling shengshu 玉靈聖書
yulou 玉樓
yulu 語錄
Yunguang dong 雲光洞
Yunguang ji 雲光集
yuniu 玉扭
Yunji qiqian 雲笈七籤
Yunqing 允卿
Yunxi 雲溪
Yunxi an 雲溪菴
Yunxi bilu 筠溪筆錄
Yunxi ji 筠溪集
yunyou 雲遊
Yunzhong lü 雲中錄
Yuqing 玉清
Yuquan yuan 玉泉院

yuqun 羽裙

Yuxi 玉溪

Yuxian gong 遇仙宮

Yuxian qiao 遇仙橋

Yuxian ting 遇仙亭

Yuyang 玉陽

Yuyang 餘姚

yuzhe 愚者

Yuzhen 玉枕

zahua 雜話

zan 讚

zan 贊

zaohua 造化

zashu 雜書

zating 雜聽

zei 賊

zeiren 賊人

Zeng 曾

zhai 齋

zhaichang 齋場

Zhaiwei ji 摘微集

zhang 杖

Zhang Boduan 張伯端

Zhang Haogu 張好古

Zhang Jiyu 張繼禹

Zhang Lintong 張臨潼

Zhang Shentong 張神童

Zhang Wanfu 張萬福

Zhang Yan 張閻

Zhang Yuchu 張宇初

Zhangzong 章宗

Zhao 趙

Zhao Daojian 趙道堅

Zhao Fuyang 趙復陽

Zhao Jiugu 趙九古

Zhao Liaozhen 趙了真

Zhao Wuxuan 趙悟玄

Zhao Xujing 趙虛靜

Zhao Youqin 趙友欽

Zhao Zhou 趙州

Zhaoxian 趙縣

Zhaozhou 趙州

Zhe 嚞

Zhen'gao 真誥

Zhenchang 真常
zhendao 真道
zheng 正
Zheng 鄭
Zhengding 正定
Zhenglong 正隆
zhengming dashi 證明大師
zhengming shu 證明書
zhengong 真功
zhengshi 證師
Zhenguang 真光
Zhengyang 正陽
Zhengyi 正一
zhengzuo 正坐
Zhenhai 鎮海
zhenjing 真經
zhenren 真人
Zhenxian yulu 真仙語錄
Zhenxian zhizhi yulu 真仙直指語錄
zhenxin 真心
zhenxing 真行
zhenyi 真意
Zhenyou 貞祐
zhike 知客
Zhiming 智明
Zhiyang 芝陽
zhizu 知足
Zhongdu 中都
Zhongfu 中孚
zhonggong 中宮
Zhongguo daojiao xiehui 中國道教協會
Zhongguo guojia tushuguan 中國國家圖書館
Zhonghe ji 中和集
Zhonghua daozang 中華道藏
Zhonghuang jing 中黃經
zhongji 中極
Zhongji jie 中極戒
Zhongli Quan 鍾離權
zhonglou 重樓
Zhong-Lü 鍾呂
Zhongnan 終南
Zhongnan neizhuan 終南內傳
Zhongnan shan ji 終南山記
Zhongnan shan Zuting xianzhen neizhuan 終南山祖庭仙真內傳

zhongri 終日
Zhongtong 中統
zhongxi 踵息
Zhongyi 忠翊
zhongyuan 中元
Zhou 周
Zhou Deqing 周德清
Zhou Xuanjing 周玄靖
zhu 主
zhu 注/註
zhu 竹
zhu 銖
Zhu Xi 朱熹
zhu'an 主庵
zhuan 傳
Zhuangzi 莊子
zhubo 主鉢
zhuhuo 主火
zhuo 拙
zhuo 濁
zi 子
zi 字
Zigong 紫宮
ziran 自然
ziran yuanqi 自然元氣
Ziwei 紫微
Ziwei yuan 紫薇院
Ziyuan 子淵
zizai 自在
zong 宗
zongri 縱日
zu 祖
Zuilu du 觜盧都
zuobo 坐鉢
zuobo 坐鉢
Zuowang lun 坐忘論
zuowang 坐忘
Zuqiao 祖竅
Zuting 祖庭

Bibliography

Acker, Peter. 2006. *Liu Chuxuan (1147–1203) and His Commentary on the Daoist Scripture Huangdi yinfu jing*. Wiesbaden: Harrassowitz Verlag.

Akizuki Kan'ei 秋月觀英. 1958. "Zenshin seiki sekibatsubo kō" 全真清規責罰榜考. *Bunka* 22.5: 33–52.

Ang, Isabelle. 1993. "Le culte de Lü Dongbin des origines au début du XIVe siècle." Ph.D. diss., Université Paris VII.

Bai Ruxiang 白如祥, ed. 2005a. *Quanzhen dao wenhua congshu: Wang Chongyang ji* 全真道文化叢書: 王重陽集. Jinan, Shandong: Qi-Lu shushe.

———, ed. 2005b. *Quanzhen dao wenhua congshu: Tan Chuduan, Liu Chuxuan, Wang Chuyi, Hao Datong, Sun Buer* 全真道文化叢書: 譚處端、劉處玄、王處一、郝大通、孫不二集. Jinan, Shandong: Qi-Lu shushe.

Baldrian-Hussein, Farzeen. 1984. *Procédés secrets du joyau magique*. Paris: Les Deux Océans.

———. 1986. "Lü Tung-pin in Northern Sung Literature." *Cahiers d'Extrême-Asie* 2: 133–69.

———. 1990. "Inner Alchemy: Notes on the Origin and Use of the Term *Neidan*." *Cahiers d'Extrême-Asie* 5: 163–90.

Baryosher-Chemouny, Muriel. 1996. *La quete de l'immortalité en Chine: Alchimie et payasage intérieur sous les Song*. Paris: Editions Dervy.

Belamide, Paulino. 2002. "Self-cultivation and Quanzhen Daoism, with Special Reference to the Legacy of Qiu Chuji." Ph.D. diss., University of Toronto.

Benn, James. 1998. "Where Text Meets Flesh: Burning the Body as an Apocryphal Practice in Chinese Buddhism." *History of Religions* 37.4: 295–322.

———. 2007. *Burning for the Buddha: Self-immolation in Chinese Buddhism*. Honolulu: University of Hawaii Press.

Berling, Judith. 1987. "Bringing the Buddha Down to Earth: Notes on the Emergence of the Yü-lu as a Buddhist Genre." *History of Religions* 27.1: 56–88.

Bokenkamp, Stephen. 1990. "Stages of Transcendence: The *Bhūmi* Concept in Taoist Scripture." In *Chinese Buddhist Apocrypha*, edited by Robert E. Buswell Jr., 119–47. Honolulu: University of Hawaii Press.

———. 1991. "Taoism and Literature: The *Pi-lo* Question." *Taoist Resources* 3.1: 57–72.

———. 1997. *Early Daoist Scriptures*. Berkeley: University of California Press.

———. 2002. "Foreword" to Robert Ford Campany's *To Live as Long as Heaven and Earth*. Berkeley: University of California Press.

Boltz, Judith. 1987. *A Survey of Taoist Literature, Tenth to Seventh Centuries*. Berkeley: Institute of East Asian Studies.

Buswell, Robert. 1993. *The Zen Monastic Experience*. Princeton, NJ: Princeton University Press.

Cahill, Suzanne. 2006. *Divine Traces of the Daoist Sisterhood: Records of the Assembled Transcendents of the Fortified Walled City*. Cambridge, MA: Three Pines Press.

Cai Meibiao 蔡美彪. 1955. *Yuandai baihua bei jilu* 元代白話碑集錄. Beijing: Kexue chubanshe.

Campany, Robert F. 2002. *To Live as Long as Heaven and Earth: A Translation and Study of Ge Hong's Traditions of Divine Transcendents*. Berkeley: University of California Press.

Chan Hok-Lam. 1975. "Wang O (1190–1273)." *Papers on Far Eastern History* 12: 43–70.

———. 1993. *The Fall of the Jurchen Chin: Wang E's Memoirs on Ts'ai-chou under the Mongol Siege (1233–1234)*. Stuttgart: Franz Steiner Verlag.

Chavannes, Edouard. 1904. "Inscriptions et pieces de chancellerie chinoises de l'époque mongole." *T'oung Pao* 5: 357–447.

———. 1908. "Inscriptions et pieces de chancellerie chinoises de l'époque mongole." *T'oung Pao* 9: 297–428.

Ch'en, Kenneth. 1964. *Buddhism in China: A Historical Survey*. Princeton: Princeton University Press.

Chen Bing 陳兵. 1985 "Jindan pai Nanzong qiantan" 金丹派南宗淺探. *Shijie zongjiao yanjiu* 4: 35–49.

———. 1986. "Yuandai Jiangnan daojiao" 元代江南道教. *Shijie zongjiao yanjiu* 5: 66–80.

———. 1988. "Qingdai Quanzhen dao Longmen pai de zhongxing" 清代全真道龍門派的中興. *Shijie zongjiao yanjiu* 2: 84–96.

———. 1992. "Mingdai Quanzhen dao" 明代全道. *Shijie zongjiao yanjiu* 1: 40–51.

Chen Junmin 陳俊民. 1984. "Quanzhen daojiao sixiang yuanliu kaolue" 全真道教思想源流考略. *Zhongguo zhexue* 1984.1: 140–68.

Chen Minggui 陳銘珪 (1824–1881). 1974. *Changchun daojiao yuanliu* 長春道教源流. Taibei: Guangwen shuju.

Chen Yaoting 陳燿庭. 2003. *Daojiao liyi* 道教禮儀. Beijing: Zongjiao wenhua chubanshe.

Chen Yingning 陳櫻寧. 1934. *Sun Buer nüdan shizhu* 孫不二女丹釋註. Shanghai: Yihuo tangshan shuju.

Chen Yuan 陳垣 (1880–1971). 1962 (1941). *Nan Song chu Hebei xin daojiao kao* 南宋初河北新道教考. Beijing: Zhonghua shuju.

———. 1988. *Daojia jinshi lue* 道家金石略. Edited by Chen Zhichao 陳智超 and Zeng Qingying 曾慶瑛. Beijing: Wenwu chubanshe.

Chen Yuming 陳宇明. 2003. *Huashan: Dongtian fudi* 華山: 洞天福地. Xi'an: Shaanxi lüyou chubanshe.

Chenivesse, Sandrine. 1997a. "A Journey to the Depths of a Labyrinth-Landscape: The Mount Fengdu, Taoist Holy Site and Infernal Abyss." In *Mandala and Landscape*, edited by A. W. MacDonald, 41–74. New Delhi: D.K. Printworld.

———. 1997b. "Le mont Fengdu: Lieu saint taoïste émergé de la géographie de l'audelà." *Sanjiao wenxian* I: 79–86.

———. "Fengdu: Cité de l'abondance, cite de la male mort." *Cahiers d'Extrême-Asie* 10: 287–339.

Cleary, Thomas. 1978. *The Sayings and Doings of Pai-chang*. Los Angeles: Zen Center Publications.

———. 1986a. *The Taoist I Ching*. Boston: Shambhala.

———. 1986b. *The Inner Teachings of Taoism*. Boston: Shambhala.

———. 1987. *Understanding Reality*. Honolulu: University of Hawaii Press.

———. 1989a. *The Book of Balance and Harmony*. San Francisco: North Point Press.

———. 1989b. *Immortal Sisters: Secret Teachings of Taoist Women*. Boston: Shambhala.

———. 1991. *Vitality, Energy, Spirit: A Taoist Sourcebook*. Boston: Shambhala.

———. 2000. *Taoist Meditation: Methods for Cultivating a Healthy Mind and Body*. Boston: Shambhala.

Conze, Edward. 1973. *The Perfection of Wisdom in Eight Thousand Lines and Its Verse Summary*. Bolinas: Four Seasons Foundation.

———. 1975. *The Large Sūtra on Perfect Wisdom*. Berkeley: University of California Press.

Davis, Edward L. 2001. *Society and the Supernatural in Song China*. Honolulu: University of Hawaii Press.

De Bruyn, Pierre-Henry. 2000. "Daoism in the Ming (1368–1644)." In *Daoism Handbook*, edited by Livia Kohn, 594–622. Leiden: Brill.

———. 2004. "Wudang shan: The Origins of a Major Center of Modern Taoism." In *Religion and Chinese Society*, edited by John Lagerwey, 553–90. Hong Kong: Chinese University Press.

———. 2010. *Le Wudang shan: Histoire des récits fondateurs*. Paris: Éditions Les Indes savantes.

Despeux, Catherine. 1988. *La moelle du phénix rouge*. Paris: Guy Trédaniel, Éditions de la Maisnie.

———. 1990. *Immortelles de la Chine ancienne: Taoïsme et alchimie féminine*. Puiseaux: Pardès.

———. 1994. *Taoïsme et corps humain: Le Xiuzhen tu*. Paris: Guy Trédaniel.

———. 2000. "Talismans and Sacred Diagrams." In *Daoism Handbook*, edited by Livia Kohn, 498–540. Leiden: Brill.

Despeux, Catherine, and Livia Kohn. 2003. *Women in Daoism*. Cambridge, MA: Three Pines Press.

Ding Ding 丁鼎et al., eds. 2007. *Kunyu shan yu Quanzhen dao* 崑嵛山與全真道. Beijing: Zongjiao wenhua chubanshe.

Ding Fubao 丁福保 (Ting Fu-pao), ed. 1939. *Foxue da cidian* 佛學大辭典. 16 vols. Beijing: Wenwu chubanshe.

Ding Huang 丁煌. 2000. "The Study of Daoism in China Today." In *Daoism Handbook*, edited by Livia Kohn, 765–91. Leiden: Brill.

Dumoulin, Heinrich. 1994 (1988). *Zen Buddhism: A History*. Vol. 1: India and China. Translated by James W. Heisig and Paul Knitter. New York: Simon and Schuster Macmillan.

Ebrey, Patricia B. 1995 (1981). "Master Ch'ung-yang's Fifteen Precepts for Establishing the Teaching." In *Chinese Religion: An Anthology of Sources*, edited by Deborah Sommer, 199–203. New York and Oxford: Oxford University Press.

Ebrey, Patricia Buckley, and Peter N. Gregory, eds. 1993. *Religion and Society in T'ang and Sung China*. Honolulu: University of Hawaii Press.

Eskildsen, Stephen. 1989. "The Beliefs and Practices of Early Ch'üan-chen Taoism." M.A. thesis, University of British Columbia.

———. 1990. "Asceticism in Ch'üan-chen Taoism." *B.C. Asian Review* 3-4: 153–91.

———. 1992. "Early Quanzhen Taoist Views on Causes of Death and Disease." *B.C. Asian Review* 6: 53–70.

———. 1998. *Asceticism in Early Taoist Religion*. Albany: State University of New York Press.

———. 2001. "Seeking Signs of Proof: Visions and Other Trance Phenomena in Early Quanzhen Taoism." *Journal of Chinese Religions* 29: 139–60.

———. 2004. *The Teachings and Practices of the Early Quanzhen Taoist Masters*. Albany: State University of New York Press.

Esposito, Monica. 1993. "La Porte du Dragon: L'école Longmen du Mont Jin'gai et ses pratiques alchimiques d'après le *Daozang xubian* (Suite au canon taoïste)." Ph.D. diss., Université de Paris VII.

———. 1997. *L'alchimia del soffio*. Roma: Ubaldini.

———. 2000. "Daoism in the Qing (1644–1911)." In *Daoism Handbook*, edited by Livia Kohn, 623–58. Leiden: Brill.

———. 2001. "Longmen Taoism in Qing China: Doctrinal Ideal and Local Reality." *Journal of Chinese Religions* 29: 191–231.

———. 2004. "The Longmen School and Its Controversial History during the Qing Dynasty." In *Religion and Chinese Society*, edited by John Lagerwey, vol. 2, 621–98. Hong Kong: Chinese University of Hong Kong.

———. 2005. "Shindai dōkyō to mikkyō: Ryūmon seijiku shinshū 清代道教と密教—龍門西竺心宗." In *Sankyō kōshō ronsō* 三教交涉論叢, edited by Kunio Mugitani 麥谷邦夫, 289–338. Kyoto: Jinbun Kagaku Kenkyūjo.

———. 2009. "Yibu Quanzhen Daozang de faming: *Daozang jiyao* ji Qingdai Quanzhen rentong" 一部全真道藏的发明: 道藏辑要及清代全真认同. In *Wendao Kunyushan* 问道昆嵛山, edited by Zhao Weidong 赵卫东, 303–43. Jinan: Qilu shushe.

Foulk, T. Griffith. 2004. "*Chanyuan qinggui* and Other 'Rules of Purity' in Chinese Buddhism." In *The Zen Canon*, edited by Steven Heine and Dale Wright, 275–315. Oxford and New York: Oxford University Press.

———. 1987. "The Ch'an School and Its Place in the Buddhist Monastic Tradition." Ph.D. diss., University of Michigan.

———. 1993. "Myth, Ritual, and Monastic Practice in Sung Ch'an Buddhism." In *Religion and Society in T'ang and Sung China*, edited by Patricia Ebrey and Peter Gregory, 147–208. Honolulu: University of Hawaii Press.

Franke, Herbert, and Denis Twitchett, eds. 1994. *The Cambridge History of China*. Vol. 6: Alien Regimes and Border States, 907–1368. Cambridge: Cambridge University Press.

Franke, Herbert, and Kok-lam Chan. 1997. *Studies on the Jurchen and the Chin Dynasty*. Brookfield, Vermont: Ashgate Publishing Company.

Gardner, Daniel K. 1991. "Modes of Thinking and Modes of Discourse in the Sung: Some Thoughts on the Yü-lu ('Recorded Conversations') Texts." *Journal of Asian Studies* 50.3: 574–603.

Goossaert, Vincent. 1997. "La création du taoïsme moderne: l'ordre Quanzhen." Ph.D. diss., École Pratique des Hautes Études, Section des Sciences Religieuses.

———. 1999. "Entre quatre murs: Un ascète taoïste du XIIe siècle et la question de la modernité." *T'oung-Pao* 85: 391–418.

———. 2000. "Poèmes taoïstes des cinq vielles." *Études Chinoises* 19.1–2: 249–70.

———. 2001. "The Invention of an Order: Collective Identity in Thirteenth-Century Quanzhen Taoism." *Journal of Chinese Religions* 29: 111–38.

———. 2002. "Starved for Resources: Clerical Hunger and Enclosures in Nineteenth Century China." *Harvard Journal of Asiatic Studies* 62.1: 77–133.

———. 2004. "Counting Monks: The Quanzhen Clergy, 1700–1950." In *Religion and Chinese Society*, edited by John Lagerwey, vol. 2, 699–771. Hong Kong: Chinese University of Hong Kong.

———. 2007. *The Taoists of Peking, 1800–1949: A Social History of Urban Clerics*. Cambridge, MA: Harvard University Press.

Goossaert, Vincent, and Paul Katz. 2001. "New Perspectives on Quanzhen Taoism: The Formation of a Religious Identity." *Journal of Chinese Religions* 29: 91–94.

Gregory, Peter N., and Daniel A. Getz Jr., eds. 1999. *Buddhism in the Sung*. Honolulu: University of Hawaii Press.

Guo Zhan 郭旃. 1983. "Quanzhen dao de xingqi ji qi yu Jin wangchao de guanxi" 全真道的興起及其與金王朝的關係. *Shijie zongjiao yanjiu* 3: 99–107.

Hachiya Kunio 蜂屋邦夫. 1972. "*Chōyō shinjin kinkan gyokusa ketsu* ni tsuite" <<重陽真人金關玉鎖訣>> について. *Tōyō bunka kenkyūjo kiyō* 58: 75–164.

———. 1989. "Dan Chōshin no shōgai to shisō" 譚長真の生涯と思想. *Tōyō bunka kenkyūjo kiyō* 115: 41–122.

———. 1990. *Dōkyō no genjō* 道教の現状. Tokyo: Kyuko shosha.

———. 1992. *Kindai dōkyō no kenkyū—O Chōyō to Ba Tanyō* 金代道教の研究—王重陽と馬丹陽. Tokyo: Tōkyō daigaku Tōyō bunka kenkyūjo hōkoku.

———. 1998. *Kin Gen jidai no dōkyō: Shichijin kenkyū* 金元時代の道教：七真研究. Tokyo: Tōkyō daigaku Tōyō bunka kenkyūjo hōkoku.

Hackmann, Heinrich. 1920. "Die Mönchsregeln des Klostertaoismus." *Ostasiatische Zeitschrift* 8: 141–70.

———. 1931. *Die dreihundert Mönchsgebote des chinesischen Taoismus*. Amsterdam: Koninklijke Akademie van Wetenshapen.

Hahn, Thomas. 2000. "Daoist Sacred Sites." In *Daoism Handbook*, edited by Livia Kohn, 683–708. Leiden: Brill.

Hartill, David. 2005. *Cast Chinese Coins: A Historical Catalogue*. Victoria, BC: Trafford Publishing.

Hawkes, David. 1981. "Quanzhen Plays and Quanzhen Masters." *Bulletin de l'École Française d'Extrême-Orient* 69: 153–70.

Hendrischke, Barbara, and Benjamin Penny. 1996. "The 180 Precepts Spoken by Lord Lao: A Translation and Textual Study." *Taoist Resources* 6.2: 17–29.

Herrou, Adeline. 2005. *La vie entre soi: Les moines taoïste aujourd'hui en Chine*. Nanterre: Société d'Ethnologie.

Homann, Rolf. 1976. *Pai wen p'ien, or, The Hundred Questions: A Dialogue between Two Taoists on the Macrocosmic and Microcosmic System of Correspondences*. Leiden: Brill.

Hou Wailu 候外盧, ed. 1957–63. *Zhongguo sixiang tongshi* 中國思想通史. 5 vols. Beijing: Renmin chubanshe.

Hu Fuchen 胡孚琛, ed. 1995. *Zhonghua daojiao da cidian* 中華道教大辭典. Beijing: Zhongguo shehui kexue chubanshe.

Hu Fuchen 胡孚琛, and Lü Xichen 呂西琛. 1999. *Daoxue tonglun: Daojia, Daojiao, Xianxue* 道學通論: 道家、道教、仙學. Beijing: Shehui kexue wenxian chubanshe.

Hu Qide 胡其德.1990. "Menggu diguo chuqi de zhengjiao guanxi" 蒙古帝國初期的政教關係. Ph.D. diss., National Taiwan Normal University.

———. 2001. "Wang Chongyang chuang Quanzhen jiao de beijing fenxi" 王重陽創全真教的背景分析. *Taiwan zongjiao xuehui tongxun* 8 (May 2001): 26–33.

Hua Tongxu 華同旭. 1991. *Zhongguo louke* 中國漏刻. Anhui: Anhui kexue jishu chubanshe.

Hucker, Charles. 1985. *A Dictionary of Official Titles in Imperial China*. Stanford: Stanford University Press.

Idema, Wilt. 1993. "Skulls and Skeletons in Art and on Stage." In *Conflict and Accommodation in Early Modern East Asia: Essays in Honor of Erik Zürcher*, edited by Leonard Blusse and Harriet Zurndorfer, 191–215. Leiden: Brill.

Jagchid, Sechin. 1980. "Chinese Buddhism and Taoism during the Mongolian Rule of China." *Mongolian Studies* 6: 61–99.

Jing Anning. 1996. "The Eight Immortals: The Transformation of T'ang and Sung Taoist Eccentrics during the Yuan Dynasty." In *Arts of the Sung and Yuan*, edited by Maxwell K. Hearn and Judith G. Smith, 213–30. New York: Metropolitan Museum of Art.

Kaelber, Walter. 1979. "Tapas and Purification in Early Hinduism." *Numen* 26.2: 192–214.

———. 1989. *Tapta Marga: Asceticism and Initiation in Vedic India*. Albany: State University of New York Press.

Katz, Paul R. 1996. "Enlightened Alchemist or Immoral Immortal? The Growth of Lü Dongbin in Late Imperial China." In *Unruly Gods: Divinity and Society in China*, edited by Meir Shahar and Robert P. Weller, 70–104. Honolulu: University of Hawaii Press.

———. 1999. *Images of the Immortal: The Cult of Lü Dongbin at the Palace of Eternal Joy*. Honolulu: University of Hawaii Press.

———. 2001. "Writing History, Creating Identity: A Case Study of *Xuanfeng qinghui tu*." *Journal of Chinese Religions* 29: 161–78.

Kirkland, Russell. 1997. "The Historical Contours of Taoism in China: Thoughts on Issues of Classification and Terminology." *Journal of Chinese Religions* 25: 57–82.

———. 2000. "Explaining Daoism: Realities, Cultural Constructs, and Emerging Perspectives." In *Daoism Handbook*, edited by Livia Kohn, xi–xviii. Leiden: Brill.

———. 2002. "The History of Taoism: A New Outline." *Journal of Chinese Religions* 30: 177–93.

———. 2004. *Taoism: The Enduring Tradition*. London and New York: Routledge.

Kim Sung-hae. 2006. "Daoist Monasticism in Contemporary China." In *Chinese Religions in Contemporary Societies*, edited by James Miller, 101–22. Santa Barbara, CA: ABC-CLIO.

Kohn, Livia. 1987. *Seven Steps to the Tao: Sima Chengzhen's Zuowanglun*. St. Augustin/Nettetal: Monumenta Serica Monograph 20.

———, ed. 1989. *Taoist Meditation and Longevity Techniques*. Ann Arbor: Center for Chinese Studies, University of Michigan.

———. 1991. *Taoist Mystical Philosophy: The Scripture of Western Ascension*. Albany: State University of New York Press.

———. 1993. *The Taoist Experience*. Albany: State University of New York Press.

———. 1995. *Laughing at the Tao: Debates among Buddhists and Taoists in Medieval China*. Princeton: Princeton University Press.

———. 1997. "The Date and Compilation of the *Fengdao kejie*: The First Handbook of Monastic Daoism." *East Asian History* 13: 91–118.

———. 1998. *God of the Dao: Lord Lao in History and Myth*. Ann Arbor: Center for Chinese Studies, University of Michigan.

———. 1999. *God of the Dao: Lord Lao in History and Myth*. Ann Arbor: Center for Chinese Studies, University of Michigan.

———, ed. 2000a. *Daoism Handbook*. Leiden: Brill.

———. 2000b. "Chinese Religion." In *The Human Condition*, edited by Robert Cummings Neville, 21–47. Albany: State University of New York Press.

———. 2001. *Daoism and Chinese Culture*. Cambridge, MA: Three Pines Press.

———. 2003a. *Monastic Life in Medieval China: A Cross-Cultural Perspective*. Honolulu: University of Hawaii Press.

———. 2003b. "Monastic Rules in Quanzhen Daoism: As Collected by Heinrich Hackmann." *Monumenta Serica* 51: 1–32.

———. 2004a. *The Daoist Monastic Manual: A Translation of the Fengdao kejie*. Oxford and New York: Oxford University Press.

———. 2004b. *Cosmos and Community: The Ethical Dimension of Daoism*. Cambridge, MA: Three Pines Press.

———. 2008. *Chinese Healing Exercises: The Tradition of Daoyin*. Honolulu: University of Hawaii Press.

———. 2009. *Introducing Daoism*. London and New York: Routledge.

Kohn, Livia, and Russell Kirkland. 2000. "Daoism in the Tang." In *Daoism Handbook*, edited by Livia Kohn, 339–83. Leiden: Brill.

Komjathy, Louis. 2002. *Title Index to Daoist Collections*. Cambridge, MA: Three Pines Press.

———. 2003a. "Daoist Texts in Translation." http://www.daoistcenter.org/advanced.html. Posted on September 15, 2003. Accessed January 23, 2012.

———. 2003b. "Daoist Teachers in North America." http://www.daoistcenter.org/advanced.html. Posted on September 15, 2003. Accessed January 23, 2012.

———. 2003c. "Daoist Organizations in North America." http://www.daoistcenter.org/advanced.html. Posted on September 15, 2003. Accessed January 23, 2012.

———. 2004. "Tracing the Contours of Daoism in North America." *Nova Religio* 8.2 (November): 5–27.

———. 2006. "Qigong in America." In *Daoist Body Cultivation*, edited by Livia Kohn, 203–35. Cambridge, MA: Three Pines Press.

———. 2007a. *Cultivating Perfection: Mysticism and Self-transformation in Early Quanzhen Daoism*. Leiden: Brill.

———. 2007b. "Quanzhen Alchemical Practice as Documented in the *Dadan zhizhi*." Unpublished article.

———. 2008a. *Handbooks for Daoist Practice (Xiudao shouce* 修道手冊). 10 vols. Hong Kong: Yuen Yuen Institute.

———. 2008b. "Mapping the Daoist Body: Part I: The *Neijing tu* in History." *Journal of Daoist Studies* 1: 67–92.

———. 2009. "Mapping the Daoist Body: Part II: The Text of the *Neijing tu*." *Journal of Daoist Studies* 2: 64–108.

———. 2010. "Living in Seclusion: Early Quanzhen Eremitic Poetry." Unpublished article.

———. 2011a. "Daoism: From Meat Avoidance to Compassion-based Vegetarianism." In *Call to Compassion: Religious Perspectives on Animal Advocacy*, edited by Lisa Kemmerer and Anthony J. Nocella II, 83–103. New York: Lantern Books.

———. 2011b. "The Daoist Mystical Body." In *Perceiving the Divine through the Human Body: Mystical Sensuality*, edited by Thomas Cottai and June McDaniel, 67–103. New York: Palgrave Macmillan.

———. Forthcoming. *The Daoist Tradition: An Introduction*. London and New York: Bloomsbury Academic.

Koyanagi Shikita 小柳司氣太. 1934. *Hakuunkan shi (Baiyun guan zhi)* 白雲観志. Tokyo: Tōhō bunka gakuin Tōkyō kenkyūjo.

Kubo Noritada 窪德忠. 1967. *Chūgoku no shūkyō kaikaku—Zenshin kyō no seiritsu* 中國の宗教改革—全真教の成立. Kyoto: Hōzōkan.

———. 1968. "Prolegomena on the Study of the Controversies between Buddhists and Taoists in the Yuan Period." *Memoirs of the Research Department of the Toyo Bunka* 26: 39–61.

Lagerwey, John. 1992. "The Pilgrimage to Wu-tang shan." In *Pilgrims and Sacred Sites in China*, edited by Susan Naquin and Chün-fang Yü, 293–332. Berkeley: University of California Press.

———, ed. 2004. *Religion and Chinese Society*. 2 vols. Hong Kong: Chinese University Press.

Lai Chi-tim. 2003. "Daoism in China Today, 1980–2002." In *Religion in China Today*, edited by Daniel L. Overmeyer, 107–21. Cambridge and New York: Cambridge University Press, 2003.

Lau, D. C. 1984. *Mencius*. 2 vols. Hong Kong: Chinese University Press.

———. 1992 (1983). *Confucius: The Analects*. Hong Kong: Chinese University Press.

Li Yangzheng 李養正. 1993. *Dangdai zhongguo daojiao* 當代中國道教. Beijing: Zhongguo shehui kexue chubanshe.

———. 2000. *Dangdai daojiao* 當代道教. Beijing: Dongfang chubanshe.

———. 2003. *Xinbian Beijing Baiyun guan zhi* 新編北京白雲觀志. Beijing: Zongjiao wenhua chubanshe.

Li Yuanguo 李遠國. 1991. *Zhongguo daojiao qigong yangsheng daquan* 中國道教氣功養生大全. Chengdu: Sichuan cishu.

Li Zhitian 李志添et al. 2007. *Xianggang daotang keyi lishi yu chuancheng* 香港道堂科儀歷史與傳承. Hong Kong: Zhonghua shuju.

Little, Stephen, with Shawn Eichmann. 2000. *Taoism and the Arts of China*. Berkeley: University of California Press.

Liu, Xun (Liu Xun). 2004a. "Visualizing Perfection: Daoist Paintings of Our Lady, Court Patronage, and Elite Female Piety in the Late Qing." *Harvard Journal of Asiatic Studies* 64.1: 57–115.

———. 2004b (2006). "Immortals and Patriarchs: The Daoist World of a Manchu Official and His Family in 19th Century China." *Asia Major* 17.2: 161–218.

Loon, Piet van der. 1984. *Taoist Books in the Libraries of the Sung Period*. London: Ithaca Press.

Major, John S. 1993. *Heaven and Earth in Early Han Thought*. Albany: State University of New York Press.

Marsone, Pierre. 1999. "Le Baiyun guan de Pékin: Épigraphie et histoire." *Matériaux pour l'étude de la religion chinoise—Sanjiao wenxian* 3: 73–136.

———. 2001. "Accounts of the Foundation of the Quanzhen Movement: A Hagiographic Treatment of History." *Journal of Chinese Religions* 29: 95–110.

———. 2010. *Wang Chongyang (1113–1170) et la fondation du Quanzhen: ascètes taoïstes et alchimie intérieure*. Paris: Institut des Hautes Études Chinoises (Collège de France).

McRae, John. 1992. "Encounter Dialogue and the Transformation of the Spiritual Path in Chinese Ch'an." In *Paths to Liberation: The Mārga and Its Transformations in Buddhist Thought*, edited by Robert Buswell and Robert Gimello, 339–369. Honolulu: University of Hawaii Press.

Miller, James. 2003. *Daoism: A Short Introduction*. London and New York: Oneworld.

———, ed. 2006. *Chinese Religions in Contemporary Societies*. Barbara, Calif.: ABC-CLIO.

Min Zhiting 閔智亭. 1990. *Daojiao yifan* 道教儀範. Beijing: Zhongguo daojiao xueyuan bianyin.

Min Zhiting 閔智亭, and Li Yangzheng 李養正, eds. 1994. *Daojiao da cidian* 道教大辭典. Beijing: Huaxia chubanshe.

Min Zhiting 閔智亭 et al. 2000. *Xuanmen risong zaowan gongke jing zhu* 玄門日誦早晚功課經注. Beijing: Zongjiao wenhua chubanshe.

Mori Yuria 森由利亞. 1992. "*Taigen shinjin ken'iroku* ni mieru Ō Gyokuyō no shin'itan" <<體玄真人顯異錄>> に見える王玉陽の神異譚. *Tōyō tetsugaku ronsō* 1: 186–203.

———. 2003. "Zenshin zahachi—Gen Min Shin no Zenshinkyō girei o chūshin ni" 眞座鉢—元明清の全眞教儀礼を中心に. In *Tōhōgaku no shinshiten* 東方学の新視点, edited by Fukui Fumimasa 福井文雅, 459–97. Tokyo: Goyō shobō, 2003.

———. 2005. "Shinchō Zenshin-kyō no denkai to Ryoso fukei shinkō" 清朝全真教の伝戒と呂祖扶乩信仰. In *Ajia bunka no shisō to girei* アジア文化の思想と儀礼, edited by Fukui Fumimasa hakushi koki / taishoku kinen ronshū kankōkai 福井文雅博士古稀・退職記念論集刊行会, 441–61. Tokyo: Shunjūsha.

———. 2006. "Shō Yobu no Ryoso fukei shinkō to Zenshin-kyō" 蔣予蒲の呂祖扶乩信仰と全真教. In *Dōkyō kenkyū no saisentan* 道教研究の最先端, edited by. Horiike Nobuo 堀池信夫 and Sunayama Minoru 砂山稔, 82–108. Tokyo: Taiga shobō, 2006.

Mote, F. W. 1999. *Imperial China 900–1800*. Cambridge, MA: Harvard University Press.

Mou Zhongjian 牟鐘鑒et al. 2005. *Quanzhen qizi yu Qi-Lu wenhua* 全真七子與齊魯文化. Jinan, Shandong: Qi-Lu shushe.

Nan Huaijin 南懷瑾. 1962. "Yuandai Quanzhen dao yu Zhongguo shehui" 元代全真道與中國社會. *Xin tiandi* 1.6: 12–16.

Nattier, Jan. 1992. "The Heart Sutra: A Chinese Apocryphal Text?" *Journal of the International Association of Buddhist Studies* 15.2: 153–223.

Needham, Joseph et al. 1959. *Science and Civilisation in China*, vol. III: *Mathematics and the Sciences of the Heavens and the Earth*. Cambridge: Cambridge University Press.

———. 1974. *Science and Civilisation in China*, vol. V: *Chemistry and Chemical Technology*, part 2: *Spagyrical Discovery and Invention: Magisteries of Gold and Immortality*. Cambridge: Cambridge University Press.

———. 1976. *Science and Civilisation in China*, vol. V: *Chemistry and Chemical Technology*, part 3: *Spagyrical Discovery and Invention: Historical Survey, from Cinnabar Elixirs to Synthetic Insulin*. Cambridge: Cambridge University Press.

———. 1980. *Science and Civilisation in China*, vol. V: *Chemistry and Chemical Technology*, part 4: *Spagyrical Discovery and Invention: Apparatus, Theories and Gifts*. Cambridge: Cambridge University Press.

———. 1983. *Science and Civilisation in China*, vol. V: *Chemistry and Chemical Technology*, part 5: *Spagyrical Discovery and Invention: Physiological Alchemy*. Cambridge: Cambridge University Press.

Overmyer, Daniel L., ed. 2003. *Religion in China Today*. Cambridge and New York: Cambridge University Press.

Ōzaki Masaharu 尾埼正治. 1986. "The Taoist Priesthood: From Tsai-chia to Ch'u-chia." In *Religion and Family in East Asia*, edited George DeVos and T. Sofue, 97–109. Berkeley: University of California Press.

Pas, Julian, ed. 1989. *The Turning of the Tide: Religion in China Today*. Hong Kong: University of Hong Kong Press.

Poceski, Mario. 2004. "*Mazu yulu* and the Creation of the Chan Records of Sayings." In *The Zen Canon: Understanding the Classic Texts*, edited by Steven Heine and Dale S. Wright, 53–79. Oxford and New York: Oxford University Press.

Pregadio, Fabrizio. 1996. "Chinese Alchemy: An Annotated Bibliography of Works in Western Languages." *Monumenta Serica* 44: 439–76.

———. 2000. "Elixirs and Alchemy." In *Daoism Handbook*, edited by Livia Kohn, 165–95. Leiden: Brill.

———, ed. 2008. *The Encyclopedia of Taoism*. 2 vols. London and New York: Routledge-Curzon.

Pregadio, Fabrizio, and Lowell Skar. 2000. "Inner Alchemy (*Neidan*)." In *Daoism Handbook*, edited by Livia Kohn, 464–97. Leiden: Brill.

Qian Mu 錢穆. 1966. "Jin-Yuan tongzhixia zhi xin daojiao" 金元統治下之新道教. *Rensheng* 31.3: 2–5.

Qiao Yun. 2001. *Taoist Buildings*. Wien, Austria: Springer-Verlag Wien New York.

Qing Xitai 卿希泰, ed. 1995 (1988–1995). *Zhongguo daojiao shi* 中國道教史. 4 vols. Chengdu: Sichuan renmin chubanshe.

de Rachewiltz, Igor. 1962. "The *Hsi-yu lu* by Yen-lu Ch'u-ts'ai." *Monumenta Serica* 21: 1–121.

Rand, Christopher. 1979. "Li Ch'üan and Chinese Military Thought." *Harvard Journal of Asiatic Studies* 39: 107–37.

Red Pine. 2004. *The Heart Sutra*. Berkeley, CA: Counterpoint Press.

Reiter, Florian C. 1981. "The Soothsayer Hao Ta-t'ung (1140–1212) and His Encounter with Ch'üan-chen Taoism." *Oriens Extremus* 28.2: 198–205.

———. 1984a. "Ch'ung-yang Sets Forth His Teachings in 15 Discourses: A Concise Introduction to the Taoist Way of Life of Wang Che." *Monumenta Serica* 36: 33–54.

———. 1984b. "The 'Scripture on the Hidden Contracts' (Yin-fu ching): A Short Survey on Facts and Findings." *Nachrichten der Gesellschaft für Natur- und Volkerkunde Ostasiens* 136: 75–83.

———. 1988. *Grundelemente und Tendenzen des religiösen Taoismus: Das Spannungsverhältnis von Integration und Individualität in seiner Geschichte zur Chin-Yüan und frühen Ming Zeit.* Münchener Ostasiatische Studien 48. Stuttgart: Franz Steiner.

———. 1990a. "A Chinese Patriot's Concern with Taoism: The Case of Wang O (1190–1273)." *Oriens Extremus* 33.2: 95–131.

———. 1990b. *Leben und Wirken Lao-Tzu's in Schrift und Bild: Lao-chün pa-shih-i-hua t'u-shuo.* Würburg: Königshausen & Neumann.

———. 1993. "A Praise of the Buddha by the Taoist Patriarch Qiu Chuji and Its Source." *Zeitschrift des deutschen morgenländischen Gesellschaft* 143: 179–91.

———. 1994. "How Wang Ch'ung-yang (1112–1170) the Founder of Ch'üan-chen Achieved Enlightenment." *Oriens* 34: 497–508.

———. 1996. "The Ch'üan-chen Patriarch T'an Ch'u-tuan (1123–1185) and the Chinese Talismanic Tradition." *Zeitschrift des deutschen morgenländischen Gesellschaft* 146.1: 139–55.

———. 1997. "The Blending of Religious Convictions and Scholarly Notions in the Life of the Taoist Patriarch Liu Ch'u-hsuan (1147–1203)." *Zeitschrift der Deutschen Morgenländischen Gesellschaft* 147: 425–60.

———. 1998. *The Aspirations and Standards of Taoist Priests in the Early T'ang Period.* Wiesbaden: Harrassowitz.

Ren Farong 任法融. 1993a. *Daode jing shiyi* 道德經釋義. Xi'an: Sanqin chubanshe.

———. 1993b. *Huangdi yinfu jing shiyi* 黃帝陰符經釋義. Xi'an: Sanqin chubanshe.

Ren Jiyu 任繼愈, ed. 2001 (1990). *Zhongguo daojiao shi* 中國道教史. 2 vols. Beijing: Zhongguo shehui kexue chubanshe.

Ren Jiyu 任繼愈, and Zhong Zhaopeng 鍾肇鵬, eds. 1991. *Daozang tiyao* 道藏提要. Beijing: Zhongguo shehui kexue chubanshe.

Roth, Harold. 1999. *Original Tao: Inward Training (Nei-yeh) and the Foundations of Taoist Mysticism.* New York: Columbia University Press.

Scarry, Elaine. 1985. *The Body in Pain: The Making and Un-Making of the World.* Oxford and New York: Oxford University Press.

Schipper, Kristofer. 1975. *Concordance du Tao-tsang: Titres des ouvrages.* Paris: Ecole Française d'Extrême-Orient.

———. 2000. "Taoism: The Story of the Way." In *Taoism and the Arts of China*, by Stephen Little, 33–55. Chicago/Berkeley: Art Institute of Chicago/University of California Press.

Schipper, Kristofer, and Franciscus Verellen, eds. 2004. *The Taoist Canon: A Historical Companion to the Daozang.* Chicago: University of Chicago Press.

Seidel, Anna. 1969. *La divinisation de Lao tseu dans le Taoïsme des Han.* Paris: Publications Ecole Française d'Extrême-Orient.

Shandong sheng Wendeng shi zhengxie 山東省文登市政協. 2005. *Zhongguo daojiao mingshan: Kunyu shan* 中國道教名山：崑崳山. Beijing: Zongjiao wenhua chuban she.

Shiga Ichiko 志賀市子. 2002. "Manifestations of Lüzu in Modern Guangdong and Hong Kong: The Rise and Growth of Spirit-Writing Cults." In *Daoist Identity*, edited by Livia Kohn and Harold Roth, 185–209. Honolulu: University of Hawaii Press.

Skar, Lowell. 2000. "Ritual Movements, Deity Cults and the Transformation of Daoism in Song and Yuan Times." In *Daoism Handbook*, edited by Livia Kohn, 413–63. Leiden: Brill.

———. 2003. "Golden Elixir Alchemy: The Formation of the Southern Lineage and the Transformation of Medieval China." Ph.D. diss., University of Pennsylvania.

Soothill, William Edward, and Lewis Hodous. 1995 (1937). *A Dictionary of Chinese Buddhist Terms.* London: Kegan Paul.

Stewart, Charles, and Rosalind Shaw, eds. 1994. *Syncretism/Anti-Syncretism: The Politics of Religious Synthesis*. London and New York: Routledge.

Strachotta, Fritz-Günter. 1997. *Religiöses Ahnen, Sehnen und Suchen: Von der Theologie zur Religionsgeschichte. Heinrich Friedrich Hackmann 1864–1935*. Frankfurt and New York: Peter Lang.

Sun Kekuan 孫克寬. 1968. *Yuandai daojiao zhi fazhan* 元代道教之發展. Daizhong: Donghai (Tung-hai) University Press.

———. 1981. "Yü Chi (1272–1348) and Southern Taoism during the Yuan Period." In *Chinese under Mongol Rule*, edited by John D. Langlois Jr., 212–53. Princeton: Princeton University Press.

Suzuki, D. T., and Paul Carus. 1973 (1906). *Treatise on Response & Retribution*. La Salle, IL: Open Court.

Tanahashi, Kazuaki, ed. 1985. *Moon in a Dewdrop: Writings of Zen Master Dōgen*. San Francisco: North Point Press.

Tang Guizhang 唐圭璋. 1979. *Quan Jin Yuan ci* 全金元詞. 2 vols. Beijing: Zhonghua shuju.

Tao Bingfu 陶秉福, ed. 1989. *Nüdan jicui* 女丹集萃. Beijing: Beijing shifan daxue.

Tao, Jing-shen. 1976. *The Jurchen in Twelfth-Century China: A Study of Sinicization*. Seattle: University of Washington Press.

Tillman, Hoyt Cleveland, and Stephen H. West, eds. 1995. *China under Jurchen Rule*. Albany: State University of New York Press.

Tsui, Bartholomew P. M. 1990. "The Transmission of the Taoist Complete Perfection Sect in South China." *Jingfeng* 33: 248–57.

———. 1991. *Taoist Tradition and Change: The Story of the Complete Perfection Sect in Hong Kong*. Hong Kong: Hong Kong Christian Study Center on Chinese Religion and Culture.

Unschuld, Paul. 1985. *Medicine in China: A History of Ideas*. Berkeley: University of California Press.

———. 2003. *Huang Di Nei Jing Su Wen: Nature, Knowledge, Imagery in an Ancient Chinese Medical Text*. Berkeley: University of California Press.

Valussi, Elena. 2003. "Beheading the Red Dragon: A History of Female Inner Alchemy in China." Ph.D. diss., School of Oriental and African Studies, University of London.

Waley, Arthur. 1931. *The Travels of an Alchemist: The Journey of the Taoist Ch'ang-ch'un from China to the Hindukush at the Summons of Chingiz Khan*. London: Routledge and Kegan Paul.

Wang Yucheng 王育成. 2003. *Mingdai caihui Quanzhen zongzu tu yanjiu* 明代彩繪全真宗祖圖研究. Beijing: Zhongguo shehui kexue chubanshe.

Wang Zongyu 王宗昱, ed. 2005. *Jin-YuanQuanzhen jiao shike xinbian* 金元全真教石刻新編. Beijing: Beijng daxue chubanshe.

Ware, James. 1966. *Alchemy, Medicine, and Religion in China of A.D. 320: The Nei P'ien of Ko Hung*. New York: Dover.

Watson, Burton. 1964. *Han Fei Tzu: Basic Writings*. New York: Columbia University Press.

———. 1968. *The Complete Works of Chuang Tzu*. New York: Columbia University Press.

Welch, Holmes. 1967. *The Practice of Chinese Buddhism, 1900–1950*. Cambridge, MA: Harvard University Press.

Welch, Holmes, and Anna Seidel, eds. 1979. *Facets of Taoism*. New Haven, CT: Yale University Press.

Wilson, Verity. 1995. "Cosmic Raiment: Daoist Traditions of Liturgical Clothing." *Orientations* (May): 42–49.

Wong, Eva. 1990. *Seven Taoist Masters: A Folk Novel of China*. Boston: Shambhala.

———. 1992. *Cultivating Stillness: A Taoist Manual for Transforming Body and Mind*. Boston: Shambhala.

———. 1994. *Lao-tzu's Treatise on the Response of the Tao*. San Francisco: HarperCollins Publishers.

———. 1998. *Cultivating the Energy of Life: A Translation of the Hui-ming ching and Its Commentaries*. Boston: Shambhala.

———. 2000. *The Tao of Health, Longevity, and Immortality: The Teachings of Immortals Chung and Lü*. Boston: Shambhala.

Wong Shiu-hon (Huang Zhaohan) 黃兆漢. 1988. "Qiu Chuji de *Panxi ji*" 丘處機的<<磻溪集>>. In *Daojiao yanjiu lunwen ji* 道教研究論文集, edited by Wong Shiu-hon, 183–210. Hong Kong: Chinese University Press.

Wu Lu-ch'iang and Tenney L. Davis. 1932. "An Ancient Chinese Treatise on Alchemy Entitled Ts'an T'ung Ch'i." *Isis* 18: 210–89.

Xingyun (Hsing Yun) 星雲, ed. 1989. *Foguang da cidian* 佛光大辭典. 8 vols. Beijing: Beijing tushu guan chubanshe. http://sql.fgs.org.tw/webfbd/. Accessed January 23, 2012.

Xue Ruizhao 薛瑞兆and Guo Mingzhi 郭明志. 1995. *Quan Jin shi* 全金詩. Originally compiled by Yuan Haowen 元好問. 4 vols. Tianjin: Nankiai daxue chubanshe.

Yanagida Seizan 柳田聖山. 1983. "The 'Recorded Sayings' Texts of Chinese Ch'an Buddhism." Translated by John R. McRae. In *Early Ch'an in China and Tibet*, edited by Whalen Lai and Lewis Lancaster, 185–205. Berkeley: Asian Humanities Press.

Yang, Der-ruey. 2003. "The Education of Taoist Priests in Contemporary Shanghai, China." Ph.D. diss., London School of Economics and Political Science.

Yao Congwu 姚從吾. 1959a. "Jin-Yuan Quanzhen jiao de minzu sixiang yu jiushi sixiang" 金元全真教的民族思想與救世思想. In *Dongbei shi luncong* 東北史論叢 (Collected Essays on the History of the Northeast), edited by Yao Congwu, vol. 2, 175–204. Taibei: Zhengzhong shuju.

———. 1959b. "Yuan Qiu Chuji nianpu" 元丘處機年譜. In *Dongbei shi luncong* 東北史論叢 (Collected Essays on the History of the Northeast), edited by Yao Congwu, vol. 2, 214–76. Taibei: Zhengzhong shuju.

———. 1966. "Chengji sihan xinren Qiu Chuji yu zhejian shi duiyu baoquan zhongyuan zhuantong wenhua zhi gongxian" 成吉思汗信任丘處機這件事對於保全中原傳統文化之貢獻. *Wenhua zhixue bao* 15: 209–307.

Yao Tao-chung. 1977. "The Historical Value of the Ch'üan-chen Sources in the Tao-tsang." *Sung Studies Newsletter* 13: 67–76.

———. 1980a. "Ch'üan-chen: A New Taoist Sect in North China during the Twelfth and Thirteenth Centuries." Ph.D. diss., University of Arizona.

———. 1980b. "Ch'üan-chen Taoism and Ch'üan-chen Drama." *Journal of the Chinese Language Teachers Association* 15: 41–56.

———. 1986. "Ch'iu Ch'u-chi and Gingis Khan." *Harvard Journal of Asiatic Studies* 46: 201–19.

———. 1995. "Buddhism and Taoism under the Chin." In *China under Jurchen Rule*, edited by Hoyt Tillman and Stephen West, 145–80. Albany: State University of New York Press.

———. 2000. "Quanzhen—Complete Perfection." In *Daoism Handbook*, edited by Livia Kohn, 567–93.

Yifa. 2002. *The Origins of the Buddhist Monastic Codes in China: An Annotated Translation and Study of the Chanyuan qinggui*. Honolulu: University of Hawaii Press.

Yoshioka Yoshitoyo 吉岡義豐. 1952. *Dōkyō no kenkyū* 道教の研究. Kyoto: Hōzōkan.

———. 1958–1976. *Dōkyō to Bukkyō* 道教と佛教. 3 vols. Tokyo: Nihon gakujutsu shinkō kai.

———. 1979. "Taoist Monastic Life." In *Facts of Taoism*, edited by Holmes Welch and Anna Seidel, 220–52. New Haven, CT: Yale University Press.

You Zian 游子安, ed. 2002. *Daofeng bainian: Xianggang daojiao yu daoguan* 道風百年: 香港道教與道觀. Hong Kong: Penglai xianguan daojiao wenhua ziliao ku.

Zhan Shichuang 詹石窗. 2001. *Nansong Jin Yuan daojiao wenxue yanjiu* 南宋金元道教文學研究. Shanghai: Shanghai wenhua chubanshe.

Zhang Guangbao 張廣保. 1995. *Jin Yuan Quanzhen dao neidan xinxing xue* 金元全真道內丹心性學. Beijing: Sanlian shudian.

———. 2000. *Tang Song neidan daojiao* 唐宋內丹道教. Shanghai: Shanghai wenhua chubanshe.

Zhang Zheng 張錚. 1992. "Gendai dōkyō no ichi kōsatsu: *Genfū keikai roku* wo megutte" 元代道教の一考祭—<<玄風慶會錄>>ゑめぐって. *Chūgoku gaku kenkyū* 11: 29–36.

Zhao Weidong 趙衛東, ed. 2005a. *Quanzhen dao wenhua congshu: Ma Yu ji* 全真道文化叢書: 馬鈺集. Jinan, Shandong: Qi-Lu shushe.

———, ed. 2005b. *Quanzhen dao wenhua congshu: Qiu Chuji ji* 全真道文化叢書: 丘處機集. Jinan, Shandong: Qi-Lu shushe.

———, ed. 2009. *Wendao Kunyushan* 問道昆嵛山. Jinan, Shandong: Qilu shushe.

Zhao Yi 趙益. 1999. *Qiu Chuji* 丘處機. Nanjing: Jiangsu renmin chubanshe.

Zheng Suchun 鄭素春. 1987. *Quanzhen jiao yu Da Menggu guo dishi* 全真教與大蒙古帝室. Taibei: Xuesheng shuju.

———. 1995. "L'école taoïste Quanzhen sous la dynastie Yuan." Ph.D. diss., École des Hautes Études.

Zhou Shiyi. 1988. *The Kinship of the Three, According to the Book of Changes*. Changsha: Hunan jiaoyu.

Zhu Yueli 朱越利. 1994. "*Panxi ji* chuangzuo shijian kao" <<磻溪集>>創作時間考. *Wenxian* 4: 34–55.

Index

Milky Way, 276, 346

Min Lanyun. *See* Min Yide

Min Yide, 9, 14, 302

Min Yuxi. *See* Min Zhiting

Min Zhiting, 13, 17, 302

ming. See life-destiny

Ming dynasty, 7, 12–14, 16, 174, 223

Mingdao ji, 263

Minghe yuyin, 14, 295–96

mingmen. See Gate of Life

Mingzhen jing, 354–55

Mingzhen ke, 354

mirror, 58, 204

miyu wupian. See secret instructions in five sections

monastic hall, 316, 320, 342, 345

monastic manuals, 12–13, 22, 103, 295–303; translation of, 303–60. *See also* specific texts

monastic paraphernalia, 334–36, 343–44, 358–59

monastic registry, 307

monastic regulations, 7. *See also* precepts

monasticism, 5–9, 11, 24, 218, 221, 295–360, 369. *See also* asceticism; eremiticism; renunciation

Mongols, 5, 221, 260, 265. *See also* Yuan dynasty

monkey-mind, 43, 46, 49, 63, 95

moon, 39–40, 46–47, 50–52, 57, 60, 83, 89, 181, 185, 193, 197, 211, 213, 235, 261, 269, 282

mountains, 4, 35, 39, 43, 46, 52, 57, 59, 61–62, 78, 80, 83, 94, 108–9, 157–58, 161, 180, 195, 215, 228, 248, 256–57, 259, 261, 278, 280, 318, 346–47, 366

mozhao. See silent illumination

Muping, 3, 68, 70, 77

Mysterious Female, 129, 163, 180, 369

Mysterious Gate, 49, 316, 344

Mysterious Movement. *See* Xuanfeng

Mysterious Pass, 32, 36, 167, 369

mysterious pivot. *See* pivot

Mysterious Tenuity, 322

Mysterious Yellow, 267

mysteriousness, 38, 43, 46–47, 52, 75, 109, 131, 139, 171, 173, 180, 182, 184–85, 187, 196, 212, 229–30, 245, 271, 279, 283, 285, 311, 318, 342, 352, 371

mysticism. *See* mystical experience

mystical experience, 2, 16, 21–22, 30, 277, 285, 287

naming system, 7, 223

Nanbo Zikui, 67

Nanchang, 174

Nanhua zhenjing. See Zhuangzi

Nanjing, 247, 278

Nanke, 52, 226

Nanshi, 2

Nanyang, 249

Nanzong, 174

Narrow Ridge, 130, 134, 137

Nei riyong jing, 18–19

neidan. See internal alchemy

neiguan. See inner observation

Neijing tu, 13

Network Heaven. *See* Luotian

Niejia, 240

Nilong Kuqin, 283

Nimanggu Wujie, 253

Nine Cavities, 60, 119–20, 174, 195, 209–10, 369

Nine Empyreans, 205

Nine Heavens, 152

Nine Lineages, 240

Nine Obscurities, 62

Nine Palaces, 143

Nine Precepts for Female Perfected, 103, 358

Nine Subterrains, 35

Nine Vapors, 309

Ninghai, 3, 68, 70, 90, 173, 187, 224–25, 228, 268, 271–72, 274, 286, 288, 290

Niwan, 51, 138, 339

no-mind, 40, 83, 85–87

nonaction, 41, 51, 81–82, 86–87, 107, 160, 186, 189, 207–8, 240, 304, 311, 316, 321, 343, 365, 369

Nonbeing, 38–39, 44–45, 49, 56, 64, 87, 106, 178, 181–82, 188–89, 196, 204, 207, 212, 215, 238, 258. *See also* emptiness; Void

nondissipation. *See* conservation

Northern Dipper, 56, 119, 163, 165

Northern School. *See* Quanzhen

nüdan. See female alchemy

nüguan, 10

numinosity, 17, 21, 36, 50, 52, 55, 58–59, 61, 64, 73, 87, 170, 174, 176–77, 193, 195, 203–5, 207, 214, 265, 270, 281–82, 313, 328, 330, 341, 370

numinous abilities, 184, 312, 365, 372, 372

Numinous Tower, 314

Nüqing, 331–32, 334

Nüyu, 67